Politics in China

Politics in China

An Introduction

THIRD EDITION

Edited By William A. Joseph

OXFORD

UNIVERSITY PRESS

OXFORD
UNIVERSITY PRESS

Oxford University Press is a department of the University of Oxford. It furthers
the University's objective of excellence in research, scholarship, and education
by publishing worldwide. Oxford is a registered trade mark of Oxford University
Press in the UK and certain other countries.

Published in the United States of America by Oxford University Press
198 Madison Avenue, New York, NY 10016, United States of America.

CIP data is on file at the Library of Congress
ISBN 978–0–19–087071–3 (pbk.)
ISBN 978–0–19–087070–6 (hbk.)

9 8 7 6 5 4 3 2 1

Paperback printed by Sheridan Books, Inc., United States of America
Hardback printed by Bridgeport National Bindery, Inc., United States of America

To my Sino-Mentors,

John Wilson Lewis (1930–2017) and Harry Harding

子曰、學而時習之、不亦說乎

The Master said, "To learn something, and then to put it into practice at the right time: is this not a joy?"

Confucius, *The Analects, Chapter 1, Verse 1*

Translated by Simon Leys, Norton, 1997

Contents

Illustrations

MAPS

FIGURES AND TABLES

Acknowledgments

In the most immediate sense, this project began when Oxford University Press invited me to submit a proposal for an introductory textbook on Chinese politics about ten years ago. But its true origins go back to the summer of 1966, when I took my first college course on China in summer school at the University of California, Berkeley. My academic interest in China had been piqued during my freshman year at Cornell by events unfolding in Beijing (we called it "Peking" then) as the Red Guards—university students like myself—were challenging professors about their political views and methods of education during the very early stages of China's Great Proletarian Cultural Revolution. It was a tumultuous time on American campuses (Cornell and Berkeley were epicenters) and also on European college campuses, and the youthful rebellion against authority in China seemed to many young people to be part of a global generational movement.

The news from the People's Republic of China (we called it "Communist China" or "Red China" then) reaching Western audiences in the mid-1960s was, at best, piecemeal and sketchy because of Cold War hostilities and the PRC's self-imposed isolation from much of the world. It would be quite a few years before the terrible destructiveness of the Cultural Revolution and the atrocities committed by the Red Guards would become widely known and well-documented.

By then, I was immersed in Chinese Studies. I had been intellectually captivated by that summer-school course, taken at Berkeley, with the incomparable Benjamin I. Schwartz of Harvard. When I returned to Cornell for my sophomore year in the fall semester of 1966, I took the plunge into learning Chinese. I also began my study of Chinese politics with Professor John Wilson Lewis. What an extraordinary time that was to be learning—and teaching—about Chinese politics! I still vividly recall Professor Lewis's lecture on why the philosophical debate that had raged a few years before in China over whether "one divides into two" or "two unites into one" was crucial to understanding Chairman Mao Zedong's ideological motives for launching the Cultural Revolution. John became my undergraduate advisor, and I was very fortunate to be able to continue my study of Chinese politics with him at Stanford, where I completed an MA in East Asian Studies and a PhD in political science. I also benefited enormously in my training at Stanford as a China Watcher, political scientist, and teacher from the guidance and inspiration provided by Harry Harding. I dedicate this book with deepest gratitude to my academic mentors, John Wilson Lewis (1930-2017) and Harry Harding.

At Oxford University Press, I am much indebted to David McBride, editor-in-chief for the Social Sciences, and Emily Mackenzie, associate editor, for their support and encouragement during the many stages of this book from conception to publication. Jeremy Toynbee, project manager at Newgen, did a terrific job of sheparding this edition through the production process.

The contributors are what make this book unique. Each is a broadly trained China scholar and practitioner of her or his discipline (mostly political science); but each is also a specialist in the study of the particular subject of the chapter of which he or she is the author or co-author. It has been a pleasure and an honor to work closely with them, and I want to thank them for being part of this project. I learned a great deal from them, as I have from so many other colleagues in the China field.

The contributors and I are very grateful to the following China scholars for their valuable comments on the chapters in this and earlier editions of this book: Marc Belcher, Edward Friedman, Thomas B. Gold, Merle Goldman, J. Megan Greene, David M. Lampton, Kenneth Lieberthal, Barrett McCormick, Kevin J. O'Brien, Margaret Pearson, Benjamin Read, Michael Sheng, Wenfang Tang, and several anonymous reviewers.

Wellesley College, my home institution for four decades, sits on the shores of Lake Waban—which the beloved Chinese writer and Wellesley alumna (MA, 1923), Bingxin, affectionately called "Weibing Hu" 慰冰湖 —"The lake that comforts Bing." For me, the college has been a beautiful and supportive academic setting in which to ponder and teach about the ever fascinating subject of Chinese politics.

As editor, I assume full responsibility for any and all errors. I invite readers to send comments and corrections directly to me at wjoseph@wellesley.edu.

William A. Joseph
Wellesley, MA
May 2019

Contributors

ROBERT BARNETT is based at Pembroke College, Cambridge, and is an Affiliate Researcher at King's College, London. He founded the Modern Tibetan Studies Program at Columbia University in New York, directed the program from 1999 to 2018, and has taught at Columbia, Princeton, INALCO (Paris), and IACER (Kathmandu). He ran an independent research project on contemporary Tibet in London from 1987 to 1998. His books and edited volumes include *Conflicting Memories,* with Benno Weiner and Françoise Robin (2019); *Tibetan Modernities: Notes from the Field*, with Ronald Schwartz (2008); *Lhasa: Streets with Memories* (2006). His writing includes studies of Tibetan politics, cinema, television, religious regulations, social management, women politicians, and contemporary exorcism rituals. He runs a number of training programs in Tibet on ecotourism, small business skills, and is a frequent commentator on Tibet and nationality issues in China for the media.

GARDNER BOVINGDON is associate professor in the Departments of Central Eurasian Studies and International Studies, and adjunct associate professor of Political Science at Indiana University. A specialist on nationalism, identity politics, and historiography with a geographical focus on Central Asia, he has published a number of journal articles and book chapters on these topics. His book, *The Uyghurs: Strangers in Their Own Land*, was published in 2010.

JACQUES DELISLE is the Stephen A. Cozen Professor of Law and professor of political science at the University of Pennsylvania, where he also serves as the director of the Center for East Asian Studies and deputy director of the Center for the Study of Contemporary China. He is the director of the Asia Program at the Foreign Policy Research Institute. His scholarship, which has appeared in many international affairs journals and law reviews, focuses on domestic legal and legal-institutional reform, the relationship of legal development to economic and political change, and the roles of law in addressing crises in China; the PRC's engagement with the international legal order; and Taiwan's international status and cross-Strait relations. He is the coeditor of *China's Global Engagement: Cooperation, Competition, and Influence in the 21st*

Century (2017), *The Internet, Social Media, and a Changing China* (2017), and *China's Challenges: The Road Ahead* (2014).

BRUCE GILLEY is professor of political science in the Mark O. Hatfield School of Government at Portland State University. His research centers on the comparative and international politics of China and Asia as well as the comparative politics of democracy and political legitimacy. He is the author of *China's Democratic Future* (2004) and *The Right to Rule: How States Win and Lose Legitimacy* (2009).

WILLIAM HURST is associate professor of political science at Northwestern University. He is the author of *The Chinese Worker after Socialism* (2009) and *Ruling Before the Law: The Politics of Legal Regimes in China and Indonesia* (2018), as well as coeditor of *Laid-off Workers in a Workers' State: Unemployment with Chinese Characteristics* (2009) and *Local Governance Innovation in China: Experimentation, Diffusion, and Defiance* (2015). His ongoing research focuses on the political economy of land and development in Mainland China, Indonesia, Malaysia, and Taiwan.

WILLIAM A. JOSEPH is professor of political science at Wellesley College and an associate in research of the John King Fairbank Center for Chinese Studies at Harvard University. He is the author of *The Critique of Ultra-Leftism in China* (1984) and editor or coeditor of *New Perspectives on the Cultural Revolution* (1991), *China Briefing* (1991, 1992, 1994, 1997), *The Oxford Companion to Politics of the World* (2nd ed., 2001), *Introduction to Comparative Politics: Political Challenges and Changing Agendas* (8th ed., 2018).

JOAN KAUFMAN is the senior director for academic programs at the Schwarzman Scholars Program, Lecturer on Global Health and Social Medicine at Harvard Medical School, and a member of the Council on Foreign Relations. She was previously the director of Columbia University's Global Center for East Asia, based in Beijing, and associate professor at Columbia University's Mailman School of Public Health, distinguished scientist at the Heller School for Social Policy and Management, Brandeis University, founder and director of the AIDS Public Policy Program at Harvard's Kennedy School of Government, and China team leader for the International AIDS Vaccine Initiative. She has lived and worked in China for more than fifteen years for the Ford Foundation and the UN, was a Radcliffe Fellow at Harvard, and a Soros Reproductive Health and Rights fellow. Dr. Kaufman teaches, works, and writes on AIDS, gender, international health, infectious diseases, reproductive health, health sector reform, and health governance issues with a focus on China

JOHN JAMES KENNEDY is professor of political science and director of the Center for East Asian Studies at the University of Kansas. His research focuses on rural, social, and political development including village elections, tax reform, family planning, and rural education. He frequently returns to China to conduct fieldwork and collaborate with Chinese colleagues in Northwest China. Prof. Kennedy is the co-author (with Yaojiang Shi) of *Lost and Found: the 'Missing Girls" in Rural China* (2019). He has also published a number of book chapters as well as articles in journals such as *Asian Survey, China Quarterly, Journal of Peasant Studies, Journal of Chinese*

Political Science, Journal of Contemporary China, Asian Politics and Policy, and *Political Studies.*

RICHARD CURT KRAUS is professor emeritus of political science, University of Oregon. He is the author of *Class Conflict in Chinese Socialism* (1981), *Pianos and Politics in China* (1989), *Brushes with Power: Modern Politics and the Chinese Art of Calligraphy* (1991), *The Party and the Arty* (2004), *The Cultural Revolution: A Very Short Introduction* (2012), and coeditor of *Urban Spaces: Autonomy and Community in Contemporary China* (1995).

CHENG LI is director and senior fellow at the Brookings Institution's John L. Thornton China Center. Dr. Li is the author/editor of numerous books, including *Rediscovering China: Dynamics and Dilemmas of Reform* (1997), *China's Leaders: The New Generation* (2001), *Bridging Minds Across the Pacific: The Sino-US Educational Exchange* (2005), *China's Changing Political Landscape: Prospects for Democracy* (2008), *China's Emerging Middle Class: Beyond Economic Transformation* (2010), *China's Political Development: Chinese and American Perspectives* (2014), Chinese *Politics in the Xi Jinping Era: Reassessing Collective Leadership* (2016), and *The Power of Ideas: The Rising Influence of Thinkers and Think Tanks in China* (2017). He is the principal editor of the Thornton Center Chinese Thinkers Series published by the Brookings Institution Press.

SONNY SHIU-HING LO is professor and deputy director (Arts and Sciences) in the School of Professional and Continuing Education at the University of Hong Kong. His new books include *China's New United Front Work in Hong Kong* (forthcoming, with Steven Hung and Jeff Loo), *Interest Groups and the New Democracy Movement in Hong Kong* (2018), and *The Politics of Controlling Organized Crime in Greater China* (2016).

KATHERINE MORTON is the chair and professor of China's International Relations at the University of Sheffield. Her research addresses the domestic and international motivations behind China's changing role in the world and the implications for foreign policy and the study of International Relations. Prior to her appointment at the University of Sheffield she was the associate dean for research at the College of Asia and the Pacific, Australian National University, and a Senior Fellow in the Department of International Relations. She has published widely on the environment and climate change, global governance, transnational security, food security, maritime security, and the South China Sea. Her current book project examines the likely impacts of China's rising international status upon the evolving system of global governance.

SHELLEY RIGGER is Brown Professor of East Asian Politics at Davidson College. She has been a visiting researcher at National Chengchi University in Taiwan and a visiting professor at Fudan University in Shanghai. She is the author of three books on Taiwan: *Politics in Taiwan: Voting for Democracy* (1999),*From Opposition to Power: Taiwan's Democratic Progressive Party* (2001); and *Why Taiwan Matters: Small Island, Global Powerhouse* (2011) as well as articles on Taiwan's domestic politics, the national identity issue in Taiwan-China relations and related topics.

R. KEITH SCHOPPA is Doehler Chair in Asian History emeritus at Loyola University, Maryland. He has authored many books and articles, including, most recently, *In a Sea of Bitterness: Refugees during the Sino-Japanese War* (2011). His book *Blood Road: The Mystery of Shen Dingyi in Revolutionary China* (1996) won the 1997 Association for Asian Studies' Levenson Prize for the best book on twentieth-century China, and he is also the author of textbooks on modern China and East Asia. He has received fellowships from the National Endowment for the Humanities, the American Council of Learned Societies, and the John Simon Guggenheim Memorial Foundation.

CHRISTIAN SORACE is assistant professor of political science at Colorado College. He is the author of *Shaken Authority: China's Communist Party and the 2008 Sichuan Earthquake* (2018) and coeditor of *Afterlives of Chinese Communism: Political Concepts from Mao to Xi* (forthcoming). His new research focuses on comparative urbanization, crisis, and temporality in Ulaanbaatar, Mongolia, and Inner Mongolia, China.

FREDERICK C. TEIWES is emeritus professor of Chinese Politics at the University of Sydney. He is the author of numerous works on Chinese Communist elite politics during the Maoist era, including *Politics and Purges in China* (1979), 2nd ed., 1993), *Politics at Mao's Court* (1990), *The Tragedy of Lin Biao* (1996), *China's Road to Disaster* (1999), and *The End of the Maoist Era* (2007) (the latter three studies coauthored with Warren Sun). During the past decade he and Dr. Sun have published revisionist studies of the early post-Mao period, notably *Paradoxes of Post-Mao Rural Reform* (2016). He thanks the Australian Research Council for generous research support over many years.

TYRENE WHITE is professor of political science at Swarthmore College. She is the author of *China's Longest Campaign: Birth Planning in the People's Republic, 1949–2005* (Cornell University Press, 2006), and many articles on rural politics and population policy in China. She is the editor of *China Briefing: The Continuing Transformation* (2000) and coeditor of *Engendering China: Women, Culture, and the State* (1994). Her current research examines China's regulatory politics in comparative perspective and the causes of China's fertility decline in the 1970s.

FENGSHI WU is senior lecturer in the Asia Institute, the University of Melbourne. She specializes in environmental politics, state-society relations, and global governance with the empirical focus on China and Asia. She was a visiting fellow at the Harvard-Yenching Institute (2008-2009) and a graduate fellow of the American Academy of Political and Social Sciences (2004). Her recent academic works have appeared in *China Journal, VOLUNTAS, China Quarterly, Journal of Environmental Policy and Planning,* and *Journal of Contemporary China.* She recently edited the book *China's Global Conquest for Resources* (2017) on China's overseas investment in and acquisition of natural resources.

GUOBIN YANG is the Grace Lee Boggs Professor of Communication and Sociology at the Annenberg School for Communication and Department of Sociology at the University of Pennsylvania. He is the author of *The Red Guard Generation and Political Activism in China* (2016) and *The Power of the Internet in China: Citizen Activism*

Online (2009). His *Dragon-Carving and the Literary Mind* (2003) is an annotated English translation of *Wenxin Diaolong*, the Chinese classic of rhetoric and literary theory. He has edited or coedited four books, including *China's Contested Internet* (2015), *The Internet, Social Media, and a Changing China* (with Jacques deLisle and Avery Goldstein, 2016), and *Re-Envisioning the Chinese Revolution: The Politics and Poetics of Collective Memories in Reform China* (with Ching-Kwan Lee, 2007).

DAVID ZWEIG is professor emeritus, Division of Social Science, at The Hong Kong University of Science and Technology HKUST, and director, Transnational China Consulting Limited (HK). He is vice president of the Center on China and Globalization (Beijing). He is the author of four books, including *Freeing China's Farmers* (1997), *Internationalizing China: Domestic Interests and Global Linkages* (2002), and *China's Brain Drain to the United States* (1995), and coeditor of *Sino-China Energy Triangles: Resource Diplomacy under Hegemony* (2015). His current book project focuses on the reverse migration of Chinese talent.

Abbreviations

ACWF	All-China Women's Federation
BRI	Belt and Road Initiative
CAC	Cyberspace Administration of China
CC	Central Committee
CCP	Chinese Communist Party
CCRG	Central Cultural Revolution Group
CCTV	China Central Television
CCYL	Chinese Communist Youth League
CMC	Central Military Commission
CMS	Cooperative Medical Scheme
CNNIC	China Internet Network Information Center
CPSU	Communist Party of the Soviet Union
DPP	Democratic Progressive Party
ELG	Export-Led Growth
GAPP	General Administration of Press and Publication
HIV/AIDS	Human Immunodeficiency Virus/Acquired Immune Deficiency Syndrome
HKSAR	Hong Kong Special Administrative Region
HLLAPCs	Higher-Level Agricultural Producer Cooperatives (Collectives)
IMF	International Monetary Fund
KMT	Kuomintang
LegCo	Legislative Council
LLPAPCs	Lower-Level Agricultural Producer Cooperatives (Cooperatives)
LSG	Leading Small Group
NCNA	New China News Agency (Xinhua)
NPC	National People's Congress
PAP	People's Armed Police
PBSC	Politburo Standing Committee
PLA	People's Liberation Army
PRC	People's Republic of China

ROC	Republic of China
SAR	Special Administrative Region
SARS	Severe Acute Respiratory Syndrome
SASAC	State-owned Assets Supervision and Administration Commission
SCNPC	Standing Committee of the National People's Congress
SEZ	Special Economic Zone
SMEs	Small- and-Medium Enterprises
SOE	State-Owned Enterprise
SAPPRFT	State Administration of Press, Publication, Radio, Film, and Television
TAR	Tibet Autonomous Region
TVE	Township and Village Enterprise
USSR	Union of Soviet Socialist Republics
VRA	Villager Representative Assembly
WTO	World Trade Organization
XPCC	Xinjiang Production and Construction Corps (*bingtuan*)
XUAR	Xinjiang Uyghur Autonomous Region

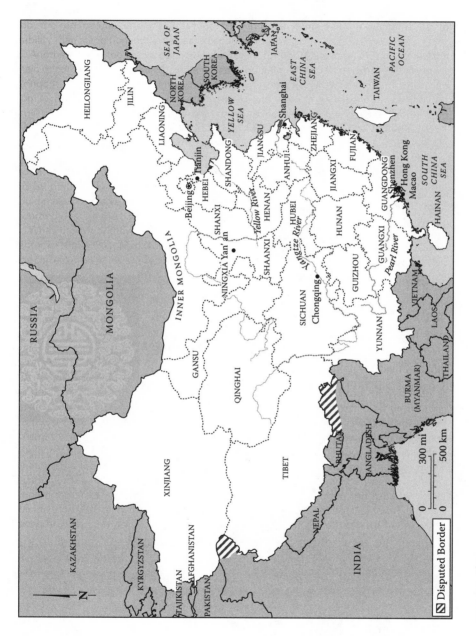

MAP 0.1 China

Politics in China

Introduction

1

Studying Chinese Politics

WILLIAM A. JOSEPH

In 1978, the **People's Republic of China (PRC)** was one of the world's poorest countries, and the standard of living for the vast majority of the population had improved only slightly in the nearly two decades since the PRC was founded. China was also diplomatically isolated, barely engaged in the international economy, and little more than a regional military power.

Today, China is the world's second largest and most dynamic major economy. Over the last forty years it has experienced "the fastest sustained expansion by a major economy in history"[1] that is widely hailed as a "miracle"[2] (see Figure 1.1). During that time, more than 800 million people have been lifted out of poverty that even in the early 1990s was recognized as "one of the biggest improvements in human welfare anywhere at any time."[3] The PRC is now the world's largest trading nation, and its export and import policies have an enormous impact in literally every corner of the globe. It is a rising power that is challenging the United States for global influence and a key member of all important international organizations. The Chinese military is world class, with a formidable arsenal of nuclear weapons, a rapidly modernizing oceangoing navy, and on the cutting edge of cyberwarfare.

But prior to the beginning of its remarkable rise to relative economic prosperity and international prominence, the PRC experienced a series of national traumas. In the late 1950s and early 1960s, China went through the deadliest famine in human history, caused largely by the actions and inactions of its political leaders during the **Great Leap Forward**. Not long after that catastrophe, over the decade from 1966 to 1976 when China went through the **Great Proletarian Cultural Revolution**, there was first a collapse of central government authority, which pushed the country to

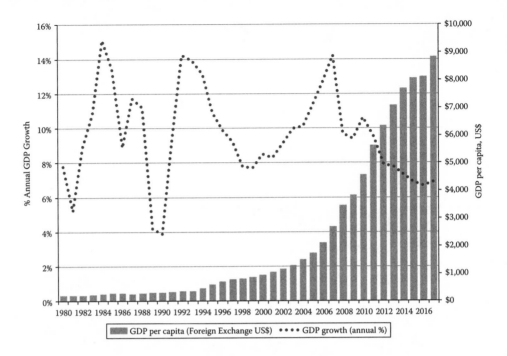

FIGURE 1.1 China's Economic Growth 1980–2017

Note: GDP per capita is given in its foreign exchange value since purchasing power parity data were not available before 1993. In PPP, China's GDP per capita in 2017 was about $16,800.

Source: World Bank Development Indicators

the brink of (and in some places actually into) civil war and anarchy, a reign of terror that tore at the very fabric of Chinese society, and a vicious and destructive assault against traditional culture, followed by destabilizing power struggles among the top leadership.

The famine and political chaos occurred during the period when Mao Zedong was chairman of the **Chinese Communist Party (CCP)** and the undisputed and largely indisputable leader of the People's Republic from its founding in 1949 to his death in 1976. The Maoist era was not without its accomplishments (which are discussed in this book), but overwhelming scholarly opinion is that it was, as a whole, a disaster for China, economically, politically, culturally, environmentally, and in other ways. The emergence of China as a global power that we are witnessing today did not begin until the early 1980s, with the onset of the post-Mao economic **reform era** under the leadership of Deng Xiaoping who, along with Mao Zedong, ranks as the most influential Chinese political leader of modern times. Deng and the other leaders who have followed Mao in power have taken the country in a very un-Maoist direction, with spectacular economic results and many other profound changes. The political story of China's incredible journey from Mao to now is one of the central themes of this book.

But one thing about China has not changed since the founding of the People's Republic on October 1, 1949: the CCP has never been seriously challenged as China's ruling party. There have been sporadic protests by students and peasants, labor unrest, ethnic uprisings, and deep pockets of dissent and discontent, but all have been quelled before they could become threatening to the CCP's hold on power. The party itself has been through internal purges and almost inexplicable ideological and policy turnabouts.

Communist rule has not only survived in China; by many measures, it has thrived. The CCP appears to maintain a firm grip on power while most other communist regimes have long perished from this earth. The *hows* and *whys* of this fundamental political continuity is another main theme of this volume. One part of the answer to this question is that it is the Chinese Communist Party itself that has presided over China's recent economic success, which has won the party a great deal of popular support, reflecting a strong desire among many sectors of the population for political stability and continuity. Nevertheless, the prospects for continued CCP rule is a hotly debated topic among political scientists who study contemporary China.

There is much greater freedom in many parts of Chinese society today than there was during the Mao era, which is another source of the party's staying power. Nevertheless, the PRC is still regarded by most outside observers as having one of the world's most repressive political regimes. For example, the *Economist*, a highly respected British weekly magazine, ranked China at 130 out of 167 countries on its 2018 "Index of Democracy," which is based on measures of "electoral processes and pluralism," "functioning of government" (which includes corruption), "political participation," "political culture," and "civil liberties."[4]

The contradiction between China's increasingly open society and globalized economy, along with its still-closed authoritarian political system, raises other fascinating questions for students of Chinese politics and comparative politics in general:

- What does the Chinese experience say about the kind of government best able to promote rapid economic development? Is a strong, authoritarian regime required for such a task?
- How has the CCP been able to resist the pressures for democratization that usually accompany the social, economic, and cultural changes that modernization brings? Will it be able to continue to do so in the future?

These questions, too, are addressed, directly and indirectly, in many chapters in this book.

The next part of this introduction provides a brief overview of the land and people of China (see Box 1.1) in order to set the geographic and demographic contexts of Chinese politics. Then comes a discussion of what I call the four faces of contemporary China—China as China; China as a **communist party-state**; China as a developing country; and China as a rising power—that are offered as ways to frame the analysis of contemporary Chinese politics. This is followed by a review of the major approaches that have been used by political scientists to study politics in China. Finally, the chapter concludes with a summary of the organization of the book and the content of its chapters.

BOX 1.1 WHERE DID "CHINA" COME FROM?

The first use of the name "China" in English in reference to the country has been traced to 1555 CE. The term is believed to have come via Persian and Sanskrit in reference to the ancient Qin (pronounced "chin") kingdom in what is now northwest China and whose capital lay at the eastern end of the Silk Road that connected East Asia, Central Asia, the Middle East, and ultimately Europe. The king of Qin became the founder of China's first imperial dynasty in 221 BCE by bringing neighboring kingdoms under his control and is therefore known as China's first emperor.

The Chinese term for China is *Zhongguo*, which literally means "Middle Kingdom." This name dates from the sixth century BCE, several centuries prior to the unification of the Chinese empire, and even then was meant to convey the idea of being the center of civilization, culture, and political authority. The Qin emperor was the first political leader to be able to claim the title of ruler of the entire Middle Kingdom.

The term "Sino" is also often used to refer to China, as in "Sino-American relations." Scholars who specialize in the study of China are called "sinologists." Sino comes from the Latin for China (*Sinae*).

CHINA: A GEOGRAPHIC AND DEMOGRAPHIC OVERVIEW

Geography is the multifaceted study of physical space on the surface of the earth, and demography is the study of the size, composition, distribution, and other aspects of human population. In all countries, there is a close relationship between geography and demography, and both have important implications for politics and policy making. In China, as one of the world's largest countries in terms of physical space and the largest in terms of population, this is especially the case.

China is located in the far eastern part of the Asian continent usually referred to as East Asia, which also includes Japan and the two Koreas: the communist Democratic People's Republic of Korea (North Korea) and the capitalist democracy, the Republic of Korea (South Korea). China shares land borders with fourteen countries, the longest being with Russia and Mongolia in the north, India in the west, and Myanmar (Burma) and Vietnam in the south. China's eastern border is made up almost entirely of an 11,200-mile-long (18,000 km) coastline along the western edge of the Pacific Ocean. The country stretches for about 3,200 miles (5,200 km) from east to west, and 3,400 miles (5,500 km) from north to south.

In terms of total area, China (5.6 million sq mi/9.6 million sq km) is a bit smaller than the United States, making it the fourth largest country in the world, with Russia first and Canada second. China's population is about 1.39 billion; India is second with 1.30 billion people and is expected to surpass China in population in 2022.

Although China and the United States are quite similar in geographic size, China's population is about four and half times that of the United States. Therefore, China, with 374 people per square mile, is much more densely populated than the United States, which has 86 people per square mile. Both countries have large areas that are sparsely populated or uninhabitable. By comparison, India, which is only about a third the geographic size of China, has more than 1,000 people per square mile and has very few areas with low population density. China has about 18 percent of the world's population but only 7 percent of its arable land—that is, land used for planting edible crops.[5] Feeding its people is—and long has been—a central challenge for the Chinese government.

Like the United States, China is a land of great geographic and climatic contrasts, but China tends to have greater extremes. One of the world's largest deserts (the Gobi) and the highest mountains (the Himalayas, which include Mount Everest—or as it is called in Chinese, *Chomolungma*) are located in the far western part of the country. Climate varies from semitropical in the southeast to subarctic in the northeast, which borders on Russian Siberia. Most of the country is much more temperate. **Beijing** (China's capital city) is located at about the same latitude in the Northern Hemisphere as New York.

One way to think about China's geography is to imagine a 2,000-mile line cutting diagonally across the country from just north of Beijing to the PRC's border with Burma in the far southwest (see Map 1.1). The area to the east of this line early on became part of the Chinese empire and is referred to as **China Proper**. China Proper accounts for about one-third of China's total territory and is largely populated by the ethnic group to which the vast majority of Chinese people belong, the **Han**, a term taken from the name of Imperial China's second **dynasty,** which lasted for more than four centuries (206 BCE–220 CE) and is considered the early golden age of Chinese civilization.

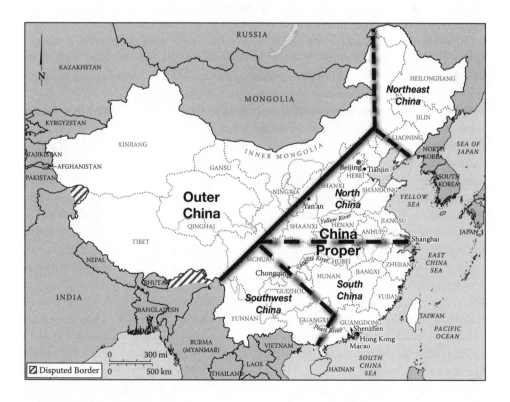

MAP 1.1 China's Major Regions

China Proper can itself be divided into several geographic regions. The three **provinces** (Heilongjiang, Jilin, and Liaoning) of the **Northeast**, historically referred to as Manchuria, have vast tracts of forestland, but this region was also once the PRC's industrial heartland; now much of it is considered China's rust belt because of the closing of aged, inefficient factories and high unemployment. The area that stretches from just north of Beijing to the **Yangtze River**, which flows into the East China Sea near Shanghai, is referred to as **North China**. Agriculturally, this is a one-crop-a-year growing area with some similarities to the American Plains states. **South China** is the region that lies below the Yangtze and is warmer and wetter than the north, and these conditions allow for rice farming and, in some areas, year-round cultivation. Almost the entire coastal area of China Proper, from north to south, has become industrialized during the country's recent economic development spurt. China's population is also heavily concentrated along the eastern coastline and the adjacent provinces of China Proper. Around 90 percent of the Chinese people live in this area, which is only about 40 percent of the country's total land area.

To the west of the imaginary diagonal line lies **Outer China**. Outer China geographically comprises about two-thirds of the country, but it is very sparsely populated. Most of the region was incorporated into the Chinese empire during its later periods, particularly in the seventeenth and eighteenth centuries, and is home to most of China's non-Han **ethnic minorities**, including **Tibetans, Uyghurs**, and Mongols. The **Great Wall** of China was begun by China's first emperor more than two thousand years ago and expanded through many other dynasties largely as a fortification to keep non-Han peoples out of China—a strategy that failed twice in Chinese history, once when the country was conquered by the Mongols in 1279 CE and again when it was overtaken by the **Manchus** in 1644 CE. Today, Han make up 91.5 percent of the PRC's population, with the other 8.5 percent divided among fifty-five ethnic minority groups that range in size from about sixteen million (the Zhuang) to under four thousand (the Lhoba).

The other major geographic and demographic divide in China is that between the urban and rural areas. China developed large and, for the times, very advanced cities early in its imperial history. When Marco Polo visited the country in the thirteenth century, he marveled at the splendor of its cities and the system of canals that linked them for commercial and other purposes. From his experience, there was nothing comparable in Europe.[6] But until very recently, China had always been a largely rural society. At the time of the founding of the PRC in 1949, only about 10 percent of the total population lived in urban areas. At the end of the Maoist era in 1976, the country was just 20 percent urbanized. Economic development since then has led to a major population shift, and in 2011, for the first time in its history, more than half of the people in China were living in cities.

China has about 160 cities with a population of more than one million (the United States has nine). By 2025, that number will grow to about 220, and, by 2030, more than a billion people in China will live in urban areas. The PRC's largest cities are Shanghai, China's financial center (24.2 million), and Beijing, its political capital (21.7 million). In both of these megacities, as in most urban areas in China since the 1980s, there has been a massive influx of people—more than 260 million—from the countryside in search of jobs and a better life. In Beijing and Shanghai such migrants—referred to as the **floating population**—make up more than 40 percent of the population. This is just one way in which urban-rural boundaries are shifting in the People's Republic, which, in turn, reflects geographic and demographic transitions with enormous political implications.

Administratively, the PRC is a **unitary state**, which means that the national government has ultimate authority over all lower levels of government (see Figure 1.2). The United Kingdom and France also have this form of government, in contrast to federal systems, such as the United States and Canada, in which there is significant sharing of power between the national and subnational levels of government.

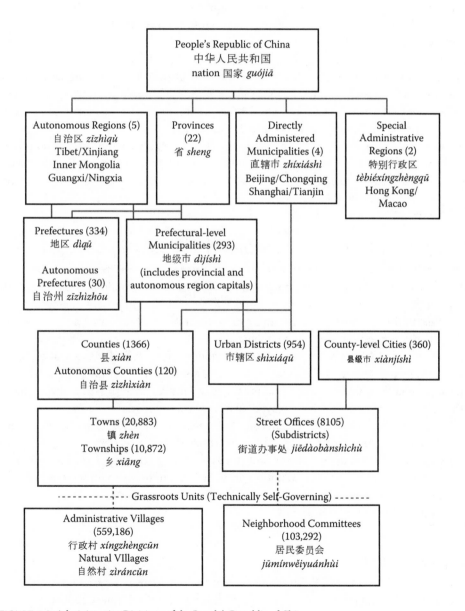

FIGURE 1.2 Administrative Divisions of the People's Republic of China

The PRC has twenty-two provinces (similar to states in the United States), four cities that are considered the equivalent of provinces and are directly administered by the central government (Beijing, Shanghai, Tianjin, and Chongqing), and five **autonomous regions** (Guangxi, Inner Mongolia, Ningxia, **Tibet**, and **Xinjiang**—all located in Outer China) with large concentrations of ethnic minority groups. Autonomous regions do have limited autonomy when it comes to some cultural and social policies, but they are completely under the political and military control of the government in Beijing.

There are also two **special administrative regions** (SAR) of the PRC: the former British colony of **Hong Kong**, which reverted to Chinese sovereignty in 1997, and **Macao**, a former Portuguese possession that became an SAR of the PRC in 1999. The SARs do have considerable political and economic autonomy, although ultimate control over their affairs lies in Beijing.

The island of **Taiwan**, located a little more than one hundred miles off the coast of southeastern China, is a politically contested area. It became part of China in the mid-seventeenth century but fell under Japanese control from 1895 until 1945. When the CCP won the **Chinese Civil War** in 1949, its rivals, the **Nationalist Party (Kuomintang** or Guomindang) fled to Taiwan, where, with U.S. support, they were able to establish a stronghold. Despite many political changes on both the mainland and the island and closer economic ties between the two in the intervening years, Taiwan still remains a separate political entity, although Beijing claims that it is rightfully a province of the PRC.

FOUR FACES OF CONTEMPORARY CHINA

Hopefully, readers have already gotten the sense that Chinese politics is extremely important in today's world, and perhaps they will also find it immensely fascinating. But Chinese politics is quite complex and can be more than a bit confusing to someone new to the subject—and often to experts, as well! Not only are the stages of political change that China has gone through in modern times full of twists and turns—a very involved and convoluted (and somewhat unbelievable) plot line, one might say, if we were talking about a novel; and for those unfamiliar with the Chinese language, the cast of characters that have played or now plays influential roles in Chinese politics can also be somewhat bewildering. Furthermore, the PRC has a type of political system—a communist party-state—about which most readers know very little, in terms of its structure of power and policy-making process. As readers progress through the chapters in this book, it might be helpful, in order to understand China's unique political development and current politics, to keep in mind what can be called the "four faces" of contemporary China.

China as China

By China as China, I mean taking note of the influence of the Chinese past and culture on politics in the PRC. In the broadest and boldest strokes, Chinese political history can be broken down into three periods: the **imperial period** of dynastic monarchy (221 BCE–1912 CE); the **republican period** (1912–1949), characterized by weak central government, powerful regional **warlords**, several stages of civil war, and the brutal invasion and occupation by Japan that started World War II in the Pacific; and the **communist period** (1949 to the present) that began with the victory of the CCP in the civil war and continues through the present day.

But Chinese *cultural* history dates back to well before the beginning of the imperial period in 221 BCE. Human beings have lived in the area that is now called China for more than a million years. The first dynasties—systems of hereditary rule over specific geographic areas—appeared as small, independent kingdoms more than four thousand years ago. The earliest artifacts of Chinese material culture, such as exquisite bronze and jade vessels, are from this period. Chinese as a written language took shape in the Shang dynasty (1600–1046 BCE) as inscriptions etched on "oracle bones" made from turtle shells and animal scapula for the purpose of divination and record-keeping (see Box 1.2.)

The imperial period in Chinese history began in 221 BCE when a number of separate kingdoms were brought under the authority of the king of Qin, who is known as the first emperor of a unified China. The **Qin dynasty** lasted less than twenty years, giving way to the much-longer-lived Han, as noted earlier. But the Chinese empire founded by Qin endured for more than two thousand years, through the rise and fall of more than a dozen different dynasties, until it was overthrown by a revolution and replaced by the Republic of China in 1912 CE.

The philosopher-scholar Confucius, whose ethical, social, and political teachings are the foundation of Chinese culture, lived in 557–479 BCE, centuries before the founding of the Qin dynasty. In fact, the emperor Qin was profoundly suspicious of Confucian scholars and ordered many of them executed and their books burned. He favored a school of philosophy called **Legalism**, which advocated harsh laws rather than Confucian education and morality as the basis for maintaining the ruler's authority and commanding the obedience of his subjects. Later dynasties restored the prominence of **Confucianism** and imbedded it in the very structure of imperial Chinese society and government. Over the millennia, Legalism and other schools of thought combined with and influenced the evolution of Confucianism. Today, not

---

BOX 1.2 A VERY BRIEF CHINESE LESSON

Chinese is spoken by more people than any other language in the world. Yet "Chinese" really comprises many dialects, some of which are so different from one another that they are mutually incomprehensible and are considered by linguists to be separate languages, as different, for example, as French is from Italian. About 70 percent of China's population speaks Mandarin, which is the dialect of Chinese spoken mainly in the northern, central, and southwestern parts of the country, as their native tongue. Other major dialects include Wu (a subdialect of which is spoken in the area that includes China's largest city, Shanghai) and Cantonese, which is the dialect native to the southern coastal region adjacent to Hong Kong.

(Continued)

BOX 1.2 (Continued)

But people who speak different Chinese dialects share the same written language. For example, Mandarin and Cantonese speakers cannot understand each other in face-to-face conversations or on their cell phones, but they can communicate by email and read the same newspapers or books because written Chinese is made up of characters rather than phonetic letters. These characters, which have evolved over time from symbolic pictures, depict meaning more than sound, so that speakers of various Chinese dialects often pronounce the same written character very differently. There are about 50,000 different Chinese characters, although basic literacy requires knowledge of only about 4,000 because the vast majority of characters are archaic and have fallen out of common usage.

Chinese does not have an alphabet; both the meaning and the pronunciation of Chinese characters can only be learned by memorization. Like many of the world's other languages—including Arabic, Greek, Hebrew, Japanese, and Russian—that do not use the Roman alphabet on which English is based, Chinese characters must be "Romanized" (or "transliterated") if English speakers are to have any idea how to pronounce them. The most common way of Romanizing Chinese is the pinyin (literally, "spell sounds") system used in the PRC. But because linguists have differed about how best to approximate distinctive Chinese sounds using Roman letters, there are still several alternative methods of Romanizing Chinese.

This book and most other English-language publications use the pinyin Romanization for Chinese names, places, and phrases, with a few exceptions for important historical names where an alternative Romanization is commonly given. In most cases, a word in pinyin is pronounced as it looks. However, there are a few pinyin letters that appear in Chinese terms in this book for which a pronunciation guide may be helpful:

"x" is pronounced "sh" (e.g., Deng Xiaoping; Xi Jinping)
"z" is pronounced "dz" (e.g., Mao Zedong)
"q" is pronounced "ch" (e.g., Emperor Qin; Qing dynasty)
"zh" is pronounced "j" (e.g., Zhongguo, the Chinese word for "China")
"c" is pronounced "ts" (e.g., Empress Dowager Cixi)

A couple of important points about Chinese names: In China (as in Japan and Korea), the family name (for instance, Mao) comes before the personal, or given, name (for instance, Zedong). Some people interpret this as a reflection of the priority given to the family or the group over the individual in East Asian culture. Chinese people who have immigrated to the United States or other countries often adapt their names to the "Western" order of personal names before family names. For example, "Li" is the family name of one of the contributors to this volume, Dr. Cheng Li of the Brookings Institution; in China, he is known as Li Cheng.

Chinese has relatively few family names: There are just about only 3100 surnames in common use in China today among the Han majority; in the United States, 63 million different surnames were reported in the 2010 census, of which about 275,000 were used by more than 50 people.

The most common family name in the PRC is Wang; there are more than 93 million Wangs in China, followed by 92 million with the family name Li, and 88 million Zhangs. On the other hand, there is an almost infinite variety of given names in Chinese, which often have descriptive meanings such as "beautiful bell" (Meiling) or "bright and cultivated" (Bingwen).

only are the areas encompassed by **Greater China** (the PRC, Taiwan Hong Kong, and Macao) considered to be part of the Confucian cultural region but so, too, are Japan, Korea, Singapore, and Vietnam, all of which were deeply influenced by the spread of many aspects of Chinese civilization.

This book focuses on Chinese politics during the communist era (with one chapter on the earlier periods) and mostly on very recent decades. From that perspective, we are concentrating our attention on but a tiny slice (see Figure 1.3) of the grand span of China's political history. It should come as no surprise that such a long and rich history should be considered when trying to understand almost any aspect of China today, including its politics.

But it is not just the imperial past or Confucian culture that should be taken into account when studying contemporary China. The revolution that brought the CCP to power and the radicalism of the Maoist era may seem far removed from the rapidly modernizing and rising power that China is today. But as one leading scholar of Chinese politics, Elizabeth J. Perry, has observed, "China's stunning economic strides in the reform era can only be understood against the backdrop of a revolutionary history that remains highly salient in many respects."[7] In fact, she goes further and argues that legacies of the CCP's revolutionary past—notably its practice of the politics of divide-and-rule when dealing with those who may oppose it—are a significant part of the answer to the question set out earlier about the durability of communist power in China.

The government of the PRC places great emphasis on nationalism in its messages aimed to audiences both at home and abroad. It expresses pride in the antiquity, greatness, and uniqueness of Chinese culture and civilization, as well as in as its growing stature in world affairs. Chinese nationalism, with its roots in the past, is an important issue not only in the PRC's foreign policy but also in Chinese domestic politics.[8]

The CCP also bases its claim to continue ruling China in part on having rescued the country from a century of humiliation at the hands of foreign imperialism that

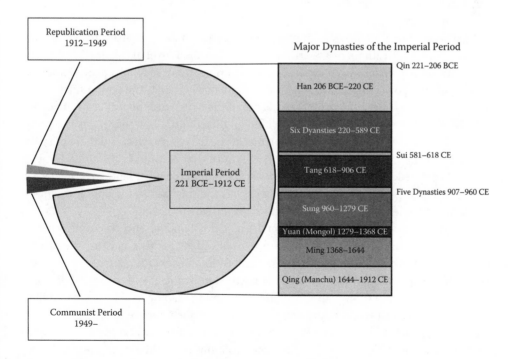

FIGURE 1.3 Major Periods in Chinese History from Imperial Times to the Present

lasted from the middle of the nineteenth century to the mid-twentieth century.[9] Beginning in the 1830s, China suffered a series of devastating military defeats and other humiliations by Western powers intent on expanding "free trade" to East Asia. Prior to this momentous encounter with Europe and America, China considered itself to be the cultural (and by extension, the political) center of its known world, able to repel or absorb any challenge to the superiority of its civilization.

The shattering of this worldview was one of the most important ingredients in the decline and collapse of China's two-thousand-year-old imperial system in the early twentieth century and the country's turn toward the revolutionary process that led to the rise of the CCP and the establishment of the People's Republic in 1949. The CCP's claim to have been the protector of China's national sovereignty from the 1950s to the present is one of the most powerful sources of its political legitimacy.

Scholars disagree on the extent to and ways in which China today is shaped by its imperial history, traditional culture, experience of imperialism, and revolutionary heritage. But none would deny that the past and the knowledge, memory, and imagination of China's long history play a prominent role in contemporary Chinese politics.

China as a Communist Party-State

In the early 1980s, about two dozen countries in Africa, Asia, Europe, and Latin America, with more than one-third of the world's population, were ruled by communist parties. Today, there are only five countries with an *unelected* ruling communist party: China, Cuba, Laos, North Korea, and Vietnam.[10] Despite many important differences, past and present communist party-states have several things in common as a unique type of political system.

First, as the term "party-state" implies, the communist party controls the state, that is, the formal institutions of government at the national level and below. The party and state are organizationally separate—for example, there may be a prime minister who heads the government and a general secretary who heads the communist party. But it is the party that is ultimately in charge of the state, and the leader of the communist party is the most powerful individual in the country. In a sense, it is the party that makes policy and the state that implements the party's policies, and there is a web of ways in which the communist party makes sure that it controls the state. For example, key state leaders, such as the prime minister and the president, are also always top communist party officials, and the party has the final say in the appointment of important state leaders at all levels of the government.

Second, the party-state proclaims, at least formally, adherence to some variant of an **ideology** based on **Marxism-Leninism** and declares that it is committed to leading the country in building **socialism** and ultimately creating a truly egalitarian communist society. This is taken to be the party-state's official and exclusive ideology in guiding policy and framing political life. Competing ideologies are considered illegitimate and even subversive, and are, therefore vigorously suppressed.

Third, the communist party sees itself as a **vanguard party** and asserts the right to exercise the leading role over society, the economy, the military, culture, and most other aspects of life because only the party, which is made up of a relatively small ideologically advanced minority of the population, is said to be able to lead the country toward socialism and **communism**. The CCP has around 90 million members, which is a little over 6 percent of the total population, or about 8 percent of the age-eligible (over age eighteen) population.

Fourth, as an extension of its exclusive ideology and leading role in society, the communist party claims to govern in the interests of all the people, and therefore holds a monopoly on political power that precludes any meaningful opposition or contestation from other political parties or organizations. The party's definition of which groups fit into the category of the "people" may shift over time—as it often has during the history of the CCP and the PRC. This is important because the people are those who support socialism and the party, while those who oppose them are labeled as "enemies of the people." One of the roles of the ruling communist party is to exercise control over these enemies through the **dictatorship of the proletariat** or, as it is called in China today, the **people's democratic dictatorship**.

Fifth, communist party-states are particularly concerned with their authority over the economy because economic growth is so critical to advancing the cause of socialism and building a strong nation. There are times when communist party politics and ideology may have a negative influence on economic growth (as during much of the Maoist era in China). And some communist party-states may greatly reduce the role of the party-state in the economy, and even introduce extensive elements of free-market **capitalism** (as in China today). But the party's claim to a leading role in determining the country's economic destiny remains a defining feature of a communist party-state.

Communist party-states have diminished greatly in number since the height of the Cold War, and those few that remain, other than North Korea, are markedly different from the kind that Stalin and Mao built. And China's political system is certainly in a time of transition (another theme of this volume), with great scholarly debate (including among scholars in China) about where it may be headed. But Chinese politics must still be described and analyzed within the communist party-state framework, as it reflects the essential structure of and distribution of power in the PRC's political system.

China as a Developing Country

Despite its astounding economic growth over the last few decades, China is still a developing country. It may have the second largest economy in the world as measured by total Gross Domestic Product (GDP),* but, by many other measures, it is much poorer and less modern than the United States, Japan, and the countries of the European Union. In 2011, China was reclassified by the World Bank from being

---

* In this book, GDP is usually given as calculated according to **purchasing power parity** (PPP), which provides a better sense of the standard of living in a particular country by comparing what goods and services actually cost locally. The other way of calculating GDP is by foreign exchange currency rates based on the U.S. dollar, and is often referred to as nominal GDP. The difference between the two can be quite dramatic, especially when presented in per capita terms. For example, China's exchange-rate-based GDP per capita in 2017 was about US$8800; calculated by PPP it was a little over US$16,800. When PPP figures are not available, GDP is given (and noted) as based on exchange rates.

a lower-middle-income country to an upper-middle-income one, a category that includes Brazil, Mexico, Russia, and South Africa, among others.[11] This was an important economic milestone, but the PRC faces many challenges in adjusting its model of growth if it is to make the more difficult transition to becoming a high-income country.[12] Table 1.1 provides an idea of China's level of development in comparison with some of the world's other large countries.

China faces many of the same challenges that other developing countries do: raising living standards and bringing better health care, education, and other social services to its citizens. It has done a quite remarkable job of lifting hundreds of millions of its citizens out of absolute poverty in recent decades, but the average standard of living is quite low and tens of millions—hundreds of millions by some measures – still are very poor. It is also facing other dilemmas of development such as glaring inequalities between the more prosperous and the poorer regions of the country, particularly between the urban and rural areas and the coastal and inland regions and also balancing economic growth and environmental concerns. The PRC very much sees itself as part of the developing world and as speaking and acting on behalf of the shared interests of the less developed countries in various international forums, such as the United Nations. Indeed, as noted later, it thinks its model of development has much to offer other countries that are struggling to overcome poverty.

But China also has some important advantages when it comes to economic development. It has had for more than forty years a variation of what political scientists refer to as a **developmental state**, that is, a government that sets its highest priority on—and effectively uses its power to promote—economic growth.[13] This is in sharp contrast with many developing countries that are classified as **predatory states,** where political power is used to further private, rather than national interests.

China certainly has a very big problem with corruption (as several chapters note). Still, the government of the PRC and the CCP have, overall, a remarkable record in promoting or at least presiding over economic growth and modernization since the early 1980s. China's other development advantages include a generally well-educated and healthy labor force and abundant natural resources, although its rapidly growing economy has generated a demand that exceeds domestic supplies of oil, coal, lumber, and other commodities, all of which are now imported in very large quantities.

There is considerable irony in the fact that the PRC has been considered as a model for Third World development at two very different times and in two very different ways since 1949. The Maoist model was much praised from the mid-1960s through the early 1970s. At that time, China was seen as a trailblazer in such areas as providing preventive health care and at least basic education to almost all its people, paying attention to rural development and limiting the "urban bias" endemic to most other developing countries, promoting gender equality, creating structures for worker participation in management, basing policy choices on a national commitment to the common good, and breaking dependency on the international economy through promoting self-reliance. This model was embraced by many—including some China scholars in the United States and elsewhere[14]—before the huge and tragic human cost and the less than stellar economic performance of the Maoist experiment became widely known beginning in late 1970s.

TABLE 1.1 China's Economic Development in Comparative Perspective

	China	United States	Russia	Brazil	India	Nigeria
World Bank Classification	Upper Middle Income	Upper Income	Upper Middle Income	Upper Middle Income	Lower Middle Income	Low Income
Total GDP (Exchange Rate)	$12.24 trillion	$19.39 trillion	$1.58 trillion	$2.06 trillion	$2.60 trillion	$375.8 billion
Total GDP (PPP)	$23.24 trillion	$19.40 trillion	$3.65 trillion	$317 trillion	$9.45 trillion	$1.08 trillion
GDP per capita (PPP)	$16,800	$59,500	$25,500	$15,500	$7,100	$5,900
Average Annual GDP Growth (2008–2017)	8.3%	1.4%	1.2%	1.6%	7.0%	4.4%
Gross Domestic Product by composition	agriculture: 8.3% industry: 39.5% services: 52.2%	agriculture: 0.9% industry: 18.9% services: 77.0%	agriculture: 4.7% industry: 32.4% services: 62.3%	agriculture: 6.2% industry: 21.0% services: 72.8%	agriculture: 15.4% industry: 23.0% services: 61.5%	agriculture: 21.6% industry: 18.3% services: 60.1%
Life expectancy at birth in years	male: 72.96 years female: 77.27 years	male: 76.19 years female: 81.17 years	male: 64.04 years female: 76.02 years	male: 69.48 years female: 76.74 years	male: 66.38 years female: 68.7 years	male: 49.35 years female: 55.77 years
Infant mortality—number of deaths per 1000 live births	male: 15.16 female: 15.25	male: 6.55 female: 5.22	male: 8.04 female: 6.29	male: 23.16 female: 16.34	male: 43.28 female: 46.08	male: 77.98 female: 67.66
Internet use per 100 people	38.3	77.9	49.0	45.0	10.1	28.8
Human Development Index* (closest to 1.0 is higher) and world ranking out of 189	.754/86	.924/13	.816/49	.759/79	.627/130	.532/157

Note: Figures are for 2016–18 or most recent year available. Sources: CIA World Factbook; World Bank World Development Indicators; United Nations Human Development Program

And now, in the early decades of the twenty-first century, China's unprecedented economic success since the 1980s has led to a lot of talk about a new Chinese model that has much to offer other Third World countries. As the PRC's current leader, Xi Jinping put it in a major speech in October 2017, China is "blazing a new trail for other developing countries to achieve modernization. It offers a new option for other countries and nations who want to speed up their development while preserving their independence; and it offers Chinese wisdom and a Chinese approach to solving the problems facing mankind."[15] That model involves a combination of a vibrant market economy with a prominent role for the government in economic policy making, investment, and control of major industries, integration into the global economy, including attracting large-scale foreign investment, and maintaining the political and social stability conducive to making this all possible. Critics point out that the PRC also has a very repressive authoritarian government and that its economic miracle has come at the cost of severe environmental degradation and a sharp rise in inequality.[16]

China as a Rising Power

There is broad scholarly, political, and public opinion consensus that the rise of China to great power status is one of the most important developments in global politics over the last two decades. China's rise is certainly well underway, as measured by its mounting global economic clout, military might, and diplomatic influence.

China's growing power is changing the terrain of international relations in both theory and practice. A new acronym, **BRICS**, which stands for Brazil, Russia, India, China, and South Africa, emerged in the early 2000s and made its way into the vocabulary of international relations to reflect the growing influence of the world's largest emerging economies. Among the BRICS countries, China is widely regarded as the showcase.[17] There is also little doubt that the PRC is now the dominant power in East Asia, having surpassed America's ally, Japan, in influence, even if Japan is a far richer country than China.

But the impact of China's rise goes far beyond the emerging economies and a shifting **regional power hierarchy** in East Asia. We are talking here of the very rare historical event of the ascendancy of a new superpower. The rise of the PRC is often compared to that of Britain in the nineteenth century and the United States in the twentieth, and it is not uncommon to hear or read that the twenty-first century will be the Chinese century.[18]

Many scholars and diplomats have noted the shift from a post–Cold War unipolar world, in which American power was unrivaled, to an emerging bipolar world in which the United States is learning to share center stage with China. Sino-American relations are considered by many knowledgeable observers to be the most important bilateral relationship in world politics today. Indeed, when leaders from the world's twenty largest economies—the Group of 20 (G-20)—met in London in early 2009 to discuss the international financial crisis, particular attention was paid to the words and actions of the "Group of Two," or "G-2"—the United States and China—as the countries most crucial to dealing with the situation. Since then, the term G-2[19] and the idea behind it that the world's most important status quo power and foremost rising power should work together to address the major issues facing the interna- tional economic system has caught on in some circles and been hotly contested by others who think that in an era of globalization, it overemphasizes the influence of any singular bilateral relationship and exaggerates the extent of cooperation possible between China and the United States because of their vastly different economic (and political) systems and levels of economic development.[20]

If there is little debate about the fact of China's rise as a world power, there is a lot of controversy among scholars, politicians, journalists, and others about what this means to the United States, East Asia, and the world. One side in this debate argues that the rise of China is threatening to American interests and a destabilizing factor in regional and international affairs. Those who are part of the "China Threat" school urge the United States and other countries to be wary of China's intentions and prepare for the worst, even war.[21] They express alarm, for example, at the PRC's vigorous development of a "blue water" navy with battleships and aircraft carriers that can sail for long periods of time far from the country's coastal waters.

The other side in this debate sees China's global ascendency as another chapter in the rise (and fall) of great powers, which has occurred throughout much of history. They understand that China's rise will create challenges for other countries, partic- ularly the United States, but they see these as an incentive for healthy competition, rather than a source of potentially disastrous military or economic conflict. They see many areas of mutual interest between the United States and the PRC and many opportunities for cooperation that could be of potential benefit to the whole world; they also emphasize China's use of **soft power**, or noncoercive influence through means such as diplomacy and foreign aid, more than its reliance on or development of the mostly military instruments of hard power.[22]

APPROACHES TO THE STUDY OF CHINESE POLITICS

Like China itself, the study of Chinese politics has gone through dramatic changes since the founding of the People's Republic in 1949.[23] Indeed, as one might expect, political changes in China have often led to changing approaches to studying Chinese politics.

The first generation of American scholars to focus on politics in the PRC were not permitted to travel to China and had little access to materials of academic interest due to Cold War hostilities. Many of these scholars spent time in Hong Kong, which was then still a British colony, conducting interviews with refugees from the China mainland and scouring valuable, yet relatively meager, collections of local Chinese newspapers and a hodgepodge of official documents held by research centers devoted to the study of contemporary China. Although most of this pioneer generation had fairly strong Chinese language skills (often honed in Taiwan), they still had to rely heavily on translations of PRC radio broadcasts provided by organizations like the Central Intelligence Agency (CIA) and the British Broadcasting Corporation (BBC) for news about what was happening in China, since very few Western reporters were permitted on the mainland.

Given the limits on research, these first-generation scholars tended to study large issues in Chinese politics. They produced numerous works that remain classics in the field, such as *Leadership in Communist China* (John Wilson Lewis, 1963), *Cadres, Bureaucracy, and Political Power in Communist China* (A. Doak Barnett, 1967), and *The Spirit of Chinese Politics* (Lucian W. Pye, 1968).

Once détente and normalization in Sino-American relations set in during the 1970s, scholarly access to China gradually opened up. Subsequent generations of specialists in Chinese politics have been able to carry out field research, work in archives, conduct surveys, interview people in all walks of life, including government and communist party officials, and engage in collaborative projects with colleagues in the PRC. There is now a literal flood of research material available from the PRC, such as books by Chinese academics, memoirs by important political figures, uncountable newspapers and journals, as well as massive amounts of data and statistics. There are still restrictions on scholarly activity (both for Chinese as well as for foreign researchers), and some subjects remain taboo because of their political sensitivity. Occasionally, a foreign scholar is accused of crossing the line between academic work and "spying" and may be detained for a while before being expelled from the country. The PRC has also banned American scholars whose work has been judged to be politically objectionable from traveling to China. In any case, the study of Chinese politics is a rich and dynamic field of scholarship that continues to attract superb graduate students, which bodes well for the future of this very important subject.

Not only have the methods and materials for studying politics in China evolved greatly over the last seven decades, but so, too, have the approaches, models, and topics that scholars employ and emphasize in their analysis. These can be broadly grouped into the following categories:

- elite politics
- factional politics
- informal politics
- bureaucratic politics
- center-local relations
- political institutions and processes
- political development
- political economy
- political culture
- ideology
- state-society relations
- policy- and event-centered studies
- comparative studies

While each of these approaches has been especially popular among scholars at certain times, all of them are still in the mix when it comes to studying Chinese politics, and most are reflected in the chapters in this book.

Elite Politics

Because so much of China's history in the twentieth century was dominated by towering political figures, it is not surprising that scholars have often focused on the country's top leaders in studying Chinese politics. Through much of the 1950s and 1960s, a so-called Mao-in-Command model of analysis reflected the extraordinary power of the Chairman of the CCP in determining the country's domestic and foreign policies. In the 1980s and 1990s, it was Deng Xiaoping who was clearly the PRC's paramount leader, even though he never held the highest formal offices in the party or the government. Deng's first two successors, Jiang Zemin (1992–2002) and Hu Jintao (2002–2012), had neither the personal clout of Mao and Deng. Current leader, Xi Jinping, who took over in 2012, has moved to consolidate power in his own hands, but even he is constrained by institutions and interests that have developed during China's decades of modernization and globalization. Nevertheless, power remains highly concentrated in the upper echelons of the CCP, particularly in the two dozen or so members of the party's top organizations. Therefore, many China specialists still take an elite-centered approach—sometimes called **Beijingology**[24]—to analyzing Chinese politics, closely studying who's who in the leadership, the formal documents issued by the central authorities, and the debates in journals containing articles by intellectuals and policy specialists who serve as advisers to party-state leaders.[25]

Factional Politics

This is really a subcategory of the elite approach to studying Chinese politics, but the emphasis is on divisions, or factions, within the ruling communist party leadership. **Factions** are groups of individuals who are united by some common bond and whose purpose is to maximize their power, especially that of their leader. Factions may be motivated by shared ideology, policy preferences, institutional interests, personal loyalties, or simply the desire for power. All political parties have factionalism to one degree or another. In the case of the CCP, high-stakes factional politics has deep roots and, during the Maoist era, led to extensive internal purges and vicious vendettas that wracked Chinese politics from the 1950s through the mid-1970s. Factionalism remains an important feature of leadership politics and policy making in the PRC, although it usually plays out in a much more routine and institutionalized manner that may cost officials their jobs, but no longer their lives, nor does it engulf their entire families.[26]

Informal Politics

Factional politics is a type of informal politics that involves power relationships outside of the constitutional institutions and processes of the state. It is not governed or regulated by formal rules or laws and is often seen as reflecting traditional, rather than modern aspects of politics. In fact, informal politics is frequently said to be a means of resistance to, or a way of overcoming the inefficiencies of, the modern state.

Political scientists have long noted the importance of various kinds of informal politics in China, especially in the form of *guanxi,* or "connections" among individuals that are, for example, based on family bonds, native place, school ties, military unit, or a network of shared friends. *Guanxi* has deep roots in Confucian culture, which places great emphasis on personal relationships.[27]

A related type of informal politics studied by China scholars is **patron–client relations**, which involve exchanges between a more powerful patron and a less powerful client. The patron may offer resources (such as land or a job) or protection to the client, while the client provides various services, including labor, personal loyalty, and political support to the patron. Patron–client relations are particularly potent in rural China, where the forces of tradition remain strong.[28] Kinship groups and folk-religion temple associations are another source of informal politics that has been identified as very influential in Chinese **villages**.[29]

Bureaucratic Politics

The bureaucratic politics model of Chinese politics seeks to explain policy outcomes by looking at the interaction of officials in different, and often competing, government agencies who are mostly motivated by their organization's interests.[30] In this sense, it might be considered a variant of the factional model, with the common bond among members being their positions in a specific part of the bureaucracy. The bureaucrats' goals may include enhancing their organization's authority, increasing its budget, or protecting its administrative turf. What's important is that individual political behavior is determined by the individual's place in the bureaucracy.

One of the first goals of the CCP when it came to power in 1949 was to rebuild the Chinese state, which had been weakened and torn apart by more than a century of rebellion, revolution, world war, and civil war. The CCP did so with quite astounding speed and effectiveness; it also created a state that had greater control over the country's vast territory and reached deeper into the most basic levels of society, particularly the rural villages, than any government in Chinese history. As discussed earlier, the kind of political system they constructed—a communist party-state on the Soviet model—is, by definition, a highly bureaucratized and centralized one that seeks to exercise authority not just over the economy but also over many or even most other areas of society. This, in turn, requires a huge and powerful bureaucracy. In such an institutional environment, bureaucratic politics can become entrenched and intense. Scholars who take this approach to studying Chinese politics also often point to the deep and lingering influence of the legacy of bureaucratic government that was one of the distinguishing features of China's imperial system.[31]

Center-Local Relations

Another approach to the analysis of Chinese politics focuses on the relations between national and local levels of the party-state. In China, "local" refers to any of the several levels of administration below the center (based in the capital, Beijing), including provinces, cities, rural **towns**, and villages. China has a long tradition of a strong central government, reaching far back into imperial times, but it also has a tradition of powerful centrifugal forces due to its historical patterns of development and regional variations. At times in its not so distant past, the country has disintegrated politically, most recently in the early twentieth century during the so-called **Warlord Era,** when real power was in the hands of more than a dozen regional strongmen rather than in the central government in Beijing. As noted earlier, the PRC is a unitary state in which the national government has ultimate authority over lower levels. Even so, ever since the founding of the country, leaders in Beijing have had to contend with recalcitrance, obstruction, opposition, and even outright resistance from subordinate authorities when it comes to the implementation of party-state policies. The **market reform** of the economy has led to a decentralization of both power and resources, and center-local relations is a timely and significant topic in the study of Chinese politics.[32] Some scholarly work focuses explicitly on local politics and provides a very valuable look at how the party-state operates at the level where most officials work and most citizens engage their political system.[33]

Political Institutions and Processes

Many studies of China by political scientists focus on specific institutions of the party-state. For example, there are studies of the CCP, of the **National People's Congress** (the PRC's legislature), and the **People's Liberation Army** (which encompasses all branches of China's military).[34] Other studies describe and analyze specific political processes, such as the **mass mobilization campaigns** that were a hallmark of the Maoist era (and have not altogether disappeared), elections for village leaders in rural China, the rise of the internet (especially blogs) as a form of political participation by netizens in the PRC, and litigation pursued by individuals who seek redress for environmental damages through the court system.[35]

A variation on these approaches to analyzing Chinese politics can be found in studies that ask questions about **state-building**, which is the construction of institutions and processes at the national and local levels designed to carry out various government functions, such as taxation or the delivery of social services.[36] This may be most crucial in the formative years of a new nation (the early 1950s for the PRC), but it is also a challenging task for a country going through a period of major transformation, as is now the case with China.

Political Development

In this context, political development refers to the process of change within a political system or the transformation from one type of system to another within a country. China has experienced particularly, and perhaps uniquely, dramatic political change over the last century. Changes that occurred before the CCP came to power are largely, but not entirely, within the purview of historians rather than political scientists.[37]

Some political development studies of the PRC analyze the evolution of the Chinese communist party-state from one form of nondemocratic regime to another. At the height of Mao's rule, China's political system approximated the totalitarian model first used to describe Nazi Germany under Hitler and the Soviet Union under Stalin. **Totalitarianism**, as the name implies, is a form of government that presumes the right of total control over almost every aspect of society and life, including thought and reproduction, and seeks to dissolve as completely as possible the autonomy of the individual.

There is a lot of scholarly debate about the totalitarian model and its applicability to Maoist China. But there is consensus that since the 1980s, the PRC has evolved towards a much less intrusive party-state, which has been variously referred to by political scientists as "revolutionary authoritarianism," "consultative authoritarianism," "soft authoritarianism," and "Market-Leninism,"[38] all of which are meant to convey that the CCP, while maintaining a very firm grip on political power has, at the same time, greatly reduced the scope of its authority, particularly in economic matters.

A relatively recent trend in the study of Chinese political development concerns the progress toward and prospects for democratization in China. This is another area in which there is vigorous academic (and political) debate that reflects divergent views about whether China is ready for democracy or even whether democracy is right for China.[39]

Political Economy

Political economy as a subfield of political science is concerned with the interaction between politics and the economy (how one influences the other), and especially with the role of the state versus the market in "governing the economy."[40] These have been matters of great importance and contention in Chinese politics since the 1950s. Mao Zedong used his near absolute power to steer the PRC forcefully in the direction of his radical vision of socialism and communism and away from both the bureaucratic Soviet model and the "capitalist road" down which he had concluded some of his closest comrades were leading the country. The results of Mao's discontent about China's economic direction were the disastrous Great Leap Forward (1958–1960) and the murderous Great Proletarian Cultural Revolution and its aftermath (1966–1976).

Since the late 1970s, Chinese leaders have remade the PRC economy into one that is almost the mirror opposite of that pursued by Mao, although still subject to the ultimate political authority of the CCP leadership and with a powerful state-controlled sector. China's spectacular economic growth is a testament to the wisdom of their policy choices (or at least their willingness to let go of the economy), but one of the major challenges they face in the early decades twenty-first century is to keep the economy growing not just for the sake of the livelihoods of the Chinese people but also because the party's political legitimacy now hinges heavily on its record of economic success.[41]

Political Culture

Political culture refers to the attitudes, values, and beliefs that people have about politics, which, in turn, shape their political behavior and how they perceive their relationship to political authority. In the case of China, scholars who have taken a political culture approach emphasize the enduring influence of Confucianism and other traditions in contemporary Chinese politics. More specifically, they stress attitudes such as deference to authority, the tendency toward an imperial style of rule on the part of government officials, a preference for an ordered hierarchy of power and a fear of disorder or chaos, the priority attached to the group rather than the individual, and an emphasis on duties over rights.

Although influential in the 1950s and 1960s as a way to understand Chinese politics, the political culture model was criticized by many scholars because of its alleged ethnocentric biases and oversimplification. Although it fell out of favor for much of two decades, it has regained adherents who apply a sophisticated and nuanced understanding of Chinese culture and history to explaining what is unique about politics in China.[42] Some China specialists draw attention to aspects of the Confucian tradition, such as reverence for education, advancement by merit, and the strength of community ties, as a partial explanation for the PRC's economic achievements as well as those of Taiwan, Hong Kong, South Korea, and Singapore.[43] This is rather ironic since in earlier times other aspects of Confucianism were given as reasons why China fell behind the West in terms of industrialization.

Ideology

Ideology can succinctly be defined as a systematic and comprehensive set of ideas and beliefs that provide a way of looking at and understanding the world or some aspect of it. A political ideology addresses such fundamental questions about power as: Who should have power? How should it be organized, distributed, and used? What are the ultimate goals for which power is used? In every political system, leaders are guided in their actions by ideology. As noted earlier, one of the defining characteristics of a communist party-state is a formal commitment to some variant of Marxism-Leninism as the country's guiding ideology. The PRC is no exception; in fact, the case could be made that ideology has been an especially important and virulent variable in Chinese politics.

Maoist campaigns such as the Great Leap Forward and the Cultural Revolution were largely driven by ideology. Post-Mao China is rightly seen as much less ideological in its politics and policy making, and the party has drastically revised what communism means in China today. But ideology still matters as the foundation of the political culture of China's leadership and their approach to governing. It also marks the formal boundaries of what is politically permissible in the PRC. Some political scientists continue to study Mao's ideology (formally called "**Mao Zedong Thought**") both because of its uniqueness as a variant of communism and because of its impact on China. Others examine communist ideology in China as it has evolved since Mao and its role in legitimizing the profound policy changes the country has experienced and the continuing rule of a communist party.[44] In fact, there are those who argue that the CCP's ideological adaptability is one of the reasons it has been able to hold on to power.[45]

State-Society Relations

Political science traditionally focused mainly on the formal institutions and agents of government—the state and state actors—as the most important units of analysis. This is still an influential approach to the study of politics in general, sometimes referred to as "bringing the state back in" or the "new institutionalism,"[46] and the state—or in the case of China, the party-state[47]—figures prominently in the work of many political scientists.

Some China scholars concentrate on relations between the party-state and various components of the society over which its exercises power. These may be classes (such as industrial workers and peasants), noneconomic groups (for example, intellectuals, artists, and youth), and groups defined by other forms of **collective identity** (including religion, ethnicity, and gender).

The key questions in this state-society approach are: What impact does state policy have on the group in question? How does the state gain compliance for those policies from members of that group? How does society respond to state demands or press its own demands on the state? Under what conditions is the state regarded as legitimate by various groups under its authority, and under what conditions is that legitimacy challenged or rejected? What forms of resistance to state power do social groups take? These have been, and remain, big questions in the study of Chinese politics. In fact, they are becoming increasingly crucial as Chinese society becomes more complex through the processes of modernization and globalization, both of which have given rise to new social groups such as private entrepreneurs and a middle class.[48] Citizen protests against the state have also become an important, if still constrained, feature of China's political landscape, which have drawn considerable attention from scholars who take a state-society approach to the study of the PRC.[49]

The concept of **civil society** is relevant here. The term is generally taken to mean the formation and operation of private organizations and associations composed of civilians who join together to pursue a common purpose *other than the direct pursuit of political power* and which operate independently of government authority. Civil society can be composed of an almost infinite variety of types of associations, ranging from trade unions to religious groups, sororities and fraternities to professional organizations (e.g., for medical doctors or political scientists), charities and nongovernmental organizations—and even, as in one famous study, bowling leagues.[50] Many political scientists see the vigor of civil society as an important indicator of the health of a democracy. On the other hand, nondemocratic regimes tend to be wary of too much autonomy for private associations lest they develop political aspirations. The Maoist party-state managed to largely obliterate civil society in China. Civil society has reemerged to a limited degree in the more open social space of contemporary China, which has led scholars to gauge (and debate) both the scope of its autonomy and its potential for planting the seeds of democratization.[51]

Policy- and Event-Centered Studies

There are numerous important works on Chinese politics that focus either on a particular policy issue or on a specific event in the history of the People's Republic. These works most often draw on one or more of the approaches or models discussed earlier for their analytical framework. For example, one study of health policy in the PRC applies the state-centered, or institutional approach,[52] while another on population policy combines the political economy and state-society relations approaches.[53] Similarly, there are works on the Great Leap Forward that stress bureaucratic politics,[54] Mao's decisive role,[55] or state-society relations.[56] Even when there are contending approaches among scholars about how to best analyze a specific policy or event, the result is most often vigorous academic debate that enhances our overall understanding of that aspect of Chinese politics.

Comparative Studies

China is exceptional in many ways, but the study of Chinese politics can be greatly enriched by making comparisons with other countries.[57] The PRC has often been compared to both the Soviet Union and post–Soviet Russia because of their shared experience as communist party-states and post–Cold War transitions.[58] Comparisons with India—as another continental-sized developing country— have also gathered considerable scholarly attention.[59] And because of their cultural connection, intertwined history, and geographical proximity, political and economic developments in China and Taiwan are frequently compared.[60] Some studies compare specific issues, institutions, and events in China with those in other countries in order to better understand the similarities and differences between the cases.[61]

The Contribution of Other Disciplines

Finally, a word should be said about the important contributions of disciplines other than political science to the study and analysis of Chinese politics. Most China scholars have had at least some interdisciplinary training and consider themselves to be area- or country-specialists as well as specialists in their specific discipline. China is literally too big, its history too long, its culture too deep, and its society (including its politics) too complex to be analyzed with a set of tools from just a single academic discipline. Most of the contributors to this volume are political scientists, but they would readily acknowledge (and many do so in their reference notes and suggested readings) how much they have learned about China from colleagues in a wide variety of fields such as history, sociology, anthropology, economics, art history, and language and literature. The other contributors (a historian, a public health specialist, a law professor, and a sociologist) would likewise recognize not only the insights they have gained from political science but from many other disciplines as well.

THE ORGANIZATION OF THE BOOK

This is a rather unusual introductory textbook about Chinese politics. There are several superb single-authored texts on this subject written by some of the leading scholars in the field.[62] The authors of the chapters in this book are China scholars who are also experts on the aspect of Chinese politics covered in that chapter.

The chapter topics are those most often taught in introductory courses on politics in China. You will note that there is not a chapter on China's foreign policy. This is, of course, a topic of great importance, particularly in light of the emphasis we have put on the rise of China as a world power. But it is usually the case that Chinese foreign policy is taught as a separate course or as part of a course on the international relations of East Asia. It is fairly ambitious for an instructor to try to cover both Chinese domestic politics and foreign policy in a single course. (Imagine trying to do that for the United States!) Several of the chapters in this book do, however, touch on aspects of China's international relations as they bear on the topic at hand.

Most chapters contain boxes that are set off from the main body of the text. These are meant to highlight and provide details about particularly important individuals, events, policies, or other topics that will enhance the reader's understanding of the main subject of the chapter. Following the main chapters of the book, there is a timeline of modern Chinese political history and a glossary of key terms. The key terms are printed in bold in their first appearance in the text.

Part I: The Political History of Modern China

The first three chapters following this introduction are analytical chronologies of Chinese history from imperial times to the present. Chapter 2, "From Empire to People's Republic" (R. Keith Schoppa), briefly discusses premodern Chinese history but focuses mostly on the period from the late eighteenth through the mid-twentieth centuries. It traces the surprisingly rapid and radical decline of—as well as the ultimately futile efforts to save—the last Chinese dynasty (the **Qing**). The author then turns his attention to the overthrow of the Qing dynasty and the imperial system in the Revolution of 1911, the founding of the Republic of China in 1912, the disintegration of the Republic in the Warlord Era of the 1920s, and the brief period of relative stability and progress under the leadership of Chiang Kai-shek and the Nationalist Party in the decade from 1927 to 1937.

This is followed by a discussion of the origins of the CCP and the rise to power within the party of Mao Zedong, the onset of civil war between the Nationalists and the Communists, which ended in 1949 with the victory of the CCP, the establishment of the People's Republic, and the flight of the Nationalists to Taiwan. In the final section of the chapter, the author offers an analysis of why the CCP won the civil war, and why the Nationalists lost—obviously very crucial questions, given the impact of the outcome of the conflict, not just on Chinese history but on world history as well.

Chapter 3, "Mao Zedong in Power (1949–1976)" (Frederick C. Teiwes) mostly covers the period during which Chairman Mao wielded nearly absolute authority in Chinese politics from the founding of the People's Republic until his death. But it also discusses in some detail the process by which Mao Zedong consolidated power in the CCP in the 1940s since that had such a strong influence on the way he exercised power after the founding of the PRC in 1949.

The early years of communist rule in China were marked by considerable successes, particularly in the areas of initial industrialization and raising health and education standards, but they also saw a tightening of the party's grip on society and the first post-1949 political fissures within the CCP's top leadership. In the latter part of the 1950s, Mao took a sharp leftward turn ideologically that had a profound effect on politics and policy in the PRC, most notably in the Great Leap Forward (1958–1960), a utopian push for accelerated economic development that plunged the country into famine and depression, and the Great Proletarian Cultural Revolution that began in 1966 and led to a terribly destructive period that combined elements of a witch hunt, a crusade, an inquisition, armed conflict, and cutthroat palace politics. The author not only describes *what* happened during this dramatic and fateful era but also *why* it happened, as well as offering a perspective on how we should evaluate the overall influence and legacy of Mao Zedong, who was surely one of the most important and complex political figures in modern times.

Chapter 4, "Deng Xiaoping and His Successors (1976 to the Present)" (Bruce Gilley), takes up the chronology of Chinese politics from the aftermath of Mao's death through the first decades of the twenty-first century. The central theme here is the political context of the phenomenal economic transformation of China during the last three-plus decades. This transformation was possible only because of the improbable political resurrection and consolidation of power by Deng Xiaoping, who became China's top leader about a year after Mao's death, despite the fact that he had been purged during the Cultural Revolution for spearheading policies that the Chairman concluded was leading the PRC away from it communist goals. Deng presided over the implementation of reforms that moved China toward a globalized **market economy**, although one with strong state involvement.

Deng's greatest crisis came in the spring of 1989 when hundreds of thousands (some estimated that the crowd peaked at over a million) of people gathered in and near **Tiananmen Square** in the center of Beijing to protest about a variety of issues, including government corruption and soaring inflation, as well as demanding greater political freedom. Deng and most of China's other key leaders decided to use massive force to end the demonstration, resulting in the so-called **Beijing Massacre** of June 4, 1989, in which a still-unknown number of civilians were killed by the Chinese army. Deng died in 1997, and his successors, Jiang Zemin (in power from 1989 to 2002), Hu Jintao (in power 2002–2012), and Xi Jinping (in power since 2012) have continued the combination of economic reform and unchallengeable communist party rule that has been the basic pattern of Chinese politics in the post-Mao era.

Part II: Ideology, Governance, Law, and Political Economy

The second part of the book consists of four chapters, which focus on broad aspects of Chinese politics important for understanding how the PRC has been and is governed.

Chapter 5, "Ideology and China's Political Development" (of which I am the author) discusses how communism (Marxism-Leninism) first came to China in the early twentieth century and its growing influence in shaping the course of the Chinese revolution. It explores how, in the 1940s, Mao Zedong's adaptation of Marxism-Leninism became the ideological orthodoxy of the CCP and the essential components of Mao Zedong Thought (as it is formally called). The chapter examines how Mao Zedong Thought influenced Chinese politics and policy during the Maoist era. There is a brief review of how Mao Zedong Thought is now officially evaluated and selectively embraced by the CCP in a country that has, in so many ways, become the obverse of what the Chairman believed should be the ideological direction of the PRC.

The chapter then turns to the topic of **Deng Xiaoping Theory**, which is said by the CCP to have been its guiding ideology in leading China into the era of market reform and opening to the world and is notable for the ideological justification it provides for introducing large elements of capitalism into a country still governed by a communist party. Both Jiang Zemin and Hu Jintao went to considerable lengths to put their personal stamps on party ideology by adapting Deng Xiaoping Theory to changing historical circumstances. In 2017, Xi Jinping's contribution to the party's ideology was elevated to be on a par with Deng's and, some argue, even with Mao's, a move that was part of a broader effort by Xi to consolidate his personal power. The chapter concludes with an exploration of contending ideologies in China today and the role of Chinese communist ideology in contemporary Chinese politics.

Chapter 6, "China's Communist Party-State: The Structure and Dynamics of Power" (Cheng Li), first provides a description of how the political system of the PRC is organized and functions in governing the country. This chapter looks at the key institutions and offices of both the CCP (the party) and the PRC (the state) and the multiple and multifaceted connections between them that ensure that the state remains under the authority of the party. It then looks at the relationship between the party and the army, which has been a matter of central concern to the CCP since it became a contender for national power in the late 1920s. Just as the PRC is a party-state, the People's Liberation Army is first and foremost a party-army whose core missions are to protect both the country and the power of the CCP.[63]

The author follows this with an analysis of several important dynamics in Chinese politics that illuminates how the political system works at the top and provides some guidance for understanding how the party-state might evolve in the near future. These include the changing composition of the membership of the CCP, the routes to power for aspiring leaders, and the growing influence of business entrepreneurs and lawyers. He then takes up the crucial issue of the balance and tension between power exercised by an individual leader and the constraints on that leader imposed by institutions of the party-state. While the trend in Chinese politics in the post-Mao era has been in the direction of institutionalization, Xi Jinping appears to have moved back in the direction of strongman rule, especially as he began his second term as party leader in 2017.

In chapter 7, "China's Legal System," the author (Jacques deLisle) provides an analysis of the role of law in China's politics and governance. He emphasizes both the notable progress toward the establishment of a modern legal system and the limitations placed by the party-state on the development of the rule of law that would protect individual liberties and act as a check on the exercise of political power. The most significant legal reform has been in the areas of economic and administrative law. The former (e.g., laws enforcing contracts) has been especially important as part of China's move toward a market economy, while the latter has provided some accountability for state institutions and officials—although the CCP is not directly subject to such laws. There have also been important reforms in criminal law, but China still has a very harsh criminal justice system in which nearly 100 percent of cases that come to trial result in convictions. Numerous offenses are subject to the death penalty and those found guilty of capital crimes are usually executed very soon after conviction if the mandatory appeal process does not succeed.

The author also discusses several "gaps" in China's legal system that provide a way of understanding the mixed record in law-related reform, such as the "implementation gap," which means that many laws are not effectively enforced, and the "interregional gap," which refers to the fact that laws are not applied consistently in different parts of the country. The chapter concludes with an assessment of the forces that are working for and against deeper legal reform in the PRC.

Economic policy making is one of the most crucial tasks of any government, and economic performance is a major standard by which citizens judge their government. It also influences nearly every other aspect of politics. Chapter 8, "China's Political Economy" (David Zweig), examines the PRC's economic development strategies set by the CCP leadership and implemented by the state machinery. Since this is one of the ways in which China has changed most dramatically in recent decades, the author provides a brief overview of the Maoist political economy that prevailed before the beginning of the reform era in the late 1970s. He then lays out the stages and strategy of economic reform begun by Deng Xiaoping, followed by a discussion of a series of issues that lie at the heart of the political economy of contemporary China such as economic reform in the rural areas, the decline of the public and growth of the private sector, the tension between market forces and the still-heavy hand of the party-state in the economy, the ambitious plan to make the PRC into a world-leading high-tech economy by 2025, the problem of corruption, and China's rapidly expanding involvement in the global economy. The chapter concludes with observations about the major economic challenges facing China's leadership under Xi Jinping.

Part III: Politics and Policy in Action

The first two chapters in Part III of the book look at Chinese politics in the geographic and demographic dimensions of rural and urban China, while the following chapters present five case studies of issues that are particularly important in the political life of the PRC.

Chapter 9, "Rural China: Reform and Resistance" (John James Kennedy) focuses on politics in the countryside, where a little more than 40 percent of the Chinese people (nearly 600 million) *technically* live—technically, that is, because as many as 250 million of those rural residents have migrated to the cities in search of better economic opportunities. The impact of such a massive population outflow on rural China is one of the topics discussed in this chapter.

The author begins by describing the administrative organization of the Chinese countryside and how that fits into the overall party-state structure of the PRC. He then pays particular attention to politics in China's villages, of which there are about 600,000. In recent decades, village governance in China has changed dramatically, with the introduction of competitive elections for leaders and the formation of **villager representative assemblies**. The chapter describes and evaluates just how democratic these trends are along with the relationship between elected village officials and the village communist party leader, who is still the most powerful person on the local level. He also discusses women in village politics, concluding that even though they are majority in many rural communities because of male outmigration, they seem to have hit a "bamboo ceiling" when it comes to their roles in local government. He then looks at the next level up in rural administration, that of the town, which has a major influence on the fifteen to twenty villages under its jurisdiction. The final major section of the chapter takes up the important issue of unrest in the Chinese countryside, which has been growing significantly as rural people take action to protest against corrupt officials, unscrupulous land grabs, polluting factories, and other matters they find harmful to their interests.

Chapter 10, "Urban China: Changes and Challenges" (William Hurst and Christian Sorace) begins by giving some historical background on the development of Chinese cities and setting the context of urban politics and policy in contemporary China. The following sections examine different types of cities in the PRC and how they are governed. The chapter then discusses the rise in the number of urban unemployed that resulted as state-owned enterprises have been shut down, streamlined, or privatized since the 1990s and the "floating population" of rural migrants, who now make up a sizable portion of the inhabitants of many Chinese cities. Together these two marginalized groups form the largest segment of the PRC's urban underclass. The authors then consider the status and political views of two groups who are among the most privileged sectors of China's urban society: the new, upwardly mobile middle class of professionals and entrepreneurs and university students. The concluding section of the chapter explores some of the most critical challenges confronting China's cities, including pollution, inequality, and the need for effective urban planning to keep pace with population growth and modernization.

The final five chapters in this part of the book are case studies of significant areas of public policy in the PRC. Chapter 11 (Richard Curt Kraus) concerns policies toward the arts and culture. Although the nature and extent of censorship has changed greatly since Mao was in power, and the arts are, in many ways, flourishing in China, culture is one of the areas of life in which the CCP still claims the right to exercise a "leading role," enforcing limits on freedom of expression if its watchdogs feel a certain and undefined ideological or political line has been crossed. In fact, Xi Jinping has reiterated that the arts should serve socialism and be under the firm leadership of the CCP.

The environmental desecration that has been a severe downside of China's economic miracle is the subject of chapter 12 (Katherine Morton and Fengshi Wu). Maltreatment of the environment is, ironically, one the things that the Maoist and reform eras in China have in common. The chapter discusses the causes and most egregious consequences of China's environmental crisis, its international implications, the government's response, and the growth of grassroots environmental activism in the PRC. The authors also assess the progress and the limitations of the reform of China's current environmental policy and the possibilities that the country will shift toward a model of **sustainable development**.

Chapter 13 on public health (Joan Kaufman) takes note of the extension of basic health care to the vast majority of the Chinese people that counts as one of the major achievements of the Maoist era. But the focus of the chapter is on trends in public health policy during the reform era, particularly the impact of marketization and privatization and recent efforts by the Xi Jinping administration to address some of the larger public health challenges of a rapidly urbanizing and aging China. The author stresses the importance of the **Severe Acute Respiratory Syndrome (SARS)** crisis in 2003 in opening the eyes of the PRC leadership to the flaws in the country's healthcare system. The chapter also looks at the evolution of China's policy toward HIV/AIDS and the government's largely commendable efforts to get on top of the epidemic by greatly improving detection and providing better treatment for those with the virus.

The issue addressed in chapter 14 (Tyrene White) is population policy in the PRC. It looks in detail at China's former **one-child policy**, which is probably among the most widely known and controversial undertakings—both at home and abroad—of the Chinese government. Among the questions that this chapter addresses are: When and why did China's leaders become so concerned about the rate of population increase in the country that they decided to implement the most restrictive and intrusive family planning policy in history? What were the components of the one-child policy, and how did it evolve over time? Why was it so effective in urban areas but not in rural areas, where it met with significant resistance? And where it was effective, did it have the positive effect on development that is claimed by Chinese leaders? Why did they decide it phase it out in 2016 and allow couples to have two children? The chapter then examines the implications of two long-term demographic consequences of the one-child policy: the unnatural gender imbalance of more males than females in certain age cohorts and the rapid "graying" of China as the over-sixty-five portion of the population has grown much faster than the youngest groups.

Chapter 15 focuses on "Internet Politics" in the PRC—an important topic that is new to this edition. As the author (Guobin Yang) observes, "The internet is one of the big China stories in the past two-plus decades." Not only has the number of internet users gone up exponentially, but the social, economic, and political impacts of this technological transition have also been profound. The chapter describes the history of the internet in China, the evolution of new forms of online association (including social media) and online activism by China's netizens (including antiregime protests and cybernationalism), and institutions and methods used by the party-state to govern and control the internet.

Part IV: Politics on China's Periphery

The final section of this book is titled "Politics on China's Periphery." This is not meant in any sense to convey that the areas or topics covered are only of peripheral, or minor, importance in understanding Chinese politics. They are, in fact, of central importance and are peripheral only in the geographic sense that they concern places that are on the periphery, or edges, of the People's Republic. Three of these areas—Tibet, Xinjiang, and Hong Kong—are formally administrative parts of the PRC, although Tibet's and Xinjiang's status as autonomous regions is quite different from that of Hong Kong as a special administrative region of the PRC. The fourth area—Taiwan—is not under the control of the PRC and acts, in many ways, as an independent country, although Beijing still insists that it is rightfully part of China.

The first two chapters (16 and 17) in this section are, respectively, on Tibet (Robert Barnett) and Xinjiang (Gardner Bovingdon). Both Tibet and Xinjiang are autonomous regions of the PRC located in the far western part of the country. As noted in the earlier discussion of geography, autonomous regions are areas, equivalent in administrative status to provinces directly under the central government, and which have a high concentration of ethnic minority population and are allowed some leeway to adopt certain national policies to their culture and customs while remaining firmly under the political and military authority of Beijing. Tibet and Xinjiang are the two largest, if sparsely populated, territorial units in the PRC, and both lie along strategically important borders; both regions have also been the site of substantial ethnic conflict and challenges to the central government. The situation in Tibet has been particularly volatile and has gained widespread international attention because of the visibility and prominence of the **Dalai Lama**, the spiritual leader of Tibetan Buddhism who has been in exile from Tibet since 1959. The majority of the population in Xinjiang is Muslim, and the largest ethnic group among them is the Uyghurs, who have very strong religious and cultural ties to the Islamic nation-states and peoples of Central Asia. There is palpable tension between Uyghurs and Han Chinese in Xinjiang, and recent incidents of unrest have led to a severe crackdown by the party-state on the Uyghur population under Xi Jinping.

Chapter 18 (Sonny Shui-Hing Lo) is about Hong Kong, which was a British colony from the mid-nineteenth century until 1997, when it was returned through negotiations to Chinese sovereignty. In contrast to Tibet and Xinjiang, Hong Kong is a densely populated but territorially tiny part of the PRC. It is also one of the world's great financial centers with a vibrant free market capitalist economy—and by far the richest part of the PRC. Hong Kong is officially a Special Administrative Region (SAR) of the PRC and has significant degrees of self-government and some important aspects of democracy. How these are exercised in practice and the tensions this creates in Hong Kong politics and with Beijing—which has the final say in matters related to the SAR—is a major theme of this chapter.

The subject of chapter 19 (Shelley Rigger) is Taiwan. The PRC claims sovereignty over this island, which is just a bit farther from the Chinese mainland than Cuba is from the United States. But, in fact, Taiwan has not been under the PRC's control since the end of the Chinese Civil War in 1949. At that time, the losing side in the conflict—the Nationalists under Chiang Kai-shek—were able to retreat to Taiwan and, with U.S. support, establish a viable political system and economy separate from the mainland. The author describes the transition that Taiwan has made since then from an authoritarian regime to a multiparty democracy with one of the highest standards of living in East Asia. After decades of hostile estrangement, Taiwan and the PRC have recently developed commercial and other ties. The future of Taiwan-China relations is a hot political topic on both the island and the mainland—and of strategic importance to the region and the United States. And, as the author emphasizes, politics in Taiwan (with a population about the same size as that of Australia) is interesting and important on its own terms.

CONCLUSION

For many decades, the observation, "Let China sleep. For when she wakes, she will shake the world," has been attributed to Napoleon Bonaparte, emperor of France, who was said to have uttered these words in the early nineteenth century when looking at a map of Europe and Asia. It is often cited as reflecting the emperor's early prescience about the rise of China as a global power. In fact, there is no record that Napoleon actually made this comment, although he is known to have wanted to learn about the Middle Kingdom both during his education as a soldier and while in exile: In 1817 he is reported to have "'asked a thousand questions respecting the Chinese, their language, customs, etc.,'"[64] of a British explorer who was on his way to China.

Even though Napoleon may never have said it, the image of China as a sleeping giant capable of making waves in the world when it wakes has caught on in both the public imagination and in print since at least the middle of the twentieth century. In 1949, a book titled *China Shakes the World* was published.[65] It was written by Jack Belden, one of the very few Western journalists allowed to cover the CCP during the war against Japan and the civil war against the Nationalists. Belden's message was that what was happening then in China—the anticipated victory of the CCP—was destined to be of global significance. But the book appeared at a time when most Americans had little interest in China, which they had given up for lost to chaos and communism. With the onset of the "Red Scare" in the United States, Belden's book gained hardly any attention and soon went out of print.[66]

In 2006, another book with the same title, *China Shakes the World*, was published.[67] But it appeared at a time of enormous international and American interest in the PRC. The author, James Kynge, was also a journalist in China, and his bottom-line message was not that much different from Belden's, which each sought to capture in the title of their books. Both Belden and Kynge were right—China *was* shaking the world—although Kynge's book, with the subtitle *A Titan's Rise and Troubled Future—and the Challenge for America*, was a much greater commercial success than Belden's; it won the *Financial Times* 2006 Business Book of the Year Award.

Whether or not China's rise can be seen as "shaking" the world, there is no doubt that what goes on in the People's Republic has a profound impact on global affairs. The editor and authors of this book hope that their contributions help readers better understand China's modern political history and contemporary politics and why these are matters that should command the attention of anyone who wants to be an informed citizen of the twenty-first century.

NOTES

1. "Overview," The World Bank in China, Apr. 19, 2018, http://www.worldbank.org/en/country/china/overview

2. See Justin Yifu Lin et al., *China's Economic Miracle: Development Strategy and Economic Reform*, rev. ed. (Hong Kong: Chinese University of Hong Kong, 2013); and Susan Shirk, "China's Economic Miracle," in *China, Fragile Superpower: How China's Internal Politics Could Derail Its Peaceful Rise* (New York: Oxford University Press, 2007), 13–33.

3. "When China Wakes," *Economist*, Nov. 28, 1992, 15.

4. "Democracy Index 2018: Me too? Political participation, protest and democracy," The Economist Intelligence Unit, http://www.eiu.com/topic/democracy-index

5. 11.3 percent of China's land is arable, compared to 16.8 percent in the United States and 52.8 percent in India.

6. See Jonathan Spence, *The Chan's Great Continent: China in Western Minds* (New York: W. W. Norton, 1998), 1–18. For an argument that Marco Polo never made it as far as China, see Frances Woods, *Did Marco Polo Go to China?* (Boulder, CO: Westview Press, 1998).

7. Elizabeth J. Perry, "Studying Chinese Politics: Farewell to Revolution?," *China Journal* 57 (Jan. 2007): 5.

8. See Howard W. French, *Everything Under the Heavens: How the Past Helps Shape China's Push for Global Power* (New York: Knopf, 2017); and Peter Hays Gries, *China's New Nationalism: Pride, Politics, and Diplomacy* (Berkeley: University of California Press, 2005).

9. See Paul A. Cohen, "Remembering and Forgetting National Humiliation in Twentieth-Century China," in Paul A. Cohen, *China Unbound: Evolving Perspectives on the Chinese Past* (New York: Routledge, 2003), 148–184.

10. In recent years, Cyprus, Nepal, and Moldova have had ruling communist parties that were *elected into* power in multiparty states. Communist party-states such as China do not permit free, multiparty elections. On Nepal's communist party, see Box 5.2, "Maoism Outside of China" in chap. 5.

11. The World Bank, Country and Lending Groups, http://data.worldbank.org/about/country-classifications/country-and-lending-groups.

12. See opening remarks by Robert B. Zoellick, World Bank Group president, at the Conference on "China's Challenges for 2030: Building a Modern, Harmonious, and Creative High-Income Society," Beijing, Sept. 3, 2011, http://www.worldbank.org/en/news/speech/2011/09/03/china-challenges-for-2030-building-modern-harmonious-creative-high-income-society.

13. See Phil Deans, "The People's Republic of China: The Post-Socialist Developmental State," in *Developmental States: Relevancy, Redundancy or Reconfiguration?*, ed. Linda Low (Hauppauge, NY: Nova Science Publishers, 2004), 133–146; and Katelyn DeNap, "China and the Developmental State Model," *US-China Business* Review, May 12, 2017, https://www.chinabusinessreview.com/china-and-the-developmental-state-model.

14. See The Committee of Concerned Asian Scholars, *China! Inside the People's Republic* (New York: Bantam Books, 1972); Michel Oksenberg, ed., *China's Developmental Experience* (New York: Academy of Political Science, Columbia University, 1973); Victor Nee and James Peck, eds., *China's Uninterrupted Revolution: From 1840 to the Present* (New York: Pantheon Books, 1975); and Ross Terrill, ed., *The China Difference* (New York: Harper Collins, 1979).

15. Xi Jinping, "Secure a Decisive Victory in Building a Moderately Prosperous Society in All Respects and Strive for the Great Success of Socialism with Chinese Characteristics for a New Era," (speech, delivered at the 19th National Congress of the Communist Party of China, Oct. 18, 2017), http://www.xinhuanet.com/english/special/2017-11/03/c_136725942.htm

16. Joshua Kurlantzick, "China's Model of Development and the 'Beijing Consensus,'" *China US Focus*, Apr. 29, 2013, https://www.chinausfocus.com/finance-economy/chinas-model-of-development-and-the-beijing-consensus

17. See Kenneth Rapoza, "Face It, China Totally Owns the BRICS," *Forbes*, Sept.1, 2017, https://www.forbes.com/sites/kenrapoza/2017/09/01/china-owns-the-brics/#642de44978f0

18. See Martin Jacques, *When China Rules the World: The End of the Western World and the Birth of a New Global Order*, 2nd ed. (New York: Penguin, 2009); and Oded Shenkar, *The Chinese Century: The Rising Chinese Economy and Its Impact on the Global Economy, the Balance of Power, and Your Job* (Philadelphia, PA: Wharton School Publishing, 2004).

19. The idea of a G-2 originated with Zbigniew Brzezinski, an international relations scholar and national security advisor to President Carter, in "The Group of Two that could change the world," *Financial Times*, Jan. 13, 2009, https://www.ft.com/content/d99369b8-e178-11dd-afa0-0000779fd2ac; see also Robert Kahn, "China and the United States: A G2 Within the G20," *Global Economics Monthly*, Council on Foreign Relations, Apr. 2016, https://cfrd8-files.cfr.org/sites/default/files/pdf/2016/04/GEM%20April%202016.pdf

20. For critiques of the G-2 concept, see Richard C. Bush, "The United States and China: A G-2 in the Making?", Brookings Institution, Oct. 11, 2011, http://www.brookings.edu/research/articles/2011/10/11-china-us-g2-bush; and Elizabeth C. Economy and Adam Segal, "The G-2 Mirage: Why the United States and China Are Not Ready to Upgrade Ties," *Foreign Affairs*, May/June 2009.

21. See Michael Pillsbury, *The Hundred-Year Marathon: China's Secret Strategy to Replace America as the Global Superpower* (New York: St. Martin's Griffin, 2016); and Peter Navarro, *The Coming China Wars: Where They Will Be Fought and How They Can Be Won* (Upper Saddle River, NJ: FT Press, 2008). For a more nuanced analysis of possible military conflict between the U.S. and the PRC, see Graham Allison, *Destined for War: Can America and China Escape Thucydides's Trap?* (Boston: Houghton Mifflin Harcourt, 2017).

22. See Thomas J. Christensen, *The China Challenge: Shaping the Choices of a Rising Power* (New York: W. W. Norton, 2016); and Edward S. Steinfeld, *Playing Our Game: Why China's Rise Doesn't Threaten the West* (New York: Oxford University Press, 2010).

23. For reviews of the evolution of the study of Chinese politics, see Sujian Guo, ed., *Political Science and Chinese Political Studies* (New York: Springer, 2012); Kenneth Lieberthal, "Reflections on the Evolution of the China Field in Political Science," in *Contemporary Chinese Politics: New Sources, Methods, and Field Strategies*, ed. Allen Carlson et al. (New York: Cambridge University Press, 2010), 266–278; Richard Baum, "Studies of Chinese Politics in the United States," in *China Watching: Perspectives from Europe, Japan and the United States*, ed. Robert Ash, David Shambaugh, and Seiichiro Takagi (New York: Taylor & Francis, 2006), 147–168; and Lowell Dittmer and William Hurst, "Analysis in Limbo: Contemporary Chinese Politics Amid the Maturation of Reform," in *China's Deep Reform: Domestic Politics in Transition*, ed. Lowell Dittmer and Guoli Liu (Lanham, MD: Rowman & Littlefield, 2006), 25–46.

24. The term "Beijingology" is an adaptation of "Kremlinology," which refers to efforts to understand politics in the Soviet Union (and, to a somewhat lesser extent, Russia today) by analyzing the words and actions of the top leaders who work in the compound of buildings in Moscow called the Kremlin. For a critique of the limits of this approach to the analysis of elite politics in contemporary China because of the lack of verifiable empirical information about what goes on in the upper reaches of power in the PRC, see Jessica Batke and Oliver Melton, "Why Do We Keep Writing About Chinese Politics As if We Know More Than We Do?", *ChinaFile*, Oct. 16, 2017, http://www.chinafile.com/reporting-opinion/viewpoint/why-do-we-keep-writing-about-chinese-politics-if-we-know-more-we-do.

25. See "China Reality Check Event: On the Road to the 19th Party Congress: Elite Politics in China Under Xi Jinping," Panel Discussion, Center for International and Strategic Studies, May 17, 2017, https://www.csis.org/events/road-19th-party-congress-elite-politics-china-under-xi-jinping; and many of the articles in *China Leadership Monitor*, Hoover Institution, Stanford University, a quarterly online journal that largely focuses on elite politics in the PRC, https://www.hoover.org/publications/china-leadership-monitor.

26. See Victor C. Shih, *Factions and Finance in China: Elite Conflict and Inflation* (New York: Cambridge University Press, 2003). The influence of leadership factions (or coalitions) on Chinese politics is a central theme of chap. 6 by Cheng Li in this volume.

27. See Lucian W. Pye, *The Dynamics of Chinese Politics* (Cambridge, MA: Oelgeschlager Gunn & Hain, 1981).

28. See Jean Oi, "Communism and Clientelism: Rural Politics in China," *World Politics* 32, no. 2 (Jan. 1985): 238–266, and her book, *State and Peasant in Contemporary Chin: The Political Economy of Village Government* (Berkeley: University of California Press, 1989).

29. See Lily L. Tsai, *Accountability without Democracy: Solidary Groups and Public Goods Provision in Rural China* (New York: Cambridge University Press, 2007).

30. See Hongyi Lai and Su-Jeong Kang, "Domestic Bureaucratic Politics and Chinese Foreign Policy," *Journal of Contemporary China* 23, no. 86 (2016): 294–313; and Kenneth G. Lieberthal and David M. Lampton, eds. *Bureaucracy, Politics, and Decision Making in Post-Mao China* (Berkeley: University of California Press, 1992).

31. See Harry Harding, *Organizing China: The Problem of Bureaucracy, 1949–1976* (Stanford, CA: Stanford University Press, 1981).

32. See John Donaldson, ed., *Assessing the Balance of Power in Central-Local Relations in China* (New York: Routledge, 2016); and Thomas P. Bernstein and Xiaobo Lü, *Taxation without Representation in Contemporary Rural China* (New York: Cambridge University Press, 2003).

33. See Juan Wang, *The Sinews of State Power: The Rise and Demise of the Cohesive Local State in Rural China* (New York: Oxford University Press, 2017); Joseph Fewsmith, *The Logic and Limits of Political Reform in China* (New York: Cambridge University Press, 2013); and Pierre Landry, *Decentralized Authoritarianism in China: The Communist Party's Control of Local Elites in the Post-Mao Era* (New York: Cambridge University Press, 2012).

34. See David L. Shambaugh, *China's Communist Party: Atrophy and Adaptation* (Berkeley: University of California Press, 2008); Kevin J. O'Brien, *Reform Without Liberalization: China's National People's Congress and the Politics of Institutional Change* (New York: Cambridge University Press, 1990); and You Ji, *China's Military Transformation* (New York: Polity, 2016).

35. See Gordon Bennett, *Yundong: Mass Campaigns in Chinese Communist Leadership* (Berkeley: Center for Chinese Studies, University of California, 1976); and Tyrene White, *China's Longest Campaign: Birth Planning in the People's Republic, 1949–2005* (Ithaca, NY: Cornell University Press, 2006); Baogang He, *Rural Democracy in China The Role of Village Elections* (New York: Palgrave Macmillan, 2007); Guobin Yang, The Power of the Internet in China: Citizen Activism Online (New York: Columbia University Press, 2009); (Stanford, CA: Stanford University Press, 2007); and Rachel E. Stern, *Environmental Litigation in China: A Study in Political Ambivalence* (New York: Cambridge University Press, 2013).

36. See Elizabeth Remick, *Building Local States: China during the Republican and Post-Mao Eras* (Cambridge, MA: Harvard University Asia Center, 2004).

37. For an example of a study by a political scientist of political development in China in the 1920s and 1930s, see Suisheng Zhao, *Power by Design: Constitution-Making in Nationalist China* (Honolulu: University of Hawaii Press, 1996).

38. Perry, "Studying Chinese Politics: Farewell to Revolution?," 5; Harry Harding, *China's Second Revolution: Reform after Mao* (Washington, DC: Brookings Institution, 1987), 200; Minxin Pei, "China's Evolution Toward Soft Authoritarianism," in *What if China Doesn't Democratize? Implications for War and Peace*, ed. Edward Friedman and Barrett L. McCormick (Armonk, NY: M. E. Sharpe, 2000), 74–95; Marc Blecher, *China against the Tides: Restructuring through Revolution, Radicalism and Reform*, 3rd ed. (New York: Continuum Books, 2009), 72.

39. See Jean-Pierre Cabestan, *China Tomorrow: Democracy or Dictatorship* (Lanham, MD: Rowman and Littlefield, 2019); Andrew J. Nathan, Larry Diamond, and Marc F. Plattner, *Will China Democratize?* (Baltimore: Johns Hopkins University Press, 2013); and Daniel Bell, *The China Model: Political Meritocracy and the Limits of Democracy.* (Princeton, NJ: Princeton University Press, 2015). Also see the debate in *Foreign Affairs* (Jan./Feb. 2013) between Eric X. Li ("The Life of the Party: The Post-Democratic Future Begins in China") and Yasheng Huang ("Democratize or Die") and TED Talks and Blogs follow-ups at: http://blog.ted.com/2013/07/01/why-democracy-still-wins-a-critique-of-eric-x-lis-a-tale-of-two-political-systems/.

40. The term comes from Peter A. Hall, *Governing the Economy: The Politics of State Intervention in Britain and France* (New York: Oxford University Press, 1986). It is also one of the four themes applied to the study of comparative politics in Mark Kesselman, Joel Krieger, and William A. Joseph, eds., *Introduction to Comparative Politics*, 6th ed. (Boston: Wadsworth/Cengage, 2012).

41. There are numerous studies by political scientists that focus on political economy issues. For a listing of some of these, see the suggested readings at the end of chap. 8 by David Zweig in this volume.

42. See Yang Zhong, *Political Culture and Participation in Urban China* (London: Palgrave MacMillan, 2018); Jeffrey N. Wasserstrom and Elizabeth Perry, eds., *Popular Protest and Political Culture in Modern China*, 2nd ed. (Boulder, CO: Westview Press, 1994). Among the most early important works that take the political culture approach to Chinese politics are those of Lucian Pye, for example, *Asian Power and Politics: The Cultural Dimensions of Authority* (Cambridge, MA: Harvard University Press, 1988). See also Peter R. Moody, "Political Culture and the Study of Chinese Politics," in *Political Science and Chinese Political Studies: The State of the Field*, ed. Sujian Guo (New York: Springer, 2013): 37–60.

43. See Ezra F. Vogel, *The Four Little Dragons: The Spread of Industrialization in East Asia* (Cambridge, MA: Harvard University Press, 1991); and Daniel A. Bell, *China's New Confucianism: Politics and Everyday Life in a Changing Society* (Princeton, NJ: Princeton University Press, 2008).

44. For a list of suggested readings on the subject of the ideology of the CCP, including Mao Zedong Thought, see chap. 5 by William A. Joseph in this volume.

45. See Heike Holbig, "Ideology after the End of Ideology: China and the Quest for Autocratic Legitimation," *Democratization* 20, no. 1 (2013): 61–81; Bruce J. Dickson, *The Dictator's Dilemma: The Chinese Communist Party's Strategy for Survival* (New York: Oxford University Press, 2016); and John W. Lewis and Xue Litai, "Social Change and Political Reform in China: Meeting the Challenge of Success," *China Quarterly* 176 (Dec. 2003): 926–942.

46. Peter B. Evans, Dietrich Rueschemeyer, and Theda Skocpol, *Bringing the State Back In* (New York: Cambridge University Press, 1985); and B. Guy Peters, *Institutional Theory in Political Science: The New Institutionalism*, 2nd ed. (New York: Continuum, 2005).

47. See Kjeld Erik Brodsgaard and Zheng Yongnian, eds., *Bringing the Party Back In: How China is Governed* (Singapore: Marshall Cavendish Academic, 2004).

48. See Fengshi Wu, ed., "Special Issue: Evolving State-Society Relations in China," *China Review* 17, no. 2 (June 2017); Tony Saich, "State-Society Relations in the People's Republic

of China Post-1949," *Brill Research Perspectives in Governance and Public Policy in China* 1, no. 1 (2016): 1–54; and Theresa Wright, *Accepting Authoritarianism: State-Society Relations in China's Reform Era* (Stanford, CA: Stanford University Press, 2010).

49. See Theresa Wright, *Popular Protest in China* (New York: Polity 2018); Yongshun Cai, *Collective Resistance in China: Why Popular Protests Succeed or Fail* (Stanford, CA: Stanford University Press, 2010); and Kevin J. O'Brien, ed., *Popular Protest in China* (Cambridge, MA: Harvard University Press, 2008).

50. Robert D. Putnam, *Bowling Alone: The Collapse and Revival of American Community* (New York: Simon & Schuster, 2000).

51. See Sara A. Newland, "Innovators and Implementers: The Multilevel Politics of Civil Society Governance in Rural China." *China Quarterly* 233, no. 22 (Mar. 2018): 22–42; Jessica Teets, *Civil Society under Authoritarianism: The China Model* (New York: Cambridge University Press, 2016); and Bin Xu, *The Politics of Compassion: The Sichuan Earthquake and Civic Engagement in China* (Stanford, CA: Stanford University Press, 2017).

52. Jane Duckett, *The Chinese State's Retreat from Health: Policy and the Politics of Retrenchment* (New York: Routledge, 2010). Another study of China's health-care system in the 1970s took the bureaucratic approach; see David M. Lampton, *Health, Conflict, and the Chinese Political System* (Ann Arbor: Michigan Papers in Chinese Studies, 1974).

53. White, *China's Longest Campaign*.

54. David Bachman, *Bureaucracy, Economy, and Leadership in China: The Institutional Origins of the Great Leap Forward* (New York: Cambridge University Press, 1991).

55. Frederick C. Teiwes and Warren Sun, *China's Road to Disaster: Mao, Central Politicians, and Provincial Leaders in the Unfolding of the Great Leap Forward 1955–1959* (Armonk, NY: East Gate Book, 1998).

56. Ralph A. Thaxton Jr., *Catastrophe and Contention in Rural China: Mao's Great Leap Forward Famine and the Origins of Righteous Resistance in Da Fo Village* (New York: Cambridge University Press, 2008).

57. For a recent call for scholars of Chinese politics to be more comparative in their approach, see William Hurst, "Treating What Ails the Study of Chinese Politics," Chinoiserie, Sept. 15, 2017, https://www.chinoiresie.info/treating-what-ails-the-study-of-chinese-politics/

58. See Minxin Pei, *From Reform to Revolution: The Demise of Communism in China and the Soviet Union* (Cambridge, MA: Harvard University Press, 1998); and Maria Repnikova, *Media Politics in China: Improvising Power under Authoritarianism* (New York: Cambridge University Press, 2017), which includes a comparative analysis of media politics China with that in the Soviet Union and contemporary Russia.

59. See Prasenjit Duara and Elizabeth J. Perry, *Beyond Regimes: China and India Compared* (Cambridge, MA: Harvard University Asia Center, 2018) and Delia Davin and Barbara Harriss-White, *China-India: Pathways of Economic and Social Development* (London: British Academy, 2014).

60. See Kristen Looney, "The Rural Developmental State: Modernization Campaigns and Peasant Politics in China, Taiwan and South Korea" (PhD Department of Government, Harvard University, 2012); and Bruce Gilley and Larry Diamond, eds., *Political Change in China: Comparisons with Taiwan* (Boulder, CO: Lynne Rienner, 2008).

61. See William Hurst, *Ruling before the Law: The Politics of Legal Regimes in China and Indonesia* (New York: Cambridge University Press, 2018); Dorothy J. Solinger, *From Lathes to Looms: China's Industrial Policy in Comparative Perspective, 1979–1982* (Stanford, CA: Stanford University Press, 1991); Dorothy J. Solinger, *States' Gains, Labor's Losses: China, France, and Mexico Choose Global Liaisons, 1980–2000* (Ithaca, NY: Cornell University Press, 2009); and Felix Wemheuer, *Famine Politics in Maoist China and the Soviet Union* (New Haven, CT: Yale University Press, 2014).

62. For example, Blecher, *China against the Tides;* Sujian Guo, *Chinese Politics and Government: Power, Ideology and Organization* (New York: Routledge, 2012); June Teufel Dreyer, *China's Political System*, 9th ed. (New York: Longman, 2014); Elizabeth Freund Larus, *Politics and Society in Contemporary China* (Boulder, CO: Lynne Rienner, 2012); Kenneth J. Lieberthal, *Governing China: From Revolution to Reform*, 2nd ed. (New York: W. W. Norton, 2003); and Tony Saich, *Governance and Politics of China*, 3rd ed. (New York: Palgrave Macmillan, 2011).

63. Ankit Panda, "M. Taylor Fravel on How the People's Liberation Army Does Military Strategy," *The Diplomat*, Jan. 30, 2019, https://thediplomat.com/2019/01/m-taylor-fravel-on-how-the-peoples-liberation-army-does-military-strategy/

64. Andrew Roberts, *Napoleon: A Life* (New York, Penguin, 2015), 791–792. An earlier biographer noted that for the young Napoleon "Anything relating to India, China, and Arabia had a particular charm for him," Thomas E. Watson, *Napoleon: A Sketch of His Life, Character, Struggles, and Achievements* (New York: Macmillan, 1907), 38.

65. Jack Belden, *China Shakes the World* (New York: Harper, 1949). The book was republished in 1970 by Monthly Review Press and in 1989 by New World Press. The other classic book from a similar time and on a similar topic is Edgar Snow, *Red Star Over China* (New York: Random House, 1938; repr. Grove Press, 1994).

66. Parts of the quote attributed to Napoleon have been used in numerous titles of books and articles about China since the 1980s; see Nicholas D. Kristof and Sheryl Wudunn, *China Wakes: The Struggle for the Soul of a Rising Power* (New York: Times Books/Random House, 1994); Yu Guangyuan, *Deng Xiaoping Shakes the World: An Eyewitness Account of China's Party Work Conference and the Third Plenum*, ed. Steven I. Levine and Ezra F. Vogel (Norwalk, CT: EastBridge, 2004); and "When China Wakes," *Economist*, Nov. 28, 1992. In 2014, Xi Jinping used the "China as a sleeping lion" quote and attributed it to Napoleon in a speech in France, "Xi Jinping Looks Ahead to a New Era in China France Relations," cited in Elizabeth Economy, *The Third Revolution: Xi Jinping and the New Chinese State*. (New York: Oxford University Press, 2018), 186.

67. James Kynge, *China Shakes the World: A Titan's Rise and Troubled Future—and the Challenge for America* (Boston, MA: Houghton Mifflin Harcourt, 2006).

SUGGESTED READINGS

China Brief, The Jamestown Foundation, https://jamestown.org/programs/cb/

China Leadership Monitor, The Hoover Institution, https://www.hoover.org/publications/china-leadership-monitor

Economy, Elizabeth. *The Third Revolution: Xi Jinping and the New Chinese State.* New York: Oxford University Press, 2018.

Fenby, Jonathan. *The Penguin History of Modern China: The Fall and Rise of a Great Power, 1850 to the Present*, 3rd ed. New York: Penguin Global, 2019.

Goodman, David S. *Handbook of the Politics of China*. Northampton, MA: Edward Elgar Publishing, 2016.

Grasso, June, Jay Cornin, and Michael Kort. *Modernization and Revolution in China: From the Opium Wars to the Olympics.* 5th ed. New York: Routledge, 2017.

Kenley, David. *Modern Chinese History*. Ann Arbor, MI: Association for Asian Studies, 2012.

Mitter, Rana. *Modern China: A Very Short Introduction*. 2nd ed. New York: Oxford University Press, 2016.

Ogden, Chris. *Handbook of China's Governance and Domestic Politics*. New York: Routledge, 2012.

Rudolph, Jennifer, and Michael Szonyi. *The China Questions: Critical Insights into a Rising Power*. Cambridge, MA: Harvard University Press, 2018.

Schell, Orville, and John Delury. *Wealth and Power: China's Long March to the Twenty-first Century*. New York: Random House, 2013.

Schoppa, R. Keith. *Revolution and Its Past: Identities and Change in Modern Chinese History*. 4th ed. New York: Routledge, 2019.

Shambaugh, David. *China's Future?* New York: Polity, 2016.

Shambaugh, David, ed. *The China Reader: Rising Power*. New York: Oxford University Press, 2016.

Shirk, Susan. *China: Fragile Superpower*. 2nd ed. New York: Oxford University Press, 2019.

Shue, Vivienne, and Patricia Thornton. *To Govern China: Evolving Practices of Power*. New York: Cambridge University Press, 2018.

Wasserstrom, Jeffrey M. *The Oxford Illustrated History of Modern China*. New York: Oxford University Press, 2016.

Wasserstrom, Jeffrey M., and Maura Elizabeth Cunningham. *China in the 21st Century: What Everyone Needs to Know*. 3rd ed. New York: Oxford University Press, 2018.

Wu, Weiping, and Chris Frazier. *The SAGE Handbook of Contemporary China*. Thousand Oaks, CA: Sage Publishing, 2018.

SUGGESTED WEBSITES

CIA World Factbook: China
https://www.cia.gov/library/publications/the-world-factbook/geos/ch.html
China Daily (PRC) National Affairs
http://www.chinadaily.com.cn/china/governmentandpolicy
China File (Asia Society)
http://www.chinafile.com/
China in the News (William A. Joseph, Wellesley College)
http://chinapoliticsnews.blogspot.com/

PART I
Political History

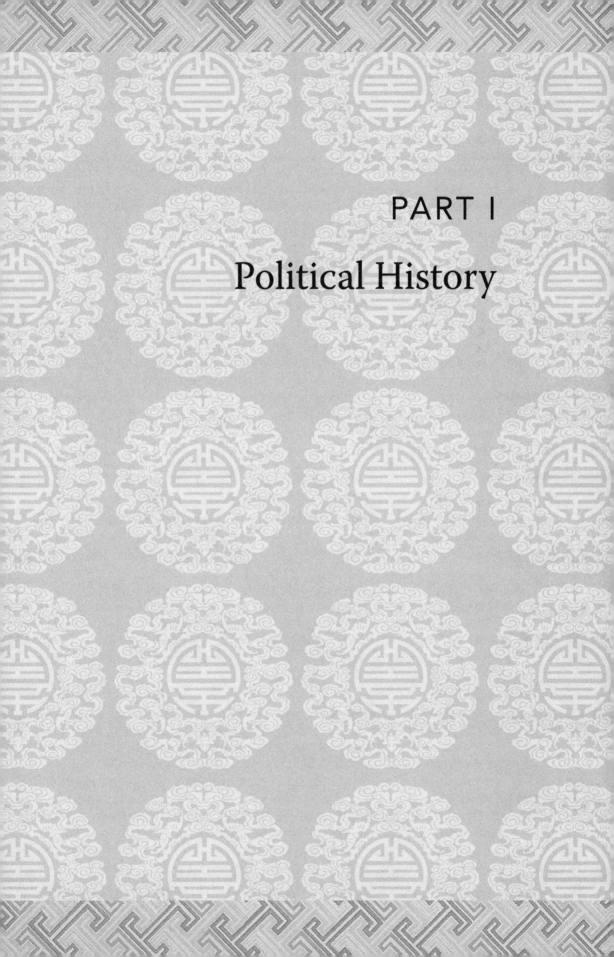

From Empire to People's Republic

R. KEITH SCHOPPA

The Chinese empire was born amid the turmoil and wars of the second century BCE. In the first two dynastic regimes, the Qin (221–206 BCE) and the Han (202 BCE–220 CE), several patterns emerged that would persist throughout the empire until it was overthrown by a revolution in 1912 and beyond. First, when the brutal leader of the Qin state, known historically as Qin Shi Huangdi (literally, "first emperor of Qin"), established a centralized empire, he momentarily put to rest the political centrifugal forces endemic in Chinese feudalism; relations between center and region and/or locality remained, however, an ongoing troublesome issue throughout the empire and the Republic (1912–1949). Tensions between center and locality continue to be problematic in early twenty-first century China in the wake of the economic reforms begun in the 1980s.

Second, while Qin Shi Huangdi tried to burn all books dealing with history, literature, or philosophy, the Han dynasty began to rally around the ideas and approach to governance of Confucius (Kong Fuzi), who had lived in the late fifth century BCE (see Box 2.1). The Han instituted a rudimentary **civil service examination system** with a strong emphasis on testing mastery of Confucianism. By the Song dynasty (960–1279), the examination had become the jewel in the crown of the imperial Chinese government. It provided political, social, ideological, and cultural unity for China's complex diversity of regional and local cultures. Those who passed the examinations became government officials and the social elite. While the Confucian-based exam was abolished in 1905, in the early twenty-first century the Chinese government established Confucius Institutes around the world to promote the learning of Chinese language and culture.

BOX 2.1 CONFUCIUS ON GOVERNMENT AND POLITICS

Confucius (551–479 BCE) was an ancient Chinese philosopher whose ideas have had an enduring impact on Chinese culture and history. Much of his philosophy is concerned with politics and government, and like other great political thinkers, such as Plato, Confucius focuses on the "good" state that he believes will be the best way for society to be organized and governed. His teachings, including the following observations on political matters, are found in *The Analects of Confucius*, which were compiled by the philosopher's disciples in the generations after his death.

2.3   The Master said: "Lead them by political maneuvers, restrain them with punishments: the people will become cunning and shameless. Lead them by virtue, restrain them with ritual: they will develop a sense of shame and a sense of participation."

12.19   Lord Ji Kang asked Confucius about government, saying, "Suppose I were to kill the bad to help the good: how about that?" Confucius replied: "You are here to govern; what need is there to kill? If you desire what is good, the people will be good. The moral power of the gentleman is the wind; the moral power of the common man is grass. Under the wind, the grass must bend."

12.11   Duke Jing of Qi asked Confucius about government. Confucius replied: "Let the lord be a lord; the subject a subject; the father a father; the son a son." The Duke said: "Excellent! If indeed the lord is not a lord, the subject not a subject, the father not a father, the son not a son, I could be sure of nothing anymore—not even of my daily food."

12.7   Zigong asked about government. The Master said: "Sufficient food, sufficient weapons, and the trust of the people." Zigong said: "If you had to do without one of these three, which would you give up?"—"Weapons."—"If you had to do without one of the remaining, which would you give up?"— "Food; after all, everyone has to die eventually. But without the trust of the people, no government can stand."

21   Someone said to Confucius: "Master, why don't you join the government?" The Master said: "In the Documents it is said: 'Only cultivate filial piety and be kind to your brothers, and you will be contributing to the body politic.' This is also a form of political action; one need not necessarily join the government."

13.13   The Master said: "If a man can steer his own life straight, the tasks of government should be no problem for him. If he cannot steer his own life straight, how could he steer other people straight?"

From *The Analects of Confucius*, translated by Simon Leys (New York: W. W. Norton, 1997), 6, 8, 56, 57, 58, and 62.

A third pattern that appeared in the late Han dynasty was the continual interaction between Han Chinese within the Great Wall (which began to be constructed in the Qin dynasty) and non-Han peoples of the steppe beyond the Wall—Mongols, Manchus, and Turkic groups, especially Uyghurs. Over the centuries, the peoples beyond the Wall, defined by their mobility in herding flocks, raided and even invaded China within the Wall, home to a more sedentary society of farmers. At times of greater Chinese strength, the Han Chinese pushed farther into steppe lands. From the late thirteenth century on, the interaction between the Han and non-Han peoples became more of an ongoing "dialogue" of power, with these outsiders ruling parts of North China from the late eleventh century, and with the Mongol Yuan dynasty (1279–1368) and Manchu Qing dynasty (1644–1912) ruling all of China. The heritage of these relationships is the early twenty-first-century Chinese government's ambivalence in its policies toward ethnic minorities.

Late imperial China reached its zenith of wealth and power during the reign of the Manchu emperor, Qianlong (1736–1795), in a period known as **High Qing**. Mid-eighteenth-century military campaigns in central Asia brought the empire six million square miles of new territory, and China made Tibet its protectorate. In the foreign policy dubbed the **tributary system** by Western scholars, countries in South, Southeast, and East Asia sent gifts and performed the **kowtow** (*ketou*—literally, "knock head") before the Chinese emperor as a symbolic ritual acknowledging the tributary states' subordinate status. Exceptional government leadership created an age of economic prosperity marked by agricultural commercialization and diversification along with the importation of crops from the New World. An indication of this remarkable time was the Qianlong emperor's four cancellations of annual taxes during his reign because the government was so fiscally wealthy. Prosperity brought greater elite wealth, new occupational opportunities, new markets and commercial relationships, and from 1749 to 1790, a 70 percent increase in population to 301 million. It is not surprising that in the late eighteenth century, the number of people fascinated with China ("Sinophiles") in Europe and the recently established United States grew, impressed with China's "enlightened despotism," meritocracy (a ruling elite based upon the examination), and material culture. Historians have recently focused on the Qing regime, not only for its rule in China but as the leader of a multiethnic empire—establishing effective rule over Turks, Tibetans, and Mongols, and other groups as well.[1]

THE DECLINE OF THE IMPERIAL STATE

Amid the glories of High Qing in the late eighteenth century were, unfortunately, many signs of decline and danger. Military campaigns and the suppression of rebellions, especially the religious-based White Lotus Rebellion (1796–1804), eroded state wealth. A weakening economy and military did not bode well for continuing successes. The emperor's patronage of He Shen, his corrupt personal favorite at the court in the 1780s and 1790s, opened the floodgates to widespread venality as the courtier parleyed his position into bureaucratic influence and great wealth. His corruption proliferated far beyond his clique to every administrative level. Like a cancer on the body politic, it metastasized into widespread corruption that robbed economic resources and undermined popular respect for the dynasty. The population surge, a sign of growing wealth, ironically posed the greatest long-term danger: the Chinese system of partible inheritance (where inheritance was divided among a family's sons) meant that land per capita shrank markedly. Poverty and bankruptcies rose. The increasingly fiscally strained government had difficulty providing charitable relief and public works for the people, two keys for insuring respect and support for the regime.

China also faced a growing threat from Western empire-building nations, propelled by the alliterative triad of merchants, missionaries, and the military. Chinese culture frowned on commerce with outsiders, seeing itself as being the "Middle Kingdom" (*zhongguo*) and "everything under Heaven" (*tianxia*) and therefore self-sufficient in all important things. But pressure from the West prompted China to allow trade at the southern city of Guangzhou under a modified tributary arrangement, where the Chinese government orchestrated the music to which Westerners danced. Westerners bought teas and silk; but because they offered nothing the Chinese wanted (such as woolen textiles for a tropical climate!), Great Britain, in particular, suffered from an unfavorable trade balance with China—until it began to smuggle in opium. Why this drug became such an addiction among the Chinese is still unclear, but the number of chests of opium smuggled into China increased exponentially in the first decades of the nineteenth century—at least as measured by the extent of drug addiction and related currency outflow and soaring inflation. When the Chinese emperor sent an imperial commissioner who used strict measures to quash the smuggling, Great Britain saw it as a cause for war.

In the **Opium War** (1839–1842) Great Britain exacted China's humiliating defeat and forced on it the **Treaty of Nanjing**, the first of many such agreements, called the **unequal treaties** because China gave all . . . yet received nothing. This war opened a century of aggression by Western nations against China, transforming the Middle Kingdom into a semicolony, subject to the demands of many foreign nations. The treaties opened trading ports along the coast and along the Yangtze River, where foreign settlements were carved into existing Chinese cities; some Chinese then came to be ruled by foreigners. These settlements installed **extraterritoriality** with consular jurisdiction under which an accused foreigner would be tried for a crime in a Western, not a Chinese, court. Although Chinese who worked with or were converted by Westerners were not covered by extraterritoriality, Westerners, because of their special legal status, often tried to use their power to protect their Chinese business agents (compradors) or their religious converts. In addition, China lost its right to control and collect its own tariffs. It could not regulate foreign ships' entries into inland waterways, the loss of an important right for any sovereign nation. China's tributary system was nullified: ambassadors of foreign states could now reside permanently in Beijing.

The open propagation of Christianity was guaranteed by the unequal treaties. This meant that missionaries could go anywhere, could purchase property for churches and schools, and could proselytize at will. Though the impact of late Qing missionaries was complex, on the whole it was an unhappy one. The political landscape was studded with episodes of violence sparked by the actions of culturally arrogant missionaries who believed they alone had the "Truth"; at core, these episodes were spawned by the cultural imperialism of the missionaries and the tenacious cultural chauvinism of the Chinese.

The nineteenth century was also ravaged by domestic rebellion. The **Taiping Rebellion** (1851–1864), the largest uprising in world history, devastated much of East Central and South China, reached militarily into most provinces, and killed an estimated twenty million people. Incubated in an area marked by ethnic rivalry, unemployment, and poverty, and forged into a utopian crusade based on a bastardized

Christianity, the rebellion (turned would-be dynasty) was a major threat to traditional Chinese culture. It promised to dethrone Confucianism and the family as cultural hallmarks, raise the status of women, institute primitive economic communism, and replace social hierarchy with equality (see Box 2.2). Though many elements caused its demise, including its poor administration, its inability to fulfill its promises to the people, and a leadership that politically cannibalized itself, its coup de grâce came from Beijing-authorized provincial armies that were formed and led by Han Chinese officials who were concerned about the rebellion's cultural threat. The rebellion's destruction is almost unfathomable; in the populous and prosperous Jiangnan (the Lower Yangtze) region, the population, which stood at sixty-seven million in 1843, plummeted to forty-five million half a century later.

BOX 2.2 THE TAIPING PLAN FOR REORGANIZING CHINESE SOCIETY FROM LAND SYSTEM OF THE HEAVENLY DYNASTY (1853)

The division of land must be according to the number of individuals, whether male or female; calculating upon the number of individuals in a household, if they be numerous, then the amount of land will be larger, and, if few, smaller. . . . All the fields in the empire are to be cultivated by all the people alike. If the land is deficient in one place, then the people must be removed to another. . . . Thus, all the people in the empire may together enjoy the abundant happiness of the Heavenly Father, Supreme Lord, and Great God. There being fields, let all cultivate them; there being food, let all eat; there being money, let us all use it so that nowhere does inequality exist, and no man in not well fed and clothed.

All men and women, every individual of sixteen years and upwards, shall receive land, twice as much as those of fifteen years of age and under. . . . Throughout the empire the mulberry tree is to be planted close to every wall, so that all women may engage in rearing silkworms, spinning the silk, and making garments. Throughout the empire every family should keep five hens and two sows. . . . At the time of harvest every sergeant shall direct the corporals to see to it that of the twenty-five families under his charge each individual has a sufficient supply of food, and, aside from the new grain each may receive, the remainder must be deposited in the public granary . . . for the whole empire is the universal family of our Heavenly Father.

[T]he sergeant must keep an account of money and grain figures in a record book. . . . For every twenty-five families there must be established one public granary and one church where the sergeant must reside. Whenever there are marriages, or births, or funerals, all may go to the public granary; but a limit must be observed, and not a cash be used beyond what is necessary. Thus, every family which celebrates a marriage or a birth will be given one thousand cash and a hundred catties of grain. This one rule is applicable throughout the empire. In the use of all things, let there be economy, to provide against war and famine. . . . In every circle of twenty-five families, all young boys must go to church every day, where the sergeant is to teach them to read the Old Testament and the New Testament, as well as the book of proclamations of the true ordained Sovereign. Every Sabbath the corporals must lead the men and women to the church, where the males and females are to sit in separate rows. There they will listen to sermons, sing praises, and offer sacrifices to our Heavenly Father, the Supreme Lord and Great God.

From J. Mason Gentzler, *Changing China: Readings in the History of China from the Opium War to the Present* (New York: Praeger, 1977), 54–58.

The decades of the 1850s into the 1870s saw other areas raked by rebellions as well. The first phase of the Robin Hood–like Nian rebellion in North China (1853–1868) was primarily extended **guerrilla warfare**. Chinese scholar-officials again dealt successfully with the rebels' challenges, copying the rebels' own strategy of employing scorched-earth tactics while building fortified settlements to keep rebels away from the masses. The rebellion's second phase was mostly a struggle between cavalries that ranged across the North China plain; Han officials suppressed it as well.

Two Muslim rebellions in Southwest (1855–1873) and Northwest China (1862–1873) had different dynamics. In the southwest's Yunnan province, the key struggle (the Panthay rebellion) was between the interloping ethnic Han Chinese, who moved in to seize the mines, and the Chinese Muslims (called Hui), who had for many years controlled mining in the province. Massacre followed by countermassacre marked the bloody affair; siege warfare ended in the murders of all caught inside city walls. Unlike the Taiping and the Nian, the Qing regime used their own military forces, not those under the leadership of Han civilian officials. The dynamic of the rebellion in the northwest, in contrast, was more religious/ideological, with the leaders of a new sect charting the way. Like the Panthay, this rebellion featured vicious and brutal siege warfare. Another Han scholar-official led in quelling the movement in a bloody five-year campaign.

TO SAVE AN EMPIRE

One impact of these devastating foreign and domestic crises facing the Qing dynasty in the mid-nineteenth century was the financial exhaustion of the government. Already by 1850—after the Opium War but before any of the rebellions—the Qing government was taking in only about 10 percent of what it was spending. It followed that the reconstruction work after the rebellions—such as rebuilding bridges, fixing irrigation works, and reclaiming devastated farmland—could not be undertaken by the central government, but that local elites had to take over any reconstruction if it was going to occur in their areas. In other words, the crises that were wracking the Chinese state, in the end, had to be solved by Han leaders of Chinese society rather than the Manchu-led central state. Or, seen another way, the center was losing power to the provinces and localities; it was the old center-locality tension that events brought once again to the fore.

Leaders of the so-called **Self-Strengthening Movement** argued that Western technology (particularly armaments and ships) should be used to protect Chinese traditions. Under the slogan, "Western learning for its use, Chinese Learning for its essence," they argued that Western technology would serve as the techniques ("means") by which Chinese traditions ("ends") could be protected and preserved. What they did not seem to understand is that ultimately the "means" always affect the "ends." While self-strengthening involved a multipronged effort in the spheres of diplomacy, education, and technology, advances in military technology were usually taken as a measure of successful self-strengthening, for they were most clearly related to defense. In this regard, the main fruits of the self-strengtheners' labor were an arsenal built near Shanghai and a shipyard at Fuzhou, one of the first five treaty ports established by the Treaty of Nanjing. These institutions were established by the same Han scholar-officials who had quelled most of the rebellions. Although self-strengtheners did not call for major institutional change in the imperial government, they did establish the *Zongli Yamen* (Office for General Management), a kind of foreign ministry, to oversee many diplomatic, educational, and technological efforts.

The self-strengtheners continually had to fight those conservatives in the imperial court who argued that contact with the West was contaminating, and that Chinese traditions must be revivified; for the most part, these were men who were overwhelmed by fears of change and what that change would portend for the traditional Chinese world and their own lives.

Even as Chinese debated their proper actions, foreign threats and crises did not abate. In the twenty-one years from 1874 to 1895, China lost control of the Ryukyu Islands (Liuqiu in Chinese), Vietnam, and Korea, its three most important tributary states, that is, states that most frequently dispatched missions to the Middle Kingdom. Aggressive actions by Japan in the first and third instances and by France in the second pointed to a new wave of imperialism in the closing quarter of the nineteenth century. The losses of Vietnam to France (1883–1885) and of Korea to Japan (1894–1895) had significant national security implications.

It was the **Sino-Japanese War** (1894–1895) that was most shocking to the Chinese: the huge land empire of China had been militarily humiliated by the Japanese, a people whom the Chinese had denigrated as "dwarf bandits." In the war with Japan, China lost the island of Taiwan and, if three European countries had not stepped in, the Liaodong Peninsula in southern Manchuria would have been lost as well. In 1897 and 1898, in an even more ominous development, Western nations demanded the right to "lease" areas of China for from twenty-five to ninety-nine years. Russia, Great Britain, France, and other Western powers queued up to "carve up the Chinese melon" by establishing spheres of influence where they could extract mineral resources, build and operate rail lines, and engage in many other kinds of profitable activity.

During this crucial period, the most powerful leader in China was the Empress Dowager Cixi, the widow of the Xianfeng emperor (r. 1850–1861), who had ruled as regent for child emperors from 1861 to 1891, and after that as a meddler in the rule of her nephew, the Guangxu emperor. Cixi was, for the most part, a strong backer of conservative political forces in the imperial government.

In the contexts of the defeat by Japan and the leasehold mania, a movement to reform state institutions emerged full-blown in the summer of 1898 after brewing for three years in the provinces. The rationale for this change was set down by the scholar-official Kang Youwei, who reinterpreted classical Confucian texts in a quite revolutionary way—all with a view of supporting radical institutional change. Gaining support from the Guangxu emperor, Kang provided the policy agenda; in the summer of 1898, in what is known as the **Hundred Days Reform**, the emperor issued more than a hundred decrees calling for institutional innovations in many arenas. These included revamping the examination system and establishing a national school system; restructuring the government and abolishing sinecure posts; modernizing the police, military, and postal systems; and setting up new institutions to promote agriculture, commerce, and industry (see Box 2.3). However, the reforms thoroughly threatened the political establishment and the power of the empress dowager. Cixi therefore

BOX 2.3 MEMORIAL FROM KANG YOUWEI TO THE GUANGXU EMPEROR ON REFORM (1898)

A survey of all states in the world will show that those states which undertook reforms become strong while those states which cling to the past perished. The consequences of clinging to the past and the effects of opening up new ways are thus obvious. If Your Majesty, with your discerning brilliance, observes the trends in other countries, you will see that if we can change, we can preserve ourselves; but if we cannot change, we shall perish. Indeed, if we can make a complete change, we shall become strong, but if we make only limited changes, we shall still perish. If Your Majesty and his ministers investigate the source of the disease, you will know that this is the right prescription.

Our present trouble lies in our clinging to old institutions without knowing how to change. In an age of competition between states, to put into effect methods appropriate to an era of universal unification and laissez-faire is like wearing heavy furs in summer or riding a high carriage across a river. This can only result in having a fever or getting oneself drowned.

It is a principle of things that the new is strong but the old weak; that new things are fresh but old things rotten; that new things are active but old things static. If the institutions are old, defects will develop. Therefore there are no institutions that should remain unchanged for a hundred years. Moreover, our present institutions are but unworthy vestiges of the Han, Tang, Yuan, and Ming dynasties; they are not even the institutions of the [Manchu] ancestors. . . . In fact, they are the products of the fancy writing and corrupt dealing of the petty officials rather than the original ideas of the ancestors. Furthermore, institutions are for the purpose of preserving one's territories. Now that the ancestral territory cannot be preserved, what good is it to maintain the ancestral institutions?

Nowadays the court has been undertaking some reforms, but the action of the emperor is obstructed by the ministers, and the recommendations of the able scholars are attacked by old-fashioned bureaucrats. . . . Rumors and scandals are rampant, and people fight each other like fire and water. A reform in this way is as ineffective as attempting a forward march by walking backward. . . . Your Majesty knows that under the present circumstances reforms are imperative and old institutions must be abolished . . . . . . As to the republican governments of the United States and France and the constitutional governments of Britain and Germany, these countries are far away and their customs are different from ours. . . . Consequently I beg Your Majesty to adopt the purpose of Peter the Great of Russia as our purpose and to take the Meiji Reform of Japan as the model of our reform. The time and place of Japan's reform are not remote and her religion and customs are somewhat similar to ours. Her success is manifest; her example can easily be followed.

From J. Mason Gentzler, *Changing China: Readings in the History of China from the Opium War to the Present* (New York: Praeger, 1977), 86–87.

opposed them and staged a coup d'état, putting the emperor under house arrest and executing those reformers who did not flee Beijing in time.

Despite this failure, the reforms and their ideological base were important in China's political development. Kang's call for institutions undergirded by and infused with Western ideas began to stimulate, as nothing had before, an interest in Western things beyond guns and ships. It might be said that Kang's work began to prime the pump of greater change. Perhaps more significant, Kang's reinterpretation of Confucianism was crucial in bringing China into the modern world, in effect, undercutting Confucianism itself. Before, Confucianism had been *the* Way, an unquestioned article of faith, but Kang had turned it into an ideology among other ideologies. When Confucianism became simply an ideology, it could, for example, be seen as a tool legitimizing the elevation of certain groups (fathers, husbands, parents, elder brothers, males in general) and demeaning others (sons, wives, women in general, all children, younger brothers). Thus, though it was an unintended consequence, Kang's work was the first step in dethroning Confucianism as the unchallenged basis of Chinese culture. It was also an important precursor to the "New Policies" adopted by the Qing regime in the first decade of the twentieth century in a last-ditch effort to save the dynasty.

But sadly the Qing did not move toward reform until they were pounded by one more wretched and seemingly quite insane episode. The decline of the traditional state was punctuated at century's end by the tragic **Boxer Uprising** (1898–1900) in North China. These rebels were called Boxers because of their martial arts rituals, which allegedly brought them invulnerability. The Boxers, mostly peasant young men and women, particularly targeted Chinese Christian converts and foreign missionaries. They attacked the converts (because of the special privileges that they often enjoyed) and the missionaries (because they refused to allow converts to participate in traditional Chinese festivals and offended Chinese customs and beliefs in other ways). Alarmed Western nations pressed Cixi to suppress the Boxers and made plans to intervene. Instead, at this time of political, cultural, and international crisis, the Empress Dowager became an active ally of the Boxers: "China is weak," she allegedly said, "the only thing we can depend upon is the hearts of the people."[2]

In the end, Western and Japanese forces marched on Beijing to suppress the Boxers, and the Chinese government, in what seems an episode from the theater of the absurd, declared war on all eight nations (Germany, Russia, France, Japan, the United States, the United Kingdom, Italy, and Austria-Hungary). In the face of the Western offensive, most Boxers simply disappeared into the northern Chinese countryside, while Cixi fled to the western city of Xi'an. The foreign powers forced the Qing court to sign a peace treaty called the **Boxer Protocol** in September 1901. Of all the Protocol's humiliating provisions, the most disastrous for China was a staggering indemnity to pay the cost of the war for the foreign powers, which proved a crushing burden to the imperial government's already crippled economy.

THE 1911 REVOLUTION

The last decade of Manchu rule in China ended with a tidal wave of reformist and revolutionary activity, the degree and rate of which varied from place to place throughout much of the country. The decade was marked by a surge of urban nationalism, driven by fears of national dismemberment by the British in Tibet, the Russians in Mongolia, and the French in parts of Southwest China. Chinese in various provinces rose together to try to recover "rights" taken by the imperialists through the unequal treaties and other means, especially their ownership and control of railroads. Newspapers and magazines that focused on current developments proliferated. Cities were being paved, lighted, and better policed. With these changes came the spiraling of wide-ranging reformist efforts to deal with social ills—opium smoking, gambling, and foot binding. Once subordinated social groups, especially women and the youth, began to emerge as social and political players. Chinese living overseas, still motivated by native place loyalties, played an increasingly active role in China's developments, sending money for specific reformist and revolutionary goals and investing in China's cities.

In this context, the Empress Dowager moved to make major reforms. In August 1905, after an unsuccessful attempt to create a dual educational structure that combined modern schools with the traditional examination system, she ordered the outright abolition of the civil service examination—arguably the single most revolutionary act of twentieth-century China. The exam system had been the chief conveyor of traditional Confucian orthodoxy and the recruiting source for political and social elites for millennia. With the examination system gone, there was no way to promulgate an official ideology. Indeed, there was now no ideology of state in China. Furthermore, the source for the recruitment of officials and political and social elites in general was a giant question mark. There was now simply no way to stop the tides of change. Military reforms led to the founding of a modern army, the New Army, organized by the longtime official Yuan Shikai, with academies producing well-trained cadets inculcated with patriotic ideas. The government departments, called Boards, in place since the Tang dynasty, were transformed into modern ministries.

Perhaps the most surprising change was Cixi's championing of a constitutional government in 1908. Chinese leaders had interpreted the victory of Japan over Czarist Russia in the Russo-Japanese War (1904–1905) not only as the first victory of an Asian nation over a European nation but also as the victory of a constitutional power over an authoritarian monarchy. In 1906, the Qing court sent missions abroad to study constitutional systems in Japan, Europe, and the United States. For the court, Japan's constitutional monarchy seemed a relevant and advantageous system for China to emulate. For one thing, it would shore up the Qing regime as it structured a more "modern" political system. While the system would set up representative bodies in the provinces and localities, where elites would presumably flex their political muscles, such a system also potentially provided a vehicle for the Qing court to regain some of the political power that had devolved to provinces and localities in the late-nineteenth-century postrebellion reconstruction.

In August 1908, Cixi announced a projected constitutional calendar, which would be fully realized by 1917. Representative bodies at township, county, and provincial levels began to be formed from 1909 to 1913. These bodies provided forums in which to debate, demand, and legislate. Had Cixi lived, she might have been able to lead China into that new system, but she died in November 1908, a day after the death of the thirty-seven-year-old Guangxu emperor, who died without an heir. She had arranged for a three-year-old member of the royal family to succeed Guangxu. The regents of the child emperor seemed incapable of dealing with what became obstreperous provincial and national assembly elites and whose own foot-dragging on the pace of reform antagonized many Han Chinese.

Japan was not just the model for China's developing constitutionalism, but the rapidly modernizing nation was also a school for young Chinese intellectuals. China began sending students to Japan in the late 1890s, with numbers soaring from two hundred in 1899 to thirteen thousand in 1906. Students formed politically oriented associations, many of them based on provincial native places. Seeing Japan's developing modernity and its role as a growing world power in the context of China's weakness, these students asked what was wrong with China. The answer more and more frequently was "the Manchus," the ethnic group that had controlled China for more than two and a half centuries. Among these students, strong anti-Manchu feelings developed. In 1905, Sun Yat-sen (Sun Zhongshan in *pinyin*), a medical doctor turned full-time revolutionary who had spent part of his youth in Hawai'i, established the Revolutionary Alliance in Tokyo. It called for overthrowing the Manchus and establishing a republic. Other revolutionary organizations sprang up as well.

Motivated by anti-Manchu nationalism and a deep sense of things gone terribly wrong for the country, revolutionaries rose up in October 1911 in a series of largely unplanned and uncoordinated actions that culminated in the **1911 Revolution.** These revolutionaries were not closely associated with Sun—indeed, he was fund-raising in Denver, Colorado, at the time. Fighting soon raged between the Qing and revolutionary forces. Yuan Shikai, the founder of the New Army, emerged as the political broker in the struggle. An assertive and powerful dynastic official and a Han Chinese who had faithfully served the Manchu Qing dynasty, Yuan had had no experience with and had not even announced support for republicanism in China, but a political deal committed the presidency of the new Republic to him if he engineered the Qing abdication. Part of the reason that Sun and other revolutionary leaders acquiesced to Yuan was the widespread fear that continued fighting might tempt some imperialist powers to make hay out of the unrest for their own advantage.

The reality was that the signs of ever more threatening imperialism were everywhere. Two examples suggest the range of imperialist tentacles at that point in the early twentieth century. First, in the month the revolution erupted, the Chinese government defaulted on its Boxer indemnity payments. The British Foreign Office, meeting with representatives from the Hong Kong and Shanghai Banking Corporation, agreed that in order to secure their loans, they would have to take control of crucial institutions in the Chinese government. The second example shows Western treaty "rights" in China as supreme: because an earlier agreement had declared that China could not interfere in the soybean trade, one provincial governor could not stop the export of soybeans from his province, even at a time when people were dying from famine.

The Qing dynasty abdicated on February 12, 1912, and was replaced by the Republic of China. White flags were flown as a sign that Han Chinese rule had been restored in the overthrow of the ethnic outsiders. But it was more than a "restoration." Despite the lack of major social and economic change in its aftermath, this *was* a revolution—for when the revolutionaries overthrew the Manchus, they also destroyed the imperial system that had existed since 221 BCE.

POSTMORTEM: WHY THE EMPIRE FELL

There was nothing inevitable about the demise of the Chinese empire. Along the way, people, parties, governments, and nations made countless existential choices and decisions about the direction they wanted to travel; if other choices had been made, the destination might well have been different.

If the Qing regime had been able to position itself fully in the vanguard of progressive change (as indeed it tried to do in the first decade of the twentieth century), the 1911 Revolution might not have been the outcome that it was. The Qing dynasty (and with it, the empire) fell for several crucial reasons. Important was a mind-set in late imperial society and politics that revered and valued the power of traditional cultural tenets and processes. Specifically, this meant a strong sense that what had made Chinese civilization great must not be forsaken, diminished, or tampered with. Doing so, in essence, would have been nothing less than forsaking, diminishing, and tampering with what it meant to be Chinese. The most fundamental issue, then, was protecting Chinese political, social, and cultural identity when various threats were seen as challenging it. Change in any basic form could only be adopted if roots for it could be found in the past. Thus, although the two late Qing reform efforts—self-strengthening and institutional reform in the 1890s—found different kinds of roots on which to base their programs for change, they were both constrained by their interpretations of Chinese civilization and culture.

In this sense, "reform" was not nearly as viable an option as it was in Japan. While the Japanese emperor, as the direct descendant of the Sun Goddess, reigned, he did not rule in day-to-day affairs. That job since the late twelfth century had been taken by the *shogun*, the chief political and military leader of the country. This duality of leadership provided the relatively smooth transition to reform in the Meiji Restoration in 1868. Once the shogun's policies were seen to be leading Japan into dangerous straits, especially in his ineffective response to the Western threat, it was logical that those interested in change would look to the divine emperor as the foremost embodiment of the Japanese Way. When the Meiji reformers "restored" the emperor to his rightful place and ended the shogunate, they could advance the government toward reform in the very name of restoring the past. Because its emperor was truly the source of ultimate power, China had no such "simple" choice and thus had to go through mental and spiritual agonies when entertaining any change from traditions of the past.

In the first decade of the twentieth century, the Manchus themselves began to move away from the traditional frameworks and ways, but they too were saddled with questions of their own identity. They could not deal effectively with Han Chinese challenges to their ethnicity. In the end, attacks on the Manchus became part of the arsenal of those who wanted to destroy the imperial institution and establish a republic.

Apart from the Chinese view of its central and special place in the world, there were historical and existential realities that prevented the Chinese from responding aggressively to new challenges. In the late nineteenth century, the central bureaucratic state structure was still based on a Tang dynasty (618–907 CE) model. A bureaucracy is often weighted down with realities of inefficiency, waste, and delay; and the Chinese bureaucratic model was no exception: communications and decision-making could move at a snail's pace. Almost ironically, however, another reason for systemic inertia was that the Chinese government was minimalist in both scale and function. Scholars have shown that the number of county magistrates, known as "father-mother officials" for their importance in ruling and for setting the tone of governance at the lowest level of imperial administration, remained almost completely the same over time from the eighteenth century until the twentieth century despite huge increases in the population.[3] In 1700, there were 1,261 counties and magistrates; in the late nineteenth century, 1,303. The population in 1700 was about 150 million, while in 1900, it was about 420 million. Thus, the average number of people that a magistrate served in each county was about 119,000 in 1700, but was more than 320,000 in 1900. By contrast in China in the early twenty-first century there are county officials for about every 2,000 people. In other words, even had the central government been able to initiate programs of change, the local government structures would have made it unlikely that they could be undertaken effectively.

But such programs would not have been possible in any event because the Qing government was bankrupt. Already in the 1850s, it was not taking in enough revenue to make ends meet. The reconstruction costs for the calamitous rebellions that raked over most areas of China in the mid-nineteenth century and the costly challenges of Western and then Japanese imperialism in a series of wars would have required immense economic reserves and a government capable of using them. But the empty coffers of the central government tied the hands of policy makers. For this reason, from at least the 1860s on, Beijing had to rely on provincial and local governments to be the agents of reconstruction, a reality that saw more and more power devolving to elites in provinces and localities. In the end, the coming together of all these factors made more and more likely the collapse of the imperial order and a revolution to replace it with a republic.

THE EARLY REPUBLIC

The Republic of China got off to a rousing democratic start in the winter of 1912–1913 with elections to the National Assembly. Sun Yat-sen turned his Revolutionary Alliance into a political party, the **Kuomintang (KMT)**[4] or Nationalist Party, to vie with a number of other hopeful parties. Although there were gender, age, educational, and economic qualifications for voting and serving in office, the elections went remarkably smoothly, given no history of electoral government in China's past. They were ironically the high point of electoral democracy in the twentieth and twenty-first centuries on the Chinese mainland and in Taiwan until the 1980s. The Nationalists won about 43 percent of the vote, a plurality among the multiple parties: with 269 of the 596 House of Representative seats and 123 of the 274 Senate seats, they would control 45 percent of the seats in each house. The Nationalist Party leader Song Jiaoren, believed to be headed to the prime ministership under President Yuan Shikai, planned to leave for Beijing from Shanghai in March 1913, but he was shot dead at the Shanghai train station. Who ordered his assassination has never been finally determined, though much of the evidence points to people associated with Yuan.[5]

Conferring the presidency of the republic on Yuan Shikai turned out to have been a huge mistake. Yuan was indeed concerned with modernizing the Chinese state, but he thought that a republican government was too unwieldy to produce focused modernization. Yuan targeted the republic as a system and its components for destruction. Song was simply the first hit.

After republican revolutionaries rebelled against Yuan in the summer of 1913 because of his other high-handed actions, the president did not slow down in his efforts to dismantle the republic. In November 1913, he outlawed the Nationalist

Party. In February 1914, he abolished the representative assemblies established in the last decade of Qing rule—at all levels, from county to province to nation. Then he announced his plan to become "Grand Constitutional Emperor" and thus reinstate the monarchy and take the throne. In late 1915 a rebellion blazed up out of Southwest China to move against the would-be emperor. Yuan died suddenly in June 1916 of natural causes before he could found a new dynasty, but his death plunged the young Republic into political chaos.

THE AGONY OF WARLORDISM

As long as Yuan Shikai was alive, he was able to control the generals who had been trained under his command in the New Army. With his death, the destructive genie of military struggle was unloosed; the struggle among these provincially-based generals, now referred to as "warlords," produced one of the most disastrous and chaotic periods in modern Chinese history.

The goal of each warlord was to take control of Beijing and its government institutions in order to be recognized as president of the Republic. Governmental institutions in the 1920s became pawns in the warlords' struggles. The concerns of civilian politicians and bureaucrats focused increasingly on keeping their positions and maintaining their own political power, frequently cultivating connections with warlords. In this context, corruption tended to become a crucial dynamic and often decided policies and elections. The most famous case was that of Cao Kun, who won the presidency in 1923 by bribing national assemblymen with 5,000 silver dollars each to vote for him. In the decade from 1916 to 1926, referred to as the **Warlord Era**, the Republic of China had six different presidents and twenty-five cabinets. The high hopes of 1912 and early 1913 lay in shambles: the hopes of establishing a republican ethos—carrying the voice of the people into the institutions of government—were aborted.

Instead, it was the ethos of the military and militarization that carried the day. There was a wide spectrum of warlord types. Some probably had the abilities, character, and potential to lead the Chinese nation. Wu Peifu, for example, had a traditional civil service degree, was a graduate of the Baoding Military Academy, and was a student of the Buddhist canon and the Confucian classics. Both Feng Yuxiang and Yan Xishan were able reformers in the areas they held, the latter often called the "Model Governor" in Shanxi province. But other warlords were simply outrageous thugs, wreaking terror and havoc in the areas they controlled. Easiest to mock was Zhang Zongchang, the "Dog-Meat General," whose Shandong troops were notorious for their practice of "opening melons"—that is, splitting skulls—and for stringing human heads on telegraph poles, all in order to elicit "respect" for their brutal power.

Those warlords who were serious about trying to gain national power were involved in shifting coalitions, often armed by Western nations, who hoped "their" warlord would come out on top and then offer them advantages. These coalitions fought major wars in north China in 1920, 1922, 1924, and 1925, while many smaller conflicts erupted throughout the country. These were bloody wars, not merely minor skirmishes and political posturing. For many Chinese, the main scourge of the times was what the warlords did to pay for the weapons and supplies their armies needed. One means was outright and outrageous taxation: every conceivable item, service, or situation bore extraordinarily high taxes, from consumer goods to licenses to everyday situations (getting married, owning a pig, going to a brothel). Land taxes were collected far in advance, in some areas up to a decade ahead. The other warlord strategy for getting needed money was to force farmers to plant opium, since that crop brought in huge profits. The tragic irony of this was that in the late Qing, the cultivation of opium had been eliminated in most areas. The acreage of cultivated land devoted to opium production was at 3 percent from 1914 to 1919; but it skyrocketed to 20 percent from 1929 to 1933. The Western powers that had first brought opium to China had long gotten out of the trade. In sum, the warlords, who arose in the context of growing nationalism in the early twentieth century, came to be the antithesis of nationalism. They rendered the Republic of China an empty shell.

THE MAY FOURTH MOVEMENT

In the midst of this military and political chaos emerged an intellectual and cultural revolution that would change China's political destiny. Though Confucianism in the political and educational realm had been dethroned, it retained its stranglehold on Chinese society. Confucian social bonds elevated the status and power of age over youth, of males over females. In one of his strongest metaphors, the famous writer Lu Xun argued that something had to be done to awaken the Chinese to the destructiveness of traditional culture.

Lu Xun's metaphor is this: Imagine an iron house without windows, absolutely indestructible, with many people fast asleep inside who will soon die of suffocation. But you know since they will die in their sleep, they will not feel the pain of death. Now if you cry aloud to wake a few of the lighter sleepers making those unfortunate few suffer the agony of irrevocable death, do you think you are doing them a good turn? But if a few awake, you can't saythere is no hope of destroying the iron house.[6]

During the New Culture Movement, the old verities, which formed the iron house, slowly began to collapse. Slogans like "Down with Confucius and sons" filled the press and echoed in street demonstrations. The journal, *New Youth*, which began to be published in 1915, offered a forum for students to discuss issues and called on youths to take charge of their lives and world. A language revolution was part of this **New Culture Movement**. Written literary Chinese (*wenyan*), a difficult grammatical form that was an obstacle to increasing the rate of literacy among the people, was discarded in favor of the vernacular (*baihua*), where the written language was the same as the spoken language, a style that facilitated the spreading of public literacy. Beijing University's new chancellor, Cai Yuanpei, set out beginning in 1916 to make the university the laboratory to shape the new culture. He brought professors to the university campus with wide-ranging ideas—from radical and liberal to conservative and reactionary—and then gave them complete academic freedom to debate all issues and possibilities for the most appropriate cultural route ahead.

The emphasis on individualism was greater in this period than in any of modern China's history; its goal was to cast off ideological shackles of patriarchy and family authority. Two imaginary characters, "Mr. Democracy" and "Mr. Science," became watchwords of the cry for progress during this time.

The New Culture Movement took place in the larger context of the **May Fourth Movement** (ca. 1915–1924), which has been called both China's Renaissance and its Enlightenment.[7] The movement added a powerful political dynamic to the pivotal events of the era. Its name came from a student demonstration in Beijing on May 4, 1919, to protest the decision at the Versailles Peace Conference to let Japan keep the former German leasehold in Shandong province that it had taken in World War I's opening days. Japan's claim to this territory had been agreed to via secret treaties with the Allied powers during the war. China's position on the matter was weakened because the government in Beijing had itself in 1915, admittedly under duress, agreed to Japan's **Twenty-One Demands,** which gave the Japanese empire many "rights" in China, much like the leaseholds the Qing had given other nations in the late 1890s.

The Beijing demonstration of May 4, 1919, was the first salvo in a nationwide protest, which successfully pressured China's delegates at Versailles to refuse to sign the peace treaty. This political "victory" gave rise to two alternative strategies for the remaking of Chinese culture and the nation. In the struggle between the proponents of these alternatives, the May Fourth Movement would come to be shattered. One approach held that the new China could best be constructed through direct, even violent political action; its proponents pointed to the impact of the Beijing demonstration and others, especially in Shanghai, that had direct and desired political results. These proponents of political action argued that other changes, for example, cultural advances, would follow once the political system was changed. They contended that unless the foundation of the current political system—warlords bolstered by imperialists—was destroyed, nothing would ever change in China because such conservative forces would always hold the balance of power and impede further progress.

Those who proposed the alternative approach contended that any meaningful political change could only be built upon cultural change, through a process that was more evolutionary than revolutionary. They argued that if the culture was not changed, then even if the current cast of political power-holders was ousted, similar groups with deep roots in traditional culture would simply take their place. This group attacked various political "isms," like socialism, Marxism, and **anarchism,** which claimed to offer overarching systemic blueprints of a holistic way out of China's predicament. Instead, led by pragmatists, they favored solutions to specific problems; in the words of American-educated scholar Hu Shi, "liberation means liberation from this or that institution, from this or that belief, for this or that individual; it is liberation bit by bit, drop by drop."[8] The results of this approach would be a long time coming, which seemed to many a dangerous prospect, given China's internal weakness and especially the external threats posed by imperialist nations. For many Chinese, the persistently urgent question after 1919 became how to build national power as quickly as possible so as to forestall deepening national humiliation and perhaps even dismemberment.

THE BIRTH OF THE CHINESE COMMUNIST PARTY

As the realization of China's plight became more widespread, the "ism" of Marxism-Leninism received increasing attention for its potential to deal with China's multiple problems, particularly after the successful 1917 communist revolution in Russia and the founding of the Soviet Union in 1922. Intellectuals and journalists formed Marxist study groups in Shanghai and Beijing. Agents from the Moscow-based **Comintern (Communist International)** made contact with these groups and formally organized the Chinese Communist Party (CCP) in July 1921. Because of the tiny number of CCP members (only fifty to sixty in 1921), Comintern agents pushed the CCP to join with the largest and best-known "bourgeois" party, Sun Yat-sen's Nationalists, which had remained in opposition to the warlord-dominated Republic from its political base in the southern province of Guangdong. Comintern agents also met and wooed Sun, who at this point was willing to accept help from whatever source. He eventually agreed to link up the KMT with the CCP in a **united front** through a "bloc within" system, where the two parties would not combine organizationally but individual CCP members could also join the Nationalist Party. Throughout the years of the united front, the CCP was directed by the Comintern and ultimately by the Soviet leader V. I. Lenin until his death in 1924, and then by Joseph Stalin.

The Comintern agent Mikhail Borodin, who emerged as a major force in these political developments, pushed to restructure the loosely organized parliamentary-like KMT on the Leninist model of "**democratic centralism**." In this model, along which the CCP was already organized, a façade of democratic-style discussion in party ranks is trumped by the decision-making of a centralized leadership. Borodin was also instrumental in the establishment of a KMT army, the results of a realistic recognition that attaining the party's political goals in the militarized culture of the time required armed forces of its own. The party thus established a military academy at Whampoa (Huangpu in *pinyin*) near Guangzhou. Its commandant was a relatively young officer, Chiang Kai-shek (Jiang Jieshi, in *pinyin*), who at the time was not a member of Sun's inner circle.

While the new Nationalist Party constitution and army had Borodin's fingerprints all over them, the party's central ideology was Sun's own **Three Principles of the People**: nationalism, democracy, and socialism (see Box 2.4). The achievement of nationalism meant uniting the country by eliminating warlords and imperialists. The attainment of democracy would come only after a period of party tutelage of the Chinese masses in the ways of democracy. The specific policy aims in Sun's concept of socialism ("people's livelihood") were somewhat ambiguous. Sun did not buy into the CCP position that China's central socioeconomic problem was the uneven distribution of wealth; rather, he argued that the central problem was the "grinding poverty" of the Chinese people. His solution: equalization of land ownership (without specifics), the development of government-owned enterprises (fitting the traditional model of socialism), and a tax on the increase in the value of landed property (the "unearned increment"—since whoever owned the land did nothing to earn the amount of the increased land value over time).

BOX 2.4 THE THREE PRINCIPLES OF THE PEOPLE, SUN YAT-SEN (1924)

Nationalism. In view of the ruthless exploitation of China by foreign powers, China is in fact a subcolony, a status that is much worse than that of a colony. . . . China has concluded unequal treaties with many countries all of whom, because of the existence of these treaties, are China's masters. Today our urgent task is to restore our lost nationalism and to use the combined force of our 400 million people to avenge the wrongs of the world. . . . Only when imperialism is eliminated can there be peace for all mankind. To achieve this goal, we should first rejuvenate Chinese nationalism and restore China's position as a sovereign state.

Democracy. There is a difference between the European and Chinese concept of freedom. While the Europeans struggle for personal freedom, we struggle for national freedom. As far as we are concerned, personal freedom should never be too excessive. In fact, in order to win national freedom, we should not hesitate to sacrifice our personal freedom. The revolutionaries in Europe and America are fond of saying that men are born equal. . . . But is it really true that men are born equal? No stretch of land is completely level; nor are two flowers exactly identical. Since there is no such thing as equality in the sphere of nature, how can there be equality among men? True equality . . . has nothing to do with equality of achievement; it merely means that all people in a democratic society should enjoy the same political rights.

Among the popular rights in a democracy the foremost is the right to vote . . .; besides the right to vote for officials, the people should also have the right to recall them.

Insofar as the enactment of legislation is concerned, the people should have the right of initiative, as well as the right of referendum. Only when people have these four rights . . . can they be said to have direct control over their government or to enjoy full democracy.

People's Livelihood. The purpose of social progress cannot be more than the realization of the utmost good for the largest number of people in the society, and such realization lies in the harmonization, rather than conflict, between different economic interests.

What is the basic fact about China? It is the grinding poverty of the Chinese people. . . . The so-called disparity in wealth is really a disparity between the poor and the extremely poor, since all Chinese are undeniably poor.

Different countries have different ways of solving their land problem. . . . The true solution of our land problem is to make sure that farmers own the land which they till; land ownership by tillers is in fact the final goal of the principle of people's livelihood. Though China does not have "great landlords" in the Western sense, more than 90 percent of the farmers till land they do not own. This is a serious problem. Unless this problem is solved, it is senseless to talk about the principle of people's livelihood.

From Dun Jen Li, *The Road to Communism: China since 1912* (New York: Van Nostrand Reinhold, 1969), 115–125.

By the mid-1920s, the KMT had become increasingly polarized. Rightists in the party argued that the Soviets had too much power in Chinese affairs and that the CCP bloc within should be discontinued. Leftists, on the other hand, supported some CCP social and economic aims. Sun was temporarily able to keep the lid on these differences, but his death from liver cancer in March 1925 opened the floodgates of factional bitterness. Intraparty rivalry only worsened in the aftermath of the killings of Chinese protestors by British troops in Shanghai and Guangzhou in May and

June 1925, acts that galvanized the deepening sense of national peril. The country erupted in demonstrations, street marches, and some violence in their anger against imperialists. In August a leader of the KMT left wing was gunned down, with some in the party's right wing implicated. From November 1925 to January 1926, a right-wing faction met in Beijing to disparage both the CCP and the left wing; in March 1926, they held their own party congress while the CCP and KMT left wing had met separately in January. The united front had disintegrated.

Suspicious of CCP aims, Commandant Chiang struck out at the Communists at Whampoa in March 1926, but he sacked only a relatively small number. Throughout the factional struggle, Stalin continued to call for the CCP to work with the Nationalists. Four months later Chiang began the **Northern Expedition**, a long-planned two-pronged military campaign (one headed to Wuhan in central China, the other to Shanghai on the coast) to unite the country by getting rid of warlords and imperialists. When armies associated with the Left (the CCP and left-wing KMT) began to mobilize farmers and workers as they reached their initial destination of Wuhan, Chiang's hostility to the Communists intensified. He took Shanghai in late March 1927, with much help from CCP-led labor unions and leftist organizations. But, in early April, Chiang had his forces attack union headquarters and leftist groups. In the ensuing bloodbath, sometimes referred to as the **White Terror**, hundreds were killed and thousands fled in panic. Even after the Terror had begun, Stalin from Moscow claimed that although the purge showed Chiang's true political color, the CCP should continue to work with the Kuomintang left; CCP General Secretary Chen Duxiu commented that these orders from Stalin were "like taking a bath in a toilet."[9]

The KMT left wing broke with the CCP in early summer 1927, with Borodin and the other Comintern agents fleeing for their lives. The White Terror spread over the country well into 1928; it broke the back of the CCP. In the fall of 1927, there were several desperate attempts by Communists to rise up, but they were all bloodily suppressed. In August 1928, Chiang Kai-shek reached Beijing and, at least on the map, had unified China for the first time since the death of Yuan Shikai in 1916.

THE NANJING DECADE

On the verge of national victory in 1927, Chiang had declared that the capital of the Republic of China would be in the central Chinese city of Nanjing (which means "southern capital") in order to be closer to his base of political power. The period from 1927 to 1937, when the Japanese invasion forced Chiang and his government to flee and abandon the capital, is known as the **Nanjing Decade**. Beijing, which means "northern capital," was renamed Beiping, or "northern peace."

Even under the best conditions, Chiang would have had to struggle mightily to overcome or even begin to solve China's many problems during the Nanjing Decade. But he had to confront extraordinary difficulties. His power lay in three positions: head of state, chairman of the Nationalist Party, and commander in chief of the army, but there were challenges to his control of all three. "Residual warlordism" remained a problem; during the Northern Expedition, Chiang had co-opted, rather than defeated, warlords. They challenged him in four wars from March 1929 to September 1930. Furthermore, the KMT itself was not unified; it was split among factions vying for power; disgruntled party officials aligned themselves with residual warlords and continued to make trouble. Chiang, who was usually called "Generalissimo" because of his command of the national army, did not firmly consolidate his power in the party until after 1935. He himself received his main backing from the Whampoa Clique, men who owed him personal loyalty from the days when he was their military commandant. The active core of the clique was an organization called the **Blue Shirts**, many of whom saw **fascism**, the ideology chosen by Germany and Italy at the time, as the way to restore China.

Another military challenge was a revived Communist movement in southeast China. From 1931 to 1937, Japan also became an aggressive military threat in the northeast—before its outright invasion of China proper in 1937. From October 1928, when he assumed power as head of state, until October 1934, Chiang's forces were involved in or on the brink of actual warfare forty-five of the seventy-two months— about 62.5 percent of the time. In 1934, six years after he had taken power, he firmly controlled just seven of the eighteen provinces; when the Japanese invaded in summer 1937, fully one-third of the provinces were still beyond Chiang's control. He thus faced huge obstacles in being able to reconstruct China in effective fashion.

Chiang Kai-shek emerged as heir to the long line of self-strengtheners, focusing on crucial infrastructure for defense and further modernization of the Republic of China. But lack of funds blocked almost all accomplishment or even significant progress; the economic difficulties confronting the government were debilitating. The worldwide depression made it especially hard to make headway in modernizing projects. In addition, the Republic had an insufficient and poorly structured tax base. The government gave up national claims to the land tax, since levying it effectively after so many years of war required a national census for which there was neither time nor money. So, by default, national revenues came from tariff duties (nonsensical, at a time of having to import many items to build industries) and from regressive excise taxes on commodities for which the poor had to pay a larger percentage of their income than the wealthy. By 1937, China, with a population of five hundred million, had less industrial production than Belgium, which had eight million people. "China had the same mileage of modern highways as Spain, one-third of the telegraph lines in France, and less railroad mileage than the state of Illinois."[10]

Like Yuan Shikai, Chiang saw state-building as a top-down process. He was determined to have the Kuomintang state penetrate more deeply into society than had the imperial state, utilizing a system of townships, wards, villages, and urban neighborhoods, alongside the traditional *baojia* **system** of group mutual surveillance in which households were organized to keep watch on their communities and each other. But lack of effective administration and control prevented its successful realization. In culture, Chiang attempted a return to the past, resurrecting Confucianism as part of his **New Life Movement** to revive traditional virtues and cultivate civic virtue. The Blue Shirts became his standard-bearers in the campaign of the New Life Movement, which essentially became a war against the legacy of the May Fourth Movement. The Generalissimo made it clear: "In the last several decades we have in vain become drunk with democracy and the advocacy of free thought. And what has been the result? We have fallen into a chaotic and irretrievable situation."[11] He said it most clearly in 1932: "The Chinese revolution has failed."[12]

THE RISE OF MAO ZEDONG

Born in 1893 into a peasant family in the central province of Hunan, Mao Zedong had been a founding member of the CCP who, as a "bloc within" member of the KMT, had been active during the Nationalist Revolution in organizing peasant associations. Driven underground in the cities and to southeast mountainous areas by the White Terror of 1927–1928, the CCP rebuilt in the countryside. It was there that Mao Zedong began his rise to power within the party. He worked closely with the military figure Zhu De, who built the **Red Army**. Even while most of the party was in the rural mountains, CCP headquarters remained underground in Shanghai and was run by former students educated in the Soviet Union. As traditional Marxists, they believed that the revolution would be engineered by the urban industrial **proletariat**; it made sense to them to keep the party center in the city. Mao and Zhu developed a **base area** on the border of Jiangxi and Fujian provinces. In late 1931, it became known as the Chinese Soviet Republic, or the **Jiangxi Soviet***.

During this period, the CCP experimented for the first time with **land reform** and implementing **class struggle.** Given that 80 to 85 percent of China's population were peasants and that there were relatively few urban workers, Mao began to see the peasants, rather than the proletariat, as key to revolutionary success. For land reform, Mao divided peasants into rich, middle, and poor categories. Although the largest group by far was the poor peasants, what constituted each group varied according to locale and to the particular people who made the categories; these groupings were not hard and fast—and they were always subject to reevaluation. Once people had been labeled, land would be confiscated from landlords and sometimes from rich peasants, and then distributed to poor and middle peasants and hired laborers. Obviously, the rankings turned people's worlds upside down: landlords lost all their land, while poor peasants overnight received the land resource they had never had.

But the capriciousness of class rankings and re-rankings alienated many people in the base area. The category of rich peasant was a political hot potato; it was defined in different ways, and policies toward rich peasants varied by location. In some areas, rich peasants were grouped with other peasants and seen as allies of the revolution. In other areas, they were put in the category of exploiters along with landlords. In one wave of radicalism from June to October 1933, many formerly designated middle peasants were reclassified as landlords and had their land confiscated. In another re-classification from October to December 1933, many landlords were relabeled middle peasants. In one county, out of 3,125 households, 1,512 (48 percent) were reclassified from landlord and rich peasants to middle and even poor peasants. Then early in 1934, rich peasants again fell under bitter attack. With such rapid changes, a peasant might be a middle peasant in May, a landlord in October, and a poor peasant in

---

* The term *soviet* is a Russian word literally meaning *council* and is used to refer to a type of political organization in which power is in the hands of the workers.

December—all without any change in economic status whatsoever. The confiscation of land and the reclassifications sparked frequent violence and unrest.

In the end, Mao called a temporary halt to land reform, partly because it was antagonizing too many people at a time when the CCP needed all the support that it could attract but also because of the lack of unity among the party elite. Although the CCP center had moved from Shanghai to the Jiangxi Soviet in the 1930s, the leadership remained in the hands of the USSR-trained party **cadres** and the Comintern representative assigned to China. There were other smaller Communist base areas in central China that had their own programs and policies; the CCP at the time was thus not a monolithic movement but was diverse and polycentric.

The reborn CCP frightened Chiang Kai-shek. Between 1930 and 1934, he launched five **extermination campaigns** against the Jiangxi Soviet. Three of the first four failed because of faulty and weak military strategy; the other failed when the Generalissimo had to pull out his troops in the wake of Japan's invasion of Manchuria. Only the fifth succeeded, when his forces adopted better strategy: constructing a network of roads to maintain supply lines and building blockhouses to tighten the noose around the soviet. To save themselves, about eighty-six thousand Communists fled, on a 370-day forced march of about six thousand miles: the fabled **Long March**. Pursued by Jiang's troops and bombers, they marched over snow-covered mountain ranges and through quicksand-like bogs. About eight thousand survived to reach **Yan'an** in Shaanxi province in China's remote northwest. En route, Mao began his climb to the top as party leader.

Once the marchers reached Yan'an, Mao admitted that the Long March and what led to it were a worse defeat than the White Terror in the late 1920s. But in orthodox party history the Long March is treated as a great victory, a verdict that came in part because of those heroes who survived the brutal natural and human forces, even though those survivors numbered less than 10 percent of those who marched. For the survivors it was a story of triumph over superhuman odds, and it produced among the survivors, especially Mao himself, a sense of mission and destiny. Indeed, until the late 1990s, veterans of the Long March monopolized the political leadership of the People's Republic.

THE WAR WITH JAPAN, 1931–1945

In contrast to the difficulties that dogged China in its efforts to build a modernizing nation state, Japan, beginning in 1868 with the **Meiji Restoration,** in which power fell to determined reformers ruling in the emperor's name, had seemed to be almost immediately successful, industrializing rapidly and adopting a constitution in little more than two decades. Already in the early 1870s some Japanese leaders had begun casting lustful eyes on the Asian mainland, in the beginning at Korea in particular. Japan proceeded to "open" Korea with an unequal treaty in 1876; and for the next eighteen years the Japanese pitted themselves against China for realizing the predominant role on the Korean peninsula. Korea had been China's closest tributary state, and China did not want to give up its long-standing interests there. Japan had won control over Korea as a result of its defeat of China in the Sino-Japanese War

(1894–1895). Between 1905 and 1910, Japan swallowed Korea piece by piece; Korea became, along with Taiwan, another spoil of war, a formal part of the Japanese empire. Japan increased its interests on the mainland, specifically in Chinese Manchuria, with its war against Russia (1904–1905).

Japan showed its determination to move more aggressively into China proper with the **Twenty-One Demands** in 1915. One group of those demands cut particularly deeply into Chinese sovereignty: it required that the Chinese attach Japanese advisers to the key governmental executive, military, financial, and police bodies—in effect, making China a protectorate of Japan. Although Yuan Shikai was compelled to sign the Demands, the Japanese in the end dropped these flagrantly arrogant conditions. But Japan insisted that it be allowed to hold on to parts of Shandong province after the war, a decision, as noted earlier, that led to the May Fourth incident in 1919. The Japanese also pushed Koreans to move into Manchuria to increase the numbers of its people in the Chinese territory, which Japan saw increasingly as its own. Japan's objectives in the area were furthered in the 1910s and 1920s through collaboration with the Manchurian warlord Zhang Zuolin. But the Japanese were not sure they could trust Zhang, so the Japanese military blew up his train and killed him in June 1928.

From 1928 until 1931, Chiang Kai-shek tried to expand Chinese interests in Manchuria, building railroads to compete with those of the Japanese. A series of seemingly minor incidents over water rights and boundary disputes ratcheted up tensions between Korean and Chinese farmers in Manchuria. Japanese newspapers exaggerated the importance of the incidents, declaring them examples of China's "disrespect" for Japan—which helped fuel anti-Chinese riots in both Japan and Korea. The Japanese military command in Manchuria also magnified the situation into a towering threat to the Japanese position in the area. In this frame of mind, Japanese field officers, without the agreement or even knowledge of the military authorities or the government in Tokyo, blew up a length of track on Japan's South Manchuria Railroad in September 1931, blamed it on the Chinese, and, in "retaliation," launched a full-scale military assault on the Chinese forces and quickly took full control of Manchuria.

The Chinese did not resist; appeasement of Japan was a pattern that Chiang Kai-shek would follow for six more years. The irony was heavy: Chiang had come to power riding the wave of nationalism. And he had begun to recover some unequal treaty system "rights": tariff autonomy, reduction of numbers of foreign concessions, and negotiations over extraterritoriality (finally achieved in 1943). But he was unwilling to resist the Japanese as, over the next several years, Japan established a puppet state in Manchuria (Manchukuo) with China's last Manchu emperor on the throne; attacked Shanghai by air for six weeks in early 1932; advanced into several provinces of Inner Mongolia; and made demands, seized territory, and took China's sovereign rights in northern China.

Generalissimo Chiang did little except to explode verbally against his own Nineteenth Route Army when it dared to resist Japan in the Shanghai attack. Chiang argued that he did not resist the Japanese because his army was not yet strong enough, and, to his mind, the CCP was a greater threat to China. According to Chiang, "The Japanese are a disease of the skin; the Communists are a disease of the heart."[13] Obviously, a heart problem is more serious and needs to be treated first, unless, of course, the skin disease was a malignant melanoma, an apt analogy given Japan's malevolent actions in China.

Chiang's appeasement stirred a loud and vigorous chorus of dissent from all across the country—from party leaders, journalists, students, and average citizens. Chiang responded in his White Terror mode: making arrests, engineering assassinations, raiding university dormitories, and closing campuses. A government decision in December 1935, which basically handed eastern Hebei province with the cities of Beiping and Tianjin over to the Japanese, gave rise to a student movement whose protest demonstrations and rallies spread beyond cities to rural areas as well. National Salvation Associations, which were established across the nation, called for the removal of Japanese troops and puppet governments in Manchukuo and East Hebei.

In this politically volatile context a bizarre episode, the **Xi'an Incident**, occurred in December 1936. Chiang's top general, former Manchurian leader Zhang Xueliang, whose main military assignment was to keep the Communists bottled up in the Yan'an area, kidnapped the Generalissimo while he was in the northwestern city of Xi'an, which is not far from Yan'an. Zhang held Chiang until he agreed to another united front with the CCP to fend off Japan. Although after he was freed, Chiang claimed that he made no such commitment; when Japan next directly challenged China in July 1937, he ended his policy of appeasement and at last resisted the outright Japanese invasion and formed, at least in name, an anti-Japanese united front with the CCP.

In the war, Chiang's government traded space for time, retreating from Nanjing, first to the nearby city of Wuhan, then to Chongqing in the far southwestern province of Sichuan, where it remained until war's end. Sichuan and neighboring Yunnan province came to be called **Free China**, that is, the part of China under Nationalist Party authority that was controlled by neither the Japanese nor the Communists. Retreating along with the government were tens of millions of civilians; schools and factories were floated into the interior on barges. Though the main refugee corridor was westward along the Yangtze River, millions of others fled to the south and southwest. By October 1938, much of Eastern China, containing the major industrial cities and much of the best cropland, had fallen to the Japanese army.

The Japanese invasion was marked by rampant and gratuitous atrocities to terrorize the population. The most infamous of these was the **Rape of Nanjing** in late 1937, during which the Chinese have estimated that two hundred thousand to three hundred thousand were killed and tens of thousands raped. In several provinces of China, the Japanese military also used chemical warfare (poison gas) and biological warfare (spreading diseases like bubonic and pneumonic plague and cholera) against the civilian population. Despite the atrocities, Chinese collaboration with Japanese military occupiers was common; although later Chinese condemned these people as traitors, those who continued to live in occupied areas had to continue with their lives in some fashion even under the Japanese sword. Not all Chinese could flee to Free China: the ill, elderly, pregnant, and poor were groups that could not easily become refugees. A national collaborationist regime was established at Nanjing in March 1940 under the longtime Kuomintang leader Wang Jingwei, who had been a close associate of Sun Yat-sen. Wang came to be regarded as a national traitor by both the KMT and the CCP.

With the attack on Pearl Harbor in December 1941, the United States became China's ally in the war against Japan. Their joint goal was to strengthen Chiang Kai-shek's position sufficiently to win back eastern China, which could then be used as a base from which to bomb Japan. But logistical problems were severe: Chiang's regime in remote Chongqing was cut off from its supply lifelines and had to make do with supplies and armaments that were airlifted in. Further, bad relationships between the Generalissimo and General Joseph Stilwell, the top U.S. military commander assigned to work with Chiang, helped to thwart that strategy, and Nationalist Chinese forces remained in Chongqing until the war ended in 1945 and the government of the Republic of China returned to Nanjing.

The war's legacy for China was tragic. About twenty million Chinese were killed, almost sixteen million of which were civilian casualties. Scorched earth policies—blowing up dikes and bridges and destroying railroads and roads—used by the Chinese resistance to slow Japanese aggression destroyed much of the infrastructural gains that Chiang had accomplished during the Nanjing Decade.

One of the most destructive legacies of the war was a malignant inflation. Whereas prices increased about 40 percent during the war's first year, from the time of the attack on Pearl Harbor in 1941, they shot up more than 100 percent each year. Thus, something that cost about 1 **yuan** in 1937 would have cost 2,647 yuan in 1945. Nothing erodes the political support of a people for its government faster than inflation, especially the marauding type of inflation China faced during and after the war. The inflation led to the hoarding of commodities, creating scarcities and ever higher prices, corruption that reached new heights, and ravaged standards of living.

But the Chinese Communists benefited enormously from the war. At war's end there were nineteen Communist base areas in North China, and the CCP governed an area that spread across roughly 250,000 square miles. Mao claimed that there were 1.2 million CCP members by the end of the war. Communist military forces had increased almost tenfold from 92,000 in the beginning to 910,00 in 1945. The war of resistance against Japan gave the Communist movement breathing room from Chiang Kai-shek's obsessive efforts to exterminate it. It also gave the CCP the time to expand its popular support in several ways: through its own nationalistic appeal to the Chinese people by fighting the Japanese; its policies of mass mobilization; and its insistence that the Eighth Route Army (its main army) respect and even help the masses.

CIVIL WAR

Even before Japan surrendered, attention in China began to shift from the war to the postwar reality of an intensely polarized Chinese political world. The united front did not work effectively, especially after an incident in January 1941, when Kuomintang troops in the New Fourth Army opened fire on Communist troops, killing three thousand and wounding many more. During the first years of the war against Japan, thousands migrated to Yan'an, the CCP's base, where Mao consolidated his political and ideological domination of the party. He was formally elected Chairman of the Chinese Communist Party **Politburo** in 1943 and of the **Central Committee** in 1945.

While in Yan'an, Mao also worked to adapt Marxism-Leninism to China's situation, emphasizing peasants as key to the revolution. At Yan'an, the party devised policies that would guide it for decades to come. These included the **mass line,** a leadership style of relying on and actively using input from the masses in decision-making. The CCP under Mao also devised a strategy for the "re-education" of those party cadres was who were recalcitrant to follow or who opposed the official "line." The goal was to change their minds. This involved a process called a **rectification campaign,** which included the cadres attending small-group sessions in which they studied documents the party selected; writing detailed self-criticisms; being criticized in mass meetings; and confessing their errors. If there were no confessions, the party might isolate the targeted cadres, apply various psychological pressures, and/or send the cadre to do hard labor among the peasantry. Finally, as part of the repertoire of party's strategic policies, the revolutionary roles of art and literature were defined by Mao at a 1942 forum:

> In the world today all culture, all art and literature belongs to a definite class and party. Art for art's sake, art that stands above class and party . . . or politically independent art do not exist in reality. . . . Proletarian art and literature are part of the whole proletarian revolutionary cause . . . therefore, the party's work in literature and art occupies a definite and assigned position in the party's revolutionary work as a whole.[14]

The United States attempted to mediate in the CCP-KMT dispute but to no avail; it was never an impartial broker, for it continued to aid the Nationalists with arms and supplies. When General George Marshall ended his failed mission to broker peace in China in January 1947, it was only a matter of time before the parties' intransigence turned into civil war. In one of the largest wars of modern times, Chiang Kai-shek's Nationalists held huge initial advantages in quantity of men and materiel: its forces numbered about three million soldiers with roughly six thousand artillery pieces; the CCP, on the other hand, had armies of about one million and just six hundred artillery pieces. The Nationalists did win the early battles in 1946; but the Communists regrouped in Manchuria, launching a campaign to isolate the major cities. Chiang then blundered badly, sending half a million of his best troops to Manchuria before consolidating his control south of the Great Wall. The Communists quickly transformed the Manchuria theater into islands of isolated KMT-controlled cities in a Communist sea. Instead of pulling out, Chiang began costly airlifts. He used, for example, his entire military budget for the last half of 1948 to supply one city for two months and four days.

By mid-1948, the numbers of Communist troops were roughly equal to those of the KMT and they had more artillery pieces, many of the new troops coming through defection or surrender and the weapons captured from the fleeing enemy. The Communist victory in Manchuria was disastrous for the KMT: Chiang lost 470,000 of his best troops, who were killed, defected to the Communists, or became prisoners of war. Essentially, the KMT had lost the civil war even before the main battles shifted to China proper.

The decisive battle for central China came at the battle of Huai-Hai in Shandong and Jiangsu provinces from October 1948 to January 1949. Communist party leaders showed themselves to be superior strategists. For leadership positions and strategic advice, Chiang was partial to Whampoa graduates and downplayed the roles and views of others. In this case, he did not follow the advice of former militarily knowledgeable warlords to make a stand at a more favorable place along the Huai River. He chose instead to stand at the railroad center of Xuzhou, where his forces were exposed on three sides. Furthermore, Chiang personally insisted on directing the battle, even though he was two hundred miles away from the fighting. Communist forces annihilated Chiang's troops: he lost half a million men and almost all of his mechanized units. By early 1949, China north of the Yangtze River was mostly in Communist hands, and in April, they took the Nationalist capital in Nanjing. Although sporadic fighting continued in the south and west until the end of the year, on October 1, 1949, Chairman Mao Zedong declared the founding of the People's Republic of China and renamed its capital Beijing. In December, Generalissimo Chiang Kai-shek and the government of the Republic of China fled to Taiwan.

POSTMORTEM: WHY THE COMMUNISTS WON

Although the military struggle was decisive in determining the outcome of the Chinese civil war, underlying political and economic factors were crucial. Chiang never attempted to reach out to non-KMT groups or to liberalize politics in areas under his authority. When the opportunity came to expand his base by joining with the Democratic League, a party formed by an unusual coalition of old-line militarists and Western-style political liberals in 1944, Chiang did not even seriously consider it. Instead, he arrested or had assassinated many of its key figures before totally outlawing the Democratic League in October 1947. Chiang's government became known for its incompetence and its corruption. He may not have been corrupt personally, but many members of his family and close associates were deeply involved in graft and other shady dealings to enrich themselves.

The most crucial reason for the failure of the KMT was the ravaging inflation that undermined both the economy of the Republic and public support for Chiang's regime. By 1945, the government's revenue was covering only one-third of its expenses. Chiang's answer was simply to print more money, a "solution" that added more fuel to fires of inflation. The exchange rate for Chinese *yuan* to U.S. dollars stood at 7,000 to 1 in January 1947 and 45,000 to 1 just seven months later. Prices in July 1948 were three million times higher than in July 1937. Inflation itself was demoralizing to the Chinese people, but even more so was having "a government with neither the will nor the ability to do anything but watch over the deterioration of the nation's urban economy."[15] In the end, the economic collapse was total, engulfing the rural economy as well.

By late 1947 and 1948, the very fabric of rural society seemed to be unraveling. Banditry, the traditional sign of feeble political control and deteriorating economic conditions, was pervasive. . . . Landlords fled the countryside for the relative

security of walled towns. . . . Ordinary peasants, too, abandoned the farms, becoming recruits to the growing ranks of the hungry and destitute, many of whom
died in the streets and alleyways of cities. . . . 10 million people were threatened with
starvation in 1948; 48 million—about one of every ten Chinese—were refugees. . . .
The most desperate reportedly sold their wives and daughters—in 1946, the price of
fifteen- and sixteen-year-old girls in [Zhejiang] was said to be 4,000 yuan.[16]

The outcome of the Chinese civil war was not only determined by KMT failures
and losses; the CCP did not win the struggle simply by default. The Communists were
obviously successful in terms of military strategy. But that was only part of the equation that equaled victory. The main elements of its success were the party's ability
to mobilize the masses to join their cause and its generally pragmatic approach in
dealing with local situations.

The most important element of the CCP's mass mobilization strategy was class
struggle, used in both base areas and guerrilla zones under their control. During the
war against Japan, class struggle was the vehicle to reduce rents, taxes, and interest,
and carry out land reform. The party sent work teams to villages to mobilize peasant
associations to challenge village elites. It is clear that the "rise of peasant associations
fundamentally changed rural power relations,"[17] and won the CCP massive popular
support. A second wave of mass organizing in the base areas concentrated on setting
up women's and workers' associations as part of mobilizing the population for war.

Mobilizing the masses was slow and difficult work. The first hurdle for a work team
sent to a village was to gain the trust of the people in a culture based on personal
connections. If the mobilizers were from the village or had close ties to residents of
the village, the effort would be easier. In situations in which the work team members
had no connections to the village, cadres had tough, sometimes intractable problems.
Mobilizers had to have networking skills and, as a matter of course, had to spend a
great deal of time winning the confidence of the community by cultivating new social
ties and building grassroots networks. Only after they had succeeded in this work
could they move on to mobilizing the population in various organizations for action,
such as land reform.

The timing of the CCP's mobilization efforts varied by locale. In some bases in
North China, the efforts were underway by 1939 and 1940; in others, they were not
begun until 1943 or 1944. In central China bases, they started in 1941. Class struggle
became most tangible in the **struggle meeting**, which was "the most intense, con-
densed form of peasant mobilization."[18] These often-violent meetings were launched
in North China against local despots by 1942 but did not begin in central China until
late 1943. Party cadres targeted the village bosses and landlords and encouraged the
expression (often explosion) of latent peasant anger against them, which was not easy
to do. The traditional relationship between peasants and local elites, where peasants
"knew their place" and were careful not to antagonize those in power, had to be overcome. Allaying peasant fears about throwing off these old relationships was a formidable task. The staged struggle meetings were pivotal in "shattering mass apathy
and passivity and disrupting what former solidarity had existed among targets and
community."[19]

In the period from 1946 to 1948, class struggle became the means to carry out radical land reform, the same policies the CCP had attempted and abandoned in the Jiangxi Soviet in the early 1930s. Party leaders argued that the inauguration of land reform during the civil war was important because it was the best way to mobilize the masses against attacks by Nationalist forces. When the party began the land reform campaign, a main dynamic of struggle meetings was vengeance against elites and even middle and poor peasants who had collaborated with the Japanese.

A party directive in March 1946 instructed party cadres to stay out of the land-reform process and leave it to peasant associations, which could themselves expropriate and redistribute land and property; it was a policy that actually encouraged extremism among the masses, which often led to the killing of landlords and other violent acts. By 1948, the party pulled back on the "leftist excesses" that had both symbolized and encouraged the extremism that had become the hallmark of the land reform process. Party leaders wanted to move away from the frequent killings of landlords and rich peasants, from taking land from middle peasants, and from attacking commercial and industrial enterprises.

In the mobilization that occurred alongside land reform, men formed militia units, peasant associations spearheaded army recruiting, women's associations managed surveillance posts, local self-defense units transported supplies and ammunition, and cultural teams did propaganda work. The continual CCP emphasis was on the connection between land reform and mobilization of the masses in support of party policy. The process of mass mobilization brought people to the party and gave them a shared purpose with the party and its undertakings, a crucial element in the party's overall success.

Finally, an important factor in Communist revolutionary success was its pragmatic strategy that varied according to place and time. One size did not fit all when it came to revolutionary strategies and approaches. Not every attempt at mobilization succeeded; sometimes the party failed. Sometimes contingencies gave the CCP their success. But, generally, when they achieved success, it came because party cadres understood the specific locale: its natural environment; its social, economic, and political structures, networks, and relationships; and its particular needs and grievances. Then, it carefully built coalitions with local leaders to mobilize the local populace on issues of significant concern and import to that particular area.

In the end, successful military and political strategies, marked by pragmatism about local situations, brought Communist success. The trajectory from empire to a Republic to the People's Republic was unpredictable and violent. Unfortunately, most of the first thirty years of Communist rule in China saw a continuation of those trends.

NOTES

1. See, for example, Peter C. Perdue, *China Marches West: The Qing Conquest of Central Eurasia* (Cambridge, MA: Harvard University Press, 2005); and C. Patterson Giersch, *Asian Borderlands: The Transformation of Qing China's Yunnan Frontier* (Cambridge, MA: Harvard University Press, 2006).

2. Quoted in John K. Fairbank, Edwin O. Reischauer, and Albert M. Craig, *East Asia: The Modern Transformation* (Boston: Houghton Mifflin, 1965), 397, 400.

3. H. Lyman Miller, "The Late Imperial Chinese State," in *The Modern Chinese State*, ed. David Shambaugh (Cambridge: Cambridge University Press, 2000), 34.

4. *Kuomintang*, which literally means "National People's Party," is an older form of romanization. In *pinyin*, it is *Guomindang* (GMD). Both romanizations are commonly used in scholarly writing. Kuomintang (KMT) is used in this book to refer to the Nationalist Party founded by Sun Yat-sen partly because that is how the party, which is currently the governing party in Taiwan, still refers to itself in English.

5. See "The song of Song: The death of a revolutionary," *Economist*, Dec. 22, 2012.

6. Lu Hsun [Xun], "Preface to the First Collection of Short Stories, 'Call to Arms,'" in *Selected Stories of Lu Hsun* (Beijing: Foreign Languages Press, 1972), 5.

7. See, for example, Jerome B. Grieder, *Hu Shih and the Chinese Renaissance: Liberalism in the Chinese Revolution, 1917–1937* (Cambridge, MA: Harvard University Press, 1970); and Vera Schwarz, *The Chinese Enlightenment: Intellectuals and the Legacy of the May Fourth Movement of 1919* (Berkeley, CA: University of California Press, 1986).

8. Quoted in R. Keith Schoppa, *Revolution and Its Past* (Upper Saddle River, NJ: Pearson Prentice Hall, 2006), 176.

9. Quoted in C. Martin Wilbur, *The Nationalist Revolution in China, 1923–1928* (Cambridge, MA: Harvard University Press, 1983), 131.

10. Schoppa, *Revolution and Its Past*, 213.

11. Lloyd Eastman, *The Abortive Revolution* (Cambridge, MA: Harvard University Press, 1974), 42.

12. Eastman, *Abortive Revolution*, 1.

13. Theodore H. White and Annalee Jacoby, *Thunder Out of China* (Cambridge, MA: Da Capo Press, 1980; 1st ed., 1946), 129.

14. Bonnie S. McDougall, ed., *Mao Zedong's "Talks at the Yan'an Conference on Literature and Art": A Translation of the 1943 Text with Commentary* (Ann Arbor: University of Michigan Center for Chinese Studies, 1980), 75. An official translation of this document, which makes some changes from the original, can be found at https://www.marxists.org/reference/archive/mao/selected-works/volume-3/mswv3_08.htm

15. Suzanne Pepper, "The KMT-CCP Conflict, 1945–1949" in *Cambridge History of China*, vol. 13, *Republican China, 1912–1949*, pt. 2, ed. John K. Fairbank and Albert Feuerwerker (Cambridge: Cambridge University Press, 1986), 742.

16. Lloyd Eastman, *Seeds of Destruction* (Stanford, CA: Stanford University Press, 1984), 81–82.

17. Ch'en Yungfa, *Making Revolution: The Communist Movement in Eastern and Central China* (Berkeley: University of California Press, 1986), 221.

18. Ch'en Yungfa, *Making Revolution*, 220.

19. Schoppa, *Revolution and Its Past*, 279.

SUGGESTED READINGS

Averill, Stephen. *Revolution in the Highlands: China's Jinggangshan BaseArea*. Lanham, MD: Rowman & Littlefield, 2005.

Coble, Parks. *Facing Japan: Chinese Politics and Japanese Imperialism*. New York: Cambridge University Press, 1991.

Cohen, Paul A. *China Unbound: Evolving Perspectives on the Chinese Past.* New York: Routledge Curzon, 2007.

Cohen, Paul A. *History in Three Keys: The Boxers as Event, Experience, and Myth.* New York: Columbia University Press, 1997.

Cohen, Paul. *Speaking to History: The Story of King Goujian in Twentieth-Century China.* Berkeley, CA: University of California Press, 2009.

Eastman, Lloyd. *The Abortive Revolution: China under Nationalist Rule, 1927–1937.* Cambridge, MA: Harvard University Press, 1974.

Feuerwerker, Albert. *State and Society in Late Eighteenth Century China.* Ann Arbor: University of Michigan Press, 1992.

Fogel, Joshua, ed. *The Nanjing Massacre in History and Historiography.* Berkeley: University of California Press, 2000.

Herschatter, Gail. *Women and China's Revolutions.* New York: Routledge, 2018.

Lary, Diana. *China's Republic.* New York: Cambridge University Press, 2007.

Lary, Diana. *The Chinese People at War: Human Suffering and Social Transformation, 1937–1945.* New York: Cambridge University Press, 2010.

Levine, Steven. *Anvil of Victory: The Communist Revolution in Manchuria: 1945–1948.* New York: Columbia University Press, 1987.

Lovell, Julia. *The Opium War: Drugs, Dreams and the Making of China.* New York: Picador, 2011.

Meyer-Fong, Tobie. *What Remains: Coming to Terms with Civil War in 19th Century China.* Stanford, CA: Stanford University Press, 2013.

Mitter, Rana. *Forgotten Ally: China's World War II, 1937–1944.* New York: Houghton Mifflin Harcourt, 2013.

Platt, Stephen R. *Autumn in the Heavenly Kingdom: China, The West and the Epic Story of the Taiping Civil War.* New York: Knopf, 2012.

Rhoads, Edward J. M. *Manchus and Han: Ethnic Relations and Political Power in Late Qing and Early Republican China.* Seattle: University of Washington Press, 2000.

Rowe, William T. *China's Last Empire: The Great Qing.* Cambridge, MA: Harvard University Press, 2012.

Schoppa, R. Keith. *Blood Road: The Mystery of Shen Dingyi in Revolutionary China.* Berkeley: University of California Press, 1995.

Schoppa, R. Keith. *In a Sea of Bitterness: Refugees During the Sino-Japanese War.* Cambridge, MA: Harvard University Press, 2011.

Spence, Jonathan. *God's Chinese Son: The Taiping Heavenly Kingdom of Hong Xiuquan.* New York: W. W. Norton, 1996.

Taylor, Jay. *The Generalissimo: Chiang Kai-shek and the Struggle for Modern China.* Cambridge, MA: Harvard University Press, 2009.

Tuchman, Barbara. *Stillwell and the American Experience in China, 1911–1945.* New York: Grove Press, 2001.

Wakeman, Frederic E. Jr. *Spymaster: Dai Li and the Chinese Secret Service.* Berkeley: University of California Press, 2003.

Westad, Odd Arne. *Decisive Encounter: The Chinese Civil War, 1946–1950.* Stanford, CA: Stanford University Press, 2003.

Zou, Rong. *The Revolutionary Army: A Chinese Nationalist Tract of 1993.* Translated by John Lust. The Hague: Mouton and Co., 1968.

3

Mao Zedong in Power (1949–1976)

FREDERICK C. TEIWES

Chairman Mao Zedong was the absolute ruler of China from the founding of the People's Republic on October 1, 1949, to his death on September 9, 1976. Under his leadership the communist regime achieved initial successes followed by two decades of wrenching failures, most notably the Great Leap Forward (1958–1960) and the Cultural Revolution (1966–1968), and periods of partial, tortured recovery. During these final two decades Mao's prestige was adversely affected among the public and even sections of the Chinese Communist Party (CCP), but his authority never wavered. Despite claims during the Cultural Revolution that he had been opposed by various party leaders, claims unfortunately echoed in much academic writing, every clear order from the Chairman was obeyed, however destructive to national, party, or individual leader's interests.

What is more remarkable than the oft-noted formulas of "no Mao, no Great Leap" and "no Mao, no Cultural Revolution," is that even after the disastrous effects of these movements became clear to the great majority of the CCP elite, they were curbed only when Mao decided that the costs were too great. Equally if not more telling, continuing (if watered down) aspects of Cultural Revolution radicalism persisted during the last period of Mao's life from 1972, when his health was extremely fragile, including his final two months when he was in a virtual coma. Only with the Chairman's death did his surviving colleagues turn decisively against his policies but not against his sacrosanct position as the founding father of the country.

Mao's power derived precisely from his accepted position as the father of the nation, a status culturally enhanced as the "severe and brilliant" founding emperor of a new dynasty.[1] For broad sections of the population, both as a result of a genuine perception of the new order and incessant official propaganda, Mao had overturned an exploitative social system, brought peace and order, launched economic construction, and, above all, expelled the foreign powers and restored China's national dignity. For top CCP leaders and lower-level officials and cadres, Mao was the strategic genius whose leadership converted the party's seemingly hopeless, or at best extremely marginalized, situation into the unimaginable victory of 1949. For such communists, opposing Mao was simply out of the question. Much more significant than any calculation of the futility of any challenge was the Chairman's moral authority: whatever his errors, Mao's achievements could not be ignored, as his brilliance, in the elite's view, had created the revolutionary success that gave meaning to their life endeavors. To deny Mao would have amounted to denying themselves.

While Mao's authority was beyond challenge, the Chairman himself was jealous of his power and wary of possible threats, sometimes readjusting the distribution of authority among institutions and individuals to reinforce his own dominance. At worst, notably during the Cultural Revolution, he showed signs of paranoia, but overall he evinced supreme confidence. Unlike Stalin, who generally stayed close to the levers of power in the Kremlin, Mao toured the provinces regularly, often at critical turning points returning to Beijing (or convening leadership councils elsewhere) to enforce his views on his colleagues. In the chronological discussion that follows, the changing distribution of power at Mao's hand and his fluctuating views of his colleagues are examined. This is related to a larger issue concerning Mao's method of rule—he was both the great unifier of the CCP and, in his later years, the figure who ripped the party apart.

In addition to shifting approaches to power, Mao's policies varied greatly. Two broad tendencies can be identified: the "revolutionary romantic" and the pragmatic.

"Maoism" is often equated with "revolutionary romantic" endeavors, the Great Leap above all others, when, in fact, the flesh-and-blood Mao had a highly pragmatic side. From his earliest days as a radical intellectual in the late 1910s he promoted both sweeping visions of a powerful China and the practicality required to achieve it, with pragmatism dominating for the majority of his career. Even in his most radical periods, Mao intermittently adopted pragmatic, rational approaches to specific issues.

Another aspect of Mao's rule is that, like any leader, he had particular interests in specific policy areas, with significant consequences for the sectors concerned. Most broadly, Mao took responsibility for the overall course of the revolution, for the ideology and goals of the regime. He also believed he had a special understanding of rural China, and he played a direct role in overseeing the transformation of agriculture. This was in sharp contrast to economic policy, an area where Mao confessed a lack of understanding and, apart from his disastrous Great Leap program, largely stayed aloof. Finally, the Chairman kept an iron grip on foreign and military policy. In this latter regard, a crucial concern of his leadership was relations with the Soviet Union. For Mao was not simply a Chinese nationalist or committed Marxist; he and the CCP were part of the international communist movement headed by Moscow. The development of this complex and often tense relationship had an enormous impact on People's Republic of China (PRC) domestic as well as foreign policy.

This chapter first briefly examines the background to the establishment of the PRC—Mao's position within the CCP, the structure of leadership power, the party's policy orientation, and the resources the regime-in-waiting possessed on the eve of taking power. It then analyzes five distinct periods involving different political dynamics, policy programs, and impacts on Chinese society, before concluding with an overall assessment of Mao and his rule. As the discussion unfolds, readers should keep in mind the question of how and why Mao changed over these years, and whether, as is sometimes claimed, there was an underlying causality connecting the earlier Mao with the destructiveness of his later years.

MAO'S RISE TO POWER, 1935–1949

Contrary to official CCP histories, Mao did not assume leadership of the party in 1935 during the Long March. Instead, this was a gradual process that was only completed a decade later. The fundamental reason for Mao's rise to power during this period was the successful political, military, and diplomatic policies he designed for the dual struggles against the Nationalists (Kuomintang) and the Japanese. These policies contributed to CCP survival from the seemingly hopeless position of the early Long March, were crucial to developing substantial communist power in base areas behind Japanese lines while outmaneuvering the Nationalists within the ostensible anti-Japanese united front, and then led to the stunning, much quicker than expected victory in the civil war of 1946–1949.

But the solidification of Mao's power also reflected other developments. Ironically, given tensions soon apparent in Mao's independent tendencies and his unwillingness to sacrifice CCP forces for Soviet priorities, one of the most crucial was Stalin's endorsement of his leadership in late 1938. Stalin's decision was apparently based on the calculation that as a strong capable leader, Mao was preferred over the historically pro-Moscow, but less politically successful "Returned Student" faction of CCP leaders. Another major factor was the development of, and through the rectification campaign of 1942–1944, the party's indoctrination in a new ideological canon, Mao Zedong Thought, an ideology that both supported his policy approach and sanctified his person as a significant Marxist theorist. Finally, a series of organizational steps completed the process—notably a 1943 decision giving Mao the authority to personally decide critical matters, and the formation of a new Maoist leadership at the Seventh **Party Congress** in 1945 in Yan'an, the town in Shaanxi province that served as party headquarters in 1937–1947.

The key to Mao's political ascent, though, was the pragmatic ideology and policy that produced revolutionary success. In ideological terms, despite some theoretical pretension, Mao Zedong Thought was intensely practical and oriented toward contemporary problems. The focus was on concrete Chinese conditions, as exemplified in Mao's famous dictum that Marxism-Leninism was the arrow, but its significance was in hitting the target of the Chinese revolution. Another seminal concept was "truth from facts"—that theory must never blind leaders from the reality of the situation. In concrete terms this led to cautious military policies, as befit the weaker forces of the CCP, and flexible rural policies that pushed mild or more far-reaching social reforms according to prevailing conditions and the party's needs.

Overall, as reflected in the rectification campaign's heavy criticism of the "left lines" of the late 1920s and early 1930s, Mao's cautious policies could be considered "rightist" in that, by and large, he avoided unnecessary struggles, sought to maximize the united front of potential allies, and bided his time until the balance of forces shifted to the CCP's favor. Also significant was that, notwithstanding the undercurrent of tensions with Stalin, Mao's theoretical claims were modest, the Soviet Union's role as the leader of the communist world was never questioned, and Stalin's writings were part of the curriculum studied during the CCP rectification campaign. Furthermore, in particular areas where the CCP had little experience, such as urban policy, when communist forces moved into cities in the Northeast from 1946, careful attention was given to Soviet precedent. Mao's pragmatism extended to both accepting the international communist order led by Moscow and utilizing what appeared to be valuable foreign experience.

One of Mao's greatest achievements in the 1935–1945 decade was to fashion a unified party. In contrast to the bitter and often violent inner-party factionalism of the early 1930s, Mao created a unified leadership around his person and policies, a process that was not based on advancing over the broken bodies of opponents, as often claimed, but instead on a shrewd process of garnering broad support. Apart from the crucial matter of propagating a successful revolutionary strategy, Mao accomplished this by moderate treatment of former political opponents, eschewing a **Politburo**[*] made up of or even including his own closest supporters, but instead drawing widely on talent and from representatives of different party constituencies or "mountaintops" to staff key positions. He also presided over a flexible and consultative policy process that devolved responsibility as required by a decentralized war situation, and where policies could be argued by his colleagues in a diluted form of "collective leadership," what has been called the "**Yan'an Round Table**,"[2] even as Mao retained the final say.

Of particular importance was his sensitivity to the various constituencies in the party, something seen in the promotions to the number two and three positions in the CCP. Liu Shaoqi, the leader most associated with the party's urban underground or "white area" forces, who although closest to Mao in criticism of past "leftist" excesses had limited personal connection to him, became the widely acknowledged successor. Zhou Enlai, a leader of higher status in the party's early days with extensive military and political connections who had been a political opponent of Mao's in the early 1930s, but one careful to maintain as positive relations as possible, assumed the critical political and diplomatic roles he would retain until his serious illness in the 1970s. (See Table 3.1)

More extensive than specific Politburo appointments was the broad distribution of power among the "mountaintops" of the decentralized party structure—the top generals of various armies, the leaders of base areas where the CCP had established viable governing structures and garnered popular support, and leading figures of the underground struggle. Thus, in addition to belief in the revolutionary cause,

[*] The Politburo (or Political Bureau) at that time (ca. 1945) consisted of thirteen members and was headed by Mao; it was outranked only by the five-man Secretariat also chaired by Mao. In 1956 the size of the Politburo was expanded to twenty-three, and a new top organization, the Standing Committee, with six members, was established, again headed by Mao. Although the memberships fluctuated in size over time, the Politburo and its Standing Committee remain the most powerful leadership bodies of the CCP.

TABLE 3.1 Top Leaders of China from 1949 to 1976

Name (Birth/Death)	Key Titles and Dates	Comments
Mao Zedong (1893–1976)	• CCP Chairman (1945–1976) • PRC President (1949–1959) • Military Commission Chairman (1949–1976)	One of the founders of the Chinese Communist Party in 1921. Assumed a position among the top leadership of the CCP in 1934–1935 during the Long March, although not elected Chairman of the Politburo until 1943 and of the Central Committee until 1945. The absolute ruler of China from the founding of the PRC in 1949 until his death in 1976. Still revered in China despite acknowledgement of his serious mistakes.
Zhou Enlai (1898–1976)	• PRC Premier (1949–1976) • PRC Foreign Minister (1949–1958) • CCP Vice-Chairman (1956–1969, 1973–1976)	Long March veteran. Headed the machinery of government after the founding of the PRC. Key role in détente with United States in early 1970s. Valued by Mao as a skilled administrator and diplomat, but not particularly respected by the Chairman. Some regard Zhou as a moderating influence during the Cultural Revolution; others see him as an obsequious underling to Mao, who nevertheless became increasingly unhappy with Zhou in 1973–1974.
Liu Shaoqi (1898–1969)	• PRC Vice-President (1949–1959) • PRC President (1959–1966) • CCP Vice-Chairman (1956–1966)	Most significant leader of CCP "white area" forces operating in urban areas and behind enemy lines during the civil and anti-Japanese wars. Regarded as Mao's successor from the 7th CCP Congress in 1945 until he was purged as a "capitalist roader" during the Cultural Revolution. Died in detention. Posthumously rehabilitated in 1980.
Deng Xiaoping (1904–1997)	• CCP General Secretary (1956–1966) • CCP Vice-Chairman (1975–1976, 1977–82) • Vice-Premier (1952–1966, 1973–1976, 1977–1980) • Military Commission Chairman (1981–1989)	Long March veteran. One of Mao's favorites in the post-1949 CCP leadership until the Cultural Revolution, when he was ousted as a "capitalist roader" but protected from physical harm by Mao. Returned to leadership positions in 1973 after making self-criticism, but removed a second time in 1976 for political mistakes. Again returned to the leadership in mid-1977, about nine months after the arrest of the Gang of Four. Consolidated power in stages after late 1978, becoming China's paramount leader in early 1980. See also Table. 4.1, chap. 4, this book.
Chen Yun (1905–1995)	• CCP Vice-Chairman (1956–1966, 1978–1982) • PRC Vice-Premier (1949–1966, 1979–1980)	Veteran revolutionary who became one of China's leading economic planners after 1949. Architect of successful economic recovery and development policies in 1949–1957. Criticized by Mao as too cautious during Great Leap Forward in 1958, but called back by him in 1959 and 1962 to deal with severe economic difficulties. Again criticized by Mao in 1962 as "always a rightist," and remained on the sidelines until late 1978 when he played a key role in altering the CCP's leadership equation. Subsequently had a major influence on economic policy, initially supporting reform but increasingly cautious and conservative from the mid-1980s. See also Table. 4.1, chap. 4

TABLE 3.1 *(Continued)*

Name (Birth/Death)	Key Titles and Dates	Comments
Lin Biao (1907–1971)	• CCP Vice-Chairman (1958–1971) • PRC Vice-Premier (1954–1966) • PRC Defense Minister (1959–1971)	Long March veteran, and one of the CCP's greatest military leaders during the civil and anti-Japanese wars. A Mao favorite, he became defense minister in 1959 following the dismissal of Peng Dehuai for criticism of the Great Leap Forward. Mao chose Lin as his successor at the start of the Cultural Revolution, an appointment written into the 1969 CCP constitution. Mao grew increasingly unhappy with Lin over a number of bizarre matters starting in 1970. Lin and other members of his family were killed in a plane crash while trying to flee China after an alleged (but unlikely) failed coup attempt against Mao.
Jiang Qing (1914–1991)	• Deputy Director, Central Cultural Revolution Group (1966–1969) • Member, CCP Politburo (1969–1976)	Former movie actress who married Mao in Yan'an in 1939. Kept on the political sidelines until the early 1960s when Mao called on her to counter bourgeois influences in the arts. She took on increasingly powerful roles during the Cultural Revolution and its aftermath. She and three of her radical colleagues were arrested after Mao's death in 1976, denounced as the Gang of Four, and accused of plotting to seize power. Sentenced to life in prison, where she committed suicide in 1991.
Hua Guofeng (1921–2008)	• CCP Chairman (1976–1981) • PRC Premier (1976–1980) • Military Commission Chairman (1976–1981)	Chosen by Mao to succeed Zhou Enlai as premier in January 1976 in a move that caught everyone by surprise. Had worked in support of Deng's program in 1975, but was seen as a beneficiary of the Cultural Revolution. Played the decisive role in the purge of the Gang of Four, becoming CCP Chairman by unanimous Politburo decision. Worked largely cooperatively with Deng in 1977–1978 in eliminating the influence of the Cultural Revolution, but from the end of 1978 was gradually undermined by his lack of Party seniority. Removed from key posts in 1980–1981. See also Table 4.1, chap. 4, this book.

the wide sharing of the spoils of power among the party elite deepened the commitment of the disciplined forces that soon defeated the larger, better equipped but factionalized armies of the Kuomintang. Of course, this could not eliminate all perceptions of unfairness concerning the distribution of power, particularly the belief of some army and base area leaders that they were the crucial actors in the CCP's success and that the underground or "white area" leaders were less deserving of rewards. This, however, was a latent tension that did not become significant until the first major post-1949 power struggle, the Gao Gang affair in 1953–1954; for now, different groups had a vested as well as an ideological interest in success, and for that unity was essential.

A final factor to be noted in Mao's unification of the party was that while it involved intense psychological pressure in indoctrinating leaders and ordinary cadres alike in Mao's political line, Mao's program contained an explicit "organizational line" that promised a break with the violent party practices of the past (in which he too had played a prominent role): patient education would replace the "ruthless struggles and merciless blows" of the early 1930s.[3]

Despite excesses, notably the so-called rescue campaign in 1943 that, under the direct leadership of Politburo security chief Kang Sheng, involved the torture and imprisonment of thousands of party members accused of disloyalty or subversion and for which Mao, who bore ultimate responsibility, apologized, this approach was mostly honored, earning Mao further loyalty and resulting in deeper commitment to the CCP's cause. While future rectification movements after 1949 would cause trepidation, leaders and ordinary cadres generally accepted that ideological self-examination was an appropriate method of enforcing the party's policies, and if excesses did occur they would be corrected, yet again demonstrating the greatness of the party and Mao. This conviction began to fray from the late 1950s, but it remained surprisingly robust to the end of Mao's life.

Two aspects of the situation in the years immediately preceding the establishment of the PRC should be mentioned: the expectation of a seamless shift from a rural-based revolution to an urban-oriented state-building approach, and the vast diversity of conditions facing the communists as they seized national power. While hopeful Westerners regarded the communists as mere agrarian reformers, a view also darkly hinted at by Stalin, who doubted the Chinese party leader's communist credentials, Mao and his colleagues were good Marxists. For all their indebtedness to the rural revolution that "surrounded the cities," they ultimately saw the rural phase as a necessary prelude to a modernizing program to create a "rich and powerful" China, a program that had to embrace an industrializing society. As Mao put it in mid-1949, "The serious task of economic construction lies before us. We shall soon put aside some of the things we know well and be compelled to do things we don't know well."[4]

This transition, however, would have to occur in a regionally fragmented China, where not only did conditions differ significantly from area to area in social, economic, and even ethnic terms, but also the CCP's strength and local history varied enormously. The fundamental difference was between, on the one hand, the base area regions of North China where "the countryside surrounded the cities," that is, the rural revolution that initiated the reform of village society, built up the political and military forces that defeated the Nationalists on the battlefield, and took over the cities of that region and the Northeast, and, on the other hand, the vast areas south of the Yangtze River, where communist forces were weak to nonexistent, a straightforward military seizure of the cities took place, and CCP cadres fanned out from the cities to bring the first stages of land reform to the villages.

Under these conditions, daunting problems faced Mao's new regime. Chinese society and polity were fragmented, public order and morale had decayed, a war-torn economy suffered from severe inflation and unemployment, and the country's fundamental economic and military weakness created monumental obstacles to the goal of national wealth and power. Yet the CCP's revolutionary experience bequeathed the new regime some potent resources. A unified leadership around an unchallenged leader, a leader whose authority was being elevated to an even more imposing level as a dynastic founder, promised strong nonfactionalized direction from the top. The pragmatic nature of Mao's policies in navigating the difficult currents of political and military struggle indicated an ongoing approach of dealing in realities. A disciplined party organization, although small for a huge country and short in critical skills, provided the core of an effective administration. Added to this, the population's positive anticipation of the prospects of peace, order, and economic development gave the new regime support during what would come to be regarded, albeit with considerable exaggeration, as the PRC's "golden years."

MAO AS ALL-POWERFUL CHAIRMAN OF THE BOARD, 1949–1956

"The Golden Years"

This initial period of the PRC was, in the party's own terms, a great success. The economy was restored more or less on schedule by 1953, before beginning rapid growth along the lines of Soviet-style central planning. All of the country except for Taiwan, Hong Kong, and Macau had been brought under Beijing's control by 1951. Through skillful diplomacy and especially by fighting the world's foremost power to a stalemate in the **Korean War**, China's national pride and international prestige had grown significantly. After a period of careful reassurance to the general populace and key groups, the CCP began to penetrate society and establish totalitarian control through organizational measures that reached into urban neighborhoods and villages. The party also used political campaigns that embodied Marxist notions of class struggle and targeted specific groups, including rural elites, the bourgeoisie, intellectuals, and presumed counterrevolutionaries, whether to attack those considered hostile to the regime, often using chilling violence, or to indoctrinate those who could be won over to the party's cause. Economic gains translated into general popular support, while those who benefited from land reform, such as poor peasants, and activists, who secured positions in the expanding industrial structure, were even more supportive of the regime.

Land reform, a priority socioeconomic program of the new regime, was basically implemented from 1950 to 1952. This program, which had been carried out in the base areas of North China during the revolutionary struggle, was now extended to virtually the entire country, notably the "newly liberated areas" south of the Yangtze. Since the PRC was, economically and socially, in the pre-socialist stage of "**New Democracy**," the movement confiscated and redistributed landlord land to peasants on the basis of individual ownership. The initial approach laid down by the agrarian reform law of June 1950 was mild; its main objective was to advance the economy by "freeing rural productive forces" rather than aiding the village poor. But the approach was radicalized by late 1950 as resistance developed in the villages. Now class struggle and mass mobilization were emphasized, with poor peasants assuming village leadership and landlords humiliated, with perhaps one to two million alleged exploiters executed. A substantial redistribution of land to poor and middle (more productive but not rich) peasants occurred, but the most significant outcome of land reform was the destruction of the old rural power structure.

From 1953 the party moved steadily toward the Marxist objective of the **socialist transformation** of the economy and society. This process had its twists and turns, producing considerable yet quite containable popular discontent during its "high tide" in 1955–1956, but the result not only achieved the ideological objective, it also extended the party's political and economic control, and with it the leadership's sense of a fundamental breakthrough. According to Mao at the Eighth CCP Congress in fall 1956: "We have gained a decisive victory in the socialist revolution [and] our Party is now more united, more consolidated than at any time in the past."[5]

As the new emperor, Mao's authority was absolute, but his manner of rule was less intrusive or disruptive than in any subsequent period of the PRC. Although imposing his views in a small albeit crucial number of cases, generally Mao served as the chairman of the board, allowing his more specialist colleagues, notably Premier Zhou Enlai and economic czar Chen Yun, to shape programs in the areas of their special competence, with Mao largely acting as a synthesizer and arbiter of policy decisions. Mao continued the consultative style of the 1940s, acknowledged his own lack of expertise, and reflected his relatively centrist position on the issues of the day. In contrast to the full-blooded Maoism of the Great Leap or Cultural Revolution, Mao's ideological position up to 1956 was largely the orthodox Marxism that saw socialist victory in terms of seizing ownership of the forces of production, and his political task was the relatively incremental one of adjusting the pace of socialist transformation. Even in the relatively few cases in which he imposed his views, his approach was systematic and rational, the process involved considerable discussion and efforts to persuade his colleagues, and although his initiatives were bold and impatient, they were still in many respects moderate.

To a large extent, Mao's less intrusive role was due to the focus on economic development and the broad elite consensus that China should follow the Soviet model, a position Mao fully shared. As Mao subsequently declared, "Since we had no experience we could only copy the Soviet Union and our own creativity was small."[6] This overstated the case for various areas, notably rural policy, where Mao oversaw considerable adjustments from Soviet precedent, but on key matters including economic strategy and methods, military modernization and government institutions, extensive borrowing and even blind copying of Soviet practices occurred with the aid of Soviet experts.

Such excessive copying undoubtedly frustrated Mao, and at the same time he endured tense relations with Stalin during negotiations in Moscow for the 1950 Sino-Soviet alliance and subsequently over the Korean War. Chinese entry into the Korean conflict was the first case in which Mao, after some vacillation, enforced his personal view, overcoming fears of an apparent majority of the Politburo that getting involved would jeopardize China's security and economic recovery. In any case, in his relations with the Soviet Union, Mao accepted Stalin's and subsequently Moscow's leadership of international communism. He swallowed some bitter pills in the 1950 treaty, such as the imposition of joint Sino-Soviet stock companies that allowed Soviet exploitation of Chinese resources, and despite some theoretical innovations he largely stayed within the Stalinist version of Marxism-Leninism, as graphically suggested by his nocturnal visits to the Beijing residence of the Soviet ambassador for ideological tutorials. Clearly, any dealings with Stalin involved considerations of international politics where Mao took personal control, but the acknowledgment of broad Soviet ideological authority only added to the weight of Russian pronouncements on building socialism. And on core economic planning issues, Mao's role was relatively limited.

Meanwhile, power was being redistributed within the CCP. This involved less the rise or fall of individuals (as the main power holders remained members of the **Central Committee**[*] elected in 1945, with all the various mountaintops still represented) than their reshuffling and the establishment of new institutions. The key aspect was the centralization and civilianization of power over the 1950–1954 period. Given the diverse conditions facing the CCP in 1949, an initial period of regional administration based on the various armies that took control of different areas was logical. Large regional Military-Administrative Committees and subordinate military control committees were established, but this was a transitional arrangement from the first. Army commanders initially playing key roles in regional governments were gradually transferred to strictly military positions. Indeed, from the start the key leaders in five of the six large regions were basically civilians, including Deng Xiaoping in the Southwest.[7] The principle Mao demanded during the revolutionary period that "the party commands the gun, and the gun must never be allowed to command the party"[8] was again enforced. Another aspect of centralization concerned Mao personally. While his authority was never in question, he enhanced his administrative control in 1953 by requiring that he sign off on all Central Committee documents.

With the new 1954 state constitution and other organizational changes, a permanent institutional structure was in place: the party was in overall control and primarily concerned with political movements, particularly in the rural areas; the **State Council** headed the expanding state bureaucracy and took charge of economic policy; and the reorganized **Central Military Commission (CMC)** oversaw the **People's Liberation Army (PLA)**. Mao as party, state, and CMC chairman was at the top of all three pillars of power, although, significantly, Zhou Enlai as premier was crucial in state administration and, along with Chen Yun, economic policy. Finally, the new structure reaffirmed Mao's control of the military and his now personalized principle that "the party commands the gun." Both Liu Shaoqi (Mao's presumptive successor) and Zhou Enlai were excluded from the CMC. The Chairman and his favored junior colleague, Deng Xiaoping (who also assumed a key role as CCP secretary-general, charged with overseeing the party's day-to-day business), were the only civilians on the reorganized CMC. At the same time, virtually all the leading generals promoted to the highest rank of marshal in 1955 took on strictly military responsibilities.[9] Although six of the ten marshals were elected to the Politburo in 1956, it is clear that in the entire period from then until the Cultural Revolution began in the mid-1960s, the military played a limited, generally minimal role in civilian affairs.

At the leadership level the most important redistribution of power concerned the transfer of leading regional figures to key positions in Beijing in 1952–1953: a development picturesquely referred to at the time as "five horses enter the capital." Deng Xiaoping was one of those horses, but the "leading horse" was the Northeast leader

---

[*] The Central Committee of the CCP is larger, but less powerful than the Politburo. In 1945, there were forty-four full members and thirty-three alternates. Mao was elected Chairman of the Politburo in 1943, and of the Central Committee in 1945, hence the title, "Chairman Mao." The Central Committee was expanded greatly in size over the years that the CCP has been in power. In 2019, it had 376 full and alternate members.

Gao Gang, another favorite of Mao's. This resulted in turf battles, as Gao's new assignment as head of the State Planning Commission apparently produced tension with both Zhou Enlai and Chen Yun over economic policy.

But the main disruptive impact was a much more fundamental challenge to leadership unity. In late 1952 to early 1953, Gao had several private conversations with Mao in which the Chairman expressed dissatisfaction with Liu Shaoqi and Zhou Enlai as too cautious concerning the pace of socialist transformation. Even more ominous, according to Gao's secretary, in summer 1953 Mao raised the issue of Liu's possibly traitorous activities in the Northeast in the late 1920s, and tasked Gao with investigating the matter. Gao then began to lobby other key leaders, including Deng Xiaoping and Chen Yun, with an aim to securing their support for a challenge to Liu and/or Zhou. He particularly argued that as a CCP leader in the so-called white areas under Kuomintang control, Liu did not deserve his high position, while he, Gao, represented the red "base areas." Mao's attitudes and motives were opaque, and other leaders did not know how to respond. After some hesitation, Chen and Deng approached Mao and reported on Gao's lobbying. Mao's reaction was to lure Gao into taking further steps in his plotting against Liu and Zhou, turn on him for disrupting party unity, and reaffirm Liu Shaoqi's position as the Chairman's successor. Gao, apparently believing he had been betrayed by Mao, committed suicide. The end result was that the first significant challenge to party unity since the consolidation of Mao's leadership had been repulsed, while the Chairman's all-powerful ability to determine the fate of his subordinates had been reemphasized, and his ultimate aims and attitudes remained uncertain. In the end, Mao opted for leadership unity and stability—on this occasion.

The Transition to Socialism

In policy terms, the key turning points in the early 1950s concerned the pace of the transition to socialism: the **general line** for the transition in 1953, and the "high tide" of agricultural **cooperativization** in 1955. In both cases the initiatives to move faster came from Mao, while Liu Shaoqi and other leaders advocated a slower pace. Given the outcomes achieved, Mao's interventions were viewed within the CCP as successful, and (together with his decision on the Korean War) as further proof of his unmatched strategic insight. In neither case, however, was Mao's position wildly radical. Prior to the fall of 1952, the consensus CCP position was that the "New Democracy" period of communist rule in China, which allowed multiple forms of economic ownership, including private property, would last for ten to twenty years, and *only then* would the transition to socialism begin.

Now, however, Mao pressed for a more ambitious schedule whereby the transition would start almost immediately, but the process itself would be gradual. When the general line was laid down by Mao unilaterally in June 1953, it stipulated that socialist transformation would be completed "within a period of ten to fifteen years or a bit longer," and warned against "errors either of 'left' deviation or of right deviation."[10] In the buildup to the general line, analogous to his handling of the Gao Gang affair, elements of both Mao's awesome power and reasonableness were present. Mao caused individual panic in early 1953 by criticizing Finance Minister Bo Yibo's tax policies as "beneficial to capitalism," yet Bo suffered only a mild career setback. In the summer of 1953, moreover, despite his impatience over the speed of transformation, Mao backed the softer, more pragmatic approach to commercial capitalists advocated by Chen Yun over the harsher preferences of Gao, who urged faster movement toward the nationalization of commerce.

Similar phenomena can be seen concerning the implementation of the transition to socialism in the countryside. Following the conclusion of land reform, the party took the first major step in that direction in 1953–1955 by gradually establishing **lower-level agricultural producer cooperatives** made up of twenty-five to fifty families. Land, although still technically owned by the farmers, as well as tools and draft animals, were pooled; agricultural production was under the direction of cooperative officials. Members were paid partly on the basis of how much work they did and partly according to how much property they had contributed to the **cooperative**.

After two years of fluctuating development in the cooperativization movement, during which Mao again warned his comrades about going too fast (left deviation) or too slowly (right deviation), a consensus emerged at the start of 1955, with Liu Shaoqi and CCP Rural Work Department Director Deng Zihui most prominent, that a limited contraction of the number of existing cooperatives was necessary after overexpansion in 1954. Mao accepted this, but by the spring of 1955, based on his own investigations, he became concerned that this policy, by loosening state control of agriculture, was undermining the state procurement of grain needed to feed the cities, and was also contributing to class polarization in the countryside, as some families were getting quite a bit richer than others. This led Mao to argue for a relatively modest increase in the number of cooperatives. While this was formally accepted by the party leadership in May, Mao pressed for further increases in June and July, which all of the highest leaders apparently accepted. Deng Zihui, however, argued against Mao's latest proposal, leaving his colleagues in the Rural Work Department astonished that he dared to "offend Chairman Mao merely over hundreds of thousands of cooperatives."[11]

Mao rejected Deng Zihui's advice and subjected him to criticism as a "right deviationist," yet Deng retained his position, although his career was more adversely affected than that of Bo Yibo. What was significant was that in turning on Deng Zihui, the Chairman had raised an economic question to a political one, and although his latest proposal on the cooperatives was still far from radical, his rhetoric mobilized the party apparatus into an intense campaign mode. This resulted in the "high tide" that by the end of 1956 had basically formed the whole countryside into **higher-level agricultural producers cooperatives, or collectives**. Not only were these much larger—250 families—than the earlier cooperatives, but the collective also now owned the land, and peasants were paid only according to their labor. Only a small portion of the collectively owned land was set aside for private cultivation. This was a far more radical outcome than Mao's mid-1955 plan, which had only called for establishment of lower-stage (less socialist) cooperatives in *half* of China's villages by spring 1958. But since the achievement of agricultural **collectivization** was a key socialist goal, Mao's intervention to speed things up was seen by his comrades as more evidence of his superior insight and inspirational leadership.

The practical consequence of collectivization was to entrench further party control of China's vast countryside. In addition to the organization of individual households into collective units, other measures deepening totalitarianism in the rural areas were strict controls on population movement, in effect limiting peasants to their villages, and the implementation in 1954–1955 of the state monopoly on grain and other agricultural products. This monopoly both guaranteed the food supply for the cities and thus the PRC's industrialization program, and placed in the hands of the regime the food that would be sold back to the countryside to meet basic livelihood needs. The misuse of this power would become a critical contributor to the Great Leap Forward famine in a few years' time.

The "high tide" in agriculture was soon followed by the similarly rapid socialist transformation of industry and commerce. By early 1957, the nationalization of these sectors was basically complete and private ownership largely eliminated from the urban economy. At about the same time, an effort had been undertaken to significantly increase the pace of economic development, an effort later regarded as the "little leap forward." But all of these programs produced dislocations in the economy, and measures were taken to relax the pace of change starting in the spring of 1956.

At a late April meeting of the Politburo, however, Mao said that he wanted to increase the already high rate of investment, despite mounting evidence that the economy could not effectively absorb it. Although there was an almost unanimous Politburo preference for a more restrained policy, the meeting dutifully approved Mao's wishes. Zhou Enlai, however, went to see Mao a few days later to argue against the decision and, after a temper tantrum, Mao agreed. The incident not only demonstrated that the Chairman responded to rational argument but also, despite the earlier attacks on Bo Yibo and Deng Zihui, that even a cautious leader like Zhou Enlai was willing to approach him, believing that Mao's consultative leadership style still applied. Similarly, pragmatic adjustments were made in other areas in 1956–1957, notably increasing the scope of private peasant production within the collective framework and reestablishing a limited rural free market.

Mao and the leadership as a whole did not regard such scaling back as defeats, but rather as sensible adjustments in the context of the overwhelming—and much more quickly achieved than anticipated—victory of socialist transformation. This, as previously noted, was orthodox Marxism. With the economic structure transformed and private property in both city and countryside largely abolished, there was now not only the basis for socialist modernization but also the class enemy no longer had the wherewithal to challenge the regime. To be sure, there were still opposing political and ideological tendencies, or contradictions, in socialist society, but these were nothing to worry about. As Mao put it in early 1957, "large scale, turbulent class struggles have in the main come to an end."[12]

In this context, party priorities set by the Eighth Party Congress and its aftermath were to shift to economic construction and handling "**non-antagonistic contradictions** among the people." In other words, most problems in China could be resolved through discussion, debate, persuasion, and other noncoercive means. The populace was believed to fundamentally support the CCP, as well as possessing creative skills that the regime should enlist, but at the same time, it was believed that society had legitimate grievances that the party should alleviate. In this context, Mao sought to encourage the expression of different opinions, including complaints about regime shortcomings. This was famously expressed in Mao's spring 1956 slogan addressed to intellectuals in particular: "let a hundred flowers bloom, let a hundred schools of thought contend." In 1956, this by and large produced only tepid academic discussion, but the following year a more determined effort by Mao set in motion a series of policy failures with ultimately catastrophic consequences for the PRC. While never intended to weaken party control, the policy line of the Eighth Congress would have mitigated the harsh edges of totalitarianism if implemented, but instead, just the opposite happened.

EXPERIMENTS AND DISASTERS, 1957–1960

The Hundred Flowers Movement and the Anti-Rightist Campaign

Three major developments followed the declaration of fundamental victory at the fall 1956 Eighth Party Congress—the **Hundred Flowers Movement** in the first half of 1957, the **Anti-Rightist Campaign** in the summer and fall, and the Great Leap Forward that emerged in late 1957 and extended into 1960. These movements were interconnected; Mao played an initiating role in each, and the Hundred Flowers and Great Leap were virtually unique experiments in the history of international communism, drawing Soviet puzzlement and criticism as a result. The Anti-Rightist Campaign and Great Leap in particular had dire consequences that left deep scars on society. These campaigns grew out of the 1956 consensus on giving priority to economic development, but the originally envisioned concessions to society of the Hundred Flowers soon gave way to increasing emphasis on class struggle against perceived enemies of the revolution. Finally, notwithstanding Mao's decisive role in each campaign, the Hundred Flowers Movement and Anti-Rightist Campaign both had broad support in the top leadership, albeit with more reservations in the former case. But even with widespread initial enthusiasm in the elite and populace, the third movement was fundamentally a case of "no Mao, no Great Leap."

Leadership consensus existed on the assumption underpinning the Hundred Flowers that the party should solicit feedback from the public. But encouraging open criticism of the government, which was only mildly encouraged in 1956, was always fraught with difficulty and met resistance from lower-ranking officials who were vulnerable to direct criticism in their work units. Facing this resistance, Mao began to push for a more vigorous Hundred Flowers in February 1957. The response from intellectuals who had been subject to various ideological remolding campaigns since 1949 was cautious, but under repeated official urging, by May an outbreak of extensive criticism of the regime unfolded. In fact, much of this criticism remained guarded and was along the themes Mao himself had set, but bitter attacks on lower-level cadres plus comparatively rare extreme statements attacking the party and even Mao himself caused deep concern within the CCP.

By mid-May, without admitting it, Mao realized he had miscalculated and began to plan for a counterattack on the critics. For several weeks he waited to "lure the snakes out" (something erroneously thought by many to have been his plan from the beginning), and then in early June launched a systematic attack in the form of the Anti-Rightist Campaign against those who had spoken out.

What was significant about the Anti-Rightist Campaign was its intensity and scope, a profound intensification of the regime's totalitarian impulse. It was conducted in all official organizations, it deeply touched intellectuals and other segments of the urban population in particular, and it resulted in the extensive use of the "rightist" label that would curse people so designated for the rest of the Maoist era, as well as the widespread sending of "rightists" to the countryside for reform through labor. Even more fundamentally, the campaign sent a chill of fear through society, something hitherto not felt on such a broad basis. In the early years of the PRC, although there had been many threatening movements directed at particular groups, for those not directly affected there was the sense that these efforts were justified, or in any case not personally relevant. Now fear was much more widespread, with an intimidating effect for the future.

Nonetheless, the Anti-Rightist Campaign initially seemed designed to restore the status quo ante, the situation of unchallenged party dominance without major policy readjustments. The broad thrust of the moderate economic policies that had prevailed since the "little leap" continued into the early fall of 1957, and there were no signs of a redistribution of power among either leading institutions or individuals.

However, various developments created pressure on existing economic policy. At one level, the perceived unreliability of intellectuals as a result of the Hundred Flowers called into doubt the assumption that specialists could be relied on as a key "positive factor" for economic development. Also, the assumption of society's support of the regime that underpinned the relaxation of 1956–1957 was undermined by waves of industrial strikes and substantial peasant withdrawals from poorly performing collectives—something that led to socialist education efforts among workers and peasants in the summer of 1957 to bring them back in line with party policy. Finally, the pace of economic growth, particularly in agriculture, lagged behind expectations. Thus, there was a basis for an altered approach to development. These considerations fed into Mao's fundamental desire to transform China into a powerful industrializing state at the quickest possible pace.

Other factors also came into play in pushing policy in a more radical direction. One was the ever-significant relationship with the Soviet Union. At the policy level, without any intention of straying from the broad parameters of the Soviet model, by 1956 CCP leaders focused on the differences between Soviet and Chinese conditions and the need for appropriate policy adjustments, something equally persuasive to an economic specialist like Chen Yun and to Mao, who offered the most systematic statement of the need for readjustment in April 1956.[13]

Furthermore, by the time Mao attended the fortieth anniversary of the Bolshevik revolution in Moscow in November 1957, he had shed any latent sense of inferiority to Stalin, who had died in 1953. Indeed, Mao felt superior as an international communist leader to Stalin's successor, Nikita Khrushchev. He also believed that China had attained a new status by mediating between the Soviets and Eastern Europe first during the Polish October that brought Poland a degree of autonomy from Moscow, and then following the crushing of the Hungarian revolution in 1956 by the Soviet army. Mao thought that the Russians had handled both matters badly.

There was also a sense of growing optimism and competitiveness in the communist world, generated by rapid Soviet economic advances and Moscow's technological breakthroughs with the *Sputnik* satellite and intercontinental ballistic missile in 1957. Mao's reaction was to declare that internationally "the east wind is prevailing over the west wind," and thus match Soviet boasts that they would overtake the United States economically in fifteen years with the claim that China would overtake Britain in the same period. In terms of international communist politics, Mao strongly affirmed Soviet leadership while in Moscow, which undoubtedly facilitated a Soviet promise to provide the PRC with nuclear weapons technology. Subsequently, despite an overlay of competing national pride and some suspicion, in March 1958, Mao declared "complete support" for every recent Soviet foreign policy initiative.

Meanwhile, following the Moscow meeting, the CCP called for significant increases in production, and the idea of a Great Leap Forward was first propagated. Yet these developments were to pale in comparison to what actually emerged in the first half of 1958.

The Great Leap Forward

A psychological factor was also arguably at play in the new turning point. After a period of virtually unbroken success since assuming unchallenged leadership of the CCP in the 1940s, Mao suffered his first notable failure with the Hundred Flowers. Seemingly unable to accept personal responsibility and seeking a new success, Mao undertook an unusually personal initiative in pushing the Great Leap, much to the surprise and consternation of his colleagues. Beginning in January 1958 he convened a series of ad hoc meetings that led to drastically increased production targets, including a frenzy in June that doubled the national steel target over 1957's actual production, a process that typified the extremism of the Great Leap that led to such disastrous consequences (see Box 3.1).

In this process, several drastic changes took place in Mao's leadership style and the distribution of power within the CCP. Mao now took personal control of the economy, the area in which he subsequently acknowledged he had no particular understanding. He complained that in the past the Politburo had become a mere "voting machine" that simply endorsed the policies of Zhou Enlai, Chen Yun, and others, and he went on to subject these leaders to severe criticism.

In attacking their 1956–1957 policies, Mao not only overlooked his own consistent approval of those policies, he also made the specious assertion that those policies were responsible for the "rightist" onslaught during the Hundred Flowers Movement. In sharp contrast to the situation in the spring of 1956, when Zhou approached Mao on the question of overinvestment, the premier was now denied the right to speak on economic matters and considered resigning. The overall result was a fundamental change from the first eight years of the regime, when a diluted form of collective leadership existed. Now any leader, no matter how prestigious, could be shunted aside at Mao's whim; it had truly become a situation in which no one dared challenge the Chairman's word.

BOX 3.1 THE GREAT LEAP DISASTER

While precise contours are not and cannot be known given incomplete and unreliable official records and continuing political sensitivity, the Great Leap Forward was without doubt Mao's and the CCP's greatest catastrophe. Demographic efforts to estimate "unnatural deaths" due to starvation generally place the number from around twenty-five million to as high as the mid-forty millions. Moreover, when depressed birth rates are taken into account, the total "lost population" is estimated at between fifty million and seventy-six million. "Unnatural deaths" also resulted from beatings and other forms of violence as cadres enforced Great Leap policies; the numbers are unclear but significant, perhaps in the hundreds of thousands.

Although quickly assuming the utopian goal of a rapid transition to communism, the underlying objective of the Great Leap program was economic development at a rate far exceeding anything achieved in world history. This goal had broad support among the populace, officials down to the grassroots, and high-ranking leaders whose doubts were mitigated by faith in the Chairman. But the economic strategy was deeply flawed. The extreme reliance on mass mobilization devalued expert knowledge that might have moderated outlandish targets and methods. A case in point was the vastly increased steel target that could be met only by "backyard furnaces," which melted down household implements for a crude form of steel that turned out to be useless. This fit the larger strategy of "walking on two legs," the rapid development of all sectors simultaneously that siphoned off peasant labor to industrial projects and resulted in depressed agricultural production. Drastic decentralization to the provincial and lower levels also had a major disruptive effect. With central planning agencies largely stripped of their powers, a breakdown of national economic coordination resulted.

Incoherent economic policies notwithstanding, political factors were at the core of the disaster. Structurally, lower-level officials looked upward for policy guidance and clues about the political atmosphere, while always bearing in mind the rule of thumb that it was better to make "leftist" mistakes than those of the "right." In the context of the Great Leap, these factors were extremely potent with Mao personally articulating wild policies at the start, and the impact of the Anti-Rightist Campaign providing a warning to officials at all levels not to appear less than fully committed to the Leap. This mindset had devastating consequences. With unrealistic targets laid down at the top and recklessly increased by lower levels, expressions of doubt or failure to meet the targets were often brutally punished as rightist deviations. When by early 1959 it became increasingly difficult to meet state grain procurement targets, this was not regarded as due to production shortfalls but as the private hoarding of grain, requiring a struggle campaign. The tragedy accelerated in the winter of 1959 following the Lushan conference dismissal of Defense Minister Peng Dehuai as a "right opportunist" for criticizing the Great Leap. Seeking harvests that didn't exist, state procurement often became a violent process of seizing whatever grain could be found in the households of starving peasants.

Apart from the deadly interaction of the procurement mechanism and false understanding of the real situation in the countryside, several specific policies worsened conditions. One was the continued exporting of grain as famine conditions deepened in 1959–1960. Part of this was due to the need to export in order to generate the foreign exchange necessary for modern inputs from abroad; another was Mao's insistence on meeting and even speeding up contracted exports to the Soviet Union as the Sino-Soviet conflict intensified. The Soviet cutoff of aid to China in 1960 was officially claimed to be partly responsible for the disaster, but Mao's desire not to lose face in dealing with Moscow was of much greater significance.

Even more detrimental was favoritism to the cities, a basic aspect of CCP policy since 1949, but now it resulted in deadly consequences. Although malnutrition occurred in urban areas, the cities were basically spared starvation as a conscious act of official policy. When the top leaders finally grasped the seriousness of food shortages from late 1959, provinces were instructed to meet their procurement quotas regardless of local conditions in order to guarantee supplies for Beijing and other major cities, a policy known by mid-1961 as "saving the cities at the expense of the villages." At its lowest ebb, the regime understood that a food crisis in urban centers was a greater threat to stability than starvation in the dispersed countryside.

Another key to the catastrophe was the failure to report accurate information up the chain of command that would have revealed production shortfalls or exposed starvation. Stringent measures were taken to prevent any information concerning famine leaking from local jurisdictions, whether to relatives elsewhere or the party center in Beijing. But provinces did send investigation teams to gain realistic assessments, and the deteriorating situation was increasingly known by provincial leaders from 1959, with some acting to alleviate the situation. While no province was immune to starvation, vast differences in suffering existed due to the action or inaction of the relevant leaders. A rough estimate indicates that about 58 percent of all "unnatural deaths" occurred in only three provinces led by particularly extreme exponents of Mao's radical policies. A courageous leader could make a massive difference, as in a Shandong county where no famine deaths were recorded despite the high death rate in the province as a whole.

What did Mao know? As the depth of the crisis became understood at the party center in 1960–1961, Mao would complain that he had been duped by lower levels. Mao was correct in a limited sense; only in early 1960 did reports of severe starvation reach the center. Yet it was Mao's Great Leap line and his warnings against rightist deviations that inhibited telling the awful truth. Moreover, as early as spring 1958 Mao received reports of food shortages, and subsequently of a few starvation cases, but these were treated as isolated and temporary, and no serious efforts to address the underlying causes were undertaken. As in traditional times, many peasants blamed the malfeasance of local officials and believed the emperor would save them if he knew. Mao did not know the extent of the devastation he had caused until late in the tragedy, but his actions and attitudes had created the disaster.

The culturally resonant, and since 1949 incessantly propagandized, view of Mao as concerned with the people's welfare was one reason why the Great Leap devastation did not produce widespread unrest. Despite intense popular dissatisfaction, small-scale rioting, the appearance of counterrevolutionary organizations, and even isolated armed rebellions, there was no serious threat to the regime. The combination of official indoctrination, the legacy of past suppression campaigns, the forceful involvement of public security forces, the system of close social control, and the contrast between a relatively modernized state apparatus and any potential opposition lacking the capacity to act outside a given locality meant resistance could not succeed. The totalitarian system was strong enough to prevail in this crisis.

A consequence of both Mao's turn against the leaders of the State Council's economic ministries and the Great Leap approach of relying on mass mobilization rather than technical expertise was that the party apparatus now assumed the key organizing role in economic development. With this came the further elevation of one of Mao's favorite colleagues, Deng Xiaoping, who as CCP general secretary exerted intense pressure on lower-level officials to meet fanciful targets. Mao's continuing favoritism was reflected in his spring 1959 remark at the very time of Liu Shaoqi's long-foreshadowed elevation to state chairman—the position equivalent to president of the PRC that Mao had held since 1949—that while he himself was the "main marshal," Deng was the "vice marshal."[14] Deng played key roles in the various stages of the Great Leap: the initial escalation of targets in the first half of 1958, the extreme radicalism of the summer and fall, and the "cooling off" phase from late 1958 until the summer of 1959; overall he bore major responsibility for some of the worst aspects of the movement.

In each phase, Mao was the key player. After forcing the dramatic escalation of steel targets in June 1958, Mao was again at the center of events at the leadership's annual summer meeting in the coastal resort city of **Beidaihe** that saw not only the further escalation of targets but also the nationwide launching of the **people's commune** movement that virtually eliminated private property in the countryside and created larger (five thousand to twenty-five thousand families) and more radical forms of collective living, as well as promising a quick transition to full **communism** within a very few years. This extremism was arguably fed by Mao's newly contentious relations with the Soviet Union, caused mainly by his resentment of proposals from Moscow for joint military facilities on Chinese soil that he took as disrespecting PRC sovereignty. Meanwhile, Moscow openly criticized claims that would have China reach communism not only in a ridiculously short time but also before the senior communist state.

Ironically, it was the Chairman who was the first of the top leaders to speak out against the radical excesses of the summer and fall, resulting in late 1958 in a significant lowering of industrial targets, moderated policy concerning the people's communes, and the relegation of the transition to communism to a more distant future. While this indicated that Mao still retained some pragmatic sensibilities, more significantly it demonstrated that none of his colleagues was willing to risk the Chairman's ire, even as excesses ran riot and the first signs of extended famine emerged, until he had spoken.

While the policy tendency in the first half of 1959 was largely one of "cooling off," it was inhibited by two factors. The first overarching factor was Mao's ambivalence about slowing down the Leap. Although he temporarily enlisted Chen Yun in mid-1959 to provide some control over the economy, Mao was unwilling to entertain any fundamental reconsideration of *his* Great Leap. Related to this was the fact that with the undercutting of the role of the centralized economic ministries, policy implementation rested with provincial party authorities, and these leaders varied considerably, from extreme radicalism to a more measured if still highly ambitious approach. In this Mao generally sided with the more cautious local leaders, but he was periodically excited by the claims of the radicals, some of whom even considered Mao's efforts to deflate their wild claims about their achievements in leaping forward as "rightist," and he never insisted on bringing them back to reality. Nevertheless, when the party leadership convened in July 1959 for a meeting at Lushan—another scenic spot, but this one located in the high cool mountains of central China—Mao's signals indicated an intention for a further retrenchment of the Leap, and he called for an open discussion of the problems facing the regime.

The **Lushan Conference** was a truly seminal event in the history of the CCP, although it can also be seen as an extension of the harsh pressures that Mao brought on his colleagues at the early 1958 meetings. The hopes of many leaders for a further readjustment of Leap policies were shattered when Minister of Defense Peng Dehuai wrote a "letter of opinion" to Mao that was highly critical of Great Leap shortcomings.

Although Peng—a Long March veteran, a marshal of the PLA, and the commander of Chinese forces in the Korean War—attributed errors in the Leap to the failure of others to implement the Chairman's directives correctly, Mao was deeply offended. Peng's effort was a clumsy misreading of Mao's psychology: whereas Peng's aim was to prod Mao into taking further steps in the direction of slowing the Leap that he had already signaled, the Chairman interpreted it as a personal challenge.

Other leaders, including those with difficult political relations with Peng, attempted to calm the situation, but to no avail, as Mao insisted on Peng's dismissal and began an intense campaign against "right opportunism"—this time aimed at targets in the party—that frightened officials from addressing problems, especially the catastrophic food situation, and intensified radical policies. This took matters further than in early 1958 in terms of how differences within the leadership were handled; now leaders earning Mao's displeasure were not merely criticized and sidelined, they were subjected to even harsher denunciation and dismissed from office. More tragic was that Mao's new lurch to the left at this time was a key factor in deepening the famine that would eventually account for anywhere from twenty-five million to more than forty-five million peasant lives, with perhaps 60 percent of them lost from winter 1959 to winter 1960 following Lushan. Significantly, throughout this drama and despite the military's concern for the famine's impact on the morale of peasant troops, there was no PLA position on the Leap nor concerted support for Peng after Mao acted.

Although there was grumbling within the top leadership over Mao's arbitrariness at Lushan, the Chairman remained unchallenged. Much as they had been in the last half of 1958, other leaders were tentative in the extreme, even as evidence of much more severe disasters accumulated in late 1959 and the first half of 1960. Mao, as before, was ambivalent about how to respond, calling for remedial measures but still endorsing high targets in mid-1960. Significantly, it was only in the fall of 1960 when Mao personally ordered a concerted effort to combat the Leap's excesses that a systematic retreat from the Great Leap began. It was also the period when Mao began his own retreat to the so-called "second front" of leadership, an arrangement whereby he concerned himself with matters of ideology and overall political direction, while other leaders on the "first front" assumed responsibility for the daily administration of the party and state. This involved no lessening of Mao's authority, although in the circumstances it meant leaving the task of cleaning up the mess he had created to Liu Shaoqi, Zhou Enlai, Deng Xiaoping, and others.

THE LIMITS OF RECOVERY, 1961–1965

The crisis created by Mao's failed Great Leap Forward was the deepest in PRC history. As the famine worsened, widespread demoralization affected cadres and population alike, the social order declined, and black markets and superstitious practices multiplied. Throughout 1961, a series of measures were implemented to cope with the situation: drastic cuts in excessive investment; shifting resources to agriculture and consumer industries; ending radical decentralization to enhance economic coordination; adjusting commune organization to increasingly vest authority in production teams, the smallest rural unit; allowing peasants private plots and free markets;

emphasizing material incentives in both urban and rural areas; restoring the authority of factory managers and technical personnel; and appealing to intellectuals by indicating that providing expertise alone (rather than being **red and expert**) was enough to demonstrate political loyalty.

In key functional areas, party documents laying down systematic policies were drafted, each under the direction of a party leader with relevant expertise. Mao approved each document, but overall leadership on the "first front" was provided by Liu Shaoqi. Mao's attention was focused on the further deteriorating relations with the Soviet Union and on the broader problem of reorienting the regime from the excessive high-pressure approach of the Great Leap to one emphasizing **inner-party democracy** and cautious policy-making, the "truth from facts" approach of the revolutionary period whereby careful investigation and research were required before decisions were made.

The depth of the crisis, as well as the damage to Mao's personal prestige, was evident at the **7,000 cadres conference** in January–February 1962. An undercurrent of discontent with the Chairman was present at this massive gathering of officials from different institutions and administrative levels, to the extent that Mao felt it necessary to offer a self-criticism. In many respects this was very restrained, and he reasserted the correctness of the Great Leap policy line. But Mao acknowledged responsibility for the current situation, declared that he was subject to the will of the majority (in the restricted sense that if everyone disagreed with him he would concede the point), and admitted that the party had been unable to "regularize a whole set of guiding principles" during the Leap in contrast to the "fully persuasive" policies of the Soviet model period.[15]

What was particularly striking was the fact that the leadership rallied around the Chairman. Although Peng Zhen, the Beijing mayor, suggested that even Mao had made mistakes (the boldest statement of any leader in the 1949–1976 period, but one that largely echoed Mao's self-criticism), Peng had earlier emphasized that "if we don't support him who can we support?"[16] Other leaders, including Deng Xiaoping, went well beyond this to fulsome praise of the Chairman. The most egregious cheerleader for the Chairman was another long-term Mao favorite, Lin Biao, the PLA marshal who had replaced Peng Dehuai as minister of defense after Lushan and who would come to play a crucial role in the Cultural Revolution.

The most important speech to the conference was the official report by Liu Shaoqi. Liu also sought to protect Mao by assuming overall responsibility as the top leader on the "first front." Liu's report was approved by Mao, who, in addition, encouraged Liu to supplement the report with oral remarks. But the report and especially the oral remarks were a particularly systematic critique of the Great Leap, and included a reference to the claims of peasants in some areas that disasters were 70 percent manmade. In sharp contrast to his appreciation of Lin Biao's fawning speech, Mao seemingly took umbrage at the bluntness of Liu's assessment, claiming a number of years later that Liu's performance during the "rightist deviation" of 1962 gave him "food for thought" concerning the reliability of his successor. In the context of the moment, given the severity of the problems facing the PRC, Mao had little immediate recourse and retreated further onto the "second front." He departed from Beijing, leaving Liu to organize additional measures to overcome the crisis.

This task was undertaken at another February work conference that concluded the situation was even more dire than previously believed, with the economy "on the verge of collapse." A series of measures followed: on Liu's recommendation Chen Yun was once again placed in charge of the economy; new sharp cutbacks in construction and investment were enforced; and most importantly, with Chen, Deng Zihui, and Deng Xiaoping arguing for concessions to small-scale farming, production quotas were assigned to individual households rather than collective units, and beyond that, even full-fledged private farming was tolerated in extensive areas of the country. Mao had given ambiguous support to this approach at the start of this process. But its underlying spirit, as captured by Deng Xiaoping's comment in a July 1962 speech on restoring agricultural production that "it does not matter if it is a white cat or a black cat, as long as it catches mice" was inevitably too much for the Chairman. This became clear in July as Mao, regarding the measures taken since February as a sign of panic, began to criticize a wide range of policies, starting with the retreat from collective agriculture, and the leaders who had backed them.

The Chairman's undiminished authority was clear. He not only reversed policies by rescinding the household-based farming system in the countryside and calling a stop to other concessions, he branded Chen Yun as "always a rightist" and removed Chen from any real power, a situation that would last until November 1978. Mao's awesome power extended beyond demoting individuals: he not only dismissed Deng Zihui but also disbanded the party center's Rural Work Department. Even higher figures were chastened as well, with Mao criticizing Liu Shaoqi for paying too much attention to Chen Yun and establishing an "independent kingdom." In this context Liu suddenly and drastically changed course to back Mao's view, while Deng Xiaoping hastily removed his **cat theory** from the record and emphasized the collective economy.

Although Mao had halted the retreat, he did not provide a clear direction for future policy. One thing was clear, though: while not disowning the Great Leap, neither was he calling for a return to the radicalism of the Leap program; the collective sector in the rural economy would be boosted, but only in its most moderate form. Mao's lack of clarity about the future was most strikingly reflected in his attempt at the September 1962 Central Committee **plenum**[*] to reorient the overall ideological guideline of the regime with the clarion call, "Never forget class struggle."

While Mao urged party leaders to talk of class struggle every day, this was not much of a guide to concrete action. As he himself put it, work and class struggle were "two different kinds of problems [and] our work must not be jeopardized just because of class struggle."[17] The inherent uncertainty that this indicates was reflected in various ways as the economy and society gradually recovered over the next three years. In the reconstruction of a more regular institutional order as the mobilization approach was largely abandoned, the government's role in the economy was enhanced, but it did not assume the same dominant role it held in the modern sector under the centralized Soviet model. Ad hoc economic arrangements prevailed, as no truly comprehensive plan emerged; significantly, in December 1964, Zhou Enlai observed that

---

[*] A plenum, or plenary session, is a meeting of the Central Committee, normally held annually between the elections to that body by the National Party Congress, which now convenes every five years. No plenum was convened between fall 1962 and August 1966, however.

"there are still large unknown areas and a great many unfamiliar phenomena [in our understanding of socialist construction]."[18]

The major mass mobilization movement of the period, the rural **Socialist Education Movement** of 1962–1966, which was aimed at ideologically reinvigorating village cadres and combating corruption and other backward phenomena, was not implemented universally but instead reached only about one-third of China's villages. And the overall party line was unclear, with various pragmatic and experimental economic programs implemented, but with more radical political themes, as reflected in the ongoing national campaign to study Mao's Thought proceeding on a parallel if sometimes intersecting track.

The net result in 1963–1965 was a politics of ambiguity, and at the core of this ambiguity was the relationship of Mao to his colleagues on the "first front." As demonstrated by his actions in the summer of 1962, Mao was all-powerful, but he remained on the "second front" and, his complaints and reservations concerning Liu Shaoqi notwithstanding, left his putative successor in charge of the daily running of the party and state. Mao was now more remote from his colleagues, often outside the capital, but still able to intervene decisively at any point. The real problem for the collective leadership on the "first front" was the Chairman's ambiguous attitudes, and how to be sure that they were in accord with his wishes. Their response was overwhelmingly collegial—rather than compete for Mao's favor by exaggerating differences among themselves, Liu and other leaders sought to come to a consensus position that they believed was acceptable to Mao, and then present it to him. This apparently worked in the overwhelming majority of cases, with the Chairman signing off on even those policies that would be denounced as "revisionist"—a betrayal of Marxism-Leninism— during the Cultural Revolution. But on occasion Mao astonished his colleagues by rejecting their carefully constructed proposals.

The most dramatic case concerned the drafting of a new **Five-Year Plan** for the economy in 1964. After carefully reviewing and adjusting the draft plan in accord with their perception of Mao's wishes, Liu, Zhou Enlai, and the planners were dumbfounded by his angry reaction that labeled their efforts as "practicing [Kuomintang ideology]," in a disparaging reference to the political party of the CCP's archenemy, Chiang Kaishek. In a display of raw power, the Chairman not only forced changes in the document but also sidelined the State Planning Commission, creating a "small planning commission" of more junior officials to take over the planning function.

A related aspect of the politics of ambiguity affecting top leaders and subordinate officials alike was that the Chairman periodically expressed unhappiness with some policy or situation and demanded action. The bureaucracies always responded, sometimes drawing Mao's explicit approval, sometimes his tart comments about the inadequacy of the response. There was no certainty that any of these responses indicated a completely satisfied or totally disapproving Chairman, however.

A case in point was education, an area where substantial shifts to the left were made in terms of politicizing the curriculum, increasing the access of workers and peasants to tertiary education, and reforming teaching methods. Still, a major requirement of "work" in education—meeting China's needs for advanced human capital—also had to be addressed. Liu Shaoqi took personal control of the issue and came up with a "two track" solution that supported regular academic education but at the same time vastly expanded vocational training. While Mao appeared well-disposed to the approach at the time, during the Cultural Revolution it was attacked as a typical example of Liu's **revisionism** that condemned the masses to inferior education while training a new bourgeois elite.

A final ambiguous aspect of the period concerned the increasing prominence of the People's Liberation Army. The army, which maintained a strong program of political indoctrination under the slogan of "politics in command," became a model for emulation throughout society with the "learn from the PLA" campaign in 1964. A feature of the PLA's political approach was lavish praise of Mao's Thought, with Defense Minister Lin Biao pushing an early version of *Quotations from Chairman Mao*, known in the West as "The Little Red Book," that would become ubiquitous during the Cultural Revolution.

Other signs of increased military prominence were a more active role in cultural affairs and the transfer of a significant number of PLA officers to staff new military-style political departments in civilian institutions. Yet there is little evidence that any of this involved a significant redistribution in institutional power. The scope and role of the transferred officers is unclear, but the limited evidence available suggests that they were absorbed into their new civilian organizations and began to adopt the perspectives of those organizations. More fundamentally, there is little evidence that the PLA was interested in assuming a civilian role, with Lin himself warning against usurping the power of civilian party committees. The explanation and significance of the army's enhanced status lay with Mao—his appreciation of the PLA's virtues as a politicized army and Lin's promotion of the Mao Zedong Thought, and his unhappiness with what he saw in the rest of the party-state and society as a whole.

Mao's unhappiness went beyond dissatisfaction with bureaucratic responses to his concerns or doubts about the performance of his top colleagues. Looking at the society around him that had been so deeply traumatized by the failures of the Great Leap, Mao saw signs of a possibly degenerating revolution: widespread corruption and self-seeking behavior, significant social inequality, and the emergence of what he called a "new bourgeois" privileged stratum that benefited disproportionately from China's socialist system. In focusing on these developments, Mao was profoundly influenced by developments in the Soviet Union. Relations with Moscow had continued to deteriorate since the late 1950s: international disagreements and an escalating ideological polemic drove the relationship to the brink of a split, while the Soviets retaliated to Chinese provocations by reneging on the promised nuclear weapons assistance in 1959, and by withdrawing their experts who had long played such an important role in the PRC's modern sector during the economic crisis in 1960. With the split on the verge of being formalized, Mao went beyond an analysis of Moscow's revisionist foreign policies, which preached peaceful coexistence with the United States, to ask how a communist party could author such policies.

The answer was that the Soviet Union had degenerated internally, due to its party leadership being usurped by a revisionist leading clique, first under Stalin's successor, Nikita Khrushchev, and then Leonid Brezhnev. Mao authorized a detailed polemic in 1963–1964 (in which Deng Xiaoping played a leading role in drafting) making the point that, in fact, capitalism had been restored in the Soviet Union. For Mao, the emergence of Soviet revisionism raised the fear that if the first socialist state could degenerate, what would prevent China from following suit? Mao could only offer some orthodox prescriptions—for example, maintaining the **dictatorship of the proletariat** by which the party-state actively suppressed class enemies, affirming and enforcing party leadership, unfolding mass movements, and conducting repeated socialist education campaigns. But what if the CCP's own leading core was ideologically suspect?

By the start of 1965, Mao harbored growing doubts about Liu Shaoqi, subsequently claiming that he had decided in January that Liu had to go. The immediate factor, according to Mao, concerned differences over the conduct of the Socialist Education movement, something he linked to his earlier "food for thought" over Liu's performance in 1962. In fact, their differences over socialist education were relatively limited and reflected more Mao's shifting position than any major confrontation. One can only speculate about Mao's "real" motives: hitherto repressed resentment over Liu's speech to the 7,000 cadres conference; a paranoid fear that he was somehow losing power to Liu, who was exerting dynamic leadership on the "first front"; or a latent distrust of someone who was a rough contemporary but had never been personally close to him.

It is ironic that Mao turned on Liu; of all top leaders in this period, Liu was most prone to adopting left-leaning tendencies, something that distinguished him from the ever-favored Deng Xiaoping, who notwithstanding complete loyalty subtly distanced himself from the more radical of Mao's interventions, yet who would be treated much better during the Cultural Revolution. In any case, by 1965, Liu, ranking vice-chairman of the CCP, chairman (president) of the PRC, and for more than a decade, the communist leader regarded certain to be Mao's successor, was a marked man. The main reason may have been that Mao perceived Liu as a threat, believed he was promoting or allowing revisionist policies to take hold, or had simply decided that, as the man in charge on the "first front," Liu had to take responsibility for the negative trends in the regime and society. Liu's fate would be sealed in the early stages of the Cultural Revolution.

GREAT DISORDER AND HARSH RETRIBUTION, 1966–1971

The Great Proletarian Cultural Revolution Begins

The Cultural Revolution, which began with secretive, obscure preparations in 1965, in reality lasted for only two years, from mid-1966 to summer 1968, despite post-Mao claims of a "Cultural Revolution decade" from 1966 to 1976.[19] Throughout this period and into its aftermath, Mao had a clearer idea of what he was against than what he envisioned would emerge from the tumult. He also demonstrated a deep misunderstanding of the forces he had unleashed. While ostensibly seeking revolutionary purity with such Delphic instructions as "fight self," "make revolution," and "destroy the old and establish the new," Mao's destruction of predictable authority structures left many people, notably rebel activists who supported him, struggling to maintain their own self-interests in fluid and threatening circumstances. Through it all, Mao was central and aloof. He could change the direction of the movement at any point, but he operated from Olympian heights and set no comprehensive or coherent overall policy line.

One of the first signs of the impending storm that was to become the Cultural Revolution was a late 1965 critique of a historical play about an intemperate emperor, written by a leading cultural figure close to the Beijing mayor, Peng Zhen, and soon attacked as a thinly veiled criticism of Mao. By the spring of 1966, Peng had been implicated in this alleged smear against the Chairman and purged, followed soon after by the formal launching of the movement with the issuing of the "Circular of the Central Committee of the Communist Party of China on the Great Proletarian Cultural Revolution" on May 16, 1966. This document, known as the **May 16 Directive**, declared an all-out struggle against "those representatives of the **bourgeoisie** who have sneaked into the party, the government, the army, and various cultural circles" and were "counterrevolutionary revisionists" whose aim was to "seize political power and turn the dictatorship of the proletariat into a dictatorship of the bourgeoisie."

A central feature of this new movement was the rupturing of the remaining leadership unity, the Yan'an Round Table that, even after the demise of Gao Gang and the ouster of Peng Dehuai, still left the overwhelming proportion of the 1945 leadership in key positions in 1965. By 1965, moreover, Mao increasingly focused on what he saw as the revisionist tendencies of Chinese society, and felt the need for some kind of new revolutionary experience, especially for the generation of young "revolutionary successors" who had not experienced the real thing. He further contemplated new methods to shake up the system, something reflected in Liu Shaoqi's June 1966 remark that "I [have never] in the past come across our party using this form of rectification."[20]

Most fundamentally, as the movement unfolded it became clear that, at least temporarily, in order to achieve his revolutionary goals, the Chairman was willing to destroy the party organization that had been the glue of the system and the vehicle of his past successes. Perceptively characterized by Stuart Schram as a "natural Leninist" for most of his career,[21] Mao now cast aside tight organizational control for the "great disorder" that he envisioned as leading to a revolutionized regime and society. During these years, the movement oscillated through a number of phases, alternately more radical or more constrained, changes ultimately reflecting Mao's judgment that disruption had gotten out of hand and had to be dampened down, or that efforts to control the chaos were undermining the very purpose of the Cultural Revolution, thus requiring a new upsurge of radicalism. The result was a perverse form of totalitarianism: without organizational control, rebellious elements would be able to attack the party; but the shifting views of the supreme leader could undermine that control and drastically affect any part of society.

The Red Guards

The first manifestation of the breakdown of Leninist order was the emergence of the **Red Guards** in Beijing high schools and universities beginning in June 1966 (see Box 3.2). Initially guided by **work teams** sent by the central authorities, student Red Guard groups formed and harshly criticized preexisting school and university authorities. Adopting Mao's rebellious spirit, various Red Guards exercised considerable autonomy, in some cases clashing with the work teams. By midsummer, with the work teams withdrawn, Red Guards became the leading force on campuses. Red Guard behavior included writing **big character posters** pasted on walls attacking campus officials and national figures; ransacking homes to destroy traditional and "bourgeois" property; and abusing, beating, and even killing teachers. After million-strong rallies in Beijing's **Tiananmen Square**, in the fall Red Guards from the capital and other cities began to "exchange revolutionary experiences" by traveling throughout China, thus placing great strain on the country's transportation system. At the same time, factional conflicts developed among Red Guard organizations, reaching violent dimensions in 1967–1968 that Mao would call "civil wars."

Throughout 1966–1968, various forms of violence surfaced, whether Red Guard beatings and killings of suspect teachers or individuals of bad class origin in the community, armed clashes of opposing Red Guard and rebel groups, or the revenge of the authorities when given license to crack down on disruption (something that became even more ferocious after mid-1968). The total number of deaths from this orgy of violence is unknown, but a figure in excess of one million is plausible, with the inevitable damage to social interaction and disruption of the economy immense.

During those two years there were also critical shifts in institutional authority—notably the destruction of the party-state apparatus, but they did not involve an unambiguous investiture of power in alternative institutions. Rather, all remained fluid, uncertainty existed throughout, and Mao stood above everything, even when he refused to give clear orders.

In the earliest period, the so-called Fifty Days of June–July 1966, overall authority for conducting the Cultural Revolution remained with the Politburo leadership of Liu Shaoqi and Deng Xiaoping, but the waters were muddied by Mao's creation in May of the **Central Cultural Revolution Group (CCRG)** with special responsibility for the movement. The CCRG was effectively, if not formally, led by Mao's wife, Jiang Qing,[22] who had been called from the political sidelines by her husband in the early 1960s to counter bourgeois influences in the arts. Most of the other members of the CCRG were, like Jiang Qing, ideological radicals who had been on the margins of the elite, although several figures of Politburo rank, notably Yan'an security chief Kang Sheng and Mao's former secretary Chen Boda, also played important roles. Who better to mount a challenge to the party establishment?

Clearly, while new Cultural Revolution organizations like the CCRG played their roles, institutional power was now thoroughly eclipsed by Mao's personal authority. This was enhanced by Mao's personality cult, something dating from his consolidation of power in the 1940s but eased at the Chairman's own initiative in the early 1950s, before being taken to new heights during the Great Leap Forward. Now, however, a virulent cult emerged that greatly surpassed all previous manifestations, with loyalty dances and many other quasi-religious phenomena deeply penetrating everyday life.

BOX 3.2 THE RED GUARD MOVEMENT

The Red Guard movement was one of the best known but inadequately understood aspects of the Cultural Revolution. With the campaign beginning in the educational sphere, high school and university students became the movement's first activists, later copied by "revolutionary rebels" in government institutions and factories. These students provided some of the Cultural Revolution's most riveting images, for example, excited adoration of Mao during the summer of 1966 rallies at Tiananmen Square, and the cruel abuse of campus authorities, including professors, and leading party-state officials paraded through the streets in dunce hats. By 1967 the violence let loose by significant numbers of Red Guards against such targets and "bad class elements" in society had been overtaken by brutal clashes among Red Guard factions. Understanding the sources of factionalism and the larger politics of the Red Guard movement is not easy; for a nationwide phenomenon, involving millions of students, remarkably little is known for the vast majority of the country. Existing studies largely focus on high schools in the southern city of Guangzhou and on the campaign in Beijing's universities.

Two broad explanations have been advanced for Red Guard factionalism: a sociological approach arguing that interests based on status and political networks in the pre-1966 academic structure and broader society determined factional affiliation, and a more political interpretation emphasizing conflicts that emerged during the course of the movement itself. Reflecting the tendency for two opposing factions or factional alliances to appear in organizations and localities, the sociological explanation (most clearly documented for Guangzhou high schools) portrays a conflict of "rebel" Red Guards from middling class family backgrounds involving neither exploiters nor the exploited (e.g., intellectuals, professionals), who were disadvantaged by CCP policies, and as a consequence attacked party leaders, versus "conservative" Red Guards from "red" class backgrounds (e.g., party officials, factory workers), who both benefited from party policies and formed part of the school political structure as Communist Youth League members, and were thus more supportive of the establishment. Of course, no Red Guard organization labeled itself "conservative," and pro-establishment attitudes had to be tempered by the radical ethos of the Cultural Revolution. But, according to these studies, students joined Red Guard factions on the basis of interests that were present before the movement began.

The political interpretation, which takes into account charismatic student leaders and the ideas and passions of Red Guard activists seeking to interpret and realize Mao's objectives, focuses on the interests created as Red Guards interacted with the environment of the Cultural Revolution. This explanation is largely based on events in Beijing's elite universities, events necessarily unique because of the role of leading CCP figures in the unfolding of the movement there. This raises the question of to what extent the movement was, as many Red Guards bitterly came to believe, simply the result of manipulation by elite politicians. The short answer is that the CCRG was deeply involved and sometimes determined the outcome of factional fights, but the Red Guard movement also had a dynamic of its own and spun out of control.

Contrary to Mao's claim that work teams sent by the central authorities to the universities had suppressed the Cultural Revolution during the so-called "Fifty Days" in June–July 1966, most teams implemented their understanding of Mao's wishes through harsh attacks on university authorities that gained Red Guard support regardless of social status. The work teams, however, clashed with militant students, not over Cultural Revolution aims but over the teams' efforts to tightly control the movement.

When the teams were withdrawn, the majority of Red Guards who had cooperated with them became, ironically, the leading force on campus, but the militant minority demanded reversals of the negative political labels they received from the work teams

(Continued)

> **BOX 3.2 (Continued)**
>
> during the "Fifty Days." As tensions escalated, the CCRG backed the militants and undercut the power of the conservative majority.
>
> Then, as the Cultural Revolution extended into government organizations in January 1967, the victorious militant Red Guards linked up with "revolutionary rebels" in ministries responsible for their universities before 1966. In the confusion that followed during the struggle to "seize power" in ministries, opposing city-wide Red Guard alliances formed. This was a struggle for political advantage and to avoid losing to bitter enemies, not over different views of the movement's direction or reflecting contrasting class backgrounds. As internecine violence unfolded after January in much of China, the Red Guards played no further useful role for Mao, eventually leading to his dismantling the movement in summer 1968 and dispatching these urban youths to temper themselves in the countryside.

A key feature of the period was that all leaders were in the dark concerning the Chairman's ultimate intentions, as seen in Liu's lament, cited earlier, concerning his bewilderment over Mao's new form of rectification. Liu had attempted to conduct the movement with the traditional rectification method of sending work teams to Beijing's high schools and universities to guide the Cultural Revolution as it unfolded on campuses, and this gained Mao's approval, albeit somewhat elusively. The uncertainty was not limited to the established inner circle of leaders; the radical members of the CCRG also defended the work teams in June, although they changed their tune in July, arguably because of a clearer understanding of Mao's intentions. In any case, when Mao returned to Beijing after an extended period outside the capital in late July 1966 and criticized the work teams as suppressing the Cultural Revolution rather than furthering it, a new stage was set. The work teams were withdrawn; Liu and Deng, as the central sponsors of the work teams, were in trouble; and the authority of the party as a whole had been damaged.

A Central Committee plenum in August 1966 laid down a set of guidelines for the Cultural Revolution, which were inherently contradictory, both asserting overall party authority and encouraging student rebellion. Moreover, change in the top leadership inevitably contributed to uncertainty. The disgraced Liu was replaced by the loyal Lin Biao as Mao's designated successor. The Politburo **Standing Committee** was significantly enlarged and its internal pecking order revamped, and most provocatively, Mao authored a big-character poster that clearly attacked Liu for adopting "the reactionary stand of the bourgeoisie."

Yet the future extent of the Cultural Revolution's destruction could not have been imagined. The movement was to steer clear of the productive sectors of the state and society, and Mao indicated it would be wound up in about three months. But following several months of increasing strife on campuses and student incursions into the community, as well as escalating attacks on individual leaders, in the late fall of 1966 the fateful decision was taken to extend the movement into factories and the countryside. This placed extra stress on provincial, municipal, and ministerial authorities that now came under intensified rebel attack. Soon the entire party structure collapsed.

Power Seizures and Revolutionary Committees

The next stage of the Cultural Revolution began with the seizure of power by rebel forces in the so-called January [1967] revolution in Shanghai. In fact, this was a largely peaceful seizure by the leading radical figures of the emerging Shanghai power structure, who significantly were also members of the CCRG. The venture thus carried Mao's authority from the outset, something rare in the power seizures by radicals that followed in other parts of the country. After a brief experiment with a radically decentralized power structure called the "Shanghai commune" that Mao rejected as lacking sufficient authority to suppress counterrevolution, **Revolutionary Committees** emerged as the new government in Shanghai and elsewhere, and in the absence of a viable party structure became the organ of local power.

While the unusual circumstances in Shanghai meant that civilian leadership prevailed, the Revolutionary Committee model established in other municipalities, provinces, lower-level jurisdictions, and institutions of various kinds, including schools and factories, promoted a "three-way alliance" of PLA representatives, "revolutionary cadres" (experienced officials from the previous regime who possessed necessary administrative skills and were judged sufficiently reformed), and "mass representatives," the latter reflecting the contending rebel factions in the area or organization concerned, with the military generally dominant. The process of forming the Revolutionary Committees was drawn out, intensely contested, with top leaders—notably Zhou Enlai—engaged in efforts to negotiate agreements among sharply opposed and, in some cases, intractable factions. Indeed, the final provincial Revolutionary Committees were established in September 1968 only after Mao had called a halt to the Cultural Revolution.

From the outset, the disruption accompanying power seizures was resisted by top leaders who had not been toppled in 1966. The most famous instance was the so-called February [1967] adverse current, a conflict involving seven Politburo-level vice premiers and PLA marshals who, apparently seeing an opening in Mao's recent criticism of the radical excesses of the early Cultural Revolution, confronted leading members of the CCRG over the accelerating chaos. After a sharp argument, Mao sided with the radicals, warning the vice premiers and marshals that "whoever opposes the CCRG will meet my resolute opposition."[23] Mao then suspended the Politburo as a policy-making body, leaving the CCRG, an organization that was growing rapidly from a small group of radical party intellectuals into a substantial bureaucracy, as one of the two authoritative bodies at the party center.

The other body, established at the same time as the CCRG in May 1966, was the arguably even more powerful **Central Special Case Examination Group**. Similar to its sister institution, it grew from a small group investigating the Peng Zhen case to a large bureaucratic organization with a nationwide network seeking incriminating evidence of traitorous activity by high-level figures. It thus became the organ of an inner-party inquisition that directed the ferreting out, arrest, and torture of suspect Central Committee members and other officials. While leading radical figures Jiang Qing and Kang Sheng played particularly notorious roles, many other leaders were drawn in, the ever-reliable Zhou Enlai performed the penultimate supervisory role, and Mao of course had the ultimate power to focus or curb the group's activities.

The institution whose domestic power grew markedly during the Cultural Revolution was the PLA. The army was not only the leading force in most of the newly established Revolutionary Committees, it was also the authority responsible for maintaining law and order before and after the committees were set up. But the result was not a true military takeover, or something the army itself welcomed. In 1967–1968 responsible PLA commanders, who were often attacked and their armories raided by rebels, found themselves engaged in bloody struggles with disruptive groups without clear authority from above, and were sometimes rebuked or ousted as a result. Most army leaders wanted the military to disengage from politics and return to national defense duties. Willing or not, the PLA remained at the center of the political structures that evolved from the summer of 1968 after Mao, disappointed by the petty but violent factionalism of the Red Guards, effectively called a halt to the Cultural Revolution by ordering a crackdown on disruptive rebel groups and the dispersal of troublesome Red Guards to the countryside, with perhaps twenty million urban-bred young rebels "sent down to the villages and up to the mountains" to live, work, and learn among the peasants. Emphasis had thus further shifted to the restoration of order, a task that was mainly the responsibility of the PLA.

The Aftermath of the Cultural Revolution

In addition to achieving unprecedented representation on the Politburo and Central Committee at the Ninth Party Congress in April 1969 (the first full party congress since 1956), the military had an even firmer grip on provincial Revolutionary Committees as prominent rebels from 1966–1968 were removed from power or marginalized, and it equally dominated the new party committees that were restored during institutional rebuilding in the provinces and lower administrative levels in 1970–1971. Meanwhile, PLA representatives had played a key stabilizing role in government ministries during factional fighting in 1967–1968, and a substantial number of military officers now became leaders of party core groups as the state structure reemerged as functioning organizations in 1970–1973.

This period also saw harsh, indeed murderous campaigns targeting troublesome rebel elements or others who had earned the displeasure of local authorities during the Cultural Revolution, as well as ordinary criminals, imaginary counterrevolutionaries, and the usual suspects with bad class backgrounds. The **cleansing of class ranks campaign** in 1968–1969, together with subsequent suppressions in 1970–1972, probably killed at least 1.5 million people. These campaigns were clearly authorized by Mao, although his available statements advocated a degree of restraint. The PLA, as the ultimate source of local authority in most places during this time, actively participated in the bloodletting or stood by and watched. Overall, since 1966 more deaths resulted from suppression by the authorities than from Red Guard violence, with its scope increasing dramatically from the second half of 1968.

Somewhat paradoxically, this period also saw a moderation of radical Cultural Revolution policy trends. These policy adjustments were modest, and mostly aimed at restoring order and predictability in the economy and administration—and there was no questioning of the central concept of the Cultural Revolution.

In addition, there was a significant change in PRC foreign policy that had domestic political implications. In August 1968, the Soviet Union invaded Czechoslovakia to crush yet another democratic movement, proclaiming the Brezhnev doctrine that asserted Moscow's right to intervene in other socialist states. This led to escalating tensions on the Sino-Soviet border in early 1969, a result of which was that Mao not only undertook feverish war preparations but also began the process of rapprochement with the United States as a way to protect China from the Soviets. The PLA still could not escape its unwanted political tasks, but the focus of the institution was turning back to its basic defense function.

All of this took place in the context of the emergence of an unusual political lineup at the top of the CCP, one marked by peculiarities that went well beyond dismantling the Yan'an Round Table. The new Politburo, consisting of twenty-one full members elected at the Ninth Party Congress in April 1969, contained less than half of the full 1956 members, and of that half nearly half again were elderly leaders without any real function. Liu Shaoqi had been declared a counterrevolutionary in 1968, expelled from the party, and subsequently died from physical abuse. Deng Xiaoping had been labeled a **capitalist roader**, removed from all his party and government posts, but with Mao's protection, he was not expelled from the party as the radicals undoubtedly wanted and was sent to work in a farm machinery repair shop on a rural people's commune.

Meanwhile, the new Politburo was filled out by CCRG radicals with marginal political qualifications, led by Jiang Qing; regional military commanders; and central military leaders close to Lin Biao, including Lin's wife. A key figure in the new lineup was Zhou Enlai, valued (but not particularly respected) by Mao as a skilled administrator, reliable political surrogate, and diplomatic negotiator, a role that became especially important in the new post-1968 foreign policy context. In short, with this diverse group, whatever capacity that previously existed for collective influence on Mao had totally dissipated. Yet the election of a new Politburo and Central Committee, together with the subsequent piecemeal reconstruction of a central party apparatus, marked a step toward institutional regularity, and the CCRG, the de facto power center of the last three years, suspended operations in September 1969.

The Fall of Lin Biao

The strangest aspect of the new leadership equation was the role of Lin Biao. Although long a Mao favorite and arguably the CCP's greatest general, and widely accepted within the elite as a top Politburo leader, Lin was a curious choice as Mao's successor in that he was in poor health and, crucially, had little interest in power or domestic affairs. He sought to avoid political elevation but could not refuse Mao's designation. Once installed as the successor, Lin played as minimal a role as possible, generally invisible in public after the massive Red Guard rallies in the summer of 1966, and avoided strong advocacy within the leadership. Moreover, his actual views were comparatively moderate, as indicated to staff and family in private, and as reflected on the rare occasions when he expressed a personal preference in leadership exchanges. Nevertheless, to the public he was a staunch supporter of the Cultural Revolution, as befit his position as the Chairman's successor, a position written into the new 1969 party constitution.

Mao's motives in selecting Lin as the successor in 1966 are unclear, but probably involve some combination of having the Minister of Defense at his side to guarantee PLA support, long-standing favoritism toward Lin and appreciation for his role in promoting the Mao cult, and the fact that of all the members of the Politburo Standing Committee, Lin was the only one not tarnished by the perceived revisionist tendencies of domestic policy. In any case, Lin's modus operandi was simply to endorse whatever position Mao took and avoid any personal initiative.

Unfortunately for Lin, this was not sufficient, in part because his ambitious wife, Ye Qun, and central military subordinates became involved in disputes with Jiang Qing and other civilian radicals. Lin was dragged into the conflict during a confrontation at the Lushan Central Committee plenum in the summer of 1970; Mao decided in favor of Jiang Qing, and over the next year Mao applied pressure to Lin's "camp," demanding self-criticisms of Lin's associates, which were invariably judged inadequate. Mao did not openly disown Lin, but he denied him a personal audience, and eventually in the summer of 1971 indicated he wanted some kind of (unspecified) showdown with his successor.

Meanwhile, Lin's twenty-six-year-old son, a high-ranking air force officer despite his age, engaged in discussions with other young officers that may have included wild ideas concerning a military coup, and possibly an assassination attempt against Mao, but which do not appear to have involved Lin Biao himself (see Box 3.3). With Mao returning to Beijing from the south for the showdown, Lin, his wife, and son fled toward the Soviet Union in September under still mysterious circumstances, their plane crashing in the Mongolian desert, killing all aboard. Contrary to what would be expected following the demise of a threatening opponent, Mao went into a physical and emotional tailspin, seemingly unable to accept that a favored colleague, even one facing criticism and uncertainty, would desert him.

MAO'S LAST STAND, 1972–1976

The Lin Biao affair was a critical turning point in Chinese politics during the Maoist era. Despite Lin's private skepticism about the movement, he was identified with the Cultural Revolution and with Mao as the Chairman's personally chosen and constitutionally mandated successor. When Lin was publicly denounced as a traitor, doubts about the Cultural Revolution that had grown both within the populace and the party elite during the increasingly destructive course of the movement inevitably intensified. Mao was acutely aware of widespread dissatisfaction with the movement, whether by people who saw it as a reign of terror, by officials bent on revenge after being attacked by rebels, or even by those who felt its objectives were good but that it did not have to be carried out in such a violent and chaotic manner.

On several occasions from 1972 to 1976 the Chairman observed that he had "[only] accomplished two things in my life, [and while few would have reservations concerning the defeat of Chiang Kai-shek], the other matter was to launch the Cultural Revolution [that] few support [and] many oppose."[24] In countering such attitudes

BOX 3.3 THE LIN BIAO AFFAIR

The Lin Biao affair, also known as the September 13 [1971] incident, after the date Lin's plane crashed while fleeing China, remains the CCP's most mysterious leadership conflict. Unlike virtually all other leaders who suffered during Mao's last two decades, there has been no serious official effort to reexamine Lin's case, much less "reverse the verdict" on him. This is probably due to the fact that, unlike other victims of the "Cultural Revolution decade" who were attacked as revisionists, Lin was a major beneficiary of the Cultural Revolution, despite his reluctance to play the role of Mao's chosen successor and his doubts about the movement, and thus he became a symbol of the excesses rejected by the post-Mao leadership. Beyond that, the sheer bizarreness of the claims concerning Lin, the likelihood that key "evidence" was fabricated, and the difficulty of presenting a clear good vs. evil narrative arguably contributed to a decision to ignore the case, leaving the story concocted in 1972 as the official version.

There is little to suggest significant reservations on Mao's part concerning succession arrangements in the year following the Ninth Congress in 1969. In the spring of 1970, however, with a new state constitution on the agenda, Mao declared he did not want to serve as state chairman, a position equivalent to that of PRC president, which had been vacant since the purge of Liu Shaoqi. But Lin Biao and other leaders, including Zhou Enlai, continued to advocate that Mao take the post, presumably pandering to Mao's vanity (something also apparent in Lin's claim that Mao was a genius). Bizarrely, these issues fed into tensions between Lin's followers in the central PLA command, and Jiang Qing's civilian radicals, who had meddled in military matters.

A confrontation erupted at the August–September 1970 Lushan plenum. With radical leader Zhang Chunqiao singled out as a target by Lin's supporters, intense criticism directed at Zhang came from well outside Lin's group. Although it was not Lin's intent, by venting their spleen at one of the Cultural Revolution's main protagonists, many participants were undoubtedly expressing their true feelings about the movement. This was certainly Mao's perception: he sided with Zhang and Jiang Qing, equating opposition to Zhang Chunqiao with opposition to himself, that is, to his Cultural Revolution.

Over the next year Mao brought increasing pressure to bear on Lin's followers, notably Chen Boda, Mao's former secretary and CCRG leader who had clashed with Jiang and Zhang before aligning with Lin's "camp," and the "four generals" who led the PLA's service arms. Mao took organizational measures to dilute Lin's military authority, launched a criticism campaign against Chen, labeling him a "phony Marxist" who had pushed the genius issue, and subjected the generals to extended criticism. But Mao's intentions were unclear, and Lin seemed uneasy but resigned to his political fate in summer 1971 when news came that Mao wanted to deal with him upon the Chairman's return to Beijing.

Earlier in March, Lin's son, Lin Liguo, an air force officer himself, had discussed his father's situation with other young officers, discussions later represented as planning for a military coup aimed at Mao. In the official version, this was Lin Biao's plot, something doubtful given its amateurish nature, and post-Mao investigations determined that none of the "four generals" had any knowledge of it. Finally, with Mao's return imminent, panic seized Lin's household, Lin Liguo may have initiated new wild discussions about assassinating Mao, and just before midnight on September 12, Lin, his wife (Ye Qun), and son fled by plane toward the Soviet Union. According to Lin's surviving daughter, her father, drowsy from sleeping tablets, was virtually kidnapped by Ye Qun and Lin Liguo. Whatever the truth, Mao reportedly stopped preparations to shoot down Lin's aircraft, commenting that "Rain has to fall, girls have to marry, these things are immutable, let them go."

Mao would not accept criticism of the concept of the Cultural Revolution, but he acknowledged that much had gone wrong in practice: "the overall assessment [of the Cultural Revolution is] basically correct, [but there are] some shortcomings. Now we must consider the deficient aspects. It is a 70/30 distinction, 70 percent achievements, 30 percent mistakes."[25] During the last years of his life Mao made concerted efforts to correct the "30 percent mistakes" so that the movement could be consolidated, but the Cultural Revolution per se remained sacrosanct.

The Chairman's fragile health (he turned eighty in December 1973) and even greater remoteness from his leading colleagues after the death of Lin Biao affected the politics of the period. Mao's health was extremely poor in 1972, improved only somewhat in 1973–1974, and began to decline sharply in 1975, finally leaving him in a virtual coma in the summer of 1976. He was out of Beijing for nine months from July 1974 to April 1975, but even when in the capital, access to him was highly restricted, resulting in considerable authority for those leaders who did see him and could convey his views. In this regard, remarkable influence was exercised by relatives who had access, for most of the period his niece (together with his interpreter—the "two ladies"), and much more significantly his nephew, Mao Yuanxin, from the fall of 1975, figures who both conveyed information about the highest leadership to Mao and carried back his orders, which were reflexively obeyed. As before, Mao's ambiguous views complicated the lives of those entrusted with running the state, but the difficulty was magnified by his deteriorating condition and isolation.

Reflecting his contradictory objectives of both correcting and defending the Cultural Revolution, Mao placed contending forces on the Politburo. On the one hand, there were key pre-1966 leaders, most notably Premier Zhou Enlai and Deng Xiaoping, who, after submitting a self-criticism to Mao, had been recalled from internal exile in 1973 and was reinstated in his position as vice-premier and subsequently in January 1975 as vice-chairman of the CCP and effective leader of the "first front." On the other hand, Mao had given Politburo positions to leading Cultural Revolution radicals. including Jiang Qing and her CCRG associates, Shanghai propaganda officials Zhang Chunqiao and Yao Wenyuan; they were joined in 1973 by the young Shanghai factory cadre and Cultural Revolution rebel Wang Hongwen. While much of the history of this period has been written in terms of conflict between this so-called **Gang of Four** (a term bestowed by Mao during one of his periods of displeasure with the radicals) and the old guard headed by Zhou and Deng, this distorts the reality in several ways.

Most fundamentally, this interpretation paints the dynamics of the period as determined by the struggle between these ideologically opposed groups, with Mao doing little more than intervening periodically in the conflict to tip the scale in one direction or the other. In fact, Mao determined *every* turning point during the period according to his own goals and placed major restrictions on Politburo conflict by demanding party unity. Although the Chairman was delusional if he believed these contentious forces could cooperate on a lasting basis to carry out his intention of rescuing key aspects of the Cultural Revolution—and he did at one point envisage a leadership team of Wang Hongwen and Deng Xiaoping—Mao was able to enforce periods of cooperation or at least quiescent relations between the groups.

Finally, by the time of the Lin Biao affair, Mao had also introduced into the higher echelons of the party elite a number of younger leaders who had served in the provinces before the Cultural Revolution. Those he promoted had been beneficiaries of the Cultural Revolution in the sense of attaining higher office than would have been possible without the movement, but they were drawn from the party apparatus and acculturated in its ways. Rather than being a third force between the old guard and radicals, as is often assumed, this group of new younger central leaders were sympathetic to Zhou and Deng in political and in policy terms, most fundamentally because of their respect for party seniority—one of the strongest factors holding the system together before 1966, but one shattered by the Cultural Revolution. The problem was that this group, like both the radicals and old guard, had to tailor their advocacy and actions in accord with Mao's views of the moment.

Over the 1972–1976 period, Chinese politics went through a number of alternating phases, phases that were longer and more coherent than those during 1966–1968, and which crucially occurred in a more stable if still volatile and developing organizational context. In 1972, while attempting to blame the excesses of the Cultural Revolution on Lin Biao, Mao authorized a critique of "ultra-left" practices that had disrupted the economy, culture, education, and science, and initiated rehabilitations of leaders dismissed during the Cultural Revolution. While these moderating measures have been identified with Zhou Enlai, who indeed played the leading role in managing the process, the political decision came from Mao, as reflected in the fact that until late in the year the radicals were largely silent concerning this trend.

Moreover, in the delicate area of leadership rehabilitations, Mao's direct personal imprint was clear on a case-by-case basis—most notably the return to office of Deng Xiaoping in early 1973. This critique of "ultra-leftism" was an extension of the policy drift away from Cultural Revolution excesses over the previous two to three years. But the measures themselves were quite limited, and no overall ideological justification was provided. When the radicals felt the need to speak out against this policy drift toward the end of 1972, their advocacy was tentative. And even after Mao signaled in December 1972 that the critique had gone too far by declaring in a 180-degree ideological turn that Lin Biao was in fact an "ultra-rightist" and a "swindler like Liu Shaoqi," official policy largely continued in the new moderate direction well into 1973.

In any case, Mao concluded that the ideals of the Cultural Revolution had been diluted, and he moved to reassert them at the Tenth CCP Congress in the summer of 1973. This could be seen in the rhetoric of the new party constitution that, among other things, praised the rebellious spirit of the Cultural Revolution by inserting Mao's observation that "going against the tide is a Marxist-Leninist principle," and in the astonishing elevation of model rebel Wang Hongwen as Mao's successor.

By the start of 1974, abetted by his growing unhappiness with Zhou Enlai, ostensibly over foreign affairs issues and concerns with the PLA's political reliability, Mao intensified his effort to reemphasize the essence of 1966–1968 by launching a "second Cultural Revolution," which was formally called the "**Criticize Lin Biao and Confucius**" (i.e., oppose "ultra-rightism") campaign. This campaign targeted Zhou (indirectly) and the PLA and produced considerable economic, social, and organizational disruption over the first eight months of the year, but this level of disruption was nowhere near the scale of the real Cultural Revolution.

Even though Zhou was under severe stress as he battled cancer, he was able to contain the movement's damage to a limited degree, including tentative moves to repair economic disruption. Moreover, independent of the Premier, leading generals were reshuffled and criticized, but not purged, while overall very few important officials were actually removed from office. Much more quickly than in 1966–1968, Mao called a halt to the campaign in August 1974: "The Cultural Revolution has already lasted eight years. It is now time to establish stability. The entire Party and the army should unite."[26]

Mao had now created a new turning point that set in motion the most serious effort during this period to consolidate the Cultural Revolution by dealing with what he had acknowledged were the "30 percent mistakes" of the movement. Several measures showed clearly Mao's intention. One was his directive on stability and unity, plus a second on the priority of developing the national economy. He also appointed Deng as de facto head of government replacing the ill Zhou in the fall of 1974, and aimed several pointed criticisms at the radicals in 1974–1975. The State Council was reorganized in January 1975, which further restored the machinery of government and placed it in a decisive position to implement the consolidation effort. By mid-1975, Mao had vested full authority in Deng that allowed for a much more comprehensive approach to rectifying Cultural Revolution problems than Zhou was able to implement in 1972.

Yet throughout this time, Deng was dependent on Mao's continuing favor, something indicated by the careful attention that some of Deng's key advisors paid to Mao's works—and indeed by Deng's own study of those works at a time when he was deeply engaged in a wide range of policy issues. Deng was able to dominate the Politburo in this period because he had access to Mao and had gained the Chairman's approval of his efforts. This support left Deng all the more dumbfounded when in the fall of 1975, he suddenly learned of Mao's discontent with his actions.

The central figure in turning Mao against Deng was not any member of the Gang of Four but his thirty-four-year-old nephew, Mao Yuanxin. A leading official in Liaoning, one of the most radical provinces, Mao Yuanxin complained to his uncle about various aspects of Deng's policies, but the core complaint was that Deng fundamentally showed little support for goals of the Cultural Revolution. Following a series of meetings mandated by Mao in November that criticized some of Deng's closest collaborators in the consolidation effort, a campaign to "beat back the right deviationist wind to reverse correct verdicts" of the Cultural Revolution in education unfolded, and Deng was gradually stripped of authority, despite three self-criticisms. Like Lin Biao before him, Deng's pleas for an audience with the Chairman fell on deaf ears.

The Death of Zhou Enlai

Deng had already been effectively removed from power before the death of Zhou Enlai, who had been premier of the PRC since its founding, in January 1976, but the new leadership alignment was confirmed only at the start of February. At that time, to everyone's surprise, one of the relatively young and little known leaders elevated by Mao to the Politburo in 1973, Hua Guofeng, was named acting premier and placed in charge of the party center, meaning he had Mao's support and confidence. Now the campaign against "right deviationist winds" spread to other spheres, ministry leaders were attacked and sidelined, and rebel activities spread in the localities. But, as in 1974, despite significant economic and social disruption, this was again a pale reflection of 1966–1968, with Mao advocating keeping the movement under party control and Hua managing to curb the more threatening developments.

It was against this background in early April 1976 that an incident occurred that reflected the volatile political situation (see Box 3.4). Hundreds of thousands of Chinese citizens took the occasion of the annual festival to pay respects to deceased ancestors to gather in Tiananmen Square for a remarkable and spontaneous demonstration of their affection for the recently departed Zhou Enlai. The Premier had a rather mythologized reputation as a truly honest and selfless leader who stood with the people. The Tiananmen gathering turned into a protest that reflected the popular sentiment at the failure of the party-state to properly honor Zhou Enlai following his death, something for which Mao bore primary responsibility, and the gathering also expressed deep undercurrents of dismay at the latest resurfacing of Cultural Revolution radicalism.

The Politburo was particularly distressed when they learned about thinly veiled criticisms of Mao himself that appeared in the poems and posters of the masses who had gathered at Tiananmen Square. Due to a clumsy decision driven by Jiang Qing to remove the wreaths that honored Zhou, people rebelled, overturned a police vehicle, and burned an official command post on the edge of the Square. The Square was finally emptied with a brief spasm of violence, but, despite popular belief, relatively few people were injured and no one died, and by the end of the year most of those imprisoned had been released.

In retrospect, the overall restraint of the authorities in the face of, what was up to then, the largest spontaneous mass protest in the history of the PRC, is striking. Moreover, the degree of initiative taken by the Politburo in handling the situation was unusual as a result of Mao's fragile health, but even in this situation the leadership absolutely accepted his directives when conveyed by Mao Yuanxin.

Two significant consequences resulted from the Tiananmen Incident of April 1976. First, Hua Guofeng was promoted to premier of the State Council (the "acting" part of his title was removed) and the unprecedented position of CCP first vice-chairman, unambiguously becoming Mao's successor, thereby removing any lingering claims of the worker rebel Wang Hongwen. Second, Deng Xiaoping was blamed for instigating what was labeled as a "counterrevolutionary incident," formally stripped of all his posts, and placed under house arrest. Yet, as he did during the Cultural Revolution, Mao again protected Deng, shielding him from physical threat and stipulating the retention of his party membership. Arguably the most telling aspect of the entire affair was the preoccupation of the leadership with sustaining Mao's prestige within the party and among the people in general. Even as he lay in a coma a few months later, and despite real fears that the radicals would somehow use the Chairman's legacy to seize power after his death, Mao's Cultural Revolution remained sacrosanct, even among the more moderate leaders, until his death. Such was the fealty owed to the founder of the regime.

Paradoxically, during Mao's last years the institutions of the party-state were gradually strengthened, but politics was overwhelmingly shaped by the interactions of a small number of leaders looking to an increasingly frail Mao. Indeed, the progress

BOX 3.4 THE TIANANMEN INCIDENT, 1976

The death of Premier Zhou Enlai on January 8, 1976, produced genuine grief within the Chinese population. Of all Chinese leaders, Zhou had the image of a caring figure concerned with the well-being of the people, an image enhanced by his perceived moderation since the outbreak of the Cultural Revolution. If Mao was god, Zhou was the people's friend. Although Zhou received official honors following his passing, the tribute in no way matched popular feelings. Moreover, mourning activities were restricted, the mourning period was curtailed, and the media shifted its emphasis to attacking "right deviationist winds," code words for the policies of Zhou and Deng Xiaoping.

While the Gang of Four was prominent in these measures, Mao was responsible for the relative denigration of the Premier. Mao declined to attend any memorial events despite appeals from top leaders, denied Zhou the accolade of "great Marxist," and as a result inhibited inclinations within the political elite to expand praise of the dead Premier. Apart from his long-standing low opinion of Zhou's political-ideological merits and jealousy over the Premier's high domestic and international reputation, Mao believed Zhou never truly supported the Cultural Revolution, and that the push for mourning activities represented disapproval of the movement.

Over the next two and a half months, resentment simmered over Zhou's treatment, resentment amplified by the upsurge of anti-rightism, which was also perceived as involving esoteric attacks on the Premier. In late March, a series of demonstrations that featured attacks on the Politburo radicals took place in Nanjing. News of this development reached Beijing and fed into the underlying pressure that had been growing since mid-March with the approach on April 4 of Qingming, the festival for honoring the dead, an occasion that allowed the public to express respect for Zhou and resentment over his treatment.

From April 1 to Qingming, hundreds of thousands of people visited Tiananmen Square, exceeding one million on the day itself. Large numbers of wreaths honoring Zhou were brought to the Square, and beyond that posters, poems, and impromptu speeches lauded the Premier, but many attacked the radicals, with some targeting the regime and Mao, although not by name.

The Politburo was thus in a quandary, facing the conflicting pressures of managing a volatile situation on the Square, allowing appropriate homage to the Premier, and protecting Mao's prestige and the sanctity of his line. Moreover, as a consequence of Mao's rapidly deteriorating health, more key decisions were taken by the Politburo independent of Mao than was ever the case in previous crises. The crucial decision, pushed through by Jiang Qing following reports of how strongly she was being attacked by protestors, was to remove the wreaths despite an informal understanding that they could stay for several days. This occurred overnight following Qingming, but as news of the removal spread on April 5, several tens of thousands of outraged people gathered on the Square. With the situation deteriorating, the Politburo turned to Mao for instructions. As conveyed by his nephew, Mao called for persuasion to get people to leave the Square, but force if that failed. In sharp contrast to Deng Xiaoping's solution to the second Tiananmen incident on June 4, 1989, however, this was to be nonlethal force (fists and clubs), and the actual violence on the night of April 5 was limited in scope, duration, and bodily harm.

Deng made in developing the consolidation program in 1975 before he lost Mao's favor was not based on gathering a range of institutional or interest group backing, as is sometimes argued, but on Mao's indications of support for his efforts. Despite their clear preferences and pressing circumstances, the leaders of the central economic and planning bodies moved with extreme caution until receiving some sign from Mao. Also, the PLA not only went back to the barracks, as was undoubtedly the military's preference, but when ordered by the Chairman in December 1973 to rotate to different regions with virtually no personal staff before facing sharp criticism over the following months, regional commanders who had ruled their areas since 1967 meekly complied.

The key power relationships at the Center were again determined by Mao's preferences, requirements, and personal attitudes. The Chairman's choice of Wang Hongwen as his successor following the demise of Lin Biao, was particularly odd, based not on close knowledge of Wang but apparently because Wang fit Mao's conception of a "revolutionary successor": a Cultural Revolution activist, young, and with a background combining worker, peasant, and soldier experiences. It would be a choice that Mao came to regret in the cold hard light of actual performance, and Wang eventually lost his successor status to Hua Guofeng after Zhou Enlai's death in January 1976.

Much more personal, and reflecting forty-five to fifty years of sustained personal interaction, were Mao's sharply different attitudes to Zhou Enlai and Deng Xiaoping. Zhou was never ousted by Mao, and he was valued by the Chairman for his skills, loyalty, and utter reliability. But Mao had long looked down on Zhou's political and ideological credentials, and arguably felt uneasy with Zhou's approximate equality in age and party seniority. Also, in the last period of their lives, Mao resented the high regard in which Zhou was held, both domestically for his policy moderation and internationally, where Zhou was widely hailed for his role in United States-China rapprochement. Thus, in 1973 Mao twice launched rhetorical attacks on Zhou for foreign policy errors that were at best exaggerated, at worst bogus. Most cruelly, in November–December of that year, Mao demanded intense Politburo criticism of the seriously ill Premier, attacks that all leaders dutifully participated in, Deng included.

In contrast, although twice removed from office for alleged ideological mistakes, the younger Deng had always been one of Mao's favorites, received his highest praise, and was protected when out of power. Mao's behavior of being "bad to Premier Zhou but nice to Deng Xiaoping" was graphically reflected in late 1973 when Deng, as required, joined in the harsh criticism of the Premier. When informed of this, an excited Chairman happily exclaimed "I knew he would speak," and wanted Deng brought to him immediately.[27]

An even more intense relationship concerned Mao and his wife, Jiang Qing, although they had not lived together for many years and she had limited access to him during this last period. On the one hand, Jiang Qing faithfully carried out the radical edge of Mao's Cultural Revolution line. In addition, she was entwined in his personal prestige because of their relationship that dated back to Yan'an. On the other hand, Jiang Qing's abrasive personality and policy excesses undermined her effectiveness as a member of the central leadership, causing the kind of disunity that Mao repeatedly railed against in these years. There are also many indications of marital tensions between the two.

Thus a peculiar dynamic existed: when criticizing the Gang of Four, Mao's barbs were overwhelmingly directed at his wife for matters of her personal style rather than her political orientation, which he shared to a considerable extent. She was strongly protected politically by Mao—a condition of Deng's return to work in 1973 was that he would not oppose Jiang Qing. Even when the Chairman's own criticisms of Jiang Qing created an opportunity to attack her, other leaders held back. Clearly Jiang's special status as Mao's wife shaped and distorted leadership politics.

In this setting of peculiar personal judgments, shifting policy preferences, and a basic incompatibility between trying to save the Cultural Revolution by correcting its excesses while affirming the rebellious essence of the movement, Mao left a seriously weakened regime when he died on September 9, 1976. The Chinese communist party-state he had founded was contending with a new upsurge of disruption, a long list of ignored national needs, mounting tensions among the masses, and sharply divided leadership councils.

Nevertheless, Mao had also left the elements that would quickly right the ship, including a battered but still coherent cadre force that desired order and respected discipline. Most crucial was that, virtually by accident, Mao had designated as his final, if transient successor, Hua Guofeng, someone who both had the legitimate authority to act by virtue of the Chairman's selection and, against many expectations, was prepared to take the decisive action of arresting the Gang of Four in October 1976, a bold step that paved the way for the restoration of the pre-Cultural Revolution political system (see Box 3.5). But the larger story of the dramatic and unexpected developments of the post-Mao period is a matter for the next chapter.

MAO IN POWER: AN ASSESSMENT

In 1981, the CCP released a **Resolution on Certain Questions in the History of Our Party Since the Founding of the People's Republic of China** as the authoritative (and still largely upheld) assessment by the post-Mao leadership of the party's achievements and shortcomings since 1949. The resolution declared that "Comrade Mao Zedong was a great proletarian revolutionary [who] made gross mistakes during the 'Cultural Revolution,' but [on the whole] his contributions far outweigh his mistakes." Even his mistakes during that chaotic period were allegedly those of a tragic figure who sought to advance the revolutionary cause but "confused right and wrong and the people with the enemy."[28]

Although this official assessment is grotesque given that Mao's personal policy excesses cost anywhere from thirty million to fifty million or more lives (particularly as a result of the Great Leap Forward for which he was also assigned some blame), when the statement is stripped of rhetoric and the need to make excuses for the founder of the regime, in some respects it has a certain validity. In particular, the resolution presents a chronology not dissimilar from that provided in this chapter: an initial period through 1956 of solid achievement in the regime's own terms; the pre-Cultural Revolution decade where, notwithstanding some achievements, serious "leftist" errors affected politics and the economy; and Mao's final decade of chaos and inadequate efforts to repair the damage.

What were the causes of the major turning points during the Maoist era, and what do they tell us about Mao's rule?

BOX 3.5 THE ARREST OF THE GANG OF FOUR

The bitter divisions between the radical Gang of Four and the moderate forces led by Hua Guofeng in mid-1976 deepened as the Chairman's life slipped away following the Tiananmen incident. To a large extent, the regime was paralyzed, with no one willing to challenge Mao's anti-rightist political line: the Gang pushed radical ideological themes but had limited impact on concrete policies; the senior revolutionaries, who had largely been relegated to the sidelines, fretted about possible dangers to the country and themselves personally if the radicals seized power once Mao passed away, but they essentially took no action; while Hua deflected radical initiatives without challenging the anti-rightist rhetoric. The deep distrust and fear intensified further following the Chairman's death in early September.

Among moderates, including those like Hua who held active posts, and the old revolutionaries who mostly lacked formal power, there was a palpable fear that the Gang would indeed attempt to seize power, with their administrative proposals, ideological slogans, and a couple of (wrongly understood or imagined) troop movements seen as evidence of possible planning for a coup. In reality, the radicals undertook no concrete planning for a coup, either in the months before Mao's death or throughout September. The radicals essentially had no political strategy except to continue to push the Cultural Revolution line, seek to maintain a radicalized political environment, and wait and see how Hua as the designated successor would perform. In truth, this fit the larger pattern of the Gang of Four's political performance during Mao's last years: they never had a coherent strategy for power, as their position was totally dependent on the Chairman's inconstant blessing, and there were sufficient suspicions and animosities among the four to prevent a serious coordinated effort.

Nevertheless, a possible power seizure was deeply feared by moderate leaders, so they were faced with "solving the Gang of Four problem." Even if there were no coup attempt, Hua realized there was a real question of how the system could function efficiently if leadership councils were engaged in an ongoing bitter ideological dispute. In the end, it was Hua Guofeng who decided the Gang had to be dealt with and played the decisive role throughout.

Of the old revolutionaries, Marshal Ye Jianying and Vice Premier Li Xiannian were brought into the planning by Hua, with Ye in particular playing a Mafialike consigliore role as key adviser and serving as a conduit to other elders on the sidelines, more to reassure them that things were under control than to secure any active participation in measures to foil the radicals.

The issue became how to eliminate the radicals' political influence, and while the legal method of calling a Central Committee meeting to vote them off the Politburo was canvased, it was considered too unpredictable, given the stacking of the body with political unknowns at its last election in 1973. Instead, the four were summarily arrested on the night of October 6, 1976. There had been a coup, but one implemented by Hua Guofeng and his moderate associates, not the radicals.

This outcome was enormously popular within the remaining leadership, causing excited celebrations well into the night following the arrest and for weeks afterward. It also gained broad popular support, with the masses for once genuinely enthusiastic about a sudden change in leadership fortunes. And it provided great support for Hua's temporary legitimacy as Mao's successor. While Hua's contribution was progressively obscured after 1981, in the official summary of his life upon his death in 2008, the CCP ultimately acknowledged that Hua Guofeng had been the "decisive leader" in crushing the Gang of Four, thus making possible the launching of the era of reform that led to China's spectacular economic growth.

From early on in his career Mao was a visionary, a strategic genius, a realistic revolutionary, a nationalist, and a dedicated Marxist. From early days he also saw himself as a leader of great destiny, and he was always acutely attentive to his personal power, but it was power for great purposes. Mao could also capture the popular and elite imagination, whether for the universally approved "standing up" to foreign imperialists and national unification, or, before everything went wrong, the Great Leap's pursuit of unprecedented economic growth.

For all his talent, Mao's successes before 1949 owed much to circumstances, notably the Japanese invasion and incompetence of Chiang Kai-shek's Nationalists. He also built successfully on Marxist ideology and the organizational backbone of a Leninist party. After 1949, Mao initially benefited from an already tested program for state-building based on the Soviet model. Mao's great achievement was to enlarge upon these circumstances by developing broad-based party unity, a form of quasi-collective leadership allowing significant leadership discussion, and a pragmatic, often cautious approach to policy. Together this produced the unimaginable victory of 1949, and also sustained the party's further successes to the mid-1950s.

Paradoxically, the seeds of later disasters can be found in the victory of 1949. Most fundamentally, Mao's power, while uncontested within the party as long as successes continued during the struggle for national power, became unchallengeable upon coming to power and would remain so for rest of his life. His emperor-like authority was unmistakable in the Gao Gang case and the handling of agricultural cooperativization, even as he maintained the semblance of collective leadership. In many senses, leadership politics under the Chairman was like the highly personalistic court politics of imperial China that could be altered into more arbitrary forms at any time of the emperor's choosing. For much of the initial period up to 1956, Mao left alone certain areas (notably the economy) in which he recognized his limitations, but his ability to intervene was clear.

In addition, the fact of virtual nationwide success during the CCP's first period in power subtly diluted the need for pragmatism, although this developed slowly, given the Korean War and the residual threat from the Nationalists on Taiwan. Without the threats of stronger enemies inside China, by the early 1950s caution was less necessary in the pursuit of ideologically prescribed social change, and overly ambitious policies surfaced. Moreover, the accomplishments of these years created a sense of infinite optimism in Mao about the capacity to shape the national landscape, something that by 1958, in the words of the CCP's official 1981 Resolution on Party History, fed Mao's "smug and impatient" arrogance as he launched the Great Leap Forward.

The Great Leap reflected a serious erosion of the factors that had underpinned Mao's earlier successes—a loss of pragmatism in demanding ever more impractical objectives, personally taking over the economy despite his lack of understanding, and creating so much political pressure and raising the stakes so high that no one dared "say him nay." This shift can be seen as a product of Mao's ambition for China's rapid advance toward development and prosperity. It was also a product of failure, particularly that of the Hundred Flowers Movement in 1957 from which Mao concluded that fulfilling his ambitions would require a new strategy. The Hundred Flowers was also Mao's first significant setback in two decades, and the new strategy for development, the Great Leap Forward, held out the promise of escaping the shadow of that setback.

But the new strategy failed, too, and with even more terrible consequences. The collapse of the Great Leap created a novel situation for Mao, one in which he had no clear idea of what to do. He relinquished day-to-day control of the party-state but retained ultimate power while searching for explanations and scapegoats for what had gone wrong. By the early 1960s Mao was increasingly focused on class struggle against enemies of his revolution, and he began to worry that the revisionism he saw in the Soviet Union might be China's future. Again, he could not develop a coherent response to this danger and approved various pragmatic proposals from his colleagues to repair the damage caused by the Great Leap. He also upheld the fundamental principle of party leadership, and despite reservations about certain individuals left most of the Yan'an Round Table leaders in place—until 1966.

The Cultural Revolution was the result of a complex mix of policy dissatisfaction, paranoia, and personal vindictiveness, and a genuine desire to somehow re-revolutionize society that led Mao into totally uncharted waters. The Great Leap, though it had been a disaster, was based on a program, was carried out by the party organization and the established leadership, and sought objectives that were at least comprehensible to the public. None of this applied to the Cultural Revolution, with the party dismantled as an institution, leadership unity in ruins, and an approach that did not simply lack pragmatism but barely had any coherent objectives beyond managing the chaos it had created. Through all this Mao was prepared to accept enormous social, economic, and human costs in pursuit of a revolutionary purity he could hardly define. Even when he attempted, in his last years, to save the Cultural Revolution by correcting its shortcomings and introducing realistic policy objectives, he refused to give up the implausible dream of a modernizing state that was authoritarian yet allowed rebellion against any signs of revisionism.

Moreover, during the entire decade from the start of the Cultural Revolution until his death, Mao broke with the principle of party seniority that had underpinned CCP rule, instead introducing in idiosyncratic manner marginal figures like Wang Hongwen and Jiang Qing into the highest leading bodies, a situation that could not outlast his life. Indeed, Mao's actions during his final decade did not simply create havoc for the lives of the Chinese people, they fundamentally attacked the interests of the vast majority of the communist party elite that had come to power with him in 1949. By doing this, Mao created the conditions that would lead those members of that elite who survived him to thoroughly reject both the means and the ends of his Cultural Revolution, even though they could not bring themselves to repudiate the Chairman himself.

While it is tempting to conclude with Lord Acton's famous observation that "power tends to corrupt, and absolute power corrupts absolutely," Mao's case is more complex. Although having many of the accoutrements and vices of an emperor, and engaging in personal vindictiveness, even in his last decade Mao indicated (however selectively) some personal remorse and protected individual old comrades, none more significantly than Deng Xiaoping, who would, with some irony, ultimately emerge as post–Mao China's dominant leader.

Mao's sin was less corruption than hubris, his belief that he was "alone with the masses" and had a special understanding of the needs of the revolution and the Chinese people. No one and no costs should stand in the way of his pursuit of those visions, and he could not accept responsibility when that pursuit led to disastrous consequences, which, in his view, were ultimately someone else's fault. Mao Zedong was only able to do this because of the absolute power he had accumulated through the combination of his record of revolutionary success, the centralizing forces of the Leninist party organization that he built, and the authoritarian strain in traditional Chinese political culture.

In speaking of the mistakes of the Great Leap Forward, the 1981 Resolution on the History of the CCP since 1949 said, "Although Comrade Mao Zedong must be held chiefly responsible, we cannot lay the blame on him alone for all those errors." In other words, the entire party leadership let him do it. More broadly, we can conclude that Mao's failures and their catastrophic consequences during the period of his rule were uniquely personal, but they were also the result of the CCP regime's totalitarian essence.

NOTES

1. At the time of his dismissal in 1959, Minister of Defense Peng Dehuai referred to Mao by noting that "the first emperor of any dynasty was always severe and brilliant." "Peng Teh-huai's Speech at the 8th Plenum of the 8th CCP Central Committee (Excerpts)" (August 1959), in *The Case of Peng Teh-huai, 1959–1968* (Kowloon: Union Research Institute, 1968), 36, 427.

2. This term was first used to describe the core of CCP leadership around Mao that formed in the Yan'an base area in the 1940s by Roderick MacFarquhar in *The Origins of the Cultural Revolution,1: Contradictions Among the People 1956-1957* (New York: Columbia University Press, 1974), 3.The shattering of the "Yan'an Round Table" was a major theme in all three volumes of MacFarquhar's *The Origins of the Cultural Revolution*, the other two being 2: *The Great Leap Forward 1958-1960* (1983) and 3: *The Coming of the Cataclysm 1961-1966* (1997).

3. *Selected Works of Mao Tse-tung*, vol. 3 (Peking: Foreign Languages Press, 1965), 208–210.

4. *Selected Works of Mao Tse-tung*, vol. 4 (Peking: Foreign Languages Press, 1961), 422.

5. *Eighth National Congress of the Communist Party of China*, vol. 1, *Documents* (Peking: Foreign Languages Press, 1956), 7.

6. "Talk at Expanded Central Committee Meeting" (January 1962), in *Joint Publications Research Service*, no. 52029, 13.

7. In the post-1949 period Deng primarily performed civilian roles, but he was regarded as a great military figure of the revolution who was only passed over as a marshal in 1955 because of his leading civilian functions. Deng's military prestige would play a major role in his post-Mao authority as the party's "paramount leader."

8. *Selected Works of Mao Tse-tung*, vol. 2 (Peking: Foreign Languages Press, 1965), 224.

9. The only exception was PLA Marshal Chen Yi, who served as foreign minister from 1958 to the Cultural Revolution.

10. *Selected Works of Mao Tsetung*, vol. 5 (Peking: Foreign Languages Press, 1977), 93–94.

11. Frederick C. Teiwes and Warren Sun, eds., *The Politics of Agricultural Cooperativization in China: Mao, Deng Zihui, and the "High Tide" of 1955* (Armonk, NY: M. E. Sharpe, 1993), 13.

12. *Selected Works of Mao Tsetung*, vol. 5, 395.

13. "On the Ten Major Relationships" (April 1956), in *Selected Works of Mao Tsetung*, vol. 5, 284–307.

14. Frederick C. Teiwes and Warren Sun, *China's Road to Disaster: Mao, Central Politicians, and Provincial Leaders in the Unfolding of the Great Leap Forward, 1955–1959* (Armonk, NY: M. E. Sharpe, 1999), 149.

15. Frederick C. Teiwes, *Politics and Purges in China: Rectification and the Decline of Party Norms, 1950–1965*, 2nd ed. (Armonk, NY: M. E. Sharpe, 1993), lviii, 370–371.

16. Teiwes, *Politics and Purges*, xxxvi; and Roderick MacFarquhar, *The Origins of the Cultural Revolution 3: The Coming of the Cataclysm 1961–1966* (New York: Columbia University Press, 1997), 157–158.

17. Teiwes, *Politics and Purges*, 385.

18. *Main Documents of the First Session of the Third National People's Congress of the People's Republic of China* (Peking: Foreign Languages Press, 1965), 15.

19. For a critical discussion of the appropriate periodization of the Cultural Revolution, see Jonathan Unger, "The Cultural Revolution at the Grass Roots," *China Journal* 57 (2007): 113–117. While the issue has been whether "Cultural Revolution" should apply to 1966–1968/69 or to the entire 1966–1976 decade, as in official PRC usage, three periods can be distinguished: (1) 1966–1968, when party control collapsed in the face of popular turmoil; (2) 1969–1971, which saw severe state repression in an effort to restore order; and (3) 1972–1976, when political trends alternated between moderate and radical phases, but at all times with considerably less violence and/or disruption compared to the preceding periods.

20. Roderick MacFarquhar and Michael Schoenhals, *Mao's Last Revolution* (Cambridge, MA: Belknap Press, 2006), 63.

21. Stuart R. Schram, *The Political Thought of Mao Tse-tung*, rev. ed. (New York: Praeger Publishers, 1969), 55.

22. For more on Jiang Qing, see Ross Terrill, *Madame Mao: The White-Boned Demon*, rev. ed. (Stanford, CA: Stanford University Press, 1999).

23. Frederick C. Teiwes and Warren Sun, *The Tragedy of Lin Biao: Riding the Tiger during the Cultural Revolution, 1966–1971* (London: C. Hurst & Co., 1996), 76.

24. Frederick C. Teiwes and Warren Sun, *The End of the Maoist Era: Chinese Politics during the Twilight of the Cultural Revolution, 1972–1976* (Armonk, NY: M.E. Sharpe, 2007), 595.

25. Teiwes and Sun, *The End of the Maoist Era*, 3.

26. Teiwes and Sun, *TheEnd of the Maoist Era*, 186. Here Mao rhetorically extended the Cultural Revolution from 1966 to the present, but as we have seen the movement was over in mid-1968.

27. Teiwes and Sun, *The End of the Maoist Era*, 20, 110. The statement concerning being bad to Zhou and good to Deng by Politburo member Li Xiannian was applied to the "two ladies" who served as Mao's liaison to the leadership, but clearly they were simply carrying out his wishes.

28. "Resolution on Questions in Party History Since 1949," *Beijing Review* 27 (1981): 29, 23. The full text of the Resolution can be found online at http://www.marxists.org/subject/china/documents/cpc/history/01.htm.

SUGGESTED READINGS

Bachman, David M. *Bureaucracy, Economy, and Leadership in China: The Institutional Origins of the Great Leap Forward*. New York: Cambridge University Press, 1991.

Brown, Jeremy, and Matthew Johnson, eds. *Maoism at the Grass Roots: Everyday Life in China's Era of High Socialism*. Cambridge, MA: Harvard University Press, 2015.

Cheek, Timothy, ed. *The Cambridge Critical Introduction to Mao*. New York: Cambridge University Press, 2010.

Domenach, Jean-Luc. *The Origins of the Great Leap Forward: The Case of One Chinese Province*. Boulder, CO: Westview Press, 1995.

Esherick, Joseph W., Paul G. Pickowicz, and Andrew G. Walder, eds. *China's Cultural Revolution as History*. Stanford, CA: Stanford University Press, 2006.

Forster, Keith. *Rebellion and Factionalism in a Chinese Province: Zhejiang, 1966–1976*. Armonk, NY: M.E. Sharpe, 1990.

Gao, Wenqian. *Zhou Enlai: The Last Perfect Revolutionary*. New York: Public Affairs, 2010.

Gao, Yuan. *Born Red: A Chronicle of the Cultural Revolution*. Stanford, CA: Stanford University Press, 1987.

Jin, Qiu. *The Culture of Power: The Lin Biao Incident in the Cultural Revolution*. Stanford, CA: Stanford University Press, 1999.

Kraus, Richard Curt. *The Cultural Revolution: A Very Short Introduction*. New York: Oxford University Press, 2012.

Li, Zhisui. *The Private Life of Chairman Mao: The Memoirs of Mao's Personal Physician*. London: Chatto & Windus, 1994.

Lubell, Pamela. *The Chinese Communist Party and the Cultural Revolution: The Case of the Sixty-One Renegades*. New York: Palgrave, 2002.

MacFarquhar, Roderick. *The Origins of the Cultural Revolution*. 3 vols. New York: Columbia University Press: vol. 1, *Contradictions among the People 1956–1957* (1974); vol. 2, The *Great Leap Forward 1958–1960* (1983); vol. 3, *The Coming of the Cataclysm 1961–1966* (1997).

MacFarquhar, Roderick, Timothy Cheek, and Eugene Wu, eds. *The Secret Speeches of Chairman Mao: From the Hundred Flowers to the Great Leap Forward*. Cambridge, MA: Harvard Council on East Asian Studies, 1989.

MacFarquhar, Roderick, and Michael Schoenhals. *Mao's Last Revolution*. Cambridge, MA: Belknap Press of Harvard University Press, 2006.

Pantsov, Alexander V., with Steven I. Levine. *Mao: The Real Story*. New York: Simon & Schuster, 2012.

Perry, Elizabeth J., and Li Xun. *Proletarian Power: Shanghai in the Cultural Revolution*. Boulder, CO: Westview Press, 1997.

Short, Philip. *Mao: A Life*. New York: Henry Holt, 2000.

Spence, Jonathan. *Mao Zedong: A Penguin Life*. New York: Viking, 1999.

Teiwes, Frederick C. *Politics and Purges in China: Rectification and the Decline of Party Norms, 1950–1965*. 2nd ed. Armonk, NY: M.E. Sharpe, 1993.

Teiwes, Frederick C. *Politics at Mao's Court: Gao Gang and Party Factionalism in the Early 1950s*. Armonk, NY: M. E. Sharpe, 1990.

Teiwes, Frederick C., and Warren Sun. *China's Road to Disaster: Mao, Central Politicians, and Provincial Leaders in the Unfolding of the Great Leap Forward, 1955–1959*. Armonk, NY: M. E. Sharpe, 1999.

Teiwes, Frederick C., and Warren Sun. *The End of the Maoist Era: Chinese Politics during the Twilight of the Cultural Revolution, 1972–1976*. Armonk, NY: M.E. Sharpe, 2007.

Teiwes, Frederick C., with Warren Sun. *The Formation of the Maoist Leadership: From the Return of Wang Ming to the Seventh Party Congress*. London: Contemporary China Institute Research Notes and Studies, 1994.

Teiwes, Frederick C., and Warren Sun. *The Tragedy of Lin Biao: Riding the Tiger during the Cultural Revolution, 1966–1971*. London: C. Hurst & Co., 1996.

Thaxton, Ralph G. *Catastrophe and Contention in Rural China: Mao's Great Leap Forward Famine and the Origins of Righteous Resistance in Da Fo Village*. New York: Cambridge University Press, 2008.

Walder, Andrew G. *China Under Mao: A Revolution Derailed*. Cambridge, MA: Harvard University Press, 2015.

Walder, Andrew G. *Fractured Rebellion: The Beijing Red Guard Movement*. Cambridge, MA: Harvard University Press, 2009.

Yang Jisheng. *Tombstone: The Great Chinese Famine, 1958–1962*. Translated by Stacy Mosher and Guo Jian; edited by Edward Friedman, Guo Jian, and Stacy Mosher. New York: Farrar, Straus and Giroux, 2012.

4

Deng Xiaoping and His Successors (1976 to the Present)

BRUCE GILLEY

The period of Chinese political history since 1976 represents China's return to its long quest for wealth and power.[1] In this period of reform, China has picked up the pieces from the disastrous consequences of the Mao era and resumed a trajectory of development that had been abandoned in the early-1950s. China remains an authoritarian regime, but it has become a more institutionalized and regularized one, and one that no longer deserves the label "totalitarian." The Chinese Communist Party (CCP) remains committed to the preservation of its power, but it has abandoned the aim of totally controlling and transforming Chinese society.

Yet it is easy to draw too sharp a distinction between the reform era and the pre-reform era. Many things have changed in the reform era, but many others have not. China's official ideology retains its references to Mao Zedong Thought, and Mao's portrait remains ubiquitous in the country—on the currency, in trinket shops, and most notably over Tiananmen Square in Beijing, the large space that dominates the seat of government. Party leadership remains the central and unchallengeable principle of political life in the PRC. And, despite extensive privatization, the party continues to view state ownership of strategic sectors of the economy—airlines, banks, energy suppliers, and even automobiles—as essential. Revolutionary mass mobilization campaigns continue to be practiced—although in a more managed manner than under Mao—by the CCP periodically to achieve policy objectives or enforce ideological compliance.[2]

Beyond these longitudinal comparisons with China's own recent history, two sets of cross-country comparisons are useful for understanding China's era of "reform and opening" (*gaige kaifang*) that began under the leadership of Deng Xiaoping and continued with his successors. The first is comparison with rapid industrialization in other Asian countries. Japan's Meiji-era (1868–1912) period of "wealthy country and strong arms" (*fukoku-kyōhei*) is perhaps the earliest example of this. An even more relevant parallel can be found with the post-1949 Republic of China regime on Taiwan under the Nationalist Party (see chap. 19). There, an authoritarian state was transformed through economic liberalization and rapid growth, which eventually resulted in a political opening for democracy in the 1980s. A similar economic and political transformation occurred in South Korea. From the perspective of culture, East Asian economic success has been deeply rooted in the work ethic associated with the region's entrepreneurial spirit. What was missing on the Chinese mainland before the reform era was an efficient, stable, and market-friendly government to unleash that spirit. There is today a great debate on how well China's experience fits with the developmental trajectories of other East Asian states, including the links between modernization and democratization in Taiwan and Korea.[3]

The second comparative perspective is with other communist and postcommunist states. In Eastern Europe and the Soviet Union, communist party-states began experimenting with decentralization, market prices, and expanded foreign trade in the 1950s and 1960s in response to the failures of highly centralized Stalinist economic policy. But those changes did not save the regimes from collapse in the late 1980s and early 1990s, after the threat of Soviet intervention against anti-party movements was lifted. In some places, such as Central Asia and Russia, authoritarianism resurfaced after the collapse of communism, often with strong nationalist dimensions. From the perspective of comparative communism, China is an important case in which a communist party has successfully carried out and adapted to market reforms.[4] This success has, in turn, been a crucial factor in the survival of communist rule in the PRC at a time when democracy has spread throughout most other parts of the world.

Thus, China's reform era, fascinating in its own terms, can be even more richly studied as a case of comparative East Asian development and comparative communist politics. These comparative perspectives can be very helpful to understanding the dramatic divergence between contemporary China's rapid and radical economic transition and its less radical political transition, which lies at the heart of many of the most important challenges that the PRC faces today.

THE ORIGINS OF THE REFORM ERA

At the time of Mao's death in September 1976, the damaging effects of his rule were palpable in nearly every aspect of life in China. Society was so weakened and fractured by the Chairman's repeated campaigns that the party-state remained de facto totalitarian in spite of lessened repression in the early 1970s. Government institutions had been damaged or suspended by the Cultural Revolution. For example, the **National People's Congress**, China's parliament, had not met in full session since 1964. Economic growth had barely kept pace with population growth for much of the Mao era, despite a brief recovery in the early 1960s. An estimated 74 percent of China's population lived in poverty in 1976. Beijing's streets were nearly as empty of traffic as those of modern-day Pyongyang, North Korea's capital.

The arrest of the Gang of Four orchestrated by Mao's immediate successor as the CCP chairman, Hua Guofeng, and his political allies in October 1976 made the reform era possible by removing from power the radical leaders who advocated a strict adherence to Maoist policies. In the two years between then and the landmark meeting of the party leadership in December 1978 (the **Third Plenum**) when Deng Xiaoping's newly consolidated power was clearly on display and the first road map of economic reform was laid out, there were, in retrospect, many signs of things to come.

In 1977–1978, local cadres in some of China's poorest regions illegally divided the communal land among private households and contracted with them for output quotas to be turned over to the collective, letting them keep or even sell anything produced above the quota. These practices were condoned by the provincial leadership and tolerated by the central authorities, even though decollectivization wouldn't become official policy until the early 1980s.[5]

There were also some telling signs of liberalization in culture and education in 1977. A ban on the "bourgeois" works of Beethoven was lifted to mark the 150th anniversary of the composer's death, allowing the Central Symphony Orchestra to perform his works for the first time since 1959. University entrance examinations were held for the first time since 1965. The first example of a genre of writing that would come to be known as "wound literature," which dealt with the sufferings under Mao, appeared in the official periodical *People's Literature*. The Yugoslavian president and communist party leader Josip Tito visited Beijing in a sign of the early post-Mao leadership's interest in Tito's decentralized type of "market socialism," which had led Yugoslavia to be excommunicated by the world communist camp by Moscow in 1948 and Tito to be denounced by Beijing as a traitor to Marxism-Leninism. Shortly after Tito's visit, the influential *Guangming Daily* newspaper ran an editorial arguing that workers should be paid bonuses for higher output or better work, while a meeting of provincial agriculture leaders made similar arguments for rural labor.

The key event that had profound and lasting consequences for China was the political resurrection of Deng Xiaoping in 1977 (see Table 4.1), who had been purged the previous spring by Mao for his alleged role in the April 1976 "Tiananmen Incident" (see chap. 3). Deng resumed his posts as PRC vice premier and CCP vice chair as a part of a deal brokered between the party's two ideological factions, the "whateverists" who were loyal to "whatever policy decisions" Mao made and "whatever instructions" he gave, and the "pragmatists," who argued that "practice is the sole criterion of truth" when formulating policies.[6]

Party chairman Hua Guofeng, as Mao's chosen successor, was affiliated with the **whateverist faction,** although he tended to emphasize the more moderate form of Maoism. Deng's return to power gave the **pragmatist faction,** led by the Long March veteran and senior economic planner Chen Yun, the chance to press its case without fear of retribution, as Deng was known to sympathize with that group. Throughout 1978, the two factions engaged in arcane debates about topics such as rural labor management and commune accounting policies. While both sides agreed with Hua Guofeng's suggestion to make economic development rather than class struggle the primary task of the party, they differed on how to go about it. Borrowing from the experiences of reform communism in Eastern Europe, Chen Yun's faction worked hard to discredit the blind adherence to Mao's Stalinist economic policies. Drawing

TABLE 4.1 Top Leaders of China Since 1976

Name (Birth–Death)	Key Titles and Dates	Comments
Hua Guofeng (1921–2008)	• CCP Chairman (1976–1981) • PRC Premier (1976–1980) • Central Military Commission Chairman (1976–1981)	Mao's designated successor, Hua was instrumental in the arrest of the Gang of Four, unintentionally paving the way for the rise of reformers led by Deng Xiaoping. Generally supportive of economic reforms in 1977–1978, he was pushed aside by Deng and Chen Yun and was removed from key posts in 1980–1981. Out of respect for Mao, Hua was still given a seat on the CCP's Central Committee until 2002. See Table 3.1 in chap.3 of this book.
Deng Xiaoping (1904–1997)	• CCP Vice Chairman(1977–1982) • PRC Vice Premier (1977–1980) • Central Military Commission Chairman (1981–1989)	Long March veteran who overthrew the weak Hua Guofeng and launched China's reform movement. "Core" of the "Second Generation" (after Mao). Deng is widely revered in China for his role in steering economic reforms, but his legacy is clouded by his role in ordering the 1989 Tiananmen Massacre. See Table 3.1, in chap.3 of this book.
Chen Yun (1905–1995)	• CCP Vice-Chairman (1956–1966, 1978–1982) • PRC Vice-Premier (1949–1966, 1979–1980)	Veteran revolutionary who became one of China's leading economic planners after 1949, though in and out of favor with Mao. Re-emerged as a key leader in late 1978 with a major influence on economic policy, initially supporting reform but increasingly cautious and conservative from the mid-1980s. See Table. 3.1 in chap.3 of this book.
Hu Yaobang (1915–1989)	• CCP Chairman (1981–1982) • CCP General Secretary (1982–1987)	Protégé of Deng Xiaoping. Played a key role in rehabilitating Cultural Revolution victims, promoting political reforms, and arguing for liberal policies in Tibet. Demoted by Deng Xiaoping in 1987 for soft-time on democracy protests. His death sparked the 1989 Tiananmen Square movement. Officially rehabilitated in 2005.
Zhao Ziyang (1919–2005)	• PRC Premier (1980–1987) • CCP General Secretary (1987–1989)	Protégé of Deng Xiaoping. Pioneer of market-oriented economic reforms and proponent of democratizing political reforms. Purged after the Beijing Massacre in June 1989, Zhao became even more pro-democratic in his long period under house arrest.
Jiang Zemin (b. 1926)	• CCP General Secretary (1989–2002) • PRC President (1993–2003) • Central Military Commission Chairman (1989–2004)	Jiang oversaw China's recovery from Tiananmen by promoting economic reforms and rebuilding ties to the United States. "Core" of the "Third Generation," Jiang was the first PRC leader to step down voluntarily and peacefully when he handed over power to Hu Jintao in 2002.
Hu Jintao (b. 1942)	• CCP General Secretary (2002–2012) • PRC President (2003–2013) • Central Military Commission Chairman (2004–2012)	Hu sought to address issues of social justice, redistribution, and welfare. But without major political reforms, those efforts faced stiff opposition. "Core" of the "Fourth Generation," Hu displayed little personal charisma.
Xi Jinping (b. 1953)	• CCP General Secretary (2012–) • PRC President (2013–) • Central Military Commission Chairman (2012–)	When Xi, the "core" of the "Fifth Generation" of CCP leaders came to power in 2012–2013, he was seen as an avid economic reformer and competent administrator who would overcome the sclerosis of China's governance system. But he has taken steps to both recentralize the Chinese economy and consolidate his own personal power at the expense of the norms of collective leadership that has prevailed in PRC elite politics for decades. He has also presided over a more assertive foreign policy in pursuit of China's great power ambitions.

upon a thirty-year repertoire of policies, ideological concepts, and institutions that had been used to limit the ravages of Mao, Chen effectively isolated and discredited the whateverists' hopes of continuing even a more moderate version of Mao's economic policies. It was Chen who revived the Sichuanese adage first used by Deng to justify modest market reforms in rural areas in 1962 that got him into political trouble with Mao: "It doesn't matter whether a cat is black or white as long as it catches mice," clearly implying that economic policies should be judged only on whether they increased production, not on whether they conformed to some abstract ideological litmus test.

At a month-long CCP Central Work Meeting in November–December 1978, Chen warned that "commune party secretaries will lead the peasants into the cities demanding food" if the party did not reform rural policies to boost production. Deng, who missed the opening of the conference while on a state visit to Southeast Asia, returned to find that a consensus had developed between the pragmatists and the whateverists on the need for management reform, international opening, and abiding by "objective" (meaning market-based) economic laws.

The Third Plenum of the CCP Central Committee in December was "a final turning point" that "allowed a fundamental departure from the economic and other policies of the Cultural Revolution."[7] The emphasis on economic development was reiterated, while rural communes were given greater autonomy and the right to experiment with incentive pay. Political institutions were to be rebuilt. Mass movements were to be abandoned. Many prominent victims of Maoism were to be rehabilitated, and the April 1976 "Tiananmen Incident" was declared patriotic rather than counterrevolutionary.

The pragmatists were helped by an eruption in late 1978 of political posters along a 200-meter stretch of wall on Chang'an Boulevard, west of Tiananmen Square in Beijing, which came to be known as **Democracy Wall**, where the mistakes of Mao and the dangers of the "whateverist" faction were widely debated by Chinese citizens. Once the posters started criticizing Deng and questioning his commitment to political reform, he ordered the suppression of Democracy Wall in early 1979 and the arrest of many of the activists. One of the most articulate activists, Wei Jingsheng, who had written an essay titled "The Fifth Modernization" that called for democracy to be added to the officially proclaimed "Four Modernizations" in agriculture, industry, science and technology, and national defense,[8] was imprisoned for eighteen years before being allowed to go to the United States for medical treatment in 1997.

What ultimately tipped the balance in favor of reform was Chen Yun's effective critique in 1979 of Hua Guofeng's overly ambitious ten-year plan (1976–1985) of economic modernization, which already showed signs in 1978–1979 of being a repeat of the Great Leap mentality of setting unreasonably high production targets. Under pressure to produce more oil, for instance, a newly bought Japanese oil rig sank while being hastily towed into position in China's Bohai sea in November 1979 with a loss of seventy-two lives. Chen's counterproposal for "readjustment, reform, correction, and improvement" of the economy had sounded a decisively cautious and pragmatic tone.

After this, Hua was gradually eased out of power, first being removed from the position of PRC premier in 1980 and then as party chairman in 1981. Out of respect for Mao's legacy, Hua—now referred to simply as "Comrade Hua" rather than as "wise leader Chairman Hua"—retained a seat on the Central Committee until 2002. After all, Hua had supported the arrest of the Gang of Four and endorsed the shift to economic development—aspects of his life officially recognized when he died in 2008. With his removal, the balance of power in the top party organizations came to rest firmly in the hands of Deng Xiaoping, Chen Yun, and others strongly committed to abandoning Maoist economics.[9]

THE REFORM ERA BEGINS

Conventional views that China reformed its economy first and its political system second are mistaken. Indeed, in many ways political changes preceded and were the necessary condition for important economic ones. The party's repudiation of "class struggle" as its primary objective in late 1978 opened the door for many important political changes. During the 1980s, nearly five million people wrongfully accused of political mistakes and persecuted since the founding of the PRC, including 1.6 million intellectuals, were exonerated. A law passed in 1979 expanded the direct popular election of people's congress delegates from the **township** to the **county** level. Voting was reinstituted within the party, and cadres were allowed to see the text of policies before being asked to approve them. Village government also became more accountable with the passage in 1987 of a law allowing villages to elect their own leaders, who would enjoy wide autonomy in village affairs. Within a decade, most of the country's nearly one million villages would elect their own leaders (see chap. 9). The term "political reform" was formally introduced into the modern lexicon of the PRC in a speech given by Deng in 1980. Deng slammed "bureaucracy, over-concentration of power, patriarchal methods, life tenure in leading posts, and privileges of various kinds" within the party-state leadership.[10]

The repudiation of the Maoist era (see chap 3) was made most clear with the passage in 1981 of a resolution on the mistakes made by Mao and the party since the leftward turn of 1957—a kinder but similar rebuke to Khrushchev's denunciation of Stalin in 1956. It accused the Chairman of smugness, impatience, bad judgment, and being out of touch, although it said his merits exceeded his faults. Earlier drafts had been more scathing, but Deng had to tread carefully on the PRC's founder and its founding mythology. As part of efforts to reinvigorate the ranks of the CCP, in 1982, Deng set up a **Central Advisory Commission** as an organization with little power to ease elderly senior leaders into retirement. He also launched a program of fast-tracking promising young cadres who had college educations and good administrative skills. Among the beneficiaries of this program was an obscure foreign trade official named Jiang Zemin, who was promoted to vice minister of electronic industry and membership on the Central Committee in 1982; another was an equally obscure party-state bureaucrat working in the hinterlands, Hu Jintao, who was made second secretary of the Communist Youth League and an alternate (nonvoting) member of the Central Committee the same year. A final beneficiary was Xi Jinping, the son of a veteran party leader purged by Mao, who was sent to Zhengding county in Hebei province as deputy party secretary. These three would go on to become successors to Deng as the top leaders of China. Courts were revived as semi-independent bodies, although party committees continued to make the final decision on major cases, and the party retained its control of judicial appointments.[11] The role of the legal system in the PRC political system was boosted with the passage in 1989 of the Administrative Litigation Law, which for the first time allowed citizens to sue the government (see chap. 7). At the top level, military members of the Politburo fell from 57 percent in 1977 to 10 percent by 1992.

With the political obstacles cleared, China entered upon a new era of "reform of the economy and opening to the world" in the early 1980s (see chap. 8). In essence, this boiled down to increasing the role of market forces while reducing government planning in the economy and inserting China more fully in the global economy. Ideologically, it was conceived of not as an abandonment of socialism but as a better pathway toward achieving it. The party declared that China was in the primary stage of socialism (see chap. 5), under which a flourishing capitalist economy was a prerequisite for a later move to total state ownership. Mao was said to have tried to skip or compress this inevitable stage of historical development by jumping too quickly to the collectivization of agriculture and the nationalization of industry in the 1950s. It could be said that, in Deng's view, a good communist first needed to be a good capitalist.

Formally, party-state leadership in the 1980s was under two relatively young protégés of Deng Xiaoping. Zhao Ziyang, who had overseen market-oriented rural experiments as party leader of Deng's native Sichuan province, replaced Hua Guofeng as premier of the State Council in 1980. Hu Yaobang, who had been head of the Communist Youth League prior to the Cultural Revolution, succeeded Hua Guofeng as the chairman of the CCP, with the title of the party leader being changed shortly thereafter to "general secretary" in order to disassociate the position from Chairman Mao's abuses of power. But Deng was clearly the power behind the throne or, as he was called, China's "paramount leader." The one top formal position that he did keep for himself until November 1989 was chair of the Central Military Commission (CMC), which made him the commander in chief of China's armed forces.

China was fortunate in seeking to unravel a planned command economy that had fewer political and bureaucratic supporters than in the Soviet Union and other communist states. A full 69 percent of China's labor force in 1978 was engaged in agriculture (versus just 22 percent of the Soviet Union's labor force in 1975, when party leaders there were attempting unsuccessfully to loosen the powers and perquisites of industrial bureaucrats). Most Chinese farmers hated Soviet-style collective agriculture.[12] This made it comparatively easy to introduce household contracting in place of communes, which were virtually eliminated by the end of 1982.

One of the key innovations in this period was the spread of **township and village enterprises**—rural factories owned and operated by local governments that competed head-on in the opening market economy with inefficient state factories and provided employment for excess rural labor. The 1980s was the "golden era" for

China's rural economy. Per capita rural incomes increased nearly six fold between 1980 and 1990.

Urban and industrial reforms were a tougher nut to crack—as the leaders of Eastern Europe's disappointing attempts at "market socialism" had discovered. The CCP leadership was particularly wary of a repeat of the worker protests in Poland in 1980 that had led to the resignation of the head of the Polish communist party and to the recognition of a new independent workers' movement, Solidarity. China's strategy with **state-owned enterprises (SOEs)** was to gradually let the small and medium-sized ones sink or swim, hoping that laid-off or underpaid workers would find jobs in a growing private sector. The state-owned sector's share of national industrial output fell from 78 percent in 1978 to 55 percent by 1990, bringing China to the brink of an era in which the state sector would be an archipelago of strategically controlled large state enterprises in a sea of private business.

Annual GDP growth between 1978 and 1988 averaged 10 percent, twice the average of the previous two decades, and GDP per capita doubled, a remarkable feat for any country. But this came with a cost. After decades of virtually state-fixed prices for all commodities, China's consumer prices began creeping up as price reforms took hold and as the central government, facing a declining tax base from state enterprises, printed more money to finance its investments. Corruption, meanwhile, which had been widespread but petty and mostly invisible in the Mao era, became more lucrative and more visible, especially among the party elite with the market reforms. Deng's own son, Deng Pufang, established the Kanghua Development Company (whose Hong Kong subsidiary was memorably called the Bring Fast Company). It signed lucrative **joint ventures** with foreign firms and property deals amid widespread allegations of corruption.

As for unemployment, as state-owned enterprise reforms began to take hold, workers lost their jobs in growing numbers—especially in the industrial heartland of the three Northeastern provinces that had been industrialized under Japanese colonialism. Chinese officials struggled to invent euphemisms to describe the plight of laid-off workers—"awaiting assignment" (*daiye*) was the most popular. Unemployment insurance was launched in 1985, but it was a pittance compared to the perquisites of the **iron rice bowl** of state socialism, which included cradle-to-grave benefits as well as guaranteed lifetime employment. The CCP's main newspaper, *People's Daily*, proclaimed in 1988 that unemployment was normal and beneficial during the "primary stage of socialism," noting that tens of millions of state employees had spent their work days getting paid for "playing poker or chess, watching television, or racing on bicycles." The question was how the party would deal with the political consequences of these dramatic changes.

THE LIMITS OF POLITICAL REFORM

From the very beginning, Deng was careful to make clear that there were limits to political reform. In response to the 1979 Democracy Wall protests, Deng had articulated the so-called **Four Cardinal Principles**. These entailed a commitment to socialism, to the dictatorship of the proletariat, to CCP leadership, and to Marxism-Leninism-Mao

Zedong Thought (see chap. 5). In other words, the CCP was determined to remain in charge in the era of reform and opening up: "What kind of democracy do the Chinese people need today? It can only be **socialist democracy**, people's democracy, not bourgeois democracy, individualist democracy," Deng said.[13] This meant that there would be a more codified, rules-based political system than that under Mao, but one that was still firmly under the control of the communist party.

A new constitution was promulgated in 1982 that formally reinstated the notions of equality before the law, along with basic rights including religious belief, speech, press, assembly, and demonstration. But these and other rights were contingent on a duty to uphold the "the security, honor, and interests of the motherland." The constitution also declared that "The socialist system is the basic system of the People's Republic of China" and that "Sabotage of the socialist system by any organization or individual is prohibited," which, in effect, gave the party-state enormous unchecked leeway in deciding when and how to exercise its power. The rights to free movement and to strike were not included, as they had been in earlier PRC constitutions, and the radically participatory **Four Big Rights**—speaking out freely, airing views fully, holding great debates, and writing big-character posters—that were part of the 1975 Cultural Revolution constitution were removed.

Yet the economic reforms, political reforms, and international opening launched under Deng Xiaoping's leadership in the 1980s emboldened Chinese society. Graphic novels, rock music, and action films flooded into the hands of consumers. The "father of Chinese rock and roll," Cui Jian, became the balladeer of this generation of youth with his 1986 song "Nothing to My Name" (*Yi Wu Suo You*), which would inspire youth with its antimaterialistic message. Increased openness to the outside world, along with looser controls on domestic publications, gave birth to a generation of youth enamored with the West and with studying abroad. Between 1978 and 2007, more than one million Chinese students would go abroad to study, only 30 percent of whom ever returned.[14]

Alongside the growth of pop culture and consumerism were some serious critiques of the party-state, especially in the realm of literature. Author Bai Hua's 1981 screenplay *Unrequited Love (Ku lian)* was a scathing portrayal of how intellectuals and artists had been treated by the CCP; in one scene, the daughter of an artist who (like Bai Hua) was persecuted during the Anti-Rightist Campaign and the Cultural Revolution, asks her father, "Dad, you love our country, but does this country love you?"

Such pointed questions were too much for Deng and other top party leaders. Bai Hua and his screenplay were denounced, and campaigns were launched, first against the **spiritual pollution** (1983–1984) caused by certain, mostly foreign, influences and then against **bourgeois liberalization**, (1986–1987), which was a way of saying that some people had taken the reforms too far and crossed into the forbidden "bourgeois" zone of challenging the principle of party leadership.

The antibourgeois liberalization campaign had a particularly important impact on the course of Chinese politics. Deng believed that Hu Yaobang, the party general secretary, had not dealt firmly enough with the dissent, especially in handling rather small-scale student demonstrations for faster political reform in late 1986 to early 1987, and ousted him, although he remained a member of the Politburo Standing Committee. Deng chose Zhao Ziyang, the premier, to take over as party general secretary in January 1987. Zhao had been given much of the credit for the successful implementation of the economic reforms and, up to that point, had toed the correct political line, even chiming in loudly in denouncing the dangers of bourgeois liberalization.

However, Zhao's interest in political reforms went far beyond what Deng envisaged. Working through a number of new think tanks in Beijing universities and research institutes, and more directly through an official Central Research and Discussion Group on Political Reform, Zhao gave his blessing to studies of bold political changes. Thus, despite Hu's demotion, China's citizens continued to consider political liberalization and the critique of CCP autocracy as valid topics for public discussion. As inflation soared in late 1988 due to leadership paralysis over price reforms, the stage was set for large-scale demonstrations demanding that the party-state undertake bolder economic and political reform.

TIANANMEN 1989

In the spring of 1989, intellectuals in China published three open letters calling for the release of political prisoners who had been jailed following the Democracy Wall movement of 1979. The airing of the letters helped to create a mood of free expression and party vulnerability, a mood already rising as a result of the clear split in the leadership between reformers led by Zhao and hard-liners led by Premier Li Peng, who had taken over that position when Zhao had replaced Hu Yaobang as general secretary in 1987. It was Hu's death on April 15, due to a heart attack suffered a week earlier during a Politburo meeting, that lit this tinderbox. Within hours of the announcement of his death, thousands of students from several Beijing universities who regarded the late leader as a champion of deeper political reform began to converge on Tiananmen Square with flower wreaths and poems of condolence—just as students had done in April 1976 to commemorate the death of Zhou Enlai in January of that year.

In the following two months, China was shaken by the largest mass protest against the state since 1949. The **Tiananmen Movement** spread to 341 of China's cities (three-quarters of the total) and was joined by a hundred million people, a third of the urban population at the time. In Beijing, staff associations from the National People's Congress, China Central Television, and the Chinese Navy and other party-state organizations joined in with their own banners. As the movement continued through the end of May 1989, the Beijing Autonomous Workers Federation was established with the tacit support of the official All-China Federation of Trade Unions. About the only groups that did *not* take part in the 1989 protest were top CCP leaders and the peasants.

Zhao was tolerant of the movement, commenting in internal meetings that it reflected reasonable demands for stronger anticorruption measures and faster democratization. But party elders like Deng and his fellow **Eight Immortals** (including Chen Yun) who had fought in the civil war and been among the leading founders of the People's Republic were aghast at the challenge to party authority. As the protests persisted into late May, party elders and hard-liners, like Premier Li Peng, allied against Zhao, now accused of the same ideological and political mistakes as Hu Yaobang.

The way was paved to implement the Eight Immortals' decision to end the demonstrations by force. Estimates of the number of civilians killed when PLA soldiers were brought into Beijing to clear the streets near Tiananmen of protestors on the night of June 3 and the morning of June 4, 1989, range from a few hundred to several thousand. The exact toll is unknown since the Chinese authorities have never given an accounting.[15] Party rhetoric in the months following the massacre, justifying the suppression of what was (and still is) called counterrevolutionary political turmoil, was reminiscent of the Maoist-style propaganda that China had supposedly left behind. Zhao Ziyang was removed as general secretary and stripped of all his official positions in late June. He was placed under house arrest, where he remained, except for a few closely escorted excursions, until his death in 2005.

Outrage about the Beijing Massacre was widespread but could only be obliquely expressed. The official logo for the Asian Games in Beijing in 1990, when looked at from the back, was a blood-splattered "6–4" (the shorthand for the June 4 massacre), while the words "Down with Li Peng, End People's Rage" were embedded diagonally in a poem carried in the *People's Daily* in 1991.

The fate of Zhao Ziyang and the Tiananmen Movement continue to be unhealed wounds, and whatever the regime says about the protestors, they continue to be remembered with sympathy both inside and outside the party. Every year as June 4 approaches, the authorities take extra precautions to ensure that no public commemorations of the Tiananmen Movement take place (see Box 4.1).

ECONOMIC RECOVERY AFTER TIANANMEN

The person that Deng tapped to fill the post of party general secretary, Jiang Zemin, was a bona fide economic reformer but, unlike Hu or Zhao, without politically liberal instincts. After being promoted to the fringes of the central leadership during Deng's youth drive in the early 1980s, Jiang, who was trained as an electrical engineer before embarking on a career in the party-state bureaucracy, went on to become mayor and then party chief of Shanghai, where he was credited with doing a good job on both the economic and political front, including skillful handling of the pro-democracy protests in that city. Plucked suddenly from his perch in Shanghai in June 1989 to take on the top formal position in the party hierarchy, Jiang said he felt like he was standing "at the brink of a large precipice."[16]

Deng hoped that the Tiananmen crackdown would not slow down economic reforms. But the purge of Zhao Ziyang and those said to sympathize with him—plus the sudden collapse of communist regimes in Europe between 1989 and 1991—led to the ascendance of economic hard-liners under Premier Li Peng. In 1989–1990, they engineered a wrenching reversal of the trend of economic reform through a combination of austerity (tightening up on wages and prices as well as on investment and credit funds for business expansion), recentralization (all investment decisions reverted back to the provincial or central level), and attempts to rebuild state-owned

BOX 4.1 WHY DID THE TIANANMEN MOVEMENT FAIL?

Why did the Tiananmen protests of 1989 fail to overthrow the ruling Communist Party in China as had similar movements in Eastern Europe? Many answers have been offered. One reason is that the movement never intended to overthrow the party in the first place, advocating only tougher anticorruption measures, better living standards for students, and non-system-threatening political reform. Yet virtually every democracy movement starts in this way before the logic of its own protests against an authoritarian system leads in an unplanned and haphazard way to democratization. China's 1989 protests were no different, and indeed party leaders in their own discussions appeared well aware of the democratic implications of the protests.

Another explanation is bad luck. Unlike other postrevolutionary authoritarian states, for example, several of communist China's "founding fathers" were still alive in the form of the "Eight Immortals" of the CCP, including Deng Xiaoping who took charge during the crisis. Had they already died, Zhao Ziyang might have retained power and been allowed to initiate a process of real democratization (which he would later tell a friend was his intention). Also, the liberal chairman of the National People's Congress, Wan Li, happened to be out of the country when the protests erupted, making it easier for the Eight Immortals to neutralize the parliament's sympathies with the protests.

Yet the protests also enjoyed a lot of good luck, especially the international media coverage from journalists who arrived to cover a state visit by Mikhail Gorbachev in May and then stayed on to cover the protests. Luck and contingency seem to have acted both for and against the protestors.

Some have argued that the protests leaders misplayed their hand. To some, the student leaders were too extreme. They openly humiliated Premier Li Peng during a televised meeting on May 18, for instance. Others, ironically, have argued that the student leaders were too deferential. For example, three students kneeled in Confucian obeisance to the state on the steps of the Great Hall of the People to present a petition on April 22. Students gathered in the center of Tiananmen Square on the fateful night of June 3–4 and sang the communist anthem, *The Internationale*. Others have said the students displayed too much disdain for the nascent worker movements that sought to join them, confining them to security duties in the square and ignoring their livelihood issues in favor of political ones.

Similar arguments have been made about Zhao Ziyang. For some, his tacit admission of a leadership split on the movement when expressing sympathy for its aims in a speech to Asian Development Bank governors in Beijing on May 4 was an imprudent move that rankled party elders who might have been more tolerant otherwise. To others, Zhao was too timorous. Unlike Boris Yeltsin, who faced down an attempted hard-line backlash in 1991 by mounting tanks and standing with the protestors outside the Russian parliament, Zhao simply bid a teary farewell to the students in Tiananmen Square on May 19 and then sheepishly went home to live out his life in silence.

Given that such arguments seem to work both ways, more recent analysis has focused on *structural* explanations. Only a decade into post-Mao reforms in 1989, Chinese society remained relatively poor and disorganized, while the state retained a hard edge of Leninist intolerance and military might, not to mention organizational effectiveness. Moreover, China remained largely immune to the sorts of foreign pressures that, for instance, had encouraged democratization in Taiwan and South Korea, and it lacked the proximity to democratic neighbors that provided great support for the anticommunist democracy movements in Eastern Europe. In this view, the cards were stacked heavily against the movement's success. It would have taken nearly miraculous luck and leadership to overcome those obstacles. In the event, Zhao and the protestors of 1989 were not up to that task.

(Continued)

BOX 4.1 (Continued)

Yet still another answer can be offered: the Tiananmen protests did *not* entirely fail. Tiananmen was followed by even faster economic and social liberalization and continued incremental political changes. The scars of 1989 inside the party led to a new search for popular support, especially in the wake of the collapse of the Soviet Union in 1991. When alleged transcripts of the leadership were published as *The Tiananmen Papers* in 2001, it caused a sensation in China, a reminder of the lingering widespread sympathies with the movement. The fact that the memoirs of Deng, premier Li Peng, and the Beijing municipal party secretary at the time, Chen Xitong, all seek to distance themselves from the bloodshed and show their sympathy with the "patriotic" students reflects how far the movement shifted debate even inside the party elite. As the acclaimed Chinese filmmaker Jia Zhangke, who was graduating from high school in 1989, told the *New Yorker* magazine in 2009: "Although it failed, it didn't really fail because it took freedom and democracy, individualism, individual rights, all these concepts, and disseminated them to many people, including me."

The CCP took those lessons to heart after 1989, seeking to avoid the fate of the East European and Soviet communist parties by initiating reforms that would reestablish its legitimacy and avert a repeat of the Tiananmen movement. So far it has succeeded. China's current youth barely know about the events of 1989 and, with their newfound prosperity, generally don't care. The erasure of this collective memory was documented in the 2015 book *The People's Republic of Amnesia: Tiananmen Revisited* by a former BBC correspondent in China. By then, most of the founders of the Tiananmen Mothers movement of bereaved parents of students killed in 1989 had died or been silenced.

enterprises. Economic growth slowed to 4 percent in both years, a drop of more than a half in the average annual rate since the reform era began in 1978.

Deng, in a last gasp, became convinced that China had to press ahead with reform and opening by the collapse of the Soviet Union in 1991. What finally turned the tables was his dramatic **Southern Inspection Tour** (*Nanxun*) in early 1992, in which he decamped from Beijing for central and southern China, where the country's most notable economic progress had taken place.[17] During his tour, he gave a series of speeches with ringing endorsements of the bold and successful economic reforms in the areas he visited, saying bluntly, "Development is the absolute principle" and warning the party of the danger of being "overcautious" in promoting reform. "Like a boat sailing against the current," he told his audience "we must forge ahead or be swept downstream."[18] He also conveyed a barely concealed threat that those who did not support reforms should quit the leadership.

Party conservatives, particularly Premier Li Peng, fearing they would be deposed by Deng, began frantically issuing documents in support of reform. The signal given to provincial and local leaders was *invest, invest, invest*. Economic growth and foreign investment surged. At the national party congress held in October 1992, the CCP formally committed itself to building a **socialist market economy**, replacing the "socialist planned commodity economy" that had been touted as the official aim of economic reform since 1984—a slight change in wording with momentous significance for the economic miracle to come because of the use of the word "market."

Like his speech to the December 1978 plenum launching the reform era, Deng's Southern Inspection Tour was more the culmination than the beginning of a policy battle. But the very public imprimatur of his remarks had a galvanizing effect on economic actors throughout the country. The 1990s became boom years for China's economy, and the economic proceeds allowed party leaders still steeped in Stalinist traditions to launch a series of gargantuan new projects like the Shanghai Pudong economic zone, the **Three Gorges Dam** along the Yangtze River, and the Qinghai-Tibet Railway. At the same time, the state sector's share of urban employment plummeted from 60 percent in 1990 to 35 percent by the year 2000, as hurried privatizations were arranged. In signs of just how far reform and opening up went in the 1990s, stock exchanges—the epitome of a market economy—were established. In 1992, official diplomatic relations were established with booming capitalist South Korea, China's sworn enemy from the Korean War. South Korea quickly became one of the PRC's major trading partners.

Subnational levels of governments enjoyed a degree of autonomy unprecedented in the history of the PRC. Many provincial **people's congresses** in 1993 rejected governor candidates proposed by the central government. Vice Premier Zhu Rongji complained that he lost fifteen pounds hammering out a tax reform package with the provinces in 1994. China also tied its fate to the future global trading system by joining the **World Trade Organization** in 2001 after fifteen years of negotiations; as a result, the PRC agreed to open its economy even more widely to international business. It also began a rapid sell-off of public housing in urban areas.

As has historically been the case during the takeoff stage of a country's economic modernization, including the industrial revolutions in Europe and the United States, China's 1990s boom created losers as well as winners. As the initial gains of rural decollectivization wore off, agricultural incomes stagnated. Antitax riots by ten thousand farmers in Sichuan's Renshou county in 1993 were the first indicator of a malaise spreading through the countryside. Unemployment among former state sector workers rose dramatically—Western economists estimated that China's urban unemployment rate was 11.5 percent in 2000, compared to the official rate of 3 percent, meaning that about thirty million unemployed people languished in cities. A popular joke went that "Mao asked us to plunge into the countryside, Deng asked us to plunge into business, and Jiang asked us to plunge into the ranks of the unemployed."

Between 1994 and 1997, a series of four **Ten Thousand Character Letters** (*wanyanshu*) critical of the direction reform was taking were issued in the form of underground pamphlets. The authors of the letters, CCP writers associated with the party ideological magazine *Mainstream (Zhongliu)*, complained of the decline in the state sector, rising foreign and private investment, and the declining hold of communist ideology over society. This group of critics was referred to as China's "New Left." Jiang Zemin successfully beat back these attacks, including by shutting down *Mainstream* in 2001: he thus ironically came to power in part by shutting down a reformist publication (the *World Economic Herald*) during the Tiananmen-inspired protests in 1989 and then stayed there by shutting down an antireformist one.

THE JIANG ZEMIN ERA (1992–2002)

Jiang Zemin was widely dismissed as a weak transitional figure when he came to power in the wake of the Tiananmen crisis of 1989. By the time Deng Xiaoping died in 1997, Jiang was fully in charge of the party-state and the military, and he more than proved his mettle in the following decade.

One of Jiang's most decisive acts came in April 1999. The CCP's loss of moral authority among its traditional constituents was dramatically highlighted by a protest that year around the **Zhongnanhai** leadership compound near Tiananmen by an estimated ten thousand adherents of a hitherto obscure spiritual organization, called **Falun Gong** (literally, "Law Wheel Practice"). Complaining about the government persecution and disparagement of the group in the nearby port city of Tianjin, the protestors dispersed after only one day. But the event unsettled a leadership with its eerie parallels to the religiously inspired and hugely destructive Taiping Rebellion of 1850–1864 (see chap. 2) that had taken over half of China and was often cited as a critical factor leading to the collapse of the Qing dynasty in 1911.

Jiang Zemin took the lead in getting a bare majority of the other top leaders to vote to ban the group as a subversive cult, leading to a decade-long suppression movement, one of whose unintended consequences was to create by far the best-organized and most committed source of opposition to CCP rule outside China itself. But inside China, the Falun Gong crackdown was thorough and effective, with many of its practitioners sent to labor camps.[19] The party had been alarmed at Falun Gong's ability to organize such a large protest at the symbolic and actual center of its power and by the popularity of the counternarrative to the official ideology that the movement offered. The harsh crackdown was also likely intended to send a strong message to others about the futility of challenging party authority.[20]

Jiang's rule can be seen as ushering in the era of relatively consensual elite politics in China after the volatile strongman rule of Mao and Deng. Under Jiang, each leadership faction, defined more by geographical base, personal ties, and institutional affiliation than by policy or ideological differences, got its fair share of appointments (described by a new slang word, *baiping*, or "to arrange evenly"), and policy making became more institutionalized. In 1998 Jiang banned the very lucrative business activities of the PLA, which ran the gamut from selling weapons to running brothels, shutting off this source of independent income and forcing it, in the words of a classical stratagem of rule in imperial China, to "rely on the emperor's grain."

Jiang's era also accelerated the era of **socialist legality** in China's politics (see chap. 7). In 1997, the state constitution was amended to say the PRC "is governed according to the law and aims to build a socialist country under the rule of law." The "legalization" of the CCP party-state under Jiang was an important part of the transition from the charismatic dictatorships under Mao and Deng in which the wishes and whims of the leaders had more authority than the law.

The PRC government promulgated one law or regulation after another that sought to create a legal framework for both its expanding market economy and also for its most repressive policies. Examples of the legalization of repression that has become staple of the party-state from the Jiang era to that of Xi Jinping include a state security law to deal with peaceful dissent (1993), a **martial law** act to deal with mass protests

(1996), regulations to limit and control domestic NGOs (1998), an antisecession law to threaten Taiwan about any moves toward independence (2005), regulations preventing Tibetans from recognizing their own living Buddhas (2007), a national security law criminalizing any perceived threat to the party or its policies (2015), and regulations governing foreign NGOs (2017).

Just as market reforms in the 1990s gave rise to a New Left in the PRC, political reforms gave birth to a New Right political current, which borrowed from traditional Chinese tenets of meritocracy, legalism, and hierarchy to advocate a new form of party dictatorship called **neo-authoritarianism**. The New Right, to which Jiang Zemin was quite sympathetic, argued for elitist rule by **technocrats** who combined high levels of education in technical fields with substantial experience in the party-state bureaucracy, a strong military, and continued market economics mixed with national corporate champions. A typical representative of this line of thinking was the Beijing University professor Pan Wei, a University of California at Berkeley PhD graduate, who argued for a "consultative rule of law" system modeled on British-colonial Hong Kong and Singapore. Singapore's (staunchly anticommunist) ruling People's Action Party was a model for emulation—a ruling party that tolerated a symbolic opposition, promoted a market economy, and ruled by legal edicts enforced by pliant courts. To some outsider observers, the New Right represented something that looked more likely to result in a polarized "bureaucratic-authoritarian" regime such as those of Latin America in the 1960s and 1970s.[21]

This main trend of legalized, technocratic authoritarianism was challenged by some democratizing pressures. In 1998, a **China Democracy Party** was established as an official and open opposition party by Tiananmen-era activists and, remarkably, was initially given permission to register as an NGO in Zhejiang province. By March 1999, the CDP boasted twenty-nine nationwide branches and eighty-three core leaders. But Beijing's tolerance ended as the CDP started to spread, and by the end of the year the organization was banned and twenty-six of its leaders were put behind bars.

Activists at the local level also continued to press for political change. In 1998, Buyun township (the lowest level of formal government above the village in the hierarchy of rural administration), in Sichuan province, held the first **direct election** for its township head, a position that was legally supposed to be appointed by the township people's congress with oversight from the local party organization. This "illegal" direct township election triggered a dozen copycat experiments in the following decade, which higher level authorities soon stopped. (see chap. 9).

During his final year in office, Jiang codified the ideological rationale for his economic program. His so-called **Three Represents** (*sange daibiao*) theory became the party's newest guiding slogan and was inserted into the party constitution in 2002 on the eve of Jiang's retirement as general secretary. In claiming that the CCP should represent the advanced forces of the economy (including private entrepreneurs), modern culture, and the vast majority of the Chinese people, the Three Represents legitimized the party's shift away from its worker-peasant constituency and more orthodox Marxism. (see chap. 5).

The result of the Three Represents was that the CCP was no longer challenged mainly by the middle class, the educated, nationalistic youths, and intellectuals, as it had been in the 1980s. These groups flourished under Jiang's rule and, for the most

part, became staunch supporters of the regime and the party's main de facto constituency. Instead, it was the poor—the urban proletariat and the less well-off among the
rural population—along with unreconstructed radical and Marxist intellectuals who
became increasingly dissatisfied with the direction being taken by party-state.

Overall, Jiang Zemin could claim to have steered China from a period of threatened
re-Stalinization after Tiananmen to irreversible economic liberalization and political institutionalization. President Bill Clinton bluntly told Jiang during a visit to the
United States in 1997 that his policies with respect to human rights and democracy
were "on the wrong side of history." Yet, the regime that Jiang rescued remains firmly
in power.

ENGAGING THE WORLD AFTER TIANANMEN

The 1980s had been a honeymoon period between China and the West. Deng had
toured the United States in 1979, even donning a ten-gallon hat at a Texas rodeo.
Western countries began selling small amounts of military equipment to China as
part of their informal alliance against the Soviet Union. The protestors in Tiananmen
in 1989 had erected a statue called the Goddess of Democracy that strongly resembled
the Statue of Liberty, which reflected the esteem in which the United States was held
by many at the time.

But after Tiananmen, Western nations imposed sanctions on China, including
a ban on military sales. The Tiananmen generation was officially and effectively
besmirched at home as stooges of foreign forces intent on weakening China and the
party. The party-state began espousing traditional cultural nationalism. The writings
of Confucius were promoted in 1994, and the PRC attempted to expand its influence
overseas through **soft power** by launching cultural promotion agencies located in
host universities in other countries; these agencies were called Confucius Institutes in
2004, and similar organizations in grade schools were called Confucius Classrooms.
By 2017, there were 525 Confucius Institutes located on every continent, including 110
in the United States.[22]

Rising cultural nationalism in China, coupled with post–Cold War American
global hegemony, created the conditions for rising tensions between China and the
West, particularly the United States. A popular book published in 1996 called *China
Can Say No* argued for a get-tough approach to the West, echoing the title of a similar
book published in Japan in 1989 A series of run-ins—the inspection in Saudi Arabia
of the Chinese cargo ship *Yinhe* in 1993 following U.S. allegations that it was shipping
chemical weapon components to Iran, Western politicking in 1993 to deny China the
2000 Olympic Games (China eventually won the 2008 games), the U.S. dispatch of an
aircraft carrier battle group in response to PLA missile tests off Taiwan in 1995–1996,
the accidental NATO bombing of the Chinese embassy in Belgrade in 1999, the col-
lision between an American spy plane and a Chinese fighter jet off the south coast of
China in 2001, and harassment by Chinese boats of a U.S. Navy submarine detection
ship in waters off the PRC island province of Hainan in 2009—brought nationalist
emotions to the fore among the Chinese public.[23]

Nonetheless, in the end, Jiang took the strategic view that Beijing's road to great
power status ran through Washington, DC. He paid an official state visit to the United

States in 1997, and President Bill Clinton did likewise to China the following year. Jiang and Clinton were attempting to build a "constructive strategic partnership" between the two nations. But the CCP found that it could not simultaneously encourage nationalism at home as the basis of regime legitimacy while at the same time aligning itself with the United States. This led to a period of U.S.-China rivalry that would shape world politics into first decades of the twenty-first century.

THE HU JINTAO ERA (2002–2012)

Hu Jintao, like Jiang Zemin, had been one of the beneficiaries of Deng's plan to fast-track the promotion of well-educated and competent young cadres in the early 1980s. During that decade, Hu, a hydroelectric engineer by training, served successively as party secretary of two poor western regions—Guizhou and Tibet. His willingness to accept the tough assignments and to maintain order when protests erupted in Tibet in early 1989 stood him in good stead with his mentor, Song Ping, one of the party elders whom Deng put in charge of choosing the new Politburo that would be installed at the CCP congress in 1992.

Aware of the dangers of a botched succession to the party leadership after Jiang, particularly if Deng had died by then (as turned out to be the case), Song convinced Deng to anoint a presumptive successor to Jiang at the congress. This would settle the post-Jiang succession in advance. Hu Jintao was the one who got the nod because of his strong record of accomplishments as a technocrat and his fealty to party orders. In the years after his 1992 appointment to the Politburo Standing Committee, Hu was showered in titles to indicate his status as the successor-in-waiting: vice president of the PRC, vice chairman of the Central Military Commission, and head of the **Central Party School**, the highest-level institution for training CCP leaders. He was designated as the "core" of the fourth generation of party leadership, following Mao, Deng, and Jiang, who had, respectively, been the cores of the first, second, and third generation of party leaders since the founding of the PRC in 1949. His elevation in 2002 to the position of party general secretary (and in 2003 to PRC president and in 2004 to chair of the military commission) was thus known a decade in advance. Two five-year term limits established for the state presidency as part of the institutionalization of succession procedures meant that it was also clear that Hu would serve until 2012.

Perhaps the single most important fact about Hu Jintao was that he was the only top leader of reform China who did *not* suffer under Mao. Deng Xiaoping, Hu Yaobang, Zhao Ziyang, Jiang Zemin, and even the current head of the party, Xi Jinping (who was sent to do manual labor in the countryside during the Cultural Revolution), all did to one degree or another. During his ten-year stint in power from 2002 to 2012, Hu was thus more responsive to the New Left critique of Jiang's policies and initiated measures to redress the questions of social justice and environmentally sustainable development. Hu's so-called **Scientific Outlook on Development,** which emphasized a shift toward more equitable and sustainable growth and included his conception of a **harmonious socialist society** and commitment to "putting the people first" (*yiren weiben*) were written into the party constitution as one of the CCP ideological guides to action in 2007 (see chap. 5). Health insurance was significantly expanded. Tough new rules on industrial safety were introduced, which cut annual coal mine deaths in half to 3,200 in 2008. As a sign of a new seriousness in the crackdown on official graft, Chen Liangyu, the party chief of Shanghai, Jiang Zemin's political base, was jailed for eighteen years for corruption involving property deals and investment funds. A new National Bureau of Corruption Prevention was established with greater autonomy and authority—at least on paper—than its ineffective predecessor body.

In 2006, a forty-eight-year-old head tax on peasant families with land under cultivation was abolished. Hu's administration accelerated the loosening of the household registration system, (*hukou*), which had stringently restricted rural to urban migration during the Mao era (see chap. 9). It also initiated policy changes that eliminated one of the most egregious procedures used by police to detain citizens for extended periods without formal charges—"custody and repatriation" (*shourong qiansong*)— and brought more procedural controls to another, called "reeducation-through-labor" (*laojiao*) (see chap. 7).

The emphasis on sustainable and equitable development led to new forms of citizen activism. In the first years of Hu's rule, sixty-one environmental groups in Yunnan province sought to block the planned construction of thirteen small dams along the Salween (Nu) river and a large one at the confluence of three rivers at Hutiaoxia Gorge.[24] Urban protests—against an ethylene plant in Chengdu, against a paraxylene plant in Xiamen, and against the extension of a high-speed train railway in Shanghai—also gathered steam under Hu's new approach. The central government's environmental watchdog was upgraded to ministerial status as the new Ministry of Environmental Protection in 2008.

One of the key documents of the Hu era was the 2004 resolution issued by a party plenum on strengthening the "governing capacity" of the party. For the first time, the CCP admitted that the 1949 revolution was no longer a sufficient basis on which the party could claim to be the legitimate ruler of China. "The party's governing status is not congenital, nor is it something settled once and for all," read the preamble to the document. By officially raising the question of defining the CCP's legitimacy as an ongoing task rather than a historically established fact, the resolution stirred an outpouring of discussion among political elites about how the CCP could continue to earn the support of China's people. The party's rapid and relatively successful response to the global economic recession that began in 2008 (see chap. 8) helped it to avert what might have been a serious challenge to its legitimacy.

But in all these areas, Hu's attempts to develop a more sustainable and equitable model of Chinese development ultimately foundered on the lack of serious efforts to disperse political power from local party organizations. Hu's populism did not extend to democratic elections. True to his Leninist sympathies, Hu emphasized an improvement in **inner-party democracy** instead, in which party members would vote on such things as policies and appointments. When a group of three hundred intellectuals, activists, and scholars in China issued a blueprint for democratic reforms under the title **Charter 08** in 2008 (mimicking the ultimately successful Charter 77 democratic movement in the former Czechoslovakia), its leading signatories were detained and sometimes jailed. Among those imprisoned was Liu Xiaobo, who won the Nobel Peace Prize in 2010 and died of untreated cancer while serving an eleven-year prison sentence in 2017.[25]

Hu also showed less interest than his predecessor in boosting China's place in the world—even though that place expanded considerably on his watch, especially with the exposure provided by the flawlessly executed 2008 Beijing Olympics. As befitted a politician who made his career in inland areas, Hu's focus was on internal problems, and he made no major efforts to improve relations with the United States or regional neighbors. This meant that China's foreign policy direction seemed adrift, veering between a "smile diplomacy" aimed at reassuring the world of Beijing's "peaceful rise" and a sometimes more aggressive posture. One of Hu's last acts as party chief in 2012 was to formally inaugurate China's first aircraft carrier, the *Liaoning*, a refurbished Soviet Union ship that had been towed rudderless and engineless from Ukraine in 1998, an event that can, in retrospect, be seen as an initial step in the PRC's continuing modernization and expansion of it naval power.

What was Hu's legacy? His pathway to power—selected for obedience and a firm hand and then groomed over a long period in which caution and consensus were key—left him ill-equipped for the challenges of reform. While Jiang can claim to have rescued China from the trauma of Tiananmen, Hu inherited a China that needed more than mere stability. In his somber final report to the party, Hu admitted that China's development was "unbalanced, uncoordinated, and unsustainable" and that social problems had "increased markedly" on his watch. China's share of the global GDP rose from 8 percent to 15 percent on his watch. But the private sector shrunk as a contributor to GDP as Hu poured money into the state sector. The image that many Chinese most closely associate with the Hu Jintao era is that of work crews quickly removing twisted passenger rail cars dangling from a viaduct after a high-speed railway crash in 2011 that killed forty and symbolized the still pervasive pre-occupation with often hastily implemented gargantuan projects and the censorship of photos or discussion of the accident that lay beneath his promotion of a "harmonious socialist society." The era of Hu Jintao was like that of the ineffective leadership in the Soviet Union under Leonid Brezhnev (communist party chief from 1964 to 1982). In one common joke that reflects the perception of how unimaginative he was in exercising his power, Hu complains to an aide that the speech he just made took three times as long as it was supposed to, "That's because I handed you three copies," the aide replies. This may be an unduly harsh judgement of his accomplishment, but there was a wide recognition by 2012, when Hu's term as party general secretary was set to end, that China needed dramatically different leadership to revitalize the country.

XI JINPING TAKES CENTER STAGE

The man chosen to succeed Hu Jintao was Xi Jinping, who as the son of a revolutionary "party elder" is considered a CCP **Princeling**, had been groomed for power since at least 1997 (see Box 4.2). While Xi's succession in 2012 was largely a formality having been signaled five years earlier, the handover of power was significant in several respects. For one, because he was not promoted to the CCP's top body, the Politburo Standing Committee, until 2007 at the start of Hu's second term, he came into office as party general secretary in 2012 having less association with his predecessor's

BOX 4.2 WHO IS XI JINPING?

Xi Jinping, born in 1952, is the son of a guerrilla organizer of communist armies in China in the 1930s, Xi Zhongxun (1913–2002). The elder Xi went on to join China's post-1949 leadership. But like many he was purged by the paranoid Mao, enduring various forms of hard labor and house arrest between 1962 and 1977. As a result, Xi Jinping was targeted as the offspring of a political pariah in the early years of the Cultural Revolution, and in 1968, at the age of sixteen, he was sent to work on a remote rural commune, where he remained for seven years. He joined the Communist Youth League in 1971 and the CCP in 1974.

When the elder Xi was rehabilitated after Mao's death, Xi Jinping's career took off. He graduated in chemical engineering from Beijing's Tsinghua University, China's premier institution of science and technology, in 1979, and took a series of assignments in local party and government organizations beginning in 1982. There he won high marks as an economic reformer with a personal touch. His father was again purged from the Politburo in 1986 for defending Hu Yaobang's tolerant attitude toward student protestors, yet Xi Jinping's career was unaffected. As early as 1997, the party leadership had Xi in mind for future promotion when it added him to the Central Committee as an "over-quota" alternate member after he failed to secure enough votes from delegates to a party congress to win one of the 150 regular alternate seats.

Rising rapidly through the ranks, he became governor of prosperous Fujian province in 2000. During plans for the 2002 leadership succession that brought Hu Jintao to power, consideration was given to promoting Xi to the Politburo to indicate that he was the future leader. But the plan was abandoned because it was seen as binding the party's hands too far in advance. By mid-2007, a consensus had developed around Xi as the "core" of the "fifth generation" leadership that would replace Hu Jintao's "fourth generation" in 2012. Xi was appointed to the nine-member Standing Committee directly from the Central Committee and without having served on the Politburo, an unusual "two-step" move up the ranks. A few months later he was made PRC vice president, a largely ceremonial post used to signal that he was to be Hu's successor as general secretary. When that took place in November 2012, Xi became the first CCP leader who was not chosen by an "elder" (*yuan lao*) of the party, a term that refers to those who joined before 1949 and later rose to prominent positions in the Mao era. Deng had personally chosen Xi's predecessors, Jiang Zemin and Hu Jintao. In March 2013, Xi became president of the PRC, a position that has been simultaneously held by the CCP general secretary since 1992. He is the first top leader of the country to be born after the founding of the PRC. He is also a relatively cosmopolitan figure who mixes easily in international business and government circles. His daughter, Xi Mingze, attended Harvard University under an assumed name.

Xi was seen as the strongman needed by China in order to realize its great power ambitions. When he first came to power many observers thought he would be an avid economic reformer and competent administrator who would overcome the sclerosis of China's governance system. But he has taken steps to both recentralize the Chinese economy and consolidate his own personal power at the expense of the norms of collective leadership that had prevailed in PRC elite politics for decades. One of the clearest signs of this was his decision to revise the Chinese constitution in 2018 to eliminate the two five-year term limit for state president, which would be a key part of a plan to remain in power beyond 2022/2023 when precedent would dictate he should step aside for a new and younger leader.

In addition to his undergraduate degree, Xi was awarded a doctorate in politics and Marxist theory (with a dissertation on rural marketization) from Tsinghua, where he was enrolled from 1998 to 2002 in an in-service postgraduate program while concurrently serving in party and government positions in several provinces. Large parts of his dissertation appear to have been copied from other works, including lengthy sections that differ little from the published works on the same topic by a junior academic at Tsinghua, Liu Huiyu, who was assigned to help him during his "studies." She was later promoted to a senior position at Fujian's Jiangxi University, where she is in charge of "library materials" among other assignments.

Xi's views on political reform are cautious, perhaps a legacy of his father's suffering as a "liberal" on political issues. He believes that cadres should be popular and uncorrupt, but he has not gone beyond official doctrine in advocating any changes to the way they are chosen. He was tolerant of mass citizen protests against development projects that erupted during his brief tenures as party chief of Zhejiang province and Shanghai. But he did not initiate new forms of public consultation. Xi appears to favor meritocratic despotism over messy democracy.

Xi is a robust nationalist. On a visit to Mexico in 2009, he warned that "some well-fed foreigners, with nothing else to do, keep pointing fingers at us." China, he said, had ceased exporting revolution as it had in the Maoist era, conquered poverty at home, and refrained from interfering in the affairs of other countries in the reform era. "What is there to criticize?" he wondered. His nationalism is shared by his wife, Peng Liyuan, a popular singer with the rank of major general in the People's Liberation Army who serenaded troops in Tiananmen Square in 1989 shortly after they massacred protestors ; she has a special ballad she sings to commemorate the military units that invaded the Tibetan capital of Lhasa in 1959. When the relatively obscure Xi first came to power, the joke went: "Who is Xi Jinping? He is Peng Liyuan's husband." By his second term in office (2017–2022) a new joke reflected the dashed hopes that he had inherited his father liberal tendencies: "I heard that Xi Jinping is the son of a Party elder!" "Yes, you are right. He is the son of Mao Zedong."

administration. This meant he could promote more distinctive policies. In addition, unlike Hu, who had to wait for two years after becoming the CCP general secretary to be given the position of chair of the Central Military Commission, Xi took over as head of the CMC at the same time he became party chief, further strengthening his hand.

A Chinese saying has it that "a new leader will begin by lighting three bonfires," and Xi was handed a golden opportunity to ignite one by the ignominious fall of his one-time rival for the top party post, Bo Xilai, in mid-2012. A charismatic and telegenic "princeling" son of an esteemed early member of the CCP and important PRC leader, Bo became Minister of Commerce in 2004 and then a Politburo member and party chief of Chongqing in 2007, where he initiated a brutal crackdown on criminal gangs and revived Maoist sloganeering. Bo styled himself as a hard-nosed corporate leader willing to take on entrenched interests. In 2011, Bo's wife, Gu Kailai, murdered a British family friend over a personal financial dispute. Asked to cover up the murder, the Chongqing chief of police fled to a U.S. consulate seeking protection, a major political embarrassment for China. In 2012, Gu was sentenced to death (suspended for two years and commutable to life imprisonment depending on her behavior). Bo was found guilty of bribe-taking, embezzlement, and abuse of power and sentenced to life in prison in 2013. Bo's fall from power provided Xi Jinping with an opportunity to show that the CCP took top-level corruption and abuses of power seriously.

Over the next three years, four more Politburo members were purged by Xi, including Hu Jintao's former top-policy advisor, who had tried to cover up the death of his son in a crash of his Ferrari in Beijing that also killed one woman passenger and seriously injured another. The official *People's Daily* quoted one of Xi's allies in 2016 as saying that the group of five Politburo members had collectively sought to "seize party and state power," a formulation not applied to top party leaders since the Cultural Revolution. Senior party officials began to regularly assert that Xi had "saved the party," "saved the country," and "saved socialism" with his decisive action. According to one high-ranking official, "They had high positions and great power in the party, but they were hugely corrupt and plotted to usurp the party's leadership and seize state power."[26]

One of the hallmarks—and most popular policies—of Xi's administration has been its unprecedented campaign against official corruption. Using the party's antigraft apparatus, the **Central Commission of Discipline Inspection**, the campaign has targeted high-ranking leaders (so-called "tigers") and rank-and-file party cadres ("flies"). During Xi's first five years in office, more than 150 senior officials, in addition to 70 military officers, and a dozen executives of major state-owned corporations were investigated, indicted, tried, or convicted. To put that in perspective, in the entire reform era from 1982 to 2012, only 50 senior officials were convicted for corruption. Under Xi, seventeen members of the Party's Central Committee were also purged for corruption (normally only one to two are purged every five years). In the lower ranks of the Chinese Communist Party (CCP), 250,000 members were indicted on corruption-related criminal charges. The anticorruption campaign has also been a means for Xi to purge some of his political rivals (like Bo Xilai) and malcontents within the party leadership.

While Hu's first domestic trip as CCP general secretary was to an old Maoist revolutionary base in the poor north, a month after coming to power Xi headed to the booming southern city of Shenzhen abutting Hong Kong, echoing Deng's tide-turning 1992 Southern Inspection Tour. There he outlined a two-pronged vision of China's future: a flourishing market economy that avoided the "closed and ossified old path" of state-led bureaucratic management alongside a renewed commitment to communist party leadership and ideology. In a leaked speech that he made at the time, Xi emphasized the importance of a unified top leadership, a loyal military, and a full embrace of Marxism-Leninism, including important aspects of Mao Zedong Thought, if the CCP were to survive attempts to undermine party rule: "The Soviet Union's communist party had proportionally more members than us, but when it was threatened, nobody was man enough to stand up and resist." He also asked rhetorically, "Why did the Soviet Union disintegrate? Why did the Soviet Communist Party collapse? An important reason was that their ideals and beliefs had been shaken."[27]

Indeed, Xi has taken significant steps to reassert party authority in numerous spheres of life in the PRC. For example, the space for civil society has been significantly has been reduced on his watch. Like Russia's Vladimir Putin, Xi views citizen's organizations independent of state control as sign of Western interference or political opposition. The tightening of constraints on civil society has focused on three groups in particular: lawyers engaged in "rights protection" cases (see chaps.6 and 7); environmental NGOs which had long been given significant space in China because they were seen as useful to the state (see chap. 12); and foreign-funded NGOs, particularly those from Hong Kong and Taiwan.

The party has also ramped up the subjugation of China's booming Christian community to party authority. Bibles were pulled from retail shelves and banned from online sellers in 2017, while several Christian megachurches in the southeastern provinces were demolished. Beijing also forced the Vatican to back down on their sixty-year dispute when Pope Francis in 2018 accepted two state-appointed bishops for China's official Catholic Church. Since 1958, the communist Party had appointed 190 "bishops" who lacked the necessary imprimatur of the Vatican. The party's already harsh treatment of its Muslim minorities in the western provinces went beyond the normal controls on personnel and education to include a ban on new "Arab-style" mosques, as well as other outward manifestations of the faith (see chap. 17). As Xi Jinping put it in his report to the 19th Party Congress in 2017, "[R]eligions in China must be Chinese in orientation and provide active guidance to religions so that they can adapt themselves to socialist society."[28] Nationalism had replaced official atheism as the basis of the CCP's religion policy.

A one-sentence addition to the PRC constitution in March 2018 captured Xi's intent to strengthen party control over Chinese society. In paragraph 2 of Article 1 of the Constitution, which states that "The socialist system is the basic system of the People's Republic of China," the following was added: "The defining feature of socialism with Chinese characteristics is the leadership of the Communist Party of China." Prior to this amendment, the leadership communist party was mentioned only in the document's preamble. By including it in such a prominent place in the body of the state constitution for the first time, the party is clearly signaling that its political preeminence is not to be doubted or challenged.

Since becoming general secretary Xi has also moved to consolidate his personal power to an extent that, some observers argue, harkens back to the days of Mao.[29] One very early boost to this end was the agreement of the party leadership in 2012 to shrink the Standing Committee of the Politburo back down to its usual size of seven from its nine-member composition of the Hu Jintao era. The upshot of this was that Xi had more control over the party's most powerful body, a shift that was reflected within the PRC government by a reduction in the number of cabinet-level departments in 2013.

In March 2018 China's rubber-stamp legislature, the National People's Congress, amended the PRC constitution, removing the two-term (ten year) limit on the state presidency imposed by Deng in 1982 and then applied informally to the party general secretary when the two positions were linked in 1993. The abolition of the formal two-term limit came as a bombshell to scholars of China's politics who had argued that the CCP had solved the common authoritarian problem of leadership succession by institutionalizing a formal process for changing leaders. It also meant that Xi, if he stayed on, would violate an informal post-Tiananmen norm that Politburo leaders should be sixty-eight or younger when appointed to the body (Xi will turn sixty-nine in 2022). The measure was not extended to other senior state posts that had two-term limits and was thus interpreted as an amendment specifically for Xi to remain "president for life." "The people love their dear leader," *China Central Television* explained in a barrage of propaganda promoting Xi's continued rule.[30]

The expectation that Xi would continue to rule beyond the end of his second term in 2022 was strengthened by the fact that no presumptive successor-in-waiting from the younger "sixth" generation of leader was appointed to the Politburo Standing Committee in 2017 at the party congress that marked the beginning of Xi's second term as general secretary. In the two previous leadership transitions, an heir apparent was designated at the start of the serving general secretary's second term in office. The fact that this didn't happen at a similar time in Xi's tenure, means that he likely will choose his own successor without a party process or consensus when he eventually steps down. According to the *People's Daily*, Xi ditched the internal "straw poll" voting system among the CCP elite instituted by Hu Jintao to choose the party's top leaders, believing it was subject to various kinds of malpractice, including vote-buying. Instead, he put in place a top-down process based on "face-to-face interviews, investigation and study." [31] The upshot of this change was that it gave Xi a significant amount of personal sway in the leadership selection process and even in the choice of his own successor.

Xi has further cemented his grip on power by personally taking charge of a variety of policy issues. He assumed the role of managing the economy that would normally be the responsibility of the premier, Li Keqiang, as well as making himself the head of **leading small groups** on national security, foreign policy, and cyberspace governance (for the latter, see chap. 15.) Xi used his position as chair of the Central Military Commission to implement a wide-ranging reorganization of the People's Liberation Army, which consists of all of the PRC's armed forces service branches. In 2016, he was named commander in chief of the military, a title that no other top CCP leader, including Mao and Deng, had assumed.

On the ideological front, shortly after becoming the party leader in 2012, Xi began espousing his idea of the **China Dream** (*zhongguo meng*) that embodied his vision for what he hoped to accomplish during his administration. That vision involves a combination of a much higher standard of living for the country and the ascent of China to greater power status, or as he put it "the rejuvenation of the Chinese nation.[32] This was a first step toward staking his claim to shaping Chinese communist ideology as each of his predecessors from Mao to Hu had done. As he began his second term in October 2017, his contributions to that ideology were codified as **Xi Jinping Thought for a New Era of Socialism with Chinese Characteristics** and written in to the party constitution as the latest installment of the CPC's guide to action.[33] Deng Xiaoping, Jiang Zemin, and Hu Jintao had to wait until they were out of power to have their thinking enshrined in this way (see chap. 5).

Furthermore, Xi has been referred to with the special term *lingxiu*, meaning "revered leader," a term last used for Mao. This represented a reversion to the cult and clout of the individual leader and another step away from collective leadership that Deng had sought hard to promote. Xi has justified such accolades by noting that the People's Republic went through two formative stages of roughly thirty-years each— the Mao era and the reform era—before his own accession in 2012, which marked the start of a third decisive era in China's development. This formulation has led to speculation that he is planning a thirty-year era of his own that would last until 2042.

As with his counterpart "president for life" in Russia, Vladimir Putin, Xi showed that a major motivation for his continuation in power was to turn the external dimension of the "China Dream" into reality. One aspect of this was creating China-owned for-eign policy initiatives that did not require Beijing to ride the coattails of Western powers. The first stage of the **Belt and Road Initiative** (BRI) for expanded economic integration between China and its Central and South Asian neighbors—and eventu-ally beyond—announced in 2013 was one example (see chap. 8). By delinking China's world status to its relations with the United States in particular, Xi seemed inclined to follow the path of Putin who gambled that his people would accept the economic costs of sanctions as long as their national pride swelled. A second aspect of this was to reconfigure China's approach to relations with its Southeast Asian neighbors, which had long been characterized by a search for cooperation and compromise. Under Xi, China's militarization of disputed islands in the South China Sea acceler-ated while its assertion of maritime claims in the area became more robust. Again, Xi was gambling that the Southeast Asian nations would accept the new dispensation, just as Putin guessed that Europe would accept Russia's 2014 annexation of Crimea.

CONCLUSION

China's trajectory since 1978 has reflected the twin impulses of economic dynamism and authoritarian politics. How long the CCP can continue market-based economic reform without undermining its base of power is the most widely debated topic among observers of Chinese politics. There is no doubt that life has become vastly better for most Chinese during the reform era. Real per capita income in purchasing-power equivalent terms rose from just $300 in 1980 to nearly $20,000 by 2019 (about one-third that of the U.S.). Hundreds of millions have been lifted from absolute pov-erty to at least a minimally secure standard of living. Infant mortality for children under one year old, probably the most reliable indicator of material progress, fell from forty-eight per one thousand live births in 1980 to eight by 2017, roughly twice as fast as the global average decline in that same indicator over the same period. The reform era has brought a long period of relative stability and growth (with the exception of the Tiananmen setback) to China. Chinese politics seems to have passed beyond the cycles of crisis and recovery that characterized the Mao era.

Still, there are palpable signs of deep discontent as reflected in rural and urban protests as well as online discussion forums about the quality of life, the commit-ment to public service rather than personal gain of party-state officials, and the overall responsiveness of the political system. Most senior Chinese leaders, including Xi Jinping, not only send their children to be educated abroad but also keep ample stores of assets in the hands of family members abroad. In order to survive in power, the CCP needs to constantly reinvent itself to maintain the expectation that things will continue to get better for the ordinary person, not just economically, but politi-cally as well.

What are the broader implications of the reform era for the study of modern China? As noted in chapter 1, during the Mao era many scholars felt that politics in China was best analyzed by the use of highly state-centered models. For example, the theory of totalitarianism saw China as the kind of state that attempted to control all aspects of society, indeed as a country where the separation of society from the party-state barely existed. Or there was "Beijingology," the China Watchers version of analyzing Soviet politics known as Kremlinology, with its focus on trying to decipher what goes on in the highly secretive top levels of leadership—a more nuanced and informed version of which is still used today to study Chinese politics.

Four decades into the reform era, these extreme versions of the state-centered theory are no longer appropriate to explain political processes or outcomes in China. At the very least, the political system has become multifaceted, if not pluralistic, and its various constitutive parts—including local governments, people's congresses, judges and lawyers, the military, **mass organizations**, state enterprises, bureaucrats, journalists, public intellectuals, and party members—more openly contest for political influence. Beyond the boundaries of the state, new forms of civil associations have emerged in China—such as homeowners' associations, independent business associations, and environmental groups—with the potential to shape policy outcomes. As a result, state-society models that focus on the interactions between state and society can now be usefully applied to some questions about politics in China.

Yet the ability of independent social forces to influence policy is still deeply constrained in a system where communist party leadership remains an unchallengeable principle of political life. Comparative analyses of China's politics continue to stress what has <u>not</u> changed in the political system, especially in a world where many states around the world have in recent decades been moving in a more democratic direction.

The People's Republic of China, in other words, is a remarkable lesson in the autonomy of politics—why politics cannot be reduced to economic conditions or changes. The Chinese Communist Party created China's economic miracle with early political reforms, managed the consequences with a judicious mixture of repression and accommodation, and rebuilt party-state institutions and ideologies to ensure they would remain compatible with rapid socioeconomic development while sustaining CCP rule. In this sense, it seems that Mao's theory of "politics in command" of social change and economic growth[34] is one part of his legacy that remains firmly embedded in China four decades into the otherwise very un-Maoist era of reform and opening up.

NOTES

1. See Orville Schell and John Delury, *Wealth and Power: China's Long March to the Twenty-first Century* (New York: Random House, 2013.)

2. See Elizabeth J. Perry, "From Mass Campaigns to Managed Campaigns: Constructing a 'New Socialist Countryside,'" in *Mao's Invisible Hand: The Political Foundations of Adaptive Governance in China*, ed. Sebastian Heilmann and Elizabeth J. Perry (Cambridge, MA: Harvard University Press, 2011), 1–29.

3. See, for example, Andrea Boltho and Maria Weber, "Did China Follow the East Asian Development Model?," in *State Capitalism, Institutional Adaptation, and the Chinese Miracle*, ed. Barry Naughton and Kellee Tsai (New York: Cambridge University Press, 2015), 240–264.

4. Thomas P. Bernstein, "Resilience and collapse in China and the Soviet Union," in *Why Communism Did Not Collapse: Understanding Authoritarian Regime Resilience in Asia and Europe*, ed. Martin K. Dimitrov (New York: Cambridge University Press, 2013), 40–66.

5. See Frederick C. Teiwes and Warren Sun, *Paradoxes of Post-Mao Rural Reform: Initial Steps Toward a New Chinese Countryside 1976–1981* (New York: Routledge, 2016).

6. The full loyalty oath of the whateverists was "We will resolutely uphold whatever policy decisions Chairman Mao made, and unswervingly follow whatever instructions Chairman Mao gave," which was included in a joint editorial of the CCP main propaganda organs published on Feb. 7, 1977. The motto of the Pragmatists, "Practice is the sole criterion of truth" was the title of an article published in another party organ on May 11, 1978.

7. Barry J. Naughton, *The Chinese Economy: Adaptations and Growth*, 2nd ed. (Cambridge, MA: MIT Press, 2018), 88.

8. See Merle Goldman, "The Reassertion of Political Citizenship in the Post-Mao Era: The Democracy Wall Movement," in *Changing Meanings of Citizenship in Modern China*, ed. Merle Goldman and Elizabeth J. Perry (Cambridge, MA: Harvard University Press, 2002), 159–186; and Wei Jingsheng, "The Fifth Modernization," http://afe.easia.columbia.edu/ps/cup/wei_jingsheng_fifth_modernization.pdf.

9. For more on Chen Yun, see David M. Bachman, *Chen Yun and the Chinese Political System* (Berkeley: University of California Institute of East Asian Studies, 1985); and Nicholas R. Lardy and Kenneth Lieberthal, eds., *Chen Yun's Strategy for China's Development: A Non-Maoist Alternative* (Armonk, NY: M. E. Sharpe, 1983).

10. Deng Xiaoping, "On the Reform of the System of Party and State Leadership," Aug. 18, 1980, http://en.people.cn/dengxp/vol2/text/b1460.html

11. See, for example, Randall Peerenboom, *China's Long March Toward Rule of Law* (New York: Cambridge University Press, 2002).

12. See Kate Xiao Zhou, *How the Farmers Changed China: Power of the People* (Boulder, CO: Westview Press, 1996).

13. See "Uphold the Four Cardinal Principles," http://english.peopledaily.com.cn/dengxp/vol2/text/b1290.html.

14. See David S. Zweig, *China's Brain Drain to the United States* (Berkeley, CA: East Asian Institute, China Research Monograph, 1995).

15. There is a large body of scholarly and popular literature about the Tiananmen Movement and the Beijing Massacre. See "Suggested Readings" at the end of this chapter for a few recommended titles. Two books, based on materials smuggled out of China, reveal the inner workings of the party leadership during the crisis. One book, *The Tiananmen Papers* (New York: Public Affairs, 2002) is largely the minutes of meetings of the top leaders, while *Prisoner of the State: The Secret Journal of Premier Zhao Ziyang* (New York: Simon & Schuster, 2009) contains transcripts of recordings made by the ousted party general secretary.

16. See Bruce Gilley, *Tiger on the Brink: Jiang Zemin and China's New Elite* (Berkeley: University of California Press, 1998).

17. See Suisheng Zhao, "Deng Xiaoping's Southern Tour: Elite Politics in Post-Tiananmen China," *Asian Survey* 33, no. 8 (Aug. 1993): 739–756; and the website "Southern Tour Legacy," at http://www.globaltimes.cn/SPECIALCOVERAGE/Dengssoutherntour.aspx.

18. Deng Xiaoping, "Excerpts from Talks Given in Wuchang, Shenzhen, Zhuhai, and Shanghai," Jan. 18–Feb. 21, 1992, in *Selected Works of Deng Xiaoping*, vol. 3 *(1982–1992)*. (Beijing: Foreign Languages Press, 1994), http://english.peopledaily.com.cn/dengxp/vol3/text/d1200.html.

19. See James Tong, *Revenge of the Forbidden City: The Suppression of the Falungong in China, 1999–2008* (New York: Oxford University Press, 2009); and David Ownby, *Falun Gong and the Future of China* (New York: Oxford University Press, 2008).

20. Vivienne Shue, "Legitimacy Crisis in China?," in *State and Society in 21st Century China: Crisis, Contention and Legitimation*, ed. Peter Hays Gries and Stanley Rosen (New York: Routledge, 2004), 24–49.

21. See, for example, Guillermo A. O'Donnell and David E. Apter, *Modernization and Bureaucratic-Authoritarianism: Studies in South American Politics* (Berkeley: University of California Press, 1979).

22. See "Confucius Institute Online" at http://english.hanban.org/. See Randy Kluver, "Chinese Culture in a Global Context: The Confucius Institute as a Geo- Cultural Force," in *China's Global Engagement: Cooperation, Competition, and Influence in the 21st Century*, ed. Jacques deLisle and Avery Goldstein (Washington, DC: Brookings Institution, 2017).

23. On the role of nationalism in Chinese politics, see Peter Hayes Gries, *China's New Nationalism: Pride, Politics, and Diplomacy* (Berkeley: University of California Press, 2004).

24. See Andrew C. Mertha, *China's Water Warriors: Citizen Action And Policy Change* (Ithaca, NY: Cornell University Press, 2008).

25. See Liu Xiaobo, *No Enemies, No Hatred: Selected Essays and Poems*, ed. Perry Link (Cambridge, MA: Harvard University Press, 2013).

26. Wendy Wu and Choi Chi-yuk, "Coup Plotters Foiled: Xi Jinping Fended off Threat to 'Save Communist Party,'" *South China Morning Post*, Oct. 19, 2017, http://www.scmp.com/news/china/policies-politics/article/2116176/coup-plotters-foiled-xi-jinping-fended-threat-save

27. "Leaked Speech Shows Xi Jinping's Opposition to Reform," *China Digital Times*, Jan. 27, 2013, https://chinadigitaltimes.net/2013/01/leaked-speech-shows-xi-jinpings-opposition-to-reform/

28. Xi Jinping, "Secure a Decisive Victory in Building a Moderately Prosperous Society in All Respects and Strive for the Great Success of Socialism with Chinese Characteristics for a New Era," report delivered at the 19th National Congress of the Communist Party of China, Oct. 18, 2017, http://www.xinhuanet.com/english/special/2017-11/03/c_136725942.htm

29. Roderick MacFarquhar, "The Red Emperor," *New York Review of Books*, Jan. 18, 2018.

30. See, "How China's Media Sold Xi Jinping's Power Grab" (video), *New York Times*, Feb. 28, 2018, https://www.nytimes.com/video/world/asia/100000003926677/who-is-xi-jinping.html.

31. Alice Miller, "The 19th Central Committee Politburo," *China Leadership Monitor* 55 (Winter 2018), https://www.hoover.org/research/19th-central-committee-politburo.

32. Xi Jinping, "Achieving Rejuvenation of the Chinese Dream," Nov. 29, 2012.

33. Chris Buckley, "China Enshrines 'Xi Jinping Thought,' Elevating Leader to Mao-Like Status Image," *New York Times*, Oct. 24, 2017, https://www.nytimes.com/2017/10/24/world/asia/china-xi-jinping-communist-party.html.

34. Jack Gray, "Politics in Command: The Maoist Theory of Social Change and Economic Growth," *Political Quarterly* 45, no. 1 (Jan. 1974): 26–48.

SUGGESTED READINGS

Baum, Richard. *Burying Mao: Chinese Politics in the Age of Deng Xiaoping*. Princeton, NJ: Princeton University Press, 1994.

Brooke, Timothy. *Quelling the People: The Military Suppression of the Beijing Democracy Movement*. New York: Oxford University Press, 1998.

Economy, Elizabeth C. *The Third Revolution: Xi Jinping and the New Chinese State*. Oxford University Press, 2018.

Gilley, Bruce. *Model Rebels: The Rise and Fall of China's Richest Village*. Berkeley: University of California Press, 2001.

Heilmann, Sebastian, and Elizabeth J. Perry. *Mao's Invisible Hand: The Political Foundations of Adaptive Governance in China*. Cambridge, MA: Harvard University Press, 2011.

Johnson, Ian. *The Souls of China: The Return of Religion after Mao*. New York Pantheon, 2017.

Li, Cheng. *Chinese Politics in the Xi Jinping Era: Reassessing Collective Leadership*. Washington, DC: Brookings Institution Press, 2016.

Minzer, Carl. *End of an Era: How China's Authoritarian Revival is Undermining Its Rise*. New York: Oxford University Press, 2018.

Overholt, William H. *China's Crisis of Success*. New York: Cambridge University Press, 2018.

Pei, Minxin. *China's Crony Capitalism: The Dynamics of Regime Decay*. Cambridge, MA: Harvard University Press, 2016.

Teiwes, Frederick C. and Warren Sun, *Paradoxes of Post-Mao Rural Reform: Initial Steps Toward a New Chinese Countryside 1976–1981*. New York: Routledge, 2016.

Vogel, Ezra. *Deng Xiaoping and the Transformation of China*. Cambridge, MA: Harvard University Press, 2011.

Zhang, Liang, Andrew J. Nathan, and E. Perry Link. *The Tiananmen Papers*. New York: Public Affairs, 2002.

PART II
Ideology, Governance, and Political Economy

5

Ideology and China's Political Development

WILLIAM A. JOSEPH

WHAT IS IDEOLOGY AND WHY IS IT IMPORTANT?

One of the most influential early studies of politics in the People's Republic of China (PRC) was Franz Schurmann's *Ideology and Organization in Communist China*, which was published in 1966, just as the Cultural Revolution was unfolding.[1] As the title suggests, Schurmann identified ideology and organization—and the relationship between them—as the keys to understanding what was both unique and comparative (especially with the Soviet Union) about China's political system as it had evolved in the first decade-and-a-half of communist rule. Schurmann's observation is still valid, despite how much has changed about Chinese politics. This chapter focuses on ideology, specifically what can generically be called "Chinese communism," while the following chapter describes and analyzes the organization of the Chinese communist party-state.[*]

Ideology is one of the most hotly contested concepts in the social sciences. For our purposes, a simple definition will do. An ideology is a systematic or comprehensive set of values and beliefs ("ideas") that provides a way of looking at and understanding the world or some aspect of it. Our concern is with *political* ideology, which consists

[*] A note to instructors and readers: Some might find it useful to read parts of this chapter in conjunction with other chapters in this book with which they coincide in terms of the period in Chinese political history being discussed, as follows: "What is Ideology and Why it is Important," "Communism," and "Marxism-Leninism Comes to China" with the latter sections of chap. 2; "Mao Zedong Thought" with chap. 3; and "Chinese Communism after Mao" and "Conclusion" with chap. 4.

of ideas about power and how it should be distributed, organized, and used, including the goals to which it is directed. Furthermore, ideology has action consequences by shaping political behavior, particularly of leaders who have the power to translate ideology into policy. In this sense, ideology shapes what is sometimes referred to as the **operational code** of decision-making elites.[2]

To be sure, political behavior is determined by many factors, and ideology may well serve as a mask or rationalization for preserving the power and privileges of a particular group (including an economic class or political party).[3] But to dismiss it as irrelevant to understanding how leaders use their power in shaping national agendas and formulating concrete policies is to ignore one of the most central facts of politics across time and space.[4]

The word "ideology" took on a rather negative connotation during World War II and the Cold War: it came to be seen as something "they" (our enemies) have and "we" don't. Ideology is, in fact, woven into the political fabric of every society. In some cases, including democratic capitalist countries, ideology is relatively latent; that is, it is less publicly visible and less formally proclaimed, and contestation among ideologies is permitted or even encouraged (although there are always limits). In other systems, ideology is a much more overt part of political life. As noted in chapter 1, the existence and enforcement of an official ideology based on Marxism-Leninism is one of the defining characteristics of a communist party-state like the PRC: the ruling party bases its claim to power largely on its role as the only rightful interpreter of the values and the beliefs that will guide the nation to its ideologically determined goals. Serious challenges to the ruling ideology are proscribed and suppressed as threats to the security of the nation and the well-being of the "people."

Ideology has figured very visibly in Chinese politics throughout the history of the Chinese Communist Party (CCP), both before and after it came to power in 1949. It motivated the formation and shaped the victory of the revolutionary movement, fueled power struggles, large and small, within the party from the 1920s on, and guided leaders in making policies and taking initiatives that have brought both progress and disaster to the country. For all the profound transformations that have taken place in China over the past four decades, including the move toward a market economy, the CCP still affirms allegiance to Marxism-Leninism and proclaims in the opening paragraph of the preamble of its constitution that "The Party's highest ideal and ultimate goal is the realization of communism."[5] Indeed, it is the ideological adaptability and its political manifestations that help explain the remarkable longevity of the PRC as one of the world's few remaining communist party-states.[6]

The next two sections of this chapter discuss Marxism and Leninism, the ideological foundations of all forms of communism, including that of the CCP. Following a brief transitional discussion of how Marxism-Leninism first came to China in the early twentieth century, the longest section of this chapter is devoted to an analysis of the ideology of Mao Zedong and the ways in which it is a distinctive variation of communist ideology. Not only did Maoist communism have a profound impact on China's political development during the era of his rule in the PRC (1949–1976), but China's post-Mao leaders have sworn fealty to certain core principles of Maoism, regardless of how un-Maoist many of their policy initiatives have been. The chapter concludes with an examination of ideology in China after Mao: the CCP's assessment of Maoist ideology; the contributions of Deng Xiaoping, Jiang Zemin, Hu Jintao, and the CCP's current leader, Xi Jinping, to Chinese communism; and some of the alternative ideologies that are supplementing or contending with communism in the People's Republic today.

COMMUNISM

Marxism

Marxism is one of the most complex, controversial, and consequential philosophies in human history. The purpose here is only to highlight those points of Marxism that are most relevant for understanding the development of communist ideology in China from its introduction in the early twentieth century to the present. In fact, these points can be considered as common ground for all "Marxists" or "communists," although they may disagree—sometimes violently—over what these ideas mean in practice.

The essence of Marxism is *class analysis*. Marxists see the world and its development over time through the lens of social classes and the economic systems that give rise to them. In particular, they emphasize the struggle between the rich and the poor, the exploiters and the exploited, and the dominant and the subordinate classes. As Karl Marx (1818–1883) and Friedrich Engels (1820–1895), his close collaborator, wrote in the opening line of *The Communist Manifesto* (1848), "The history of all hitherto existing society is the history of class struggles."[7]

Based on years of study, Marx concluded that from ancient times to his lifetime and beyond, the truly major turning points in history were revolutions—which he called "the locomotives of history" ("The Class Struggle in France," 1849)—in which a ruling class that hindered further human progress—particularly economic progress—was overthrown by a rising class that would take the lead in moving humankind forward to the next, higher stage of its destined development. According to Marxism, history, propelled by class struggle and revolution, unfolds in a series of stages marked by increasing levels of economic development. From the Marxist perspective, this path to progress is scientific and inevitable.

For example, feudalism in England was followed by capitalism when the lords of the manor were displaced as the ruling class by the owners of industries and businesses (capitalists) in a revolutionary process, which began to unfold in the sixteenth and seventeenth centuries and led to the Industrial Revolution and the expansion of capitalism. The same process turned peasant serfs into the industrial working class, or the **proletariat**.

The timing of revolutions in any particular society is determined largely by its level of economic development and class struggle. Marx concluded that the time and place in which he lived—mid-nineteenth-century Western Europe—was ripe for communist revolution. Capitalism had been a magnificent achievement in terms of economic modernization and other areas of human advancement. But it was also a brutally exploitative system in which the capitalist owners of private property (also referred to in Marxism as the "bourgeoisie") literally profited from the labor of the proletariat.

Capitalism, in fact, depended on the complete political, cultural, and economic domination and subjugation of the proletariat.

Marx identified the proletariat as the most oppressed class in all of human history—and therefore the most revolutionary. He concluded that by the late nineteenth century, history had come down to a final life-and-death class struggle between the proletariat and the bourgeoisie. Revolution was inevitable, as was the triumph of the proletariat. In this sense, Marxism is *a theory of proletarian revolution*.

For Marx, this was the final **class struggle** of history because, once they came to power, the proletariat would abolish private property, and the capitalist class would cease to exist. Indeed, when all property was public property, classes would cease to exist, and the history of all *thereafter* existing society would be a history without class struggles. Communism—a truly classless utopia—would be achieved, and humankind would enter into an era of *equality, cooperation, and abundance*. These are the essential elements of the communist society that Marxist revolutionaries have envisioned as the ultimate goal of their actions.

This revolutionary transformation from capitalism to communism would not be completed in a short period of time. After the political overthrow of the bourgeoisie and the capitalist system, there would have to be a transitional stage of undetermined length. Marx called this transitional phase the "lower stage of communism," but it is more commonly referred to as **socialism**. During the transition from capitalism to socialism, proletarian political power would be used to create the conditions for moving on to the "higher stage" of communism. But unlike any of history's previous transformations, this would be an evolutionary, rather than a revolutionary, process. The progress of evolution from socialism to communism would be measured by the increasing material wealth of society and the deepening of communist values, such as selflessness and devotion to the common good, among the people.

Marxism became a political ideology when it was adapted as the basis of the guiding principles and program of self-proclaimed revolutionary movements. The first of these was the Communist League founded in 1847 by Marx and Engels, among others. It was for the Communist League that Marx and Engels wrote *The Communist Manifesto* as an accessible distillation of the Marxist analysis of historical development and the political program of communism. Its most famous phrase, "Workers of the World Unite!" was a clarion call to the proletariat to launch the revolution that would destroy capitalism and begin the transition to socialism.

Marx's ideas were strongly challenged in his lifetime, not only by those who feared his call for communism but also by many who proclaimed themselves to be revolutionaries as well. His radical writings and political activities got him expelled from France (twice) and Belgium before he settled in London in 1849. The strongest challenge to him came from another anticapitalist revolutionary, Mikhail Bakunin (1814–1876), the Russian theorist who advocated a radical version of egalitarian self-governance called anarchism and criticized Marx for being too authoritarian in his leadership of the communist movement in Europe.

Marx did not live to see a proletarian revolution under the banner of Marxism come to power. That wouldn't happen until the 1917 Russian Revolution, and its leader, V. I. Lenin, would not only preside (if briefly before his death) over the first government committed to the realization of socialism and communism, but his theories would also become the foundation of the second and, in some ways, more politically influential branch of Marxism known as Leninism.

Leninism

Marxism is a *theory of history* that establishes the claim that the proletariat is destined to lead humankind in a revolution to overthrown capitalism and create a socialist and then a communist society. Leninism is, in essence, a *theory of revolutionary organization*. It builds on Marxism, but it also adds a new, more practical dimension that deals with the actual seizure and exercise of power by a revolutionary communist organization.

Lenin (1872–1924) was set on the path to becoming a revolutionary following the execution of his elder brother in 1887 for involvement in a plot to kill the czar of Russia. He later became a lawyer and was introduced to Marxist theory during his student years. He joined a small Marxist group in the mid-1890s, and his political activism got him exiled to Siberia for a few years; he subsequently traveled widely in Russia and Europe. He rose to a position of leadership in the Russian Social Democratic Labor Party, which was the most important Marxist organization in Russia at the end of the nineteenth century. In 1903, Lenin led the party's more radical "Bolshevik" ("Majority") faction in taking control of the organization.

After a failed attempt at revolution in 1905, Lenin spent the years until 1917 in Europe, mostly in Geneva, but remained an influential leader of the Bolshevik movement in Russia. He returned to Russia a few months after a revolution—in which the communists were just one of the leading parties—overthrew the czar in February 1917. In October, the Bolsheviks seized power from a noncommunist provisional government, which had been set up after the ouster of the czar. From then until his death in 1924, Lenin was the head of the government of the country that was renamed the Union of Soviet Socialist Republics (USSR), or Soviet Union, and the organization that became the Communist Party of the Soviet Union (CPSU).

This brief review of Lenin's life as a revolutionary is important to understanding the context of his writings that form the foundation of Leninism. "Leninism" was not a term that Lenin himself used (the same with Marx and "Marxism") but was coined posthumously by one of his communist comrades when his theories were elevated to join Marxism as the guiding ideology of the Soviet Union. In fact, what is generally described as "Leninism" derives as much, if not more, from how revolutionaries that followed him, including Stalin and Mao, expropriated and adapted his ideas rather than from what Lenin actually did or wrote.[8]

Lenin wrote at length on the issue of how a communist party could best be organized to achieve its political objectives, especially in his 1902 pamphlet, *What Is to Be Done?* He criticized those who favored an open organization that would recruit members widely, particularly among the proletariat. This approach, Lenin argued, was dangerous for two reasons: First, it would make the party highly vulnerable to infiltration and repression by the Czarist authorities; second, it would dilute the ideological integrity of the party by admitting people who did not fully grasp Marxist theory or were not fully committed to the revolution.

Lenin's solution to this dilemma was to insist that the communist organization be a vanguard party, that is, one composed only of professional revolutionaries, many of whom would be nonworking class intellectuals—like himself—who had embraced Marxism. It would be the vanguard—the leading edge—of the proletarian revolution with the mission to mobilize and lead the working class to seize political power.

To survive, the communist organization not only had to be highly selective in its membership but also secretive and disciplined. The party would operate according to the principle of **democratic centralism**: debate and the free exchange of ideas would be encouraged while a matter was up for discussion (democracy); but once a decision had been reached by the leadership, discussion stopped and all members were bound to follow without hesitation or dissent (centralism). Lower levels of the organization had to follow the orders of higher levels, and the minority had to follow the majority.

The Leninist theory (and practice) of a vanguard party of the proletariat is an adaptation of (or departure from) Marxism in at least two major ways. First, it substitutes a *political party* claiming to represent the interests of the proletariat for the proletariat itself as the leading force of the revolution. Marx and Engels, like Lenin, had also seen an important role for bourgeois intellectuals who had become communists—again, like themselves—in providing ideological guidance to the revolution. But they had more faith that the proletariat would rise up in to take the lead in the revolution when the time was right.

Second, Leninism reflects the idea that a largely agrarian country with relatively little industry and a small proletariat, such as Russia in the late nineteenth century, could, in fact, begin the process of a communist revolution through the agency of a vanguard party. Both of these Leninist adaptations of Marxism would have great appeal to aspiring revolutionaries in nonindustrialized countries, including China.

Lenin saw the vanguard communist party as the best type of revolutionary organization to seize political power. But it also became the model for all communist organizations after seizing power when they became the ruling party. In Lenin's book, *State and Revolution* (1917), he expanded significantly on an important idea put forth by Marx: the **dictatorship of the proletariat**. This was to be the form of the political system put in place after the communist party took power in the country and that would prevail during at least the early stages of the transition to socialism. "The proletariat," Lenin declared, "needs state power, a centralized organization of force, an organization of violence, both to crush the resistance of the exploiters and to lead the enormous mass of the population . . . in the work of organizing a socialist economy." The communist party was to be this "centralized organization of force" and would exercise the dictatorship of the proletariat in the revolutionary state.

Lenin stressed the need for a ruling communist party to remain vigilant against the possibility of a counterrevolution, especially at a time when capitalist enemies surrounded the country. Lenin, like Marx, believed that the state would "wither away" once communism was achieved; but before that time came, the power of the state (and the communist party) would have to increase in order to protect and promote the interests of the proletariat. It is this model of a vanguard party, based on the principle of democratic centralism and exercising some variation of the dictatorship of the proletariat, that is being conveyed when a communist party, such as the CCP, is referred to as a Leninist party, or the PRC as having a Leninist political system.

The other main ingredient of Leninism that we should take note of is its theory of imperialism. Basically, Lenin's thesis on imperialism was that the most advanced capitalist countries had been able to avert proletarian revolution at home in the late nineteenth century, at least temporarily, by exploiting their colonies and other less developed areas of the world that were in the pre-capitalist stage of history and using the wealth gained through such exploitation to overcome the economic crises inherent in capitalism. These areas, in turn, became the weakest link in the global capitalist chain because of the extreme exploitation they suffered. Communists could find fertile ground for a revolution led by a vanguard party in these weak links, even though they were far from the level of economic and class development that Marx had said was a prerequisite for building socialism. Lenin had in mind Russia as the weak link of capitalism most ready for revolution in the first decades of the twentieth century, but his ideas on imperialism were one of the main factors in drawing nationalist leaders and intellectuals in the Third World to Marxism-Leninism, including the founders of the CCP and Vietnam's communist leader, Ho Chi Minh.

After coming to power, the vanguard communist party would use its centralized authority to promote rapid economic development that would allow the country to achieve rapid industrialization without capitalism. As Lenin said in a speech in 1920, "Communism is Soviet power plus the electrification of the whole country" (*Collected Works*, vol. 31, 496–518). Lenin's vanguard communist party not only substitutes itself and does the historical work for a weak proletariat class in making revolution in a pre-industrial society, but it also takes the place of a weak capitalist class in achieving industrialization. Thus, Leninism allowed for the acceleration of the Marxist trajectory of history. With the right degree of revolutionary consciousness and the right kind of revolutionary organization, communist power and socialist society became possible for a country without having to wait for and experience the long, painful stage of capitalism to unfold. This, too, was a powerful message to would-be communist revolutionaries in the less-developed parts of the world.

In some ways, these theoretical and organizational innovations by Lenin more or less turned Marxism on its head. But they also became foundational pillars of Marxism-Leninism as the guiding ideology of communist movements in China and elsewhere during the twentieth century.

MARXISM-LENINISM COMES TO CHINA

Chapter 2 described the **May Fourth Movement** of 1919 and the founding of the CCP in 1921. These two events paved the way for the introduction of Marxism-Leninism into China and its emergence as the country's dominant revolutionary ideology.

Socialist ideas had been influential among some Chinese intellectuals since early in the twentieth century, including not only Marxism but also "non-Marxist socialisms."[9] These schools of thought shared common ground with Marxism in the belief that society would be better if it were organized according to egalitarian principles of collective, rather than private, property, cooperation rather than competition, and power, both economic and political, in the hands of the producers rather than exploiters. But they differed from Marxism (and particularly later with Leninism) over how these lofty goals were to be achieved and what forms they would take when put into practice.

The May Fourth Movement steered some Chinese intellectuals toward more radical variations of socialism in their desperate search for solutions to China's internal and external crises. A few, inspired by the success of the Russian Revolution in 1917 and the anti-imperialist stand of the new Soviet government, began to look more seriously at the ideological and organizational model offered by Marxism-Leninism. These newly converted Marxist-Leninists were guided in establishing the CCP in 1921 by agents of the Moscow-based Comintern (Communist International) who had been sent to China to help promote revolution. The CCP organization was, from the beginning, structured as a vanguard party along Leninist (or Bolshevik) lines. As the party grew, it enforced both ideological and political discipline on its members, which soon squeezed out those advocating alternative non-Marxist-Leninist versions of socialism.

MAO ZEDONG THOUGHT

Chapters 2 and 3 discussed the gradual rise of Mao Zedong in the hierarchy of CCP leaders during the civil war against Chiang Kai-shek's Nationalist Party and his emergence as the undisputed head of the party during the Yan'an period. It was in **Yan'an** that Mao also consolidated his ideological domination of the Chinese communist movement.

The CCP first formally proclaimed **Mao Zedong Thought** as its guiding ideology in the party constitution of 1945, which was promulgated in Yan'an toward the end of World War II. The process of enshrining and giving official primacy to Mao's theories had begun a couple of years earlier. The rectification campaign of 1942 had eliminated Mao's major opponents, and in the spring of 1943, he was elected chairman of the party Politburo, a position he literally held until his last breath on September 9, 1976.

It was a conscious decision of the party leadership in 1945 to use the term Mao Zedong Thought (*Mao Zedong sixiang*) as the designation for Mao's contribution to communist ideology.[10] They could have chosen—and did consider—other terms, including what would be translated as "Maoism" (*Mao Zedong zhuyi*), but that particular rendition had a foreign connotation, as in the Chinese translation for Marxism-Leninism (*Makesi zhuyi, Liening zhuyi*). Mao Zedong Thought was chosen as an unmistakable statement that Mao's thinking was neither derivative of nor subordinate to Marxism-Leninism but embodied the successful **Sinification** of Marxism-Leninism. Sinification refers to the process of being absorbed or deeply influenced by Chinese culture, society, or thought. In 1938, Mao had cited adapting

the European ideology of Marxism-Leninism to China's particular situation as a critical step in the revolutionary process (Report to the Sixth Plenum of the Central Committee of the Chinese Communist Party).[11]

After the founding of the People's Republic in 1949, the relationship of Mao Zedong Thought to Marxism-Leninism—and the "true" meaning of Mao Zedong Thought itself—would become a matter of both spirited ideological contention and ferocious, even violent political struggles within the CCP. But the general formulation that Mao Zedong Thought is the integration of the "universal truths" of Marxism-Leninism with the "concrete practice" of the Chinese revolution thus became the CCP's standard formulation early in the Maoist era and remains so today.

The universal truths of Marxism refer to class struggle as the key to understanding the development of human history and the belief in the inevitable downfall of capitalism and the triumph of socialism-communism. For Leninism, it is the theory of the vanguard proletarian party that will lead the revolution and the nation. It is Mao's adaptation and elaboration of these universal truths to Chinese circumstances that form the essence of Mao Zedong Thought. As Franz Schurmann put it, Marxism-Leninism is the "pure ideology" part of Chinese Communism, while Mao Zedong Thought is the "practical ideology."[12]

There has been a very vigorous academic debate among China scholars about the extent to which Mao Zedong Thought is based on Marxism-Leninism.[13] One side argues that the core of Maoism is faithful to the fundamental principles of that ideology. The other side concludes that Mao's Thought, while employing communist terminology and rhetoric, deviates so sharply from Marxism-Leninism that it should be considered as an entirely different school of political thought, one more deeply influenced by other sources, such as Chinese philosophy and culture. Some see Mao Zedong Thought as an innovative amalgamation of Marxist-Leninist and Chinese characteristics. Others see it as an utter betrayal or perversion of Marxist ideas. Then there are those who portray Mao as having no ideology or guiding principles other than the pursuit of personal power at any cost.[14]

What are the distinguishing features of Mao Zedong Thought, which is often referred to outside of China as "Maoism," and how have these features influenced China's political development?

The Role of Peasants in the Revolution

First, and most fundamentally, what is distinctive about Maoist Marxism is its designation of the peasants as a leading force in advancing China's communist-led revolution. As noted earlier, Marx saw socialism and communism as the result of a proletarian revolution that would take root in and spring from the factories and cities of advanced industrial capitalist societies. Marx had little positive to say about peasants and rural society. He regarded the peasantry as among the most exploited classes in capitalist society, but one that history had passed by on its march toward industrialization and urbanization—and socialism.

Marx once called the peasantry "a class of barbarians standing halfway outside of society, a class combining all the crudeness of primitive forms of society with the anguish and misery of civilized countries" (*Capital*, vol. 3, pt. 6, chap. 47) and compared peasant society to "a sack of potatoes" (*The Eighteenth Brumaire of Louis Bonaparte*, 1852) because of its lack of cohesion and class consciousness, both of which he saw as prerequisites for revolutionary action. *The Communist Manifesto* (1848) actually applauds capitalism for having "subjected the countryside to the rule of the towns. It has created enormous cities, has greatly increased the urban population as compared with the rural, and has thus rescued a considerable part of the population from the idiocy of rural life."

Lenin was somewhat more optimistic about the revolutionary potential of the peasantry in Russia. He thought rural dwellers—particularly the poorest peasants—could be valuable allies of the proletariat in seizing power. But, like Marx, he was skeptical that they could see beyond their desire for "freedom and land" to the ultimate goals of socialism, including the abolition of private property (*The Proletariat and the Peasantry*, 1905).

Mao, drawing on his own rural roots, went quite a bit farther by identifying the peasantry as playing a leading role in bringing the revolutionary movement to power, concluding from his own investigations in his home province of Hunan in early 1927 that

> In a very short time, in China's central, southern and northern provinces, several hundred million peasants will rise like a mighty storm, like a hurricane, a force so swift and violent that no power, however great, will be able to hold it back. They will smash all the trammels that bind them and rush forward along the road to liberation. They will sweep all the imperialists, warlords, corrupt officials, local tyrants and evil gentry into their graves. Every revolutionary party and every revolutionary comrade will be put to the test, to be accepted or rejected as they decide. There are three alternatives. To march at their head and lead them? To trail behind them, gesticulating and criticizing? Or to stand in their way and oppose them? Every Chinese is free to choose, but events will force you to make the choice quickly. ("Report on an Investigation of the Peasant Movement in Hunan," March 1927)

Mao went on to make the case that the poorest peasants, which he estimated at 70 percent of the rural population, were "the most revolutionary group" and "the vanguard in the overthrow of the feudal forces," by which he meant the landlord class that had dominated rural society for millennia. He then put the center of gravity of China's struggle squarely in the countryside by claiming that to "overthrow these feudal forces is the real objective of the national revolution."

Mao's rural strategy of "surrounding the cities from the countryside" gradually became the dominant approach of the CCP after Chiang Kai-shek's attacks against the party in the late 1920s drove them out of the urban areas into the countryside and then forced them to undertake the Long March to the hinterlands of Yan'an in the mid-1930s.

But this strategy was not without opposition from within the CCP, especially from party leaders who had been trained in more orthodox Marxism in Moscow. It also was not endorsed by Stalin, who had become head of the Soviet Communist Party and the Comintern following Lenin's death in 1924. Although Stalin eventually gave Mao crucial support in his bid to lead the CCP, the Soviet leader was skeptical of a communist revolution based on mobilizing the rural masses. He ordered the Chinese Communists to stay in the urban-based united front with the KMT in 1927 even when it became apparent to many that Chiang Kai-shek was preparing a bloody purge of the communists. He later referred to Mao as a "cave Marxist" who hid in the countryside of Yan'an rather than fighting in the cities.[15]

China scholars have reached very different conclusions, and argued with great intensity, about whether Mao's views of the role of the peasantry in China's revolution constitute a profound break with orthodox Marxism or merely an adjustment in strategy to accommodate circumstances that left him and the communist party no real choice. There is no dispute that Mao exhibited a certain kind of political genius in recognizing that peasants would, out of necessity, be the leading force in the struggle to gain power. But he never abandoned the orthodox Marxist assumption that the industrial proletariat was the leading class and the peasants a subordinate partner in the revolutionary coalition whose ultimate goal was to bring socialism and modernization to China. Nevertheless, Maoism is a distinctive variant of Marxism in the degree to which it puts a positive emphasis on the rural factor in influencing the revolution both before and after the acquisition of power.

Peasants and the Building of Socialism

After the founding of the People's Republic, Mao, at many times and in various ways, continued to express and act on his ideological view that the peasantry had a special role in bringing about revolutionary change. The most dramatic—and ultimately tragic—example was his decision to launch the Great Leap Forward in 1958. As discussed in chapter 3, the purpose of the Leap was to recalibrate China's approach to building socialism away from the bureaucratic Soviet-style five-year-plan model, with its strong urban bias to a mass-mobilization strategy of economic development that would "walk on two legs" in benefiting both city and countryside and promoting both industry and agriculture. The goal of all this was to reduce and eventually eliminate the difference between peasants and proletarians as a critical step toward the realization of communism. Furthermore, the vanguard of the Leap into communism would be the peasants, and its most revolutionary thrust would be in the rural areas with the founding of the radically egalitarian people's communes. It was also among the peasantry that the Leap took its most terrible toll in the tens of millions who perished because of famine, illness, and mistreatment by communist cadres.

The **Cultural Revolution**, although it was to be a "great proletarian" movement and was a largely urban phenomenon in its first phases, had roots in Mao's concerns in the early 1960s about the growing inequality and cadre corruption in the rural areas that had resulted from the policies sponsored by Liu Shaoqi and Deng Xiaoping to promote recovery from the ravages of the Great Leap Forward. And in the late 1960s, when the Chairman became disenchanted with the factionalism and internecine violence of the urban youth who made up the Red Guards, he sent more than twenty million of them "down to the countryside and up to the mountains" where they could be reeducated by the peasants about what it really meant to make revolution.

Yet, to a certain extent, Mao was ambivalent about the role of the peasantry in the building of socialism. He retained a somewhat utopian view about the revolutionary enthusiasm of the rural folk and the political purity of the countryside. He was also concerned about the corrupting influences of city life. But his vision of the socialist (and communist) future was not a pastoral one. He wanted the rural areas to modernize with the goal of overcoming what he called the "Three Great Differences" between industry and agriculture, town and country, mental and manual labor. Like Marx and Lenin, he believed that the ultimate objective of seizing political power and building socialism was to unleash the productive forces and usher in an era of modernization, which would lead to unprecedented bounty. But Mao Zedong Thought does ascribe to the rural peasants a much more vital role as a revolutionary force in achieving those ends.

Leninist Populism

The Leninist theory of revolution is based on the assumption that the masses cannot lead the revolution on their own but must be mobilized and directed by a vanguard communist party. Mao was, at bottom, a faithful Leninist, but throughout his political life his thinking and his action reflected a deep populist streak. Populism is an approach to politics that claims to represent the interests of ordinary people, particularly against predatory elites whose own wealth and power depends on a status quo that disadvantages the vast majority.[16] It also expresses a deep faith in the wisdom of the masses and the power of the "people" as a political force and, in some variations, a "widely-held belief in popular sovereignty."[17]

One of Mao's first important political essays, written while he was just beginning to learn about Marxism-Leninism, was called, "The Great Union of the Popular Masses" (1919). This essay resounds with populist themes in its call to action against all the woes that plagued China in the tumultuous decade after the fall of the Qing dynasty. After observing that "the decadence of the state, the sufferings of humanity, and the darkness of society have all reached an extreme," he wrote:

> Where is the method of improvement and reform? Education, industrialization, strenuous efforts, rapid progress, destruction and construction are, to be sure, all right, but there is a basic method for carrying out all these undertakings, which is that of the great union of the popular masses. If we look at the course of history as a whole, we find that all the movements which have occurred throughout history, of whatever type they may be, have all without exception resulted from the union of a certain number of people. A greater movement requires a greater union, and the greatest movement requires the greatest union.[18]

Mao rails time and again in this essay against "the union of powerful people" that has caused the abject misery of so much of humankind. At this early time in the pre-Marxist stage of his life, he calls only for "reform and resistance," not revolution, and the perspective is clearly one in which the heretofore powerless masses will, on their own, undertake the struggle for justice without the need for vanguard party.

Once he was a committed Marxist-Leninist, Mao's faith in the masses was tempered, if not wholly tamed, by his belief in the CCP as the vanguard of the revolution. But he often seemed torn between the two poles of populism and Leninism. During his ascent to power in the 1930s, he reminded his communist colleagues that the party had to "be concerned with the well-being of the masses" in order to win them over to their side; if they failed in that task, they would fail in making revolution. The party had to think of the masses not only as foot soldiers in the revolution but also as a kind of partner in a mutual cause. The people would not be swayed to join the cause by abstract ideological appeals. Rather, "if we want to win," he said in 1934,

> We must lead the peasants' struggle for land and distribute the land to them, heighten their labor enthusiasm and increase agricultural production, safeguard the interests of the workers, establish co-operatives, develop trade with outside areas, and solve the problems facing the masses—food, shelter and clothing, fuel, rice, cooking oil and salt, sickness and hygiene, and marriage. In short, all the practical problems in the masses' everyday life should claim our attention. If we attend to these problems, solve them and satisfy the needs of the masses, we shall really become organizers of the well-being of the masses, and they will truly rally round us and give us their warm support. Comrades, will we then be able to arouse them to take part in the revolutionary war? Yes, indeed we will! ("Be Concerned with the Well-Being of the Masses," 1934)

The enemy—at that time defined as "imperialism and the Kuomintang"—may have superior weaponry and shield itself in "iron bastions" like military fortifications. But if the revolutionary forces have the people on their side, then the CCP had nothing to fear and victory was assured:

> What is a true bastion of iron? It is the masses, the millions upon millions of people who genuinely and sincerely support the revolution. That is the real iron bastion which no force can smash, no force whatsoever. The counter-revolution cannot smash us; on the contrary, we shall smash it. Rallying millions upon millions of people round the revolutionary government and expanding our revolutionary war we shall wipe out all counter-revolution and take over the whole of China. ("Be Concerned with the Well-Being of the Masses," 1934)

The populist impulse in Maoism often asserted itself after 1949. In the Hundred Flowers Movement (1956–1957), Mao called on the people to criticize the party's shortcomings during its first years in power, particularly "bureaucratism" (being out of touch with the masses). At the start of the Great Leap Forward (1958–1960), which was in large measure a turn from an elite-centered model of socialist development to a radically populist one, the Chairman exclaimed that the "most outstanding thing" about China's people was that, for the most part, they were "poor and blank." This gave them "the desire for changes, the desire for action and the desire for revolution." Furthermore, he said, "On a blank sheet of paper free from any mark, the freshest and most beautiful characters can be written; the freshest and most beautiful pictures can be painted" ("Introducing a Co-operative," April 15, 1958).In the early stages of the Cultural Revolution (1966–1968) Mao literally unleashed the masses to attack authority in all its personal and institutional manifestations, including the party.

Each of these episodes not only resulted in catastrophes that inflicted great suffering on the Chinese people but also ended with a firm reassertion of Leninist authority.

These outcomes reflect both the perils of Maoist radical populism and Mao's deep ambivalence about giving power to the people.

The Mass Line

The tension between populism and Leninism in Mao's thought can clearly be seen in his theory of leadership, which is called the "mass line." Both the theory and practice of the mass line took shape during the years that the CCP spent in rural base areas from 1927 to 1945. It is a method of leadership—or "**work style**"—emphasizing that those with authority ("cadres") must always remain in close touch with those they lead. It rejects both leaderless, spontaneous action by the masses and leadership that is aloof or divorced from the masses. As Mao wrote in 1943:

> However active the leading group may be, its activity will amount to fruitless effort by a handful of people unless combined with the activity of the masses. On the other hand, if the masses alone are active without a strong leading group to organize their activity properly, such activity cannot be sustained for long, or carried forward in the right direction, or raised to a high level. ("Some Questions Concerning Methods of Leadership," 1943)

In other words, cadres have to talk and listen to the people, spend time among them, not live at a level too high above them, share their weal and woe, and avoid arrogance of any kind. In making decisions, cadres have to put into practice the key concept of "from the masses, to the masses":

> This means: take the ideas of the masses (scattered and unsystematic ideas) and concentrate them (through study turn them into concentrated and systematic ideas), then go to the masses and propagate and explain these ideas until the masses embrace them as their own, hold fast to them and translate them into action, and test the correctness of these ideas in such action. Then once again concentrate ideas from the masses and once again go to the masses so that the ideas are persevered in and carried through. And so on, over and over again in an endless spiral, with the ideas becoming more correct, more vital and richer each time. ("Some Questions Concerning Methods of Leadership," 1943)

The mass-line approach to leadership certainly does not cede all power to the people. Leaders are meant to exercise authority and expect compliance. But such authority is rooted in the masses, not in the liberal democratic sense that the leaders are ultimately accountable to the people: they are not. According to the Leninist system of democratic centralism, cadres are responsible to higher levels in the party's pyramidal chain of command, not to those below them. But the mass line is distinctive in that it does give more emphasis and life to the democratic vein in democratic centralism than does orthodox Leninism, if "democratic" is understood as connection and consultation by the leaders with the led. In this sense, the mass line might be said to be the basis of a political system with "quasi-democratic" characteristics, but always under firm party control.[19]

The Mass Line: Deviation and Innovation

The mass line was the essence of proper cadre "work style," and deviation from it was one of the deadly sins of Maoism. Tendencies toward elitism, bureaucratism, commandism, and other manifestations of a deviant work style were always to be guarded against in a vanguard party, but they became a central and abiding concern to Mao after the CCP had come to power.

On the eve of the communist triumph in 1949, Mao warned in a speech to the party leadership that "With victory, certain moods may grow within the Party—arrogance, the airs of a self-styled hero, inertia and unwillingness to make progress, love of pleasure and distaste for continued hard living." He worried that "There may be some Communists, who were not conquered by enemies with guns and were worthy of the name of heroes for standing up to these enemies, but who cannot withstand sugar-coated bullets; they will be defeated by sugar-coated bullets" in the form of the prestige, privileges, and perquisites that power brings. If the party was to achieve its goal of building a new socialist China, then cadres had "to remain modest, prudent and free from arrogance and rashness in their style of work. . . [and] preserve the style of plain living and hard struggle" that had won them the support of the masses during the civil war ("Report to the Second Plenary Session of the Seventh Central Committee of the Communist Party of China," March 5, 1949).

In the early years following the establishment of the People's Republic, Mao came to believe that his warnings had been ignored. In 1951, the **Three-Anti campaign** (anticorruption, antiwaste, antibureaucracy) was launched primarily to target cadre abuses of the mass line. The Hundred Flowers Movement had a similar thrust. The ideological restlessness that Mao exhibited throughout the remainder of his life derived from his worries—ultimately his obsession—that China was in dire danger of veering off the socialist road to communism and might well wind up instead in the clutches of capitalism. The only safeguard against this was if the vanguard party remained true to its mission, and that was possible only if its leaders stayed loyal and attuned to the people through the mass line.

One of the institutional innovations that grew out of the Cultural Revolution was the so-called **May 7th Cadre Schools**, which were designed, in part, to reinforce the mass line. The name of these "schools" was derived from the "May 7th Directive" of 1966, which was a letter from Chairman Mao (to Defense Minister Lin Biao) that called on the army to be a "big school" in which soldiers engaged in labor and studied politics as well as fulfilling their military duties. Applied to state and party cadres, this Directive led to the dispatch of hundreds of thousands of officials, on a rotational basis, from the relative comfort of their urban offices to work and live among the masses, mostly in rural communes, while also engaging in political study and self-criticism.

The May 7th Schools were an artifact of the short-lived period in which some of the radical ideas of the Cultural Revolution were actually put into practice, and, in practice, the reality of the policy frequently fell far short of its ideals. Cadres were often quartered in barracks at some distance from peasant households and worked on separate plots of land (in fact, the peasants did not want the soft-handed city slickers mucking up their crops). Nevertheless, at least the idea of the May 7th Schools embodied the centrality of the mass-line approach to leadership in Mao Zedong Thought.

Voluntarism

Voluntarism is the belief that human will ("volition") can be decisive in bringing about major historical changes. It expresses supreme faith in the power of *subjective* factors such as commitment, faith, determination, and perseverance to overcome *objective* conditions or obstacles that stand in the way of solving a problem or achieving a goal. Voluntarism also has a collective aspect in that it sees the power of human will magnified when people work together for a common cause. Many scholars see voluntarism as one of the defining characteristics of Mao Zedong Thought and as a recurring theme in both his writings and political actions.[20]

This voluntarist element in Maoism is also frequently cited as one of the main points separating it from orthodox Marxism, which puts more emphasis on the limits that objective circumstances, notably economic circumstances, place on the scope of human will and activity. For this reason, Marxism is often said to be based on "economic determinism," meaning that it is the economic structure (and the class system that derives from it) of any given historical era that determines politics, culture, philosophy, and nearly every other aspect of human society. The juxtaposition of Mao's voluntarism with Marx's economic determinism (or **materialism**) can be overstated: Marx did not discount altogether the role of human consciousness and action in shaping important events, and Mao was always an authentic Marxist in the centrality he accorded to the economic forces of production. Nevertheless, any discussion of Mao Zedong Thought and its impact on Chinese politics has to take account of its strong voluntarist thread.

The essay of Mao's that is most voluntarist in its message is also one of his shortest: "The Foolish Old Man Who Removed the Mountains." The essay comes from a speech that the Chairman gave in June 1945 at a national congress of the CCP. World War II was approaching its end, and the likelihood that the civil war against Chiang Kai-shek's Nationalists would resume was certainly on the minds of those attending this meeting.

In order to rally his comrades for the struggles ahead, Mao inserted into his speech an ancient Chinese fable. It tells the story of an old man who decides to dig away two huge mountains that are blocking his house (perhaps from access to the nearest market town?). When a neighbor calls him foolish for attempting such an obviously impossible feat, the old man replies that if he keeps digging, along with his sons, and their sons, and so on, they will eventually be able to remove the mountains, since they weren't growing any higher and each shovelful made them lower. Mao brought the fable up to the present by saying that it was the two big mountains of imperialism and feudalism that "lie like a dead weight on the Chinese people." The CCP, he said, was committed to digging them up. "We must persevere and work unceasingly," he noted, and if we "stand up and dig together" with the Chinese people, "why can't these two mountains be cleared away?" ("The Foolish Old Man Who Removed the Mountains," 1945).

Mao's invocation of this fable at that critical moment of the Chinese revolution was meant to be a ringing call to party members to keep faith in their mission and themselves despite the "objective" fact that they would soon be fighting an army much larger, better armed, and supported by the United States. There are also elements of Mao's Leninist populism in his telling of the fable: it is the combination of the Chinese people and the CCP standing up and digging together that will ensure victory.

Mao's voluntarism is sometimes analyzed as reflecting a kind of peasant utopianism with roots in his fascination with the fabled heroism of characters from ancient Chinese novels. But it can also be traced to the series of seemingly miraculous successes that he and the CCP had during their rise to power: the escape from Chiang's anticommunist "White Terror" and extermination campaigns of the late 1920s to mid-1930s; their survival of the Long March of 1934–1935; and their ability not only to survive but also to thrive in Yan'an while fighting both the Nationalists and the Japanese. The lesson that Mao drew from these experiences could certainly have been a voluntarist one, bolstered by the triumphs of the early years of CCP, such as in the land reform campaign and particularly by fighting the United States to a stalemate in the Korean War.

This voluntarist element in Maoism played out most clearly in the Great Leap Forward, in which the Chairman took the lead in a movement that proclaimed China would achieve economic miracles and reach the ranks of the advanced industrial nations in a decade or less. And how would it do this, despite the fact any "objective" assessment of the technology and resources available to China in the late 1950s would say that such a claim was foolish? By relying on the willpower, the labor, and the revolutionary enthusiasm of the Chinese people under the leadership of the CCP. It was during the Leap that the slogan, "The spirit of the Foolish Old Man is the spirit that will transform China" first became popular. Mao's "Foolish Old Man" speech of 1945 became one of his "Three Constantly Read Articles" that were emphasized and often memorized by many people during the Cultural Revolution.[21]

Even some of Mao's poetry (yes, he was a poet, and not a bad one, according to many critics) have lines and stanzas that carry a strong voluntarist message, particularly some written on the eve of the Cultural Revolution, when he was pondering his odds of launching an ideological crusade against much of the party-state establishment. Consider the following excerpt from a poem written in 1965:

> Wind and thunder are stirring,
> Flags and banners are flying
> Wherever men live.
> Thirty-eight years are fled
> With a mere snap of the fingers.
> We can clasp the moon in the Ninth Heaven
> And seize turtles deep down in the Five Seas:
> Nothing is hard in this world
> If you dare to scale the heights.
>
> —"Reascending Jinggangshan"

Contradiction

Stuart R. Schram, one of the foremost scholars of Mao Zedong Thought, has called the "theory of contradictions" the "philosophical core" of Mao's thinking.[22] It is also one of the more complex aspects of Maoism and one not easily illustrated by references to fables, poems, or slogans. In fact, the two major essays in which Mao deals most centrally with this topic, "On Contradiction" (1937) and "On the Correct Handling of Contradictions among the People" (1957), are among his longest and densest writings. Mao's ideas about **contradictions** root his ideology firmly in Marxism-Leninism, while at the same time—rather contradictorily—reflect one of his most distinctive theoretical innovations, and one that had profound consequences for Chinese politics.

Mao wrote in his 1937 essay that "contradiction exists in the process of development of all things" and that "contradiction exists universally and in all processes, whether in the simple or in the complex forms of motion, whether in objective phenomena or ideological phenomena" ("On Contradiction," 1937). What did he mean by "contradiction"? As Mao uses it, contradictions refer to things that are closely connected but are still fundamentally different or that "contradict each other" in important ways.

However, it is not just the difference between thing, but also the connection that makes for a contradiction.

It is the continuous interaction among the aspects of a contradiction that causes the development of everything—of life, nature, knowledge, culture, society. This view of the centrality of contradictions comes from an approach to philosophy called "dialectics," which dates back to ancient Greece and which was adapted by Marx as the heart of his understanding of history. For Marxists, including Mao, the most important contradiction in human society *before socialism and communism* are reached is that between classes, particularly between exploiting and exploited classes, which itself reflects contradictions in the process of economic development since without exploitation, development would not occur.

Mao, again building on Marxism-Leninism, made the distinction between two kinds of contradictions in society, *nonantagonistic* and *antagonistic*. Nonantagonistic contradictions are those in which the opposing parts have some common ground despite their differences, which may, in fact, be quite big. In such cases, the contradictions can be resolved through discussion, debate, learning, and other noncoercive means.

Mao often pointed to the contradictions between rural peasants and urban workers as parts of the revolutionary movements as an example of a nonantagonistic contradiction: both classes wanted the same fundamental thing—to overthrow their exploiters and have a "better" life—but because of their vastly different circumstances, they are bound to have differences about both the means and ends of the revolution. There could even be—given the law of contradictions, there *had* to be—contradictions within the communist party itself, but these were—at least as formulated in his 1937 essay— also nonantagonistic, for example, over whether the CCP should follow an urban or rural strategy of revolution to reach the common goal of winning national power.

Mao also referred to nonantagonistic contradictions as "contradictions among the people"—the "people" being a broad yet vague category that included all those who were on the side of the revolution. **Antagonistic contradictions**, on the other hand, are between the people and their "enemies," for example, between poor peasants and the landlords who exploit them. There is no common ground for compromise or room for debate. Such antagonistic contradictions can only be resolved through class struggle, which requires force to defeat and suppress the enemy.

Responding in the late 1920s to those who claimed that the peasants were "going too far" in their actions against landlords, Mao exclaimed,

> A revolution is not a dinner party, or writing an essay, or painting a picture, or doing embroidery; it cannot be so refined, so leisurely and gentle, so temperate, kind, courteous, restrained and magnanimous. A revolution is an insurrection, an act of violence by which one class overthrows another. ("Report on an Investigation of a Peasant Movement," 1927)

Mao noted that if left unresolved, nonantagonistic contradictions could fester and eventually turn antagonistic. Therefore one of the primary tasks of a communist party leadership was to differentiate between types of contradiction, decide which were the most important to tackle at any given point in time, and use the correct methods in handling them.

Up to this point, what has been presented as Mao's views on contradictions is pretty standard Marxist-Leninist fare. But he went much farther, in both theory and practice,. Toward the end of his 1937 essay, Mao approvingly quoted Lenin as follows: "'Antagonism and contradiction are not at all one and the same. Under socialism, the first will disappear, the second will remain.' That is to say, antagonism is one form, but not the only form, of the struggle of opposites; the formula of antagonism cannot be arbitrarily applied everywhere" ("On Contradiction," 1937). In other words, once the communist party had consolidated power and established a socialist system—including the abolition of private property and exploiting classes—there would still be contradictions, but they would be nonantagonistic contradictions "among the people" since the economic (material) basis of class antagonism would have been eliminated.

Mao soon changed his mind about the validity of Lenin's conclusion. He was deeply influenced in this by his reading of Joseph Stalin's *The History of the Communist Party of the Soviet Union: Short Course* (1935), which was translated into Chinese in Yan'an in 1938/1939.[23] The central points of the *Short Course* were that class struggle, indeed, never ceases and that the communist party must constantly be on guard against contamination by hostile forces and ideas that threaten to divert it from its revolutionary mission and dilute its revolutionary ideology.[24]

The Yan'an rectification campaign of 1942-44 (see chaps. 2 and 3), which solidified Mao's personal control of the CCP through a purge of party members deemed insufficiently loyal to the official line and intensive ideological indoctrination, was the first large-scale application of the lessons Mao learned from Stalin's *Short Course*. In 1956, Mao saw the storm of condemnation of the CCP and even of himself that unexpectedly followed his call in "to let a hundred flowers bloom, let a hundred schools of thought contend" as evidence of the persistence of antagonistic contradictions, which he deemed to be "poisonous weeds" in China's socialist society that had to be eradicated. The Chairman's Stalinist instincts were unleashed in the subsequent Anti-Rightest Campaign of 1957, a witch hunt for alleged class enemies that Frederick

C. Teiwes in chapter 3 aptly describes as "a profound intensification of the regime's totalitarian impulse."

Mao's view that antagonistic contradictions do *not* disappear with the advent of socialism but remain a mortal threat to the revolution, requiring eternal vigilance, would preoccupy him for the rest of his life. Such ideas about contradictions—seemingly abstract, philosophical musings on what makes the world go around—in fact, help us to understand why Mao Zedong became such an impatient revolutionary and why his use of power, once he had it, led to such radicalism and violence.

Class Struggle as the Key Link

By definition, an ideology has to have internal consistency or logic; in other words, the pieces have to fit together to form a coherent view of the world and guide to action. If the theory of contradiction is the "philosophical core" of Mao's ideology, a number of other ideas flow directly from that core. Perhaps none is more crucial in the whole construct of Mao Zedong Thought than the idea of "class struggle." As noted earlier, the most fundamental connection between Marxism and Maoism is the class-analysis approach to understanding history and society. But Mao Zedong Thought takes Marxist class analysis in a much more radical direction.

As discussed earlier, from the mid-1950s on, Mao was centrally concerned with the persistence, even under socialism and after the abolition of private property, of the most important of all antagonistic contradictions: class struggle, most especially that between the proletariat and the bourgeoisie, or more precisely, between proletarian and bourgeois ideology, not just in Chinese society but within the CCP itself.

In 1953, Mao was already fretting about the corrosive influence of "bourgeois ideas inside the party" ("Combat Bourgeois Ideas in the Party," 1953). His thoughts about the nature of class struggle in socialist society evolved over the next decade, reflecting his experience of the Hundred Flowers Movement, the Anti-Rightist Campaign, and the Great Leap Forward. Mao's decision to purge the defense minister Peng Dehuai as a "right opportunist" for expressing his opinion at the Lushan Conference in mid-1959 that the Great Leap should be slowed down after the first signs of famine became apparent was particularly significant: it injected the specter of class struggle into the highest echelons of the CCP leadership and represented a fundamental shift in innerparty norms for handling leadership disputes. With the deepening of his dissatisfaction about the direction in which China was headed during the post-Leap recovery, and, importantly, the hardening of his conclusions about the restoration of capitalism in the Soviet Union under Khrushchev, Mao's rhetoric about the persistence of class struggle escalated and became more urgent. (See Box 5.1.)

At a crucial party meeting in September 1962, Mao said, "We can now affirm that classes do exist in socialist countries and that class struggle undoubtedly exists" and told his comrades that "We must raise our vigilance . . . from now on we must talk about this every year, every month, every day." Yet he still cautioned them to "take care that the class struggle does not interfere with our work" ("Speech at the Tenth Plenum of the Eighth Central Committee," 1962).

BOX 5.1 THE IDEOLOGICAL ORIGINS OF THE SINO-SOVIET SPLIT

The Soviet Union was a strong supporter of the Chinese Communist Party from the time of its founding in 1921 through its first decade or so in power in the People's Republic of China. There certainly were tensions over revolutionary strategy between Soviet and Chinese communists during the course of China's civil war, and Mao Zedong did not feel well-treated or respected by Stalin when he first visited Moscow in 1949. Nevertheless, a Sino-Soviet Treaty of Friendship, Alliance, and Mutual Assistance was signed in 1950 and became the basis of massive assistance from Moscow to the PRC, mostly in the form of industrial designs, machinery, and technical advisors. The Soviets also backed the PRC in the Korean War (1950–1953).

But relations between the two communist powers began to deteriorate in the mid-1950s, after Nikita Khrushchev had succeeded Stalin as Soviet leader; by the end of the decade, they had reached the point of open rupture. There were a number of causes of the **Sino-Soviet split**, including Chinese suspicion on Soviet meddling in its internal politics; Soviet "requests" for a military presence on Chinese soil and reluctance to aid the PRC in the development of nuclear weapon; differences in foreign policy, particularly between Moscow's efforts to promote "peaceful coexistence" with the United States and Beijing's preference for confrontation with American imperialism.

Mao was also alarmed at Khrushchev's denunciation of Stalin's crimes in 1956, both because it showed disunity in the communist camp and because he feared he might suffer the same fate after his death. In 1959, the Soviets, due to their increasing displeasure with Mao's taunting rhetoric and reckless policies, withdrew all of their equipment and personnel from China, a move that had a severe negative impact on Chinese industry during the disaster of the Great Leap Forward.

When the Sino-Soviet split spilled out in public in the early 1960s, it took the form of an ideological "debate" in which each side accused the other of having betrayed Marxism-Leninism in both theory and practice. These debates—called "polemics"—were carried out in print and in speeches at international meetings and pitted the Communist Party of the Soviet Union (CPSU) against the Chinese Communist Party (CCP) in a struggle for leadership of the communist world.

Soviet polemics denounced Mao as a narrow-minded nationalist and the CCP as being peasant bandits parading under the banner of communism with no understanding of the "scientific" nature of building socialism. The CCP portrayed Khrushchev as a political bully and an ideological lightweight who had committed the ideological sin of "revisionism," or altering some of most fundamental tenets of Marxism-Leninism.

Mao also came to the conclusion that, under Khrushchev, the Soviet Union had actually abandoned socialism and restored capitalism. In July 1964, the ccp issued an "Open Letter" to the CPSU, which was called "On Khrushchev's Phony Communism and Its Historical Lessons for the World." it declared that "The revisionist Khrushchev clique are the political representatives of the Soviet bourgeoisie, and particularly of its allegedly privileged stratum . . . [that] has gained control of the Party, the government and other important organizations." This "privileged stratum" supported its decadent lifestyle by exploiting the labor of Soviet workers and farmers and was therefore behaving just like a capitalist class. This dire outcome reflected the fact that the Soviets had the wrong ideological perspective on such crucial matters as antagonistic contradictions and the persistence of class struggle in socialist society. Those points are, of course, central hallmarks of Mao Zedong Thought.

For China, the most significant impact of the Sino-Soviet split was the influence it had on Mao's decision to launch the Great Proletarian Cultural Revolution in 1966. The primary purpose of the Cultural Revolution was to forestall the spread of Soviet-style revisionism to China. Mao's main target in this struggle was Liu Shaoqi, president of the

(Continued)

By July 1964, such caution had been jettisoned. Mao proclaimed to his nephew, Mao Yuanxin, who would become one of his uncle's most ardent radical supporters, that "Everywhere there is class struggle, everywhere there are counter-revolutionary elements" and "We . . . have cases where political power is in the grip of the bourgeoisie. . . . No matter what guise they have been transformed into, we must now clean them all out" ("Talk with Mao Yuanxin," 1964). When the Cultural Revolution was launched in full force in May 1966, its targets were those "representatives of the bourgeoisie who have sneaked into the party, the government, the army, and all spheres of culture" ("May 16 Circular," 1966).

In the last months of his life, as the power struggle to succeed him as China's top leader began to heat to a feverish pitch, Mao chastised those (including Deng Xiaoping) he thought were trying to keep the country focused on its economic priorities. In the 1976 New Year's Day editorial in the CCP's most important publications, he was quoted as warning that "Stability and unity do not mean writing off class struggle; class struggle is the key link and everything else hinges on it."[25]

The ways in which Mao acted on his views about the persistence and intensity of class struggle in socialist society and especially within the communist party had momentous consequences for Chinese politics. Those views also reflect a number of important points where Mao Zedong Thought is at ideological odds with—or is at least a radical elaboration on—central elements of Marxism-Leninism.

First, consider the Maoist conclusion that a "bourgeoisie" could emerge within socialist society when, in fact, there was no longer a material basis for a capitalist class, since no property of significant worth was privately owned and no one worked for an owner of a private business, which was the case in China by the mid-1950s. For Mao, class—the basis of all Marxist theory—no longer depended on an individual's or group's relations to the means of production but was more a matter of ideas, values, goals, behavior, and particularly the way in which they exercised authority over others.[26]

This new "bourgeoisie" included those within the communist party who no longer supported the revolution but used the socialist system to enrich or empower themselves. The Yugoslav dissident Milovan Djilas called such fallen comrades "the New Class," in his classic 1957 critique of the Soviet Union and similar communist-party states.[27] Mao went a little farther: it was not just entrenched bureaucrats and party bigwigs who could fall victim to the bourgeois ideology of selfishness and individu-alism; everyone was at risk—even peasants, factory workers, and other usually stal-wart supporters of the revolution.

Similarly, in the Maoist view, the term "proletariat" no longer applied only to in-dustrial workers but to all those—be they farmers, intellectuals, cadres—who were committed to the revolution in both thought and practice. Thus, the formal name of the Cultural Revolution was the "Great *Proletarian* Cultural Revolution," the goal of which was to rid China of all manifestations of bourgeois ideology and replace it with a truly proletarian culture that all of the people would embrace. To Mao, being "pro-letarian," reflected more of an ideological standpoint than membership in a specific economic class.

The second of Mao's important elaborations on the idea of class struggle was his warning that if left unchallenged, the newly emerged bourgeoisie would eventually change China from "red" to "white"—or from socialist to capitalist. This leads to an-other of Mao's ideological innovations: the idea that socialism, once established, can degenerate and even retrogress back to capitalism. That was, in his view, exactly what had happened in the Soviet Union, and what the Cultural Revolution was designed to prevent from happening in China. The notion that such ideological retrogression was possible is contrary to more conventional Marxism, which saw history as inevitably and irreversibly moving in only one direction, toward socialism and communism.

"Permanent Revolution"

Another component of Mao Zedong Thought that logically derives from his theory of contradiction and his views on class struggle under socialism is his notion of **per-manent revolution**.[28] This is also another aspect of Maoism that many scholars argue distinguishes it from mainstream Marxism. In Mao's view, the process of revolution does not stop when the communist party seizes power, and "continuing the revolu-tion" does not just mean putting into place new institutions and policies that reflect the goals of the revolution. For Mao, permanent revolution meant there would have to be revolutions *within* the revolution if human society was going to continue to make progress. At the outset of the Great Leap Forward, Mao declared,

> I stand for the theory of permanent revolution. . . . In making revolution one must strike while the iron is hot—one revolution must follow another, the revolution must continually advance. The Hunanese often say, "Straw sandals have no pattern—they shape themselves in the making." ("Speech to the Supreme State Conference," 1958)

If the hot iron of revolution is left to cool off, it would harden and become an obstacle to change rather than its instrument. Mao's reference to the saying from Hunan (his native province) about straw sandals meant that although the purpose of the revolution (to build socialism and reach communism) is clear—as is the purpose of sandals (to protect the feet)—the actual process of achieving their purpose must be custom-made to fit the circumstances (or the feet of the wearer). The revolution that worked at one historical moment will not fit the next, so the revolution must be continually remade.[29]

Much of Mao's rule over China can be seen as an application of his theory of permanent revolution: for example, the full-steam-ahead, don't-stop-to-consolidate approach to the collectivization of agriculture, culminating in the formation of the radically egalitarian people's communes in 1958; and the all-out class warfare against the "representatives of the bourgeoisie" in the party during the Cultural Revolution.

But, in theory, Mao went even further with his views on permanent revolution. Not only would it be a feature of socialist society but would even continue into the era of communism: "Will there be revolutions in the future when all imperialists in the world are overthrown and all classes eliminated?. . . In my view, there will still be a need for revolution. The social system will still need to be changed and the term 'revolution' will still be in use" ("Speech at the Second Plenary Session of the Eighth Central Committee of the CCP," 1956). In 1962, he wrote, "The transition from socialism to communism is revolutionary. . . . The transition from one stage of communism to another is also revolutionary. . . . Communism will surely have to pass through many stages and many revolutions" ("A Critique of Soviet Economics," 1962).

Mao conceded that revolutions in the communist era "will not be of the same nature as those in the era of class struggle" ("Speech at the Second Plenary Session," 1956). How could they, since communism is, by definition, a classless society? But there would be scientific, technological, cultural revolutions—and even, he suggests, the need to "overthrow" many aspects of communist society when they impede further progress. Communism will be an era of "uninterrupted development," which will be the new form of permanent revolution ("A Critique of Soviet Economics," 1962).

In a very un-Marxist mode, Mao several times even mused that communism would not be the ultimate destination of human social development. He did not speculate on what might lie beyond communism but said that it, too, at some point "would come to an end." Even as he was preparing in March 1958 to launch China on the Great Leap Forward, with the goal of reaching communism as its objective, Mao noted that "There is nothing in the world that does not arise, develop, and disappear. Monkeys turned into humans; humankind arose; in the end, the whole human race will disappear, it will turn into something else; at that time the earth itself will also cease to exist. The earth must certainly be extinguished, the sun too will grow cold. . . . All things must have a beginning and an end" ("Talks at the Chengdu Conference," 1958).

"Seek Truth from Facts"

It may seem rather strange that a revolutionary best known for his utopian ideas and radical policies would also have a pragmatic side. But that is very much the case with Mao Zedong. Mao's pragmatism was a key part of his operational code.

One of Mao's most important essays is called "On Practice," written in 1939, in which he explores at great length the Marxist-Leninist theory of knowledge (epistemology), or how it is that human beings come to learn about the world around them and determine truth from falsehood. Mao adamantly affirms that "social practice alone is the criterion of the truth" and that only by constant reengagement with concrete reality can a person claim to have true knowledge of anything. As he colorfully put it, "If you want to know the taste of a pear, you must change the pear by eating it

yourself." He goes on to say, "If you want to know the theory and methods of revolution, you must take part in revolution" ("On Practice," 1939).

Not only was this one of Mao's guiding principles in developing his revolutionary
strategy (including guerrilla warfare), but in the mid-1960s it would also become part
of his rationale for the Cultural Revolution. One of Mao's goals for that movement
was to give the youth of China, born after Liberation in 1949 and accustomed to a
relatively easy life, an opportunity to "taste" revolution so that they would become
worthy successors to the Maoist cause after his death.

Mao was, of course, a strong believer in Lenin's point that "without revolutionary
theory there can be no revolutionary movement" (*What Is to Be Done?*, 1905). But,
in the Chairman's view, the only way to develop a *correct* theory was on the basis of
practice, and the only way to make sure that it continued to be correct was to constantly subject it to practice, and, if need be, adjust the theory so that it more correctly
reflected reality. Marxism, Mao said,

> emphasizes the importance of theory precisely and only because it can guide action.
> If we have a correct theory but merely prate about it, pigeonhole it and do not put
> it into practice, then that theory, however good, is of no significance. Knowledge
> begins with practice, and theoretical knowledge is acquired through practice and
> must then return to practice. ("On Practice," 1939)

In another context, he pronounced simply that "No investigation, no right to speak!"
("Oppose Book Worship," 1930).

In stressing the importance of practice, experience, and investigation, Mao was
arguing against those in the party leadership who approached any problem with an
absolutely fixed theory and refused to bend even if it was not working or proved
counterproductive. Such people were called "dogmatists" because they treated *their
interpretation of* Marxism-Leninism as "dogma," or as absolutely authoritative and
not to be disputed or diverged from under any circumstances. He was also refuting
the "empiricists" in the party who thought theory was of no great importance in
guiding practice but only looked to their own experiences and the empirical facts of
the immediate situation in deciding policy.

How then, according to Mao, can one strike the right balance between theory and
practice? Not surprisingly, the right balance comes from the contradiction between
the two—the unity of opposites that is the source of the development of all things.

During the period of the civil and anti-Japanese wars (1927–1949), Mao seemed
to come down on the side of practice being the most decisive factor. In two essays,
written in the 1940s, he used the phrase "seek truth from facts" (*shi shi qiu shi*) as
a capsule summary of how communists are supposed to evaluate the correctness
of their theories, and that phrase was adopted as the motto for the school to train
party leaders in Yan'an.[30] Mao did point out that communists must be "guided by the
general principles of Marxism-Leninism" when deciding what conclusions to draw
from the facts" ("Reform Our Study," 1941). But in "On Practice," he makes the rather
bold statement that "Marxism-Leninism has in no way exhausted truth, but cease-
lessly opens up roads to the knowledge of truth in the course of practice." This quote
from Mao and the slogan "seek truth from facts," were cited extensively as guiding

principles for the economic reforms that were introduced after Deng Xiaoping had consolidated power in the early 1980s. In 1988 in fitting reflection of the profound shift in the party's guiding ideology after Mao, the CCP's monthly ideological journal, which was called *Red Flag* (*Hong Qi*) during the Maoist era, was renamed *Seeking Facts* (*Qiu Shi*) in 1988.

Both chapters 2 and 3 note that one key source of Mao's success in the struggle for national power was his willingness to modify policies, such as land reform in the communist base areas, that were not working, even if that meant adjusting the way in which ideology was applied. In chapter 3, Frederick C. Teiwes discusses the "two broad tendencies" of Mao's approach to policy: "the 'revolutionary romantic' and the pragmatic." In Teiwes' view, it was pragmatism that characterized most of Mao's career as a revolutionary, but that after the Hundred Flowers and particularly with the onset of the Great Leap Forward, the romanticism took over.

But, even on the eve of the Cultural Revolution, the pragmatic Mao wrote: "Where do correct ideas come from? Do they drop from the skies? No. Are they innate in the mind? No. They come from social practice, and from it alone" ("Where Do Correct Ideas Come From?," 1963). One could conclude that the latter Mao lost touch with his own good advice to "seek truth from facts" as he became more isolated and detached from reality—in fact, as will be discussed later, that is exactly what his successors, beginning with Deng Xiaoping, did say about him.

CHINESE COMMUNISM AFTER MAO

Did Mao's death and the coming to power of Deng Xiaoping bring "the end of ideology" in the PRC and a complete renunciation of Maoism? After all, Deng and his successors, have taken the country a long way down the "capitalist road" that the Chairman decried ideologically and fought so hard to prevent. China is certainly less ideological than it was in the Mao era, but the CCP still swears allegiance to "Marxism-Leninism-Mao Zedong Thought," and that ideology—although having been reformulated in major ways—still provides the foundation of the operational code of China's leaders and defines the boundaries of what is permissible in Chinese politics.

Maoism after Mao

In 1956, Nikita Khrushchev, the leader of the Communist Party of the Soviet Union, gave a "Secret Speech" that depicted in great detail the crimes of his predecessor, Joseph Stalin. The speech sent shock waves throughout the world, particularly the communist world. It set in motion the process of "de-Stalinization" during which Stalin was literally erased from the formal history of the USSR. It culminated in the removal of Stalin's embalmed corpse from the Mausoleum in Moscow's Red Square, where it had been on display next to that of Lenin (which is still there), and its burial in a grave near the wall of the Kremlin.

Nothing so drastic has happened to Mao in post-Mao China. Too much of the history of the CCP is bound up with the legacy of Mao Zedong for his successors to repudiate him or his ideas completely no matter how far they deviate from his ideology and policies. It has been remarked that Mao was Lenin and Stalin wrapped into one—meaning that he not only led the communist party to power but that he also ruled the country for a long period. (Lenin died about six years after coming to power, while Stalin ruled the Soviet Union for nearly thirty years.) The CCP cannot totally disassociate itself from the legacy of Mao without seriously undermining its legitimacy and its claim to be China's rightful ruling party.

This was particularly true for Deng Xiaoping. He was a veteran of the Long March and was among the top leaders at the founding of the regime and backed some of Mao's most disastrous campaigns, including the Anti-Rightist Campaign and the Great Leap Forward. As chapter 3 documents, Deng was for a long time one of Mao's favorites among the top party leadership, and Mao protected him from suffering even worse harm when he was purged for ideological mistakes in both 1966 and 1976.

Yet it was politically critical for Deng to separate himself from Mao's most radical ideas and particularly from the Cultural Revolution as he undertook his program of market reform and opening the Chinese economy to the world. To that end, he engineered a nuanced reevaluation of Mao that criticized the Chairman's errors and praised his accomplishments. This reevaluation never became a "de-Maoification" campaign. As Deng put it: "We will not do to Chairman Mao what Khrushchev did to Stalin" ("Answers to the Italian Journalist Oriana Fallaci," 1980). The Chairman's embalmed remains are on solemn public display—and still attract huge crowds—in a Memorial Hall in the center of Tiananmen Square, behind which is a souvenir store selling all sorts of Mao trinkets. Maoism has also lived on in some radical communist movements in other countries (see Box 5.2).

In 1981, the CCP issued a lengthy document called "Resolution on Certain Questions in the History of Our Party since the Founding of the People's Republic of China." Chapters 3 and 4 of this book note the political significance of the Resolution. The Resolution concluded that Mao's achievements were much greater than his mistakes, and it also spends many pages providing an assessment of Mao Zedong Thought. It reaffirms that his ideology remains "the valuable spiritual asset of our party" and that "it will be our guide to action for a long time to come." The document presents an extensive catalog of the ways in which Mao "enriched and developed Marxism-Leninism, including his ideas about a rural-based revolution that involved "encircling the cities from the countryside and finally winning countrywide victory"; his contributions to military theory, particularly guerrilla warfare and the need to develop a people's army; and some of his thoughts about guiding China through the transition to socialism.

The Resolution then focuses on "three basic points," which constitute "the living soul of Mao Zedong Thought" that are of continuing relevance to the CCP in how it legitimizes its rule in China. The first is "seek truth from facts," which, as noted earlier, conveys the pragmatic side of Maoism. The second is the "mass line" as the guiding principle of the party in "all its work":

BOX 5.2 MAOISM OUTSIDE OF CHINA

In the 1960s, many student activists in the United States and Western Europe were enamored with Maoism. The Cultural Revolution, and the ideology that guided it, seemed part of a worldwide struggle against oppressive authority, crass materialism, and imperialism—including the American war in Vietnam. They saw the Red Guards as kindred spirits in rebellion against stuffy professors, uptight administrators, and out-of-touch elders in general. After all, Chairman Mao had said things like "There are teachers who ramble on and on when they lecture; they should let their students doze off. If your lecture is no good, why insist on others listening to you? Rather than keeping your eyes open and listening to boring lectures, it is better to get some refreshing sleep. You don't have to listen to nonsense, you can rest your brain instead" ("Remarks at the Spring Festival," 1964).

Little did Mao's foreign admirers know of the terror being unleashed by the Red Guards against alleged "class enemies," many of whom were physically or psychologically brutalized, or the scale of cultural destruction that the young rebels caused.

A few Maoist organizations emerged outside of China from the tumult of the 1960s. Most of these have remained on the fringes of politics in their respective countries, including the Revolutionary Communist Party, USA, which was founded in 1975, or are now defunct. In a handful of countries, self-proclaimed Maoists have engaged in armed struggle against the government, the most active being in India, Nepal, and Peru.

Maoist guerrillas have been waging an insurgency in India or several decades, mostly in the eastern part of the country. The rebels are often referred to as the "Naxalites" after the region in the state of West Bengal where the movement began in 1967. It occasionally carries out assassinations of politicians, attacks police offices to gain weapons, and robs banks. It is estimated to have 10,000–20,000 members, with bases in nearly half of India's twenty-eight states where it effectively controls large parts of the countryside. They draw supporters largely from among the Adivasi (Sanskrit meaning, "original people") who are descendants of the first inhabitants of the Indian subcontinent. The 84 million Adivasi live mostly in densely forested areas and are among the most impoverished and discriminated against groups in India—which makes them, particularly the young, receptive to the call to revolution of the Naxalites. Although India's Maoists have never seriously contended for power, they remain a source of considerable worry for the government, especially in the states where their operations are expanding.

In neighboring Nepal, a tiny nation in the Himalayan Mountains, a Maoist party actually won the most seats in parliamentary elections in April 2008. A coalition with two other parties gave the head of the Communist Party of Nepal (Maoist) enough votes to be elected as the country's prime minister. The Maoists had been fighting a violent "people's war" against Nepal's monarchy for ten years until signing a peace agreement in 2006. During the war, which claimed an estimated 13,000 lives, the rebels gained widespread support in the rural areas of Nepal, which is one of the world's poorest countries. The party's founder is Pushpa Kumal Dahal, a school teacher-turned-guerrilla fighter, better known by his revolutionary name of Prachanda ("Fierce One"). Its ideology is officially called "Marxism-Leninism-Maoism-Prachanda Path," which reflects its leader's adaptation of communist theory, notably Mao Zedong's ideas about peasant revolution, to Nepal's particular situation, such as the combination of class and caste oppression. The Chinese Communist Party did not support the Maoist insurrection in Nepal because, from China's perspective, it was a destabilizing force in that part of the world.

Once the Nepali Maoists gave up armed struggle in order to participate in the democratic process, they had to tone down some of their most radical demands, but the party remains committed to pursuing social and economic justice. They also achieved one of their most important political aims: the abolition of the monarchy. In May 2008, the

Kingdom of Nepal was renamed the Democratic Federal Republic of Nepal. Prachanda served as Nepal's prime minister for about a year before resigning in a dispute with the country's president over who had the power to appoint the army chief of staff. Since then the Maoists have continued to play a major political role as one of the largest parties in Nepal.

Prachanda drew inspiration not only from the Chinese revolution but also from another communist movement that claimed a Maoist ideological lineage: the Shining Path (*Sendero Luminoso*) in Peru. Shining Path was established in the early 1980s, declaring that all of the world's ruling communist parties at the time, including the CCP under Deng Xiaoping and the CPSU under Gorbachev, had become revisionist counterrevolutionary organizations. Shining Path remained loyal to the most radical variation of Maoist thought and practice, as developed by its founder-leader, philosophy professor Abimael Guzmán, known as Gonzalo. "Gonzalo Thought" had its roots in the writings of earlier twentieth-century Peruvian revolutionaries and embodied elements based on the country's Indian heritage and culture. Shining Path gained some support among poor peasants in the Andes, but its extremely violent, often brutal, tactics, eroded its popularity. Guzmán and other top leaders of the movement were captured in the 1990s. The organization dwindled dramatically in size but remains sporadically active in remote areas of the country.

> As the vanguard of the proletariat, the party exists and fights for the interests of the people. But it always constitutes only a small part of the people, so that isolation from the people will render all the party's struggles and ideals devoid of content [and make success impossible]. To persevere in the revolution and advance the socialist cause, our party must uphold the mass line.

The final basic point of the "living soul" of Maoism is "independence and self-reliance." This encompasses the idea that China must chart its own way and must always "maintain our own national dignity and confidence and there must be no slavishness or submissiveness in any form in dealing with big, powerful or rich countries." This may sound somewhat ironic, given the depth of China's current integration in the international economy and its rise to great power status. But the idea of self-reliance persists in the PRC's contemporary statements on the overall orientation of its foreign policy.

The Resolution also warns against adopting "a dogmatic attitude towards the sayings of comrade Mao Zedong, to regard whatever he said as the unalterable truth which must be mechanically applied everywhere." It stresses that the CCP must acknowledge that Mao made serious blunders, especially in his later years, and that some of these were guided by parts of his ideology that simply were wrong. Mao is chastised for "enlarging the scope of class struggle and of impetuosity and rashness in economic construction." These errors were, of course, the basis of the three great tragedies of Maoist China from which the post-Mao leadership wants to cut the ideological cord: the Anti-Rightist Campaign, the Great Leap Forward, and the Cultural Revolution.

Finally, as a way to depersonalize even the positive components of Mao Zedong Thought, the Resolution declares that the ideology of the CCP is "a crystallization of the collective wisdom" of the Chinese Communist Party, not the product of one person. "Many outstanding leaders of our party" made "important contributions" to "the scientific works of comrade Mao Zedong." Mao's problem was that he deviated from his own "scientific" ideas, as well as from the "collective wisdom" of the party leadership. In other words, we will all take credit for what has gone right since the founding of the PRC and the Chairman's good ideas; what went wrong, well, that was *his* fault and the result of *his* faulty ideas. This is still the official evaluation of Mao Zedong Thought in China. By establishing the principle that the guiding ideology of the CCP is the result of collective wisdom rather than the product of any single individual, the party was partly dethroning Mao but also opening up the possibilities for further "important contributions" to Chinese communism by future leaders.

Deng Xiaoping Theory

If Mao Zedong is often seen as a "revolutionary romantic" guided by a radical ideology and impervious to practical concerns, then Deng Xiaoping is, in contrast, viewed as the ultimate pragmatist who had little use for communist theory. Both are exaggerations that distort any thorough understanding of what made these two towering figures in modern Chinese history tick. As pointed out previously, Maoism has a significant pragmatic element, and the Chairman's dictum to "seek truth from facts" became an early watchword of the Deng regime and remains so today. Likewise, Deng Xiaoping did have a distinctive ideological bent that shaped his political choices and the way that he used his power.

Although he never took for himself the formal top positions in either the party or the state, Deng Xiaoping was often referred to in the Chinese media while he was alive as China's "paramount leader" and as the "architect of China's reform and opening up." After his death in 1997, **Deng Xiaoping Theory** was added into the CCP constitution, along with Marxism-Leninism and Mao Zedong Thought, as the party's guiding ideology. Deng Xiaoping Theory was said to be

> the outcome of the integration of the basic tenets of Marxism-Leninism with the practice of contemporary China and the features of the times, a continuation and development of Mao Zedong Thought under new historical conditions; it represents a new stage of development of Marxism in China, it is Marxism of contemporary China and it is the crystallized, collective wisdom of the Communist Party of China. It is guiding the socialist modernization of China from victory to victory. (General Program, Constitution of the Communist Party of China)

Building Socialism with Chinese Characteristics

Some of the central features of Deng's ideological contribution to the CCP are conveyed under the general rubric of **Building Socialism with Chinese Characteristics**. Mao, it is inferred, successfully led the communist party to power in 1949 and for the first few years in power before he began to make serious mistakes in his policies to build socialism in China. Deng picked up not where Mao had *left off* when he died in 1976, but where he had *gone wrong*, beginning in the mid-1950s with the Anti-Rightist

Campaign and the Great Leap Forward. Deng provided the CCP with the theory that correctly addressed the "basic questions concerning the building, consolidation and development of socialism in China," which is precisely where Mao is said to have failed.

Deng Xiaoping Theory gives absolute priority to economic development (under party leadership, of course)—while Mao Zedong Thought, though certainly not shunning that as a goal, put "politics in command." As Deng noted in 1984, in an off-handed slap at Mao, "What is socialism and what is Marxism? *We were not quite clear about this in the past.* Marxism attaches utmost importance to developing the productive forces. . . . One of our shortcomings after the founding of the People's Republic was that we didn't pay enough attention to developing the productive forces. Socialism means eliminating poverty. Pauperism is not socialism, still less communism" ("Build Socialism with Chinese Characteristics," 1984; emphasis added).

Building Socialism with Chinese Characteristics is the party's way of explaining in ideological terms the introduction of market reforms into China's economy and for letting aspects of capitalism (such as the profit motive and private ownership of businesses) be the driving force for the country's economic development. It is, in essence, the updated version of Deng's "cat theory," first expounded in 1962 when he said: "It doesn't matter if a cat is white or black, as long as it catches mice." He meant that the measure of success of any economic policy should be whether it leads to increased production, not whether it meet some abstract ideological standard. He expressed this view in support of allowing farmers more economic freedom as part of the effort to recover from the Great Leap Famine. Such ideas got Deng into big political trouble with Mao during the Cultural Revolution. Once he had returned to power in the late 1970s, Deng really let the capitalist cat loose and transformed the PRC's centrally planned economy into a mix of socialism and capitalism that since the 1990s has been called a "socialist market economy." The nature of that transformation and the extent of the marketization of China's economy is discussed in chapter 8.

Deng Xiaoping Theory rationalizes the adoption of a "socialist market economy" by positing that China is in the "primary," or "initial stage" of socialism. Based on the orthodox Marxist view that history inevitably passes through a sequence of stages of development, the primary stage of socialism is that which follows immediately after the political overthrow of the capitalist system. For some period of time, it would be unavoidable, in fact, absolutely necessary, to use many aspects of capitalism while building socialism. And this, it is implied, is where Mao Zedong (and his Thought) got it wrong. Although in the early 1950s, during the first period of communist rule in China, Mao said the PRC would have a mixed economy, he came to believe that the transition to socialism could happen much faster and all aspects of capitalism done away with much sooner (a reflection of his voluntarism) and began the country's full socialist transformation in 1954. In contrast, Deng is credited with correctly recognizing that socialist China, even in the late twentieth century and beyond, would have to use capitalist means to become developed enough to move on to the next stages of the socialist transition. Even more un-Maoist are some of the slogans often associated with Deng Xiaoping Theory, such as "Let some people get rich first" and "To get rich is glorious."

Deng was adamant that China would not become capitalist even if it used many aspects of a capitalist market economy to promote development. Rather, he insisted that "we can develop a market economy under socialism. . . . Developing a market economy does not mean practicing capitalism" ("We Can Develop a Market Economy under Socialism," 1979).

The critical difference between a socialist market economy and a capitalist market economy seems largely to be a matter of who has political power in the country. In Deng's view, in a capitalist country, wealthy capitalists (owners of private property) dominate both the economic and political systems. In a socialist system, political power is in the hands of the vanguard communist party that represents the interests of the "people." It is the party that will make sure that the socialist market economy does not lead to the kind of exploitation and inequalities that mar a truly capitalist system and that the market part of the economy ultimately serves the goal of building socialism and achieving communism.

The Four Cardinal Principles

If Building Socialism with Chinese Characteristics conveys the economic heart of Deng Xiaoping Theory, the Four Cardinal Principles express its political essence.[31] The phrase "Four Cardinal Principles" comes from a lengthy speech that Deng gave in March 1979 at a forum on the party's theoretical work very soon after he had consolidated his position as China's undisputed leader. In this context, "cardinal" means essential or fundamental.

The speech did not gather much attention outside of the PRC at the time because most of the world was focused on the economic changes Deng was bringing to the country. He had been named *Time* magazine's "Man of the Year" for 1978 (in the January 1, 1979, issue) and was grandly feted in an official visit to the United States in late January/early February 1979. In retrospect, the speech is one of the most important Deng ever gave, and the Four Cardinal Principles are as essential as Building Socialism with Chinese Characteristics is to understanding Deng Xiaoping Theory.

The purpose of the forum at which Deng gave this speech was to set the ideological and political guidelines for the party's shift in the focus of its work from the class struggle of the Cultural Revolution and late Maoist era to economic development. In the speech, Deng reiterated that modernization would be the party's "main task for the present and for some time to come." He then laid out what he called the Four Cardinal Principles that were "the basic prerequisite for achieving modernization":

1. Upholding the socialist road.
2. Upholding the dictatorship of the proletariat.
3. Upholding the leadership of the communist party.
4. Upholding Marxism-Leninism and Mao Zedong Thought.

Deng asserted that only by following these principles in carrying out economic reform could the party be sure that it was fostering *socialist* modernization rather than promoting capitalism, as some in the party were contending would happen if China followed Deng's path. Deng also stressed that ideological reinforcement was urgently

needed at that particular time, which coincided with the Democracy Wall movement of the late 1970s (see chap. 4). Deng warned in this speech of certain "incidents"
incited by "bad elements" who raised slogans like "Give us human rights!" and set up
organizations such as the "Democracy Forum." "Can we tolerate this kind of freedom
of speech?" Deng asked. "No Party member . . . must ever waver in the slightest on this
basic stand. To undermine any of the Four Cardinal Principles is to undermine the
whole cause of socialism in China, the whole cause of modernization."

Deng went into great detail about the meaning and importance of each of the four
principles. But they really all boil down to the principle of upholding the leadership
of the communist party. It is the party that will keep China on the socialist road; it is
the party that enforces the dictatorship of the proletariat; it is the party that interprets
the current meaning of Marxism-Leninism–Mao Zedong Thought. And about party
leadership, Deng declared:

> In the China of today we can never dispense with leadership by the Party and extol
> the spontaneity of the masses. Party leadership, of course, is not infallible, and the
> problem of how the Party can maintain close links with the masses and exercise cor-
> rect and effective leadership is still one that we must seriously study and try to solve.
> But this can never be made a pretext for demanding the weakening or liquidation of
> the Party's leadership.

The Four Cardinal Principles do not reflect the kind of sharp break with Mao Zedong
Thought that the make-way-for-capitalism emphasis of Building Socialism with
Chinese Characteristics does. In fact, the principles represent one of the clearer ide-
ological continuities between the two leaders.

The Four Cardinal Principles are very similar to the "six criteria" that Mao laid out
in the revised version of his 1957 speech, "On the Correct Handling of Contradictions
among the People" during the Hundred Flowers Movement. Mao said that these
criteria should be used to distinguish between "fragrant flowers" (nonantagonistic
contradictions) and "poisonous weeds" (antagonistic contradictions) when judging
how to treat criticism of China's political system and leaders. The key distinction was
whether the criticism was helpful or hurtful to six indisputable aspects of politics
in the PRC, including the unity of "the people of all our nationalities"; the goal of
"socialist transformation and socialist construction"; the people's democratic dictatorship; "democratic centralism"; "the leadership of the Communist Party"; and
"international socialist unity and the unity of the peace-loving people of the world."
The Four Cardinal Principles is certainly a variation on a Maoist theme, and as Mao
emphasized, "Of these six criteria, the most important are the two about the socialist
path and the leadership of the Party."

During the era of his rule, Deng Xiaoping often invoked the Four Cardinal
Principles, including in the aftermath of the Beijing Massacre in June 1989. In his
"Address to Officers at the Rank of General and Above in Command of the Troops
Enforcing Martial Law in Beijing," (June 9, 1989), Deng commented that

> It is not wrong to keep to the Four Cardinal Principles. If we have made a mistake,
> it is that we have not kept to them consistently enough and inculcated them as basic
> ideas in the people, the students and all cadres and Party members. . . . True, we

have talked about keeping to those principles, conducting ideological and political work and combating bourgeois liberalization and mental pollution. But we have not talked about those things consistently. . . . The mistake was not in the principles themselves, but in the failure to keep to them consistently enough and to do a good job in education and in ideological and political work.

The Four Cardinal Principles were written into the CCP constitution in 1992 at the same time Building Socialism with Chinese Characteristics was added, which was a prelude to the formal inclusion of Deng Xiaoping Theory as part of the CCP's guiding ideology in 1999. The principles themselves, though not the phrase "Four Cardinal Principles," were incorporated into the Preamble of the constitution of the PRC in 1993, which gave them the force of law.[32] They remain today part of the CCP's core doctrine. As the former party leader Hu Jintao remarked in his report to the 18th Party Congress in November 2012 as he was about to hand over power to Xi Jinping, "Taking the path of socialism with Chinese characteristics means we must, under the leadership of the Communist Party of China and basing ourselves on China's realities, take economic development as the central task and adhere to the Four Cardinal Principles and the policy of reform and opening up."[33]

Understanding these two aspects of Deng Xiaoping Theory—Building Socialism with Chinese Characteristics and the Four Cardinal Principles—reveals the operational code of China's communist leaders as they continue to navigate the delicate balance between promoting an increasingly open economy and keeping a firm grip on power.

Jiang Zemin and the Theory of the Three Represents

Deng Xiaoping seems to have set, intentionally or otherwise, the precedent that the top leader of the CCP has the right to make an "original contribution" to the CCP's guiding ideology that conveys the theory behind major policy initiatives of that leader's administration. Both Jiang Zemin and Hu Jintao did this, each praising and building on the contributions of his predecessors while adapting them to the priorities of the times.

Jiang's ideological innovation is called the **Three Represents**, which he first expressed during an inspection tour of Guangdong province in February 2000. He noted at the time that the CCP should always represent "the development trend of China's advanced productive forces, the orientation of China's advanced culture, and the fundamental interests of the overwhelming majority of the Chinese people."[34]

What this boiled down to was a reaffirmation of Deng's modernization program and economic reforms. But there was also an important element of innovation that was made clear only through further explication and other formulations of the Three Represents and how it was actually put into practice. During his last term in office (1997–2002), Jiang took the bold step of leading the CCP to recognize the crucial role of the so-called **new social strata** as the most dynamic force in China's economic development. The new social strata include groups that had been created during the process of market reform and internationalization, most importantly private entrepreneurs, managers, and technical staff as well as professionals, intellectuals, and others who are self-employed or work outside the public sector of the economy. The Three Represents theory was an ideological rationalization for allowing members of these strata to join the CCP. In other words, in a truly innovative and ironic adaptation of Marxism-Leninism, capitalists—as representatives of China's "most advanced productive forces"—were welcome in the Communist Party!

At a broader ideological level, Jiang's Three Represents implied that the CCP was moving to cast itself as the representative, not just of the working classes but also of "the overwhelming majority of the Chinese people." Some scholars see this as reflecting an even more profound transformation of the CCP's self-image of its role from being a "revolutionary party" committed and empowered to lead the nation toward socialism and communism to that of a "governing party," which implies a less ideological claim about its purpose and an effort to broaden its base of political support in Chinese society.[35]

As discussed in chapter 4, when Jiang Zemin began to put forth the ideas of the Three Represents, he ran into significant political opposition from conservative party leaders who were particularly unhappy with such an open embrace of private entrepreneurs (they are never officially referred to as "capitalists") by the CCP. But in the end, he and his supporters prevailed. Jiang's theoretical contributions were inscribed in the party (2002) and state (2003) constitutions, and the CCP's guiding ideology was formally dubbed "Marxism-Leninism, Mao Zedong Thought, Deng Xiaoping Theory, and the important thought of the Three Represents."

Hu Jintao's Scientific Outlook on Development

The constitutional enshrinement of the Three Represents took place at party and state congresses in 2002/2003, which were also the moments of transition in leadership from Jiang Zemin to Hu Jintao. Although there had been clear signs of political rivalry between Jiang and Hu, Hu became effusive in his praise of his predecessor and his ideological contributions. The three-volume collection of *The Selected Works of Jiang Zemin* was published with great propaganda fanfare in 2006, followed by a national campaign, aimed largely at party cadres to study Jiang's writings.

While paying due respect to the "important thought of the Three Represents," Hu also carved out an ideological niche of his own.[36] Soon after he had become CCP general secretary (2002) and PRC president (2003), Hu began to enunciate slogans and signal policy priorities with a definite populist tinge. Hu's brand of populism was very different from Mao's, which was mostly a matter of mobilizing the masses to take action in support of his agenda. In contrast, Hu was a populist in the sense of advocating policies that addressed some of the socioeconomic downsides of China's three decades of spectacular growth: inequitable income distribution among people and regions; unemployment; and inadequate public services, particularly health care. Special emphasis was placed on combating rural poverty and narrowing the vast rural-urban gap. The country's very serious environmental problems and the necessity for sustainable development were also high on Hu's agenda.

The overall goal of these policy priorities was said to be the creation of a "harmonious socialist society," the underlying assumption being that unless these issues were addressed, social and political instability would increase and lead to disharmony. The extent of protests by displaced workers, discontented farmers, and citizens angered about pollution during his years in power certainly influenced Hu's thinking.

The idea of a harmonious socialist society with its calls for "social justice" and "putting people first" was an implicit critique of Jiang Zemin's growth-at-any-cost and rather elitist economic strategy (and Deng Xiaoping's, as well). Hu faced some resistance to his effort to shift the focus of the party's work in a more populist direction from those leaders who did not want resources diverted away from the more prosperous coastal areas and modern sectors of the economy. Nevertheless, some progress in these areas was made during the Hu years, for example, in the expansion of health insurance (see chap. 13).

Hu Jintao's policy and ideological initiatives were formally endorsed at the 17th CCP Congress in late 2007. They were written into the party constitution with statements such as "The Communist Party of China leads the people in building a harmonious socialist society" added to the preamble. The more general formulation of Hu's input to the CCP's ideology is presented as the "Scientific Outlook on Development" that "calls for comprehensive, balanced, and sustainable development."

When Hu retired as general secretary at 18th CCP Congress in November 2012 his ideological embellishment was added to Chinese communism's pantheon of guiding theories with the party constitution being amended to proclaim that "The Communist Party of China takes Marxism-Leninism, Mao Zedong Thought, Deng Xiaoping Theory, the important thought of Three Represents, and the Scientific Outlook on Development as its guide to action." A full paragraph was also added to the opening section of the constitution explaining how Hu's ideas "represent the latest achievement in adapting Marxism to China's conditions."

XI JINPING THOUGHT FOR A NEW ERA

It was a few years into Hu Jintao's rule that his "harmonious society" stamp on CCP ideology became apparent. But within two weeks of taking over as party leader in late 2012, Xi Jinping started touting his vision of the "China Dream," which many observers concluded was the opening round in formulating his signature contribution to the party's guiding ideology. The China Dream was about "the rejuvenation of the Chinese nation" that would bring even greater prosperity to the Chinese people and elevate the PRC's role in the world.[37]

Throughout Xi's first term in office (2012–2017), the China Dream was one of the most consistent drumbeats in the official media. It became a mandatory subject of study for party and government officials, was written into school textbooks, and heavily featured in propaganda billboards that dotted urban landscapes throughout the country. It appeared that Xi Jinping's thinking would gradually evolve and, as it had for his two immediate predecessors, be enshrined in the party constitution when he left office in 2022.

But, as preparations for the 19th CCP Congress in the fall of 2017 that would mark the start of Xi's second term unfolded, it became apparent that there would be a break with precedent and that his signature ideology would be formally recognized at that meeting. When that happened, it was unveiled as Xi Jinping Thought on Socialism with Chinese Characteristics for a New Era, a vastly expanded version of the China Dream. Beyond its early canonization, there were a couple of other things that were quite remarkable in the choice of this designation.

First, with his personal name attached to the ideology, Xi's thinking seems to have been put on a par with Mao Zedong Thought and Deng Xiaoping Theory and well above that of his two immediate predecessors, Jiang Zemin and Hu Jintao, whose names do not appear along with their theoretical contributions. Second, by declaring his thought to define a "new era" in the history of the PRC that began when he came to power in 2012, Xi was staking a claim that his personal leadership was of historic importance to the party, the people, and the nation.

Xi views the history of the PRC up to 2012 as being divided into two major periods: the revolutionary era under Mao (1949–1976) in which China "stood up" against foreign imperialism and established its independence, and the reform era (1978–2012) under Deng Xiaoping, Jiang Zemin, and Hu Jintao that had set China on the path to economic growth and modernization. The new era with Xi in charge will build on the past successes of the earlier ones to take the PRC to the next level of economic development and national power. Its goals are that the PRC should become a "moderately well-off society" by 2021 (the 100th anniversary of the founding of the CCP) and "a modern socialist country that is prosperous, strong, democratic, culturally advanced, and harmonious" by 2049 (the 100th anniversary of the establishment of the PRC).[38] In other words, like the previous two eras, the new era for which Xi Jinping Thought is the ideological beacon guiding the party and the country will last more than three decades (2012–2049).[39]

In his three-and-a half hour long report to the 19th CCP Congress, Xi focused extensively on spelling out the content and policy implications of his ideology. This was framed by identifying the "principal contradiction"—in other words, the main issue facing the CCP—for the new era as that "between unbalanced and inadequate development and the people's ever-growing needs for a better life," which requires the party to "devote great energy to addressing development's imbalances and inadequacies, and push hard to improve the quality and effect of development." The Xi era will both accelerate the achievements and also rectify some of the shortcomings of the first thirty years of the reform era, including persisting environmental degradation and socioeconomic inequality: Xi Jinping Thought is to be the ideological blueprint for doing so.

Part of that blueprint will inform the economic policies of the PRC as it strives to reach a higher level of development (see chap. 8). There is also a very important part that falls under the rubric of "modernizing China's system and capacity for governance." This involves such goals as "securing a sweeping victory against corruption," improving the caliber of party-state officials, and strengthening the legal system. But the paramount emphasis is on enhancing and deepening the CCP's ideological influence and political control. In his report to the 19th Party Congress, Xi listed "Ensuring Party Leadership in All Work" as the number one point when enumerating "the essence and rich implications of the Thought on Socialism with Chinese Characteristics for a New Era" that every CCP member should "fully and faithfully apply . . . in all our work." He then proclaimed that "the party exercises overall leadership over all areas of endeavor—over the party, government, military, people, and intellectuals—in every part of the country."

To affirm this central point of Xi Jinping Thought, the CCP constitution was amended to say "Leadership of the Communist Party of China is the most essential attribute of socialism with Chinese characteristics, and the greatest strength of this system." And, perhaps even more significantly, the PRC constitution was amended to include a similar declaration—the first time the CCP has ever been mentioned outside of the preamble in the body of the document.

In many ways, the prominent emergence of Xi Jinping Thought is a reflection of Xi's swift and thorough consolidation of personal authority in China's party-state (see chaps. 4 and 6). He is now the PRC's most powerful leader since at least Deng—and perhaps since Mao as Deng had serious rivals during his first decade or so at the top and had to operate in an environment of collective leadership that Xi appears to have dispensed with.[40]

The CCP now declares\ that it "uses Marxism-Leninism, Mao Zedong Thought, Deng Xiaoping Theory, the Theory of Three Represents, the Scientific Outlook on Development, and Xi Jinping Thought on Socialism with Chinese Characteristics for a New Era as its guides to action." Given the current dynamics in Chinese elite politics, it would not be surprising if it was quite some while before another leader's ideological contribution is added to this already lengthy list of milestones in the evolution of Chinese communism.

CONCLUSION: IDEOLOGY IN A CHANGING CHINA

The ascendency of Xi Jinping Thought suggests that ideology still matters very much in Chinese politics. It is not simply empty rhetoric and noisy propaganda. It expresses the worldview of the CCP leadership and informs their policy choices, both at home and abroad. Under Xi, the party has assigned a high priority to the ideological education of it cadres requiring them to take courses at special schools and often convenes "theoretical work conferences" to spread the word about new wrinkles in official doctrine.

And there are campaigns to publicize ideology among the population as a whole, often in a less direct Marxist-Leninist guise, such as the campaigns to promote various types of "civilization" that the CCP says it is trying to create, including "material civilization" (modernization and economic reform), "spiritual civilization" (cultural pride, patriotism, ethical behavior, abiding by the law),[41] and, most recently "ecological civilization "(green development). The party is cast as the vanguard in the building of these civilizations and the only party that can lead the entire people of China toward a brighter future. Not exactly the same as building socialism and reaching communism under the party's wise leadership, but the idea is very similar, just packaged for broader appeal.

The CCP has also injected a strong element of nationalism into the legitimizing ideology of the party-state. Many scholars have pointed to the CCP's efforts to portray itself as the manager of China's great economic success (and the only thing standing between prosperity and great chaos) and also as the guardian of the nation's sovereignty and the promoter of its international image.[42] Whatever else one can say about the terrible costs of Mao's rule, he did found a nation that has stood on its own and greatly elevated its stature in the world. The CCP can still draw on that deep reservoir of nationalist legitimacy.

But it also can, and does, point to more contemporary signifiers of China's international status, such as the hosting of the 2008 Beijing Olympics and the 2010 World Expo or the rapt attention Xi Jinping receives when he addresses the World Economic Forum in Davos, Switzerland, an annual invitation-only gathering of influential business executives, political leaders, academics, journalists, celebrities, and other opinion makers. At times, the party-state has fanned (and then controlled) anti-Japanese or anti-American sentiment to arouse the patriotic spirit of the Chinese people. The message is clear: the CCP was the savior of the nation, and it remains the protector of its interests. This message is supplemented by official presentations of the greatness, uniqueness, and antiquity of Chinese culture and civilization.

There have been serious ideological debates within the CCP during much of the reform era. Party leaders and intellectuals on the so-called "New Left" take the position that the CCP has strayed too far from its socialist ideals, particularly egalitarianism. In contrast, the "New Right" staunchly defend the Chinese version of **neoliberalism** that favors free market-friendly policies and decries most state interventions in the economy, even to ensure more equitable outcomes. Then there are the "conservatives" who emphasize social stability, morality, political order, and economic growth.[43] This ideological debate sometimes got quite vigorous, particularly in journal articles, even if all sides agreed on the sanctity of communist party leadership. But the advent of Xi Jinping Thought as the new party orthodoxy will probably stifle or at least further marginalize such ideological debates.

The focus of this chapter has been on the *official* ideology of the CCP and how that ideology has both shaped and reflected different stages in the political development of the CCP and the PRC. But there are multiple other ideological influences that are also much in evidence in the PRC, and some of them should be noted, at least in passing, as they are likely to continue to play an important role in the politics of a rapidly changing China.

The most potent and pervasive contending ideology is probably "consumerism."[44] Can the preoccupation with buying and acquiring things of value (and increasing value) really be considered an ideology? Yes, to the extent that many people take it as a guide to action and a measure of their own value. Contrary as this is to any standard of Marxism, it is hard to deny that this is the most prevalent ideology in China today. As one scholar of Chinese culture noted, the philosophical essence of contemporary China could be conveyed as "I shop, therefore, I am."[45] A slew of other analyses of China from the 1990s to the present convey the same conclusion in catch-all phrases such as the PRC meaning the "People's Republic of Capitalism," or other characterizations like "From Communism to Consumerism," "Cashing in on

Communism," "From MAOsim to MEism," and the "Great Mall of China"[46] to describe life and values in the PRC today.

But is consumerism a *political* ideology? Not directly, but it certainly has political implications. If many of the Chinese people, and especially the growing middle class, are fixated on improving their material lives (and who can blame them after generations of deprivation?), then that is a message the ruling party has to pay heed to in order to maintain popular support, which it seems to have done. Opinion polls show that private entrepreneurs, in general, are strong supporters of the CCP and the status quo.[47]

Religion has also remerged in China as a central focus in the lives of many citizens. Estimates of the number of religious believers in China vary widely. Officially, it is given as 100 million, including Buddhists, Muslims, Taoists, and Christians. Unofficial figures run as high as 350 million, with the number of Protestants alone put at 93 million–115 million.[48] Religion is not a political ideology per se, but, as is evident in today's world, it can become highly politicized. For most of the Mao era, religious organizations were severely repressed or closely controlled by the party-state. The constraints on religion have been gradually loosened during the reform era. The PRC constitution has long affirmed freedom of religion, but with restrictive clauses such as the state only "protects *normal* religious activities" (emphasis added).

In 2007, the CCP constitution was amended to mention religion for the first time. Although the party remains officially atheist, the General Program of the CCP as laid out in the constitution now states "The Party strives to fully implement its basic principle for its work related to religious affairs, and rallies religious believers in making contributions to economic and social development."[49] But, in another sign of his determination to preempt any threat to the party's ideological hegemony, Xi Jinping has insisted that all religions must adapt to Chinese culture and socialism. As an official government report issued in April 2018 put it, religious groups should be guided "to support the leadership of the CCP and the socialist system; uphold and follow the path of socialism with Chinese characteristics; develop religions in the Chinese context; embrace core socialist values; carry forward China's fine traditions; integrate religious teachings and rules with Chinese culture; abide by state laws and regulations, and accept state administration in accordance with the law."[50]

Then there's democracy. This is an ideology that it would be hard for the communist party to incorporate or co-opt without changing its very essence. To acknowledge the rights of citizens, the accountability of leaders, the rule of law, the political competition, and a free press that are core values of democracy are inconsistent with the CCP's claim to be *the* ruling party and to exercise the "leading role" in all aspects of Chinese society.

Organized public expressions of demands for democratization have been nearly nonexistent since the Tiananmen crackdown in June 1989. The one notable exception was the effort to establish a China Democracy Party ten years later: although the founders followed the rules for registering a new organization, the leaders of the party were arrested and sent to prison for endangering state security. When Xi Jinping declares that one of his goals for PRC in the new era is for the country to become "democratic," he does not mean that China will become a multiparty democracy but a more modern form of a **socialist democracy**, which, like everything, is under the leadership of the CCP. In April 2013, shortly after he became the country's top leader, the CCP Central Committee issued a document that depicted the ideological situation in China "as a complicated, intense struggle" and warned party members to be on guard against seven "false ideological trends," including "Western Constitutional Democracy," "the West's idea of journalism," and "promoting civil society and Western-style theories of governance."[51]

The Xi Jinping era will not be a hospitable time for China's democracy advocates and activists. But given the deepening of the PRC's interdependence with the global community and the rise in the living standards and educational level of its people, it is quite likely that the time will come when the leadership of the communist party will again have to decide how to respond to the challenge of the "democratic idea."[52]

NOTES

1. Franz Schurmann, *Ideology and Organization in Communist China* (Berkeley: University of California Press, 1966).

2. Alexander L. George, "The 'Operational Code': A Neglected Approach to the Study of Political Leaders and Decision-Making," *International Studies Quarterly* 13, no. 2 (June 1969): 190–222.

3. I'd like to thank an anonymous reviewer for reminding me of this important caveat about the functions of ideology. Indeed, even Marx (and Engels) noted that the "ruling ideas" of any era "are nothing more than the ideal expression of the dominant material relationships, the dominant material relationships grasped as ideas; hence of the relationships which make the one class the ruling one, therefore, the ideas of their dominance" (*The German Ideology*, 1846).

4. For a strong argument that ideology still matters a great deal in Chinese politics – and is, in fact, essential to understanding China in the Xi Jinping era, see, John Garnaut, "Engineers of the Soul: Ideology in Xi Jinping's China, Aug. 2017, published on Sinocism, January 16, 2019, https://nb.sinocism.com/p/engineers-of-the-soul-ideology-in

5. For the full text in English of the Constitution of the Communist Party of China as amended in 2017, see http://www.china.org.cn/20171105-001.pdf.

6. See John W. Lewis and Xue Litai, "Social Change and Political Reform in China: Meeting the Challenge of Success," *China Quarterly* 176 (Dec. 2003): 926–942.

7. Quotations from the works of Marx, Engels, Lenin, Mao, Deng et al., will be cited by title and date in the text or parenthetically rather than in a reference note. All of these works are easily accessible online via such web sites as "The Marxist Internet Archive," (http://www.marxists.org/).

8. See Lars T. Lih, *Lenin Rediscovered: What Is to Be Done? In Context* (Boston: Brill, 2006).

9. See Arif Dirlik, *The Origins of Chinese Communism* (New York: Oxford University Press, 1989), chap. 1.

10. See Raymond F. Wylie, *The Emergence of Maoism: Mao Tse-tung, Ch'en Po-ta, and the Search for Chinese Theory, 1935–1945* (Stanford, CA: Stanford University Press, 1980).

11. See Stuart R. Schram, "Chinese and Leninist Components in the Personality of Mao Tse-Tung," *Asian Survey*, vol. 3, no. 6, 260.

12. Schurmann, *Ideology and Organization*, 21.

13. For one analysis of this debate, see Nick Knight, "The Marxism of Mao Zedong: Empiricism and the Discourse in the Field of Mao Studies," *Australian Journal of Chinese Affairs*, no.16. (July 1986): 7–22.

14. See, for example, Jung Chang and Jon Halliday, *Mao: The Unknown Story* (New York: Knopf, 2005).

15. Sergeï Khrushchev, *Memoirs of Nikita Khrushchev*, trans. and ed. George Shriver, vol. 3, *Statesman (1953–54)* (College Park: Pennsylvania State University Press, 2007), 405.

16. See, for example, Jan-Werner Müller, *What is Populism?* (Philadelphia: University of Pennsylvania Press, 2016).

17. Laura Grattan, *Populism's Power: Radical Grassroots Democracy in America*. (New York: Columbia University Press, 2016): 9

18. As cited in Stuart R. Schram, *China Quarterly* 49 (Jan.–Mar. 1972): 76–78.

19. Brantly Womack, "The Party and the People: Revolutionary and Post-Revolutionary Politics in China and Vietnam," *World Politics* 39, no. 4 (July 1987): 479–507.

20. See, for example, Maurice J. Meisner, *Marxism, Maoism, and Utopianism: Eight Essays* (Madison: University of Wisconsin Press, 1982).

21. Besides "The Foolish Old Man," the other two constantly read articles were "Serve the People," in which Mao lauds the sacrifice for the revolutionary cause of a common soldier, and "In Memory of Norman Bethune," in which Mao praises a Canadian doctor who came to China to aid the revolution (and died there) as an example of proletarian internationalism.

22. Stuart R. Schram, *The Thought of Mao Tse-tung* (New York: Cambridge University Press, 1989), 84.

23. Garnaut, "Engineers of the Human Soul"; Alexander V. Panstov and Steven I. Levine, *Mao: The Real Story* (New York: Simon and Shuster, 2013), 335. Panstov and Levine write that Stalin's *Short Course* "served as [Mao's] model."

24. Garnaut, "Engineers of the Human Soul." Garnaut says of Stalin's *Short Course*, "The most important lines in the book: 'As the revolution deepens, class struggle intensifies' and 'The Party becomes strong by purging itself.'"

25. Cited in Tang Tsou, "Mao Tse-tung Thought, the Last Struggle for Succession, and the Post-Mao Era," *China Quarterly*, no. 70 (1977): 518.

26. See Franz Schurmann, "On Revolutionary Conflict," *Journal of International Affairs* 23, no. 1 (1969): 36–53.

27. Milovan Djilas, *The New Class: An Analysis of the Communist System* (New York: Praeger, 1957).

28. For excellent discussions of this topic, see Nick Knight, *Rethinking Mao: Explorations in Mao Zedong Thought* (Lanham, MD: Lexington Books, 2007), 225ff.; and Stuart R. Schram, "Mao Tse-tung and the Theory of the Permanent Revolution, 1958–69," *China Quarterly* 46 (June 1971): 221–244.

29. Schram, "Mao Tse-tung and the Theory of the Permanent Revolution."

30. "On the New Democracy," 1940, and "Reform Our Study," 1941; see Deng Xiaoping, "Hold High the Banner of Mao Zedong Thought and Adhere to the Principle of Seeking Truth from Facts," *Selected Works of Deng Xiaoping*, Sept. 16, 1978.

31. In yet another twist of ideological phrasing, Deng Xiaoping Theory is often summed up as consisting of "one central task, two basic points," the one central task being economic development, and the two basic points are upholding the Four Cardinal Principles and the policy of market reform and opening to the outside world.

32. The PRC Constitution uses the phrase, "people's democratic dictatorship," rather than "dictatorship of the proletariat." This is more than semantics, but the two terms imply essentially the same thing: that there are those in society over whom dictatorship needs to be exercised.

33. "Hu Jintao's Report at 18th Party Congress," Nov. 18, 2012, http://www.globaltimes.cn/content/744880.shtml.

34. Li Yu, "Red Star Over China," *Beijing Review*, June 28, 2011, http://www.scmp.com/news/china/policies-politics/article/2110433/chinas-underground-churches-head-cover-crackdown-closes

35. Joseph Fewsmith, "Studying the Three Represents," *China Leadership Monitor* 8 (Fall 2003).

36. Heike Holbig, "Remaking the CCP's Ideology: Determinants, Progress, and Limits under Hu Jintao," *Journal of Current Chinese Affairs* 38, no. 3 (2009): 35–61.

37. "Xi Jinping, "Achieving Rejuvenation Is the Dream of the Chinese People," Nov. 29, 2012, in Xi Jinping, *The Governance of China*, vol. 1. (Beijing: Foreign Language Press, 2014): 37–39.

38. Xi Jinping, "Secure a Decisive Victory in Building a Moderately Prosperous Society in All Respects and Strive for the Great Success of Socialism with Chinese Characteristics for a New Era," report delivered at the 19th National Congress of the Communist Party of China, Oct. 18, 2017, http://www.xinhuanet.com/english/download/Xi_Jinping's_report_at_19th_CPC_National_Congress.pdf

39. David Zweig, "A New Era Dawns for Xi Jinping's China, but What Will It Mean for the Rest of the World?," *South China Morning Post*, Oct. 25, 2017, http://www.scmp.com/comment/insight-opinion/article/2116902/new-era-dawns-xi-jinpings-china-what-will-it-mean-rest-world

40. See Joseph Fewsmith, "The 19th Party Congress: Ringing in Xi Jinping's New Age," *China Leadership Monitor*, no. 55, Winter 2018, https://www.hoover.org/research/19th-party-congress-ringing-xi-jinpings-new-age

41. Nicholas Dynon, "'Four Civilizations' and the Evolution of Post-Mao Chinese Socialist Ideology," *China Journal* 60 (July 2008): 83–110.

42. See, for example, Peter Hayes Gries, *China's New Nationalism: Pride, Politics, and Diplomacy* (Berkeley: University of California Press, 2004).

43. Peter Moody, *Conservative Thought in Contemporary China* (Lanham, MD: Lexington Books, 2007).

44. Lianne Yu, *Consumption in China: How China's New Consumer Ideology is Shaping the Nation* (New York: Polity, 2014).

45. Geremie Barmé, "Soft Porn, Packaged Dissent and Nationalism: Notes on Chinese Culture in the 1990's," *Current History* 93: 584 (Sept. 1994): 270-277.

46. See, for example, the Discovery Channel TV series *The People's Republic of Capitalism* (2008).

47. Jie Chen and Bruce J. Dickson, *Allies of the State: China's Private Entrepreneurs and Democratic Change* (Cambridge, MA: Harvard University Press, 2010).

48. Sarah Cook, "The Battle for China's Spirit: Religious Revival, Repression, and Resistance under Xi Jinping," Freedom House, Feb. 2017, https://freedomhouse.org/report/china-religious-freedom; Viola Zhao, "China's Underground Churches Head for Cover as Crackdown Closes In," *South China Morning Post*, Sept. 10, 2017, http://www.scmp.com/news/china/policies-politics/article/2110433/chinas-underground-churches-head-cover-crackdown-closes

49. This was added to the Constitution of the Communist Party of China in Oct. 2007.

50. "China's Policies and Practices on Protecting Freedom of Religious Belief," Information Office of the State Council, April 4, 2018, http://www.chinadaily.com.cn/a/201804/04/WS5ac42428a3105cdcf6516251.html

51. "Communiqué on the Current State of the Ideological Sphere," Central Committee of the Communist Party of China's General Office, April 22, 2013, http://www.chinafile.com/document-9-chinafile-translation. The Communiqué is often referred to as "Document No. 9."

52. See William A. Joseph, "China," in *Introduction to Comparative Politics*, 8th ed. (Boston: Wadsworth Cengage Learning, 2018).

SUGGESTED READINGS

Dirlik, Arif, Paul Michael Healy, and Nick Knight, eds. *Critical Perspectives on Mao Zedong's Thought*. 2nd ed. Amherst, NY: Humanity Books, 1997.

European Council on Foreign Relations. "China's "New Era" with Xi Jinping Characteristics." *China Analysis*, Dec. 2017, http://www.ecfr.eu/publications/summary/chinas_new_era_with_xi_jinping_characteristics7243

Holbig, Heike. "Ideology After the End of Ideology. China and the Quest for Autocratic Legitimation." *Democratization* 20 (2013): 61–91.

Jiang Shigong. "Philosophy and History: Interpreting the "Xi Jinping Era" through Xi's Report to the Nineteenth National Congress of the CCP." *Open Times*, Jan. 2018. An Introduction by David Ownby and Timothy Cheek. Translated by David Ownby, https://www.thechinastory.org/cot/jiang-shigong-on-philosophy-and-history-interpreting-the-xi-jinping-era-through-xis-report-to-the-nineteenth-national-congress-of-the-ccp/

Joseph, William A. *The Critique of Ultra-Leftism in China, 1958–1981*. Stanford, CA: Stanford University Press, 1984.

Knight, Nick. *Rethinking Mao: Explorations in Mao Zedong's Thought*. Lanham, MD: Lexington Books, 2007.

Meisner, Maurice. *Mao Zedong: A Political and Intellectual Portrait*. New York: Polity, 2007.

Schram, Stuart R. *The Thought of Mao Tse-tung*. New York: Cambridge University Press, 1989.

Sun, Yan. *The Chinese Reassessment of Socialism, 1976–1992*. Princeton, NJ: Princeton University Press, 1995.

Wakeman, Frederic Jr. *History and Will: Philosophical Perspectives of Mao Tse-tung's Thought*. Berkeley: University of California Press, 1973.

Womack, Brantly. *Foundations of Mao Zedong's Political Thought, 1917–1935*. Honolulu: University Press of Hawaii, 1982.

Wylie, Raymond F. *The Emergence of Maoism: Mao Tse-tung. Ch'en Po-ta, and the Search for Chinese Theory, 1935–1945*. Stanford, CA: Stanford University Press, 1980.

Xi Jinping, *The Governance of China*, 2 vols. (Beijing: Foreign Language Press, 2014 and 2018.

6

China's Communist Party-State: The Structure and Dynamics of Power

CHENG LI

Ever since the founding of the People's Republic of China (PRC) in 1949, the Chinese Communist Party (CCP) has been the country's only ruling party. With the exception of a few tumultuous years during the early phases of the Cultural Revolution, the ultimate source of political power in China has always been the Communist Party. Indeed, for the past seven decades, power struggles within the CCP leadership have been the only serious instances of political contention in the country. With around 90 million members, the CCP is currently the world's largest ruling political party, and only the Korean Workers' Party of North Korea has held on to power for longer.

The CCP has made it clear that it is not willing to give up its monopoly on political power to experiment with multiparty democracy, nor do Party leaders appear interested in moving toward a Western-style system based on a separation of power between the executive, legislative, and judicial branches of government. This does not mean, however, that the CCP is a stagnant institution that has been completely resistant to political change. On the contrary, during the reform era the CCP has experienced a number of profound transformations in terms of the recruitment of party elites, institutional reforms, and ideological changes (see chap. 5 for a discussion of the latter). Furthermore, the CCP leadership today is by no means a monolithic group whose members all share the same ideology, political background, and policy preferences.

China's search for an effective mechanism of governance suited to meet the dynamism of its economy and growing pluralism of its society in the reform era has not been a smooth and linear process but rather painstakingly difficult. Under the leadership of Xi Jinping since 2012, the return of strongman politics has been widely seen—in both China and abroad—as a move backwards in the country's political institutionalization. In early 2018, Xi and the Chinese political establishment made a decision to remove an important clause from the country's constitution—added during the Deng Xiaoping era—which limits both the presidency and vice presidency to two five-year terms (see chap. 3). Undoing this restriction essentially lines Xi up to be "president for life." As a result, Xi has squandered a precious opportunity to follow the institutionalized practice of predictable transfer of power in the PRC, undermining the example set by two former presidents, Jiang Zemin in 2002 and Hu Jintao in 2012.

This constitutional amendment appears to serve not only as a coronation for Xi's long-term rule but also fundamentally weakens the collective leadership initiated by Deng. Collective leadership functions according to commonly accepted rules and norms such as bureaucratic and regional representation and intraparty elections. A central component of collective leadership involves factional checks and balances in the supreme decision-making bodies such as the CCP Politburo and its **Standing Committee** in which the top leader is supposed to be only the "first among equals."

For those who previously held more optimistic prognoses for China when Xi first came to power, this disappointing turn reveals the enduring tensions and reversibility of political trends with regard to individual rule versus institutional constraints. But it also makes students of Chinese politics appreciate or recognize—in a somewhat ironic way—the great significance of the institutional reforms, most notably political succession norms and collective leadership, initiated by Deng and experimented with during the Jiang and Hu eras. With the abolishment of term limits for the presidency, rule by a dominant strong leader has undoubtedly gained tremendous momentum, and it will not be easily replaced. Yet, intense criticism of Xi's "imperial ambition" and serious reservations about the absence of any mechanisms for political succession from Chinese liberal intellectuals and other like-minded people could constitute a major challenge to Xi.

Also paradoxically, Xi's drastic ongoing efforts to consolidate his personal power, exemplified by his holding of as many as fourteen leadership titles and positions, is not necessarily a sign of strength; rather, it can be reasonably interpreted as just the opposite. It would also be an oversimplification to define the present-day Chinese political system as one-man rule autocracy, or to assert there is a complete absence of checks and balances in the Chinese political system, at least within the party leadership itself. Even if he is inclined to do so, Xi and his team cannot replace all of the institutional regulations, rules, and norms developed during the reform era. In fact, at the 19th Central Committee held in October 2017, most of the institutional rules and norms in elite selection, including the mandatory retirement age and regional and bureaucratic representation, remained largely intact.

A fact-based critical and comprehensive assessment of the structure, organization, elite formation, and main players in Chinese politics is essential. This chapter aims to highlight both the sources of continuity in China's long-standing party-state system and some of the more recent and intriguing twists and turns in the PRC's political landscape. Using the biographical data drawn from the party and government leadership bodies formed in the 19th Party Congress in October 2017 and the 13th National People's Congress in March 2018, this chapter explores new channels for elite advancement and emerging players in leadership politics in the Xi Jinping era. An analysis of these crucial aspects of Chinese leadership politics, especially their dynamics and tensions, will not only reveal how the country is governed but will also provide an assessment of both the resilience and vulnerability of the Chinese political system as well as the future political trajectory of this emerging world power.

THE STRUCTURE OF CHINA'S COMMUNIST PARTY-STATE

The CCP describes the history of its leadership in terms of political generations. Mao Zedong is portrayed as the core of the first generation of PRC leaders, Deng Xiaoping as the core of the second, and Jiang Zemin as the core of the third. Although he was not explicitly designated as its core, instead often identified as its "monitor" or "team leader," Hu Jintao was the head of the fourth generation of CCP leaders. The current general secretary, Xi Jinping, was dubbed the core of the fifth generation in 2016, even before he began his second term as general secretary of the CCP the following year. Despite the dramatic changes in ideology and policy over the course of these generations, the CCP has always clearly maintained that it plays a "leading role" in the state and society and therefore has the right to command the government, media, legal system, and military in the interest of preserving China's socialist system.

By design, the top leaders of the CCP have concurrently held the most important positions in the state (or government) since the establishment of the People's Republic. These top state positions include president of the PRC, premier (or prime minister) of the State Council (the government cabinet), the chair of the National People's Congress (the legislature of the PRC), and chair of the Central Military Commission (CMC). Leading party officials at various levels of the state—provincial, municipal, county, and town—often concurrently serve as officials in local government organizations. The head of the party organization (the party secretary) at any level of administration is the real "boss" in local political and policy matters. For example, the city of Shanghai has both a party secretary and a mayor, but the party secretary is the one with the greater authority, although the mayor is also a high-ranking party member.

In a very real sense, the institutions of party and state are intimately intertwined. This is why political systems such as the PRC (and previously, the Soviet Union) are referred to as communist party-states (see chap. 1). The preamble to the PRC's constitution makes several references to the communist party leadership, and Article 1 describes the PRC as "a socialist state under the people's democratic dictatorship led by the working class and based on the alliance of workers and peasants." It then says "The socialist system is the basic system of the People's Republic of China. The leadership of the Communist Party of China is the defining feature of socialism with Chinese characteristics." The last sentence was added when the constitution was revised in 2018, the same time that presidential term limits were abolished. Prior to this, the document had been rather ambiguous about where supreme political power in the PRC truly lies. The new sentence made it clear that, in practice, the communist party is unequivocally in charge at all levels, and the state operates merely as the executor of decisions made by the party.

Although high-ranking Chinese leaders have sporadically called for a greater separation between the party and the state, the overwhelming trend of the last three decades, especially under the leadership of Xi Jinping, has been to consolidate party rule and revitalize the party rather than fundamentally change the communist party-state system. Two important observations can be made regarding the party-state structure in present-day China. First, the party has the power to make all of the state's most important personnel and policy decisions. Second, notwithstanding the party's leading decision-making role, many important policy discussions, as well as most activities relating to policy implementation, take place in or through *government* institutions, not CCP organizations. In order to understand the complex relationship existing between the CCP and the PRC government, it is essential to grasp the basic structure of both the party and the state.

Organization of the CCP

As indicated in Figure 6.1, party organizations exist at all administrative levels from the center in Beijing down to the 4.5 million primary, or "grassroots" units, which, according the CCP's constitution, "are formed in enterprises, rural areas, government organs, schools, research institutes, communities, social organizations, companies of the People's Liberation Army and other basic units, where there are at least three full Party members." The party's reach extends throughout the country, but power is highly concentrated at the center, particularly in the twenty-five-member Politburo (or Political Bureau) and the seven members who concurrently sit on its Standing Committee (see Table 6.1).

The Politburo and the Standing Committee are formally elected by the **National Congress of the Communist Party of China** (or National Party Congress), which convenes for about a week in the fall once every five years and is the most important political convention in the country. All delegates must, of course, be members of the communist party. There were two types of delegates to the most recent party congress, which met in October 2017: regular (2,280) and invited (74). The delegates included representatives from China's thirty-one provincial-level administrations (which includes twenty-two provinces, five administrative regions, and four large cities directly under central administration). There was also a delegation of ethnic Taiwanese who are citizens of the PRC and members of the CCP, as well as delegations from the central departments of the party, the ministries and commissions of the central government, major state-owned enterprises, China's largest banks and other financial institutions, the People's Liberation Army (PLA), and the **People's Armed Police**. Invited delegates, who are also eligible to vote, were mostly retired party elders and can be considered China's equivalent of the "superdelegates" to the Democratic Party Convention in the United States.

The Party Congress elects the **Central Committee** (currently 204 full and 172 alternate members) and the **Central Commission for Discipline Inspection** (133 members). In theory, the Central Committee then elects the party's most powerful organizations: the Politburo, the Standing Committee, and the Central Military Commission (7 members). It also elects the general secretary, which is the top position

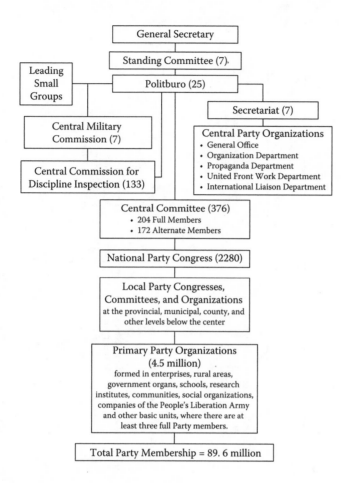

FIGURE 6.1 Organization of the Chinese Communist Party
(Number of members in parentheses is as of the 19ᵗʰ Party Congress, October 2017)

in the CCP. In practice, however, the process is top-down rather than bottom-up: the leading organizations of the party closely guide the selection of members of the Central Committee, and then present to the Central Committee a slate of candidates for the incoming Politburo and its Standing Committee for the Central Committee's "approval."

Although the CCP Constitution does not define term limits for the general secretary, the party regulations specify that party leaders undertake "no more than two full five-year terms in the same position, and three five-year terms at the same level of leadership." Based on this regulation, the general secretary of the party can serve two full terms and a leadership transition is to take place every decade. For example, Hu Jintao took over as general secretary in 2002 from Jiang Zemin, who served a full first term in that position starting 1992 and was reelected in 1997. Common practice, or the succession norms, established in the first two decades of the post-Deng era indicated that the heir apparent as party leader was to be anointed at the halfway point of the serving general secretary's term by being promoted to a number of preparatory positions, including a seat on the CCP Politburo Standing Committee, vice president

TABLE 6.1 CCP Politburo Standing Committee (elected October 2017)

Name	Other Key Positions	Year Born	Factional Affiliations	Education	Previous Provincial-Level Leadership & Other Major Experience
Xi Jinping	• CCP General Secretary • PRC President • Chair, Central Military Commission	1953	Xi Faction Elitist	• BA, Chemical Engineering, Tsinghua University (1975–1979) • PhD in Politics and Marxist Theory, Tsinghua University (via part-time studies, 1998–2002)	• PRC Vice President • Party Secretary, Zhejiang; Shanghai • Governor, Fujian; Zhejiang
Li Keqiang	• Premier, PRC State Council	1955	Tuanpai Populist	• B.A. Law (1982), Peking University • Ph.D. Economics (via part-time studies), Peking University	• Executive Vice Premier • Party Secretary, Henan; Liaoning • Governor, Henan
Li Zhanshu	• Chair, National People's Congress	1950	Xi Faction Elitist	• Received an undergraduate education in politics from Hebei Normal University in Shijiazhuang City (via part-time studies and night school, 1980–1983) • Attended the graduate program in business economics at the Chinese Academy of Social Sciences (CASS, via part-time studies, 1996–1998) • Executive Management of Business Administration from the Harbin Institute of Technology (via part-time studies, 2005–2006)	• Director, General Office of the CCP Central Committee • Party Secretary, Guizhou • Governor, Heilongjiang
Wang Yang	• Vice Premier, State Council • Chair, Chinese People's Political Consultative Conference	1955	Tuanpai Populist	• BA in public administration from the Central Party School (via correspondence courses, 1989–1992) • MA in management science from the University of Science and Technology of China in Hefei City (via part-time studies, 1993–1995).	• Party Secretary, Guangdong; Chongqing,

Name	Position	Year	Faction	Education	Notable Positions
Wang Huning	Executive Secretary of the CCP Secretariat	1955	Jiang Faction Elitist	Studied French language at Shanghai Normal University in Shanghai (1972–1977); MA in law and international politics at Fudan University (1978–1981); Visiting scholar at the U. of Iowa, the U. of Michigan, and the U. of California at Berkeley (1988–1989).	• Director, Central Policy Research Office of the CCP Central Committee • Dean, Fudan University Law School
Zhao Leji	Chair, Central Commission for Discipline Inspection	1957	Xi Faction Elitist	Received an undergraduate degree in philosophy from Peking University (1977–1980); Attended the graduate program in currency and banking at the CASS (via part-time studies, 1996–1998); Attended the graduate program in politics at the Central Party School (via part-time studies, 2002–2005)	• Director, CCP Organization Department • Party Secretary, Shaanxi; Qinghai • Governor, Qinghai
Han Zheng	Executive Vice Premier, PRC State Council	1954	Jiang Faction Elitist	Attended a two-year college program at Fudan University (1983–1985); BA in politics at East China Normal University in Shanghai (via part-time studies, 1985–1987); MA in international political economy at East China Normal U. (via part-time studies, 1994–1996)	• Party Secretary, Shanghai • Mayor, Shanghai

of the PRC, and vice chair of the CMC. With the abolishment of the term limits on the presidency in the PRC constitution in 2017, Xi Jinping will most likely change these party regulations at a party meeting during his second term (2017–2022) in order to stay in the top CCP position indefinitely.

The Central Committee convenes at least once per year in meetings called plenums or plenary sessions. Generally, all full members and alternate members attend these sessions. Top officials in CCP central organs, government ministries, provincial administrations, and the military who are not members of the Central Committee are also invited to attend the plenary sessions as nonvoting participants. Plenary sessions provide an opportunity for the announcement of new policy initiatives and major personnel appointments. For example, the Third Plenum of the Eleventh Central Committee held in December 1978 adopted Deng Xiaoping's reform and opening proposals, and this landmark meeting is often considered the turning point in CCP history from the Cultural Revolution's focus on ideology and politics to an emphasis on economic reform.

As suggested earlier, to call the process of choosing the Politburo and the Standing Committee by the Central Committee an election is something of a misnomer. These top bodies are actually selected by the outgoing Standing Committee, with considerable influence exercised by retired or retiring senior leaders. For example, Deng Xiaoping personally chose Jiang Zemin to take over the position of CCP general secretary in 1989, and Jiang Zemin played a major role in the shaping of the Standing Committee chosen in 2012.

There is intraparty competition for Central Committee seats. Since the 1982 National Congress of the CCP, the party has followed the method of "more candidates than available seats" (*cha'e xuanju*) for Central Committee elections. The 19th Party Congress[*] in 2017 chose 204 full members from 222 candidates on the ballot (8.8 percent were eliminated). In the election for alternate members of the Central Committee, they elected 172 leaders from a candidate pool of 189 (9.9 percent were eliminated).

The Central Commission for Discipline Inspection (133 members), while less important than the Central Committee, plays a crucial role in monitoring and punishing abuses of power, corruption, and other wrongdoings committed by party officials. The Commission's most serious sanction is to purge senior level officials and expel them from the party; in cases where it is determined that a crime may have been committed, the matter is handed over to the state judicial system. Lower-level party organizations, including provincial, municipal, and county-level bodies, also have discipline inspection commissions that report directly to the commission one level above them. The chiefs of the local discipline inspection commissions are usually not selected from the localities that they serve but are transferred in from elsewhere to lessen the likelihood of favoritism.

The **Secretariat** (7 members) is an important leadership body that handles the party's routine business and administrative matters. Secretariat members meet

---

[*] National Party Congresses are numbered in sequence beginning with the 1st Party Congress in 1921 that marked the founding of the CCP. Seven congresses were held between then and the founding of the PRC in 1949. The 8th Party Congress in 1956 was the first held after the CCP came to power. Because of political turmoil during the Maoist era, party congresses were convened irregularly. (Thirteen years elapsed between the 8th and 9th Party Congress, which was held in 1969.) Since 1982, party congresses have been held every five years.

daily and are responsible for coordinating the country's major events and meetings, drafting important documents, and arranging top leaders' foreign and domestic travel. By comparison, the more powerful organizations, the Politburo and Standing Committee, meet only once a month and once a week, respectively. Members of the Secretariat, like members of the Standing Committee, all live in Beijing. Some Politburo members reside in other cities, where they serve concurrently as provincial or municipal party chiefs. Of the seven members of the current Secretariat, six also serve as members of the Politburo, with one of those six (the Executive Secretary) serving on the Standing Committee.

The Secretariat supervises the work of the General Office of the CCP (its administrative coordinating body) as well as the party's four most important central departments—the **Organization Department**, the Propaganda (or Publicity) Department, the United Front Work Department, and the International Liaison Department. The current directors of the General Office, the Organization Department, and the Propaganda Department also serve on both the Politburo and the Secretariat. The Organization Department determines the personnel appointments of several thousand high-ranking leadership (or cadre) positions in the party, government, and military, as well as in large business firms, key universities, and other important institutions. These positions are part of the *nomenklatura* ("name list") system that was adopted from the Soviet communist party. Control of the cadre appointment process is one of the CCP's most important sources of power. The Propaganda Department is primarily responsible for spreading the party's message and controlling the media. The United Front Work Department deals with non-communist organizations, including the country's eight "**democratic parties**,"[†] ethnic and religious policy, and with issues concerning Taiwan, Hong Kong, and Macau. The mission of the International Liaison Department is to establish contacts with foreign political parties; it was more important and active when there were more communist parties in the world.

Among the twenty-five members of the current Politburo, eight primarily represent party organizations, nine come from government organizations, two from the military, and six from province-level administrative units. Table 6.1 lists some key information about the seven members of the Politburo Standing Committee, the most powerful leadership body in China. These individuals hold, concurrently with their positions on the Politburo Standing Committee, some of the most important offices in the party-state, including the presidency and premiership of the PRC, and the chair of China's legislature (the National People's Congress). Party General Secretary Xi Jinping serves simultaneously as president of the PRC and chair of the CMC, which has been the practice for China's top leader since the Jiang Zemin era.

In addition to these formal leadership institutions, the CCP also has a number of informal interagency executive decision-making bodies called **leading small groups** (*lingdao xiaozu*) that are focused on major functional issue areas. One estimate in late

---

† China's constitution says the PRC has "a system of cooperation and political consultation led by the Communist Party of China." In fact, China does have eight political parties other than the CCP, which are officially referred to as the "democratic parties." These parties are made up mostly of academics, scientists, writers, artists, professionals, and entrepreneurs and have a total membership of about seven-hundred thousand, must swear allegiance to the CCP, and do not compete with or challenge the CCP in any meaningful way.

2017 counted twenty-six party leading small groups.[1] Some of these are more or less permanent, while others are temporary task forces convened to deal with an immediate issue. Among the permanent leading small groups are those that cover foreign policy; national security; politics and law; finance and the economy; ideology and propaganda; party affairs; internet security and information technology; Taiwan; and Hong Kong and Macao.[2]

The main purpose of these leading small groups is to coordinate the implementation of policies across top decision-making bodies such as the Politburo, the State Council, and the CMC. Leading small groups report directly to the Politburo and its Standing Committee, and a member of the Standing Committee normally heads the most important ones. For example, Xi Jinping heads the leading groups on economics and finance, foreign affairs, national security, military reforms, internet security and information technology, comprehensively deepening reform, and Taiwan affairs.

The State Structure

The structure of PRC government is presented in Figure 6.2. China's constitution declares, "All power in the PRC belongs to the people. The organs through which the people exercise state power are the National People's Congress and the local people's congresses at different levels." People's congresses operate at every administrative level in the PRC from the national at the top to rural towns and urban districts and are the legislative branch of the government. But, like other state organizations, the congresses operate under strict party scrutiny and exercise power only as allowed by the CCP.

In rural areas, deputies to county and town people's congresses are *directly* elected by all eligible citizens in that locale, as are deputies to people congresses at the lowest level of formal urban administration, the district. Elections at all higher levels are *indirect*, meaning.deputies are elected by the people's congress at the next lowest level. For example, deputies to the National People's Congress (NPC) are elected by the people's congresses at the provincial level. (China's 560,000 villages are not considered to be a formal level of administration and have a different form of governance, which involves direct elections, as discussed in chap. 9.)

Elections for the NPC are held every five years. The current NPC, formed in 2018, has 2,980 deputies. They are not full-time lawmakers, and when the NPC is not in session, they return to their regular locations and jobs.

Deputies to the NPC are allocated according to the population of a given province. The NPC recently equalized the representation of urban and rural areas. Prior to this reform, every 960,000 rural residents and every 240,000 urban residents were represented by one NPC deputy, which gave China's cities much more clout in the legislature. The province with the smallest population is guaranteed at least fifteen deputies. Special administrative regions such as Hong Kong and Macau have a set quota of delegates, as does the PLA.

Just as the National Congress of the CCP elects party leaders every five years at its fall meeting, the NPC elects a new state leadership at a meeting in the spring following the Party Congress, although those to be elected have been predetermined

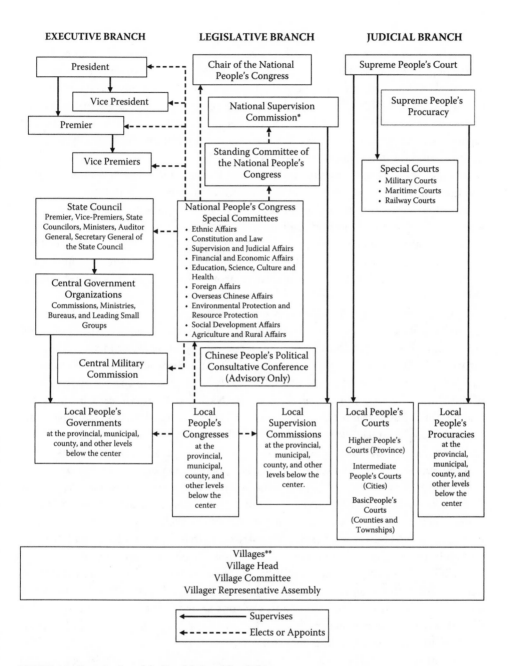

EXECUTIVE BRANCH

President

Vice President

Premier

Vice Premiers

State Council
Premier, Vice-Premiers, State Councilors, Ministers, Auditor General, Secretary General of the State Council

Central Government Organizations
Commissions, Ministries, Bureaus, and Leading Small Groups

Central Military Commission

Local People's Governments
at the provincial, municipal, county, and other levels below the center

LEGISLATIVE BRANCH

Chair of the National People's Congress

National Supervision Commission*

Standing Committee of the National People's Congress

National People's Congress Special Committees
• Ethnic Affairs
• Constitution and Law
• Supervision and Judicial Affairs
• Financial and Economic Affairs
• Education, Science, Culture and Health
• Foreign Affairs
• Overseas Chinese Affairs
• Environmental Protection and Resource Protection
• Social Development Affairs
• Agriculture and Rural Affairs

Chinese People's Political Consultative Conference (Advisory Only)

Local People's Congresses
at the provincial, municipal, county, and other levels below the center

Local Supervision Commissions
at the provincial, municipal, county, and other levels below the center.

JUDICIAL BRANCH

Supreme People's Court

Supreme People's Procuracy

Special Courts
• Military Courts
• Maritime Courts
• Railway Courts

Local People's Courts

Higher People's Courts (Province)

Intermediate People's Courts (Cities)

BasicPeople's Courts (Counties and Townships)

Local People's Procuracies
at the provincial, municipal, county, and other levels below the center

Villages**
Village Head
Village Committee
Villager Representative Assembly

Supervises
Elects or Appoints

FIGURE 6.2 Organization of the People's Republic of China

*The National Supervision Commission is on the same level of the Supreme People's Court and the Supreme People's Procuracy

** Village are technically self-governing but in fact are under the authority of party and state organizations at the town or township level..

by the party. But unlike deputies of the Party Congress, which only meets every five years, the NPC convenes in its entirety every March for a two-week session, during which deputies discuss the reports by the premier and other government leaders and approve laws and legislative regulations. The NPC has increasingly served as a venue for policy debates, although politically sensitive or controversial topics are off limits. The work of the NPC has become more substantive in terms of drafting laws and regulations and providing a venue for policy discourse, but it still basically acts as a rubber stamp for decisions made by the party leadership.

When the NPC is not in session, the **Standing Committee of the National People's Congress** (not to be confused with the much more powerful CCP Politburo Standing Committee) takes responsibility for any issues that require congressional consideration. The Standing Committee of the NPC, which generally convenes every two months for about a week at a time, is headed by a chair, who is also a member of the party Politburo Standing Committee. The NPC also appoints ten special committees to draft legislation in various areas such as economics, education, energy, and the environment.

In theory, NPC delegates are not only supposed to elect the members of the Standing Committee of the NPC but are also constitutionally entitled to elect the president and vice president of the PRC, the chair of the state Central Military Commission, the chief justice of the **Supreme People's Court**, the chief of the **Supreme People's Procuracy** (the PRC's top law enforcement official, roughly equivalent to the attorney general of the United States), and the director of the **National Supervision Commission**. The National Supervision Commission, which was first established at the National People's Congress meeting in March 2018, is the highest state anticorruption agency of the PRC, with the same administrative ranking as the Supreme People's Court and the Supreme People's Procuracy. The National Supervision Commission's operations are integrated with the CCP's Central Discipline Inspection Commission. The director of the National Supervision Commission, Yang Xiaodu, also serves as the deputy secretary of the CCDI and is a member of the Politburo. As a state organization, it has a legal basis for investigating corruption that the CCDI lacks, and its jurisdiction to investigate corruption extends to nonparty officials (see chap. 7).

The NPC is also empowered to approve the premier, who is appointed by the president, as well as the other members of the State Council and CMC. In reality, however, all of the candidates for these positions are chosen by the top party leadership. This formal process is hardly competitive. When Xi Jinping was first elected PRC president in 2013, for example, the vote was 2,952 for, 1 against, and 3 abstentions. The election for vice president was more contested: the tally was 2,839 for, 80 against, and 37 abstentions. In Xi's reelection as PRC president in 2018, he received unanimous support with 2,970 votes. One deputy voted against the candidate for vice president, Wang Qishan.

This lack of competitiveness notwithstanding, it is an interesting and fairly recent phenomenon that NPC delegates sometimes vote against some nominees for important positions in the confirmation process. For example, the nominee to head the government's environmental protection ministry in 2013 won "only" two-thirds of the vote, which probably reflected widespread public unhappiness with air pollution and other ecological problems.

The State Council is headed by the premier, and its Executive Committee consists of the premier; four vice premiers; and five state councilors, who are senior government leaders with broad responsibilities (one of the state councilors also concurrently serves as secretary-general of the State Council). The State Council currently consists of more than two dozen members, including ministers and commissioners who head functional departments such as the Ministry of Foreign Affairs and the National Health Commission, the central bank governor, and the auditor-general (who oversees the government's budget). All these minister-level leaders are members of the CCP, all except two are members of the party Central Committee, and for all their first loyalty is to the party. Like the CCP, the central government of the PRC has leading small groups and similarly-tasked committees focused primarily on economic and social issues to coordinate policy making and implementation across the vast state bureaucracy.[3]

As discussed in more detail in chapter 7, the judiciary is not a separate independent branch of government in the PRC. The CCP uses the nomenklatura system and other means of control to maintain tight oversight on all aspects of China's legal system. Some Chinese intellectuals who believe that the PRC should move toward a true rule of law system have spoken out against party interference. One such intellectual is the law professor He Weifang. In 2006, he bluntly criticized Zhou Yongkang, Minister of Public Security (who was also a member of the CCP Politburo), for his heavy-handed "oversight" of the Supreme People's Court. To Professor He, Zhou's actions exemplified the lack of a genuinely independent judicial system in the country. "There is no other country in the world," Professor He said, "in which the chief justice reports to the chief of police."[4]

The Party and the Army

The party's control over the military has been an important principle throughout the history of the CCP. In 1938, Mao Zedong declared, "Every Communist must grasp the truth, 'Political power grows out of the barrel of a gun.' Our principle is that the Party commands the gun, and the gun must never be allowed to command the Party."[5] On a few occasions, however, the PLA has intervened in Chinese politics. Examples include the 1971 "Lin Biao incident," when Minister of Defense Lin Biao pursued a failed military coup to overthrow Chairman Mao (see chap. 3), and the two years immediately following the 1989 Tiananmen crisis, when the generals of the so-called "Yang family clique"—Yang Baibing and Yang Shangkun—gained enormous power, only to be outmaneuvered by Deng Xiaoping.

Over the past decade, China's military has steadily moved away from active involvement in domestic politics. The probability that a military figure might serve as a kingmaker has become increasingly remote. In each of the last five Politburos (1997–2017) there were only two representatives of the military, and none served on the Politburo Standing Committee. Furthermore, no member of the military elite serves on the current Secretariat, which signals the further retreat of the PLA from domestic affairs and foreign policy toward a more narrow focus on military affairs.

The most important organizations for deciding military policy are the CCP Central Military Commission and the PRC Central Military Commission. Although technically the former is a party organization and the latter is part of the state structure, they are in fact different names for the same institution with identical membership. This arrangement reflects the CCP's desire to exercise its power and authority, at least formally, through the PRC's constitutional framework. In reality, however, the Central Military Commission reports to the Politburo and its Standing Committee. In other words, China's armed forces are under the command of the CCP, not the government of the PRC. Moreover, as the former general secretary, Hu Jintao, declared in 2004, the primary mission of the Chinese military is "to provide an important guarantee of strength for the party to consolidate its ruling position"[6] and new recruits in the PLA swear an oath that includes a promise "To obey the leadership of the Chinese Communist Party."[7]

The current CMC has seven members. CCP General Secretary and PRC President Xi Jinping is the chair, which effectively makes him commander in chief of China's armed forces. The two military leaders who sit on the Politburo serve as CMC vice chairmen. Other members include the minister of defense (responsible for the PLA's foreign interactions), the chief of the CMC Joint Staff Department (responsible for military operations), the director of the CMC Political Department (responsible for ideological indoctrination and personnel appointments), and the secretary of the CMC Commission for Discipline Inspection (responsible for anticorruption efforts in the PLA). Since 1992, only three civilians, Jiang Zemin, Hu Jintao, and Xi Jinping have served on the CMC. Nevertheless, the norm of a civilian party leader being in charge of military affairs seems to be well-accepted by the PLA.

Both Deng Xiaoping and Jiang Zemin delayed turning over the position of CMC chair to a relatively untested successor, holding onto the seat for a few years after they had already stepped down from their party and government posts. This created a rather strange situation in which the civilian commander in chief of China's armed forces did not hold any other position in the party or the government. In the run-up to the 18th Party Congress in 2012, there was considerable speculation that retiring general secretary, Hu Jintao, might similarly try to stay on as head of the CMC for a transition period. But Xi Jinping took over as CMC chair at the same time he was elevated to the top party position. By surrendering power to Xi, Hu set an example for a more institutionalized and complete political succession and strengthened the relationship among the party, the state, and the army.

DYNAMICS IN THE CHINESE POLITICAL SYSTEM

While the Chinese party-state institutional structure has remained more or less the same over the past seven decades, the CCP leadership in the post-Mao China recognized the need to keep abreast of the times and make necessary changes in order to stay in power. A truly durable political system should be open to new blood, new skills, and new ladders to leadership. In so doing, it is more able to evolve institutionally and politically and avoid becoming insolated and stagnant. CCP rule has been a constant over the past seven decades, but the composition of the party membership, the routes for elite advancement, and professional backgrounds of leaders have seen continual change, especially during the reform era.

The Changing Composition of the CCP

As a matter of fact, the occupational and educational backgrounds of the CCP's membership and the party's leaders have changed profoundly. The CCP has been transformed from a revolutionary party consisting primarily of peasants, soldiers, and urban workers to a ruling party with an increasing number of members from diverse areas of society.

Over the past half century, the size of the CCP has increased enormously. As shown in Figure 6.3, CCP membership has increased from about 4.5 million in 1949, when the party came to power, to 89.6 million as of mid-2018. Note that nearly half this growth has occurred since the end of the Maoist era in 1976. However, the party's total membership still constitutes a very small proportion (about 8.5 percent) of the total age-eligible (over eighteen) population. The party get about 20 million applications for new member each year. But since Xi Jinping came to power, there has been a significant slowdown in the number admitted. In 2012, there were 3.23 million new members; the next year that dropped to 2.41 million—the first decrease in a decade. In 2017, 1.9 million people joined the CCP. This reflects Xi's emphasis on improving

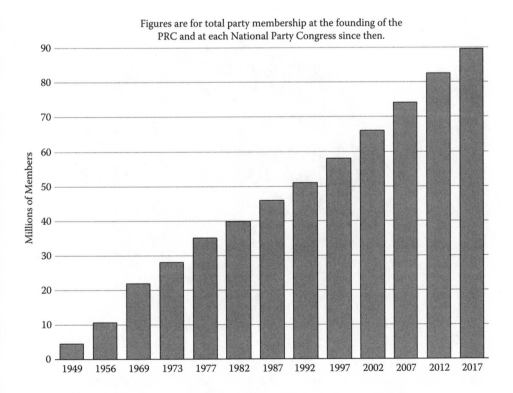

Figures are for total party membership at the founding of the PRC and at each National Party Congress since then.

FIGURE 6.3 CCP Membership (1949–2017)

the quality of party members in terms of educational levels and fealty to communist principles.[8]

Not only has the CCP grown enormously in size, but its occupational composition has also changed in dramatic ways over the past three decades. At the start of the reform era in 1981, farmers and workers—the traditional base of the communist party—made up 63.4 percent of the CCP.[9] As Figure 6.4 shows, those two groups accounted for just 36.9 percent of CCP members in 2016. Although farmers continue to constitute the largest single segment of the CCP, the current occupational composition of the party reflects the impact of modernization and the ideological reorientation of the party. For the last decade or so, the CCP has actively sought to recruit members from groups that came into existence only with the market reforms, the so-called new social strata, which includes, among others, private entrepreneurs (**Red Capitalists**), technical personnel and managers in private firms and foreign-funded enterprises, independent professionals, and the self-employed. (See the figures for a discussion of the role of private entrepreneurs in the CCP.)

In the three decades after the establishment of the PRC, elite recruitment—bringing in new leaders—was mostly based on family background (the preferred categories being peasant or worker), ideological loyalty, and political activism, rather than on educational credentials and/or managerial skills. This politicized pattern of recruitment was expressed by the idea that it was better to be "red" than "expert" during the Mao years. "Reds" were cadres who advanced their careers on the strength of their revolutionary pedigree and ideological purity, while "experts" were members of the

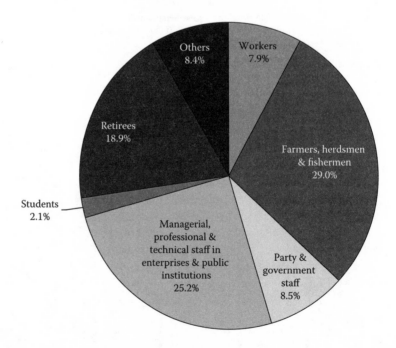

FIGURE 6.4 Occupations of CCP Members (2016)

Source: "2016 Zhongguo gongchandang dangnei tongji gongbao" [The 2016 Chinese Communist Party Public Report of Internal Statistics]. *Gongchandangyuan wang* [Website of the Members of the Communist Party], June 30, 2017, http://news.12371.cn/2017/06/30/ARTI1498810325807955.shtml

party elite who distinguished themselves by their educational credentials and technical skills.

When it came to elite recruitment and promotion, reds have traditionally almost always prevailed over experts. Thus, from 1949 through the early 1980s, the educational attainment of party cadres and members was extremely low. In 1955, for example, only 5 percent of national leaders had a junior high school education or above.[10] Even in 1985, only 4 percent of CCP members were educated beyond the high school level, and a majority (52.2 percent) had received only a primary school education or were illiterate.[11] These numbers reflect both the low value placed on educational accomplishments and technical know-how within the CCP and the relatively underdeveloped system of higher education before the reform era.

Since the reform era, the educational level of CCP members has increased significantly in the past three decades, now that "expertise" is much more valued than "redness" in the recruitment process. Still in 1998, among the 61 million CCP members, only 11 million were college graduates (17.8 percent); by 2017, 43.3 million CCP members held, at minimum, a two-year college degree, constituting 48.3 percent of the total membership.[12]

The growth in the percentage of national-level party leaders with higher education has been particularly dramatic. For example, in 1982, no member of the Politburo had completed a university education; in 2017, all except one member of the Politburo have college-level degrees, eighteen from universities, one from a military academy, and five from the Central Party School, where the training is largely political, ideological, and managerial. Twenty-two Politburo members have advanced degrees, including five PhD degree holders, for example, General Secretary-President Xi Jinping (PhD in law and political science) and Premier Li Keqiang (PhD in economics). The percentage of college-educated individuals at senior levels of leadership has significantly increased. For example, the number of college-educated top provincial leaders (party secretaries, governors, and their deputies) increased from 20 percent in 1982 to 100 percent in 2010, two-thirds had postgraduate education, usually through part-time programs, and many held PhD degrees. Their fields of graduate education were diverse, including economics, management, politics, and law, as well as engineering.[13]

The 1980s–1990s was a time of "technocratic turnover" within China's party-state leadership. In 1982, technocrats—cadres with a university-level technical or science education and work experience as an engineer or scientist—constituted just 2 percent of the Central Committee, but by 1987 they made up 25 percent of the Central Committee, and by 1997 they made up over half. All nine members of the Politburo Standing Committee elected in 1997 were engineers, including the three top leaders, General Secretary Jiang Zemin (electrical engineer), Chair of the NPC Li Peng (hydroelectric engineer), and Premier Zhu Rongji (electrical engineer). This was also true of the top three leaders elected in 2002: General Secretary Hu Jintao (hydraulic engineer), NPC Chair, Wu Bangguo (electrical engineer), and Premier Wen Jiabao (geological engineer). The representation of technocrats also rose dramatically in other high-level leadership categories; for example, in 1982, no provincial party secretaries or governors had higher-level technical education; by 2002, 74 percent of provincial party secretaries and 77 percent of governors were technocrats.[14]

Beginning with the 17th Party Congress that met in 2007, the dominance of technocrats in the Chinese leadership began to decline and the percentage of leaders with nontechnical educations started to rise sharply. The Politburo elected that year had thirteen technocrats (including eleven engineers) out of twenty-five members (52 percent), down from eighteen out of twenty-four (75 percent) in the 2002 Politburo. In the twenty-five-member Politburo formed in 2017, in terms of highest degree obtained, only two (8 percent) are technocrats. None of the Politburo Standing Committee members is a technocrat. Most of them majored in economics, political science, law, and humanities. Although Xi Jinping's undergraduate degree is in chemical engineering, he never practiced as an engineer. Late in his career, Xi received a doctoral degree in law and political science through a part-time study program.[15] Having leaders who are educated in a broader range of fields may well bring more diverse perspectives to policy making and problem-solving.

The rise of technocrats and others with higher-education degrees to dominance in the Chinese leadership over the recent decades is particularly striking considering the following three facts. First, in 2010, only 7 percent of China's labor force had a college education.[16] Second, although China was traditionally a meritocratic society in which status was largely determined by success in the imperial exams, scientific knowledge and technical competence were always subordinate to literary and cultural achievements in the Confucian worldview. Third, China's meritocratic tradition underwent an extreme reversal during the Mao era, especially during the Cultural Revolution, when professionals or "experts" were repeatedly targeted as enemies of the people.

Women are significantly underrepresented at all levels of the CCP. In 2017, women made up only 25.7 percent of total party membership, a modest improvement from 16.6 percent in 2002.[17] They are even less well-represented in the top leadership organizations and positions. There are thirty women among the 376 full and alternate members of the Central Committee (8.0 percent), but only ten of the 204 full members (4.9 percent) are women. Only one woman serves on the current 25-member Politburo, and no woman has ever served on the Politburo Standing Committee. In 2018, among the 31 provincial-level administrative units of the PRC, there was not a single woman serving as party secretary and there were only three women governors (in Inner Mongolia, Guizhou, and Ningxia).

The Main Route to the Top is through the Provinces

An analysis of the composition of the party's top bodies reveals a significant increase in the number of leaders who have advanced their careers through experience in provincial leadership posts. Since the reform era began in 1978, the most important political credential for a top leadership position has been experience as a provincial-level party secretary. Former party leader Jiang Zemin was promoted to general secretary of the CCP in 1989 from the post of party secretary of Shanghai (where he had been credited with the "successful" handling of pro-democracy demonstrations). Hu Jintao had served as party secretary in both Guizhou and Tibet before being promoted to the Standing Committee in 1992. Xi Jinping has served as governor of both Fujian and

Zhejiang province and as party secretary of both Zhejiang and Shanghai. Six of the seven members of the current Standing Committee had served as provincial party secretaries prior to their ascent to the supreme decision-making body.

The increase in the percentage of Politburo members with experience as provincial leaders since 1992 is shown in Figure 6.5. From the 14th Party Congress in 1992 to the 19th Party Congress in 2017, on average, about 65 percent of Politburo members had served as provincial/municipal party secretary and/or governor/mayor. Since two members of the Politburos hailed from the military and some members served as deputy party secretaries or vice governors, the percentage of civilians with major provincial experience was even higher.

The large representation of leaders with provincial experience in the Politburo and its Standing Committee reflects the growing power and influence of the politicians who run the country's thirty-one province-level administrative units. In addition, the central authorities try to prevent the emergence of local power bases by promoting provincial leaders to positions in Beijing and frequent reshuffling of provincial leaders.

Top CCP officials seem to be seriously concerned with ensuring regional balance in the national leadership. The party secretaries of four major cities directly under central government control (Beijing, Shanghai, Tianjin, and Chongqing) routinely serve in the Politburo. The Politburo that was elected in 2017 has at least one current member who was born and/or worked extensively in each of China's major geographic regions—the northeast, north, northwest, east, south central, and southwest. In addition, at the time of the Party Congress, there are usually six new Politburo members

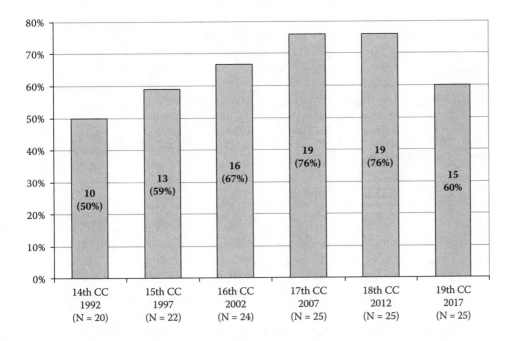

FIGURE 6.5 Politburo Members with Provincial Experience

Source: Cheng Li, "A Biographical and Factional Analysis of the Post-2012 Politburo," China Leadership Monitor, No. 41 (June 6, 2013), http://www.hoover.org/publications/china-leadership-monitor/article/148836. Updated by Cheng Li.

who have recently advanced their careers or who concurrently serve as province-level party secretaries in recently formed Politburos.

This concern for equal regional representation in the CCP's leadership organizations is even more evident in the distribution of full membership seats on the Central Committee. A strong political norm in Chinese elite recruitment since the 1997 Central Committee has been that almost every province-level administration has two full membership seats on the Central Committee, usually occupied by the party secretary and governor. Although provincial leaders are sometimes later promoted to the central government or transferred to other provinces, this distributional norm has been strictly applied at the time of Central Committee elections. Local demands for an even distribution of membership seats across provinces and regions in both the Central Committee and the Politburo have been increasingly accommodated and institutionalized by the party leadership.[18]

At the same time, top national leaders still need to accumulate political capital through close ties with some of the country's most important regions. Because of the emphasis top party elites place on leadership experience gained through serving as a party secretary in major provinces and cities, these posts are pivotal stepping stones for aspiring entrants into the top national leadership. This further enhances the political weight of local power in present-day China. But the fact that provincial leaders' career prospects depend on their superiors in Beijing speaks unambiguously to the enormous power the central party-state has over local administrations in China's still highly hierarchical, authoritarian system.

Another experience at the local level shared by many of the China's newest generation of leaders is that of having been "sent-down youth" during the Cultural Revolution. Five of the seven members of the current Politburo Standing Committee (Xi Jinping, Li Keqiang, Li Zhanshu, Zhao Leji, and Han Zheng) and nine other Politburo members were among the more than 20 million students who were sent to the rural areas to do manual labor in the late 1960s and early 1970s after Mao disbanded the Red Guard movement (see chap. 3). Xi Jinping spent 1969–1975 working in an agricultural commune in a very poor area of Shaanxi province and began his university education only after returning from the countryside. Some observers think this experience may give the leaders a deeper understanding of the difficult conditions many of China's hundreds of millions farmers still face.

New Channels for the Membership in the Politburo

The slight decline in Politburo members with experience as a provincial chief in the Politburo formed at the 19th Party Congress in 2017 (as shown in Figure 6.5), can probably be attributed to the fact that Xi Jinping has moved to broaden the fields from which elites are recruited to include think tanks, universities, and foreign affairs experts. Xi Jinping is the first leader in the PRC who has publicly endorsed the role of think tanks in enhancing the country's soft power and has promoted the building of the "Chinese new type of think tanks" as part of the country's strategic mission.[19] Xi has declared on a number of occasions in the past few years the strategic goal of developing new think tanks with Chinese characteristics. In April 2016, in an important speech delivered at the Internet and Information Security Work Conference, Xi proclaimed that China should adopt a mechanism common in many foreign countries, whereby think tanks serve as a "revolving door" (*xuanzhuanmen*) for political and intellectual elites to move between the government, enterprises, and think tanks themselves.[20]

Profiles of four key leaders who emerged at the 19th Party Congress in 2017 illustrate the new channels in the route to the top in the Xi Jinping era.

For the first time in the PRC history, someone who advanced his career entirely through universities and think tanks has become a member of the Politburo Standing Committee and is now in charge of party propaganda. Wang Huning, one of the first group of Chinese students to major in law and international politics in the post-Cultural Revolution period, taught these subjects at Fudan University for more than a decade. He served as dean of the Fudan Law School in the early 1990s before moving to Beijing, where he has worked as division head, deputy director, and then director of the Central Policy Research Center of the CCP Central Committee, a prominent party think tank, for more than two decades. He served as a key advisor to three general secretaries of the CCP—Jiang Zemin, Hu Jintao, and Xi Jinping—before becoming one of the seven members of the supreme decision-making body at the 2017 Party Congress. Wang played a crucial role in developing the trademark contributions to Chinese communist ideology for each of those three leaders, most recently Xi Jinping Thought on Socialism with Chinese Characteristics for a New Era (see chap. 5). His elevation reflects the increased importance hat Xi attached to ideological matters both within the party and the country more broadly.[21]

The leader currently in charge of China's financial affairs, Liu He, a new Politburo member and vice premier, has also advanced his career primarily through think tank work. An economist by training, in the 1990s Liu founded the Chinese Economists 50 Forum, a prestigious think tank that consists of the country's most influential economists and financial technocrats (including the former and current governors of the People's Bank, Zhou Xiaochuan and Yi Gang). Liu is the author of six books and over 200 articles. His work covers five broad research areas: the relationship between economic development and the change in industrial structure in China; macroeconomic theories; corporate governance and property rights; the new economy and the information industry; and the reform of Chinese SOEs (state-owned enterprises). These are all critical issues as the PRC adjusts its economic model from the export-led, investment-heavy approach that generating the high levels of growth in the first decades of the reform era to one based on domestic consumption, technology, and innovation (see chap. 8).

While serving as a researcher and administrator at various government think tanks such as the Research Office of the Industrial Policy and Long-term Planning Department in the State Planning Commission, the State Information Center, and the Development Research Center of the State Council, Liu He was one of the principal drafters of communiqués for key CCP leadership meetings from 2003 to 2013.[22] Partly because of his expertise in economics and finance and partly because of his strong personal ties with Xi Jinping, Liu He has now moved from serving as a think tank advisor to a government policymaker.

Xi Jinping's college classmate and roommate at Tsinghua University, Chen Xi, also entered the new Politburo at the 19th Party Congress and concurrently serves as director of the Central Organization Department—which oversees the *nomenklatura* system—and president of the **Central Party School**, the top training academy for CCP officials. After receiving a master's degree in chemical engineering from Tsinghua, Chen Xi advanced his career mainly through his academic and party/administrative work at Tsinghua, where he served as a leader in charge of student affairs; deputy party secretary of the Department of Chemical Engineering; and deputy party secretary, executive deputy party secretary, and then party secretary of the Tsinghua Party Committee.

With Xi's strong backing, Chen promoted a few of his close associates at Tsinghua and administrators of other universities to important leadership posts. The most notable examples from Tsinghua are Chen Jining, former president of Tsinghua University, who was appointed minister of Environmental Protection in 2015 and mayor of Beijing in 2017, and Hu Heping, former party secretary of Tsinghua University, who was first appointed director of the Organization Department of the Zhejiang Provincial Party Committee, then deputy party secretary of Shaanxi Province in 2015, governor of Shaanxi in 2016, and party secretary of Shaanxi in 2017. Chen Jining and Hu Heping, born in 1964 and 1962, respectively, are seen as rising stars among the next generation of leaders. With his new responsibility as Xi's chief personnel officer and president of the Central Party School, Chen Xi has a major role in shaping the elite recruitment channel and thus Xi's power base.

The elevation of Yang Jiechi, a career diplomat and the chief representative from the foreign affairs bureaucracy, to be a member of the Politburo at the 19th Party Congress reflects the growing importance of international relations to the CCP leadership in the Xi era. No representatives from China's foreign affairs apparatus had served on the Politburo in the fifteen years prior to Yang's appointment. Further, Yang is the first former ambassador to the United States to serve on this important leadership body. As a diplomat, Yang worked in the Chinese Embassy in Washington, DC twice for a total of twelve years.

It is notable that all four of these prominent leaders studied in the West early in their career. Wang Huning was a visiting scholar at the University of Michigan, the University of Iowa, and the University of California, Berkeley, in the late 1980s. Wang's elevation to the Politburo Standing Committee marks the first time in PRC history that a Western-educated **returnee** has served on this supreme leadership body. Vice premier Liu He received two master's degrees from American universities: an MBA from at Seton Hall University and an MPA from Harvard's Kennedy School of Government, where he was a Mason fellow. Chen Xi served as a visiting scholar at Stanford University in the early 1990s. Yang Jiechi studied at the University of Bath and the London School of Economics and Political Science in the early 1970s. On the 370-plus-member central committee, the percentage of foreign educated "returnees" has gradually increased from 6.2 percent in 2002, 10.5 percent in 2007, and 14.6 percent in 2012 to 20.5 percent in 2017. Most of these leaders studied in the West, especially in the United States.

Emerging Players in the CCP: Entrepreneurs and Lawyers

In terms of the occupational backgrounds of the CCP elites, two distinct groups—entrepreneurs and lawyers—have recently emerged as new and important players in the politics and socioeconomic life of the country. Like the ascendency of well-educated technocrats in the Chinese communist party-state in the 1980s, the growing influence of these groups represents another major shift in the landscape of Chinese politics.

The upward social mobility and political role of entrepreneurs—owners and managers of private businesses—is particularly momentous. Traditional Chinese society, which was dominated by the scholar-gentry class, tended to devalue merchants because they lived by making profits off others rather than through "honest" mental or manual labor. Anticapitalist bias reached its peak during the first few decades of the PRC. The 4 million private firms and stores that had existed in China prior to 1949 had all but disappeared by the mid-1950s as part of the transition to socialism. During the Cultural Revolution, anything to do with capitalism was branded poisonous, and top leaders such as Liu Shaoqi and Deng Xiaoping were purged for allegedly taking China down "the capitalist road." Small-scale private business and self-employment was not possible until the end of the Mao era, and private enterprises that could employ a large number of laborers did not exist in China until the late 1980s.

Several factors have contributed to the reemergence of entrepreneurs in the PRC. Among them are the lifting of ideological taboos against privately owned businesses; rural-to-urban migration, which created a large number of very small-scale entrepreneurs in China's cities; joint ventures between foreign and Chinese private companies; the establishment of stock and real estate markets; and the technological revolution, which has given birth to a whole new private industry. At the start of the reform era in the late 1970s, there were literally no private businesses in China. In 1989, there were 3.6 million private enterprises (with more than eight employees) and 14.5 million individually owned businesses (with fewer than eight employees) in China, employing 26.6 million people. By 2012, that number had grown to 10.9 million private enterprises and 40.6 million individual businesses with a total of nearly 200 million employees. The Chinese leadership's call for innovation and entrepreneurship in Chinese society has led to a rapid increase in the number of privately firms in recent years. At the end of 2017, China had a total of 27.3 million private firms and 65.8 million small-scale individually owned firms employing 340 million people. The private sector accounts for more than 60 percent of the PRC's GDP and 90 percent of new job creation.[23]

The rise of private entrepreneurs in terms of political influence can be traced to July 2001, when then-CCP General Secretary Jiang Zemin gave an important speech on the eightieth anniversary of the party's founding. In his speech, Jiang claimed that the party should be representative of three components of society: the advanced social productive forces, advanced culture, and the interests of the overwhelming majority. As discussed in chapters 4 and 5, Jiang's so-called "Theory of the Three Represents" was an ideological justification for the priority given to the private sector in China's economic development and for allowing entrepreneurs to be members of the communist party (the CCP still shies away from calling them "capitalists"). A 2004 official study found that 34 percent of the owners of private enterprises were members of the CCP, up from just 13 percent in 1993. Of that 34 percent, only 9.4 percent had joined *after* Jiang's 2001 speech,[24] which reflects the fact that Jiang's ideological embrace was mostly just formal acknowledgment that a large number of party members were already engaged in private business. More recent studies suggest that the proportion of private entrepreneurs who are CCP members remains at about one-third, but, interestingly, the larger the scale of the private enterprise, the more likely it is that the owner(s) are party members.[25]

Entrepreneurs and, especially, their executive counterparts in state-owned industries have just begun to acquire positions in national and local-level political leadership. A small, but increasing percent of the delegates to the national party congress are from the corporate world. At the 19th Party Congress in 2017, 148 of the 2,280 delegates (6 percent) were from the corporate sector, but, of those, just 27 were from the private sector.[26]

The entrepreneurs and executives of SOEs, especially China's flagship companies, have gradually increased their representation in the national leadership, including on the Politburo and the State Council. For example, Guo Shengkun, currently a member of both the Politburo and the Secretariat and concurrently State Councilor of the State Council, responsible for political and legal affairs, advanced his early career in the mining industry and previously served as CEO of the Aluminum Corporation of China (also known as CHALCO), the world's second-largest aluminum producer. Wang Yong, the State Councilor responsible for SOE development, advanced his early career from the aerospace industry, where he worked for twenty-three years. Wang served as vice president of the China Aerospace Electrical Group before joining the CCP Central Organization Department in 2000.

The 2017 Party Congress witnessed an interesting phenomenon: a significant number of leaders with work experience in the aerospace industry have entered the Central Committee as full or alternate members. A new term, "the cosmos club" (*yuzhoubang*), has been coined to refer to national and provincial leaders who have advanced their careers through China's aerospace industry.[27] In addition to Wang Yong, the State Councilor mentioned above, the 19th Central Committee includes seven other full members and thirteen alternates who belong to the "cosmos club," most of whom are concurrently serving in key provincial posts as governor or party secretary. Many of them are relatively young (under the age of sixty) and, given their solid political and business experience, they are well positioned for further promotion. Some of them are strong candidates for the next Politburo, which will be chosen in 2022.

For Xi Jinping, bringing the business executives of SOEs (especially those in the important industry of aerospace) into top leadership posts could serve four objectives. First, nurturing a new set of protégés hailing from China's SOEs allows Xi to diversify the composition of his power base, thereby broadening his support within the party leadership. Second, leaders from SOE and technical backgrounds are seen as "less tainted by the political bureaucracy's interests and undesirable customs."[28] Bringing in provincial leaders who are "outsiders"—with respect to both a locality and its provincial bureaucracy—allows Xi to undermine forces of localism and potential factionalism that might otherwise constrain his power. Third, former CEOs possess substantial and multifaceted business experience. Xi expects these individuals to improve the financial administration of their respective provinces and implement policies to stimulate their local economies. And fourth, Xi Jinping has long been advocating for prioritizing China's space program and the aerospace industry on both the military and civilian fronts, which he views as the best testimony to China's national strength and status on the world stage.

Wealthy private entrepreneurs have also become more visible, albeit in the less-powerful state institutions, such as the National People's Congress and its advisory body, the **Chinese People's Political Consultative Conference** (CPPCC).[‡] The net worth of the 153 deputies to the 2018 meeting of these two bodies who are listed among China's "super rich" was estimated at US$650 billion.[29] The list includes 102 billionaires, one of whom is Pony Ma, CEO of Tencent, one of the world's largest internet and technology companies. One of the "just barely" billionaires in the CPPCC was Neil Shen, a graduate of Yale University, who was named in 2018 by *Forbes* magazine as the World's Top Venture Capital Investor. By way of comparison, there were 207 millionaires, but no billionaires, in the U.S. Congress that same year. The total wealth of all the members of the House of Representatives and Senate was US$2.4 billion.[30]

Clearly, although private entrepreneurs play a much more significant role in the PRC than they did just a decade ago, there is still a long way to go before their political clout comes anywhere near matching their economic power. It is worth noting that the children of many of the top Chinese leaders are now pursuing careers in the business sector, with most working in foreign joint ventures such as investment banks in Hong Kong, rather than climbing the ladder of the CCP political hierarchy as their technocrat fathers did. If, as is likely, some of them aspire to political careers, it would represent a very different path to power, with important implications for the future of the Chinese communist party-state.

Along with the economic and political rise of entrepreneurs, there has also been an increase in the power and prevalence of lawyers in China (see chap. 7). The Maoist system was hostile to both the legal profession and the legal system. At the start of the reform era in the early 1980s, there were only three thousand lawyers in a country of over one billion people.[31] Since then, the number of registered lawyers and law school students has increased significantly. In early 2017, China had a total of 300,000 registered lawyers in about 25,000 registered law firms.[32] The legal profession remains a tiny one (especially on a per capita basis) when compared to the more than one million lawyers in the United States. But the number of lawyers in China has increased dramatically in recent years (an average of 9.5 percent annual increase over the past eight years) and will likely become even more so in the years to come. There are now more than 630 law schools and law departments in China, graduating about 100,000 students each year.[33]

---

‡ The CPPCC consists of more than two thousand members who represent a wide range of constituencies, including the CCP, China's noncommunist "democratic parties," official mass organizations (such as the All-China Women's Federation), various occupational circles (such as artists and writers, educators, medical personnel, and farmers), ethnic minorities, and religions. Although the majority of members of the CPPCC are noncommunists, the organization is bound by its charter to accept the leadership of the CCP, and it has always been headed by a high-ranking party leader. The Conference meets each year for about two weeks, concurrent with the annual session of the National People's Congress, but its function is only to advise the government; it has no legislative power of its own.

Some of China's lawyers work outside the political establishment to challenge abuses of power, including rampant official corruption, and seek to promote the rule of law and civil society at the grassroots level. While activist lawyers are an emerging factor in Chinese politics, they are still subject to regulation and persecution by the party-state. All lawyers must be licensed by the government, and the authorities often refuse to renew licenses if the lawyer in question is regarded as a "troublemaker." Under Xi Jinping there has been extensive suppression of so-call "rights lawyers" who advocate for greater legal protection for China's citizens against the arbitrary of state power and sometime take action in defense of those rights.[34]

Other lawyers work within the political or intellectual establishment and some become political leaders. The rapid rise of leaders with legal training is an important trend in Chinese politics. The percentage of full members of the CCP central committee trained in law increased from 1.7 percent in the 14th Central Committee in 1997 to 18.6 percent in the 19th Central Committee in 2017.[35] Four members of the current Politburo, including two Standing Committee members, have some training in legal studies. For example, Premier Li Keqiang received undergraduate training in law at Peking University, and Wang Huning served as dean of the law school at Fudan University. Presently, Chief Justice of the Supreme People's Court Zhou Qiang, Chief of the Supreme People's Procuracy Zhang Jun, Director of the National Supervision Commission Yang Xiaodu, and Auditor General of the State Council Hu Zhejun all hold law degrees.

An important theoretical proposition in Western studies of political elites is that the occupational identity of the leaders in a given country correlates with—and sometimes has a determining effect on—the nature of the political system. Political elites often want to leave their leadership legacy in the area in which they have a personal or professional interest. Technocrats, for example, are often particularly interested in economic growth and technological development due to their own backgrounds in these subjects. It will be interesting to watch whether the growing presence of lawyers and social scientists in the current generation of leaders will give greater attention to meaningful political and legal reform than did the preceding generations of communist ideologues, revolutionary veterans, and engineer technocrats.

INDIVIDUAL RULE VS. INSTITUTIONAL CONSTRAINTS

China's party-state has been vigorous in responding to the changing environment and potential challenges facing the CCP and the country over the past few decades. The constant efforts to recruit new blood for party membership and to broaden the channels for elite advancement help explain the remarkable survival and durability of the CCP, especially in light of the collapse of many communist regimes in the recent past. What has further differentiated reform era China from other authoritarian political systems, according to some scholars, is that the CCP has developed effective institutional mechanisms to make the party-state "more accountable, responsive, and law-bound."[36] Two of the most important institutional developments have been the establishment of (1) term limits on various levels of leadership, especially those that define the succession norms for the top leader; and (2) collective leadership, which emphasizes the power-sharing among competing factions or coalitions and their deal-making based on accepted rules, norms, and procedures.[37]

During the 19th Party Congress and the 13th National People's Congress, Xi Jinping completed the remarkable task of consolidating his power on multiple fronts—constitutional, ideological, institutional, political, and personnel (see chaps. 4 and 5). Xi's decision to abolish term limits for the PRC presidency has reversed succession norms. Many observers have concluded that politics in China has returned to strongman rule, with collective leadership having come to an end. In line with this perspective, the nature of Chinese elite politics can be characterized, once again, by old-fashioned zero-sum games and winner-takes-all competition instead of by the recent experimentation in factional negotiation and compromise. Do these perceived changes in Xi Jinping's "new era" reflect a temporary phenomenon or a broader, long-term trend in Chinese politics? Does the line-up of the current CCP leadership validate this analysis? What challenges will Xi face?

Political Succession: Lessons from the Past and Challenges for the Future

Mao Zedong wielded enormous, almost unchallengeable, personal power for most of the first three decades following the founding of the PRC in 1949 (see chap. 3). He treated succession as if it were his own private matter; discussion of any power transition for post-Mao leadership was taboo, and he eliminated two of his expected successors who had displeased him, Liu Shaoqi in 1966 and Lin Biao in 1971. The omnipresent slogan "Long Live Chairman Mao!" reinforced the illusion of Mao's "immortality." The Chairman literally held on to power until he exhaled his dying breath in September 1976. The result was a cataclysmic succession struggle that led, ironically, to Deng Xiaoping's rise to power and the reversal of most of the policies that characterized Maoist China.

During the Deng era, political succession and generational change in the Chinese leadership became a matter of public concern (see chap. 4). Yet, because of his legendary political career, no leader seriously challenged Deng's ultimate authority. Even when he did not hold any important leadership positions following the 1989 Tiananmen crisis, Deng was still regarded as China's "paramount leader." For many years during the 1990s, speculation by people in China and China Watchers abroad about when the elderly and ailing Deng would die often caused stock markets in Hong Kong and China to fluctuate wildly. Like Mao, Deng thought that who would take over after him was a decision for him alone to determine. In fact, also like Mao (though more gently), he twice removed leaders he had tapped to succeed him, Hu Yaobang in 1986 and Zhao Ziyang in 1989, because he considered both of them as being too soft on democracy protesters. But unlike Mao, Deng effectively handed over the reins of power to Jiang well before he died in 1997. In particular, with Deng's strong input, the PRC Constitution amended in 1982 established the two five-year term limits for the presidency and vice presidency, abolishing the lifetime tenure of top Chinese leaders.

Jiang Zemin had neither the charisma nor the revolutionary experience possessed by Mao or Deng. To a large extent, Jiang exercised power primarily through coalition-building and political compromise. Hu Jintao's generation of leaders relied even more on power-sharing and consensus-finding. Willingly or not, Hu often characterized his top leadership role as being "first among equals" in his generation of leaders. Under Jiang and Hu, the CCP adopted more regulations on term limits for party and government leaders at various levels. According to these regulations, an individual leader cannot hold the same position for more than two terms, and no leader can remain at the same level of leadership for more than fifteen years. Although the CCP Constitution does not specify term limits for the general secretary of the party, party regulations establish that two-term limits apply to all party leaders. In light of the recent PRC Constitution amendment to abolish term limits for the presidency, one can expect that the CCP will similarly change the party regulations to allow the general secretary of the CCP to stay in that position longer than two terms. A change of party regulations is, or course, much easier than a constitutional amendment.

Post-Deng succession norms have also included the practice of "successor-in-training." Under that norm, after the general secretary's first five-year term, he and the CCP leadership would select one or two younger leaders to be promoted to the Politburo Standing Committee (one of whom would be the successor to general secretary when the latter completes his second term). This was precisely what happened to Hu Jintao and Xi Jinping, both of whom served as an "heir apparent."

Another informal arrangement for political succession in the post-Deng era has been the phenomenon called "grandpa-designated successor" (*gedai zhiding jiebanren*), which refers to the practice of the current general secretary selecting the leader of two generations below him. Deng (second generation) not only designated Jiang (third generation) to succeed him but also Hu Jintao (fourth generation) to be the top leader to follow Jiang. Jiang similarly chose Xi Jinping (fifth generation) to take over from Hu, and Hu picked his protégé, Hu Chunhua (sixth generation), the youngest member of the current Politburo and the youngest vice premier on the State Council, to rule after Xi. The "heir apparent" is therefore by design a protégé of a proceeding top leader, not of the incumbent general secretary. To a great extent, in both the Jiang and Hu eras, the power of top leaders was constrained by other members of the Politburo Standing Committee, especially by those who represented the rival faction or coalition.

These succession norms, especially term limits for the general secretary of the party, have served as an institutional mechanism for the orderly and peaceful transition of power. This was true of the transition of Jiang to Hu in 2002 and then Hu to Xi in 2012. This kind of mechanism has multiple positive effects: for instance, consolidating the unity and solidarity of the leadership, regulating the jockeying among political elites, and providing consolation to the rival (both individual and faction) in anticipation of a future rotation to the driver's seat in the leadership. This rotation also presents the possibility that policy changes can be pursued under the next top leader, forming a "safety valve for potential popular discontent."[38]

Nevertheless, these institutional constraints on the general secretary were not without problem or deficiencies. The so-called "team of rivals" often led to factional infighting, political fragmentation, and policy deadlock. Each Politburo Standing Committee member tended to control one functional area, and thus there was poor coordination in policy implementation. The General Secretary of the party did not have enough power to counter rampant official corruption and other serious challenges. The norms for identifying a "successor-in-training" likely undermined the power and authority of the general secretary and made him become a lame duck during the entire second five-year term.

All of these deficiencies—real or perceived—in CCP political succession norms have become reasons Xi and his followers have used to justify his rapid consolidation of power and his radical change of post-Mao succession norms. The political capital that Xi gained during his first five-year term through his bold anticorruption campaign, sweeping military reforms, a popular policy agenda in environmental protection and poverty alleviation, and nationalistic and proactive foreign policy moves such as the Belt and Road Initiative (see chap. 8) apparently enabled him to abolish the term limits for the presidency and consolidate his personal power in other ways without major opposition from other party leaders.

Xi's ambition to be a Mao-like figure was evident in a number of important maneuvers on his part prior to that. During his first term, in addition to holding the top posts in the party, government, and military, Xi also chaired the newly established National Security Committee, the Central Leading Group for Comprehensively Deepening Reforms, and several central leading groups in important functional areas, including foreign affairs, finance and the economy, internet security and information technology, and military reform—for a total of fourteen top leadership positions. The Central Leading Group for Comprehensively Deepening Reforms, as some scholars have observed, has become more powerful than the State Council in socioeconomic decision making.[39] Xi's dominant power; the glorification of the Cultural Revolution-style personality cult; the purge of Sun Zhengcai, a rising star in the Politburo, on corruption charges; the decision to not select a successor-in-training at the 19th Party Congress; and the appointment of heavyweight political ally Wang Qishan (who does not even serve on the current Central Committee) to be PRC vice president; all undermine the institutional power of the Politburo Standing Committee, thereby allowing Xi to stay in power indefinitely.

The dire consequences, as critics argue, may likely include the absence of a succession principle or mechanism, greater centralization of decision making, a lack of incentives for innovative work by other leaders, and most importantly, a return to an era of vicious power struggles—a zero-sum game in which power contenders will ruthlessly engage over the years to come. One-man rule is surely not sustainable for the governance of the world's most populous country in the twenty-first century, but the real issue is what, if anything, will bring an end of this trend towards autocracy.

Institutional Rules and Factional Politics Remain

The institutional mechanisms that have been developed over the past three decades will not disappear overnight. Rules and norms, such as the regional and bureaucratic representation of seats on the Central Committee discussed earlier, the mandatory retirement age for various levels of leadership, and innerparty "more candidates than seats election," were all applied at the 19th Party Congress. The rate of change of CCP Central Committee membership has been remarkably high over the past thirty-five years (1982–2017). Newcomers have constituted an average of 64 percent at each of the five Party Congresses held during that period. The 2017 CCP Congress, which had a Central Committee turnover rate of 75 percent, also saw large membership turnovers in the other leading bodies of the CCP (see Figure 6.6). The infusion of new blood into the leadership cannot but help the party-state adapt to changing circumstances and new challenges. This could either strengthen Xi's hand or give rise to younger leaders who have concerns about the return to strongman rule in Chinese politics.

The equal regional distribution of full membership seats on the CCP Central Committee has a profound effect the relationship between the central party-state and local authorities. This shift has been hastened by the emergence of local interests politically and economically empowered by the decentralization stemming from China's market reforms. Understandably, local leaders (mainly provincial and municipal leaders) tend to side with the top national leaders who will protect or advance their interests. Politicians in areas that have benefited from the reforms want to keep the policy orientation that favors their interests, while those in disadvantaged regions favor members of the central leadership who represent a change in direction. Whichever "side" they are on, local leaders in China have a much bigger stake in—and a bigger opportunity to influence—elite politics than ever before in the history of the People's Republic.

Strongman politics also cannot eliminate factional competition. Xi's rapid consolidation of power for him and his faction within the CCP leadership is uncontroversial, but it has not yet become a winner-take-all game. Other factions who make up a rival coalition, though noticeably weakened, still occupy a significant number of seats in the most important leadership bodies.

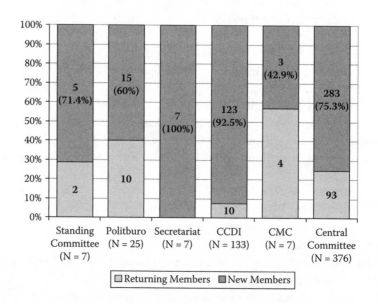

FIGURE 6.6 Membership Turnover of Top CCP Organizations 19th Party Congress (October 2017)

Note: CDIC = Central Commission for Discipline Inspection; CMC = Central Military Commission. Cheng Li's research.

In the Jiang and Hu eras, the CCP leadership was structured by an unofficial system of checks and balances between two informal political coalitions that still influences Chinese elite politics. This is not the kind of constitutional system of checks and balances that operates with the executive, legislative, and judicial branches of the U.S. government, an essential element of a truly democratic system that limits the power of any individual, party, or government institution. It is more of an intra-elite tacit agreement to share power and accommodate different interests in the policy-making process.

The two groups can be labeled the **elitist coalition,** which was born in the Jiang Zemin era and is currently led by Xi Jinping, who was a protégé of Jiang Zemin, and the **populist coalition,** previously led by former General Secretary-President Hu Jintao and now led by Premier Li Keqiang. The elitist coalition represents business interests, including state-owned enterprises, and China's more prosperous coastal regions. The populist coalition places greater emphasis on addressing economic inequalities, affordable housing, and social welfare.

Upon his ascension to the post of general secretary of the party in 2002, Hu Jintao quickly sensed that his mandate was to fix the economic disparities associated with Jiang's leadership. As a result, Hu, in partnership with Premier Wen Jiabao, used his time at the helm to promote a populist strategy under new catchphrases such as "scientific development" and "harmonious society" (see chap. 5). While some refer to the Hu–Wen years as the "lost decade" because of lack of significant progress in economic, political, and legal reform, there were, in addition to continuing high growth rates (10.5 percent per year), important gains in areas of central concerns to the populists. These included significantly expanding health-care insurance: by 2010 more than 90 percent of both the urban and rural population had at least minimal coverage.[40]

Neither the elitist nor the populist coalition is capable of-—nor really wants to— completely defeat the other. Each coalition has its own strengths, including different constituencies, which the other does not possess. When it comes to policy making, their relationship is one of both competition and cooperation. This situation is sometimes referred to as the "one-party, two-coalitions" political mechanism.[41]

These leaders of the two coalitions have distinct personal backgrounds, career trajectories, and political associations. Many of the top leaders in the elitist coalition are children of revolutionary heroes or high-ranking officials. This group of so-called **princelings** includes Xi Jinping, whose father was a close associate of Mao's and who fell afoul of the Chairman's ideological wrath in the early 1960s and later emerged as a strong proponent of economic reform, and his vice president Wang Qishan, whose father-in-law was vice premier and a Politburo Standing Committee member. The elitists have advanced their political careers primarily in Shanghai (and are sometimes referred to as the "Shanghai Gang") or other major cities or coastal provinces.

By contrast, most of the leading figures in the populist coalition, for example, Hu Jintao, Li Keqiang, and a Standing Committee newcomer, Wang Yang, come from more humble or less-privileged families. They usually had substantial leadership experience in less-developed inland provinces. For example, Hu spent most of his working life in some of the least developed provinces of China's inland region, including fourteen years in Gansu, three years in Guizhou, and four years in Tibet.

Similarly, Li served as a provincial chief in Henan, a large inland agricultural province, for many years, and Wang worked in his native Anhui province, one of the poorest in China, for almost twenty years before starting his climb toward the center of power.

Many of the prominent populist leaders also advanced their political careers through the ranks of the **Chinese Communist Youth League (CCYL)** and have therefore garnered the label *tuanpai*, literally, "league faction" (see Box 6.1). The princelings and *tuanpai* served as the core groups in the larger competing political coalitions—elitists and populists, respectively.

It is very important to note that both camps share fundamental goals: to ensure China's political and social stability, promote continued economic growth, enhance China's status as a major international player, and, most importantly, the survival of CCP rule. These common goals push the two factions to compromise and cooperate with each other more often than not. To a degree, leaders of the elitist coalition also recognize the need to allocate more resources to inland regions and help vulnerable social groups, just as the populists understand the importance of maintaining rapid economic growth to meet the rising expectations of China's entrepreneurs and urban middle class. Through popular policy initiatives and a more informal personal style—such as eating at an ordinary dumpling restaurant in Beijing[42]—Xi Jinping has been particularly effective in presenting himself as a leader of the people instead of as a princeling who cares more for the rich and powerful.

Furthermore, because the leaders of the factions differ in expertise, credentials, and experiences, they understand that they need to find common ground to coexist

---

BOX 6.1 THE YOUNG PIONEERS AND THE CCYL

The CCP has two organizations that bring together young people to learn about party ideology and policies and to engage in service projects and other activities that support party goals: the Young Pioneers and the Chinese Communist Youth League (CCYL).

Almost all students in the PRC between the ages of seven and fourteen belong to the Young Pioneers, whose official purpose is "to promote 'indoctrination of children by cultivating [positive] feelings of the Party and the socialist motherland.'" New members make the following pledge: "We take our oath under the flag of Young Pioneers: I promise to follow the lead and teachings of the CCP, to study well, to work well, to labor well—to prepare myself and sacrifice all my energy for Communism."[§]

The CCYL is an organization for people aged fourteen to twenty-eight. Its main function is to identify and foster new communist party members. At the time of its national congress in June 2018, the CCYL had 81 million members. The CCYL's mission statement refers to the organization as the "reserve army" for the Party. In addition to providing ideological training, the league runs a variety of social service programs and operates several prominent media outlets, notably the *China Youth Daily* newspaper. Membership in the CCYL does not guarantee party membership, nor is participation in the youth organization required to join the CCP. Nonetheless, being active in the CCYL can certainly facilitate becoming a full party member.

[§]Hunter Hunt, "Joining the Party: Youth Recruitment in the Chinese Communist Party," *US-China Today*, Nov. 7, 2011, http://uschina.usc.edu/article@usct?joining_the_party_youth_recruitment_in_the_chinese_communist_party_17639.aspx

and govern effectively. The *tuanpai* excel in terms of organization and propaganda and have often had experience in rural administration, especially in poor inland regions. However, they generally lack experience and credentials in some of the most important administrative areas and in relation to the handling of foreign trade, foreign investment, banking, and other crucial aspects of economic policy making. Therefore, they have to cooperate with the elitist coalition, who have strong backgrounds in economic and financial administration and have spent most of their careers in the developed coastal cities. This bipartisan collective leadership can contribute, as was the case in the Jiang and Hu eras, to a more pluralistic decision-making process through which political leaders can represent various social and geographic constituencies.

But, overall, the Xi camp and the princelings have clearly gained the upper hand in most key civilian and military organizations in the past few years.[43] Five of the seven members of Standing Committee are part of the elitist coalition, with only two from the populist *tuanpai* (see Table 6.1). Xi's protégés hold thirteen out of twenty-five seats on the Politburo, and the Xi camp now makes up the majority of the 376-member Central Committee.

The dominance of the elitist faction in the current leadership bodies, however, does not necessarily mean a return to "winner takes all" in Chinese politics at the top. It should be noted that the populist camp and *tuanpai* are still well represented in various important leadership bodies. *Tuanpai* leaders currently constitute 29 percent of the Politburo Standing Committee membership, 12 percent of the Politburo, 22 percent of the State Council, and 11 percent of the Central Committee. These numbers do not include other leaders who are inclined toward the populist coalition's policy preferences.

CONCLUSION

At a time when China confronts many tough choices, the CCP leadership may find it increasingly difficult to reach a consensus on how to manage crucial issues. Such issues include the regional redistribution of resources, an inadequate public-health system, inadequate environmental protection, ethnic tensions in Tibet and Xinjiang, relations with Taiwan, banking system reform, denuclearization and stability of the Korean peninsula, trade disputes with the United States, and territorial disputes in the East China Sea and South China Sea. This could lead to challenges to Xi's hold on power and concerns about the absence of succession mechanisms. Political paralysis over key issues could not only impede effective policy making and leadership unity, but could also dissolve into ruthless factional power struggles, perhaps even involving the military. Such a scenario could undermine the legitimacy of the political system and threaten the stability of the country at large.

China is at a crossroads in the development of a system of governance for an increasingly modern, prosperous, and globalized country. Political institutionalization, including institutionalized succession rules, some kind of checks and balances that constrain individual leaders, and a means for the representation of different interests are important parts of this. There is a tension between the need for such institutionalization and Xi Jinping's consolidation of personal power that will shape the dynamics of Chinese politics in the years ahead.

But, at bottom, this tension between individual rule and institutional constraints reflects major deficiencies in China's authoritarian political structure that are unlikely to be mitigated through a strongman's centralized power or policy adjustments. Rather, addressing these will require systematic political changes that may stretch the CCP's remarkable record of adaptability and resilience that have been critical to its survival by pointing in the direction of greater political institutionalization and democratic governance.

NOTES

1. Christopher K. Johnson, Scott Kennedy, and Mingda Qiu, "Xi's Signature Governance Innovation: The Rise of Leading Small Groups," Center for Strategic and International Studies, Oct. 17, 2017, https://www.csis.org/analysis/xis-signature-governance-innovation-rise-leading-small-groups

2. Alice Miller, "More Already on the Central Committee's Leading Small Groups," *China Leadership Monitor*, July 28, 2014, https://www.hoover.org/research/more-already-central-committees-leading-small-groups

3. Johnson, Kennedy, and Qiu, "Xi's Signature Governance Innovation."

4. *China Economic History Forum*, May 3, 2006, http://web.archive.org/web/20080604234836/http://economy.guoxue.com/article.php/8291/2. For more on Professor He's views concerning the rule of law in China, see He Weifang, *In the Name of Justice: Striving for the Rule of Law in China* (Washington, DC: Brookings Institution, 2012).

5. Mao Zedong, "Problems of War and Strategy," *Selected Works of Mao Tse-tung*, vol. 2, (Beijing: Foreign Languages Press, 1965): 224, http://archive.org/details/SelectedWorksOfMaoTse-tungVol.Ii.

6. James Mulvenon, "Chairman Hu and the PLA's "New Historic Missions," *China Leadership Monitor*, no. 27 (Winter 2009), http://media.hoover.org/sites/default/files/documents/CLM27JM.pdf

7. Peter Wood, "PLA Oath," Commentary on East Asian Security Issues & Foreign Policy, May 13, 2017, https://www.p-wood.co/2017/05/13/oaths/

8. "China's Communist Party Is Becoming Choosier about New Members," *Economist*, Nov. 23, 2017.

9. Hong Yong Lee, *From Revolutionary Cadres to Party Technocrats in Socialist China* (Berkeley: University of California Press, 1990), 291.

10. *Xinhua banyüe kan* (*Xinhua* bimonthly), Jan. 2, 1957, 89; and cited in Franz Schurmann, *Ideology and Organization in Communist China*, 2nd ed. (Berkeley: University of California Press, 1968), 283.

11. Lee, *From Revolutionary Cadres*, 302.

12. *Shijie ribao* (World Journal), June 28, 1999, A9; "CPC has 89.6 million members," *Xinhua*, July 1, 2018, http://www.china.org.cn/china/2018-07/01/content_54278031.htm

13. Alice Miller, "The New Party Politburo Leadership," *China Leadership Monitor*, no. 40 (Winter 2013): 3, 14, http://www.hoover.org/publications/china-leadership-monitor/article/137951.

14. Cheng Li, "China's Midterm Jockeying: Gearing Up for 2012 Part 1: Provincial Chiefs," *China Leadership Monitor*, No. 31 (Winter 2010): 12, http://www.hoover.org/publications/china-leadership-monitor/article/5330.

15. Miller, "The New Party Politburo Leadership."

16. "China's Labor Force Lags behind in Higher Education," *People's Daily*, May 21, 2010, http://english.peopledaily.com.cn/90001/90782/6994379.html

17. "China's Communist Party Membership Exceeds 85 million," *Xinhua*, June 30, 2013, http://news.xinhuanet.com/english/china/2013-06/30/c_132498982.htm. The 2002 figure is from http://www.chinatoday.com/org/cpc/; and also http://www.xinhuanet.com/politics/2017-06/30/c_1121242479.htm.

18. For more discussion of this development, see Zhiyue Bo, "China's New Provincial Leaders: Major Reshuffling before the 17th National Party Congress," *China: An International Journal* 5, no. 1 (Mar. 2007): 1–25; and Cheng Li, "Pivotal Stepping-Stone: Local Leaders' Representation on the 17th Central Committee," *China Leadership Monitor*, no. 23 (Winter 2008): 1–13, http://www.hoover.org/publications/china-leadership-monitor/article/5772.

19. For more discussion of the new development of the Chinese think tanks under Xi Jinping, see Cheng Li, *The Power of Ideas: The Rising Influence of Thinkers and Think Tanks in China* (Singapore: World Scientific Publishing Company, 2017), 3–56.

20. Xi Jinping, "Zai wangluo anquan he xinxihua gongzuo zuotanhui shang de jiang-hua" [Speech at the internet and information security work conference]. *Xinhua* Newsnet, Apr. 25, 2016, (http://news.xinhuanet.com/politics/2016-04/25/c_1118731175.htm).

21. See Ryan Mitchell, "China's Crown Theorist: The Rise of Wang Huning," *Foreign Affairs Snapshot*, Dec.. 4, 2017, https://www.foreignaffairs.com/articles/china/2017-12-04/chinas-crown-theorist

22. Cheng Li, *Chinese Politics in the Xi Jinping Era: Reassessing Collective Leadership*. (Washington, DC: Brookings Institution Press, 2016), 321–324.

23. The data in this paragraph come from Nicholas Kristoff, "China's Private Businesses Face Inspection," *New York Times*, Aug. 3, 1989, 68; Nicholas Lardy, *Markets over Mao: The Rise of Private Business in China*. (Washington, DC: Peterson Institute for International Economics, 2014), 70; and "China's Private Sector Contributes Greatly to Economic Growth," *Xinhua*, Mar. 6, 2018, http://www.xinhuanet.com/english/2018-03/06/c_137020127.htm

24. The United Front Department of the CCP Central Committee, *2005 nian Zhongguo siying qiye diaocha baogao* (A survey of private enterprises in 2005). See also http://www.southcn.com/finance/gdmqgc/gdmqyyrl/200502030218.htm.

25. Chinese Academy of Social Sciences, "2013 Social Blue Book," reported at http://dailynews.sina.com/bg/chn/chnpolitics/sinacn/20121219/13274074905.htm

26. "Chinese Communist Party Endorses the Spirit of Enterprise," *China Banking News*, Oct. 23, 2017, http://www.chinabankingnews.com/2017/10/23/chinese-communist-party-endorses-spirit-enterprise/

27. Geng Shenzhen, "Zhongguo zhengzhi diliudai lingdaoceng 'yuzhoubang' jueqi" [The rise of "Cosmos Club" members in the sixth generation of Chinese leaders], *Zhongyang ribao* [Central Daily], May 6, 2015; and Li, *Chinese Politics in the Xi Jinping Era*, 181.

28. Cheng Li and Lucy Xu, "The Rise of State-Owned Enterprise Executives in China's Provincial Leadership," *China and US Focus*, Feb. 21, 2017.

29. "China's 'Super Rich' Legislators Get Richer," *Japan Times*, Mar. 2, 2018, https://www.japantimes.co.jp/news/2018/03/02/asia-pacific/politics-diplomacy-asia-pacific/chinas-super-rich-legislators-get-richer/

30. David Hawkings, "Wealth of Congress: Richer Than Ever, but Mostly at the Very Top," *rollcall.com*, Feb. 27, 2018, https://www.rollcall.com/news/hawkings/congress-richer-ever-mostly-top

31. Cheng Li, "The Rise of the Legal Profession in the Chinese Leadership," *China Leadership Monitor*, no. 43 (Fall 2013), https://www.hoover.org/research/rise-legal-profession-chinese-leadership

32. Xinhua News Agency, Jan. 9, 2017, http://www.xinhuanet.com/legal/2017-01/09/c_1120275319.htm.

33. Cao Yin, "Law Graduates Facing Bleak Job Prospects," *China Daily*, Feb. 9, 2015, http://www.chinadaily.com.cn/china/2015-02/09/content_19526194.htm

34. "China: Free Rights Lawyers, Reinstate Law Licenses," Amnesty International, July 5, 2018, https://www.hrw.org/news/2018/07/05/china-free-rights-lawyers-reinstate-law-licenses

35. Cheng Li's database research.

36. Susan L. Shirk, "China in Xi's 'New Era': The Return to Personalistic Rule," *Journal of Democracy* 29, no. 2 (Apr. 2018): 22–36. See also Francis Fukuyama, "China's 'Bad Emperor' Returns," *Washington Post*, Mar. 6, 2018.

37. Li, *Chinese Politics in the Xi Jinping Era*, 7–39.

38. Mary Gallagher, "Does a Stronger Xi Mean a Weaker Chinese Communist Party?" *New York Times*, Mar. 2, 2018.

39. Shirk, "China in Xi's 'New Era.'"

40. W. C. Yip, W. C. Hsiao, W. Chen, S. Hu, J. Ma, and A. Maynard, "Early Appraisal of China's Huge and Complex Health-Care Reforms," *Lancet*, Mar. 3, 2012: 833–842.

41. For more detailed discussion of the "one party, two coalitions" mechanism, see Cheng Li, *Tongwang Zhongnanhai zhilu—Zhonggong shibada zhiqian gaoceng lingdao qunti* (The Road to Zhongnanhai: High-Level Leadership Groups on the Eve of the 18th Party Congress) (New York: Mirror Books, 2012).

42. Matt Schiavenza, "Xi Jinping Eats Some Dumplings at a Restaurant . . . and China Swoons: Why the President's Casual Lunch Resonates So Much in the Country," *The Atlantic*, Dec. 30, 2013, https://www.theatlantic.com/china/archive/2013/12/xi-jinping-eats-some-dumplings-at-a-restaurant/282719/

43. For more discussion of the princelings' victory at the 18th Party Congress, see Cheng Li, "Rule of the Princelings," *Cairo Review of Global Affairs*, no. 8 (Winter 2013): 34–47.

China's Legal System

JACQUES DELISLE

Law and the legal system have come to play large and complex roles in China during the reform era. Yet, accounts of contemporary China often suggest little role for law. They depict China's recent history as one of market-conforming and internationally engaged economic growth, resilient and adaptable authoritarian politics, and lack of rule of law, or even much rule by law.* Law has been a durable theme since Deng Xiaoping became China's paramount leader after Mao Zedong's death. In 1978, the reform era's founding charter, the Communiqué of the Third Plenum of the Eleventh Central Committee, directed that there must be laws, that the laws must be followed and strictly enforced, and that violations of law must be corrected. A key slogan of the Jiang Zemin years called for "ruling the country by law" and "building a socialist rule of law state."

Hu Jintao called the constitution the country's "fundamental" and inviolable law, and insisted that it was to be implemented by all state and private entities. He mentioned law a record number of times in his political work report to the 17th Party Congress in 2007. In 2011, Wu Bangguo, chairman of the National People's Congress (NPC), declared that construction of China's socialist legal system was basically complete. Xi Jinping's emergence as China's top leader in 2012 brought renewed insistence on law's importance. The 18th Party Congress political work report directed the party

---

* "Rule by law" refers to a system in which a principal means for regulating economic, social, political, and state behavior is legal rules—whatever their content—that are publicly known, the product of authorized processes or institutions, and applied fairly and consistently. "Rule of law" requires more, including that laws operate as a reliable constraint upon—and not serve merely as a narrow instrument of—the state or wielders of political power and, on more restrictive definitions, meet substantive standards of justice or protection of rights.

to operate "within the limits of the constitution and the law" and to uphold their authority. On the thirtieth anniversary of the 1982 PRC constitution, Xi announced that "we must firmly establish, throughout society, the authority of the constitution and the law." The 18th Central Committee's Third Plenum in 2013 pledged to "strengthen rule of law guarantees" and constrain power within a "cage" of institutions and rules. The following year, the Fourth Plenum—often called the "rule of law plenum"—declared the "rule of law" a guiding force in the Chinese Communist Party's (CCP) pursuit of major tasks. Xi included "governing the country according to law" among his "four comprehensive" goals, reiterated at the 19th Party Congress in 2017.[1]

This rhetoric has not translated fully into reality. Law's roles have remained limited and are the subject of much disagreement among observers in China and abroad. Still, some general—if uneven—patterns have emerged. The turn to law has fallen between an embrace of market-oriented economic development and continued shunning of political democracy. The party-state has invested many material resources and much political capital in laws and legal institutions. Law has been expected to play—and to some extent has played—significant roles in promoting economic development, maintaining order, and sustaining the party's rule. Law's effects have varied over time, across fields, and in different places in China. Legal development remains characterized by gaps between rule of law ideals and many of law's formal promises, on one hand, and how law functions in practice, on the other. Constituencies favoring greater reliance on law and demands for more legality create pressure for roles for law and legal institutions that are more robust and, to Western eyes, more familiar. But these forces face many impediments, ranging from practical difficulties to popular disillusionment to elite skepticism. The trajectory of legal change in China is uncertain and continues to be a test for global theories about law's role in supporting economic development and political order.

CHINA'S LEGAL SYSTEM THEN AND NOW

China's legal system has ancient roots, with the earliest legal code dating—depending on one's definition—to the Spring and Autumn Period (770–476 BCE) or the Han dynasty (206 BCE–220 CE). Debates over the role of law *(fa)*, as opposed to moral or social norms *(li)*, originated with conflicts between Confucian and Legalist views more than two millennia ago and still resonate in Chinese legal discourse today. Although laws and the legal system changed over many centuries of dynastic rule, several broad features characterized law in "traditional" China. Elaborate written codes focused primarily on criminal and, to a lesser extent, administrative matters. Punishments were imposed for acts merely analogous to those proscribed by law. Laws governing economic and other civil relations were sparse, and civil disputes were left largely to informal resolution by social institutions. Formal enforcement of law, including criminal sanctions, was a means of governance secondary to instilling Confucian norms by which people should guide their own behavior. Although officials and staff at various levels specialized in legal affairs, there was no formal separation of powers and few distinctly legal institutions. All legislative, executive, and judicial power rested, in principle, with the emperor. At the local level, the magistrate was an omnicompetent official, charged with all aspects of governing, including judicial functions. There was no legal profession, and those who offered litigation services could risk criminal punishment.

Late Qing and Republican reformers borrowed extensively from Western legal ideas. Following the political thought of Sun Yat-sen (see chap. 2), the constitution of the Republic of China adopted a five-power structure that included three Western-style branches (legislative, executive, and judicial) and two derived from Chinese tradition (a "control" organ focusing on government misbehavior, and a civil service exam organ). It also included a formally democratic system of popular sovereignty, constitutional review, and liberal citizens' rights. The basic "six laws" of the Republic drew heavily from Western models. They included substantive and procedural statutes for criminal, civil, and administrative law. Many of these laws and legal institutions were never effective in mainland China, where the Republic failed to consolidate power and suspended the constitution amid conflict with China's communist revolutionaries.

The laws and institutions established under the People's Republic of China (PRC) adapted Soviet models. The PRC adopted a constitution in 1956 based on the USSR's Stalin constitution, with principles of party rule, nominal popular sovereignty, government structures, and, if only in name, liberal individual rights. The 1956 charter is broadly similar to the 1982 constitution—the fourth in the PRC's history—that is currently in force. The early PRC regime also established legal institutions that remain in place today. Radical phases of the Mao era, especially the Anti-Rightist Campaign and, more so, the Cultural Revolution (see chap. 3), dealt heavy blows to courts and other legal institutions. Coming after a highpoint of "socialist legality" in the middle 1950s, these campaigns attacked previously officially endorsed principles of respect for law and a degree of judicial independence and legal professionalism. The Cultural Revolution's most extreme phase largely shut down legal institutions (along with many other state organs) and brought withering attacks on legal rights as a bourgeois concept and law as a malevolent means for protecting class enemies.

The current PRC legal system is one of parliamentary supremacy, with executive and judicial institutions formally subordinate to the legislature, and a unitary nonfederal state, with local lawmaking power limited to that delegated by the central state. Key legal institutions include the people's courts, the people's procuracy, and the public security apparatus. The procuracy combines the functions of investigation and prosecution of serious criminal cases with oversight of malfeasance by other government organs. Public security bureaus, under the Ministry of Public Security, serve police and internal security and social monitoring functions, but the last of these responsibilities have been substantially reduced during the reform era, and the second role has been shifted largely to a Ministry of State Security. In 2013, a National Security Commission was established—under the CCP and thus more remote from the legal system—to centralize and consolidate means for addressing internal and external security threats.

The people's courts have a four-level structure, including basic-level, intermediate, and provincial high courts, and the Supreme People's Court. Different level courts have initial jurisdiction over more or less difficult or important cases. Each court's decision is subject to non-deferential review—essentially a second trial—by a higher-level court. Courts are divided into chambers or tribunals based on subject matter (such as criminal, civil, administrative, intellectual property law, and enforcement of judgments). Under the Supreme People's Court, multiprovincial circuit courts were established in 2015 , increasing the capacity for discretionary review of provincial court decisions, and, in 2018, specialized international commercial courts were launched to handle a select set of cases, primarily related to the Belt and Road Initiative. The Supreme People's Court exercises bureaucratic, ministry-like authority over the judiciary.

Broadly similar multitiered and hierarchical structures characterize the procuracy (headed by the Supreme People's Procuracy), the legislative branch (the people's congress system, with the NPC making national laws and lower-level congresses adopting more local measures), and the executive branch (the State Council and central ministries that issue regulations and rules, and provincial and local governments that exercise delegated rulemaking powers). In the context of an anticorruption drive under Xi, a constitutional amendment and related legislation shifted the procuracy's role (and the role of the Ministry of Supervision) in addressing official corruption to a National Supervision Commission (see chaps. 6 and 8).

Courts and other legal institutions are directly and indirectly under the leadership of the party, although the extent of party intervention varies and has declined in many areas during the reform era. The party plays a central role in selecting and promoting judges and court officials, many of whom are party members. Within each court, an adjudication committee, headed by the court president, has authority to shape and override decisions by the judges who hear a case. At each level, CCP **political-legal committees** (*zhengfa weiyuanhui*) have power to oversee courts and other legal institutions. Although the role of the committees has been reduced, party leadership over the judiciary remains a key principle. Court budgets and staffing depend on the people's congress and government at the court's own level, which has contributed to a form of "home court" judicial bias known as "local protectionism." Reforms adopted in the mid-2010s moved to address these problems by centralizing court budget and judicial personal decisions to the provincial and national levels. Compared to the Mao years, legal institutions in the reform era operate in an environment of much more extensive laws and regulations, much stronger official support for principles of legality, and a much larger and more professional cohort of lawyers.

BUILDING LAW AND LEGAL INSTITUTIONS

The building of law and legal institutions during the reform era has been extensive.[2] The "complete laws" of the PRC from 1949 to 1985 fit in a single volume. Twenty years later, a much thicker tome could not contain a year's output. During the reform era, the NPC or its Standing Committee has enacted hundreds of major laws and many more lesser ones. The State Council and its subordinate commissions and ministries, and local people's congresses and governments, have adopted tens of thousands of regulations and other rules with legal effect. Many of these have been amended repeatedly to accommodate China's changing conditions and policy goals or to conform to international norms.[3]

Unlike in earlier periods, when many rules were written only in "internal" or "secret" documents that were not to be shown to those whose behavior they governed, sources of law are now publicly available. Although ambiguity and confusion persist and formal mechanisms for resolving conflicts among sources of law remain weak and rarely used, there is now a clear hierarchy: the constitution (which is in principle supreme over other laws—if not party policy—but which generally has no legal effect absent implementing legislation), national legislation, central-level regulations and rules, lesser and more local rules, and "normative documents" that do not formally have the status of law. In practice, courts and other legal decision-makers often look to the most specific, rather than the highest-ranking, source of law. Party and policy documents provide many operative rules of governance that in many other systems would be created by law.

China has opened or reopened more than six hundred law schools that have trained many lawyers (who now number more than three hundred thousand and have been increasing nearly 10 percent annually), judges (who staff more than ten thousand courts, and whose numbers—once on par with those of lawyers—have been reduced under a reform program begun in the middle 2010s to create a more elite, expert, and professional judiciary), prosecutors, and others who have taken legal training into jobs in the public and private sectors. The reform era has brought large investments in rebuilding and improving courts and prosecutorial institutions. Legislatures and regulatory bodies have enhanced their law-making and law-interpreting abilities by expanding legal staffs, upgrading skills, and turning to China's leading, often partly foreign-trained, legal scholars as advisors. Both the NPC, in its Legislative Affairs Commission and its Constitution and Law Committee (known before 2018 as the Law Committee), and the State Council, with its Legislative Affairs Office, include specialized bodies that focus on law and legal affairs.

These developments have been accompanied by large-scale propaganda, media, and outreach efforts to increase popular knowledge of law and legal rights. Although such changes are hard to measure, "rights consciousness" (awareness of legal rights and expectations that they should be protected by the state) or, at least, "rules consciousness" (knowledge of the rules that the state has promulgated and belief that they should be followed) appears to have risen markedly from low baselines among the public.[4] Business entities and citizens regularly turn to law firms (which number over twenty-five thousand), legal assistance offices (which serve the poor), or individual lawyers for legal services.

Each year, courts handle far more than ten million complaints from parties who seek redress on matters including business dealings, property and intellectual property rights, accidentally or intentionally inflicted harms, employment disputes, defamation, and divorce. Courts execute a few million civil judgments per year. Courts annually address hundreds of thousands of suits against the state for actions such as improper taking of property, imposition of fines or other noncriminal sanctions, and denial of licenses or government benefits.

Litigants' perceptions of the system vary. One study that suggested relatively positive experiences with the legal system concluded that ordinary citizens were more likely to turn to courts if someone they knew had done so effectively. Other assessments conclude that many Chinese—especially the less well-off and less educated—sue not because they expect a just or satisfactory result but because bringing suit offers hope of a moral victory and a sense of (limited) empowerment. Some research depicts deep popular disillusionment with the legal system but attributes this disaffection partly to litigants' optimistic expectations about legal remedies and disappointment with outcomes that are procedurally proper but seem substantively unjust.[5]

Although greatly reduced as a percentage from the Mao era (to around 6 percent of cases), criminal cases remain important in the work of courts. The first full-fledged Criminal Law and Criminal Procedure Law were adopted in 1979. Both underwent major revisions in the mid-1990s and significant additional changes since then, including extensive amendments to the Criminal Procedure Law in 2012. Broadly, these changes have made definitions of criminal behavior more detailed and precise, removed the most obvious vestiges of politicized justice from the Mao years, adopted measures to address problems arising from economic reform and other developments (such as financial crimes, official corruption, terrorism, and cybercrimes), and brought formal law nearer to Western or international norms of procedural fairness. High-level policy pronouncements, and a variety of court practices, have led to improved transparency in trials. Conviction rates are nearly 100 percent for cases that reach court, reflecting what critics call a de facto "presumption of guilt." Criminal trials of those who have lost political struggles—from the defeated Gang of Four leaders of the late Cultural Revolution period (see chap. 3) and Democracy Wall activist Wei Jingsheng (see chap. 4) at the beginning of the reform era to top elite-member and one-time contender for top leadership posts Bo Xilai in 2013 (see chap. 4)—have been publicized in great detail, but with ambiguous implications for the rule of law given their combination of prosecution for violations of specific criminal laws and political show trial with a preordained outcome.

Much of law's impact in reform era China lies outside formal legal institutions and procedures. On one hand, courts in exercising judicial power sometimes depart from their legal mandate to decide cases according to law, for reasons ranging from political interference and corruption to public pressure and judges' extralegal senses of justice or fairness. On the other hand through petitioning, public protests, and informal appeals to state or party authorities, aggrieved citizens invoke legal rights or point to legal rules to support their pleas for redress that officials have discretion to grant or deny.Given the complexity, unevenness, and rapidity of legal change during the reform era, overall assessments of the impact of efforts to build law and the legal system are problematic, but they can help put China's experience in comparative context. In the World Bank's "Rule of Law" governance indicator, China scores near the median globally and at the median for countries in its upper-middle-income group—a significant metric because rule of law rankings correlate with wealth, and China's per capita income falls near the middle of its income group. In the World Justice Project's Rule of Law Index, which omits a few dozen states that rank low in the World Bank index, China is at the top of the bottom third globally and around the thirtieth percentile in its income group.[6] In both indexes, China fares significantly better in economic areas of law than in political ones.

Among foreign and domestic observers, China is often seen not as an incapable regime (a problem in many developing or postsocialist countries) but as a still-formidable one that presumably could more effectively address shortcomings in its legal system if it were more committed to doing so.[7]

LAW AND CHINA'S ECONOMIC DEVELOPMENT

The most notable role for law and legal institutions during the reform era has been to support economic development—specifically, development of an economy that has transitioned from Soviet-style socialist planning toward the market, from international isolation to global engagement, and from poverty to relative prosperity.[8] Economic policies that support and reflect these transitions have been cast heavily and, for China, unprecedentedly in legal form. This agenda has been reaffirmed repeatedly, from the nascent call at the 11th Central Committee's Third Plenum in 1978 to use law to protect the ownership and decisional autonomy rights of production units, through Xi Jinping's 19th Party Congress speech associating achievement of a moderately prosperous society with the "basic" achievement of the rule of law. There are constitutional commitments to a "socialist market economy," which a 2014 Central Committee document declared to be "essentially a rule of law economy." The opening articles of many laws addressing economic matters identify economic progress as a guiding principle.

From an initial Economic Contract Law in 1981 through a comprehensive Contract Law in 1999 and in many other laws and rules, China has created an elaborate legal framework for economic actors to engage in voluntary, more market-based transactions with a widened universe of partners. Parties to agreements have gained much legal freedom to make (and forego) contracts, choose suppliers, customers, and (under the Labor Contract Law) employment relationships, negotiate terms of agreements, and operate without much constraint from the state plan. They have gained discretion in selecting procedures for resolving disputes and, in many international contracts, to choose which country's law governs.[9]

These and other laws have embodied and advanced policies to give enterprises and individuals room to pursue their own economic agendas and respond to market signals. For firms that remain owned or controlled by state organs, laws have supported greater management autonomy and insulation from intervention by government overlords. Laws have affirmed the legitimacy, and set forth the rights, of new business organizations that faced largely market environments and lacked extensive state subsidies from their inception. These entities, which have proliferated during the reform era, include township and village enterprises (see chap. 8), new types of collective enterprises, and many forms of private and foreign-invested firms. The Company Law and Securities Law, adopted in the 1990s and revised through the mid-2010s, and related laws and regulations, authorized and encouraged complex and flexible forms of ownership and modes for transferring ownership. They created legal frameworks for corporations that issue shares, including shares traded on stock exchanges that China began to establish in the 1990s, and shares that could be sold to foreigners and institutional investors. Corporate governance laws imposed duties on officers, directors, and controlling shareholders, and gave minority shareholders rights to sue.

These reforms were intended to press those who run these enterprises to exercise their powers and judgment to pursue firms' economic interests.[10]

Laws governing profits and taxation delineated more arm's-length and rule-governed fiscal relationships between firms and the state. For enterprises owned or controlled by the state, these reforms replaced complete, arbitrary, or ad hoc negotiated payments of enterprise profits to the state. Laws made taxation a principal form of legitimate state revenue extraction. These legal changes occurred alongside shrinkage of the state share of the rapidly growing economy to much less than half of GDP. Laws on bank lending, securities and futures markets, and creditor-debtor relationships mandated and facilitated more market-based, less political or policy-based, mechanisms for allocating credit and capital.

Bankruptcy law was another effort to impose market discipline, with a 1987 law superseded by a more ambitious 2006 version that promised creditors more power, reduced the state's role as gatekeeper to bankruptcy, and weakened employees' **"iron rice bowls"**—the term for de facto permanent employment and guaranteed benefits that workers in state-owned enterprises enjoyed for much of the Mao era. An Anti-Monopoly Law, adopted in 2008, targeted threats to markets from firms with dominant positions or collusive practices (sometimes pursued with the backing of state authorities). Ongoing revisions to laws and rules, and policy commitments have continued to press for deepening and extending market reforms.

But such reforms have been limited, even in principle. Laws have continued to require that contracts be consistent with the ever-shrinking state plan and vaguely defined public interests.[11] Some contracts and projects, including some large-scale undertakings by non-state-owned firms, still need somewhat discretionary government approvals. Many major enterprises have remained wholly state-owned or state-controlled, often through complex corporate structures, and thus beyond the full reach of many market-oriented laws. Reforms to bankruptcy law have been circumscribed by ongoing limits to creditors' rights and restrictions on disposition of state-owned assets. Corporate governance laws countenance CCP committees (and CCP influence on management) inside companies and retain a formal system of shareholder dominance (which, in many large companies, means control by state or party-state-connected interests), creating tensions with other legal imperatives that tell firms to maximize economic efficiency, profitability, or enterprise value. The pro-market impact of laws for equities has been limited by restrictions on access to capital markets and by the ambivalent mandate of regulators to police listed firms' misbehavior and to promote the development of stock markets.

A State Market Regulatory Administration, which absorbed the functions of the State Administration for Industry and Commerce, the General Administration of Quality Supervision, Inspection, and Quarantine, and China Food and Drug Administration (CFDA) and other agencies, was created in 2018 with an extremely broad mandate, overseeing matters ranging from food and drug safety to business registration and supervision to competition regulation and overall market supervision.

Other areas of economics-related law tell a similar tale of extensive and ongoing yet still-restricted reform. Building on earlier, related amendments to the 1982 constitution, a 2004 revision raised private property nearly to formal equality with state and collective property and mandated that takings of private property have a public purpose and provide compensation. After long delays and criticism that it undermined socialism and risked asset-stripping from state enterprises, a Property Rights Law passed in 2007, giving clearer content and higher status to rights in property, especially land.[12] Here, too, reform was limited even in the law on the books. Urban land remains owned by the state and rural land by the collective—essentially, the local state. People and enterprises have only contract-based "usufruct" rights (broadly, rights to use and derive profits from land and, to some extent, transfer their rights). The public interest required for taking land rights is ill-defined and unconstraining, and there is no requirement that compensation match market value. Problems of uncertain, weak, and uneven rights to land have been sufficiently serious that a key policy document acknowledged in 2013 that China still needed to "complete a modern property rights system" to allocate, equalize (especially between rural and urban sectors), protect, and transfer rights.

Law has acquired still-emerging roles in addressing other economically harmful behavior. Producers and sellers of defective products and others who engage in dangerous activities face legal liability under a framework that has evolved from sparse provisions in the General Principles of Civil Law (1987), through a Product Quality Law (1993, 2000) and a Consumer Rights and Interests Protection Law (1993), to a scandal-expedited Food Safety Law (2009), a full-fledged Tort Liability Law (2010) and a reaffirmation of basic principles in the General Provisions of Civil Law (2017). These laws promise those who suffer accidental or intentional harm rights to court-ordered compensation, and, in a narrow range of cases, punitive damages.[13] Environmental laws have extended legal rights to recovery to victims of pollution and have authorized nongovernmental organizations to bring public interest lawsuits.[14] Amendments in 2017 authorized the procuracy to bring public interest lawsuits on environmental and food and drug safety issues.

Laws governing international economic interactions have been important in China's opening to the outside world and have supported market-oriented reform at home. The PRC has adopted increasingly and, by the standards of large developing countries, liberal trade and investment laws. Reform-era laws dismantled restrictions on enterprises' foreign trading rights, lowered barriers to imports and exports, and pursued conformity with World Trade Organization (WTO) requirements, as China sought to enter the international trade body, and after its accession in 2001, to implement WTO obligations (see chap. 8). Key among these have been moves to bring China's intellectual property laws into line with international standards. Laws on Chinese-foreign joint ventures, wholly foreign-owned enterprises, foreign ownership of shares in—and full acquisition of—Chinese companies, and access to foreign currency have become much more flexible and foreigner-friendly throughout the reform era. Legal changes have opened more regions and economic sectors more fully to foreign investment.[15] A Foreign Investment Law, still in draft in 2018, will bring together and harmonize laws regulating this vast sector.

What market-supporting, economic development-promoting, and international engagement-expanding legal reform has wrought in practice is complex. In many cases changes in the law have occurred alongside changes in practice that have fulfilled what the law promised, profoundly transforming China's economy. In many areas of economic law, however, reforms have fallen short of their stated goals. For example, some studies have found that, especially in China's most developed areas, businesses have come to engage in more transactions with strangers and to rely less on personal connections *(guanxi)* or corruption, in part because of pressures from market competition and the law. But other analyses have found that economic reform has permitted or encouraged *guanxi* to endure as a key feature of economic transactions, and that law has made only modest progress in establishing reliably enforceable, neutral rules that allow parties to forego relational contracting in favor of making business decisions on narrowly economic grounds.[16] Limited ability to enforce court judgments has been an ongoing problem. Private enterprises complain of irregular fees and taxes or regulatory bias toward state-linked or government-favored rivals.

Although company law and corporate governance reforms, and judicial enforcement of them, have had significant effects, the state-as-owner and state-selected managers face opportunities and pressure to steer firms to ends—often politically defined ones—other than maximizing profits or shareholder value.[17] Shareholder suits to address corporate malfeasance have made only limited headway. Under Xi Jinping, there has been a push to establish more formidable CCP committees in companies to provide more oversight.

Although fiscal and financial legal reforms have brought major market-oriented changes, stock markets periodically have been rocked by scandals rooted in inadequately policed fraud by listed companies. For small and non-state-linked enterprises, access to capital from banks, stock markets, or any legally authorized channels other than retained earnings has remained limited, denying them the full benefits of legal reforms to the banking sector and often relegating them to informal "shadow banking" and other sources that have been largely outside the reach of reformed laws and that regulators have scrambled to address.[18]

Although bankruptcies have risen sharply, bankruptcy law and other financial law reforms have not subjected many large firms to much financial discipline, in some cases because state-owned or state-favored enterprises receive preferential or subsidized access to capital, often under lawful industrial policies but sometimes in tension with the letter or at least the spirit of market-oriented commercial banking laws. While labor contract laws have faced criticism for making workers too hard to fire, labor rights laws have not solved widespread problems of dangerous working conditions—sometimes leading to significant loss of life—and unpaid wages.[19]

Contract-based property rights were instrumental in the shift from collectivized agriculture to household farming, the rise of urban homeownership, and burgeoning commercial development. Still, legal rights to use land often have proved a weak defense against expropriation and transfers to developers for urban redevelopment or conversion of rural land to urban use (see chap. 8). In practice, much housing construction has depended on extralegal mechanisms, such as the so-called "minor property rights" that have been the vehicle for developing land still legally consigned to agricultural and rural uses.[20]

The growth of laws that allow people to seek compensation for damages or injuries caused by the harmful acts of others has been limited by their recent adoption, modest levels of compensation, and continuing restrictions on class action lawsuits that have been key sources of such law's impact in other countries. Other legal and institutional

features assign much of the task of addressing socially harmful activities to administrative remedies or lawsuit-preempting, state-run compensation schemes—especially
in cases involving large-scale harms such as dangerous consumer products or environmental disasters. Courts also have been criticized for going too far, awarding
damages to people who lacked good legal claims, whether out of sympathy for victims
who otherwise would go uncompensated, or under pressure from victims' angry
friends and relatives or local citizens.

In terms of the willingness and ability of courts to handle economic cases according
to law, much progress has been made in building a more educated, professional, and
capable judiciary, and increasing judicial autonomy, especially in relatively ordinary cases. More secure budgets, the Supreme People's Court's selection of "guiding
cases" to function somewhat like precedents, more centralized and intrajudiciary
mechanisms for review of judges, and other reforms have contributed to these
developments. Some studies of court behavior in ordinary commercial disputes in
more prosperous and internationally integrated areas find relatively high levels of belief among litigants that outcomes in their cases comported with the law.[21]

Yet, accounts of courts also point to serious problems. These include judicial corruption (whether bribery or trading on personal connections) and "local protectionism," which refers to courts favoring local parties, especially large or state-linked
firms. Several widespread features of China's local political economy contribute to this
pattern. Although reforms adopted in the mid 2010s promised to centralize budgets
and personal decisions, local courts have depended on local governments for their
funding, and judges on the local party for career advancement. The local party-state
relies on local companies as sources of tax revenue, profits (where local businesses
are owned by the local government), economic growth, and jobs (which are key
components in the job evaluation of local officials). Given the entanglement of local
business elites and local power holders, companies provide important political support for, and sometimes receive protection from the local party-state. Assessments
vary about how often adjudication committees and CCP political-legal committees
intervene in adjudication, and with what effect on the lawfulness of outcomes.[22]

In external economic relations, laws and legal mechanisms have contributed
to China's rise to the top ranks of recipients of foreign investment. Yet, this law-
facilitated, even law-driven, success has coincided with recurring accounts of foreign
investors facing discriminatory or opaque regulation, inadequate protection of intellectual property rights, protectionist uses of laws ranging from ostensibly health and
safety measures to antimonopoly law governing acquisitions, and much else. China
has been a uniquely high-frequency target in WTO disputes with other member
countries. In the mid-2010s US complaints about market access, coerced transfer or
theft of intellectual property, and industrial policy focusing on high technology became the focus of a heated bilateral disputes and US claims that China is violating
international legal obligations.

Despite the overarching drive for market-oriented laws that has brought dramatic changes from earlier baselines, the reform era has seen episodic, and diverse,
countertrends in the development of economic laws. The Tiananmen Crisis of 1989
was followed by a few-year pause in economic legal reform. The later Hu Jintao years
were marked by: "the state advances and the private sector retreats" *(guojin mintui)*,

which meant growing clout for large, state-linked enterprises that were less effectively constrained by the laws and had less need to rely on law and courts to protect their interests; and an emphasis on mediation over adjudication, social harmony over legal rights, and political and public interests alongside the law in courts' work. Under Xi, economic nationalism, revived roles for the party in economic affairs in general and inside enterprises, industrial policies to promote key sectors and "national champion" enterprises, and renewed talk of a Chinese development model (amid deepened skepticism toward Western capitalist paradigms) have raised concerns, or perceptions, of another period of retrenchment in rule of, or by, law for the economy.

One possible indicator of the contribution of legal reform to promoting economic development is China's remarkable success. As discussed in chapter 8, China has achieved exceptionally high growth rates, often around 10 percent annually during much of the reform era, and extensive sectoral transformation, from agriculture to industry and, then, to knowledge-intensive industries and services. Comparative studies, including ones focusing on East Asia, find significant correlation between economic development and the rule of law. China's success in attracting foreign investment may be another indicator of legal achievement. Global investors are often believed to demand—and China's law reform agenda assumed that they demanded—relatively familiar and reliable legal frameworks. Yet, some accounts portray China as an exception to any rule that legal development is a prerequisite for economic development, at least to the level China has reached. According to this view, China's economic success is a case of impressive development despite weak law, or even because of weak law, with, for example, vulnerable property rights removing potential barriers to transferring resources to more productive uses, or political commitments substituting for legal rights in creating the security of expectations needed for growth in a partly marketized economy.[23]

REGULATING THE STATE AND ITS AGENTS

China's reform era leaders have perceived that law could help address problems such as corruption, *guanxi*, parochialism (including local protectionism), abuses of power or abdication of responsibility by those wielding power, all of which can undermine economic development, produce social unrest, and threaten political stability. They also see legal reform as a way to avoid the consequences of failing to remedy badly designed or poorly executed policies. Public opinion polls, critical observers, and Chinese leaders all identify public health threats from environmental degradation and dangerous food, drugs, and products tolerated by lax legal regulation as problems that need to be addressed.[24] Well over one hundred thousand "mass incidents" of social unrest occur annually, with many focusing on official abuse or indifference, or property takings and environmental and other public safety incidents in which officials often are complicit (see chap. 9). The regime has turned to laws and legal institutions to enhance discipline, transparency, and accountability in governance and, in turn, to sustain development and avoid disorder.

Law's roles in serving these public governance ends have included elements of formally private law, which, in principle, governs relationships among individuals, enterprises, and other nonstate institutions, and rights to property. Lawsuits beginning in the 1980s sometimes involved farmers and entrepreneurs who profitably managed assets leased from their village, town, or state owners but faced efforts to extract larger payments or nullify contracts. Some suits over contracted-out agricultural or industrial assets challenged assignments of rights to cadres or other insiders on suspiciously favorable terms. Litigation by industrial and commercial enterprises has addressed breaches stemming from official lawlessness, including misdeeds by state owners or overseers, such as diverting enterprise revenues or issuing orders that prevented enterprises from fulfilling obligations. Some enterprises have engaged in opportunistic, unlawful behavior because they could expect party-state patrons to shield them from legal accountability. In such cases, courts and other institutions, when following applicable laws, have played market-supporting roles of upholding complainants' legal rights, but they also have performed policy-implementing and official-abuse-checking roles by exposing, criticizing, and punishing actions attributable to state agents that violated reform policies embodied in laws.[25]

Enterprise and company laws have addressed similar problems. Early in the reform era, local governments and state-linked parent companies were sometimes held liable for acts of sham enterprises that they had created but never provided the capital they needed to operate. Later, corporatized state-owned enterprises selling shares became the focus of cases in which behavior linked to agents of the state underlay economic disputes. For example, the abuse of the rights of private minority shareholders by state-linked majority shareholders prompted reforms to expand shareholder suits, impose duties on controlling shareholders and managers, and authorize "piercing the corporate veil" and other means to hold owners and others who exercise effective control responsible for the actions of the enterprises they dominate.

Constitutional amendments and laws on private property rights and takings, regulations on land tenure and expropriation, rules defining court jurisdiction over land disputes, and lawsuits or protests (often invoking legal rights or rules) by victims of expropriation have targeted the collusion of local authorities with developers to obtain land without adequate compensation and beyond legal and policy authorization. Although sometimes undertaken in pursuit of development, such expropriations have faced criticism for creating uncertainty in land rights, social unrest, wasteful acquisition of land that sits unused, and inefficient overinvestment in construction, as well as cheating rural communities out of much of the value of their land.

Such legal and law-invoking pushbacks have drawn much government, media, and public attention. One unusually successful example from the mid-2000s is the "nailhouse" in Chongqing where two residents resisted eviction from a home and business perched atop a spire of land in a vast construction site. They invoked principles of property rights law and brought an administrative litigation action against local authorities. Having become celebrities amid intense media coverage, they ultimately received much-increased compensation. Another example is the challenge by several prominent legal scholars to State Council regulations on housing demolition and relocation. They argued—with some success, given regulatory changes that soon followed—that the highly permissive rules were unacceptably vague and inconsistent with higher laws.[26]

China's emerging tort law (primarily addressing accidental harms) partly serves regulatory ends. Many provisions explicitly address the roles and responsibilities of state regulators. Safety scandals, born of regulatory failure, have driven moves to enforce and revise laws that address the state's shortcomings, including conflicts of interest, incompetence, corruption, and the failure to ensure the safety of the public in matters ranging from tainted food and consumer goods to poorly constructed buildings, and medical malpractice. Lawsuits by victims of environmental harm are a relatively recent addition to the toolkit for tackling one major area of regulatory weakness.

The impact of private law in checking misuses or non-uses of state power has been limited. Contract and company law reforms have not solved the problems of state-linked opportunistic or predatory economic behavior. Contemplated reforms to change the bifurcated system of land ownership in which villages own rural land and the state owns urban land, strengthen and clarify private property rights, and reduce the reliance of local government on real estate for revenue—which is a significant motivation for land seizures—reflect the continuing weakness of private law in constraining cadres whose careers still hinge heavily on local economic growth. Concerns that lawsuits might stoke, rather than slake, public discontent have coincided with decisions to quash collective litigation that jointly asserts the rights and interests of large groups. Instead, the state has preferred more ad hoc state-managed compensation funds and state sanctions as means for handling notorious mass torts, which harm many people, for example, as a result of dumping toxic waste, distributing poisoned food, or mishandling construction work.

For private law to be expected to play the public function of addressing wayward state behavior is not so surprising in China's authoritarian political context. Robust private law is a product of the reform era and has emerged in the shadow of a PRC pattern, and a longer Chinese tradition, of the dominance of public law, which governs the state and its relationship with those under its jurisdiction. Partly because the party-state has long claimed nearly unlimited authority, much of the public appears to view serious social harm—whether the **Severe Acute Respiratory Syndrome (SARS)** epidemic in 2002–2003 (see chap. 13), melamine-poisoned baby formula powder, severe air pollution, earthquake-collapsed buildings, tainted vaccines, or massive industrial accidents—as instances of the failure of rulers to fulfill their obligation to keep the people safe.

Because many nominally private law cases involve state-linked actors or actions, litigants' dissatisfaction with outcomes in lawsuits often entails disappointment, anger, or disillusionment toward the state. Many complaints about the courts are strikingly "statist," focusing on structural bias toward, or susceptibility to influence by, party or state actors and problems of local protectionism. Unjust outcomes in lawsuits against non-state parties thus can be perceived as manifesting failure or indifference by the party-state.

Reform era public law has addressed official behavior that threatens to undermine economic policies and the political stability they help provide. Administrative law has been a key mechanism for doing so.[27] Under the Administrative Litigation Law, courts adjudicate challenges to state decisions affecting citizens and enterprises in matters such as land use, business licenses, fines, government benefits, environmental harms, abuse by law enforcement authorities, and so on. Amendments in 2014 expanded the range of covered rights, giving greater scope not to apply unlawful low-level rules, and increasing the obligations of courts to accept, and administrative officials to answer, properly filed cases. The Administrative Reconsideration Law offers an informal alternative to litigation over specific actions, as well as a means to seek changes in the rules and regulations themselves. Other administrative laws provide additional means to address the ways the state offers benefits and imposes burdens, including those that affect individuals' and enterprises' economic interests and, in the aggregate, China's economy and society. More specific economic regulatory laws deal with issues such as the abuse of government power to regulate competition and the failure of officials to perform their oversight duties in consumer safety and financial regulation.

Criminal and administrative punishments for government or party functionaries are another part of the public law repertoire for checking state behavior that threatens the success of reform policies. Authorities have deployed these legal weapons, with penalties ranging up to capital punishment (see Box 7.1), most aggressively during periodic drives against corruption that began under Deng, accelerated under Jiang, abated somewhat under Hu, and surged under Xi. High officials who have faced prosecution for corruption (and, in some cases, other crimes) include the former Beijing mayor Chen Xitong in the 1990s, the Shanghai Party Chief Chen Liangyu in 2007, the Chongqing Party Secretary, the former Minister of Commerce, prominent princeling, and aspiring Politburo Standing Committee member Bo Xilai in 2013, and the former Politburo Standing Committee member and Minister of Public Security Zhou Yongkang in 2014.

Public laws also have allocated authority among state institutions to make and implement rules and decisions that affect economic development and economic rights and constrain the power of state agents. Examples include laws that structure and empower state agencies, govern lawmaking and regulatory processes, permit lawmaking input from outside the state, and so on. Among other goals, such laws seek to impose discipline and order within the party-state, to assure that pro-development principles, relevant expertise, legal and policy directives from above, and the views of approved stakeholders will shape rules governing economic and economics-relevant behavior. They aim to limit the distorting effect of parochial interests, bureaucratic resistance, governmental ineptitude, corrupt influences, and other such factors. Under Xi, rhetoric emphasizing "governing the country according to law" and saying that "Power Must be 'Caged' by the System,"[28] the establishment in 2018 of the National Supervision Commission and a Supervision Law to address corruption in conjunction with the party's Central Commission for Discipline Inspection (CCDI), and what might be called a more Leninist emphasis on a disciplined party-state, all reflect the persistence and resurgence of this dimension of public law.

Nevertheless, public law has by not solved problems of unlawful and other troubling behavior by the party-state and its agents. How far practice has fallen short of potential or promise is debatable. For example, in administrative lawsuits, plaintiffs have prevailed 20–40 percent of the time—with the rate of success generally declining after the 1990s from a level that was high by international standards. But it is difficult to estimate the underlying rate of inappropriate state action and the proportion of filed claims that are meritorious. Some studies, especially those focusing on China's most developed areas, indicate relatively high trust in the administrative litigation

BOX 7.1 CAPITAL PUNISHMENT IN CHINA

China executes many more convicted criminals than the rest of the world combined. Because details about the use of the death penalty in the PRC are considered a state secret, it is impossible to know the number of executions each year or much information about most of the cases in which capital punishment is applied. Although the number of executions has fallen during the last decade, Amnesty International estimates that it is still thousands per year.

China's criminal law authorizes the death penalty for a large number of offenses—forty-six as of mid-2018, down from a high of sixty-eight before a series of amendments that began in 2011 as part of the government's "killing fewer, killing cautiously campaign" (shao sha shen sha).[†] Capital crimes cover a wide range of offenses including: violent crimes such as homicide, rape, and kidnapping; endangering public security through actions that cause significant harm; and economic and financial wrongdoings such as large-scale embezzlement, bribery, and fraud. Since 2007, all death sentences are reviewed by the Supreme People's Court, with perhaps a third or more being reversed—in a small number of cases because the defendant was determined to be innocent—or sent back to lower courts for further proceedings.

Chinese authorities have publicized capital punishment in cases involving threats to public welfare. Examples include: State Food and Drug Administration chief Zheng Xiaoyu, convicted of taking bribes to approve possibly unsafe drugs; officers of Sanlu Dairy, which was among the companies at fault for poisoning thousands of children with milk powder that contained melamine, a toxic chemical, and groups of drug traffickers (and others) sentenced after summary multidefendant joint trials, reminiscent of the Mao era, conducted before thousands of spectators in sports stadiums in 2017.

Criminal trials in the PRC are conducted very quickly, sometimes lasting only a few hours, including in some capital punishment cases. The time from conviction to appellate and Supreme People's Court review to execution is generally quite brief. In recent years, China has moved toward lethal injection as the method of execution, though a single gunshot to the back of the head is still used. The PRC has an unusual penalty called a "suspended death sentence" or "death sentence with a two-year reprieve." After two years, such sentences are usually commuted to life in prison without the possibility of parole—and sometimes to lesser sentences—if the inmate shows good behavior.

Abroad and at home, criticism of China's extensive use of the death penalty and calls for reform or repeal have mounted. Controversial cases have intensified the critique. Examples include: Yang Jia, a man who stabbed nine police officers to death and whose execution in 2008 drew widespread condemnation because of public sympathy for someone who struck back after police had abused and beaten him, and because many thought Yang's trial was deeply flawed and his apparent mental illness made him not fully responsible; and cases of false conviction, such as Zhao Zuohai, convicted in 1999 after a dubious confession and freed a decade later when the murder victim showed up alive. In December 2016, the Supreme People's Court overturned the conviction of Nie Shubin, twenty-one years after his execution for murder because the Court ruled that he had been found guilty on the basis of insufficient evidence. As a BBC reporter observed, "Rather than a sign of the justice system's ability to right wrongs, many . . . see his exoneration as exposing continuing flaws and weaknesses in the justice system."[‡]

[†]"China's Deadly Secrets," Amnesty International, Apr. 10, 2017, https://www.amnesty.org/en/documents/asa17/5849/2017/en/
[‡]"Nie Shubin: China Clears Man 21 Years after Execution," BBC, Dec. 2, 2016, https://www.bbc.com/news/world-asia-china-38179311

system. Some accounts conclude that threatening to sue can prompt officials to reverse unlawful decisions because they fear losing and because the fact of being sued can count against them in China's complex system for evaluating officials' performance. Recent years have witnessed a growing phenomenon of claimants bringing meritless claims or falsely asserting violations of law in efforts to induce the authorities to buy off the complainants. Amendments in the mid-2010s expanded the promise of administrative law, allowing suits that challenge some underlying rules (rather than just specific administrative decisions), requiring state agencies to explain and defend their actions, and restricting the discretion of courts to avoid adjudicating properly brought claims.[29]

Other reports, especially but not only those focusing on poorer or rural areas, find futility and frustration, with local authorities' wielding influence over unskilled or pliable courts that hear cases against them, using coercive means to deter potential litigants, and retaliating against victorious ones. High rates of ostensibly voluntary withdrawal of administrative lawsuits suggest pressure on litigants or courts by local authorities. Reforms in the 2010s to require courts to give reasons for rejecting claimants' attempts to file cases recognize, and attempt to redress, related problems. The relatively small number of administrative litigation cases in China raises doubts about the law's effectiveness or perceived effectiveness. Much relevant state activity lies beyond the reach of administrative law. Even after rights-expanding amendments, administrative litigation does not include review of laws, regulations, relatively high-level rules, or many other documents that have law-like effect. Significantly, given China's political system, administrative law does not permit suits against the CCP.

Laws to punish officials have played a limited role in redressing official corruption. Although corruption is, by its nature, hard to measure, it is generally recognized to be pervasive and economically costly, and to have become more organized and large-scale and more often economically harmful in China's now relatively liberal and market-based economy than it was early in the reform era when some forms of corruption could overcome inefficiencies in a system transitioning from socialist planning. Public skepticism generally greets announced drives against corruption. Criminal punishment reaches only a tiny percentage of reported instances. The CCDI,, not the state procuracy, has been the dominant institution for addressing corruption among state officials, who are overwhelmingly party members and thus subject to party discipline. Far more common than criminal prosecution has been the extralegal process of party discipline, including *shuanggui,* the "dual regulation" that directs suspects to submit to detention, investigation, and, potentially, sanctions, such as demotion or the revocation of party membership. In cases where criminal wrongdoing is suspected, those found to have committed corrupt acts can be turned over the state judicial system where they can face significant legal punishment, including life in prison, but this has been relatively uncommon.

Critics of the party-led approach to dealing with corruption have argued for greater reliance on criminal prosecution and laws to require officials disclose assets and thereby facilitate detection of ill-gotten gains. The 2018 constitutional amendment and related legislation establishing a National Supervision Commission took a different path and have been highly controversial from a rule-of-law perspective. Taking over the procuracy's former anticorruption roles and entwined with the Party's CCDI, the commission formally has been given stature akin to a fourth branch of government and is not subject even to the weak constraints of due process, transparency, and limits to detention imposed by China's criminal procedure laws.[30]

Law has been a relatively unpromising means for addressing some major forms of party-state dysfunction. Ongoing efforts for more law-based and rule-governed allocation of authority among law-making and regulatory institutions have not overcome fragmented institutions, entrenched political interests, and the importance of informal power within the party-state.[31] Failure or laxness in following central laws and directives by those in positions of authority has been only weakly targeted by law. Despite a few relevant laws focusing on crisis situations, addressing these types of problems has remained largely the purview of less formal bureaucratic mechanisms and ideological exhortations to motivate officials to act properly and energetically. Under Xi Jinping, the party-led anticorruption drive, the controversial National Supervision Commission, and the broader migration of power from state agencies to party leading small groups, suggest a further turn away from the rule of law in curtailing official abuse of power by party and state agents.

LAW AND POLITICS: ACCOUNTABILITY AND RIGHTS

Law in reform era China has not done much to advance democracy or protect liberal political rights, nor has it been designed to do so. China's middle-tier rankings for rule of law contrast with very low standings on democracy, civil liberties, and related metrics.[32] Law arguably has functioned, and been intended to function, to help avoid, preempt, or co-opt pressure for political change that would significantly limit party-state power or increase official accountability. In facilitating market-oriented, internationally open growth, law has contributed to fulfilling one side of an implicit social contract that has helped sustain party-state rule: the regime delivers material well-being, and society does not challenge its authority. In preventing or redressing official and state-linked unlawful behavior, law may provide some degree of accountability and reduce pressure for political reform. The concern that abuse and malfeasance, left unchecked, foster discontent and demands for fundamental change is among the reasons public anger over corruption and imperious cadres so discomfits China's rulers and prompts a turn to law, along with other means, to sanction wayward officials and silence activists and dissidents.

Reforms to laws on criminal and administrative punishments have offered a means to reduce a possible source of pressure for deeper political change by softening the system's harder authoritarian edges, retrenching the pervasive reach of the party-state, and securing spheres of individual autonomy. Although criminal law has remained draconian and procedural protections for the accused weak, greater transparency, predictability, depoliticization, and, for some criminal behavior, leniency, have been incorporated in several rounds of reform to criminal law and criminal procedure since the 1990s. Notable changes included: replacing "counterrevolutionary crime," which was at least akin to "thought crime," with the still-vague offense of "endangering state security"; imposing limits on police and prosecutors, including tighter restrictions on incommunicado detentions and prohibitions on using confessions extracted by torture or evidence acquired by other illegal means; adopting a formal presumption of innocence (even though a very high conviction rate suggests a continued presumption of guilt in practice); expanding defendants' formal due-process-like rights, such as access to counsel, charges, and evidence; and eliminating prosecution based on retroactive application of new laws or analogy to existing laws that did not prohibit the accused's conduct.[33]

The noncriminal deprivation of liberty known as **"re-education through labor"** *(laojiao)*, which was imposed without judicial process by public security authorities on political dissidents and others who run afoul of officials, was amended to provide shorter maximum detentions, more definite terms, narrower ranges of offenses, and greater judicial review.[34] Amid growing scandals over abuses and mounting criticism, *laojiao* was eliminated in 2014. After the notorious 2003 Sun Zhigang incident, in which a recent university graduate was mistaken for an illegal internal migrant and was detained and killed in a "custody and repatriation" center in Guangzhou, the regulation permitting such detentions without process was canceled amid intense media coverage and challenges by leading legal scholars who argued that the regulation was unlawful or unconstitutional.[35]

At the same time, criminal law has continued to be a weapon wielded against the regime's critics and perceived threats to political and social order. In addition to the ill-defined crime of endangering state security, less obviously politically tinged offenses such as undermining social stability and public order, destruction of property, or assaults on police that occur in the context of political protests have been used to punish activists who challenge party-state authority. Charges of tax evasion have bedeviled some high-profile activists, such as the artist Ai Weiwei (see chap. 11), and NGOs that pursue political agendas and have been allowed to register as non-profit entities. The notoriously vague and much-criticized "pocket offenses" *(koudai zui)* such as "picking quarrels and provoking trouble" have been used to detain those who are seen as challenging the regime.

Principal targets of criminal prosecution and less formal measures include advocates for liberal democracy, stronger legal and constitutional restraints on government, or civil and political rights. Examples from across the reform era who have faced criminal sanctions and persecution by the party-state on such grounds include 1979 Democracy Wall activist Wei Jingsheng; prominent participants in the 1989 Tiananmen Movement; Liu Xiaobo, drafter of the 2008 liberal-democratic Charter 08 proposal for constitutional reform and 2010 Nobel Peace Prize recipient who died while imprisoned in July 2017; "rights protection" *(weiquan)* lawyers, such as the blind, self-taught lawyer-activist Chen Guangcheng, who provided legal representation for victims of land seizures, followers of heterodox religious and spiritual movements, such as Falun Gong (see chap. 4) and resisters of coercive family planning (before the single-child-family policy ended in 2015); civil society activists, including the Feminist Five who performed street theater against domestic violence and ignited the Chinese version of the #MeToo movement; and ethnic minority dissidents, especially Uyghurs and Tibetans (see chaps. 16 and 17).

Chinese criminal justice remains the object of numerous, well-documented human rights critiques.[36] Much of this criticism has focused on violations of the law by authorities. But the content of the laws has been an issue, too. For example, the criminal procedure reforms of 2012 still authorized secret detention of those suspected of crimes of endangering national security, terrorism, or large-scale corruption. Amendments in 2018 authorized trials in absentia in some corruption and national security-related cases. Government concerns about terrorism and unrest and advancements in surveillance technology have gone hand in hand with enhanced legal authority for public security and paramilitary organs, notably the People's Armed Police, especially in restive ethnic minority regions.

These factors have contributed to large-scale detentions—including hundreds of thousands of Uighurs in 2018—and the use of force to quell protests. "Black jails"—extralegal detention centers—have been used to confine petitioners who travel to Beijing, or provincial capitals, to press grievances about local authorities. Removing the legal categories of reeducation through labor and custody and repatriation have not eliminated all of the related practices. Despite reforms to relax the *hukou* system of household registration, rural to urban migrants have continued to face periodic state-sanctioned removal (see chap. 10). **Urban management officers (chengguan)**—a para-police force assigned to address minor urban crime and enforce local regulations—and other "stability maintenance" organizations came to rival the police as targets of complaints about abuses of ordinary citizens (see chap. 10).

Legal and political changes in the reform era have meant greater enjoyment of some rights related to politics. For example, citizens have much more freedom to express politically nonconformist and critical views in many contexts, including on the internet and social media (see chap. 15), and traditional media enjoy expanded, if uneven, space for critical journalism on politically salient topics. Yet, serious limits persist, in legal principle as well as in practice. Individual rights spelled out in the constitution are not operative law until they are embodied in legislation. The Supreme People's Court in 2001 broke new ground when it said courts could directly enforce constitutional rights in the case of Qi Yuling—a young woman who claimed her constitutional right to education was violated when her exam scores were stolen by another woman with the complicity of local officials. This ruling was unceremoniously "canceled" in 2008, dimming the prospect for courts to provide remedies for violations of constitutional rights.[37] Addressing a perceived threat from China's often-raucous cyberspace, Xi-era changes have authorized punishment for those who use the internet and social media to spread ill-defined "rumors" even where the audiences reached are small (as few as five thousand).

The democratic content of Chinese law is thin. The constitution contains democratic elements, including that "all power in the People's Republic of the China belongs to the people," that people's congresses will be democratically elected, and that citizens have civil and political rights similar to those found in liberal-democratic constitutions. But the constitution also declares, "The leadership of the Communist Party of China is the defining feature of socialism with Chinese characteristics" and that "Disruption of the socialist system by any organization or individual is prohibited." Its liberal and democratic provisions are among the least effective ones in a document with limited impact on party-state behavior.

One law with significant democratic content is that governing village elections (see chap. 9). Elections held under this law sometimes have allowed meaningful political participation by villagers, and provided mechanisms for monitoring local power-holders and outlets for potentially explosive discontent. Elections sometimes have removed ineffective or despised local authorities and recruited new leaders who command popular support and their superiors' confidence. In one celebrated instance in 2011/2012 in Wukan village, Guangdong, popular discontent over the subversion of election results and improper land seizures combined with a provincial leadership, which at first supported the aggrieved villagers, to create hope for a new, more democratic model of village governance under law and, in the view of some prominent commentators, direct citizen implementation of constitutional rights to property and free expression (see chap. 9). But this incident was short-lived as the party-state cracked down on Wukan activists. Such dramatic cases are very much the exception, not the rule. Although the overall record is mixed, the village election law often has failed to fulfill its mandate for open contests, and efforts to expand competitive leadership elections have not succeeded.[38]

At higher levels, democracy, and law's support for it, has been even more limited. The electoral law for local people's congresses has been at best weakly democratic, producing few heterodox candidates, fewer victories for them, and still fewer wins that survive authorities' efforts to overturn them or prevent their recurrence. The rules for selecting higher-level people's congresses provide for indirect election by lower-level congresses rather than directly by voters, and result in compliant legislative bodies. Concrete discussions of democratic reform once focused less on government offices and more on intraparty democratization and related proposed reforms, including modest expansions of pluralism at elite levels and initial steps to expand voting for leaders at the party's grassroots, but those ideas have faded.[39] Furthermore, law has played only peripheral roles in the internal governance of the party beyond exhortations to CCP members and state officials to follow the law and declarations that the rule of law ranks alongside party leadership and socialist democracy as guiding principles.

Legal mechanisms offer means for popular input into lawmaking, but generally in atomized or weakly institutionalized forms.[40] Procedures of "consultative democracy," especially on government budget issues, have developed at the local level, but they reach only a narrow range of issues and do not entail a legal right to be heard or to influence outcomes. Procedures allowing public comment on proposed regulations often draw tens of thousands of comments, but the comments are so numerous and diverse that they do little to constrain drafters who need not give reasoned responses or explanations of their decisions. The principle, reflected in the Law on Legislation, that the people should "participate" in making laws and high-level national regulations through "various channels" has resulted in occasional hearings and opportunities for countless written comments, but no regular and systematic means for public input. The aims and effects of such measures include enhancing the information about preferences and complaints among affected constituencies of the institution that receives the comments and makes the laws.

This can improve policy-making—making it more "scientific," as official sources characterize it—and can enhance the recipient organization's leverage in intraregime wrangling over policy. But that is not the same thing as legally mandated democratic participation. Overall, laws and rules defining the powers and responsibilities of state organs have tolerated, and even encouraged, highly discretionary and heavily state-managed processes of soliciting input from social and economic interest groups to people's congresses, central ministries, and provincial and local governments.

Fragmentation and weak institutionalization of popular participation extends to other aspects of law broadly related to democracy. Citizens seeking judicial redress for harm caused by state action long have been limited to challenging specific acts, not underlying laws and rules, and mid-2010s reforms still have kept all but the lowest-level rules beyond judicial review. Courts lack the power of constitutional review, which is formally vested in, but almost never used by, the NPC's Standing Committee. Many mechanisms—both lawful and not—of party and state influence over the judiciary offer potent means for keeping courts from straying from regime preferences in politically sensitive cases—a category that can include prosecution of advocates for political change, collective suits over mass torts born of regulatory failure, and much else.

Periodically, official policy has turned toward promoting legal informality and discounting rights and clear rules in favor of more ad hoc and "harmonious" resolutions. The late Hu era, for example, saw an emphasis on judicial mediation over full-fledged adjudication. Authorities also encouraged "grand mediation" *(da tiaojie)*—an impromptu process bringing together courts, other authorities, complaining parties, targets of complaints, and others in the community to address issues that threatened to erupt into social conflict.[41] Throughout much of the reform era, there has been widespread reliance on the informal process of "**letters and visits**" *(xinfang)* by which Chinese citizens can lodge complaints about abuses of power by local officials and other grievances by making a petition to the authorities. Such petitions outnumber litigated cases, avoid judicial involvement, and—especially given restrictions that have been imposed on "group petitions"—mostly involve individual pleas for redress rather than broader legal issues. Observers inside China and abroad have criticized the party-state's reliance on such informal means, for reflecting and reinforcing a mindset reminiscent of the traditional notion of seeking justice as an act of grace from a benevolent emperor, and for being inconsistent with development of the rule of law, constitutional rights, and democracy.[42]

Persisting, and at times resurgent, preferences for informality in law by China's leaders have been associated with purported, and perhaps genuine, perceptions of threats to party-state rule for which law not only failed to provide adequate answers but also seemed to be part of the problem. When citizens have mobilized in groups to invoke their legal rights and broader interests through direct action, including mass protests, regime responses typically have ranged from repression to limited accommodation, but have not included moves to institutionalize democratic participation.[43]

Under Xi Jinping, the regime has shifted to renewed calls for formal legality, with major policy documents looking anew to legal means to implement policy agendas, and pledging efforts to strengthen and professionalize legal institutions and to build support for law and the legal system within the party-state and among disillusioned citizens. But the Xi leadership's agenda for law and its view of the rule of law and party rule as fully compatible, along with its broader political ideology, imply no large role for law in fostering quasi-democratic or liberal political change.

Finally, law's limited role as a means to accommodate input by, or increase account-ability to, the public reflects an ambivalent relationship between law and democratic change, broadly defined. Mass pressure on courts—sometimes spurred by traditional and social media—has grown. Sometimes this has driven courts to follow or enforce the law. Other times it has pressed courts to decide in ways adverse to unpopular or vilified parties, such as government officials who are seen as abusing their powers or shirking their responsibilities, or in favor of popular or sympathetic ones, including ordinary citizens who have been driven to violence by official abuse or suffer from the failure of the authorities to secure public safety. Such pressure from below can influ-ence judicial outcomes even in cases where evidence is lacking and the law provides little basis for courts' rulings.[44]

"GAPS" IN CHINA'S LEGAL DEVELOPMENT

One way to understand law's mixed record in reform era China is to think of it in terms of several "gaps."[45] First, the most commonly noted, and serious, problem is an "implementation gap": the law on the books is too often not effectively put into practice. Reasons include limited resources, a still-weak culture of legality, rational decisions by parties not to pursue their rights, poor training of judges and other officials, resistance by cadres and the public, local protectionism, ideological oppo-sition, conflicting or unclear legal and policy mandates, and corruption (including in courts), among others. Weak implementation of the laws governing lawmaking is a problem as well. The multifaceted, often political processes that shape policy making and the exercise of power often remain divorced from the institutional structures and procedures prescribed in the constitution and laws. This disjunction has faded somewhat with the National People's Congress taking on a greater role in shaping legislation, and ministries and other parts of the state hierarchy relying more on laws and regulations to define and enhance their reach. Courts are also playing larger and more conventionally judicial roles, while legislative and executive mechanisms have been strengthened to resolve conflicts among sources of law and to supervise its im-plementation.[46] Under Xi, centralization of power and the migration of power to-ward party bodies (see chaps. 4 and 6) has reinvigorated concerns about practices departing from legal prescriptions. On the other hand, the Xi-era emphasis on greater discipline and control within the state and major policy documents recommitting to law and a conception of law as a key instrument of party rule suggest that those in power are paying attention to the implementation gap.

Second, some laws have been near-literal adoptions of foreign models that did not take Chinese conditions fully into account. The resulting "transplant gap"—which also contributes to implementation problems—has made such laws sometimes poorer means to desired ends than less "world class" alternatives might have been. Many economics-related laws, which tracked developed capitalist, and especially Anglo-American, models are examples. The evident motivation was to replicate the models' promotion of economic efficiency, mobilization of foreign and domestic capital, answers to problems of corporate governance, and so on. In some areas, including intellectual property law, China's WTO entry required adoption of laws meeting detailed international standards.

Such legal transplants face daunting challenges in China.[47] The national contexts of U.S. and other foreign law, including a rich history of judicial opinions, autonomous and experienced courts, expert and professional enforcement agencies, and cohorts of specialized lawyers that have given key legal terms clear meaning in their home jurisdictions, have not been replicated in the PRC. The same is true of complementary factors for economic law, such as institutional investors, non-state-linked controlling shareholders, a strong financial and business press, a pool of experienced managers to serve as independent directors, and the like, that helped give legal provisions the impact they have had in their places of origin. Prospects that this gap would close faded after the Global Financial Crisis of 2007–2008 dimmed the luster of U.S.-style economic law and regulation in China.

In more political aspects of law, the turn to external models has been more limited, and seems designed partly to answer foreign expectations and criticism and not to reflect a deep commitment to changing the legal and political system. Examples include provisions in the constitution promising rights that resemble international human rights norms, changes to obviously illiberal elements in criminal law, and pledges to pursue elements of a model of law that establishment Chinese critics characterized as unrealistically, even dangerously, Western-style. Here, the gap between promise and practice has been large, and political commitment and external pressure to close it have been weak. Under Hu and Xi, official and orthodox views have become more critical of Western legal models. Ostensibly universal values embedded in Western-style constitutionalism or laws related to human rights and civil liberties have faced increasing denunciation, at the highest levels, as not suitable for Chinese conditions (see Box 7.2 Human Rights and Law in China).

Third, Chinese law has an "interregional gap," with the rule of law generally seen as stronger, particularly in economic affairs, in more developed and cosmopolitan areas.[48] Several factors contribute to this pattern. Large, diversified economies in thriving coastal cities can reduce problematic entanglements between local officials and dominant local enterprises, which underlie local protectionism or predatory state behavior that siphons off wealth. In more fully marketized and open economies in more advanced regions, enterprises face pressure to compete on price and quality, which may reduce opportunities for law-disregarding behavior, and may lessen **rent seeking** (see chap. 8) by authorities acting as economic gatekeepers. In more open and prosperous areas, potentially wayward officials and enterprise officers face greater scrutiny and demands for law-conforming behavior from anticorruption investigators, civil or administrative lawsuits adjudicated in higher-quality courts, muckraking journalists, social media users, foreigner investors and, increasingly, Chinese who can withdraw their capital or lobby the party-state. Legal and judicial talent—and an accompanying legal culture—are thicker in the most economically advanced areas. Judges in Shanghai, Beijing, Shenzhen, and similar places have legal educational credentials, and their courts have resources and reputations, far above those of their counterparts in less-developed areas.

These regional variations among judges are broadly paralleled among officials in other law-related roles. Lawyers and law firms—especially elite and internationalized

BOX 7.2 HUMAN RIGHTS AND LAW IN CHINA

Amid intense international criticism that followed the violent suppression of the Tiananmen Movement in 1989, China officially accepted the idea of universal human rights in 1991 and has joined almost all major UN human rights treaties (although it has not ratified the International Covenant on Civil and Political Rights). The Chinese constitution's provisions on citizens' rights and duties parallel core human rights in the Covenant, including freedom of speech, of the press, of assembly, of association, of procession and of demonstration, and religion. The constitution also declares that "the state respects and preserves human rights" and that "freedom of the person of citizens of the People's Republic of China is inviolable."

Human rights NGOs such as Amnesty International and foreign governments, including the U.S. Department of State in its annual human rights country reports, regularly criticize human rights violations in China. Examples of major law-related issues raised in such criticism include:

- the persecution of political critics and dissidents, including politically motivated prosecution for offenses ranging from endangering state security to disrupting social order to destruction of property, unauthorized assembly, and tax evasion;
- limits to freedom of expression and media freedoms, including regulations authorizing press and Internet censorship, and criminal punishment for ostensibly socially harmful content of online speech;
- the use of torture and denial of due process–like protections for persons accused of crimes (despite legal reforms barring such practices), and detention without legal process, even after the abolition of reeducation through labor;
- extensive surveillance, detention, and use of coercive measures against minority ethnic groups, especially in the Xinjiang Uyghur and Tibetan Autonomous Regions, and prosecution of critics, such as the Uyghur academic Ilham Tohti, who was convicted for crimes of separatism after criticizing regime policies toward Xinjiang and calling for fuller implementation of regional autonomy laws;
- restrictions on religious freedom, including a regulatory framework for state-supervised bodies to oversee practices of Buddhism, Catholicism, Islam, (Protestant) Christianity, and Taoism, and periodic drives against underground "house churches" as unlawful organizations and spiritual groups such as Falun Gong that are legally barred as "evil cults";
- the destruction or taking of property, especially land and houses, without process or fair compensation;
- the suppression of rights protection (*weiquan*) or human rights (*renquan*) lawyers, who represent clients in human rights–related cases, including those involving resistance to coercive family planning, unlawful takings or destruction of property, participation in Falun Gong, or criminal prosecutions targeting political dissidents or fellow rights protection lawyers.

The PRC government regularly releases White Papers and makes reports to UN bodies that recite the country's accomplishments and some shortcomings in human rights, but that also reflect a different perspective from long-prevalent international norms, or, as some Chinese and other critics see it, from ethnocentric Western standards. Among the divergent views that China has pressed are that human rights include national sovereignty and economic development, measures by which the PRC has done well, and that human rights vary significantly by cultural context and type of political system, which China sees as justifying priority for economic and social rights over civil and political ones. The PRC also issues an annual report on human rights in the United States in which it highlights problems such as crime and divorce rates, racism, mass incarceration, and the influence of money in politics and other "serious abuses in the U.S. style of democracy."

ones—are similarly unevenly distributed. The five provincial-level units in China with the highest density of lawyers are all prosperous areas (Beijing, Shanghai, Zhejiang, Guangdong, and Jiangsu) and have nearly seven times the number of lawyers per capita as do the bottom and much poorer five (Tibet, Guizhou, Jiangxi, Gansu, and Qinghai).[49] Even the law on the books varies regionally, with more sophisticated, market-friendly, and international-style laws more common in more developed regions.

Intranational disparities are not necessarily bad for law's roles under contemporary Chinese conditions. The need or demand for law is likely higher in more developed places where the supply is also greater. Observers, including the prominent legal scholar Zhu Suli, have argued that eschewing the modern Western-style model of legal reform is inevitable and even advisable in the rural hinterland, where such an approach is doomed to failure and could have perverse results.[50]

A final "gap" is between a narrow instrumentalism that has characterized much of the official legal reform program and the mindsets associated with full-fledged rule of law. Overall, the reform era legal project has been consistent with a broadly Leninist conception in which laws and legal institutions are one among many complementary means to achieve substantive ends, such as rapid economic development and durable authoritarian rule, and are embraced to the extent they advance those ends. This instrumentalism was especially pronounced in the early reform era, when the turn to economic reform and the turn to law went hand in hand, and it has again gained prominence under Xi, with, for example, the key policy document from the "rule of law" plenum declaring party leadership and socialist rule of law fully consistent (*yizhi*) and mutually supportive. The question has long been how far the ruling elite ultimately will go in choosing, or acquiescing, in what many would call the requisites of the rule of law, including accepting, in principle and practice, legal limits to the party-state's autonomy and authority, even where those limits bring significant unwanted consequences for the economy or the politically powerful.

FORCES FOR, AND AGAINST, GREATER "LEGALITY"

Several factors favor movement toward greater rule by law and possible progress toward the rule of law in the PRC. First, perceived interests and preferences of members of the top elite offer significant support for legality. The instrumental case for law—including aspects that converge with foreign rule-of-law models—has persisted throughout the reform era: law is a valuable means to achieve high-priority goals of economic development, effective governance (including discipline within the party-state), and social stability; and some self-restraint by the party-state, which law can help to achieve, may serve the needs of the ruling party.[51] The 19th Party Congress even gave a tentative endorsement to the idea of constitutional review of state action. Leaders with legal training increasingly have entered the upper echelons of the party-state (see chap. 6). Li Keqiang, who became premier in 2013, has a degree in law. People with legal training and experience often—although not always—head major legal institutions, including the Supreme People's Court and the Supreme People's Procuracy. Beginning in 2013, these bodies were led, respectively, by Zhou

Qiang and Cao Jianming (succeeded in 2018 by Zhang Jun), who were regarded as supportive of pro-law agendas. Although their influence has fluctuated during the reform era, reform-minded legal intellectuals have won the ears (if less often the hearts and minds) of top leaders. They serve as counselors to key officials, participants in briefings and other channels for providing advice to the leadership, and members of the cohort of public intellectuals whose views reach China's rulers.

Although elite preferences are ambivalent and variable, the regime may have "bound itself to the mast," meaning that after years of endorsing law and legality at party congresses, central committee plenums, and in countless laws, regulations, lesser rules, and public statements, it may be impossible, or too costly, to change direction. Trying to reverse legal developments or commitments to law could risk undermining the regime's credibility with relevant audiences. Even in China's authoritarian system, elites can be expected to respond, to some degree, to societal demands for law.

Second, reform era policies and practices have created relatively small but expanding and increasingly influential constituencies of judges, lawyers, and others with legal training and functions who have institutional and professional interests, as well as intellectual and normative preferences, that support stronger, more autonomous roles for law and legal institutions. Agendas that align with these orientations, and reinforce them, have included concrete reform measures, such as basing judges' career advancement more on evaluations by superiors and less on support of local party and state authorities; shifting court budgets from local governments to the central government; expanding legal aid, pro bono work, and other "access to justice" initiatives to make the legal system more effective for ordinary citizens; requiring courts, lawmaking, and rule-making bodies to operate more transparently and to provide reasoned explanations of their decisions; requiring clearer legal authority, procedures, and opportunities for review for deprivations of liberty or property; and making good on policy commitments to protect lawyers' professional rights. More mundanely, daily work in China's courts, other state legal institutions, law firms, and enterprises has helped create habits and raised aspirations of autonomy and professionalism among China's growing pool of "legal workers."[52]

Diverse groups among Chinese lawyers have pressed, with remarkable resilience, for more fundamental legal changes. Prominent examples include: the Open Constitution Initiative (*gongmen*) and its successor New Citizens' Movement that called for constitutionalism, rule of law, civil rights, and transparency of officials' income; the two dozen lawyers who signed Charter 08, which advocated for a transition to democratic, individual rights-protecting, constitutional governance; and "rights protection" (*weiquan*) or "human rights" (*renquan*) lawyers, whose work has run the gamut from representing individual clients suffering abuse or repression by the state to dissident activism for radical political change, including an end to CCP rule.[53]

Third, societal pressure for greater legality has been rising and may continue to do so. Hopes and expectations about law and legal rights have grown, partly thanks to political space created by the long-running official embrace of law. Social demand for law and a legal system apparently have increased, arguably reflected in the millions of claimants who pursue litigation, arbitration, and mediation each year; the millions more who invoke legal norms through letters and visits, other informal appeals to party and state organs, and direct public action that ranges from peaceful marches to guerrilla street theater to violent protests; the hundreds of thousands who formally challenge the state's actions through the gradually expanding mechanisms provided by administrative law; the vast growth in the use of opportunities for public comment on proposed legislation or administrative rules; and the social discontent that accompanies perceived lawlessness by officials or state failures to enforce laws that promise to protect citizens' health, safety, or livelihoods.

If broad cross-national comparative patterns, traditional social science theories, and still-fragmentary evidence from contemporary urban China hold up, the rising social and economic status of tens of millions entering China's burgeoning middle class portends growing demand for legal protection of rights and interests. Those who have fared less well in the reform era also have been invoking legal norms or seeking legal redress, turning to law—whether out of hope or desperation—when unlawful acts threaten their precarious existence by expropriating their land, polluting their environment, terminating their employment, or taking their liberty.

Fourth, sustaining economic growth may require more developed laws and legal institutions. China's economy will become more mature and complex and economic integration with the outside world may continue to deepen. It is likely that the cost of corruption and abuse by state and non-state actors will mount, the harm done due to weak regulation (of polluters, makers of shoddy products, perpetrators of financial fraud, and so on) will accumulate, popular resentment toward official failures to follow or enforce the laws will fester.[54] Maintaining social stability may become more dependent on legality in the party-state if economic performance becomes a less reliable basis for regime legitimacy and substitutes, such as nationalism, seem inadequate. Under such conditions, the double-edged sword of stronger formal law and legal institutions may prove to be more of a useful instrument, and less of a dangerous risk, for a regime that has held chronically conflicted and oscillating views about law.

Yet, forces favoring law's growth face strong countercurrents.[55] First, reform era China's leadership, always ambivalent about further fostering development of law and legal institutions, became, at least at the level of broad ideology, more skeptical from the middle 2000s. The widely discussed and occasionally promoted "Chinese Model" of development departs from, and offers an alternative to, a Western-style paradigm, including its rule of law. In his address to the 19th Party Congress in October 2017, Xi Jinping proclaimed that "the path, the theory, the system, and the culture of socialism with Chinese characteristics have kept developing, blazing a new trail for other developing countries to achieve modernization. It offers a new option for other countries and nations who want to speed up their development while preserving their independence; and it offers Chinese wisdom and a Chinese approach to solving the problems facing mankind." The "new option" that Xi invokes, and the Xi leadership's embrace of a larger role for the state in steering the economy and promoting national champion firms, are an alternative to the Western model, including many of its political and legal features, even as other, finer-grained, Xi-era policy statements still emphasize law.

Top law-related positions periodically have been in the hands of leaders not invested, or versed, in formal legality. Prominent examples from the Hu years include: Supreme People's Court President Wang Shengjun, who had no formal legal education and called on courts to decide cases according to policy and public opinion as well as law (a policy dubbed the "three supremes"); Luo Gan, the Politburo Standing Committee member assigned to legal-political affairs, who warned that judicial independence risked a "color revolution" undermining communist rule in China, as it had in former Soviet areas; and Luo's successor Zhou Yongkang, who blamed the rise in mass incidents on people's "consciousness of legal rights" outstripping their "legal consciousness" and leading them to resort to "illegal means."

Although holders of these posts under Xi have had a much more favorable view of law, and much rhetoric and some reforms under Xi have made clear commitments to improving law and legal institutions, Xi's tenure also has brought continuation and intensification of positions less favorable to rule of law and kindred values. High-profile illustrations include: a 2013 Central Committee circular that included rule of law-related ideals such as Western constitutional democracy (including independent judiciaries) and universal values (including "Western" human rights) among seven topics inappropriate for classroom and media discussion; a law professor's article and related favorable commentary in official media that rejected constitutional governance as a bourgeois-capitalist and hollow form of democracy unsuited to China; and the 2018 constitutional amendments that, while procedurally lawful, drew criticism for removing term-limit-based restrictions on the top leader's power, writing party leadership into the constitution's substantive provisions (rather than its preamble), and shifting coercive power from the state procuracy to the more legally informal supervision commission.[56] Even Supreme People's Court head Zhou Qiang advocated resolute resistance to "erroneous" influences from the West, including constitutional democracy, separation of powers and an independent judiciary.

Second, key constituencies for law have had limited impact and faced frustration, or worse. Reformist legal scholars' public prominence and ability to reach top elite audiences have led to no more than modest real legal change. Lawyers and law firms have faced ongoing restrictions on multiplaintiff, potentially high-impact public interest litigation, and warnings and retribution, including from professional regulatory bodies, when they stray into controversial work. Even relatively restrained advocates and activists for constitutional government and other transformative rule of law reforms have suffered long or repeated prison sentences, including Xu Zhiyong, founder of the New Citizen Movement who was sentenced to four years in jail after being convicted in 2014 of "gathering a crowd to disturb public order." Rights-protection lawyers have been subjected to recurrent, severe crackdowns, and law-focused NGOs have faced harassment and state-mandated closures. Such experiences have contributed to political radicalization of some lawyers.

Third, social demand for more thoroughgoing legal reform may be limited. Despite a **new normal** of slower growth and other economic challenges (see chap. 8), the CCP's political legitimacy may continue to be sustained by successful management of the economy thereby deflecting calls for stronger law and reducing the need for more legal-rational legitimacy. Authoritarian rule, which retains much capacity to limit access to information, repress perceived enemies, and deter or co-opt potential challengers, may undercut development of effective social pressure for stronger legality. The party-state has developed an expanding repertoire of strategies for "stability maintenance" (*weiwen*) and "social management" (*shehui guanli*) that reflect its adaptability in controlling popular demands.[57] Official approaches that have embraced legal informality (such as mediation and letters and visits), ad hoc and discretionary forms of redress (rather than rights-asserting legal remedies) may preempt focal points or foundations of social pressure for formal legality. The public's sometimes disappointing experiences with, or negative perceptions of, China's existing legal system also may dampen enthusiasm for law and the rule of law more generally. (Indeed, top-level party statements have expressed growing concern about low public esteem for the judiciary.)

Fourth, a prediction that the consequences of past economic development and the requirements for future success will demand greater rule of law may prove overly deterministic and optimistic. Despite the positive cross-national correlation between the rule of law and high levels of economic development, and the historical arc of increasing wealth and increasing rule of law in now-developed countries in East Asia and elsewhere, China may sustain an alternative pattern with less of a role for law. Under Xi, China is increasingly proffering an alternative Chinese model of law and development, and seeking to shape international legal rules, including those that bear on domestic legal orders.

More than four decades after the beginning of the reform era and several years into what may be the long tenure of Xi Jinping as top leader, big questions about law's place in China's politics, economy, and society do not yet have definitive answers. It is possible that the broad, if slow and uneven, trend toward convergence with Western, international, or developed-country models of legality that has broadly characterized the reform era will continue. It may be that elite choice, constituency preferences, public pressure, functional demands, foreign influences, or other factors will push decisively in that direction. It is also possible, however, that China's CCP-led party-state will survive, and even thrive, while rejecting strong—and, in the official view, "Western," "capitalist," or non-"socialist"—forms of law and a legal system as unnecessary for the successful pursuit of essential goals, or as intolerably threatening to the maintenance of social order and political control, or as constituting key parts of a Western **"peaceful evolution"** strategy that some in the PRC see as an effort to erode and eventually end CCP rule. Rejecting movement toward a rule of law system might, indeed, contribute to regime failure and unleash more radical outcomes, one of which could be democratization. But the CCP might find a distinctive path that includes a role for law that sustains, for a long time, relatively high rates of economic growth (and, therefore, achieves relatively high levels of per capita income) and stable, undemocratic rule.

NOTES

1. The other three "comprehensives" are: (1) the construction of a moderately well-off society, (2) deepening of economic reform, and (3) strengthening party disciple. See "'Four Comprehensives' Light up the Future," *China Daily*, Jul. 17, 2017, http://www.chinadaily.com.cn/opinion/2017-07/10/content_30050292.htm

2. See generally Albert H. Y. Chen, *An Introduction to the Legal System of the People's Republic of China*, 4th ed. (New York: LexisNexis, 2011); Randall Peerenboom, *China's*

Long March toward the Rule of Law (Cambridge, UK: Cambridge University Press, 2002); Daniel C. K. Chow, *The Legal System of the People's Republic of China in a Nutshell*, 3rd ed. (New York: West, 2015).

3. See Zhu Jingwen and Han Dayuan, eds. *Research Report on the Socialist Legal System with Chinese Characteristics*, vol. 1 (Singapore: Enrich, 2013).

4. Elizabeth Perry, "A New Rights Consciousness?" *Journal of Democracy* 20, no. 3 (2009): 17–20; Lianjiang Li, "Rights Consciousness and Rules Consciousness in Contemporary China," *China Journal*, no. 64 (2010): 47–68; Peter Lorentzen and Suzanne Scoggins, "Understanding China's Rising Rights Consciousness," *China Quarterly* 223 (2015): 638–657.

5. Pierre Landry, "The Institutional Diffusion of Courts in China: Evidence from Survey Data," in *Rule by Law: The Politics of Courts in Authoritarian Regimes*, ed. Tom Ginsburg and Tamir Moustafa (Princeton, NJ: Princeton University Press, 2008), 207–234; Ethan Michelson and Benjamin L. Read, "Public Attitudes toward Official Justice in Beijing and Rural China," and Mary E. Gallagher and Yuhua Wang, "Users and Non-Users: Legal Experience and Its Effect on Legal Consciousness," in *Chinese Justice: Civil Dispute Resolution in Contemporary China*, ed. Margaret Y. K. Woo and Mary E. Gallagher (New York: Cambridge University Press, 2011), 169–203, 204–233.

6. World Bank, *Worldwide Governance Indicators*, http://info.worldbank.org/governance/WGI/#reports; World Justice Project, Rule of Law Index: China, http://data.worldjusticeproject.org/#/groups/CHN.

7. See Dali L. Yang, *Remaking the Chinese Leviathan* (Stanford, CA: Stanford University Press, 2004); also see generally Samuel P. Huntington, *Political Order in Changing Societies* (New Haven, CT: Yale University Press, 1968).

8. The analysis in this and the next two sections draws upon Jacques deLisle, "Legalization without Democratization in China under Hu Jintao," in *China's Changing Political Landscape*, ed. Cheng Li (Washington: Brookings, 2008), 185–211; "Law and the Economy in China," in *Routledge Handbook of the Chinese Economy*, ed. Gregory C. Chow and Dwight H. Perkins (Abingdon: Routledge, 2015), 255–279; and "Law and Democracy in China: A Complex Relationship," in *Democratization in China, Korea, and Southeast Asia?*, ed. Kate Xiao Zhou, Shelley Rigger, and Lynn T. White III (Abingdon: Routledge, 2014), 126–140.

9. See Jiang Ping, "Drafting the Uniform Contract Law in China," *Columbia Journal of Asian Law* 10 (1996): 245–258; Stephen C. Hsu (Xu Chuanxi), "Contract Law of the People's Republic of China," *Minnesota Journal of International Law* 16 (2007): 115–162; Larry A. DiMatteo and Chen Lei, eds., *Chinese Contract Law: Civil and Common Law Perspectives* (Cambridge: Cambridge University Press, 2017).

10. See generally Jiang Yu Wang, *Company Law in China* (Cheltenham: Edward Elgar, 2014).

11. For examples, see Christina Ebert-Borges and Su Yingxia, "Freedom of Contract in Modern Chinese Legal Practice," *George Washington International Law Review* 46 (2014): 341–371.

12. Mo Zhang, "From Public to Private: The Newly Enacted Chinese Property Law and the Protection of Property Rights in China," *Berkeley Business Law Journal* 5 (2008): 317–362; Shitong Qiao, "The Evolution of Chinese Property Law," in *Private Law in China and Taiwan*, ed. Yun-chien Chang, Wei Shen, and Wen-yu Wang (Cambridge: Cambridge University Press, 2017), 182–211; Wang Liming, *Law of Real Rights* (Getzville, NY: Hein, 2017).

13. Jacques deLisle, "A Common Law-Like Civil Law and a Public Face for Private Law: China's Tort Law in Comparative Perspective," in *Towards a Chinese Civil Code: Comparative and Historical Perspectives*, ed. Lei Chen and C. H. (Remco) van Rhee (Leiden: Brill 2012), 353–394; Mo Zhang, *Introduction to Chinese Tort Law* (Beijing: Tsinghua, 2014).

14. See Rachel E. Stern, "From Dispute to Decision: Suing Polluters in China," *China Quarterly* 206 (June 2011), 294–312.

15. Barry Naughton, *The Chinese Economy: Adaptation and Growth,* 2nd ed. (Cambridge, MA: 2007), chaps. 16–17; Hui Huang, "The Regulation of Foreign Investment in Post-WTO China," *Columbia Journal of Asian Law* 23 (2009): 187–215; Jacques deLisle, "China and the WTO," in *China under Hu Jintao,* ed. T. J. Cheng, Jacques deLisle, and Deborah Brown (Singapore: World Scientific Press, 2006): 229–292.

16. Lucie Cheng and Arthur Rosett, "Contract with a Chinese Face: Socially Embedded Factors in the Transition from Hierarchy to Market, 1978–1989," *Journal of Chinese Law* 5 (1991): 143–244; Doug Guthrie, *Dragon in a Three Piece Suit* (Princeton, NJ: Princeton University Press, 1999); David L. Wank, *Commodifying Communism* (Cambridge: Cambridge University Press, 1999); Thomas Gold, Doug Guthrie, and David Wank, eds. *Social Connections in China: Institutions, Culture, and the Changing Nature of Guanxi* (Cambridge: Cambridge University Press, 2002); Berry Kwock, Mark X. James, Anthony Shu Chuen Tsui, "Doing Business in China: What is the Use of a Contract?" *Journal of Business Studies Quarterly* 4, no. 4 (2013): 56–67; Scott Wilson, "Law *Guanxi*: MNCs, State Actors and Legal Reform in China," *Journal of Contemporary China* 17, no. 54 (2008): 25–51.

17. Nicholas C. Howson, "'Quack Corporate Governance' as Traditional Chinese Medicine," *Seattle University Law Review* 37 (2014): 667–716; Jiangyu Wang, "The Political Logic of Corporate Governance in China's State-Owned Enterprises," *Cornell International Law Journal* 47 (2014): 631–669; Donald C. Clarke, "Law without Order in Chinese Corporate Governance Institutions," *Northwestern Journal of International Law and Business* 30 (2010): 131–199; Li-Wen Lin and Curtis J. Milhaupt, "We Are the (National) Champions: Understanding the Mechanisms of State Capitalism in China," *Stanford Law Review* 65 (2013): 697–759.

18. Guanghua Yu and Hao Zhang, "Adaptive Efficiency and Financial Development in China: The Role of Contracts and Contractual Enforcement," *Journal of International Economic Law* 11 (2008): 459–494; Shen Wei, *Shadow Banking in China* (Cheltenham: 2016).

19. See Mary E. Gallagher, "'Use the Law as Your Weapon': Institutional Change and Legal Mobilization in China," in *Engaging the Law in China,* ed. Neil J. Diamant, Stanley B. Lubman, and Kevin J. O'Brien (Stanford, CA: Stanford University Press, 2005), 54–83.

20. Eva Pils, "Waste No Land: Property, Dignity and Growth in Urbanizing China," *Asian-Pacific Law and Policy Journal* 11 (2010): 1–48; Shitong Qiao, "The Politics of Chinese Land," *Columbia Journal of Asian Law* 29 (2015): 70–111.

21. See, for example, Minxin Pei, Zhang Guoyan, Pei Fei, and Chen Lixin, "A Survey of Commercial Litigation in Shanghai Courts," in *Judicial Independence in China,* ed. Randall Peerenboom (New York: Cambridge University Press, 2010), 221–233.

22. Mei Ying Gechlik, "Judicial Reform in China: Lessons from Shanghai," *Columbia Journal of Asian Law* 19 (2005): 100–137; Haitan Lu, Hongbo Pan, and Chenying Zhang, "Political Connectedness and Court Outcomes: Evidence from Chinese Corporate Lawsuits," *Journal of Law and Economics* 58 (2015): 829–861; Xin He and Yang Su, "Do the 'Haves' Come Out Ahead in Shanghai Courts?" *Journal of Empirical Legal Studies* 10, no. 1 (2013): 120–145; Yuhua Wang, "Court Funding and Judicial Corruption in China," *China Journal* 69 (2013): 43–63; Qianfan Zhang, "The People's Court in Transition," *Journal of Contemporary China* 12 no. 34 (2003): 69–100; Xin He, "Black Hole of Responsibility: The Adjudication Committee's Role in a Chinese Court," *Law and Society Review* 46, no. 4 (2012): 681–712.

23. See generally, World Bank, *Economic Development and the Quality of Legal Institutions,* http://siteresources.worldbank.org/INTLAWJUSTINST/Resources/LegalInstitutionsTopicBrief.pdf; Douglass C. North, *Institutions, Institutional Change and Economic Performance* (Cambridge: Cambridge University Press, 1990); Katharina Pistor and Philip A. Wellons (Asian Development Bank), *The Role of Law and Legal Institutions in Asian Economic Development,1960–1995* New York: Oxford University Press, 1999); Kevin E. Davis

and Michael Trebilcock, "The Relationship between Law and Development: Optimists Versus Skeptics," *New York University Law and Economics Working Papers* 133 (2008); Jacques deLisle, "Development without Democratization? China, Law and the East Asian Model," in *Democratizations: Comparisons, Confrontations and Contrasts*, ed. Jose V. Ciprut (Cambridge, MA: MIT Press, 2009), 197–232; Minxin Pei, "Does Legal Reform Protect Economic Transactions? Commercial Disputes in China," in *Assessing the Value of Law in Transition Economies*, ed. Peter Murrell (Ann Arbor: University of Michigan, 2000), 180–210; Donald C. Clarke, "Economic Development and the Rights Hypothesis: The China Problem," *American Journal of Comparative Law* 51 (2003): 89–111; Franklin Allen, Jun Qian, and Meijun Qian, "Law, Finance and Economic Growth in China," *Journal of Financial Economics* 77, no. 1 (2005): 57–116.

24. See Minxin Pei, *China's Trapped Transition: The Limits of Developmental Autocracy* (Cambridge, MA: Harvard University Press, 2006); Gordon C. Chang, *The Coming Collapse of China* (New York: Random House, 2001); Pew Global Attitudes Project, "Chinese Views on the Economy and Domestic Challenges" (Oct. 2016), http://www.pewglobal.org/2016/10/05/1-chinese-views-on-the-economy-and-domestic-challenges/.

25. See for example, David Zweig, Kathy Hartford, James Feinerman, and Deng Jianxu, "Law, Contracts and Economic Modernization: Lessons from the Recent Chinese Rural Reforms," *Stanford International Law Journal* 23 (1987): 319–364; Nicholas C. Howson, "Corporate Law in the Shanghai People's Courts, 1992–2008: Judicial Autonomy in a Contemporary Authoritarian State," *East Asia Law Review* 5 (2010): 303–442; Robin Hui Huang, "Rethinking the Relationship between Public Regulation and Private Litigation: Evidence from Securities Class Action in China," *Theoretical Inquiries in Law* 19, no. 1 (2018): 333–361; Eric C. Ip and Kelvin Kwok, "Judicial Control of Local Protectionism in China: Antitrust Enforcement against Administrative Monopoly," *Journal of Competition Law and Economics* 13, no. 3 (2017): 549–575.

26. Steve Hess, "Nail Houses, Land Rights, and Frames of Injustice on China's Protest Landscape," *Asian Survey* 50, no. 5 (2010): 908–926; Mark D. Kielsgard and Lei Chen, "The Emergence of Private Property Law in China and its Impact on Human Rights," *Asian Pacific Law and Policy Journal* 15, no. 1 (2013): 94–134.

27. John Ohnesorge, "Chinese Administrative Law in the Northeast Asian, Mirror," *Transnational Law and Contemporary Problems* 16 (2006): 103–164; Zhou Hanhua, "China's Regulatory Reforms," *University of Pennsylvania Asian Law Review* 13 (2018): 1–23.

28. Xi Jinping, "Power Must be 'Caged' by the System," in *The Governance of China*, vol. 1. (Beijing: Foreign Languages Press, 2014), 425–431.

29. For examples of diverse assessments administrative litigation in practice, see Minxin Pei, "Citizens v. Mandarins: Administrative Litigation in China," *China Quarterly*, no. 152 (1997): 832–862; Randall Peerenboom, "Globalization, Path Dependency and the Limits of Law: Administrative Law Reform and the Rule of Law in the People's Republic of China," *Berkeley Journal of International Law* 19, no. 2 (2001): 161–264; Gechlik, "Judicial Reform in China: Lessons from Shanghai"; Ji Li, "Suing the Leviathan: An Empirical Analysis of the Changing Rate of Administrative Litigation in China," *Journal of Empirical Legal Studies* 10, no. 4 (2013): 825–846; Kevin O'Brien and Li Lianjiang, "Suing the Local State: Administrative Litigation in Rural China," *China Journal* 51 (2004): 76–96; He Haibo, "How Much Progress Can Legislation Bring?: The 2014 Amendment of the Administrative Litigation Law of the PRC," *University of Pennsylvania Asian Law Review* 13 (2018): 137–190.

30. See Jamie P. Horsley, "What's So Controversial About China's New Anti-Corruption Body? Digging into the National Supervision Commission," *Diplomat*, May 30, 2018, https://thediplomat.com/2018/05/whats-so-controversial-about-chinas-new-anti-corruption-body/; Fu Hualing, "The Upward and Downward Spirals in China's

Anti-Corruption Enforcement," in *Comparative Perspectives on Criminal Justice in China*, ed. Mike McConville and Eva Pils (Cheltenham: Edward Elgar, 2013), 390–410; Melanie Manion, *Corruption by Design: Building Clean Government in Mainland China and Hong Kong* (Cambridge, MA: Harvard University Press, 2004); Andrew Wedeman, *Double Paradox: Rapid Growth and Rising Corruption in China* (Ithaca, NY: Cornell University Press, 2012); Margaret K. Lewis, "Presuming Innocence, or Corruption, in China," *Columbia Journal of Transnational Law* 50 (2012): 287–369.

31. Kenneth G. Lieberthal and David M. Lampton, eds., *Bureaucracy, Politics, and Decision Making in Post-Mao China* (Berkeley: University of California Press,1992); Andrew Mertha, "'Fragmented Authoritarianism 2.0': Political Participation in the Chinese Policy Process, *China Quarterly* 200 (2009): 995–1012; Hong Gao and Adam Tyson, "Power List Reform: A New Constraint Mechanism for Administrative Powers in China," *Asian Studies Review* 42, no. 1 (2018): 125–143.

32. See Economist Intelligence Unit, *Democracy Index 2017*, http://www.eiu.com/ Handlers/WhitepaperHandler.ashx?fi=Democracy_Index_2017.pdf&mode=wp&campa ignid=DemocracyIndex2017 (rank of 139 of 167 countries; classified as "authoritarian"); *Polity IV Project: Political Regime Characteristics and Transitions, 1800–2012*, http://www. systemicpeace.org/polity/polity4.htm (-7 on a scale where -10 to -6 is "autocracy" and +10 is "full democracy"); World Bank, *Worldwide Governance Indicators* (7th percentile in voice and accountability); World Justice Project, *Rule of Law Index* (rank of 100 out of 113 on constraints on government mower). See generally Randall Peerenboom, *China Modernizes: Threat to the West or Model for the Rest?* (Oxford: Oxford University Press, 2007); Pan Wei, "Toward a Consultative Rule of Law Regime in China," *Journal of Contemporary China* 12 (2003): 3–43; and Jacques deLisle, "Chasing the God of Wealth while Evading the Goddess of Democracy," in *Development and Democracy: New Perspectives on an Old Debate*, ed. Sunder Ramaswamy and Jeffrey W. Cason (Middlebury, VT: Middlebury College Press, 2003).

33. See generally, Ian Dobinson, "The Criminal Law of the People's Republic of China (1997): Real Change or Rhetoric?" *Pacific Rim Law and Policy Journal* 11 (2002): 1–62; Carlos Wing-hung Lo, *China's Legal Awakening: Legal Theory and Criminal Justice in Deng's China* (Hong Kong: University of Hong Kong Press, 1995); "Reforming China's Criminal Procedure" (Symposium) *Columbia Journal of Asian Law* 24 (2011): 213–364.

34. Fu Hualing, "Reeducation through Labor in Historical Perspective," *China Quarterly* no. 184 (2005): 811–830; Jiang Su, "Punishment without Trial: The Past, Present, and Future of Reeducation through Labor in China," *Peking University Law Journal* 4 no. 1 (2016): 45–78.

35. Keith J. Hand, "Using Law for a Righteous Purpose: The Sun Zhigang Incident and Evolving Forms of Citizen Action in the People's Republic of China," *Columbia Journal of Transnational Law* 45 (2006): 114–195.

36. Among the organizations regularly issue such reports are Amnesty International, Human Rights Watch, Human Rights in China, and the U.S. State Department.

37. Shen Kui, "Is it the Beginning of the Era of the Rule of the Constitution?" *Pacific Rim Law and Policy Journal* 12 (2003): 199–231; Thomas E. Kellogg, "Constitutionalism with Chinese Characteristics?" *International Journal of Constitutional Law* 7 no. 2 (2009): 215–246.

38. Kevin J. O'Brien and Rongbin Han, "Path to Democracy? Assessing Village Elections in China," *Journal of Contemporary China* 18, no. 60 (2009): 359–378; Johan Lagerkvist, "The Wukan Uprising and Chinese State-Society Relations: Toward "Shadow Civil Society," *International Journal of China Studies* 3, no. 3 (2012): 345–361; Pierre F. Landry, Deborah Davis, and Shiru Wang, "Elections in Rural China: Competition without Parties," *Comparative Political Studies* 43, no. 6 (2010): 763–790.

39. Andrew J. Nathan, *Chinese Democracy* (Berkeley: University of California Press, 1985), chap. 10; Daniel A. Bell, *The China Model: Political Meritocracy and the Limits of Democracy*

(Princeton, NJ: Princeton University Press, 2015); Suisheng Zhao, "The China Model: Can it Replace the Western Model of Modernization?" *Journal of Contemporary China* 19, no. 65 (2010): 419–436; Jacques deLisle, "What's Happened to Democracy in China?: Elections, Law and Political Reform," *Foreign Policy Research Institute E-Note* (Apr. 2010) http://www.fpri.org/enotes/201004. delisle.democracyinchina.html.

40. See generally Laura Paler, "China's Legislation Law and the Making of a More Orderly and Representative Legislative System," *China Quarterly*, no. 182 (2005): 301–318; Wang Xixin, "Administrative Procedure Reforms in China's Rule of Law Context," *Columbia Journal of Asian Law* 12 (Fall 1998): 251–277; Greg Distelhorst. "The Power of Empty Promises: Quasi-Democratic Institutions and Activism in China," *Comparative Political Studies* 50, no. 4 (2017): 464–498; Baogang He and Mark E. Warren, "Authoritarian Deliberation: The Deliberative Turn in Chinese Political Development, *Perspectives on Politics* 9, no. 2 (2011): 269–289; Wang Xixin and Zhang Yongle, "The Rise of Participatory Governance in China," *University of Pennsylvania Journal of Asian Law* 183 (2018): 24–71.

41. Fu Hualing and Michael Palmer, eds. "Mediation in Contemporary China" *Journal of Comparative Law* 10, no. 2 (2015), special issue; Jieren Hu, "Grand Mediation in China," *Asian Survey* 51 (2011): 1065–1089.

42. Carl F. Minzner, "Xinfang: An Alternative to Formal Chinese Legal Institutions," *Stanford Journal of International Law* 42 (2006): 103–179; Xin He and Yuqing Feng, "Mismatched Discourses in the Petition Offices of Chinese Courts," *Law and Social Inquiry* 41 (2016): 212–241<; He Weifang, "Constitutional Trends–The World and China" (Oct. 2009), http://boxun.com/news/gb/pubvp/2009/10/200910270945.shtml.

43. See, for example, Eva Pils, "Land Disputes, Rights Assertion and Social Unrest in China: A Case from Sichuan," *Columbia Journal of International Law* 19 (2005): 235–292; Sarah Biddulph, "Responding to Industrial Unrest in China," *Sydney Law Review* 34 (2012): 35–63; Carl F. Minzner, "Riots and Cover-Ups: Counter-Productive Control of Local Agents in China," *University of Pennsylvania Journal of International Law* 31 (2009): 53–123.

44. Benjamin L. Liebman, "Watchdog or Demagogue? The Media in the Chinese Legal System," *Columbia Law Review* 105 (2005): 1–157; Benjamin L. Liebman, "A Populist Threat to China's Courts?" in *Chinese Justice*, ed. Woo and Gallagher, 269–313; Xin He, "Maintaining Stability by Law: Protest-Supported Housing Demolition Litigation and Social Change in China," *Law and Social Inquiry* 39 (2014): 849–872.

45. This section draws on and updates Jacques deLisle, "Traps, Gaps and Law: Prospects and Challenges for China's Reforms" in *Is China Trapped, in Transition? Implications for Future Reforms* (Oxford: Oxford Foundation for Law, Justice, and Society, 2007). On implementation, see Jianfu Chen, Yuwen Li, and Jean M. Otto, eds. *Implementation of Law in China* (The Hague: Kluwer, 2002); Benjamin van Rooij, "The People's Regulation: Citizens and Implementation of Law in China," *Columbia Journal of Asian Law* 25 (2012): 116–179.

46. Keith J. Hand, "Understanding China's System for Addressing Legislative Conflicts," *Columbia Journal of Asian Law* 26 (2013): 139–265; Yan Lin and Tom Ginsburg, "Constitutional Interpretation in Lawmaking: China's Invisible Constitutional Enforcement Mechanism," *American Journal of Comparative Law* 63 (2015): 467–492; Xixin Wang, "Rule of Rules: An Inquiry into Administrative Rules in China's Rule of Law Context," in *The Rule of Law: Perspectives from the Pacific* (Washington: Mansfield Center for Pacific Affairs, 2000), 22–40.

47. See Jacques deLisle, "Lex Americana?: United States Legal Assistance, American Legal Models, and Legal Change in the Post-Communist World and Beyond," *University of Pennsylvania Journal of International Economic Law* 20 (1999): 179–308; Pitman B. Potter, "Globalization and Economic Regulation in China: Selective Adaptation of Globalized

Norms and Practices," *Washington University Global Studies Law Review* 2 (2003): 119–150; Katharina Pistor, Daniel Berkowitz, and Jean-Francois Richard, "The Transplant Effect," *American Journal of Comparative Law* 51 (2003): 163–203; Jedidiah J. Kronke, *The Futility of Law and Development* (New York: Oxford University Press, 2017).

48. See World Bank, *China-Governance, Investment Climate, and Harmonious Society: Competitiveness Enhancements for 120 Cities in China* (Oct. 8, 2006), http://siteresources.worldbank.org/ INTCHINA/Resources/318862-1121421293578/120cities_ en.pdf; and compare Randall Peerenboom, "Show Me the Money: The Dominance of Wealth in Determining Rights Performance in Asia," *Duke Journal of Comparative and International Law* 15 (2004): 75–152; Xin He, "Court Finance and Responses to Judicial Reforms: A Tale of Two Chinese Courts," *Law and Policy* 31, no. 4 (2009): 463–486; and sources cited in notes 17 and 18.

49. Jacques deLisle, "Law and the Economy in China," 269.

50. Zhu Suli, "Political Parties in China's Judiciary," *Duke Journal of Comparative and International Law* 17 (2007): 533–560.

51. Yuhua Wang, *Tying the Autocrat's Hands* (New York: Cambridge, 2015).

52. See Benjamin L. Liebman, "China's Courts: Restricted Reform," *China Quarterly* 191 (2007): 620–638; Ethan Michelson and Sida Liu, "What Do Chinese Lawyers Want?" in *China's Changing Political Landscape*, ed. Cheng Li, 310–333; Randall Peerenboom, ed., *Judicial Independence in China* (New York: Cambridge, 2010).

53. Hualing Fu and Richard Cullen, "Climbing the *Weiquan* ladder: A Radicalizing Process for Rights-Protection Lawyers," *China Quarterly* 205 (2011): 40–59; Hualing Fu, "The July 9th (709) Crackdown on Human Rights Lawyers," *Journal of Contemporary China* 27, no. 112 (2018): 554–568.

54. Jacques deLisle, "Law and China's Development Model" in *In Search of China's Development Model: Beyond the Beijing Consensus*, ed. Philip Hsu, Yushan Wu, and Suisheng Zhao (New York: Routledge, 2011), 147–165; "Law in the China Development Model 2.0," *Journal of Contemporary China* 26, no. 103 (2017): 68–84; Albert H. Y. Chen, "China's Long March towards the Rule of Law or China's Turn against Law?" *Chinese Journal of Comparative Law* 4, no. 1 (2016): 1–35.

55. See Carl F. Minzner, "China's Turn Against Law," *American Journal of Comparative Law* 59 (2011): 935–984; and Benjamin Liebman, "Legal Reform: China's Law-Stability Paradox," *Daedalus* 143, no. 2 (2014): 96–109.

56. Chinese Communist Party Central Committee Document No. 9 (Aug. 2013), http://www.mingjingnews.com/2013/08/9. html; Yang Xiaoqing, "A Comparative Study of Constitutional Governance and the People's Democratic System," *Seeking Truth*, May 21, 2013; Cheng Li and Ryan McElveen, "China's Constitutional Conundrum," Brookings Institution, Feb. 28, 2018, https://www.brookings.edu/blog/order-from-chaos/2018/02/28/chinas-constitutional-conundrum/

57. See Dali L. Yang, "China's Troubled Quest for Order," *Journal of Contemporary China* 26, no. 103 (2017): 35–53.

SUGGESTED READINGS

Chen, Albert H. Y. *An Introduction to the Legal System of the People's Republic of China*, 4th ed. New York: LexisNexis 2011.

Diamant, Neil J., Stanley B. Lubman, and Kevin J. O'Brien, eds. *Engaging the Law in China*. Stanford, CA: Stanford University Press, 2005.

Gallagher, Mary. *Authoritarian Legality in China: Law, Workers, and the State.* New York: Cambridge University Press, 2017.

He Weifang. *In the Name of Justice: Striving for the Rule of Law in China.* Washington, DC: Brookings Institution, 2012.

Hurst, William. *Ruling before the Law: The Politics of Legal Regimes in China and Indonesia.* New York: Cambridge University Press, 2018.

Liu, Sida, and Terence Halliday. *Criminal Defense in China: The Politics of Lawyers at Work.* New York: Cambridge University Press, 2016.

Ng, Kwai Hang, and Xin He. *Embedded Courts: Judicial Decision-Making in China.* New York: Cambridge University Press, 2017.

Peerenboom, Randall, ed. *Judicial Independence in China.* New York: Cambridge University Press, 2010.

Pils, Eva. *Human Rights in China: A Social Practice in the Shadows of Authoritarianism.* New York: Polity, 2018.

Wang, Yuhua. *Tying the Autocrat's Hands: The Rise of The Rule of Law in China.* New York: Cambridge University Press, 2017.

Woo, Margaret Y. K., and Mary E. Gallagher, eds. *Chinese Justice: Civil Dispute Resolution in Contemporary China.* New York: Cambridge University Press, 2011.

Yu, Keping, ed. *Democracy and the Rule of Law in China* (Leiden, Netherlands: Brill, 2010).

8

China's Political Economy

DAVID ZWEIG

Few modern societies have as "political" an economy as China. Even after forty years of market reform, bureaucrats, local and national leaders, as well as new and old government regulations, still have remarkable influence over the allocation of goods and services. Similarly, because the legitimacy of the Chinese Communist Party (CCP) depends so heavily on continuing economic growth; because expanding inequalities may threaten social stability; and because corruption has seeped deeply into the political system, economics has enormous political significance in China.

China's national leaders greatly influence the country's economic fortunes, as their preferred developmental strategies have always shaped China's trajectory. And leaders use their power to press their policy preferences. Every leadership change in China, including subtle shifts of power from one leader or faction to another, influences public policy. Without Mao's death in 1976, Deng Xiaoping would have been unable to introduce the reform era. Similarly, after coming to power in 2002, Hu Jintao and Wen Jiabao established a more balanced development strategy than their predecessor Jiang Zemin, to ameliorate the inequality that had emerged in the 1990s. Similarly, Xi Jinping has dramatically restrengthened the state's and the CCP's role in the economy, as well as propelling China's global influence through the Belt and Road Initiative (BRI). Conversely, economic difficulties undermine the authority of factions or leaders. When price reforms in the summer of 1988 triggered popular fears of inflation, the resulting run on Shanghai banks allowed conservative party leaders to attack one of the key supporters of reform, then CCP General Secretary Zhao Ziyang, who was ousted from office as part of the Tiananmen crisis in 1989.

A second component of China's "political" economy is that economic deregulation threatens the power of bureaucrats who struggle to maintain their influence. Economic planning and regulations during the Mao era had empowered millions of bureaucrats from Beijing down to the villages, giving them control over the allocation of wealth, resources, jobs, and people's right to participate in the economy. Policies that decentralized control over the economy left local officials, not the market, in control of many resources. No doubt, decades of reform and deregulation, in particular, the requirement for joining the WTO that all laws be transparent and open to public scrutiny, have undermined bureaucratic authority. Nevertheless, as of 2017, despite a booming private sector, central and local bureaucrats still controlled 33 percent of China's gross domestic product (GDP) and some sectors, such as telecommunications, are overly regulated. State banks still discriminate against the private sector when allocating loans and Xi has strengthened the role of CCP committees even in private firms.

State power also determines a country's relationship to the global economy. What balance between imports, exports, and trade restrictions is most likely to enhance national power and the pace of economic development? How tightly should economic interactions with the outside world be constrained, even if those constraints are not in conformity with international norms? As states open their economies to the world, their leaders discover that a predetermined set of international rules, norms, international organizations, trading structures, transportation networks, and pricing mechanisms limit their choices. But which of those rules can be evaded and at what price? To what extent can a country rely on the global economy for its growth? These issues, which fall under the purview of International Political Economy (IPE), shaped China's transition from a relatively isolated state with a stagnant or, at best, slowly growing economy in the Maoist era, to an economic dynamo, a trading giant, and a major investor in countries around the world.

POLITICAL ECONOMY IN THE MAO ERA

The CCP came to power in 1949 planning a moderate program of economic change, but with several pressing issues on the agenda. In 1950–1952, land reform redistributed 42 percent of arable land from richer farmers to poorer villagers. The goal was to weaken the landlord class, which had supported the Kuomintang (KMT), and repay China's peasants who fought and died on behalf of the CCP. Hyperinflation, which had undermined KMT support in the cities during the Civil War, was tamed. Under the slogan of "thirty years without change," the CCP promised to leave the private economy alone in the hope that China's small capitalist class would continue to invest in their own firms, which they did.

However, in 1953, the CCP took the first steps in a process of fast-paced change that would transform the economy when they began copying the Soviet model of industrialization. Twenty million peasants moved to the cities to become workers for an enormous number of new factories; at the same time, the CCP began to extend its reach over other parts of the economy. In the countryside, the state took control of the rural grain markets in 1953, prohibiting private trading. After land reform, some peasants had sold their holdings to local officials and former landlords, leading Mao to see the emergence of a new rural ruling class. Mao attacked this situation, in the summer of 1955, by urging local officials to press villagers to join rural cooperatives in which the land would be owned and farmed collectively. Any idea of expanding private land holdings was foreclosed. By the end of 1956, 98 percent of villagers had turned their land, oxen, and tools over to the cooperatives and were drawing their income based largely on the work they performed for the collective. Property transfer accelerated in the cities in the waning weeks of 1955 and the early part of 1956, as all capitalists, small shopkeepers, and professionals running their own businesses turned their firms over to state.

Overall, economic growth during China's First Five-Year Plan (1953–1957) was robust, averaging over 9percent per year. But growth rates fluctuated widely, for example, from 15 percent in 1956 to 5 percent in 1957, and industrial growth far outpaced that of agriculture.

In early 1958, China entered the Great Leap Forward, a period of euphoric anticipation of the advent of the communist utopia. Top-down, Soviet-style economic planning was replaced by an approach that emphasized mass mobilization and ideological appeals to achieve a dramatic breakthrough in production. Mao and other leaders argued that much larger collective farms, the "people's communes," filled with peasants possessing heightened revolutionary fervor, would bring unprecedented prosperity to the countryside.

But when production fell far short of ridiculously elevated targets, local officials, mostly out of fear that they would be accused of insufficient commitment to the Great Leap, lied, reporting highly exaggerated increases in agricultural output. Central leaders, deep in the throes of self-deception, believed the false reports and demanded that communes remit their "surplus grain" to the state to feed the cities and for export, leaving little food in the villages. When the weather soured in 1959, famine struck rural China, claiming tens of millions of lives in the poorer parts of the country. Industry and commerce were also severely affected by the irrational policies of the Great Leap, and the country plunged into an economic depression. GDP growth in 1961 was -27.1 percent and -6.1 percent in 1962.

This disaster led Mao Zedong to withdraw from day-to-day management of the economy, allowing more pragmatic leaders, especially Liu Shaoqi and Deng Xiaoping, to introduce reforms to repair the damage by reversing the extreme policies of the Great Leap. By 1963, the economy had recovered, with annual GDP growth averaging 14.1 percent in 1963–1965.

But trouble was looming. Mao, convinced that the CCP was becoming a new capitalist class, launched the disastrous Cultural Revolution in 1966 to keep the party and the country on what he considered to be the correct revolutionary road. Moderate leaders, including Liu and Deng, were purged. During the subsequent decade, radical policies greatly restricted the scope of private economic activity in both city and countryside. Although the economic consequences of the Cultural Revolution were not nearly as severe as those of the Great Leap Forward, GDP growth averaged only 3.9 percent in 1967 through 1976. Because population growth was relatively high during this period (2.4 percent per year), annual GDP growth per capita was just 1.5 percent.

During the Maoist era, which ended with the Chairman's death and the arrest of the Gang of Four in 1976, China made important strides toward industrialization and improved agricultural infrastructure, such as irrigation. Inequalities of various kinds were limited, and health and education standards significantly improved. For example, life expectancy, which in 1949 was just thirty-six years, had almost doubled to sixty years in 1976 and literacy had spread from one-fifth of the population to about two-thirds in 1980.[1] But the PRC was still an impoverished nation with a per capita GDP of about US$310 (purchasing power parity) per year in 1980.[2] Furthermore, Mao, insisting that China be economically self-reliant, moved the country toward almost complete **autarky**, which together with self-imposed international isolation during much of the Cultural Revolution, meant that, when his rule came to an end, the PRC had very low levels of foreign trade and almost zero foreign investment (see Table 8.1 and Figure 8.3).

POLITICAL ECONOMY IN THE REFORM ERA

Between 1978 and 2002, China went through five waves of reform that have literally changed almost every aspect of domestic and foreign economic policy. Yet while major reforms have been introduced across various sectors at the same time, implementation has at times been piecemeal, following a logic attributed to Deng of **"crossing the river by feeling the stones"** in contrast with post-Soviet Russia's **big bang** approach of seeking fast results through rapid fundamental changes. Importantly, many reforms were tested locally before being popularized nationally.

The first wave of reform was initiated by Deng Xiaoping almost as soon as he had consolidated power and it formally began with the Third Plenum of the 11th Central Committee in December 1978, which is marked as the start of China's ongoing era of "reform and opening up" (*gaige kaifang*). The plenum redirected national policy from the Cultural Revolution's emphasis on politics and ideology to improving the economy and people's livelihood. It introduced rural reforms, established official diplomatic relations with the United States, opened the economy to the outside world, and ended "class labels" that had divided citizens into "friends and enemies" of the state.

During this wave of reform, the people's communes were abolished, and the rural economy was decollectivized with the establishment of the **household responsibility system** in which individual families managed agricultural production (see the discussion of decollectivization later in this chapter). China also opened its economy to the outside world under an approach that can be called **segmented deregulation**,[3] where rules controlling cross-border exchanges were lifted (or deregulated) in specific locations, while in other locations business relations between China and the rest of the world remained under tight bureaucratic control. Thus, in 1979, China's leaders established four **Special Economic Zones (SEZs)** in coastal areas that had maintained links to Chinese communities overseas. The SEZs—Shenzhen, Zhuhai, Xiamen, and Shantou—were given special privileges in terms of imports, exports, labor and land policy, and the management of foreign direct investment (FDI).

The second wave of reforms emerged in 1984/1985. Fourteen coastal cities were opened to foreign trade. Scientific institutions and universities were encouraged to do business with enterprises and keep the profits, and universities were allowed to link directly with universities overseas. In the cities, efforts were made to invigorate state-owned enterprises, which were responsible for most industrial output in China. Central planning was curtailed; as long as firms fulfilled their yearly targets, which stipulated what goods they had to sell to the state and at what prices, they could produce more goods for sale at market prices. This "dual price system" expanded output and efficiency, but people who could buy goods produced at planned prices, and sell them on the free market, made a killing.

In 1987/1988, the third wave of reform opened all of coastal China to the global economy. This "Coastal Development Strategy," including the establishment of more than six thousand foreign trade companies (FTCs), marks the beginning of China's **export-led growth (ELG)**, which continues today. China's rural industry—which had expanded significantly after 1984—became a driver of China's export boom. For the next seven years, China's export growth came largely from these small- and medium-sized rural enterprises along the coast. In 1988, the State Science and Technology Commission (SSTC)—a more powerful version of a ministry of science—opened a high-tech park in the suburbs of Beijing, which also had special tax and export benefits; these zones would eventually be spread to more than fifty cities.

But in the summer of 1988, a second attempt to lift price controls on many items—the first attempt had failed in 1985—triggered a run on the banks, as people, frightened that the cost of goods would soar, withdrew their cash and bought everything off the shelves. The panic had political repercussions, undermining CCP General Secretary Zhao Ziyang, who was leading the reform effort with Deng Xiaoping's support. The power struggle, pitting conservative leaders, who wanted slower reform, against Zhao and other committed reformers, would form the political background to the crisis in Tiananmen Square that shook China to the core in May–June 1989 (see chap. 4).

The military assault on Beijing on June 4, 1989, had economic repercussions. In fall 1989, China experienced its only quarter of negative growth during the entire reform era, and a general economic slowdown lasted until 1992. In late 1989, the CCP watched with horror as communist party-states across Eastern Europe tumbled down, along with the Berlin Wall. Further shock followed the collapse of the Soviet Union in August 1991, as Mikhail Gorbachev's reforms led to the dismantling of the Soviet empire.

Deng Xiaoping learned important lessons about the political economy of a successful reform by studying communism's demise in Europe. While fear paralyzed most Chinese leaders, Deng understood that the CCP's political survival was wedded to economic growth; Gorbachev's mistake had been promoting political reform without putting more food on the tables of Soviet citizens. So, in January 1992, Deng, then well into his eighties, embarked on his "Southern Journey" to Shenzhen, next to capitalist Hong Kong, and one of China's fasting-growing cities, where he called on the people and local governments to "move faster and take greater risks" in economic reform. Though conservative opponents in Beijing suppressed his clarion call for almost two months, his exhortation to return to a path of reform struck a chord with Chinese along the coast, triggering the fourth wave in China's reform.

In the fall of 1992, the 14th Party Congress of the CCP announced that henceforth China would establish a "socialist market economy," ending once and for all the ideological debate about whether China would remain a fully planned economy or move rapidly toward one with a good measure of capitalism. This decision led to the creation of a mixed public-private economy that still characterizes China today and is often referred to as a form of **state capitalism**.[4]

China's integration into the global economy deepened during the fourth wave of reform (see Table 8.1). Whereas most foreign investment in the 1980s involved overseas Chinese investors in small enterprises, between 1993 and 1995 larger firms from Europe, the United States, Japan, along with Taiwanese investment, triggered a foreign direct investment (FDI) boom. Economic growth rates took off as local governments dusted off plans drafted in 1987/1988, but tabled in 1989, and began many new local projects.

When the fifth wave of reform ensued in 1997/1998, the CCP General Secretary, Jiang Zemin, who had recently solidified his position as China's top leader, and Premier Zhu Rongji, began the process of privatizing all but the largest state-owned enterprises (SOEs), including tens of thousands of collectively owned enterprises in the countryside. This shift was dramatically reflected in the sharp drop in the number of workers in state-owned enterprises, which fell from a peak of 112.6 million in 1995 to about 70 million in 2002/2003 (see Fig. 10.1).[5] During this wave, Jiang Zemin and Zhu Rongji halved the number of state bureaucrats and promoted the private ownership of apartments—triggering a nationwide housing boom. Tens of thousands of small and medium SOEs were taken over by their managers. Final plans were made to join the World Trade Organization (WTO), which entailed removing regulations that limited foreign access to China's domestic market, deepening China's integration into the international economy.

The Hu Jintao era (2002–2012) saw no major wave of reform, partly because Hu was a relatively weak general secretary whose efforts were thwarted by Jiang Zemin whose influence on the levers of power extended for more than five years after he stepped down. Hu and Premier Wen Jiabao focused on alleviating the excesses of the Jiang era, which had allowed for increased pollution, massive layoffs, and the decline in the social welfare of the working class due to SOE privatization, growing income and class inequalities, and a significant deterioration in the quality of rural education. China made some progress in these areas, especially in expanding the social safety net for most of the population.[6] The Hu–Wen administration also established the **State-owned Asset Supervision and Administration Commission (SASAC)**, which took over the management of all the major 170 SOEs from industry-specific ministries. A major downside of this period was official corruption, which had become endemic. All in all, by 2012, the country seemed ready for a stronger leader and a more effective central government.[7]

As discussed in chapter 4, Xi Jinping had been the successor-in-waiting since the start of Hu Jintao's second term as general secretary in 2007. When he took over five years later, expectations ran high that he would set the course for dramatic changes in China's domestic and international political economy.

Xi's credentials as an economic reformer are attributed to a remarkable document passed at the Third Plenum of the 18th Central Committee in November 2013, slightly more than a year after Xi came to power. It included 336 important initiatives across multiple sectors, including finance, housing, urban-rural relations, reform of SOEs, the role of the market, social welfare, and internationalization of the economy.[8]

However, many of those reforms have failed to materialize, moved forward very slowly, or have been contradicted by new policies in what many have seen as a zigzag policy agenda. It is now clear that Xi is deeply committed to enhancing the party-state oversight of the economy, strengthening the state sector,[9] consolidating CCP rule, and using China's growing economy to make it into a great global power, all part of fulfilling his "China Dream" (see chap. 5).

Xi's impact on China's economic development may not be clear for some time. But trends suggest only tentative steps forward on the road to further marketization in sectors such as banking and finance, with greater consolidation for the state sector in key national industries.

In any case, what is clear is that the five waves of reform from 1978 to 2001 led to dramatic economic transformations in the PRC, including: (1) a shift from a state-run economy, dominated by public ownership of all the means of production, to a mixed, socialist market economy with a prominent private sector; (2) from commune-based agriculture to decollectivization and the return of profit as the motive force in the rural economy; (3) from economic autarky to global interdependence as China became a trading powerhouse and member of the WTO; (4) from a very poor country to one with a rapidly rising standard of living; and (5) from one of the world's most equal (if poor) societies to one of the most unequal.

RURAL REFORM

Although the rural areas had been the base of power for the communist revolution, the CCP turned on the peasantry in the mid-1950s, freezing rural to urban migration through the "household registration system" (*hukou*), which has been called a Chinese equivalent of apartheid because Chinese citizens had to carry permits that restricted them to living and working in specific locations (see chaps. 9 and 10).[10] This system embedded a deep "urban bias"[11] in the PRC's development strategy in which urbanites received subsidized grain, food, and housing, retirement benefits or pensions, better-quality schools, health-care coverage, and many social amenities that turned large SOEs into welfare units. Rural residents, on the other hand, had to sell what was called "surplus" grain—which was really a part of the harvest—to the state at below cost, build their own homes, finance low-quality schools, fund their own cooperative medical program, and rely on their sons to support them in their old age. Urban bias was also reflected in the gap between the low prices paid to farmers for agricultural products and the high sales prices for urban industrial goods—what is called a "price scissors"—and may have shifted some wealth from the countryside to the cities, although some studies suggest that rural-urban inequality grew largely because of direct state investment in urban industry, not because of any price scissors.

During most of the Mao era, ideological and policy constraints undermined private economic activity. Between 1966 and 1978, village officials were pressured to limit "the tail of capitalism"—that is, private economic activity that leftists said might lead to the reemergence of capitalism in the countryside.[12] Rural markets were closed, household sideline production (such as raising pigs and chickens) was banned in some places, and private plots—5–7 percent of collective land, which had been allocated during collectivization to all villagers for their own production—were banned or placed under collective controls. Under a policy called "taking grain as the key link" (*yi liang wei gang*), the state forced communes to forgo producing higher valued products, such as fruit, vegetables, oil-bearing crops, bamboo, and fish, in order to ensure local (and national) grain self-sufficiency.

Given all these constraints on income generation in the countryside, peasant living standards barely improved in the latter Maoist period, and when Mao died in 1976, there was there was widespread support for rural reform in much of China.

Decollectivization

The story of decollectivization is the stuff of novels, reflecting the audacity of China's rural inhabitants to challenge the state. People's communes were first dismantled as a survival strategy during the Great Famine of 1959–1961 in a village in Fengyang county, Anhui province, a region rocked by very high death rates.[13] Faced with starvation at that time, villagers farmed the collective land independently. But while this action saved many lives, in 1962 Mao sacked Anhui's provincial leader for undermining collective agriculture, admonishing the CCP to "never forget class struggle."

In 1978, about two years after Mao's death, peasants in Anhui, still one of China's poorest provinces, again faced famine conditions. Fengyang's cadres and villagers signed a secret document, in blood, saying that they would again farm the collectively owned land as individual households but, this time, not tell higher-level officials. But even when the province's leader discovered what was occurring, he turned a blind eye to these steps toward decollectivization. Key figures at the center began pushing for a relaxation in agricultural policies in order to stimulate production, and through a complex interplay of forces at the central, provincial, and local levels, by the early 1980s the household responsibility system was official policy and in just a few years all of rural China was decollectivized.[14]

Land *management* was returned to each household, while the village maintained *ownership* of the land. Farmers contracted the land from the village, paying a fixed amount to the village in return. Families, not commune cadres, decided what crops to plant, how to allocate labor, and whether to consume, save, or sell what they produced. The amount of work that villagers performed and their farming skills determined their financial rewards. Households switched to higher value cash crops, enhancing their incomes, while "specialized households" engaged in larger-scale farming, animal husbandry, fishery, and other agricultural specialties. Farmers paid only a small tax. In 1979, the state also raised its price for most crops by an average of 25 percent, significantly increasing incomes in the countryside.

The rural economy boomed. While the average annual increase of the gross value of agricultural output (GVAO) between 1952 and 1978 had been 4.2 percent, between 1979 and 1984 it was 7.4 percent. The annual output of grain had risen by only

2.3 percent a year between 1952 and 1978, but this went up to 5.1 percent a year between 1979 and 1984. Between 1978 and 1984, rural household income grew by 12.4 percent annually, while urban incomes grew 6.8 percent. The quality of food in both city and countryside improved enormously because of the rural reforms.

Flush with cash, villagers demanded more durable consumer goods; while 31 percent of rural households owned a bicycle in 1978, eight years later 81 percent of households did. Only 20 percent of households owned a sewing machine in 1978; by 1985, more than 43 percent had one. As many as 80 percent of rural Chinese families renovated their homes in the 1980s, replacing mud walls with brick ones, thatched roofs with tiled ones, and dirt floors with concrete ones. With rural Chinese comprising approximately 18 percent of the world's population at the time—and with 80 percent of them significantly upgrading their homes—rural reform generated the largest housing boom in world history!

In 1984 the central government's attention turned to industrial reform. The prices of consumer and industrial goods were allowed to rise in order to stimulate the urban economy. Within a decade the countryside was again falling behind the cities in terms of economic growth, and the urban-rural income gap was even greater than it had been on the eve of decollectivization in the late 1970s (see Box 8.1).

A new tax policy introduced in 1994 compounded problems for rural China. In the 1980s, the central government's share of GDP and total investment, relative to local governments, had dropped precipitously due to economic decentralization and the increased rural GDP was mostly in the hands of farm families. The provinces and localities had become rich while the central government had grown relatively poor, undermining its ability to redistribute wealth among regions of the country in order to significantly influence China's direction of development. In response, the taxes that provinces and local governments paid to the central government were increased, leaving most rural counties without the finances to help the towns and villages under their administrative authority.

Moreover, the central government imposed new tasks on local officials, such as running schools, reestablishing health-care programs, and building new roads, without giving them adequate funds to do so.[15] To pay for these projects, local cadres forced peasants to pay arbitrary taxes and illegal fees for all kinds of activities, such as slaughtering pigs or chickens, to raise funds for new schools or roads. These "peasant burdens" led to an upsurge in rural protests in the decade after 1994 (see chap.9).

For Hu Jintao and Wen Jiabao, who led China from 2002 to 2012, creating a **new socialist countryside** became a priority.[16] As part of Hu's strategy to create a "harmonious socialist society," they hoped to establish a more sustained pattern of growth for agriculture, even as that sector continued to decline as a percentage of China's labor force and GDP (see Figure 8.1). To do so, they increased investment in rural China. The central government took responsibility for rural teachers' salaries, and all rural children were guaranteed a free education through the end of junior middle school. Rural health-care clinics and health insurance were expanded. The state also ended all agricultural taxes in China for the first time in more than two thousand years, which increased rural incomes by about 5 percent.

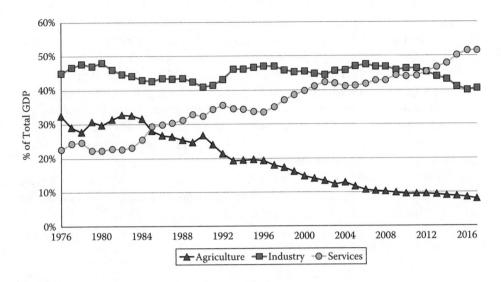

FIGURE 8.1 China's GDP by Sector of the Economy (1976–2017)

Source: National Bureau of Statistics of China

Township and Village Enterprises

In addition to decollectivization, the rapid expansion of rural **township and village enterprises** (TVEs) in 1984 was a second important source that contributed to the dramatic increase in rural incomes in the first decades of the reform era. These rural industries functioned outside the planned economy, using funds in local credit cooperatives where villagers had put much of their newly gained, disposable income. Others operated under contracts with urban SOEs, which sought to expand outside state control.

Initially, TVEs competed very effectively with SOEs. They not only had lower labor costs but were also unburdened by the welfare benefits of the so-called "iron rice bowl," which until it was discontinued in the late 1990s, guaranteed SOE employees a wide range of benefits. Thus, the TVEs took over the production of many goods, including household appliances, which had been totally dominated by SOEs. Suddenly, China's "urban bias," which had endowed city dwellers with many more perquisites than their rural cousins, became a liability in a competitive market economy.

Furthermore, TVEs had comparative advantage in cheap labor relative to Taiwan, Japan, Hong Kong, and other rapidly developing regions of East Asia, leading Prime Minister Zhao Ziyang to see them as the basis of an "export-led" strategy for China. In 1987, under his "Coastal Development Strategy," Zhao gave TVEs incentives to sell overseas, including the right to keep some of the foreign currency that they earned through exports.

By 1994, more than 50 percent of all products purchased in China by state-run foreign trade companies for export came from TVEs. Rural joint ventures with overseas investment boomed, as Hong Kong and Taiwanese firms moved into the Pearl River Delta in southern China, the Min River region in Fujian across from Taiwan, and the lower reaches of the Yangtze River. In the mid-1990s, TVEs were the fastest growing sector of the Chinese economy, expanding at rates of nearly 30 percent annually and accounting for more than two-thirds of China's increased foreign trade.[17]

While most TVEs had been owned by local governments, a wave of privatization began in 1994. TVE managers, who were part of the local power elite, took ownership of their firms through "manager buyouts" (MBO). Local governments supported this process because private firms generated more profits and taxes than collectively owned ones, while those TVEs that proved unable to make the transition from collective to private ownership were closed.[18]

By 2018, collectively owned TVEs had largely disappeared, replaced by private enterprises in the more prosperous parts of the country. Eastern China now has an industrialized countryside that covers much of the Pearl River Delta bordering Hong Kong in the south, the Yangtze River Delta west of Shanghai, as well as suburban communities all along the coast.

The Struggle over Rural Land

The state and China's peasants have long fought over land. After giving land to poorer villagers during land reform (1950–1952), the CCP reasserted control over all rural land and its products beginning in 1953, when it outlawed private grain sales. In 1956, it transferred ownership rights from individuals to the collective economy run by local officials, culminating in the creation of the people's communes in 1958 during the Great Leap Forward. Once land became "collective property," local officials gained the rights to manage it, encouraging cadres to grab land for the collective unit which they controlled. In fact, almost every new policy or campaign focusing on the countryside since the 1950s has become an opportunity for a new wave of land expropriations.

The **Great Leap Forward** (1958–1960) involved a huge land grab when the state took land for **state farms** run by the central administration and for massive irrigation projects and reservoirs. During the Cultural Revolution, local officials at the county and commune level expropriated land for rural industries and new office buildings, all under the slogan of "building socialism in a big way" (*da gan shehuizhuyi*).

Land grabs persisted into the reform era. In 1982, to prevent rural surplus labor freed up by decollectivization from flooding into the large cities, the central government called for the establishment of "rural small towns" (*xiao cheng zhen*). In one locality outside Nanjing, township leaders suddenly confiscated land owned by village collectives under their jurisdiction and let officials and friends from more distant villages move into the town.[19] In the early 1990s, urban areas across China designated large swaths of suburban land that belonged to villages for building industrial and export "development zones." Communities around China quickly set up more than eight thousand development zones and transferred control of large amounts of suburban village land to urban officials. During the building boom that followed the decision to allow private ownership of apartments in 1998, a new struggle over suburban and urban land ensued.[20]

As discussed in chapter 9, land grabs are the one of the most common causes of rural protests. These disputes arise largely because a huge gap exists between the compensation that villagers receive for giving up their use rights to the land (they cannot sell it outright) and the profits earned by local officials and development companies that create new projects on that land. One 2010 estimate by a Chinese scholar calculated that over two decades, the difference between the compensation paid to farmers and the market price of the seized land was about 2 trillion yuan (US$294 billion) for 36.3 million acres.[21]

In 2008, the government began exploring the idea of letting villagers receive compensation for transferring their "use rights" over their land to agribusinesses that would then combine the small individual plots into large farms more suitable for mechanization. This would go a long way toward addressing another major challenge facing Chinese agriculture: the small size of the average farm, 90 percent of which are less than 2.5 acres,[22] and acreage that often consists of separated parcels of land. Such small-scale, "noodle strip farming" makes mechanization and cost-efficient use of inputs nearly impossible.[23] Agribusinesses would also hire farmers at salaries far greater than what they could earn from farming as individual families. This more institutionalized process was recommended to make sure that farmers get a fair deal when they give up their land rights, which might include an urban *hukou* (residence permit) so they could legally move to a city.

If villagers were to gain legal title to the use of their land as part of this process, they could use the land as collateral for bank loans, which are difficult to get for most farmers. With this money, they could start businesses, generating new jobs and economic growth in poorer regions.

But some in the Communist Party worried that if villagers sold their land rights and took up jobs in cities or factories, they would not have land to farm if an economic crisis forced them to return to their villages, as happened during the global recession of 2008, when most of the approximately 25 million rural migrant workers in the Pearl River Delta lost their jobs in export factories and returned home to farm. Also, for leaders who remain committed to communist ideals, allowing private ownership of land is ideologically unpalatable and politically unacceptable. For these and other reasons, the party backed away from giving farmers more flexible rights to their land.

Nonetheless, the idea has reemerged in recent years. In 2014, the government began experiments in which villages in some counties divided land rights into three categories: "ownership rights," which would remain with the village, "contract rights," which would remain with the households to whom the land is contracted, and "management rights," which can be leased to others or used as collateral to secure bank loans.[24] In December 2017, it was announced that pilot programs for this policy would be expanded to more parts of the country and the reform was to be "basically completed by the end of 2021."[25]

CHINA'S CHANGING ECONOMIC STRUCTURE

In countries in early stages of development, the Gross Domestic Product (GDP) and a majority of jobs are in the primary sector: agriculture, forestry and fishing, mining, and the extraction of oil and gas. Economic modernization expands industry, services, transportation, and utilities; it can transfer labor from lower-skilled to higher-skilled jobs; and it directs investment into science, technological innovation, and education. While the shift from agriculture to industry forms the first stage of development, the growth of services in sectors such as banking, telecommunications, and health care often heralds the next step in the modernization of the economy. These changes occur through domestic investment and government policy, as well as by opening to the global economy in search of capital, technology, and markets for manufactured goods. In general, China has followed this pattern, albeit with some of its own unique characteristics.

In the early 1950s, agriculture dominated the PRC's economy. But in line with the Soviet model of development, China rapidly urbanized and industrialized. In the "largest example of technology transfer in world history,"[26] the Soviet Union helped China build 156 major infrastructure and industrial projects, sent more than 11,000 engineers and scientists to the PRC, and trained more than 28,000 Chinese technical personnel. Almost half of China's industrial investment in the first half of the decade went to support these projects. Millions of rural residents came to the urban factories, triggering what has been called the "making of the Chinese working class."[27] As a result, the Chinese economy not only recovered swiftly from the devastation of the Japanese invasion and the civil war but started down the road to industrialization.

Nevertheless, by the end of the Maoist era, China still relied heavily on agriculture, which in 1980 accounted for 30.1 percent of GDP and 68.7 percent of the work force. These numbers steadily declined once modernization and urbanization took off.

Figure 8.2 shows the volatility in the growth of China's agricultural output during the first decades of the reform era. Current policy, including land rights reform, aims

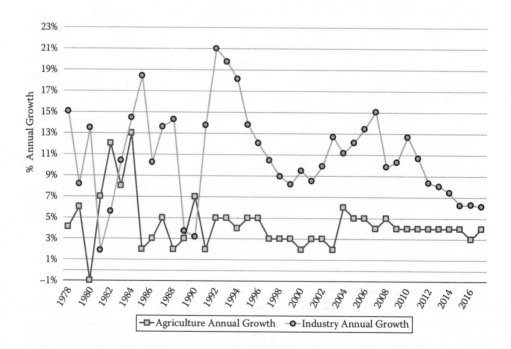

FIGURE 8.2 China's Annual Growth Rates of Agriculture and Industry (1978–2017)

Source: World Bank Development Indicators

to establish a more stable and sustained pattern of growth for agriculture to both provide a good livelihood for those who remain in farming and to ensure the country's food security.

As discussed earlier, one hallmark of the reform era in China has been the adoption of a very successful export-led growth (ELG) model. This strategy more than anything else has accelerated the transition of labor from agriculture to light industry, where most employees are rural migrants. An overemphasis on heavy industrial development—such as chemical or steel plants—and too little investment in light industry—such as textiles or electronics—during the Mao era created a scarcity of consumer goods and too few new jobs to motivate more people to move off the land. Light industry is labor-intensive, so it creates many more jobs for each unit of input than capital-intensive heavy industry; exports of light industry, produced by comparatively inexpensive labor, pay for technology imports that fuel modernization and shift the composition of GDP and the movement of labor, first from agriculture to industry, and then to services. This process is what happened in Taiwan (see chap. 19) and South Korea in their move to modernization.

Reform-minded leaders in the early post-Mao period were committed to restructuring government investment from heavy to light industry—a shift from "lathes to looms"[28]—which they did in 1979. They then laid the groundwork for export-led growth in the 1980s by investing in harbors and roads in those coastal regions that linked China to the global economy. These policies, along with decollectivization, set in motion a rapid shift in the composition of GDP and the labor force from agriculture to industry and services. In 2017, agriculture's share of GDP stood at just 7.9 percent (see Figure 8.1) and accounted for 17.5 percent of employment. The service sector now dominates both China's GDP and employment.

A Smaller, but Still Powerful, Public Sector

Since the mid-1990s, the Chinese economy has undergone a dramatic decline in the public sector. At the start of the reform era in 1978, SOEs accounted for 78 percent of industrial output, with the remainder coming almost entirely from other types of public ownership; SOEs employed about three-quarters of the urban workforce as well.

By the mid-1990s, privatization was taking hold, so by 1996, the SOEs' share of industrial output had declined to 31 percent even though they still employed close to 60 percent of urban workers. However, as the public sector remained burdened by overemployment, as well as by the "iron rice bowl," involving welfare responsibilities for tens of millions of retirees hired in the 1950s, the entire sector's profits were close to zero.

The rapidity of privatization in 1996-2000, driven in part by a hunger among local officials to pillage the public sector as it was being dismantled, led the government to try to slow it down. Particularly worrying was the pervasive tendency toward "asset stripping," whereby new owners (mostly former state-employed managers) sold the equipment and pocketed the cash, leaving the workers without jobs or any share of the enterprise's value.

Nevertheless, the government was determined to shrink the role of SOEs in the economy. In the span of less than a decade, the number of SOEs was sharply reduced and the state-employed workforce cut by about 45 million. According to one scholar of the Chinese economy, "If anything in China's transition counts as a "big bang," this was it: the rapid increase in involuntary layoffs and the dramatic downsizing of the state sector."[29] Another 20 million or so employees of collective TVEs lost their jobs to privatization, many of whom migrated to the cities in search of work, becoming the first wave of the "floating population." Altogether, in the late 1990s, 65 million Chinese workers were displaced as a result of market-oriented economic reforms. The social and political impacts of this massive, labor force dislocation in China's cities are discussed in chapters 9 and 10. At the same time, the Mao-era "iron rice bowl" that guaranteed workers lifetime employment and retirement benefits, in addition to free or highly subsidized housing, health insurance, child care, and cafeteria meals, was dismantled.

The closures, mergers, and privatization of SOEs made them more efficient and competitive by having to be more responsive to market forces. But those that remain retain enormous economic —and in some ways—political influence. As of 2016, 61.7 million workers were employed by approximately 50,000 SOEs. Eight of China's ten largest businesses are SOEs, and three of these are among the ten biggest businesses in the world.[30] Key industries, including telecommunications, steel and iron, energy and power, aviation and shipping, and defense, are totally dominated by large state firms, which are managed through the State Asset Supervision and Administration Commission (SASAC). When it was formed in 2003, SASAC oversaw 170 SOEs. As of 2017 that number had been cut to 98, again through privatization, mergers, and closures, but the combined assets of the firms under its control stood at US$25.6 trillion, more than double China's GDP.[31]

In 2015, Xi Jinping declared that state-owned enterprises were "the backbone" of the national economy and warned against "the blindness of the market," even as the country pursued deeper reform.[32] His administration has solidified state monopolies in pillar industries related to national defense, nuclear power, electricity grids, basic communication infrastructure, oil and gas pipelines, and reserves of strategic materials, such as oil, rare earths, and grain. Between 2015 and November 2016, eleven extremely large SOEs were merged to create giant national champions in key sectors whose technological strengths enhance their global competitiveness. These mergers also targeted industrial overcapacity in SOEs, which had resulted from the excessive dispersion of industrial production among state enterprises in different regions that engaged in cut-throat competition thereby reducing profits.[33]

The Rise of the Private Sector

In 1978, there were literally no private businesses in China. In 2003, twenty-five years later, there were 3.3 million private enterprises and 2.6 million small, individually owned businesses that employed only family members. By 2017, those numbers had skyrocketed to 27.3 million private enterprises and 65.8 million individual businesses. The number of employees increased nearly fourfold from 86 million in

2003 to 340 million in 2017. Private enterprises now contribute 60 percent of China's GDP and supply more than 80 percent of urban employment and over 90 percent of new jobs.[34]

The private sector's role in exports is far more important than that of SOEs, which prefer to operate in the domestic economy where they are protected from global competition. From January through April 2018, private enterprises accounted for 46.9 percent of exports, compared to just 10.9 percent for state-owned firms. Export from foreign-invested companies made up an additional 42.9 percent of the total.[35]

Privatization was first given formal ideological legitimization within the CCP in 1993, when Article 15 of the PRC's constitution was amended to replace the phrase: "The state practices economic planning on the basis of socialist public ownership" with "The state has put into practice a socialist market economy." In 1999, the private sector was enshrined in the state constitution as a key component of the national economy, overturning its previous status as a mere supplement to the state-run economy. Then in 2000, Jiang Zemin opened the door to CCP membership for private entrepreneurs as part of his theory of the **Three Represents**, which claimed that the CCP should incorporate the most advanced sectors of the Chinese economy (see chap. 5).

The Hu–Wen administration made certain that most loans related to the gigantic 2009 stimulus package went to private firms, including many small and medium enterprises. And, in a major pronouncement early in the Xi Jinping era in May 2013, Premier Li Keqiang declared that the role of the state in the economy would be further cut back and market-friendly policies would be implemented as a means to open more areas of the economy to private capital. Later that year, in his "Explanatory Notes" to a document outlining the Third Plenum of the Central Committee's major decision about deepening economic reform, Xi emphasized that the market would henceforth be the "decisive force" (*jueding xing*) in the allocation of all factors of production (capital, land, labor, natural resources), while the state would be responsible for maintaining macroeconomic stability, as in the West.[36] This formulation amplified the role of the private sector, which, since the term had first been introduced in 1992, had been called the "basis" (*jichu*) of China's socialist market economy with the state being the "decisive force."

Despite such encouraging signs, the capitalist sector of the economy remains subordinate to, and ultimately under the control of, the state. As Article 15 of the PRC constitutions says, "The State strengthens formulating economic laws, improves macro adjustment and controls and forbids according to law any units or individuals from interfering with the social economic order." Although the scope of economic planning has been greatly reduced in the reform era, China still promulgates detailed five-year plans, the most recent being the Thirteenth Five-Year Plan for 2016–2020, that set specific targets in almost all spheres of economic activity.

Xi Jinping has sought to bring the private sector under tighter party-state control in a number of ways. He has called for the strengthening of Communist Party committees in private and foreign firms. His government has made big private holding companies, run by individual tycoons, liquidate most of their assets that are unrelated to their core businesses and has launched a broad "mixed ownership" initiative that calls for SOEs to buy into large private firms in innovative sectors, such as technology.

In turn, private internet giants, such as Tencent and Alibaba, have been encouraged to buy shares in state-owned telecommunications companies.[37] As one China scholar noted in early 2017, the PRC "is far from a vibrant market economy" because of recent trends toward enhancing the role and the power of the state sector.[38]

CORRUPTION AND RENT-SEEKING

There was quite a bit of corruption in the Mao era, but because it was difficult for individuals to gain access to large sums of money, move funds abroad, or use ill-gotten gains in any conspicuous manner, it was mostly petty graft. But in the reform era, China's mix of central planning and a market-economy era has proven to be fertile soil for pervasive large-scale corruption in both the public and private sectors.

Political economists differentiate between "market facilitating" and "regime threatening" corruption, and in the 1980s and 1990s, much of the corruption was the former, through which firms circumvented regulations that impeded market flows. But in the new millennium, corruption changed. During the Hu–Wen era (2002–2012), the scale was mind-boggling. In 2007, the direct cost of corruption was estimated to be US$86 billion a year.[39] In 2011, the People's Bank of China estimated that since the mid-1990s at least 44,000 officials smuggled around US$125 billion out of China.[40]

When Xi Jinping took over as leader of the CCP in 2012, his most urgent task was to deal with this specific problem. He declared that "We must solidify our resolve, insure that all cases of corruption are investigated and prosecuted, and that all instances of graft are rectified, continue to remove the breeding ground for corruption, and further win public trust by making real progress in the fight against corruption."[41] He vowed to catch "'tigers' and 'flies'—senior officials as well as junior ones guilty of corruption."[42]

Using the CCP's Central Commission for Discipline Inspection (CCDI) and its branches at lower levels, Xi first took aim at corrupt party officials. These commissions conduct investigations of suspected wrongdoings, and, if such is proven, the guilty official may be demoted or expelled altogether from the party. If it appears a crime was committed, the case is turned over to the state judicial authorities. In that case, punishment can include long prison terms and even execution.

While some argue that an official's political ties to Xi greatly affects whether he or she is investigated for corruption, or that Xi is using the antigraft campaign to purge his political rivals, the extent of the crackdown since he came to power has been nonetheless remarkable. Between November 2012 and March 2018, more than 2.7 million party officials were investigated for corruption, over 1.5 million were punished, and 58,000 criminally tried.[43] The biggest "tiger" to get caught during this period was Zhou Yongkang, a one-time member of the Politburo Standing Committee who oversaw the country's domestic security services. In June 2015, Zhou was sentenced to life in prison after being convicted of a series of corruption charges, including bribery, abuse of power and leaking state secrets. He and close family members were said to have accepted bribes totaling around US$20 million.[44]

In his keynote address to the CCP's 19th Party Congress in October 2017, Xi declared that "Disciplinary inspections have cut like a blade through corruption and misconduct; they have covered every Party committee in all departments at the central and provincial levels. No place has been out of bounds, no ground left unturned, and no tolerance shown in the fight against corruption." "The people," he noted, "resent corruption most; and corruption is the greatest threat our Party faces. We must have the resolve and tenacity to persevere in the never-ending fight against corruption."[45]

The following March, China's parliament, the National People's Congress, established a National Supervision Commission with branches at all levels of government with broad powers to investigate corruption outside of the party, including state-owned enterprises and public institutions such as hospitals, universities, and sports organizations.[46]

Nevertheless, there is considerable skepticism in some quarters about the effectiveness of the efforts to root out corruption, which is so deeply embedded in the fabric of China's communist party-state, given the absence of a truly independent judiciary and free press.

A related issue is that the families of many of China's leaders are enriching themselves through their personal connections. In June 2012, Bloomberg News reported that Xi Jinping's extended family had investments worth about US$600 million in rare earth, real estate, and hi-tech companies. Neither Xi nor his wife or daughter held any of these assets, which were mostly controlled by his sisters and their families. In October of that year, the *New York Times* published an article that revealed that the family of then-Premier Wen Jiabao, including his mother and wife, controlled assets worth at least US$2.7 billion in financial services, construction, real estate, technology, and diamonds. In neither case was there any indication of illegal activity, but both families benefited greatly from connections with powerful people, lucrative state contracts, and favorable loans from government banks.

Such activities reflect what social scientists call "**rent-seeking**," which means the use of political power to gain ("seek") an economic advantage ("rent") that would not occur in an open market situation. Rent-seeking may be legal or illegal, so it is not quite the same as official corruption, which is, by definition, illegal, and such activity can be very costly to the economy by distorting the market through political manipulation.

Upgrading China's Economy

Many Westerners have long argued that China can only imitate, not innovate. In fact, much of China's technological upgrading to-date has relied on copying or improving Western technology acquired through a number of mechanisms, including purchases, technology transfer by returning Chinese students, purchasing equity in advanced overseas firms, enforced technology agreements with potential joint-venture partners, or even violations of intellectual property rights.

Particularly since 2006, the PRC has tried to remedy this lack of innovation. That year, the State Science and Technology Commission (SSTC) introduced the Medium- and Long-Term Plan on the Development of Science & Technology, a fifteen-year program whose key concept, "indigenous innovation," focused on advanced technologies. In October 2010, China identified seven "strategic emerging industries" that it must master to become an advanced economy. Developing leading-edge technologies would occur through investment in R&D, accumulation of cutting-edge intellectual property, setting distinct technical standards, and swapping access to the Chinese market in exchange for technologies belonging to the foreign companies. In 2013, China upped the ante by organizing a nationwide research program, with 150 research teams; the outcome was "**Made in China 2025**."

In 2014, Xi Jinping said that to upgrade its economy the PRC had to go through three transformations: "From China's speed to China's quality; from China's products to China's brands; and from 'made in China' to 'created by China.'"[47] In formally introducing the plan in March 2015, Premier Li Keqiang explained: "We will implement the Made in China 2025 strategy, seek innovation-driven development, apply smart technologies, strengthen foundations, pursue green development, and redouble our efforts to upgrade China from a manufacturer of quantity to one of quality."[48]

"Made in China 2025" was designed as a comprehensive plan to make the PRC into a global hi-tech powerhouse in areas such as advanced information technology, aerospace and aviation, new energy vehicles, railway transportation, shipping, and pharmaceuticals and medical equipment. The plan also aimed to upgrade the quality of China's industrial products to world-class standards in order to avoid the "**middle-income trap**."[49] This "trap" has been faced by most countries whose economies have in recent decades grown rapidly, overcome widespread poverty, and reached per capita GDP between US$8,500 to US$18,500, only to experience a sharp drop in growth rates, causing them to fail to reach the level of a high-income economy. The sources of this crisis include rising wages as the surplus supply of labor dwindles, falling population growth that shrinks the labor force, slower gains in productivity growth, reliance on the imitation of foreign technology, and investment bubbles (largely in property). Overcoming the middle-income trap necessitates investment in human capital, moving up the product cycle from low value-added industries to higher value-added industries, and greater competitiveness to drive innovation.

Today, China faces this dilemma. Due to the reform era, China achieved the status of an upper-middle income economy in 2011. In a talk in Beijing marking that transition, Robert B. Zoellick, president of the World Bank, commented that "In the next fifteen to twenty years, China is well-positioned to join the ranks of the world's high-income countries. That is a transition that only a handful of countries have made—and, sadly, many have failed."[50] In fact, a Bank study in 2012 found that only 13 of the 101 middle-income countries in 1960 had achieved high-income levels by 2008.[51]

For most of the reform era China has been a big part of the supply chain for hi-tech products where components produced in one country are modified or assembled somewhere else. China now aims to enhance its role in this supply chain, to the point where even the high-tech components of the product are "made in China," rather than China only being the final assembly point. And it plans to do so by creating major, new investment funds that will subsidize domestic firms to go out and purchase the foreign companies that are creating these high-tech components, thereby developing domestic capabilities for most, if not all, stages of the production process for world-class products. This policy of "indigenous innovation" and "self-sufficiency," largely supported and guided by the state, also aims to push Chinese companies to acquire core technologies through investment abroad.[52]

THE INTERNATIONALIZATION OF THE ECONOMY

The depth of China's integration into the global economy since 1978 is breathtaking. For centuries, China tried to limit foreign influences. Before the Opium War, foreign traders had to reside in Canton (Guangzhou) or other coastal towns and could deal only with trade officials and intermediaries designated by the imperial government. From 1949 and well into the 1980s, foreign merchants were permitted to buy a limited range of Chinese products at the twice-annual Canton Fair and only from twelve state-run foreign trade companies. But since 1978, China has opened its door to the world, as reflected in Table 8.1 at the end of this chapter.

As China's involvement with the international system has deepened, so, too, has the world's impact on China, as states who choose to join the global economy must negotiate the terms of their engagement with international organizations and countries that dominate global economic institutions.

China as a "Trading State"

In recent decades, China has become a quintessential **trading state**,[53] whose international commerce has dramatically increased its national power. Exports increased by leaps and bounds. Foreign trade increased from US$20 billion in 1978 to over US$4.3 trillion by 2016 (see Figure 8.3 and Table 8.1). After declines in 2015 and 2016, it rebounded in 2017. Particularly after joining the WTO in 2001, thereby increasing its access to other countries' domestic markets, China's trade between 2001 and 2014 grew at an annual rate of about 19.5 percent, far more than double the growth rate for world trade; in 2017, the growth rate was 14.2 percent. In 2012, China's imports and exports (US$3.87 trillion)) eclipsed the United States (US$3.82 trillion), making it the world's largest trading economy and the leading trading partner of 120 countries.

Trade is now one of the most important engines of China's economic growth. As a share of GDP, foreign trade jumped from 14 percent in 1978 to a peak of 60 percent in 2007 (see Figure 8.4). The 2007–2008 global financial crisis drove down Chinese exports to 45 percent of GDP and as of 2016, trade as a percent of GDP had further declined to under 35 percent. Nevertheless, the boom years of 2000–2008 filled the national coffers and increased China's foreign exchange holdings, leaving it with a massive amount of funds to invest overseas.Following the pattern set by Japan, Taiwan, and South Korea, the composition of China's exports has shifted from light industrial goods, such as clothing, footwear, and consumer electronics, to more capital-intensive ones, such as electrical machinery, transport equipment, and information and communications technology (ICT).

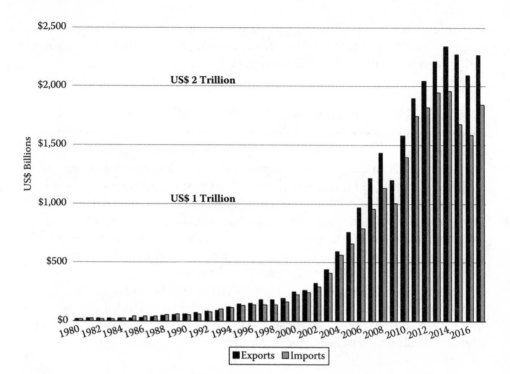

FIGURE 8.3 China's Foreign Trade (1980–2017)

Source: National Bureau of Statistics of China, Statista

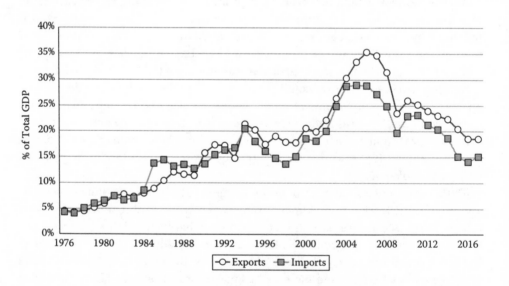

FIGURE 8.4 China's Imports and Exports as a Percent of GDP (1976–2017)

Source: National Bureau of Statistics of China

Foreign Direct Investment (FDI)

In its first efforts to attract foreign investment, the PRC targeted "Diaspora Capitalism"—overseas Chinese in Hong Kong, Macau, Taiwan, and Southeast Asia— who were eager to invest in the newly opened China. They liked China's inexpensive labor, cheap land, low taxes, and huge domestic market. They also wanted to establish projects in their families' hometowns, which would enhance their social status. Thus, most firms entering China in the 1980s were ethnic Chinese, family-run firms, investing under US$500,000 in joint ventures with local governments.

From near zero in the early 1980s, inward FDI jumped dramatically after Deng Xiaoping's "Southern Tour" in 1992, and then in anticipation of China's entry to the WTO, reaching US$46.9 billion in 2001, the year the PRC joined. It doubled to US$92.4 billion by 2007 (increasing by more than 23 percent in that year alone) but then declined to US$90 billion in 2008 due to the global financial crisis, only to quickly bounce back to record levels, reaching US$135 billion in 2017 (see Table 8.1). In 2012, China surpassed the United States as the world's top FDI destination.

Foreign investment enterprises (FIEs) have had a big impact on China's economy.[54] FIEs in the PRC, and the "ripple effect" they have through their supply chains, represented 33 percent of GDP and 27 percent of employment in China in 2013.[55] They have helped develop China's leading industries, "including industries with substantial spillovers into the local economy, export-oriented industries and industries that provide needed inputs for the rest of Chinese economy. . . . Without foreign invested enterprises, China would not have much of a computer industry, and would not have developed as extensive modern activities in chemicals, clothing, accounting, consulting and numerous other industries."[56] A case study of Chongqing shows that although this huge inland city opened up to the world well after the coastal areas, "foreign investment has helped turn what was once a relatively backward place into a modern metropolis linked to the global economy."[57]

For the first twenty years of opening up, China made all foreign investors form joint ventures with local firms—usually run by local governments—that could control the foreign investor's behavior. Nor could foreigners hold majority share in these ventures. But, after 1999, as China prepared to join the World Trade Organization (WTO), restraints eased and many new entrants to the Chinese market had no domestic partner. Furthermore, after the PRC joined the WTO in 2001, external and internal barriers to foreign investment continued to decline, as China met many of its obligations under the accession agreement.

But while foreign firms compete today on a much more level playing field than they did before China joined the WTO, many sectors of the economy that China promised to open more widely, particularly information technology (IT), telecommunications, government contracting and financial services, remain tightly regulated. According to the American Chamber of Commerce in China's annual report in 2017,[58] 59 percent of firms in the IT sector feel that foreign companies are treated unfairly, relative to domestic firms—equal treatment for foreign firms is a key obligation for countries in the WTO—with the most unfair aspect (54 percent) being "restrictions or prohibitions on market participation." The primary concern of 57 percent of firms was "inconsistent regulatory interpretations and unclear laws," with 31 percent worried about a lack of protection of intellectual property rights, which explains why many firms will not bring in their core technologies to China. In response, Chinese firms try to force their prospective joint-venture partners to transfer technology as a precondition for market access, something that 15 percent of American firms highlighted as a barrier to innovation within China. Yet, 64 percent of U.S. firms in China reported revenue growth, and 46 percent were confident that the Chinese government would further open the economy to foreigners over the next three years, while only 17 percent thought that further market opening was not going to happen. This optimism is reflected in the fact that 90 percent of the Fortune 500 list of the largest American firms maintain a presence in China.

Joining the WTO

No single act better reflects China's global economic integration than joining the World Trade Organization (WTO) in November 2001. After World War II, leaders in the West argued that the world would get richer if each country produced more of the goods in which it had "comparative advantage"—that is, what it made best and most efficiently—and then traded these goods to other states, buying in turn what other countries made best. But free trade was necessary if this idea were to work, so in 1948, the United States and its allies created the General Agreement on Tariffs and Trade (GATT), whose goal was to stop countries from using tariffs and quotas on imports to protect their local markets.

But many countries still engage in protectionism through rules or regulations that favor local companies over foreign ones in their domestic market. These restrictions are particularly troublesome for service sector industries, such as banking, insurance, and financial markets, where the West has comparative advantage. In 1995, GATT was replaced by a more powerful and intrusive WTO, which targets internal regulations that block foreign competitors *within* countries, not just "at the border."

The PRC applied to join the GATT in 1986, but numerous regulations in China that constrained foreign economic activity and the subsequent crackdown in Tiananmen Square in 1989 led to long delays. Even though Jiang Zemin cut China's tariffs dramatically throughout the 1990s, the United States, the European Union, Japan, and Canada still demanded enormous concessions from China before they would let it join the WTO. But yielding to the West on these issues weakened China's sovereignty in the eyes of strongly nationalistic intellectuals,[59] making such compromises politically risky for any leader. Moreover, while the WTO's prohibition on trade discrimination against firms from any other member country (under the concept of "most favored nation status"), its insistence that all economic regulations be made public (under the concept of "transparency"), and the rule that foreign firms must be treated just as any local firm (under the concept of "national treatment") challenged the PRC government's sovereign control over the economy. Thus, in spring 1999, when the concessions that Premier Zhu Rongji made to enter the WTO became public, he was pilloried on Chinese blogs and attacked by domestic opponents.[60] Nonetheless, by fall 1999, after making greater compromises to enter the WTO than any other country in history,[61] China's top leaders agreed to the terms, and China officially became a member of the WTO two years later,

WTO entry has had a very positive impact on China's political economy.[62] By joining the WTO, China swapped easier access to its own market for similar access by Chinese firms to the rest of the world's domestic markets. And China's booming exports after 2001 are testament to the opportunities created by WTO entry for China's competitive products. (Figure 8.3) Lower barriers to trade has also decreased smuggling, making corruption a minor issue in China's foreign trade sector as compared to other parts of the economy.

In the wake of President Donald Trump's attack on globalization as unfair to America's economy, Xi Jinping has positioned China as the stalwart of a globalized world economy. For example, in speeches at the annual gathering of some of the world's most influential people at Davos, Switzerland, in January 2017, and at other forums, Xi has pledged greater foreign access to the Chinese economy.[63]

Yet, while Xi talks the talk of furthering China's commitment to globalization, the PRC has pulled back from many commitments made under its WTO accession agreement. Its adherence to a more statist, less market-oriented economy maintains the government's influence over its links to the global economy through formal regulations, informal practice, and a variety of nontariff barriers. For example, making technology transfer a condition for market access by foreign firms, continually subsidizing Chinese export firms, failure to prosecute Chinese firms for violating intellectual property rights, and keeping certain sectors of the economy, such as telecommunications, closed to FDI, all contravene WTO rules.[64] While China claims that it considered WTO's rules when it drafted "Made in China, 2025," some people assert that parts of that plan were designed to protect Chinese firms from foreign competition as the country seeks to become a high-tech superpower.[65]

Overall, therefore, WTO has not helped foreign firms doing business in the PRC in ways that they and their governments had hoped. As a member, China has been compelled in some significant cases to open its markets in response to formal complaints. But in some of those cases, China dragged its feet long enough to create "national champions" in those sectors that could challenge foreign entrants to the Chinese economy, thereby negating the impact of its response.[66]

China's "Going Out" Strategy

Beginning in the early 1990s, China began a transition from what it called its "externally oriented economy" (*waixiangxing jingji*) that prioritized export-led growth to a new strategy known as **"going out"** (*zou qu chu*), where the state pushes China's SOEs to invest overseas.

The strategy was first articulated by Jiang Zemin at the 14th National Party Congress in October 1992 when he called for more firms to enter the international market, a diversification of trading partners, new global marketing strategies, and using overseas resources for China's exports.[67] Soon after, the State Economic and Trade Commission (SETC) selected 120 "national champions" to lead China's engagement with the world. In 1996, after returning from Africa, where he saw that Chinese technology could compete effectively in the developing world, Jiang called for research on how to mobilize SOEs to "go out." In December 1997, following the East Asian Financial Crisis,

Jiang declared the "going out" strategy a key component of national development, and in 2000, as China edged toward joining the WTO, he reflected that while the first twenty years of China's opening had emphasized inbound investment flows, the country now had the capabilities to compete globally.

The idea of "going out" was written into the CCP constitution in 2002 and speeches and reports exhorted SOEs to go abroad. In 2004, the Ministry of Commerce posted a list of countries and the resources available in those countries, where investments by SOEs would receive state bank subsidies.[68]

According to a survey in 2006 for the World Bank, the "most important" or "very important" reasons for firms to go overseas were: "market seeking" (85 percent), the search for strategic assets (51 percent), global competitive strategies (50 percent), support from the domestic government (43 percent), favorable policies of foreign governments (41 percent), making use of domestic production capacity (41 percent), resource seeking (39 percent), efficiency seeking (39 percent), tariff-jumping (36 percent), operational risk reduction (26 percent), capital risk reduction (20 percent), and pressure from domestic competitors who already were investing abroad (12 percent).[69]

China's outward nonfinancial investment in overseas businesses, manufacturing, mining, and other areas between 1990 and 2000 averaged US$2.2 billion per year, while the pre-2008 crisis annual average (2005–2007) was US$18.8 billion. Outward FDI peaked in 2016 at US$196 billion, before falling back to US$124 billion in 2017 (see Figure 8.5).[70] The total value of China's "outbound FDI" (OFDI) rose at a matching rate. In 1995 it was little more than US$17.7 billion; by 2005 it had hit US$651 billion, and by 2017, China's investments abroad had soared to almost US$1.5 trillion.[71] In 2017, the PRC had investments in 174 countries and territories.[72] Between 2005 and

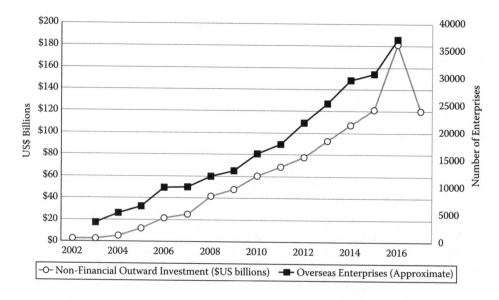

FIGURE 8.5 China's "Going Out" Strategy (2002–2017)

Source: National Bureau of Statistics of China, Statistical Bulletin of China's Outward Foreign Direct Investment (2003-2016)

2016, the top ten destinations for Chinese OFDI were the United States, Australia, Switzerland, Canada, Britain, Brazil, Russia, German, Italy, and France.[73]

Despite this growth, China remains far behind the United States in term of OFDI, which in 2017 shipped out US$342 billion, 2.75 times China's OFDI. Not surprisingly, as China is a new kid on the block in terms of OFDI, its total stock of foreign investments was about 20 percent of that of the U.S. (US$7.8 trillion), though the gap is narrowing. SOEs accounted for about 80 percent of China's OFDI in 2006, and still comprised more than a half in 2016, although the percent of private firms among all Chinese firms going out averaged 10 percent between 2003 and 2015 but jumped to 26.2 percent in 2016.

Many international observers see investment abroad by Chinese corporations as positive, not only for China but also for the world. Increased Chinese investment boosts the global economy and lets China recycle its massive foreign exchange holdings (and its massive domestic savings). Stiff competition could force Chinese firms to conform to global standards (rather than change those standards, as others worry). This should be particularly beneficial to SOEs. An article in the *Wall Street Journal* in 2008 remarked on the "quiet revolution under way in the Chinese state sector, which has produced a new generation of confident companies with global ambitions."[74]

But direct investment by SOEs creates suspicion in some countries because Chinese firms have access to Chinese government subsidies and other advantages that give them an unfair edge; sometimes, they are seen as a threat to the national security in the host country because the CEOs of major SOEs are on the CCP's Central Committee. Furthermore, Chinese state firms do not always conform to global norms of corporate responsibility, getting into trouble with overseas trade unions because of their lack of compliance with labor standards. They also pursue opportunities in countries where Western firms have chosen not to compete for political reasons, such as Sudan or Iran, creating problems for China with the United States and the European Union, which seek sanctions against these "rogue" states.

The main focus of China's "going out" strategy has been on securing the natural resources needed to fuel its rapid economic development.[75] Between 2005 and 2018, more than one-third of all China's overseas investment has been in the energy sector.[76] During the same period, the next largest sectors were transportation infrastructure, such as railroads, highways, airports, and ports (18.7 percent), real estate (9.4 percent), and metals, particularly aluminum, copper, and steel (9.0 percent).[77]

As of 2017, China surpassed the United States as the world's largest oil importer, as its thirst for oil has been largely driven by the energy demands of both domestic industry and the export economy.[78] But the demand for petroleum is increasingly being propelled by the surging growth in the number of vehicles on the road, which hit 330 million—nearly three quarters of which were passenger vehicles—in late 2018.[79]

The Belt and Road Initiative

No foreign investment strategy in the world today can match China's **Belt and Road Initiative (BRI)** (*yi dai yi lu*) in its grandiosity. [80] But this is the stuff of Xi

Jinping's China. Building on Deng Xiaoping's policy of "opening to the outside world," Jiang Zemin's "going out" strategy, and Hu Jintao's "neighborhood initiative," Xi has proposed a global strategy through which to fulfill his "China Dream," resolve the PRC's need for adjusting its economic structure, keep incomes rising, internationalize China's high-tech standards, and position China once again at the center of global development. Mobilizing all elements of the state, Party and even parts of China's civil society, such as think tanks and private businesses, Xi has intertwined China's and the world's economic development under a highly politicized, campaign-style economic movement reminiscent of the Mao era. Officials, ministries, SOEs, consulates, and embassies have all been given quotas to fulfill, while developing countries, and even some middle-income countries, have been offered funding for projects that are difficult to resist.

Xi introduced what he called the Silk Road Economic Belt concept during a visit to Kazakhstan in September 2013, and one month later, in Indonesia, he talked about constructing a "21st Century Maritime Silk Road" to promote maritime cooperation between China and the Association of Southeast Asian Nations (ASEAN). Together these two plans make up the Belt and Road Initiative.

At the Indonesian parliament, Xi also proposed establishing the **Asian Infrastructure Investment Bank** (AIIB) to finance infrastructure construction and promote regional interconnectivity and economic integration, an important component of the BRI strategy and China's own challenge to both the World Bank and the Asian Development Bank, which are respectively more attuned to U.S. and Japanese policies. The AIIB was established in January 2016 and as of mid-2018 had eighty-seven member countries.

In December 2013, at China's annual Central Economic Work Conference, Xi emphasized how the BRI could promote connectedness in the region and beyond through infrastructure. And at the subsequent meeting of the National People's Congress in March 2014, Premier Li Keqiang called for a speedup in the program and emphasized two major projects, the Bangladesh-China-India-Myanmar Economic Corridor and the China-Pakistan Economic Corridor.

In November 2014, Xi announced that China would contribute US$40 billion to a new Silk Road Fund, which would provide investment and financing for infrastructure, resources, industrial cooperation, financial cooperation, and other projects in countries along the Belt and Road. In December, China and Thailand approved a memorandum of understanding (MOU) on railway cooperation. Finally, on March 28, 2015, the National Development and Reform Commission (NDRC), Ministry of Foreign Affairs, and Ministry of Commerce jointly released an action plan on the principles, framework, and cooperation priorities and mechanisms of the BRI.

Planned Belt and Road routes would run through Asia, Europe, and Africa, "connecting the vibrant East Asia economic circle at one end and developed European economic circle at the other."[81] The Silk Road Economic Belt focuses on linking China with Europe through land routes in Central Asia and Russia. The second leg, the 21st-Century Maritime Silk Road is even more ambitious and envisions connecting the PRC with countries and continents that lie along the South China Sea, the South Pacific, the Mediterranean, and even connecting China to Europe via the Arctic Ocean.[82]

There are three drivers of this strategy.[83] First, China hopes to export its excess industrial capacity, particularly its steel. Second, China hopes to create a host of new global standards based on China's own standards in IT (5G technology), energy, and particularly high-speed railroads, which would insure that the world turns to China for this potentially important component of economic development. In fact, China's engineers will be involved in railway projects in Thailand, Indonesia, and Laos.

Finally, BRI is geopolitical. Exchanges with Central Asia will pass through Xinjiang, potentially bringing greater economic development to China's most unstable region (see chap. 17). BRI greatly strengthens ties with Pakistan, where investments in the China-Pakistan Economic Corridor total more than US$65 billion. This part of the initiative, along with BRI activities in Sri Lanka, Bangladesh, and Nepal, are generating apprehension in India, who see the BRI as an aggressive strategy which threatens to surround India through a purportedly economic program.[84]

The harbors in which China has recently invested as part of the BRI show strategic, not just economic, logic. China's ninety-nine-year lease and total control over the Sri Lankan harbor of Hambantota, at the southern tip of the island nation, could greatly enhance China's military power if it can gain the rights to dock naval vessels at this potentially key port of call in the Indian Ocean.[85] China's huge investment in the massive Gwadar deep-water port on the Arabian Sea coast of Pakistan has raised similar concerns, especially in India.[86]

Another benefit of the BRI to China is that 89 percent of all contractors in BRI projects are Chinese companies, 7.6 percent are local companies (headquartered in the country where the project takes shape), and only 3.4 percent are foreign companies.[87] And China is particularly well positioned to benefit from infrastructure projects, which are the core of BRI, because, as of 2017, seven of the largest ten construction companies in the world, by revenue, were Chinese.[88]

Many analysts worry about the economics of BRI. For example, by the end of 2014, two of China's state-owned banks that are providing credit to BRI countries already had outstanding loans to foreign borrowers of nearly US$700 billion, which on a scale is similar to the total outstanding lending of the World Bank and six regional development institutions combined. Then, as a study from the Center for Global Development noted, twenty-three of the sixty-eight countries eligible for lending under BRI are vulnerable to debt distress. Christine Lagarde, managing director of the IMF, said in Beijing that "good infrastructure can help achieve more inclusive growth, attract more foreign direct investment, and create more jobs." But she added that it was essential that the BRI "only travels where it is needed" because investing in inappropriate projects and weak fiscal management in recipient countries might "lead to a problematic increase in debt."[89] Brahma Chellaney, a vocal Indian critic of China, called the Maritime Silk Road Initiative "China's Creditor Imperialism" that "can shackle" participating countries with debt. "Just as European imperial powers employed gunboat diplomacy," he wrote, "China is using sovereign debt to bend other states to its will."[90]

Indeed, there is some blowback by recipients of China's BRI largess. Government officials in Indonesia see Chinese investors as arrogant, particularly in contrast to the Japanese, China's major competitor.[91] In July 2018, the newly elected prime minister of Malaysia, Mohamad Mahathir, suspended three BRI project worth US$22 billion that been approved by his predecessor, who is being investigated for signing off on overpriced initiatives in return for bribes.[92] The government of Myanmar has downsized plans for a US$10 billion BRI-related port they had previously approved, explaining that it should be "as lean as possible" and not lead to a situation where the country cannot repay the loans from China that are funding the project.[93] Even in Pakistan, the primary beneficiary of the BRI project, Chinese investment has stirred some resentment.[94] In December 2018, the new Pakistani government asked Beijing to end a US$2 billion coal power project.[95]

CHINA'S ECONOMIC CHALLENGES

China's economic success over the last four decades has been unprecedented. The standard of living for the vast majority of its population has improved enormously. At the start of the reform era in the late 1970s, China had little impact on the global economy. Today, it is an economic powerhouse whose trade and investment policies affect literally every corner of the world. As discussed in chapter 1, there are many who see China as a model for other developing countries.

This chapter has noted some of the major economic challenges that the PRC faces, including the imperative to adjust its economic structure if it is to avoid the middle-income trap and achieve the status of a high-income, truly prosperous society. Chapter 10 addresses the challenges of rapid urbanization in the PRC and the government's plan to move 250 million more people into cities by 2025. Chapter 12 discusses China's severe environmental crisis, which, according to one estimate, cost the country 6.5 percent of its GDP each year between 2000 and 2010 due largely to the impact on health and lost productivity when extreme pollution forced factories to shut down.[96] And chapter 14 examines the implications for China's work force of its aging society, a problem accelerated by the decades-long one-child policy.

In his speech to the 19th Party Congress in October 2018, Xi Jinping promised that his government would play "its function of adjusting redistribution, move faster to ensure equitable access to basic public services, and narrow the gaps in incomes." A property bubble has priced new apartments out of the reach of young members of China's new middle class, which could undermine support for the CCP among this key constituency.

China's economy has entered an era known as the "new normal," where growth rates will remain below 7 percent, with some predictions that growth by 2020 will drop to 4 percent.[97] While this is still an enviable rate of increase, too much money goes to the public sector, which returns less than 2 percent on capital, while the vibrant private- and foreign-owned sector remain starved for cash.[98] Creating 13.5 million new jobs a year, which was the inflow of new entrants into the economy in 2017, will remain problematic, and productivity will likely slack off.[99] The Xi administration needs to tackle China's domestic debt problem, which many analysts see as a looming crisis that could spell disaster for the Chinese economy and reverberate beyond its borders.[100] The total amount of the debt is estimated to be in the range of 260–300 percent of GDP or more.

BOX 8.1 THE CHALLENGE OF INEQUALITY IN CHINA

The Maoist model of development promoted egalitarianism as one of its major goals. Although significant gaps in income, services, and welfare persisted throughout the Maoist period (1949–1976), particularly between the urban and rural areas, there were significant achievements in promoting equality within China through land reform, the collectivization of agriculture, the nationalization of industry and commerce, the expansion of literacy and education, public health campaigns, and other policies that were part of the PRC's socialist agenda. Per capita incomes went up during these years, but only modestly, so that by the time Mao died in 1976, it could be said that the Chinese people were both relatively poor and relatively equal.

China's economic boom during the post-Mao reform era has led to a spectacular growth in national wealth, as well as improvement in the standards of living for the large majority of the population. But it has also led to the appearance of multiple and deep inequalities in the country. Several of the chapters in this book touch on this problem of inequality in the contemporary People's Republic.

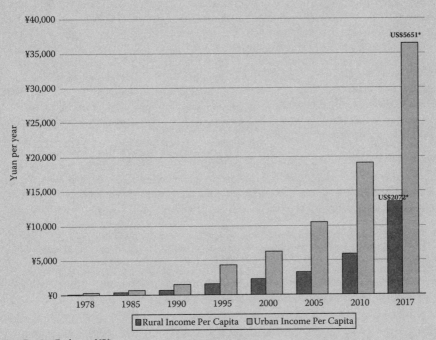

* Foreign Exchange US$

FIGURE 8.6 China's Rural-Urban Income Gap (1978–2017)

Source: National Bureau of Statistics of China

Figure 8.6 shows that when the reform era began in the late 1970s, the gap between urban and rural incomes was very small, but started diverging about a decade later, then widened rapidly over the next twenty years. There are also sharp inequalities within both rural and urban areas, with the latter becoming particularly noticeable in the different living standards of those who have done well in China's economic boom, including the

(Continued)

BOX 8.1 (*Continued*)

rising middle class, and the millions who make up China's new urban underclass, including rural migrants and the unemployed (see chap. 9).

One way to measure inequality in a country is called the **Gini Index**. It calculates the distribution of family income within a population and comes up with a composite number between 0 (perfect equality) and 1 (perfect inequality) for the country as a whole. In other words, the closer the Gini Index is to 0, the more evenly income is distributed; the closer it is to 1 the more income goes to the rich.

China's National Bureau of Statistics reported that the Gini Index in 2015 was .46. Other studies put it the range of .53–.61. To put this into perspective, the Gini Index of the United States is .45. Among the economies with the most equal income distribution are Sweden (.24) and Germany (.27), while the most unequal include South Africa (.62) and Hong Kong (.54).[*]

To measure inequality *within* China, you might consider, for example, the range in Gross Domestic Product per capita among the PRC's administrative regions. While per capita income for the country as a whole in 2017 was about $4100, regionally it varied from $9300 in Shanghai at the high end to $2400 in Tibet.[†] A study published by a team of Chinese economists in 2016 concluded that China's administrative regions have diverged into what they call "two clubs": a relatively small high-income club of areas that are mostly along the eastern coast, and a large low-income club consisting of inland regions. On average, the latter club has incomes that are only 60 percent of the former.[‡]

Research shows that most people in China are not very concerned about inequality as long as their own economic lives are improving.[§] But if there were to be a serious economic downturn that dashed expectations among a large segment of the population, that complacency could change and the country's extreme economic gaps could become a socially explosive issue.

Xi Jinping seems aware of this: in his address to the 19th Party Congress in October, 2017, he said that the principal challenge facing the PRC was its "unbalanced development" and that the party had to "continue our commitment to our people-centered philosophy of development, and work to promote well-rounded human development and common prosperity for everyone."

[*] National Bureau of Statistics Communique, Jan. 19, 2016; and CIA World Factbook
[†] "Shanghai, Beijing and Zhejiang Province Top China's New Per Capita Income List," China Banking News, Feb. 26, 2018.
[‡] Sarah Hsu, "High Income Inequality Still Festering In China," Financial Times, Nov. 16, 2018.
[§] Martin King Whyte, "China Needs Justice, Not Equality," *Foreign Affairs*, May 5, 2013.

A sizeable chunk of that debt, which is the part most vulnerable to default, is held by provincial and city governments and was incurred in the aftermath of the 2008 global recession. At that time, the state encouraged local governments to introduce many new projects to keep the economy booming and insisted that half the cost of these endeavors be covered by local governments, resulting in a precipitous increase in their debt. Since more construction enlarges the local GDP, which in turn advances the local leader's career and political interests, these officials also turned to nontraditional ways to borrow additional money to pay for more projects, including from unregulated "shadow banks" that operate outside the regular banking system and charge usurious interest rates.[101]

In recent years, the central government has initiated a series of policies to restrict local governments from borrowing more money and to help them reduce their debt.

But so far those policies have had little impact, and, as of early 2018, local government debt was growing again.[102]

China's leadership also still needs to rebalance an economy that is excessively dependent on exports. The international financial meltdown of 2007–2008 caused Chinese exports to plummet, a warning that global markets are not a reliable basis for sustained economic growth for such a large country. Moreover, as wages in China continue to rise, local and foreign-owned private firms engaged in exports will relocate production to Vietnam, Bangladesh, Cambodia, Indonesia, and other lower-cost countries. This rebalancing from a labor-intensive export-dependent economy to one based on capital-intensive industries, domestic consumption, and innovation is crucial if the PRC is to move up the ladder of the international division of labor and emerge as a strong global competitor among the world's advanced economies.[103]

China needs to shift from investment—which comes mostly from the government in things such as building infrastructure—and trade as the primary sources of economic growth to one driven more by domestic consumption. This shift will not only require Chinese firms to provide more and better quality goods for the consumer market but also that Chinese citizens spend more and save less (the opposite of America's problem). China's personal savings rate (the percentage of a person's disposable income devoted to savings rather than consumption) is among the world's highest at nearly 50 percent (in the U.S. it is under 20 percent). Confucian culture is traditionally frugal, and the experience of great economic uncertainty, especially during the Mao years, makes most PRC citizens prone to save money when they have it. Moreover, China's weak health insurance and social security systems force most Chinese to put away money to pay for unforeseen medical expenses, the rising costs of their child's education, and provide for their retirement.

In 2016, consumption's share of China's GDP (39.5 percent) moved past that of trade (37.0 percent), although this was largely because of the drop in trade volume in the wake of the Global Financial Crisis of 2008 (see Figures 8.3 and 8.4) rather than due to a major increase in the role of consumption. The rebalancing of the economy does not really require that China significantly shrink its export sector, which in the period from 2008 to 2017 accounted for 25 percent of GDP. After all, exports contribute significantly to the GDP of quite a few highly-developed countries, such as Switzerland (65.8 percent in the same period), Germany (44.7 percent), and France (28.0 percent). The challenge is to export world-class products that are not only assembled in China but are also comprised of parts made by Chinese companies—which is another of the core goals of plans to upgrade the PRC's economy.

That goal could be complicated by the trade war with China that President Donald Trump unleashed in mid-2018, which complicates the external environment that is so important for China's continued economic growth. The tariffs imposed on Chinese exports—in 2018 exports to the United States totaled nearly half a trillion US dollars—could deal a huge blow to one of the largest sectors of the PRC's economy. By strengthening the government agency that reviews the national security implications of foreign investments in American companies, the Committee on Foreign Investment in the United States (CFIUS), Trump has made it virtually impossible for Chinese high-tech firms to invest in the U.S., creating a major problem for China's IT exports, which relies heavily on inputs made in America for many of their products.

TABLE 8.1 Indicators of China's Global Integration, 1978–2016

	1978	1980	1984	1988	1990	1992	1994	1998	2001	2003	2006	2009	2012	2014	2015	2016
Total foreign trade ($US bil.)	20.6	38.1	53.6	102.8	115.4	165.5	236.6	324	509.7	851	1760.4	2207.5	3867.1	4301.5	3953	3685.6
Foreign trade as % of GDP (current prices)	9.7	12.4	16.4	25.2	29.4	33.5	42	32	38.6	51.6	64.4	43.2	45.3	41	35.8	32.9
Total exports ($US bil.)	9.8	18.1	26.1	47.5	62.1	84.9	121	183.7	266.1	438.2	969	1201.6	2048.7	2342.3	2273.5	2097.6
Exports by foreign-invested firms ($US bil.)				2.5	7.8	17.4	34.7	80.9	133.2	240.3	563.8	672.1	1022.6	1074.6	1004.6	916.8
Exports by foreign-invested firms (% of total exports)				5.2	12.6	20.5	28.7	44	50.1	54.8	58.2	55.9	49.9	45.9	44.2	43.7
Inbound foreign direct investment ($US bil.)			1.4	3.2	3.5	11	33.8	45.5	46.9	53.5	63	90	111.7	119.6	126.3	126
Foreign exchange reserves ($US bil.)	0.2	-1.3	8.2	3.4	11.1	19.4	51.6	145	212.2	403.3	1066.3	2399.2	3311.6	3843	3330.4	3010.5
Cargo handled in major coastal ports (mil. tons)	198	217	275	456	483	604	744	922	1426	2011	3422	4755	6652	7696	7846	8109
Deep-water berths in major ports (10,000 tons)		144	153	226	284	312	359	468	527	650	883	1214	1453	1633	1750	1814
Number of foreign tourists (1,000s) *	230	529	1134	1842	1747	4006	5182	7108	11226	11403	22210	21938	27192	26361	25985	28151
International air routes		18	24	40	44	58	84	131	134	194	268	263	381	490	660	739
Number of foreign-invested 5-Star Hotels**								734	833	686	570	561	492	485	442	383

Sources: National Bureau of Statistics of China, China Tourism Statistical Bulletin (various years).

*Excluding overseas Chinese and Chinese from Hong Kong and Macau.

**Statistical Bulletin of Star Hotels in China, China National Tourism Administration; foreign invested Star Hotels also include sources from Hong Kong, Macau, and Taiwan.

When Xi Jinping took over as leader of the CCP and the PRC in 2012/2013, many observers of Chinese affairs were generally upbeat about his willingness to take on many of the economic challenges facing the PRC. As he commented to President Obama in their meeting in California in June 2013, China "must deepen reforms to promote healthy and sustained economic development."[104] The outline of planned reforms that was unveiled later that fall was seen as a bold package of policies that would move the PRC further in the direction of a market economy.[105] But, as noted earlier, that does not seem to be the direction in which Xi Jinping is taking the Chinese economy. Strengthening the state-sector and party control seem to be his priorities.

The 19th Party Congress in late 2017, which marked the beginning of his second term as CCP leader, was all about enhancing Xi's power and extolling him as an ideological visionary who was leading China into a new era of prosperity and global influence, and not about the nitty-gritty or even a grand plan of reform. The meeting of the National People's Congress in March 2018 that formally reelected Xi as PRC president focused on the reorganization of the government, although, as one scholar put it, was "generally market-friendly . . . its main purpose is to create a more disciplined and accountable administration to serve as an instrument for Xi Jinping."[106] In March 2018, the Central Committee that had been chosen at the Party Congress held its third meeting, or Third Plenum. Third meetings of newly installed Central Committees have become occasions for announcing detailed economic agendas. But while "reform" was mentioned often, it came up only a couple of times in the context of economic reform. "Deepening the reform of party and state institutions," or some variation on that theme, pops up more than twenty times.[107]

China Watchers should consider various scenarios, not reach hard-and-fast conclusions or make predictions about what may or may not happen in the PRC in the future. Perhaps Xi Jinping's consolidation of his personal power and that of party-state institutions is simply motivated by a desire to rule as long and in whatever way he pleases with the result that China's economic dynamism is undermined and the country gets stuck in the middle-income trap. Or perhaps it is part of a strategy that many of his comrades at the top agree is necessary to deepen the anticorruption campaign at the grassroots and promote the political stability and institutional capacity needed to undertake bold, market-friendly reforms that will propel China to the next level of economic development. We should have a clearer notion of which of these scenarios—or another one—is unfolding by the time the CCP holds its 20th Party Congress in the fall of 2022.

NOTES

1. On life expectancy, see (for 1949) S. S. Kantha, "Nutrition and Health in China, 1949 to 1989," *Progress in Food & Nutrition Science*, 14, no. 2–3 (1990): 93–137, and (for 1976) *World Bank Development Indicators*; on literacy, see (for 1949) http://english.peopledaily.com.cn/200211/18/eng20021118_106987.shtml; and (for 1980), www.unescap.org/stat/data/statind/pdf/t8_dec04.pdf>.

2. International Monetary Fund, *World Economic Outlook 2018 Data*, http://www.imf.org/external/pubs/ft/weo/2018/01/weodata.

3. David Zweig, *Internationalizing China: Domestic Interests and Global Linkages* (Ithaca, NY: Cornell University Press, 2002), 23–48.

4. See Barry Naughton and Kellee Tsai, *State Capitalism, Institutional Adaptation, and the Chinese Miracle* (New York: Cambridge University Press, 2015).

5. China Statistical Yearbooks 1999, 2007, table 5.1.

6. See Jude Howell and Jane Duckett, "Reassessing the Hu–Wen Era: A Golden Age for Social Policy," *China Quarterly*, forthcoming.

7. A remarkable article published in Sept. 2012 at the end of the Hu–Wen era by Deng Yuwen, then deputy editor of the journal of the CCP's Central Party School, accused the retiring duo of ten major failures, several of which reflected weak economic stewardship. See Gloria Davies, "Fitting Words," chap. 7, in *Yearbook 2013: Civilising China, Australia Centre on China in the World*, https://www.thechinastory.org/yearbooks/yearbook-2013/chapter-7-fitting-words/deng-yuwen/.

8. "Decision of the Central Committee of the Communist Party of China on Some Major Issues Concerning Comprehensively Deepening the Reform," adopted at the Third Plenary Session of the 18th Central Committee of the Communist Party of China on Nov. 12, 2013, http://lawprofessors.typepad.com/files/131112-third-plenum-decision---official-english-translation.pdf.

9. See "Chinese Leaders Emphasize Efforts to Deepen SOE Reform," *Xinhuanet*, July 4, 2016, http://www.xinhuanet.com/english/2016-07/04/c_135488264.htm.

10. See Peter Alexander and Anita Chan, "Does China Have an Apartheid Pass System?" *Journal of Ethnic and Migration Studies* 30, no. 4 (2004): 609–629.

11. Michael Lipton shows that this urban bias occurs in most of the developing world. Michael Lipton, *Why Poor People Stay Poor: Urban Bias in World Development* (Cambridge, MA: Harvard University Press, 1976).

12. See David Zweig, *Agrarian Radicalism in China, 1968–1981* (Cambridge, MA: Harvard University Press, 1989).

13. Jasper Becker, "Anhui: Let's Talk about Fenyang," in *Hungry Ghosts: Mao's Secret Famine* (New York: Henry Holt, 1996), 130–149.

14. See Frederick C. Teiwes and Warren Sun, *Paradoxes of Post-Mao Rural Reform: Initial Steps Toward a New Chinese Countryside 1976–1981* (New York: Routledge, 2016).

15. See Thomas P. Bernstein and Xiaobo Lü, *Taxation without Representation in Contemporary Rural China* (Cambridge: Cambridge University Press, 2003).

16. See Kristen E. Looney, "China's Campaign to Build a New Socialist Countryside: Village Modernization, Peasant Councils, and the Ganzhou Model of Rural Development," *China Quarterly* 225 (Dec. 2015): 909–932.

17. Zweig, *Internationalizing China*.

18. James Kai-sing Kung and Yi-min Lin, "The Decline of Township-and-Village Enterprises in China's Economic Transition," *World Development* 35, no. 4 (2007): 569–584.

19. This location was one of the author's field research sites in the 1980s and 1990s.

20. David Zweig, "The 'Externalities of Development': Can New Political Institutions Manage Rural Conflict?," in *Contemporary Chinese Society: Social Conflict and Popular Protest*, eds. Elizabeth J. Perry and Mark Selden (New York: Routledge, 2000), 120–142.

21. "Rural Land Disputes Lead Unrest in China," *China Daily*, Nov. 6, 2010, http://www.chinadaily.com.cn/china/2010-11/06/content_11511194.htm.

22. Tracie McMillan, "How China Plans to Feed 1.4 Billion Growing Appetites," *National Geographic*, Feb. 2018. https://www.nationalgeographic.com/magazine/2018/02/feeding-china-growing-appetite-food-industry-agriculture/. In the U.S., the average farm is more than four hundred acres.

23. The term "noodle strip farming" comes from William Hinton, *Shenfan: The Continuing Revolution in a Chinese Village* (New York: Random House, 1994). Hinton was highly critical of the decollectivization of agriculture: "If these communities don't again 'get organized,' if they don't, in various ways, relearn how to work together, their problems can only get worse, polarization can only accelerate, and economic stagnation can only deepen. Noodle strip farming is a dead end road." Hinton, "Mao, Rural Development, and Two-line Struggle," *Monthly Review*, Feb. 1, 1994.

24. "China Focus: China Considers Revising Law for Stable Land Contracts, Easier Transfer," *Xinhua*, Oct. 13, 2017, http://www.xinhuanet.com/english/2017-10/31/c_136717775.htm.

25. "China to Expand Rural Land Ownership Reform," http://www.xinhuanet.com/english/2017-12/01/c_136793675.htm.

26. Barry J. Naughton, "The Pattern and Legacy of Economic Growth in the Mao Era," in *Perspectives on Modern China: Four Anniversaries,* ed. Kenneth Lieberthal. et al. (Armonk, NY: M. E. Sharpe, 1991), 233.

27. Andrew G. Walder, *Communist Neo-Traditionalism: Work and Authority in Chinese Industry* (Berkeley: University of California Press, 1986).

28. Dorothy Solinger, *From Lathes to Looms: China's Industrial Policy in Comparative Perspective, 1979-1982* (Stanford, CA: Stanford University Press, 1991).

29. Barry Naughton, *The Chinese Economy: Adaptation and Growth*, 2nd ed. (Cambridge, MA: MIT Press, 2018), 214.

30. Fortune Global 500, 2018, http://fortune.com/global500/list/filtered?hqcountry=China; and http://fortune.com/global500/list/.

31. Barry Naughton, "Reform of State-owned Enterprises," in *China Update 2018: China's Forty Years of Reform and Development: 1978–2018*, ed. Ligang Song and Ross Garnaut (Canberra: Australian National University Press, 2018), http://press.anu.edu.au/node/4267; and "China's US$26 Trillion State-Asset Watchdog Says More M&As to Come," *Bloomberg News*, Apr. 11, 2018, https://www.bloomberg.com/news/articles/2018-04-11/china-to-engineer-more-state-firm-mergers-to-cut-overcapacity.

32. "China's Xi Says State Industry the Backbone of Economy Amid Reforms," *Reuters News*, July 18, 2015, https://uk.reuters.com/article/uk-china-reform-industry/chinas-xi-says-state-industry-the-backbone-of-economy-amid-reforms-idUKKCN0PS07Z20150718.

33. See Wendy Leutert, "State-Owned Enterprise Mergers: Will Less Be More?" in *Big Is Beautiful? State-Owned Enterprise Mergers under Xi Jinping*," China Analysis, European Council on Foreign Relations, Nov. 2016.

34. The data in this paragraph are from Nicholas Lardy, *Markets over Mao: The Rise of Private Business in China* (Washington: DC: Institute for International Economics, 2014), 70; and "China's Private Sector Contributes Greatly to Economic Growth: Federation Leader," Mar. 6, 2018, http://www.xinhuanet.com/english/2018-03/06/c_137020127.htm

35. Regular Press Conference of the Ministry of Commerce, People's Republic of China, May 10, 2018, http://english.mofcom.gov.cn/article/newsrelease/press/201805/20180502743309.shtml.

36. Xi Jinping, "Explanatory Notes for the 'Decision of the Central Committee of the Communist Party of China on Some Major Issues Concerning Comprehensively Deepening the Reform,'" China.org.cn, Jan. 16, 2015, http://www.china.org.cn/china/third_plenary_session/2014-01/16/content_31210122.htm.

37. "China's Companies on Notice: State Preparing to Take Stakes," *Bloomberg News*, Jan. 18, 2018, https://www.bloomberg.com/news/articles/2018-01-17/china-s-communists-will-take-more-stakes-in-private-companies.

38. Yasheng Huang as quoted in "Capitalism Loses Ground in China," Columbia Business School, *Chazen Global Insights*, Feb. 16, 2017, https://www8.gsb.columbia.edu/articles/chazen-global-insights/capitalism-loses-ground-china.

39. Minxin Pei, "Corruption Threatens China's Future," *Policy Outlook*, Carnegie Endowment of International Peace, Oct. 9, 2007, https://carnegieendowment.org/2007/10/09/corruption-threatens-china-s-future-pub-19628.

40. Melinda Liu, "The Cost of Corruption," *Newsweek*, July 30, 2012, https://www.newsweek.com/cost-corruption-65625.

41. Xi Jinping, "Power Must Be 'Caged' By System," in Xi Jinping, *The Governance of China*, vol. 1 (Beijing Foreign Languages Press, 2014), 426.

42. Xi Jinping, "Historical Wisdom Helps Us Combat Corruption and Uphold Integrity," Xi Jinping, *Governance of China*, vol. 1, 424.

43. Jamie P. Horsley, "What's So Controversial about China's New Anti-corruption Body? Digging into the National Supervision Commission," *Diplomat*, May 30, 2018, https://www.brookings.edu/opinions/whats-so-controversial-about-chinas-new-anti-corruption-body/.

44. Michael Forsythe, "Zhou Yongkang, Ex-Security Chief in China, Gets Life Sentence for Graft," *New York Times*, June 11, 2015, https://www.nytimes.com/2015/06/12/world/asia/zhou-yongkang-former-security-chief-in-china-gets-life-sentence-for-corruption.html.

45. Xi Jinping, "Secure a Decisive Victory in Building a Moderately Prosperous Society in All Respects and Strive for the Great Success of Socialism with Chinese Characteristics for a New Era" (report delivered at the 19th National Congress of the Communist Party of China, Oct. 18, 2017), http://www.xinhuanet.com/english/download/Xi_Jinping's_report_at_19th_CPC_National_Congress.pdf.

46. "Revealed: The Far-Reaching Powers of China's New Super Anticorruption Agency," *South China Morning Post*, Mar. 13, 2018, https://www.scmp.com/news/china/policies-politics/article/2136949/far-reaching-powers-chinas-new-super-anti-corruption.

47. Cited in Sylvia Xihui Liu, "Innovation Design: Made in China 2025," *Design Management Review*, Feb. 22, 2016, https://onlinelibrary.wiley.com/doi/full/10.1111/drev.10349.

48. Li Hui, "Made in China 2025: How Beijing Is Revamping Its Manufacturing Sector," *South China Morning Post*, June 9, 2018, https://www.scmp.com/tech/innovation/article/1818381/made-china-2025-how-beijing-revamping-its-manufacturing-sector.

49. "Middle Income Trap," https://www.tutor2u.net/economics/reference/middle-income-trap.

50. Robert B. Zoellick, "Opening Remarks at the Conference on China's Challenges for 2030," Beijing, Sept. 3, 2011, http://www.worldbank.org/en/news/speech/2011/09/03/china-challenges-for-2030-building-modern-harmonious-creative-high-income-society.

51. Pierre-Richard Agénor, Otaviano Canuto, and Michael Jelenic, "Avoiding Middle-Income Growth Traps," *Economic Premise*, World Bank, Nov. 2012, http://siteresources.worldbank.org/EXTPREMNET/Resources/EP98.pdf.

52. Scott Kennedy, "Made in China 2025," Center for International and Strategic Studies, June 1, 2015, https://www.csis.org/analysis/made-china-2025.

53. Richard N. Rosecrance, *The Rise of the Trading State: Commerce and Conquest in the Modern World* (New York: Basic Books, 1986).

54. See Michael J. Enright, *Developing China: The Remarkable Impact of Foreign Direct Investment* (New York: Routledge, 2017).

55. Enright, *Developing China*, 3–4.

56. Enright, *Developing China*, 3–4.

57. Enright, *Developing China*, 3-4 .

58. 2018 China Business Climate Survey Report, American Chamber of Commerce in China, Jan. 2018, http://www.bain.com/publications/articles/china-business-climate-survey-report-2018.aspx.

59. Di Yingqing and Zheng Gang, "What Does China's Joining the WTO Actually Imply with Regard to China's Long-term Interests? An Analysis of the Question of China's Joining the WTO," *Gaige Neican* (Internal Reference Material on Reform) 9 (May 5, 1999), 34–38, translated in *Chinese Economy: China and the WTO*, Part 2, 33, no. 2 (Mar.–Apr. 2000), 19.

60. Margaret M. Pearson, "The Case of China's Accession to GATT/WTO," in *The Making of Chinese Foreign and Security Policy in the Era of Reform, 1978–2000*, ed. David M. Lampton (Stanford, CA: Stanford University Press, 2001), 337–370.

61. Nicholas R. Lardy, *Integrating China into the Global Economy* (Washington, DC: Brookings Institution Press, 2002).

62. See Peter Ford, "How WTO Membership Made China the Workshop of the World," *Christian Science Monitor*, Dec. 14, 2011.

63. Peter Martin and Keith Zhai, "Xi Mounts Fresh Defense of Globalization in Contrast to Trump," https://www.bloomberg.com/news/articles/2017-11-10/xi-mounts-fresh-defense-of-globalization-in-contrast-to-trump; "Chinese President Xi Jinping Stands up for Globalisation and Free Trade at Asia's Davos," http://www.scmp.com/news/china/economy/article/2141099/chinese-president-xi-jinping-stands-globalisation-free-trade.

64. Peter Buxbaum, "China Still Not Living Up to WTO Commitments," *Global Trade*, Jan. 1, 2017, http://www.globaltrademag.com/in-the-news/china-still-not-living-wto-commitments.

65. Jost Wübbeke, Mirjam Meissner, Max J. Zenglein, Jaqueline Ives, and Björn Conrad, "MADE IN CHINA 2025: The making of a high-tech superpower and consequences for industrial countries," Mercator Institute for Chinese Studies (MERICS), *Merics Papers of China*, no. 2, Dec. 2016, https://www.merics.org/sites/default/files/2017-09/MPOC_No.2_MadeinChina2025.pdf.

66. Scott F. Kennedy, "The WTO in Wonderland: China's Awkward 15th Anniversary," *Center for Strategic and International Studies* (Dec. 11, 2016) 6–7, https://www.csis.org/analysis/wto-wonderland-chinas-awkward-15th-anniversary.

67. For a report that attributes this policy's development to Jiang Zemin, see Chen Yangxiong, "Jiang Zemin 'zou chu qu' zhanlue de xingcheng ji qi zhongyao yiyi" (The formation and the great significance of Jiang Zemin's strategy of "going out"), *Zhonguo gongchandang xinwen wang* (News Network of the CCP), Oct. 10, 2008, http://theory.people.com.cn/GB/40557/138172/138202/8311431.html#.

68. Ministry of Commerce, *"Dui wai touzi guobie chanye daoxiang mulu"* (An advisory list of sectors in different countries for foreign investment), July 21, 2004, http://www.mofcom.gov.cn/ aarticle/bi/200407/20040700252005.html.

69. Joseph Battat, "China's Outward Foreign Direct Investment," *Foreign Investment Advisory Services*, World Bank (2006).

70. United Nations Conference on Trade and Development (UNCTAD) World Investment Reports for 2018. https://unctad.org/fdistatistics.

71. UNCTAD World Investment Reports for 2006 http://unctad.org/en/pages/PublicationArchive.aspx?publicationid=709) and 2017 (http://unctad.org/sections/dite_dir/docs/wir2018/wir18_fs_cn_en.pdf).

72. The *Economist* Intelligence Unit, "China Going Global Investment Index, 2017," 3, http://www.eiu.com/public/thankyou_download.aspx?activity=download&campaignid=ChinaODI2017.

73. Derek Scissors, "Chinese Investment: Revenge of the State," *American Enterprise Institute*, July 2017, 4, http://www.aei.org/publication/chinese-investment-revenge-of-the-state/.

74. Geoff Dyer and Richard McGregor, "China's Champions: Why State Ownership Is No Longer Proving a Dead Hand," *Wall Street Journal*, Mar. 16, 2008.

75. See Elizabeth C. Economy and Michael Levi, *By All Means Necessary: How China's Resource Quest is Changing the World* (New York: Oxford University Press, 2014).

76. *China Global Investment Tracker*, American Enterprise Institute, http://www.aei.org/china-global-investment-tracker/.

77. *China Global Investment Tracker.*

78. International Crisis Group, *China's Thirst for Oil, Asia Report*, no. 153, June 9, 2008, 3.

79. "Vehicle drivers exceed 400 million in China," *Xinhua*, Oct. 17, 2018, http://english.gov.cn/state_council/ministries/2018/10/17/content_281476349681232.htm.

80. The Mercator Institute for Chinese Studies (MERICS) hosts a website that tracks developments in the Belt and Road Initiative, https://www.merics.org/index.php/en/bri-tracker.

81. "Chronology of China's Belt and Road Initiative, *Xinhuanet*, http://www.xinhuanet.com/english/2016-06/24/c_135464233.htm.

82. "Full Text: Vision for Maritime Cooperation under the Belt and Road Initiative," *Xinhua*, June 20, 2017, http://www.xinhuanet.com/english/2017-06/20/c_136380414.htm.

83. Peter Cai, "Understanding China's Belt and Road Initiative," *Lowy Institute for International Policy*, Mar. 2017.

84. See Amitendu Palit, "The Maritime Silk Road Initiative (MSRI): Why India is Worried, What China Can Do," May 31, 2017, *Global Policy*, https://www.globalpolicyjournal.com/blog/31/05/2017/maritime-silk-road-initiative-msri-why-india-worried-what-china-can-do.

85. Maria AbiHabib, "How China Got Sri Lanka to Cough Up a Port," *New York Times*, June 25, 2018, https://www.nytimes.com/2018/06/25/world/asia/china-sri-lanka-port.html.

86. Drazen Jorgic, "China Pours Money into Pakistan Port in Suspected Strategic Power Push," *Sydney Morning Herald*, Dec. 17, 2017, https://www.smh.com.au/world/china-pours-money-into-pakistan-port-in-suspected-strategic-power-push-20171218-h069s1.html.

87. Jonathan Hillman, "China's Belt and Road Initiative: Five Years Later," *Center for Strategic and International Studies*, Statement before the U.S.-China Economic and Security Review Commission, Jan. 25, 2018, https://www.csis.org/analysis/chinas-belt-and-road-initiative-five-years-later-0.

88. "Top 250 Global Contractors," *Engineering News-Record*, Aug. 2017, https://www.enr.com/toplists/2017-Top250-Global-Contractors-1, cited in Hillman, "China's Belt and Road Initiative."

89. "Top 250 Global Contractors."

90. Brahma Chellaney, "China's Creditor Imperialism," Project Syndicate, Dec. 20, 2017, https://www.project-syndicate.org/commentary/china-sri-lanka-hambantota-port-debt-by-brahma-chellaney-2017-12?barrier=accesspaylog. For a call for India to join the BRI, see editorial, "Off the Road: India Cannot Sit Out B&RI," May 16, 2017, https://www.thehindu.com/opinion/editorial/off-the-road/article18459388.ece.

91. Albert Park, "The Belt and Road: From Vision to Reality," HKUST Institute for Emerging Market Societies, May 24, 2018, http://iems.ust.hk/events/talk/2018/from-vision-to-reality-how-the-belt-and-road-initiative-is-unfolding-around-the-world.

92. Stefania Palma, "Malaysia Suspends US$22bn China-Backed Projects," *Financial Times*, July 4, 2018, https://www.ft.com/content/409942a4-7f80-11e8-bc55-50daf11b720d.

93. Yuichi Nitta and Thurein Hla Htway, "Myanmar Will Ask China to Downsize Project, Minister Says US$10 Billion Port Investment Should Be 'As Lean As Possible' to

Avoid Debt Trap," *Nikkei Asian Review*, July 4, 2018, https://asia.nikkei.com/Politics/Myanmar-will-ask-China-to-downsize-project-minister-says.

94. Sarah Zheng, "Is China's US$62 Billion Investment Plan Fueling Resentment in Pakistan?," *South China Morning Post*, July 3, 2018, https://www.scmp.com/news/china/diplomacy-defence/article/2153609/chinas-us62-billion-investment-plan-fuelling-resentment.

95. Haroon Janjua, "Islamabad asks Beijing to axe US$2b coal plan," *South China Morning Post*, 17 January 2019, p. A8, https://amp.scmp.com/week-asia/geopolitics/article/2182326/cash-strapped-pakistan-asks-china-shelve-us2-billion-coal.

96. Constance Gustke, "Pollution Crisis Is Choking the Chinese Economy," *CNBC*, Feb. 11, 2016, https://www.cnbc.com/2016/02/11/pollution-crisis-is-choking-the-chinese-economy.html.

97. "How Will the Long Fall in China's Growth Impact Risks and Opportunities for Business?" https://www.conference-board.org/china-growth/.

98. Jane Cai, "Private Players Feeling Squeezed Out by Beijing's Support for State Companies," *South China Morning Post*, Oct. 4, 2017, https://www.scmp.com/news/china/economy/article/2113869/past-its-use-date-warps-chinas-antiquated-policy-picking-industry.

99. The data are from the Ministry of Human Resources and Social Security, http://www.mohrss.gov.cn/SYrlzyhshbzb/zwgk/szrs/tjgb/201805/W020180521567611022649.pdf. According to the Ministry, in 2016, the number was 13.14 million. For 2016 see http://www.mohrss.gov.cn/SYrlzyhshbzb/zwgk/szrs/tjgb/201805/W020180521567132619037.pdf.

100. Douglas Bulloch, "Why China's Looming Debt Problems Won't Stop at Its Borders," *Forbes*, May 31, 2018, https://www.forbes.com/sites/douglasbulloch/2018/05/31/while-china-is-facing-its-own-debt-crisis-it-is-also-exacerbating-others/#42f52fc3fc33.

101. See Andrew Collier, *Shadow Banking and the Rise of Capitalism in China* (New York: Palgrave Macmillan, 2017); and Kellee Tsai, *Back-Alley Banking: Private Entrepreneurs in China* (Ithaca, NY: Cornell University Press, 2004).

102. Sara Hsu, "Fears Over China's Local Government Debt Are Growing—Again," *Forbes*, Jan. 2, 2018, https://www.forbes.com/sites/sarahsu/2018/01/02/fears-over-chinas-local-government-debt-are-growing-again/#2f6b3369decf.

103. He Weiwen, "China's Economic Slowdown Is Nothing to Worry About," *China-US Focus*, http://www.chinausfocus.com/finance-economy/chinas-economic-slowdown-is-nothing-to-worry-about/.

104. Chris Buckley, "China's New President Sets up a Potential Showdown, with Himself," *New York Times*, June 21, 2013.

105. Arthur R. Kroeber, "Xi Jinping's Ambitious Agenda for Economic Reform in China," *Brookings Institution*, Oct. 17, 2013, https://www.brookings.edu/opinions/xi-jinpings-ambitious-agenda-for-economic-reform-in-china/, and David Zweig, "Breaking the Bureaucratic Blocks to Development: Reflections on China's 3rd Plenum of the 18th Central Committee," *Research Reports*, Asia-Pacific Foundation of Canada (website), Dec. 19, 2013.

106. Barry Naughton, "Xi's System, Xi's Men: After the March 2018 National People's Congress," *China Leadership Monitor* 56 (Spring 2018), 1.

107. "China Focus: 19th CPC Central Committee 3rd Plenum Issues Communique," *Xinhuanet*, Mar. 1, 2018, http://www.xinhuanet.com/english/2018-03/01/c_137006746_2.htm.

SUGGESTED READINGS

Ang, Yuen Yuen. *How China Escaped the Poverty Trap*. Ithaca, NY: Cornell University Press, 2016.

Chen, Ling. *Manipulating Globalization: The Influence of Bureaucrats on Business in China*. Stanford, CA: Stanford University Press, 2018.

Collier, Andrew. *Shadow Banking and the Rise of Capitalism in China*. New York: Palgrave Macmillan, 2017.

Economy, Elizabeth C., and Michael Levi. *By All Means Necessary: How China's Resource Quest is Changing the World*. New York: Oxford University Press, 2014.

Huang, Yasheng. *Capitalism with Chinese Characteristics: Entrepreneurship and the State*. New York: Cambridge University Press, 2008.

Kroeber, Arthur R. *China's Economy: What Everyone Needs to Know*. London: Oxford University Press, 2016.

Lardy, Nicholas R. *Markets over Mao: The Rise of Private Business in China*. Washington, DC: Institute for International Economics, 2014.

Li, Lanqing. *Breaking Through: The Birth of China's Opening-up Policy*. New York: Oxford University Press, 2010.

Li, Shi, Hiroshi Sato, and Terry Sicular. *Rising Inequality in China: Challenges to a Harmonious Society*. New York: Cambridge University Press, 2013.

Naughton, Barry. *The Chinese Economy: Adaptation and Growth*, 2nd ed. Cambridge, MA: MIT Press, 2018.

Overholt, William. *China's Crisis of Success*. New York: Cambridge University Press, 2018.

Nolan, Peter. *Is China Buying the World*? New York: Polity, 2013.

Rozelle, Scott, and Natalie Johnson. *China's Invisible Crisis: How a Growing Urban-Rural Divide Could Sink the World's Second-Largest Economy*. New York: Basic Books, 2019.

Shambaugh, David. *China Goes Global: The Partial Power*. New York: Oxford University Press, 2013.

Steinfeld, Edward S. *Playing Our Game: Why China's Rise Doesn't Threaten the West*. New York: Oxford University Press, 2010.

Teiwes, Fredrick C., and Warren Sun. *Paradoxes of Post-Mao Rural Reform*. London: Routledge, 2017.

Wedeman, Andrew. *Double Paradox: Rapid Growth and Rising Corruption in China*. Ithaca, NY: Cornell University Press, 2012.

Yueh, Linda. *China's Growth: The Making of an Economic Superpower*. New York: Oxford University Press, 2013.

Zheng, Yongnian, and Yanjie Huang. *Market in State: The Political Economy of Domination in China*. New York: Cambridge University Press, 2018.

Zweig, David. *Freeing China's Farmers: Rural Restructuring in the Reform Era*. Armonk, NY: M. E. Sharpe, 1997.

Zweig, David. *Internationalizing China: Domestic Interests and Global Linkages*. Ithaca, NY: Cornell University Press, 2002.

Zweig, David, and Yufan Hao. *Sino-US Energy Triangles: Resource Diplomacy under Hegemony*. New York: Routledge, 2016.

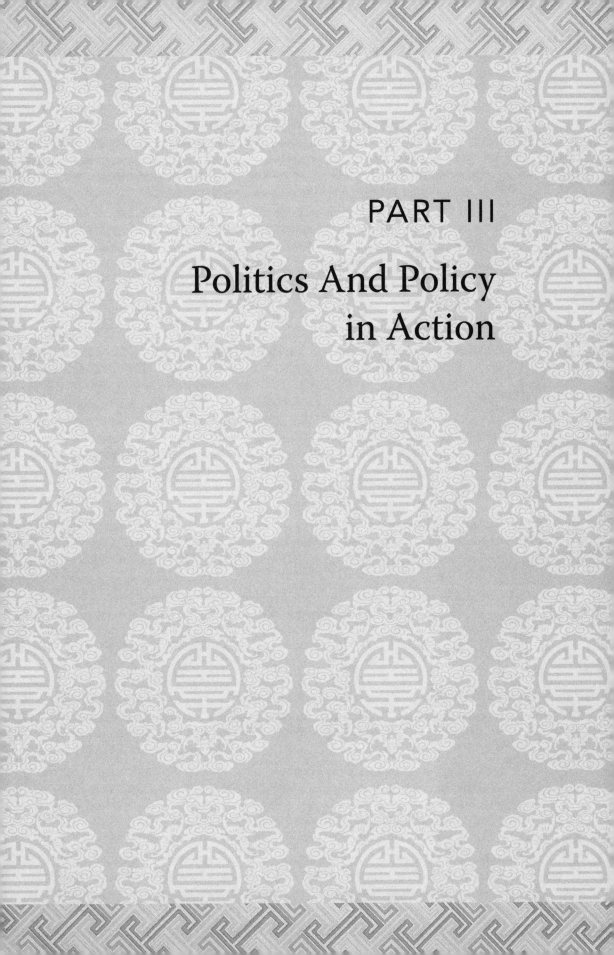

PART III

Politics And Policy
in Action

9

Rural China: Reform and Resistance

JOHN JAMES KENNEDY

From spreading grassroots democracy and rising incidents of unrest to rapid urbanization and migration to the cities, rural China has witnessed dramatic political and demographic changes over the last quarter century. New political opportunities for rural residents began with the introduction of economic reforms in the early 1980s (see chap. 8). This was critical for the central leadership because the vast majority of the population lived in the countryside. Market reforms and the abolition of the people's commune system eroded the political authority of local cadres, who, in the Maoist era, had control over the rural economic and social life, and fundamentally altered cadre-villager relations. While leaders' control over basic resources and activities has diminished, villagers' participation in political affairs has increased. With the introduction of the **Organic Law of Villagers Committees** in 1987 (revised in 1998),[1] villagers could directly elect and recall their local leaders. The quality of village elections varies across rural China, but cadre accountability by their village constituents has improved. The next step was experiments in direct elections for high authorities at the town level in 1998, but the central leadership quickly ended these experiments and scaled back the direct elections for town government heads. However, in 2012 the majority of China's population was designated as urban due to precipitous expansion of large and small municipalities as well as massive rural to urban migration. This dynamic change has reshaped social and political environment in rural China.

At the same time, since the 1990s, reported incidences of rural unrest have dramatically increased. The modes of resistance range from legal petitions to massive demonstrations that sometimes turn violent. Yet, these social disturbances do *not* threaten the central government or the Chinese Communist Party (CCP). Most incidents of rural resistance tend to be directed toward local government officials rather than the central authorities (including resistance to unfair land grabs due to expanding cities and urban development projects). Indeed, many of these resisters use national laws, such as the Organic Law and Administrative Litigation Law, to protect themselves from abusive local cadres. This has created a contradictory situation of rural unrest that has a relatively high level of support for the central leadership.

Still, unrest reflects villagers' discontent, as well as demands for greater participation in the local decision-making process. Therefore in order to maintain popular support from the rural population, the CCP leadership continues to slowly expand political reforms. The question is whether the gradual introduction of reforms is enough to satisfy rural political demands before the incidents of rural unrest become unmanageable for the central party-state.

This chapter is divided into eight parts. The first section is a brief introduction to the rural administration that comprises counties and town governments. The second part focuses on the concerns of villagers and village cadres, such as land management, local economy, taxes, and environmental protection. This includes the change in cadre-villager relations from the 1980s to the present. The third section introduces the town and township officials and how the *nomenklatura* system of cadre management shapes their incentives to fully implement central policies. The chief question for students studying the politics of rural China and political reform is this: Does the central government lack the political *will* or *capacity* to influence county and town officials? Section four focuses on the development of village elections and addresses the introduction of the Organic Law of Villagers Committees and the uneven implementation of the law. The fifth section speaks to the influence of rural to urban migration on village life and governance including those "left behind." The sixth part addresses several experiments with direct elections for town mayors and more accountable local People's Congresses. While the central leadership quickly ended early attempts at direct elections for government heads, there have been a number of less direct election methods that broaden the public participation in the cadre selection method. The seventh section focuses on rural unrest. This section will look at the various methods of rural resistance: legal means, semilegal (**rightful resistance**), and illegal actions. One key observation is that resistance and protest is associated with the uneven implementation of rural political reforms. Indeed, many large illegal protests started out as local legal attempts to get specific reforms, such as a fee reduction regulation or the village election law, fully enforced in their village. Yet, other protests are direct reaction to semilegal or illegal acts on the part of local governments and developers particularly in the case of rural land acquisitions. The final section addresses the prospects of future political reform in rural China.

RURAL ADMINISTRATIVE DIVISIONS

As discussed in greater detail in the chapter 10, China has experienced extensive urbanization in recent decades. In 1980, about 81 percent of China's population lived in the rural areas. By 2016, that percentage was down to 43 percent, and for the first time in Chinese history, fewer than half the people lived in the countryside. Nevertheless, that means more than 590 million people are still classified as rural residents, which is almost twice the total population of the United States. Moreover, there is an enormous diversity in the countryside that makes it difficult to generalize about the rural population, especially in terms of geography. From abject poverty in remote mountainous villages to industrialized villages near larger cities, the levels of wealth, access to health care, and educational opportunities vary by proximity to urban centers.

The definition of rural residents is associated with the administrative hierarchy that dramatically changed with decollectivization and the end of the communes in the 1980s. From 1958 to 1982, the administrative division below the county was the people's commune, and its subordinate units the production brigade and production team. Rural residents were citizens who lived and worked in the communes. As a result of restructuring, after 1982, communes were renamed towns or townships, brigades became villages, and production teams became small groups. In essence, this was going back to the traditional, precommunist names for these levels of social organization.

Currently, the formal administrative hierarchy of the PRC includes the national, provincial, municipal (or city), county, and the town or township levels of government (see Figure 1.2, chap. 1). Technically, rural residents are those citizens who live below the county level and whose household registration (*hukou*) is in a town, township, or village. The town or township is the lowest formal administrative level of state authority in China. Villages are not part of the formal administrative structure of the state but, according to the PRC constitution, are self-governing units.

The difference between a town and a township is the percentage of registered urban population who live in a particular locale. A town is more urbanized, with over 10 percent of the population registered as nonagricultural, while in a township more than 90 percent of the population is registered as agricultural (rural). Reflecting the trend toward urbanization, the number of towns surpassed the number of townships in 2002.[*] This process has accelerated as the government moves millions of villagers into new housing in towns and small cities (see chap. 10) in the more remote mountainous areas, they may have no more than a dozen widely dispersed households.

Figure 9.1 displays the administrative hierarchy of the People's Republic below the provincial level. Within every municipality there are a number of counties; within every county, there are towns; and below the towns are villages; and within every village there are a number of small groups. According to the 2017 *China Statistical Yearbook*, there are 152 cities at the prefectural level (the level below the province) with more than a million people.[2] The population of these municipalities can range from 10.7 million in Shijiazhuang city, Hebei province, to 2.9 million in Xining city, Qinghai province. Within every municipality there are about five to fifteen counties. There are more than 2,800 counties in China, and their population varies from under 100,000 to more than one million. County population size can vary widely even within one province. In 2016 Shaanxi province, Hu county near the provincial capital of Xian municipality had more than 600,000 residents, while the geographically larger, but more remote Ganquan county had only 90,000. Under each county, there

---

[*] To simplify the discussion of rural governance in this chapter, the term "town" will be used to refer to both towns and townships.

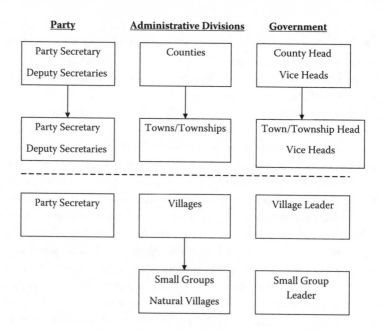

FIGURE 9.1 Party/Government Officials and Administrative Divisions Below the Provincial Level

Note: The dash line represents the lowest official administrative level (the town/township).

are about ten to twenty rural towns, and the population is usually about 20,000, but can be as large as 70,000 or as small as 7,000. There are more than 30,000 towns, and within every town there are about fifteen to twenty villages. Rural China has about 560,000 villages, formally called **administrative villages**. Village population is typically around 1,000 to 2,000 residents. Finally, within every village there are two to seven small groups or **natural villages**. While some small groups in densely populated villages near urban centers can be as large as a typical village (2,000 residents),

In order to maintain CCP influence in the large and varied rural areas, each town, county, and village has a party secretary as well as a government head. The party secretary has the most political power and makes the final policy decision at his or her respective level. Party secretaries connect higher authorities with the lower levels to ensure that policies are carried out and laws are enforced. Therefore, although the party-state is *not* a monolithic regime that can enforce its will at all times and in all places, the CCP still retains significant authority to carry out priority policies and maintain at least a minimum level of control down to the village level.

VILLAGERS AND CADRES: CHANGING POLITICAL RELATIONSHIPS

Villagers

China's villagers have a keen sense of justice. Whether it is the distribution of collective land or investment of public funds, villagers expect a fair decision from their local leaders. For example, villagers *do not* own the land they cultivate and live on.

It remains collectively owned by the village and managed by village cadres. Villagers lease land, and cadres decide how to allocate the collective land among households. For most villagers, this is *the* most crucial cadre decision because of the variation in land quality and location. Each household is allocated two to four separate plots of land, and the location of the plot can be a few yards from their back door or several miles away. Moreover, arable land is scarce. Currently less than 15 percent of land in China is cultivated. In villages where arable land is less than 50 percent, the local leaders tend to give every household a small portion of the good land. This is because villagers prefer an allocation decision based on fairness rather than efficiency (the relationship between labor and output), which would dictate that the land be allocated in larger, contiguous pieces rather than in smaller, dispersed segments. Portions of village land were readjusted every five to ten years due to demographic changes such as births, deaths, and marriages. Village cadres can also lease land to people outside the village. Rapid industrialization and urbanization have made land a very valuable commodity and the source of profit. Villagers expect leaders to protect the arable land or at least to receive fair compensation for leased land. But this situation has created enormous opportunities for corruption, such as land grabs, and has been one of the major causes of growing rural unrest.

Villagers also expect fair and transparent management of public funds, especially in the area of rural education. For villagers, the local elementary school is vital for the education of their children and grandchildren, and local cadres are responsible for construction and maintenance. Villagers rely on the local cadres to spend education funds in an efficient and honest manner that will ensure quality schooling and the safety of their children. Neglecting the maintenance or cutting corners during school construction can be disastrous. For example, the May 2008 earthquake in Sichuan province occurred in the middle of a school day, and many rural elementary and junior high schools collapsed, killing thousands of children.[3] Grieving parents asked why local government buildings remained standing while most of the schools collapsed. Thus the quality of education and the safety of their children remain a vital concern for villagers.

Villagers can also be proactive when their expectations of fairness are not met. Many rural people are unafraid to meet or even confront local cadres and town officials. Villager action can be as simple as an individual walking over to the leader's home to discuss a problem, such as road maintenance or a land lease issue. It may also be more complex, when villagers take legal action to recall an elected leader or sue a town government official in the local courts for attempting to extract excessive fees. If legal action does not resolve the problem, then some rural residents may turn to public demonstrations, such as a roadblock or a sit-in. Of course, not all villagers take political action, but most retain a sense of justice and support resistance when expectations of fairness are not met.

Village Cadres

Village cadres are community members who have leadership positions and are responsible to both villagers and higher authorities. Residents are very familiar with local cadres, since they are from families who have long lived in the village. Of course, this familiarity does not always reduce friction between cadres and villagers, nor does it increase cadre authority. Whether they are popularly elected or appointed from above, village cadres are caught in the middle between villagers and town officials, and therefore have a delicate balancing act in carrying out their jobs. Town officials depend on them to carry out national policies and local regulations. Many of these are unpopular policies, such as tax and fee collection (before 2005) or family planning (before 2015). In the 1980s and 1990s, villagers called town and village officials the "three wanting cadres": they want your money, grain, and unborn children. The last is in reference to the role that cadres play in carrying out China's strict "one-child policy" (see chap. 14). However, some village cadres did not fully carry out policies, such as the relaxing the single-child policy or the required quota of grain that had to be turned over to the state in the 1980s and 1990s. This was due to their close and mutually dependent relations with villagers.

Village committees were officially established as the governing body on the village level with the enactment of the 1982 state constitution. The constitution does not provide great detail regarding the composition and functions of the village committee. In fact, the language combines both the rural village and urban residents' committees. According to Article 111 of the constitution, "the residents' committees and villagers' committees established among urban and rural residents on the basis of their place of residence are mass organizations of self-management at the grass-roots level. The chairman, vice-chairmen and members of each residents' or villagers' committee are elected by the residents." A village committee consists of three to seven members, including the chair of the committee or village leader, vice chairs, an accountant, a female member who deals with family planning and women's affairs, and finally, a person in charge of public security. "Grass-roots level" means that the village committee is not an official administrative division of the party-state; nevertheless, committee members are still responsible for carrying out national policies on the local level.

Villages also have a communist party branch that is made up of a party secretary and two or three deputy party secretaries. According to Article 32 of the CCP constitution, "The primary Party committees in communities, townships and towns and village Party branches provide leadership for the work in their localities and assist administrative departments, economic institutions and self-governing mass organizations in fully exercising their functions and powers." The village party secretary is the most powerful political figure in the village. In many cases, one person serves as both the party secretary and the village head. This is called the "one-shoulder-carrying-two-positions" (*yijiantiao*). The reason for this combined position is to resolve the potential problem of competing village leadership between the popularly elected village leader and the party secretary who is either appointed from above or elected by village party members. According to the Ministry of Civil Affairs in 2011, 38 percent of the villager committees had the one-shoulder position.[4] The village committee is responsible for carrying out policies, but major public affairs are first approved by the party secretary. This includes financial matters and village collective enterprises.

Below the village committee are small groups or natural villages. Each small group has an elected leader, but no party secretary (see Figure 9.1). The village committee assigns small group leaders with specific duties, and, in some cases, they manage the small group's collective land.

During the Maoist era (1949–1976) and into the 1980s, local cadres had considerable control over the economic, social, and political life for most villagers. In the economic arena, village cadres managed the collective land, and they also had administrative control over access to subsidized agricultural necessities, such as chemical fertilizers and hybrid seeds. Village cadres managed collective industries, including small factories and shops; they alone decided who had access to these lucrative jobs. After the implementation of the one-child policy in 1980, local cadres were responsible for reproduction education, introducing contraceptive methods, and birth planning in their village. The village and party leaders also often act as the mediators dealing with family disputes from marriage problems to clashes between households over land.

In the 1970s and even into the mid-1980s, political campaigns were still a central part of rural life, and CCP cadres were responsible for disseminating party propaganda and educating villagers about specific policies and laws. The methods for spreading CCP information were through a village-wide public address (PA) system, village assemblies, and political study sessions. Cadres used their considerable authority over the local economy to get villagers to attend these political meetings.

The PRC constitution refers to the election of village committee leaders. However, town government officials had the last word in selecting the village leaders and committee members throughout the 1980s, and for some villages even into the 1990s. Likewise, the town party committee had the power to appoint village party secretaries. The main reason that town party and government cadres intervened in village affairs was that they relied on village cadres to carry out national mandated policies and local regulations. While village cadres in the early to mid-1980s had significant authority, they also owed their position to the town officials. As a result, both the village leader and the party secretary were more accountable to the town officials than to the villagers. This does not mean that village cadres were unresponsive to villagers. Indeed, for village cadres, improving the general welfare of the entire village could satisfy the community as well as the town officials.

By the late 1980s and the 1990s, market reforms had eroded village cadres' traditional economic and political authority. As villagers gained access to the market economy, they became less dependent on village cadres for agricultural necessities such as fertilizer and farming equipment. Moreover, there were significant changes in off-farm employment. The rise in private enterprises meant that local factories producing everything from clothing for export to small electronic goods for local retailers were built in or near the village. Rural residents could get local industrial jobs without relying solely on their personal relations (*guanxi*) with the village cadre. Urban industrialization and construction also meant greater employment opportunities outside the village.

Political campaigns and study sessions became less frequent. After cadres lost most of their authority over economic opportunities, they also lost their leverage to get villagers to attend political meetings. In fact, cadres frequently complained that villagers displayed little interest in village assemblies and study sessions, and begrudgingly admitted that the only reason people came to village assemblies was to vote in village elections once every three years. The PA system is now used for mundane matters such as announcing a missing goat or found shoes.

Despite their reduced authority, village cadres still retain a number of vital duties, including land management, family planning, economic development, maintenance of village schools, dispute mediation, and, until recent reforms, tax and fee collection. The collection of taxes and fees, also called "villager's burdens" had been one of the most contentious duties for village cadres.[5] Some of these fees were arbitrarily imposed on villagers by corrupt officials. But others resulted when central government told town and village cadres that they were responsible for implementing certain policies and projects without providing them with adequate funds to implement these mandates. Therefore, local cadres had to collect fees from villagers in order pay for projects, including family planning programs, school and village road maintenance, and irrigation works. The list of taxes and fees could be long and consisted of ten to twenty different items, such as payments to support the family members of revolutionary martyrs, village militia, family planning, and electricity. By the late 1990s, in some places, villagers were paying anywhere from 20 to 50 percent of their annual income on taxes and fees.[6] While most of the fees were legitimate, villagers worried about how and where the money was spent. For example, in one village, residents pointed out that their village road maintenance fee increased every year, but their dirt road remained in very poor condition and impassable during the rainy season.

In an attempt to reduce villager's burdens, the central government enacted the tax-for-fee reform in 2002 that eliminated all local fees at the village and town levels. All fees were abolished in favor of a single agricultural tax, and in 2005 the agricultural taxes were removed altogether, which in one form or another had been in effect for over twenty-six hundred years. While villager's financial burdens have been dramatically reduced, village committees and the town governments have become heavily dependent on funds from the county, and it has become more difficult for local cadres to provide public services, such as maintenance of local schools, health clinics, and irrigation projects. In addition, some town and county governments near urban centers have turned to land lease sales to make up for lost revenues after the tax reform.

VILLAGE ELECTIONS: GRASSROOTS DEMOCRACY?

Organic Law of Villagers Committees

The Organic Law of Villagers Committees was enacted on a trial basis in 1987 and then made into a permanent law in 1998. The Organic Law allows villagers to select three to seven village committee members and the village leader in a competitive election (see Figure 9.2). Elected cadres serve three-year terms, and there is no term limit. In 2016, 98 percent of China's 560,000 village committees were formed by direct election.[7] Villagers can recall elected leaders if over one-fifth of the eligible voters file a case to the town government for impeachment. The Organic Law also covers more than elections. It spells out village committee duties in greater detail than the constitution, including transparency in village financial affairs and public investments.

Why would top leaders of a single-party authoritarian regime introduce local democratic institutions and processes?

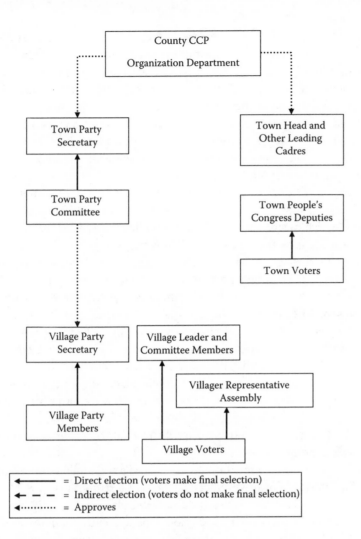

FIGURE 9.2 Selection of Village Cadres and Town Officials

The central government first introduced village elections as a mechanism for citizens to monitor the performance of village leaders and committee members, and to replace those who were incompetent or corrupt.[8] At the time, cadres in the villages were appointed by higher-level town officials. In the 1980s, one of the greatest supporters for the Organic Law was the veteran party leader and former mayor of Beijing, Peng Zhen, who was the chairman of the **Standing Committee of the National People's Congress** (NPC) from 1983 to 1988. Peng believed that relations between villagers and cadres were deteriorating and that rural discontent was rising. Elections were seen as a way to improve cadre-villager relations and policy implementation at the grassroots level. Indeed, direct elections for village leaders have more to do with administrative efficiency than with democracy. In 1985, China had over 940,000 village committees, and it was nearly impossible for authorities to keep tabs on all village cadres.[9] According to Peng, top-down monitoring of local cadres was not enough: "Who supervises rural cadres? Can we supervise them? No, not even if we had 48 hours a day."[10] Elections were designed to shift basic responsibility for cadre supervision from higher authorities to the villagers. Despite support from some top leaders, there was still opposition to direct village elections within the CCP and the NPC. A number of NPC deputies expressed their concerns that villagers were not ready to govern themselves and they did not have the "democratic consciousness" to manage elections. Other opponents said that village elections would weaken town officials by removing their authority to select village leaders. But both supporters and opponents agreed that some form of elections was needed to improve the political conditions in the countryside.

While Peng made a good case for village elections, he and his supporters still had to compromise. In 1987, the NPC passed the Organic Law of Villager Committees on a trial basis, which meant that the policy could be reversed before the Organic Law became official. In 1988, the Ministry of Civil Affairs was put in charge of carrying out the Organic Law throughout rural China, and by 1993, most villages had held at least one round of village elections. By 2016 most villages have had at least nine rounds of elections.[11] Yet, from the start the Organic Law has been unevenly implemented, which means that the quality of village elections has varied significantly across China.

The trial version of the Organic Law allowed villagers to select leaders and committee members in a competitive election, but the regulation did not specify how candidates were to be chosen. This left a large legal loophole for county and town officials to manipulate the election law to their advantage. In the first round, most elections were not truly competitive. For example, many elections had just one candidate for village leader. Consequently, some people referred to these elections as "old wine in a new bottle," meaning that the newly "elected" cadres were no different from the previously appointed ones.

One of the main reasons for the slow and uneven implementation of the Organic Law was the resistance of town officials, who had a strong incentive to manipulate the election process. This is not because town officials are inherently antidemocratic, but rather, as noted earlier, their promotion depends on the fulfillment of mandated policies set forth by the county government. In order to ensure that village committee members can be trusted to fully implement policies, especially unpopular policies such as family planning and tax collection (before 2005), town officials feel they must either appoint leaders or at least be involved in the candidate selection process. Competitive elections generally occurred only in villages where county authorities pressured town officials to fully implement the Organic Law.

Nominations and Voting

In 1998, the trial law became an official law and was revised to include a clause that ensures a villager nomination process. According to Article 14 of the Organic Law (1998), "candidates shall be directly nominated by villagers." However, the nomination process, which is one measure of election quality, still varies greatly among villages across China. In general, an open nomination process means villagers can freely nominate candidates without town or village party branch interference. That is, election outcomes are uncertain (i.e., not predetermined). The highest-quality election process is one in which villagers nominate the candidates in a village assembly. These are called "open sea" nominations. Lower-quality elections involve a nomination process in which the village party secretary or town officials select or exercise the power to approve the candidates,[12] even if these elections are competitive. In a village where the town official selected the candidates, one villager bemoaned, "Why even bother to vote? The outcome is a foregone conclusion." Nevertheless, a growing number of villages have an "open sea" nomination process, and there has been tremendous progress in the quality of elections since 1998.

These improvements include increasing use of secret voting booths and limited use of proxy votes and roving ballot boxes. Secret balloting is an important aspect of democratic elections, and Article 14 of the Organic Law guarantees access to secret voting booths on election day. In the early rounds of elections, few villages employed secret ballots, but since 1998 most villages have adopted the practice.

Proxy voting allows a single voter to cast a ballot for someone else or even for a few other people. This was an adjustment to the large-scale temporary migration that has led to a large number of people (mostly men) to leave the village to work in the city (see chap. 10). However, this practice can corrupt the electoral process if proxy voters are dishonest in casting the ballots entrusted to them. While the Organic Law does not prohibit the use of proxy votes, several provinces have banned the practice, and new restrictions are now in place, such as limiting the number of proxy votes or requiring written authorization from the absentee voter. According to the *Civil Affairs Statistical Yearbook 2009*, over 18 million or 7 percent of the voters cast a proxy vote.

Roving ballot boxes are exactly what they suggest. On election day, village cadres take a ballot box in hand and go door-to-door to collect votes, instead of having villagers attend an election assembly with secret voting booths. The idea was to accommodate rural residents who live in more remote natural villages and the elderly. But, the potential for stuffing ballot boxes and intimidating voters is obvious. As one villager in Shaanxi complained, "They collect the ballots and count them in secret, then they announce the winners days later. Who knows who really won?"[13] As with proxy voting, provinces are starting to restrict the use of roving ballots.

Village Cadre Accountability and Relations with the Party Secretary

The evidence suggests that elected leaders are more accountable to villagers than to previously appointed cadres. In fact, popular elections have changed the behavior of village cadres. Rather than looking upward to the town authorities in order to secure their position, elected cadres are more responsive to their village constituents. Some studies show that even imperfect elections can curb corrupt behavior and misuse of public funds because villagers can more easily remove elected cadres.[14] Other studies demonstrate that land management decisions of elected leaders reflect villagers' preferences for a fair reallocation.[15]

At times, elected leaders may also place villager preferences over the demand set by town officials. Indeed, a noted researcher on village elections states that "Much to the concern of township authorities, some village heads put the villager's will before that of the township authorities when they have to make a choice."[16] For example, in Ningxia province, an elected village leader refused to collect a townwide irrigation maintenance fee for the town officials because their village had no irrigation. In an interview, the town party secretary bemoaned, "I miss the days when we could just fire the guys who do not listen to us, now we have to wait until the next election."[17] His comment expressed not only his frustration with noncompliant village cadres, but also the hope that he would be able to influence the outcome of the next round of village elections.

Nevertheless, elected village leaders still have to implement policies mandated by higher levels and remain dependent on the town government for investment funds. Furthermore, in order to best serve the village, an elected leader must work well with town authorities. For instance, elected leaders can work with the town officials to help farmers get low-interest loans to build a greenhouse or buy agricultural equipment.

The Organic Law is also changing the relationship between popularly elected village leaders and the appointed (or elected only by CCP members) village party secretary in those cases where one individual does not hold both offices. Of course, party secretaries are also village residents, but their direct constituents are the minority of villagers who are members of the town party branch, even though their authority extends over the whole village.

The role of village party organization is not spelled out in the Organic Law, which leads to imprecise and overlapping areas of jurisdiction between the party secretary and the village leader. The CCP's policy is that the "party manages cadres," and according to Article 3 of the Organic Law (1998), the party organization assumes the core leadership role in the village. Therefore, the party secretary is considered the "number-one hand" in the village, and elected cadres must accept party leadership. Yet, it is well documented that many popularly elected village leaders are acting in the interest of their constituents, even if it means going head-to-head with the party secretary. A number of elected leaders are attempting to create an equal rather than subordinate relationship between the village committee and the party branch.

Villager Representative Assembly

According to Article 21 of the Organic Law, residents may establish a **villager representative assembly (VRA)** to which every five to fifteen households elect one representative (see Figure 9.2). The function of the VRAs is to monitor the work of the village committee. The Organic Law does not provide a list of specific VRA responsibilities, but counties, towns, and even villages can write up documents that detail VRA duties. For example, in some localities, the VRA is in charge of reviewing annual village budgets, investment plans, and implementation of national policies. During VRA meetings, representatives can raise questions about villagewide problems or specific constituent issues.

In some cases, the VRA will challenge a village leader's decision and even make motions to dismiss the leader or village committee members. For example, in Shaanxi province, one VRA led the fight to recall the elected village leader because they believed he misappropriated funds meant to improve and remodel the outdoor toilets for the elementary school. The leader said the accusations were baseless, but he ended up quitting over the "toilet scandal." Finally, the VRA can serve as a deliberative body, participating fully in policy-implementation decisions.

Although there are some reported cases in which VRAs seem to exert significant village authority, many scholars find that VRAs are generally less effective. The main criticism is that the VRAs, like the people's congresses at the town and county levels, are little more than rubber-stamp agencies for party-state policies. One scholar who examined a number of surveys on VRAs concluded that they are "largely ceremonial and not signs of the villager's increased decision-making power."[18] The variation in VRA authority may depend on how well the Organic Law is implemented and whether the town or county officials believe that a strong VRA is necessary. Some town officials view strong VRAs as an efficient mechanism to keep the village committee and elected leader in line, while others may prefer to keep the VRAs weak and ineffective. Nevertheless, whether they are strong or weak, VRAs have become a part of village political life.

Vote Buying and Family Clans

Villages that have an "open sea" nomination process and competitive elections may be free from town government and village party branch interference, but there are also nonparty and nongovernment community forces that can influence local elections and political life more broadly. The two common issues are vote buying and the influence of village family clans (kinship ties).

When town officials or village party secretaries manipulate the election process candidates must curry favor with the officials in order to get elected. In this case, the election outcome is decided by officials, and villagers' votes are not worth buying. However, when the election process is free from official interference, voters determine the outcome. Then the value of the vote increases. Thus candidates who are out to win at any cost will attempt to influence voters, and buying votes is one way to sway the election. The price of a vote can range from 7 RMB (US$1) to 20,000 RMB (US$2,898), and candidates have offered T-shirts, pens, and even household appliances in exchange for votes. Given the fact that village leaders' authority has eroded over the last two decades as the scope of the private economy has widened, why would a candidate spend so much money to be a village leader?

The reason is land. Leasing village land to developers can be hugely profitable for a village leader (see chap. 8) and, in recent years, vote buying has become more directly related to local land management and village leader's authority to lease collective land.[19] In an interview, one village committee member in Shaanxi admitted, "While a candidate may spend a ridiculously large sum of money to get elected, he can easily get the money back after a post-election land deal." Land, which is still managed by local cadres, is a scarce resource in rural China, particularly in areas close to a city. Developers are eager to acquire land for factories, housing developments, shopping malls, golf courses, and other ventures that promise to yield high profits. As the demand increases, so does the leasing price.

Land management is one of the most contentious issues between cadres and villagers. Due to villagers' concerns over land, vote buying can backfire. In one southern village, the incumbent leader offered about 2,000 RMB (about one-third of the average annual per capita rural income at the time) for each vote just before the election. He won. However, soon after the election, villagers discovered that the leader leased portions of the village land to local developers without giving villagers legal compensation. The compensation should have been 7,000 RMB per villager. Upon hearing the news, a group of villagers went to the leader's home and proceeded to beat him. Recognizing the corrupt behavior of the incumbent leader and wanting to ease tensions, town government officials paid the villagers 7,000 RMB each and nullified the election results.[20]

In the wake of post-Mao economic reforms, some areas of rural China have experienced a resurgence in the role of village kinship groups. Kinship groups or family clans can complicate the election process or even highjack village committees. In some villages with two or more competing organized kinship groups, town officials have intentionally appointed one representative of a clan as party secretary and the other as village leader in order to strike a balance. However, an open election process can upset the balance. Moreover, in villages with only one dominant kinship group, elections may just be a formality in which the traditional clan leadership assumes authority over the village committee as well as the party branch. While some reported cases suggest that strong kinship organizations can subvert village elections and the authority of the village committee, it is still unclear how family clans will influence the future development of grassroots democracy at the village level or even possible elections for town government heads. A study of several villages in early 2000s showed that kinship and religious groups were more important than elections in holding local cadres accountable for providing the kinds of public goods, such as paved roads and running water that villagers want and expect from their government.[21] However, as discussed later, rural to urban migration may weaken village close kinship and communal ties with these villages.

WOMEN IN VILLAGE POLITICS

Few women are elected as village committee members and even fewer are village leaders. Women are participating in elections, and in many villages there are more women voters than men. However, the female vote does not translate into more women elected to village committees. As a result, women are left underrepresented and at a political disadvantage in rural China.

Article 9 of the Organic Law states that, "Female members shall take a proper portion in the composition of villager's committees." Yet, the law does not make it clear what the proper portion of women should be on any given village committee. According to the 2016 *China Statistical Yearbook*, 28 percent of elected village committee members nationwide are women, and just over 10 percent of elected village leaders nationwide are female.[22] Even at higher administrative levels, women seem to be hitting a "bamboo ceiling."

Elected female village committee members are usually confined to roles that are considered "women's work" or are just ignored. Women's work includes checking birth quotas and disseminating contraception material, such as condoms and pamphlets on available types of contraception. Indeed, in many cases, the work of female cadres is limited to family-planning duties and not much else. Many elected women feel ineffective and overpowered by the men in the village committee. For example, in an interview, one elected female committee member said that she was proud to be elected, but felt ignored at committee meetings when she demanded more funds to improve family-planning duties. She eventually quit before her three-year term was up.[23] Without adequate representation in the village committee, serious women's issues, such as domestic violence, the high elementary and middle-school dropout rates of girls, and mental health, including the disturbing prevalence of suicide among young rural women are not addressed (see Box 9.1).

Traditional attitudes held by rural men and women prevent females from getting nominated and elected to leading cadre position. Although the economic and political reforms have altered the relationship between male cadres and villagers, political and social relations between men and women remain unequal. At issue is the pervasive belief that politics and public affairs is a man's job. A traditional saying that is still widely repeated in rural China is, "women live inside and men live outside." In many respects, rural China is still a male-dominated society, both politically and culturally. For example, the burden of family planning has fallen on rural women for contraception, sterilization, and most importantly, the pressure to give birth to sons.

TOWN GOVERNMENT

Town Cadres

Town governments are responsible for local economic development, including agricultural and rural industries, and public services such as health, education, family planning, water and land management, and security. Town staff have generally ranged from twenty to eighty officials, depending on the number of villages and villagers under their jurisdiction.

The most politically powerful individuals at the town level are the party secretary, the government head, and their several deputies (see Figure 9.1). For these town cadres, promotion to higher administrative levels depends on fulfilling policy obligations passed down from county government offices, which have, in turn, received them from higher-level provincial authorities. All personnel matters are handled through the *nomenklatura* system of cadre management (see chap. 6), which means that the appointment and promotion of "leading cadres" must be approved by the CCP organization department at the next level up the administrative hierarchy. For example, town officials are managed by the county organization department (see Figure 9.2).

BOX 9.1 SUICIDE AMONG THE RURAL ELDERLY

Early one summer morning in 2014, seventy-four-year-old Xiang Yougyu stepped outside her family home in a remote mountain village and hanged herself from an orange tree just a few feet from the front door.[†] This is not an uncommon event in villages especially for the left-behind elderly in more isolated regions of western and central China. In 2014, the United States suicide rate for older adult over sixty-five was fifteen per 100,000; in China it was thirty-five. While only 9 percent of the population in China is over sixty-five, the elderly make up 38 percent of national suicides. The suicide rates of the rural elderly are the highest, especially among older men over sixty-five.[‡] The most common methods of suicide is the ingestion of pesticides; the second is hanging.

This is a change in the demographics of suicide in China from the 1990s where the suicide rate of rural women (thirty-eight per 100,000) was among the highest in the world. One of the principal reasons for suicidal behavior among young rural women at the time was family conflict and marital problems, such as abusive mothers-in-law or violent husbands. For many rural women with little education or independent sources of income, suicide appeared to be the only way out of a seemingly hopeless situation. Although suicide is still the number one cause of injury mortality for young rural women,[§] improved social conditions and economic opportunities in urban areas have contributed to a steep decline in the suicide rate in that demographic category.[**] Ironically, the economic circumstances that reduced the suicide rate for young women may be contributing to an increase in suicide rate of rural elderly.

There were over 260 million estimated rural to urban migrants by 2017. These migrants tend to be younger adults who leave the village to find work in the cities, but they also leave behind elderly parents. Several studies suggest that rural elderly, who are empty-nesters, tend to have depressive symptoms and prevalence of major depressive episodes.[††] As opposed to urban elderly, older villagers live alone and tend to have less family and social support. In addition, there are fewer medical and mental health resources in the countryside. The suicide rate for rural adults over sixty-five in 2014 was forty per 100,000, which was double the urban rate. The gender difference for the suicide rate among the elderly is forty per 100,000 for men and twenty per 100,000 for women. In the United States, it is thirty for men and five for women.

There are also stark regional differences in the older adult suicide rates across China. In rural central rural the suicide rate per 100,000 for males over sixty-five in 2014 is sixty-seven and it is fifty-three for women.[‡‡] The suicide rates for the elderly are the highest in more remote villages with fewer resources. The rate is much lower in eastern regions where villages tend to be more developed and near urban centers where their adult children live.

The PRC government is aware of this growing problem and there are programs to improve mental health care in the rural areas especially training village and town medical clinics how to identify symptoms of depression in the elderly. This also includes elder care and rural support networks. However, the high suicide rates among rural elderly remains a serious issue that needs greater attention. As one researcher remarked in 2016, "If this was happening among college students, there would be major headlines. The rural elderly truly are China's invisible people."[§§]

[†]Kathleen McLaughlin, "Rural China Is No Country for Old People," *Science*, Apr. 15, 2016, vol. 352, no. 6283: 283.

[‡]Zhong Bao-Liang, Helen FK Chiu, and Yeates Conwell, "Rates and Characteristics of Elderly Suicide in China, 2013–14," *Journal of Affective Disorders* 206 (2016): 273–279.

[§]Lijuan Zhang et al., "Study on the Trend and Disease Burden of Injury Deaths in Chinese Population, 2004–2010," *PLos One*, 9 no. 1 (Jan. 2014): e85319, https://www.ncbi.nlm.nih.gov/pmc/articles/PMC3894968/

*Zhang Jie, Long Sun, Yuxin Liu, and Jianwei Zhang, "The Change in Suicide Rates between 2002 and 2011 in China," *Suicide and Life-threatening Behavior* 44, no. 5 (2014): 560–568.

††Zhou Liang, Guojun Wang, Cunxian Jia, and Zhenyu Ma, "Being Left-behind, Mental Disorder, and Elderly Suicide in Rural China: A Case-control Psychological Autopsy Study," *Psychological Medicine* (2018): 1–7; Wang, Guojun, Mi Hu, Shui-yuan Xiao, and Liang Zhou, "Loneliness and Depression among Rural Empty-nest Elderly Adults in Liuyang, China: A Cross-sectional Study," *BMJ open* 7, no. 10 (2017): e016091.

‡‡Zhong et al.

§§McLaughlin.

Higher authorities at the county levels therefore have a direct influence the behavior of town cadres.[24] In fact, town party secretaries and government heads are generally more responsive to higher officials one administrative level above them, rather than to central government directives or villagers under their authority. The mechanisms that these higher authorities use to control lower-level officials are the **one-level-down management system** and the **cadre exchange system**. In the one-level-down management system, officials at each level have the authority to appoint their own subordinates. For example, the head of a county government can appoint the head of the town government without seeking approval from higher authorities at the municipal or provincial levels; the same is true of party secretaries at the county and town levels. The implication of this system is that promotion or reassignment depends on the ability of the subordinate to carry out policies of his or her immediate superior. This can create highly personalized politics whereby the decision of the county officials can have direct influence on a town cadre's career.

In the cadre exchange system, leading town cadres are transferred to a different locality every three to six years. Cadre exchange does not apply to the average town bureaucrats, only to leading cadres, such as the party secretary and the town head. By limiting leading cadres to a short fixed term of office, this system is meant to prevent cadres from developing local networks that might dilute their allegiance to higher-level authorities or provide opportunities for corruption. The cadre exchange system can have a strong influence on a leading cadre's direction of accountability. For instance, if a town party secretary or government head does not fulfill his or her policy obligations to the county government after a fixed time, he or she may receive a lateral transfer to another town rather than be promoted. On the other hand, leading town cadres who successfully complete their policy obligations may be promoted to the county government. Under this system, the direction of accountability leads upward to the individual cadre one administrative level above, rather than downward toward villagers.

This combination of the one-level-down management and the cadre exchange system ensures tight control over immediate subordinates, which leads to selective policy implementation.[25] Subordinates selectively implement the policies that enhance their career opportunities, while ignoring policies that have little influence over their prospects for promotion or transfer. This partly explains the variation in local policy implementation in rural China, especially with political reforms such as village elections.

Direct Election of Town Leaders: The Next Step?

Although direct, competitive elections have become commonplace at the village level in China, party-state leaders have been much more cautious in extending such democratic practices to the next level of rural administration, the town. People's congresses at the town level are directly elected, but not the town head or other leaders. They are still mostly appointed from above (see Figure 9.2). During the National Party Congress in late 1997, the then PRC president and CCP general secretary Jiang Zemin pledged to "extend the scope of democracy at the grassroots level." This was viewed by many as an official nod to expand the direct elections for village leaders to the town level.

The first push for a more inclusive selection process for town government heads came from party leaders in Shizhong district, part of a municipality in Sichuan province.[26] The leading reformer was a female party secretary of Shizhong district, Zhang Jinming. The Shizhong party committee was having problems with town government heads, and saw more open elections as a way to improve relations between villagers and town officials.

One particularly troubled spot was Baoshi town, where the government head was dismissed for embezzling public funds. Moreover, the local economy was stagnant. Shizhong officials knew that villagers were growing dissatisfied, and the local leadership was losing political legitimacy. In an attempt to regain public confidence, the Shizhong party and government leaders, led by Zhang Jinming, implemented a breakthrough political reform in Baoshi town. They adopted a new system known as **open recommendation and selection** of town leaders in May 1998.

The process began with an objective written civil service exam for all aspirants to town offices. Then the district CCP organizational department screened potential nominees who passed the exam. The second stage was a limited vote to select the final nominees. This was not a direct election in the sense that all eligible voters in the town and villages cast ballots. But it did provide greater representation than purely indirect elections by allowing town-level people's congress deputies, village leaders and party secretaries, and village small-group leaders to vote. The balloting, vote count, and announcement of the winners occurred on the same day. Once candidates were chosen, townspeople's congress deputies voted for the town government head and other leading cadres, in accordance with the constitution.

In response to positive comments about the Baoshi elections from both central leaders and villagers, the Shizhong party and government leaders decided to move forward with direct elections for the government head of Buyun town. The combination of cues from the central leadership and villager demands from below convinced Shizhong leaders that the time was right to hold direct elections for town heads.

On December 30, 1998, residents of villages in Buyun town went to the polls to elect the head of the town government. This was the first publicized direct election for town government head in China, and it attracted considerable domestic and international media attention because such positions had previously always been appointed and subject to approval by the CCP organization department.

However, the central and provincial governments swiftly put an end to the **Buyun experiment** with town-level democracy. They denounced the direct election of town heads as unconstitutional, but their political reason behind their alarm was because such elections reduced the authority of county party leaders to manage town cadres. In 2001, the CCP Central Committee issued Document Number 12, which officially put the development of direct elections for town leading officials on hold. The document stated that direct elections for town heads, "does not accord with the constitution and the Organic Law of People's Congress and Local Governments."

According to Article 9 of the Organic Law of Local People's Congresses and Local People's Governments and Article 101 of the state constitution, the townspeople's congress deputies elect the town government head and deputy heads. The county party committee has strict control over the selection of candidates for these positions. Town government heads and party secretaries are leading cadres, and they are managed through the county CCP organizational department. Typically, the selection of candidates via the *nomenklatura* system (see chap. 6) occurs behind closed doors and only includes top party leaders in the county.

Town People's Congresses

Although town government heads are not directly elected, deputies to town people's congresses are chosen by all the voters in the area. Elected representatives to the local congress serve a three-year term. According to the Electoral Law of the People's Republic of China on the National People's Congress and the Local People's Congresses, the minimum number of deputies to a town people's congress is 40 and the maximum is 130.

Town people's congresses convene at least once a year for two or three days to approve policy initiatives put forward by the town government and ratify the budget. They are also responsible for approving government decisions regarding matters such as education, economic development and public health. Between meetings, people's congress deputies may also meet individually with town officials to discuss issues of concern to their constituents. Despite the formidable powers and functions described on paper, town congresses still play a minor role in shaping and affecting government decisions.

THE IMPACT OF MIGRATION ON CHINA'S VILLAGES

The massive rural to urban migration in recent decades has had a significant influence on the rural governance and social life in China. The outflow began in the early 1980s as a result of decollectivization and the relaxation of the household registration system that had severely restricted population movement for most of the Mao era. In 1982 there were about 6.5 million rural to urban migrants.[27] By the end of 2017 that number had reached 286.5 million.[28] Although they are often referred to as the "floating population," most recent waves of migrants are not "floating" from the villages to the cities in search of jobs but are moving to particular urban employment opportunities introduced to them by other migrants from their village.[29] This is an important distinction because when one migrant worker returns to the village with an urban job opportunity, then a number of people from the same village tend to leave at the same time.

While both adult men and women migrate out of the village, most rural migrants tend to be male. Migrating out of the village is a difficult choice for adult family members especially when they may be separated from their children and other relatives for months or even years at a time. As a result, many villages in China are "hollowed out" with only women, children, and the elderly left behind. The alarmingly high suicide rates among older adults in rural China is a reflection of this trend (see Box 9.1). In some villages, a large number of working-age women have also left for the cities, leaving a greater proportion of middle-aged and elderly women in villages compared to twenty years ago. There are an estimated 60 million "left-behind children" in rural China whose parents have left for the cities and who are now cared for by relatives—often the grandparents. The education of these children often suffers, and concern has been expressed about their psychological development and emotional well-being.[30]

Male outmigration can have a significant influence on the women left behind. The additional burden these women take on are sometimes called the "three big mountains" the mountains referring to taking care of the farm, the elderly, and their own children.[31] These women have to deal with the physical and emotional hardships of an absent husband while managing those "three big mountains."

Furthermore, although women have taken on greater household and farm responsibilities, they have not increased their representation on elected village committees. As noted earlier, the percentage of women on village committees is about 28 percent. Although there are laws and policies that aim to increase women's grassroots participation and representation, village cadres including those in the party branch , remain male dominated even when many or most of the males have migrated out of the village.[32]

Some villagers are left behind because their families have no other choice due to economic constraints, while others decide to stay in the countryside because they have viable economic opportunities in the area.[33] Villagers may work in rural industries that can boost rural incomes without leaving the countryside. Others are engaged in more profitable agriculture production, such as orchards and greenhouses, and selling the cash crops at local, regional, and even national markets. Animal husbandry, such as raising pigs, chickens, and cattle, can be lucrative rural businesses for villagers who choose to stay in the countryside. These villages are not "hollowed out." Indeed, within a single village there may be those who have migrated (still technically residents), left-behind women, elderly, and children, as well as those who choose to stay.

Rural to urban migration can also influence social services in the villages. Many agricultural communities have kinship networks or communal assistance among neighbors. Early in the reform period (1980s and 1990s), these informal networks were important for local governance and social support. However, as rural to urban migration increased, many of these tight informal village networks have deteriorated and villages have become more atomized. As a result, villages with greater proportion of outmigration tend to rely more on formal institutions for social support and services such as mediation, elderly care, and rural health insurance.[34] However, this also places greater pressure on village committees and town governments to provide social services, and in some poorer regions the villagers left behind have both reduced social networks and minimal public services to rely on.

RURAL UNREST AND RIGHTFUL RESISTANCE

Since the 1990s, researchers and journalists have closely followed reports of mounting unrest in rural China. In July 2005, the Minister of Public Security, Zhou Yongkang, said that incidences of social disturbances, such as riots and demonstrations, which are referred to as "mass incidents" (*quntixing shijian*) in China, had risen from 58,000 in 2003 to 74,000 in 2004, many of which occur in the countryside.[35] A Chinese sociologist estimated that there were more than 180,000 mass incidents in 2010.[36] There have not been any official or academic estimates of the total number of such protests since then because the party-state has decided that such information should not be made public at a time when there is a strong emphasis on "stability maintenance" (see chap. 6). Indeed, in August 2017, an activist blogger, Lu Yuyu, who had been documenting mass incidents online, was sentenced to four years in prison for "picking quarrels and provoking trouble."[37]

The large number of mass incidents might suggest that protest and discontent may put support for the CCP at risk. However, rural unrest and villagers' disapproval is directed toward village cadres or town officials, not toward the national government of the CCP; many demonstrations that end in violent clashes between villagers and the local police began as legitimate claims against local governments and then escalated into riots. So far, rural unrest does not threaten the central leadership.

Rightful Resisters

Some villagers appeal to the central government and invoke national laws when they seek redress for abuses by local cadres. This type of protest, in which villagers claim that local officials are breaking the law, is called **rightful resistance**.[38] Rightful resisters believe that the legal system and the national leadership are on their side. The central government usually permits this kind of protest, but some rightful resistance pushes the legal limits and sometimes goes beyond. While many resisters take to the streets to press their claims, others use the courts to sue local officials and government agencies to protect their interests.

Rightful resisters tend to be well informed about specific national policies or laws when they take action. The most prevalent sources of such information are watching television news, listening to the radio, and reading newspapers and magazines. The central government also provides large print, easy-to-read legal pamphlets for specific laws, such as Organic Law of Villager Committees. These can be bought at most bookstores in smaller cities such as county seats. The great increase in rural to urban migration has also contributed to the flow of information.

Sometimes villager activists stumble across a copy of a law. In one case from Hebei province, a villager activist, who went to the town government office to lodge a complaint against a village cadre, noticed a copy of the Organic Law. After reading the law and sharing the information with other villagers, he lodged a complaint against the town government for failing to allow democratic elections.[39] Thus resisters not only obtain information, but they make the crucial connection between the published law and administrative misconduct.

Rightful resisters use their knowledge about specific laws and local officials' unlawful activity to inform the village community and grab the attention of higher authorities. They may take advantage of a public event such as a Spring Festival gathering or a public performance at a village fair. Sometimes, resisters will literally use a soapbox and loud speakers at rural markets to denounce illegal actions of local officials. In order to gain a wider audience, village activists may work with local or even national journalists to publicize their discovery of official misdeeds.

The central party-state tolerates rightful resisters because they provide information about local corruption and illegal administrative acts. Corruption reflects uneven implementation of laws and weakened political capacity of the central leadership to control officials at the county and town governments. The national leadership cannot monitor all midlevel officials all the time; rightful resisters act as fire alarms so that higher authorities can identify misconduct. Still, while national leaders allow village activists to point out fires, they do not tolerate rightful resisters putting them out.

There are several legal and semilegal modes of resistance that activists can employ. These include petitions, lawsuits, noncompliance, and demonstrations. While many reports from the Western media about rural unrest focus on relatively large demonstrations that result in violent clashes with local police, most acts of rural resistance take place within the legal system.

Legal Modes of Resistance

The most common mode of legal resistance is petitioning higher authorities. This involves visiting a county government office (or an office at a higher level) to submit a letter of complaint against a local cadre or organization, such as the town government or village committee. The reasons for petitioning range from complaints about exorbitant elementary school fees and excessive irrigation charges to cadres who beat and extort villagers.

Many counties and municipalities have Letters and Visits Offices where villagers can officially lodge a complaint. Rather than going through the formal court system, petitioners are seeking official mediation through the Letters and Visits Offices to resolve issues involving local cadre abuse. Successful mediation occurs when the higher officials directly address the complaint and confront local cadres to resolve the problem. However, sometimes mediators do not mediate. Villagers and small delegations can "languish for weeks waiting for an appointment with leaders who never emerge."[40] Other unsuccessful attempts at mediation include complaints being treated politely at the office, then ignored once the petitioners return home, or authorities making decisions that are not enforced.

Individuals and even whole villages can register a specific grievance to these offices. The State Council's Regulation Concerning Letters and Visits (1995, revised 2005) allow citizens to petition as a group, but the number of representatives a group can send to the office is limited to five people. If an individual or group is dissatisfied with the ruling of the mediation at the municipal level, they can take their case to higher levels. The highest level is the Letters and Visits Office in Beijing, and a large number of citizens have taken their grievances all the way to the top. In fact, there are "petitioner's camps" where individuals or group representatives wait to be heard.

While petitioning is the most common form of legal resistance, it can be costly for villagers in term of money and their physical well-being. For many villagers, it is time-consuming and expensive to travel to the Letters and Visits offices, especially when the waiting period before one can be seen may take days or weeks. Back in the village, petitioners may be faced with threats of violence from village cadres or town officials. Consequently rightful resisters take a huge risk to get higher authorities to hear their grievances. Nevertheless, millions of petitions are received nationwide each year by Letters and Visits Offices at the county level or above. In 2005, the 1995 State Council Regulation Concerning Letters and Visits was revised to include a clause that forbids any individual or organization from retaliating against petitioners.

Another form of rightful resistance is lawsuits filed against local officials or government offices. The Administrative Procedure Law (APL) allows citizens to sue local governments for unlawful acts such as the misuse of public funds (see chap. 7). However, the law does not allow citizens to sue any party committee or party secretary. (The party has its own Central Commission for Discipline Inspection, which is charged with investigating wrongdoing by party members or organizations. See chap. 6.) Although most cases do not result in full compensation, the number of citizens using the APL to sue local officials continues to increase. In 2006, Chinese courts accepted 95,617 new administrative cases that citizens brought against government officials. In 2016, there were 225,485 cases.[41]

However, getting a case accepted by the higher courts can take time. In 2008, a fish farmer named Feng Jun from Langfang, Hebei, sued the county government's environmental agency for dereliction of duty by allowing two chemical plants to operate near his village without any environmental protection report or evaluation. In 2006, his sixteen-year-old daughter was diagnosed with cancer, and she died in 2007. That same year his twelve-year-old daughter was also diagnosed with cancer and is still being treated. His 2008 case was rejected by the county court, but Feng continued to make his case and in 2017, the municipal (intermediate) court accepted his case and his ligation moved forward.[42]

Semi-Legal and Illegal Modes of Resistance

Noncompliance is one mode of resistance that can easily go beyond the accepted limits of the law. For example, the 1993 Agricultural Law grants villagers the right to refuse to pay illegal fees. Legal fees and taxes before 2002 were authorized and posted by the town people's congresses. Any fees that are not sanctioned by the local people's congress are considered illegal, and villagers have the right to refuse payment of these illegal fees. However, villagers are not allowed to actively resist fee collectors; they are supposed to leave resolution of their complaints to the government. And they are still obligated to pay sanctioned taxes and fees. Nevertheless, some villagers invoked the law to justify "tax strikes" where they refused to pay any taxes or fees until illegal fees were eliminated in the early 2000s. In this case, villagers' use of the 1993 Agricultural Law went beyond the legal limits in order to stop cadres' illegal actions. However, these tax strikes were not without consequence. In some cases, village cadres tried to negotiate with the resistant villagers. Cadres sometimes went door-to-door to cajole villagers to pay or forcibly took items from the home, such as television sets and even beds, as payment. There were also incidents that ended in violent clashes with police.

Villager demonstrations and violent unrest are often the result of failed legal attempts to resolve grievances. In 2004, a prominent researcher for the PRC State Council made a clear connection between petitions and unrest: "villagers start by lodging complaints at the county level or higher, and doing so at the province or in Beijing is also fairly common. If the petition fails, they often turn to 'direct' resistance." On paper, demonstrations are legal. Article 35 of the PRC constitution grants Chinese citizens "freedom of speech, of the press, of assembly, of association, of procession and of demonstration." However, the October 1989 Law on Assembly, Procession, and Demonstration (promulgated in the aftermath of the Tiananmen protests) requires that all citizens who wish to demonstrate must first obtain police approval in advance. Of course, even in the United States, large demonstrations require a permit. But, in China, local police rarely grant these permits. Therefore, many of the demonstrations, road blocks, or sit-ins that begin as peaceful are broken up by police, and these confrontations between protesters and police can become violent.

Land Grabs and Local Resistance

Some of the most violent protests have been over local government land acquisitions.[43] One of the most famous cases occurred in 2011 when rural residents at Wukan village in Guangdong Province staged a villagewide protest against the local village leaders who misappropriated village land.[44] Several protest leaders filed complaints against the village leaders for selling village land without proper compensation to the residents. To stop the complaints, local police arrested several of the villagers. One of them died while in police custody and this sparked a villagewide protest involving more than 20,000 villagers. Protesters overran local government offices, and hundreds of township and county police responded with by firing tear gas and water cannons. The clash ended with police cordoning off the village and not allowing supplies to enter the area for days. The standoff ended with provincial leaders pressuring the county and town government to peacefully resolve the crisis. The protest leader, Lin Zuluan, was appointed party secretary of the village, replacing the one who had held the position for forty-two years. New village committee elections were held, and Lin was also chosen as village head. Wukan became known as China's "democracy village."

But in September 2016, Lin was arrested after complaining about continuing land grabs by a real estate development in cahoots with the county government. He was convicted of taking bribes and kickbacks and sentenced to about three years in prison as well as being given a heavy fine. When villagers protested Lin's conviction, the authorities cracked down, arresting nine vocal participants who were then sentenced to two to ten years in prison for disrupting public order, staging illegal demonstrations, disturbing traffic and intentionally spreading false information. The village was also put under tight security and pervasive surveillance.

Successful protests against land grabs require resources and competent leadership. In 2016, another village, Xialongtan, in Guangdong Province, not far from Wukan, also staged a protest against an illegal land grab. Although the severity of the corruption and scope of the land grab was similar to Wukan, Xialongtan did not receive the same media attention. A hotel was built on village land, and two other development projects were started without consulting villagers. The village leadership leased the land for 200 million yuan (over 30 million dollars) without villager compensation. Xialongtan villagers have staged several protests, but they have had little success in gaining the attention of higher authorities or the media. As one resident said, "Unlike Wukan, we've got neither financial nor competent people to lead the way."[45]

Some protests over land grabs can also become deadly. In October 2014, a clash between villagers and construction workers from a development project resulted in eight deaths: four construction workers and four villagers. Fuyou village is outside Kunming, the capital of Yunnan province, and the village leaders together with several town officials leased Fuyou land to a developer without consulting the village community. In the summer months, villagers complained to the village leader and town government that the construction site was flooding their fields ruining their crops. However, the local leaders ignored their pleas. On the morning of October 14, the villagers blocked the village entrances and barred the construction crew from entering the village and the development site. The workers soon returned with batons, shields, and anti-riot gear. The villagers responded welding farm tools and homemade gasoline bombs. By the end of the day eight were dead. In the aftermath, the provincial government arrested seventeen village and town officials for corruption as well as several village protest-leaders.[46]

These examples of protest against land grabs and demonstrations paint a picture of widespread rural discontent, but the vast majority of villagers do not protest. Most land acquisitions are mediated and local grievances tend to resolved within the village or town through villager committees or local police.

Why aren't more villagers protesting? One reason may be fear. Another may be poverty. The economic and physical costs of resistance can be high. However, even if villagers do not take to the streets, they still have a strong sense of justice and an expectation of fairness. Another possible explanation is that most disputes are being resolved at the village level. For instance, if village elections are making elected leaders more accountable to villagers, then there may be greater transparency in village financial accounts and a relatively fair management of collective land. This means that political reforms in China's countryside are helping to maintain social stability, which is one major reason they were implemented by the central government in the first place.

THE FUTURE OF POLITICAL REFORM IN RURAL CHINA

Political reform in rural China has made significant progress since the 1980s, but it is still unclear whether the current reforms are enough to deal with villagers' expectations for fairness and growing demands for greater participation in the local decision-making process. Village elections have been a relative success, but they may also contribute to rising demands for direct elections at the town level. This success has even emboldened some reform-minded mid-level officials at the county and municipal levels to introduce semidirect elections of town government heads. Nevertheless, uneven implementation and the resulting rural unrest still pose serious problems for the CCP.

Soon after the 19th National Party Congress in 2017, CCP General Secretary Xi Jinping stressed the need for deeper political reform and greater social stability. However, this was not the first time a national leader has called for political liberalization at the local level. Jiang Zemin did so in 1997, and in his political report at the 17th National Party Congress in October 2007, CCP General Secretary Hu Jintao said, "We need to improve institutions for democracy, diversify its forms and expand its channels, and we need to carry out democratic elections, decision-making, administration and oversight in accordance with the law to guarantee the people's rights to be informed, to participate, to be heard, and to oversee."[47] As Jiang Zemin's and Hu Jintao's statements spurred reformers in 1997 and 2007, it is possible that reformers working at the municipal and county levels may look for democratic cues from Xi Jinping as encouragement to move forward with their efforts to democratize rural politics, for example, trying again to win approval for the direct election of local government heads. In recent years, more rural activists have also taken advantage of the legal opportunity for self-nomination in local people's congress elections, and a number have actually won seats. Nevertheless, the continuing dominant role of the cadre management system and the authority of the party secretary over town government heads and the local people's congresses stand in the way of further democratization and accountability.

Therefore, the question remains whether the gradual introduction of reforms is enough to satisfy rural political demands before the incidents of rural unrest become unmanageable for the central government. The relative success of the limited reforms suggests that the central leadership has adapted to some of the growing demands from the rural population for a greater voice in governance. But the pace and depth of political change in rural China will have to speed up if the CCP is to maintain political legitimacy and social stability in the countryside.

NOTES

1. Organic Law of the Villagers Committees of the People's Republic of China, http://www.npc.gov.cn/englishnpc/Law/2007-12/11/content_1383542.htm.

2. *China Statistical Yearbook 2017* (Beijing: National Bureau of Statistics of China), http://www.stats.gov.cn/tjsj/ndsj/2017/indexeh.htm. Of the 152 prefectural level cities with more than a population over a million, thirteen have four or more million, forty-three have two to four million, and ninety-six are in the one to two million range.

3. Christian Sorace, *Shaken Authority: China's Communist Party and the 2008 Sichuan Earthquake* (Ithaca, NY: Cornell University Press, 2017).

4. See 2011 Civil Affairs Work Report, PRC Ministry of Civil Affairs, http://www.mca.gov.cn/article/gk/mzgzbg/201507/20150715848397.shtml

5. See Thomas Bernstein and Xiaobo Lü, *Taxation Without Representation in Contemporary Rural China* (New York: Cambridge University Press, 2003).

6. Ray Yep, "Can 'Tax-for-Fee' Reform Reduce Rural Tension in China? The Process, Progress, and Limitations," *China Quarterly* 177 (Mar. 2004): 42–70.

7. 2016 Statistical Report on Social Services Development, PRC Ministry of Civil Affairs, http://www.mca.gov.cn/article/sj/tjgb/201708/20170815005382.shtml

8. Kevin J. O'Brien and Lianjiang Li, "Accommodating 'Democracy' in a One-Party State: Introducing Village Elections in China," *China Quarterly* 162 (June 2000): 465.

9. According to the *1986 China Statistical Yearbook*, the number of village committees was 940,617. By 2013 the number has decreased to 640,000 (see O'Brien and Li Lianjiang, "Selective Policy Implementation in Rural China"). This was due to urbanization and to administrative changes such as combining villages and changes from townships to towns and towns to counties.

10. O'Brien and Li, "Accommodating 'Democracy.'".

11. *2016 Statistical Report on Social Services Development.*

12. John J. Kennedy, "The Face of 'Grassroots Democracy': The Substantive Difference between Real and Cosmetic Elections in Rural China," *Asian Survey* 42, no. 3 (May–June 2002).

13. Author interview, Mar. 2001.

14. Loren Brandt and Matthew A. Turner, "The Usefulness of Imperfect Elections: The Case of Village Elections in Rural China," *Economics and Politics* 19, no. 3 (Nov. 2007): 453–479.

15. John J. Kennedy, Scott Rozelle, and Yaojiang Shi, "Elected Leaders and Collective Land: Farmers' Evaluation of Village Leader's Performance in Rural China," *Journal of Chinese Political Science* 9, no. 1 (Spring 2004).

16. Baogang He, *Rural Democracy in China: The Role of Village Elections* (New York: Palgrave Macmillan, 2007), 110.

17. Author interview, Mar. 2001.

18. Björn Alpermann, "The Post-Election Administration of Chinese Villages," *China Journal* 46 (July 2001): 45–67. See also Sylvia Chan, "Villagers' Representative Assemblies: Towards Democracy or Centralism?," *China: An International Journal* 1, no. 2 (Sept. 2003): 179–199.

19. Zhao Tan, "Vote Buying and Land Takings in China's Village Elections," *Journal of Contemporary China* 27, no. 110 (2017): 277–294.

20. Minnie Chan, "Local Polls Put off after Corruption Charges," *South China Morning Post*, June 7, 2008, http://archive.scmcom/results.php.

21. Lily T. Tsai, *Accountability without Democracy: Solidary Groups and Public Goods Provision in Rural China* (New York: Cambridge University Press, 2007).

22. *2016 China Statistical Yearbook* (Beijing: National Bureau of Statistics of China, 2016).

23. He, *Rural Democracy in China*, 129. See also Tamara Jacka, "Increasing Women's Participation in Village Government in China," *Critical Asian Studies* 40, no. 4 (2008): 499–529.

24. Kevin J. O'Brien and Lianjiang Li, "Selective Policy Implementation in Rural China," *Comparative Politics* 31, no. 2 (Jan. 1999): 167; Maria Edin, "State Capacity and Local Agents Control in China: CCP Cadre Management from a Township Perspective," *China Quarterly* 173 (Mar. 2003): 35–52.

25. O'Brien and Li, "Selective Policy Implementation in Rural China."

26. Li Lianjiang, "The Politics of Introducing Direct Township Elections in China," *China Quarterly* 171 (Dec. 2002): 704–723.

27. Lu, M., and Y. Xia, "Migration in the People's Republic of China. ADBI Working Paper (2013) 593." Tokyo: Asian Development Bank Institute, 2016. https://www.adb.org/publications/migration-people-republic-china/

28. "Number of Chinese Rural Migrant Workers Reaches 286.5 million," *People's Daily Online*, Apr. 28, 2018, http://en.people.cn/n3/2018/0428/c90000-9455034.html.

29. Scott Rozelle, Li Guo, Minggao Shen, Amelia Hughart, and John Giles, "Leaving China's Farms: Survey Results of New Paths and Remaining Hurdles to Rural Migration." *China Quarterly* 158 (June 1999): 367–393; Zhao Yaohui. "The Role of Migrant Networks in Labor Migration: The Case of China," *Contemporary Economic Policy* 21, no. 4 (Oct. 2008): 500–511.

30. See Lijia Zhang, "One of 60 Million: Life as a 'Left-behind' Child in China," *South China Morning Post*, Jan. 21, 2018, http://www.scmp.com/week-asia/society/article/2128700/one-60-million-life-left-behind-child-china

31. Jingzhong Ye, Huifang Wu, Jing Rao, Baoyin Ding, and Keyun Zhang, "Left-behind Women: Gender Exclusion and Inequality in Rural-Urban Migration in China." *Journal of Peasant Studies* 43, no. 4 (2016): 910–941.

32. Zeng Benxiang, "Women's Political Participation in China: Improved or Not?," *Journal of International Women's Studies* 15, no. 1 (Jan. 2014): 136.

33. Jingzhong Ye, "Stayers in China's "hollowed-out" Villages: A Counternarrative on Massive Rural-Urban Migration," *Population, Space and Place* 24, no. 4 (May 2018): e2128.

34. For further explanation regarding how out migration can influence village governance see Lu, Jie, *Varieties of Governance in China: Migration and Institutional Change in Chinese Villages* (New York: Oxford University Press 2014).

35. "Ministry of Public Security Reports Rise in Public Order Disturbances in 2005," Congressional-Executive Commission on China, Jan. 30, 2006, https://www.cecc.gov/publications/commission-analysis/ministry-of-public-security-reports-rise-in-public-order

36. Tom Orlick, "Unrest Grows as Economy Booms," *Wall Street Journal*, Sept. 26, 2011, https://www.wsj.com/articles/SB10001424053111903703604576587070600504108; Alan Taylor, "Rising Protests in China," *Atlantic*, Feb. 17, 2012, https://www.theatlantic.com/photo/2012/02/rising-protests-in-china/100247/.

37. Austin Ramzy, "Chinese Court Sentences Activist Who Documented Protests to 4 Years in Prison," *New York Times*, Aug. 4, 2017, https://www.nytimes.com/2017/08/04/world/asia/china-blogger-lu-yuyu-prison-sentence-protests-picking-quarrels.html. For a detailed account of the activities of Lu Yuyu and his girlfriend, Li Tingyu, see Wu Qiang, "What Do Lu Yuyu's Statistics of Protest Tell Us About the Chinese Society Today?," *ChinaChange*, July 6, 2016, https://chinachange.org/2016/07/06/the-man-who-keeps-tally-of-protests-in-china/

38. Kevin O'Brien and Lianjiang Li, *Rightful Resistance in Rural China* (Cambridge: Cambridge University Press, 2006); Kevin O'Brien, "Rightful Resistance Reconsidered," *Journal of Peasant Studies*, 40, no. 6 (2013): 1051–1062.

39. O'Brien and Li, *Rightful Resistance in Rural China*, 39.

40. O'Brien and Li, *Rightful Resistance in Rural China*, 81.

41. Cheng Hu, "The Development of Administrative Litigation and State Compensation," in *The China Legal Development Yearbook*, ed. Lin Li and Yuwen W. Li, vol. 2 (Leiden: Brill, 2009): 2011; "In 2016, Chinese Courts Handle 225,485 Administrative Cases," *China Daily*, Dec. 21, 2017, https://www.chinadailyhk.com/articles/3/96/213/1513844879532.html

42. Yuan Suwen and Li Rongde, "Fish Farmer From 'Cancer Village' Seeks Landmark Ruling Over Dead Daughter," *Caixin Magazine*, Apr. 18, 2017; https://www.caixinglobal.com/2017-04-18/101079896.html. For an informative and entertaining depiction of one young rural woman's efforts to take legal action against a village cadre for injuring her husband, see the 1992 Chinese film *Qiu Ju Goes to Court* (or *The Story of Qiu Ju*). See also Jerome Alan Cohen and Joan Lepold Cohen, "Did Qiu Jiu Get Good Legal Advice?" in *Cinema, Law and State in Asia*, ed. Corey K. Creekmur and Mark Sidel (New York: Palgrave Macmillan, 2007), 161–174.

43. Sally Sargenson, "Violence as Development: Land Expropriation and China's Urbanization," *Journal of Peasant Studies*, vol. 40, no. 6 (2013): 1063–1085.

44. See "Wukan: China's Democracy Experiment," a six-part video series on *Al Jazeera*, Apr. 2017, https://www.aljazeera.com/programmes/specialseries/2017/04/wukan-china-democracy-experiment-170403074626458.html. For a compilation of *South China Morning Post* articles about the Wukan protests from 2011 to 2017, see https://www.scmp.com/topics/wukan

45. Choi Chi-yuk, "Neighbors of Chinese Village Protesting over Land Grabs Are Involved in Similar Disputes" *South China Morning Post*, June 22, 2016, http://www.scmp.com/news/china/policies-politics/article/1978993/neighbours-chinese-village-protesting-over-land-grabs

46. "China 'punishes 17 officials' after deadly village clash," *BBC*, Oct. 24, 2014; "Arrested Over Deadly Land Clash in Yunnan" *China Digital Times*, https://chinadigitaltimes.net/2014/10/21-arrested-deadly-land-clash-yunnan/

47. "Hu Jintao's Report at 17th Party Congress," *China Daily*, Oct. 25, 2007, http://www.chinadaily.com.cn/china/2007–10/25/content_6204667_6.htm.

SUGGESTED READINGS

Chan, Anita, Richard Madsen, and Jonathan Unger. *Chen Village: Revolution to Globalization*, 3rd ed. Berkeley: University of California Press, 2009.

Chen, Xi. *Social Protest and Contentious Authoritarianism in China*. Cambridge: Cambridge University Press, 2012.

Friedman, Edward, Paul G. Pickowicz, and Mark Selden. *Revolution, Resistance, and Reform in Village China*. New Haven, CT: Yale University Press, 2006.

Gao, Mobo C. F. *Gao Village: Rural Life in Modern China*. Honolulu: University of Hawaii Press, 2007.

Gao, Mobo C. F. *Gao Village Revisited: Whither Rural China*. Hong Kong: Chinese University Press, 2018.

Goldman, Merle, and Elizabeth J. Perry, eds. *Grassroots Political Reform in Contemporary China*. Cambridge, MA: Harvard University Press, 2007.

Jacka, Tamara. *Rural Women in Urban China: Gender, Migration, and Social Change*. New York: Routledge, 2014.

Landry, Pierre. *Decentralized Authoritarianism in China: The Communist Party's Control of Local Elites in the Post-Mao Era*. New York: Cambridge University Press, 2008.

Lu, Jie. *Varieties of Governance in China: Migration and Institutional Change in Chinese Villages*. New York: Oxford University Press, 2014.

O'Brien, Kevin J., and Lianjiang Li. *Rightful Resistance in Rural China*. Cambridge: Cambridge University Press, 2006.

Oi, Jean, and Steven Goldstein. *Zouping Revisited: Adaptive Governance in a Chinese County*. Stanford, CA: Stanford University Press, 2018.

Sargeson, Sally. "Grounds for Self-government? Changes in Land Ownership and Democratic Participation in Chinese Communities." *Journal of Peasant Studies* 45 no. 2 (2018): 321–346.

Schubert, Gunter, and Anna Ahlers. *Participation and Empowerment at the Grassroots: Chinese Village Elections in Perspective*. Lanham, MD: Lexington Books, 2012.

Takeuchi, Hiroki. *Tax Reform in Rural China: Revenue, Resistance and Authoritarian Rule*. New York: Cambridge University Press, 2014

Wang, Juan. *Sinews of State Power: The Rise and Demise of the Cohesive Local State in Rural China*. New York: Oxford University Press, 2017.

Yan Yunxiang. *Private Life under Socialism: Love, Intimacy, and Family Change in a Chinese Village, 1949–1999*. Stanford, CA: Stanford University Press, 2003.

Emily T. Yeh, Kevin O'Brien, and Jingzhong Ye, "Rural Politics in Contemporary China," special issue, *Journal of Peasant Studies* 40, no. 6 (2013).

10

Urban China: Changes and Challenges

WILLIAM HURST AND CHRISTIAN SORACE

China has long been the world's largest agrarian society, yet it also has the largest urban population in the world, and more than twice as many people live in its cities than in the entire United States. China is also, in terms of the number of people moving into cities, the world's most rapidly urbanizing country. In the late 1970s, less than 20 percent of Chinese citizens lived in urban areas; by 2018, well over half did.

This chapter will focus on: (1) the historical background and contemporary context of Chinese cities; (2) reform of urban administration in the post-Mao era; (3) urban governance; (4) rural-to-urban migration and the shifting boundaries between urban and rural China; (5) reform of the state-owned economy and the massive unemployment it has caused; (6) the rising middle class; (7) the changing lives of urban university students; (8) challenges for China's cities including pollution, inequality, and urban planning; and (9) the likely dynamics and trajectories of future reform.

BACKGROUND AND CONTEXT

Chinese cities have been among the biggest in the world since the time of the Han Dynasty (206 BCE–220 CE) and Roman Empire (27 BCE–476 CE), and several cities in China were larger than almost any in Europe during the Middle Ages. During the Qing Dynasty (1644–1911), China experienced unprecedented urbanization, producing a number of "megacities" to rival the industrial hubs of Western Europe and North America. Despite massive damage and destruction from World War II and the Chinese civil war, China's urban centers recovered quickly after 1949. Today, thirty seven of the world's one hundred largest cities are in China.

Though most Chinese cities were traditionally not especially well-planned and extremely crowded, the Chinese Communist Party (CCP) imposed its particular brand of order on them after 1949.[1] There were three key elements of the CCP's early program for urban areas: the reorganization of housing and transportation; the **work unit (danwei)** system; and the household registration (*hukou*) system.

Almost immediately upon coming to power, the CCP set about remaking the urban landscape, erecting new apartment blocks to replace packed tenements, corralling commercial activities into regulated zones, closing many markets and street stalls, widening and straightening roads, and building new highways and transit corridors. These moves were made with the goal of following the model laid down earlier in the Soviet Union. Soviet cities, and by extension, socialist cities the world over, were to be rational, modern, functional, and grand.

Though the physical environment of Chinese cities changed much throughout the 1950s and beyond, the social landscape saw an even greater transformation. After 1949, and especially after the nationalization of private business in 1956, most urbanites were employed in state-owned enterprises (SOEs) or smaller urban collectives. These, along with government bureaus and state agencies, operated as work units (*danwei*) that provided not simply jobs but also housing, health care, education, day care, pensions, restaurants, shopping, and even vacation resorts for their members. These benefits, along with permanent employment, made up the "iron rice bowl" that was a feature of urban (and to a lesser degree rural) life in Maoist China. Work units became truly all-encompassing social institutions to the extent that many came to resemble cities within cities that their residents quite literally never had to leave. Although it has undergone fundamental change in the reform era, this form of organization continues to exert an influence on Chinese urban life in the twenty-first century, especially for the millions of workers in state-owned enterprises.[2]

Finally, the household registration (*hukou*) system was established in order to keep rural residents out of cities in the 1950s (see chapter 8). The primary goal was to avoid the development of unmanageable shantytowns or slums and to ensure that villagers and city dwellers alike could be accounted for and monitored in their places of residence. Another purpose was to facilitate the expropriation of the agricultural surplus by the state to feed the cities and finance urban construction and industrialization. Under the system, all families were assigned a registration, either "agricultural" or "nonagricultural," tied to their specific place of residence. Moving anywhere, especially from rural to urban areas, was extremely difficult and often impossible.

These aspects of the Maoist order altered the social and political dynamics of Chinese cities tremendously.[3] They became rather rigid and unchanging, largely self-sufficient, well-managed metropolises. In such an environment, urbanites lived stable, well-protected, if somewhat restricted, lives. This placed city dwellers at a substantial advantage over their rural counterparts, for whom life was still precarious and fraught with shortage and deprivation.

The remainder of this chapter will discuss changes and continuities in Chinese cities in the current era of reform and opening up that began with Deng Xiaoping's emergence as China's most powerful leader in 1978. But two features of change in urban China during that period should be highlighted at the outset.

First, as noted earlier, the pace of urbanization has greatly accelerated over the past four decades with the country reaching a developmental milestone in 2011, when more of its people lived in cities than in the countryside for the first time in history. A crucial contributor to this has been a globally unprecedented scale of rural to urban migration. Since the early 1980s, more than 260 million villagers have streamed into Chinese cities. This so-called "floating population" now makes up a significant percentage of the population in some of China's biggest cities. For example, in both Beijing (21.7 million people) and Shanghai (24.2 million), migrants make up about 40 percent of those residing in the city. This demographic fact has profound implications for the future of urban China's.

Second, this initial wave of rapid urbanization was largely a spontaneous, bottom-up process in which villagers took off for the cities in search of better economic opportunities, and the government pretty much let them do so because migrant labor was desperately needed. But when Xi Jinping came to power during the 18th National Congress of the Communist Party held in November 2012, planned urbanization became one the PRC's highest priorities.

The goal was to move away from a model of urbanization based on the excessive expansion of physical urban space and shift to a "people-centered" approach focused on the quality of urban life. In March 2014, the government announced the "New-Style Urbanization Plan, 2014–2020," a multifaceted blueprint of measures to accelerate the movement of population into urban areas and the modernization of China's cities. In December 2015, for the first time in thirty-seven years, the Party convened a Central Urban Work Conference, which resulted in a new set of guidelines published on February 21, 2016, by the Central Committee and State Council. At the heart of these goals was promoting the growth of smaller cities, far from coastal metropolises, that could absorb and integrate rural migrants. At the 19th Party Congress, convened in October 2017, Party leadership emphasized a rationally managed distribution of urban centers and clusters of industrial landscapes. By 2030, policy makers expected 310 million new urban residents in China's cities. This second wave of reform-era urbanization has been for the most part a top-down, centrally planned, process.

WHAT IS A CITY?

More so than in many countries, the question of just what a city in China is comes up with astonishing regularity. Some places classified as rural county towns have nearly one million residents, with traffic congestion and tall buildings that would rival some of America's larger cities. Cities like Chongqing can formally include vast rural hinterlands larger than some European countries, with many more farmers than there are residents in the urban core. Including those rural areas, Chongqing has a total population of more than thirty million, which would make it, by far, the world's largest city; but only about eight million live in its urban districts.

Prior to the late 1980s, defining urban areas as those districts where residents were allocated nonagricultural household registrations was simple enough. Now, for a variety of reasons, including large-scale rural-to-urban migration, it has become harder. Still, there are three basic levels of city in China: county (*xian*), prefecture (*diqu*), and province (*sheng*) (see Figure 1.2 in chap. 1). County-level cities have a status equivalent to rural counties and generally tend to be small and under the jurisdiction of a larger city nearby. Prefecture-level cities are not true cities, but large regions encompassing a major city and a significant rural hinterland. In fact, since the late 1990s, nearly all of China has been organized into such "cities," which have become the dominant organizational unit between province and county. Finally, Beijing, Chongqing, Shanghai, and Tianjin are **directly administered municipalities** (*zhixiashi*) that have the status of provinces, with no intermediary institution between them and the central government.

Each class of city faces distinct issues, in part because each is governed differently in terms of its relationship to higher levels of authority. The four directly administered municipalities have mayors and Communist Party secretaries of provincial rank who are among the most important political figures in the country. They have direct links to the central government in Beijing and all the spending and revenue powers of provinces. Prefecture-level cities fall one level down the chain of governance and must bargain for resources and access doled out by provincial governments. County-level cities are at the bottom of the pile when it comes to status, resources, and access, and often have to contend with local rural areas for attention from prefectural or provincial governments.

Since 1995, a number of changes have shaken up the administrative hierarchy. The overall trend of these has been toward increasing central power at the expense of provinces and seems to be continuing, with the effect that all cities, but especially those directly administered from Beijing, are being drawn closer into the central government's orbit. The second important change has been the rising importance of the nearly three hundred prefecture-level cities as compared to other forms of subprovincial organization. Finally, even at the local level, we have seen an increasing emphasis on building state capacity—that is, the ability of the central government to exercise its authority—and increasing hierarchical control. The central government apparatus has been taking a growing role in the local urban economy, fine-tuning its regulatory and enforcement bureaus, and trying to integrate itself more deeply into urban daily life, even as citizens grow more savvy about using state actors and agencies to their own ends.[4]

Important aspects of this, especially since 2010, have been initiatives aimed at the integration of urban and rural areas (*chengxiang yitihua*) and the urbanization of villages (*chengzhenhua*), under which traditionally rural areas have been urbanized in terms of living and working spaces as well as structures and institutions of governance. For example, between 2011 and 2013, China poured more concrete than the United States did throughout the entire twentieth century.[5] But this process has not been simple or straightforward.

HOW CHINA'S CITIES ARE GOVERNED

Like all other administrative levels in the PRC, cities in China have both a state (or government) structure and a Communist Party structure. The two most powerful officials in a city are the mayor, who presides over the municipal administration, called the **people's government**, and the party secretary, who is the head of the municipal party committee and is the real "boss." In many cases, the mayor serves concurrently as the deputy secretary of the city's CCP committee.

As noted in chapter 1, China has a unitary political system in which subnational levels of administration are subordinate to the central government. The mayor and other important city officials are appointed by higher levels and must be approved by the CCP organization department as part of the PRC's *bianzhi* (or *nomenklatura*) system (see chap. 6).

The mayors and party secretaries of major cities are important national political figures who frequently rise to key positions in the party-state system. The former Shanghai mayor (and party secretary) Jiang Zemin became general secretary of the CCP in 1989 and president of China in 1993. Xi Jinping, who became general secretary of the CCP in 2012 and president of China in 2013, also once served as party secretary in Shanghai.

Cities are divided into districts (Shanghai has, for example, 16), some of which are suburban or even rural. Districts are, in turn, divided into subdistricts, or **street offices** (Shanghai has about 100), which are the lowest level of formal administration in a city. However, there is another level of urban organization, the **neighborhood (or residents') committee** (Shanghai has around 4,000), at the grassroots (like a village in the rural areas). A relatively new kind of urban organization, the *shequ* ("community") is being implemented around the country to provide some of the services to residents that were once supplied by the *danwei* and the residents' committee. In some cities, *shequ* are even starting to supplant street offices. (See Box 10.1) All these various sublevels of urban administration combine service to constituents and surveillance/security functions.

Municipal people's governments have a variety of agencies, such as education commissions and health bureaus. The chief law enforcement agency in Chinese cities is the **Public Security Bureau** (PSB), which has offices at the city and district levels. Municipal PSBs are subordinate to the central government's Ministry of Public Security. This arrangement might be compared to a situation in which city police departments in the United States were under the authority of the FBI.

As part of the party-state's emphasis on "social stability maintenance" (*weiwen*; see chap. 6), a new system of surveillance and social control, "grid management" (*wangge*), has been implemented in cities throughout the country.[6] Under this system, each neighborhood or community is subdivided into several "grid units" responsible for a group of households, supervised by a "grid captain," and run by a small staff of residents. The security functions of the grid units are to gather information proactively about people and events in the area under their jurisdiction, coordinate as needed with higher levels of authority, and provide a kind of "neighborhood watch" crime prevention. They are also designed to provide residents with better access to social services, including family planning, and to facilitate and offer venues for local conflict resolution.

In the early 2000s, every Chinese city set up an **Urban Administrative and Law Enforcement Bureau** , a para-police organization, which is charged with enforcing local ordinances involving a range of issues such as sanitation, environmental regulation, occupational safety, and licensing regulations. Uniformed but unarmed urban

BOX 10.1 MAKING NEW URBAN COMMUNITIES

After 1949, the CCP put into place a strictly hierarchical system of urban governance. Below the level of province came prefecture-level cities, which were in turn divided into districts. Districts then were broken into neighborhoods managed by street committees (or subdistricts) that each presided over several residents' committees at the very lowest level of governance (see Fig. 1.2, chap. 1). State-owned work units, though not official organs of government, frequently assumed many of the functions otherwise performed by street committees, residents' committees, or even districts—including sanitation, basic social services, and even some elements of policing. With the disintegration of China's work unit system in the reform era and the fraying of vertical ties that had bound grassroots governmental organizations, this framework became less workable.

Since the late 1990s, China has made a concerted effort to craft a new institution of local governance at the most basic level of urban society—the "community" or *shequ*. These grassroots units were explicitly intended to take over many of the political and social functions of the work unit and other institutions of street-level governance. They were staffed and funded directly by city and district governments, often recruiting personnel and appropriating funds that had previously been channeled to neighborhood-level organs. The implication was that the *shequ* would become a new all-encompassing social institution. Individuals would be associated with their *shequ*, as they once were with their work unit or neighborhood.

By 2009, *shequ* had directly replaced work units as neighborhood-level organizations in many cities and employed a few million in various positions ranging from office staff to sanitation workers and through outright featherbedding. *Shequ* have also steadily assumed increased responsibility for reemploying laid-off workers. Such *shequ*-based programs have been touted as more successful in promoting reemployment than city government labor bureaus or work units.

Some national-level mass organizations, like the All China Women's Federation, which had earlier run informal reemployment programs, have worked through the *shequ* as a mechanism not only for that purpose but also for many other functions, ranging from providing legal aid to implementing birth-planning policies at the local level. This has helped both to establish the new *shequ* model of governance and also to breathe new life into tired mass organizations like the Women's Federation.

Finally, the *shequ* has become a mechanism of social control by the party-state that may help fill the void left by the decrepit work unit system. This was especially true under the Shanghai model, which had social control as one of its primary goals. But every model of *shequ* has sought to enhance the declining capacity of local governments to head off popular discontent before it turns into contention.

By 2013, it was clear that government's primary goal of the *shequ* policy was to create a new institutional basis for social welfare and, notably, to also provide surveillance and control in China's cities, to replace the *danwei* system. If it is successful, this organizational transition could preserve or even reinvigorate many positive aspects of pre-reform urban China.

management officers (known as *chengguan*) have, however, developed bad reputations by cracking down (often brutally) on unlicensed, mostly migrant street vendors, including beating to death a watermelon seller in 2013. Onlookers have sometimes taken matters into their own hands by attacking *chengguan* in retaliation. A report by the Chinese Academy of Social Sciences found that the *chengguan* were the least popular of all government officials.[7]

China's cities also have people's congresses, which are constitutionally empowered to supervise the work of the people's government, but, in fact, have very little authority. The citywide people's congress is *indirectly* elected by members of the district-level people's congresses. Elections to the district congress are *direct*, which means that all eligible citizens who live in the district are entitled to vote for their representatives. These elections have become more competitive and lively in recent years, although they are always carried out under the watchful eye of the CCP.

STATE ENTERPRISE REFORM AND UNEMPLOYMENT

For the first twenty years of reform, state-owned enterprises remained largely unchanged from the Mao era. Only at the 15th National Party Congress in 1997 did the CCP leadership decide to implement thoroughgoing reform of the state sector and *danwei* system. Between 1997 and 2002, China moved to close insolvent SOEs, merge successful ones to create multinational corporations, and "reduce staff to increase efficiency" (*jian yuan zeng xiao*) in underperformers. The results were mixed economically but were also intensely disruptive in social and political terms. As Figure 10.1 shows, employment in SOEs started to drop sharply in the late 1990s, while urban incomes skyrocketed during that same period, reflecting the trend toward a market economy. A new urban middle class was the main beneficiary, while laid-off workers came to constitute a large proportion of the urban poor.

Although a complex process (see chap. 8), the gist of SOE reform can be summed up in a few key points. First, SOEs did not change their basic structure or practices very much from the years after the Cultural Revolution in the mid-1970s until the

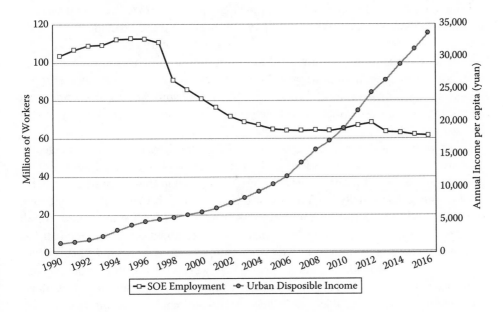

FIGURE 10.1 Urban Disposable Income per capita and Employment in State-Owned Enterprises (1990–2016)

Source: China Statistical Yearbooks

late 1990s. Second, SOEs ran up tremendous debts in the 1990s as they struggled to survive in a changing economic environment. Third, when change did come, it came quickly and harshly. Fourth and finally, the Chinese party-state has been unwilling to give up the state sector entirely, necessitating the maintenance of a large state economy in key sectors even as subsidies decline and competition increases.

By 1997, SOE debts and business losses convinced the top leadership that decisive action was needed to reform the state sector. From that year, SOEs were largely cut off from additional credit or lending, many were closed or merged, and all were strongly encouraged to reduce their workforces as a way of cutting costs and stemming losses. Little more than two decades later, China's remaining state companies are indeed in better financial shape, but they also employ far fewer workers and are much less central to urban society and the broader economy.

The greatest social impact came from the massive layoffs that SOEs implemented after 1997. In that year, SOEs employed roughly110 million workers. By 2002, the number was just over 70 million, a loss of around 40 million state sector jobs in just five years. In 2016, there were about 62 million SOE employees, a reduction of 50 million from the peak of 112 million in 1995. That's larger than the combined population of Texas and New York.

SOE layoffs propelled the decline of the urban *danwei* system.[8] Sensing that it was unrealistic to expect SOEs to keep up welfare elements of the *danwei* system after the iron rice bowl of guaranteed benefits for workers had been smashed as part of the cost reductions imposed on firms, the government offered two programs to replace the old work-unit-based system. The first, known as the *dibao* or **minimum livelihood protection** was meant to provide subsidies to all individuals with incomes below locally determined poverty lines. This theoretically egalitarian program was in fact implemented in such divergent ways across regions and localities that it exacerbated existing inequalities. In nearly all cities, the *dibao* failed to provide sufficient security to keep many workers out of desperate poverty, although it has been increased in recent years and now forms the backbone of a very rudimentary safety net.[9]

Second, the ***shequ***, or "community," has become the most important institution of urban governance for capturing laid-off workers and other potentially disruptive groups in a new formal state embrace.[10] These have had some success in reemploying and taking care of the unemployed, sometimes even in roles such as long-term jurors (*peishenyuan*) sent to work in local courts.

Faced with a bleak set of circumstances, laid-off workers have often engaged in contention against local authorities or their former employers over issues such as unpaid pensions or other unfulfilled promises made when they were let go. The official response has usually been a mix of trying to smooth things over by meeting some demands and arresting those seen as instigators of the unrest. The overall number of such protests has declined markedly since about 2007, although strikes and demonstrations by younger factory workers are not uncommon in China's cities.[11]

On balance, the situation of many current SOE workers is hopeful in that the new generation is not likely to face the layoffs their parents have endured. In fact, those lucky enough to retain SOE jobs after 2008 have seen their income increase sharply as the Chinese government spent liberally to avert the worst effects of the global recession, and lifetime employment is still a regular practice. Such good prospects are more likely to prevail in large SOEs in prosperous cities like Shanghai, but they are more uncertain in state-owned units in less advantaged regions where the decline of the state sector is likely to continue and will leave long-term scars. Given the continuing lack of geographic mobility for most Chinese urbanities, this could well contribute to deepening pockets of poverty in some cities.

CHINA'S "FLOATING POPULATION"

Though it is hard to pinpoint just who is moving where, what kind of life they lead in cities, and with what effects, a few general trends within the floating population of a quarter-billion migrants are apparent. First, most migrants are young and travel short-to-moderate distances to find work, often returning to their villages on a weekly basis or even commuting daily. Second, having reached the city, migrants face significant bias and discrimination in their daily activities and mostly end up in certain low-end jobs. Third, many of the problems migrants encounter can be tied to the persistence of the *hukou* system. Fourth and finally, migration and the remittances that migrants send home have had significant effects on village life (see chap. 9).

Although there are exceptions, the floating population generally works in jobs that are largely segregated by age and gender. For example, young women often work in service jobs, including as domestic workers, hotel and restaurant staff, or in "sweatshop" factories, while men tend to find jobs in construction and building trades.[12] This is true to such a degree that in many cities virtually all workers employed in certain jobs are migrants. Networks have also developed to recruit migrants in their home villages for specific jobs in their destination cities, and migrants from particular regions have cornered the market in certain sectors. For instance, there are scores of laundries in Beijing run by people from Chongqing's Rongchang county.

Much attention has been paid to the millions of migrants who travel hundreds of miles across China to work in the teeming metropolises of Beijing, Shanghai, and the Pearl River Delta (near Hong Kong) and manage to go home only once annually during Chinese New Year.[13] But most migrants stay closer to home. Many even commute on a daily or weekly basis from village to city. Working in the nearest—or a neighboring—prefecture-level city has certain advantages. But it also limits migrants' earnings potential and job prospects. Traveling farther afield opens up more possibilities but also carries greater costs and risks.

When they do travel to major urban centers, migrants are often shunted into particular jobs. Sometimes they will even have been recruited for a specific position. Work in restaurants, retail, and construction is common for migrants throughout China. In certain cities, migrant labor is also heavily represented in other sectors. Perhaps the most well-known are the export manufacturing firms in the Pearl River Delta that employ millions of migrant workers from various parts of China. In other cities, though, sectors like transportation draw largely on migrants. Most of their jobs, regardless of sector, come without comprehensive benefits or most forms of security and protection common to state sector or other "regular" urban jobs. A new labor law implemented in 2008 was meant to address some of these problems. It required written contracts for all employment, demanded that "informal" employees be granted at least minimal benefits previously only afforded their "formal" counterparts with urban household registrations, and empowered wronged employees to sue errant employers more easily. It is still too soon to evaluate the full impact of the law, but its passage shows that the Chinese government had at least become acutely concerned about the issues migrants confronted.

The floating population also must overcome systematic disadvantages when working in the city. These stem from lingering elements of the old *hukou* system. Most important, migrants do not have legal rights to work in permanent or formal urban jobs, or even to live in the city. Rather, they are almost always hired "off the books" in a manner similar to illegal immigrants in the United States and with a similar pattern of low wages and lack of protections. They also are unable to access subsidized urban health care systems and must pay very high out-of-pocket costs for treatment of illness or injury (even for work-related injuries in some cases). Preventive care or other routine medicine is mostly unavailable. Finally, migrants' children are unable to enroll in urban schools without a local *hukou*. This effectively forces migrants to leave their children behind, where they attend rural schools, or to allow their children to grow up without the benefits of an education. Even though some informal urban private schools have been established for migrants' children, these are generally not accredited and cannot provide the educational credentials needed to advance to the next level in China.

Many migrants in China live in **urban villages** (*chengzhongcun*) located either near the heart of the city amid skyscrapers and shopping malls or on the outskirts, where they often sit on one-time farmland that was swallowed up by urbanization. The former farmers found that they could make good money by building apartments on their leased land and renting them out to migrant workers who desperately needed housing that they could afford. Much of the construction is substandard, the dwellings are cramped, the streets are narrow, and sanitation is problematic. Local governments see them as a source of crime and other social problems and an unsightly blight on their city's modern image. One upside of the *hukou* system during the Maoist era was that it restrained the kind of massive rural-to-urban migration that created gigantic slums in many developing world cities. Urban villages are creating a new feature of China's cityscape that have been called "slums with Chinese characteristics."[14] The government's dilemma is: What to do about the urban villages? To tear them down would invite protests by tenants and landlords. To insist that they be brought up to some kind of code would price them out of the range of those who need low-cost housing.

For now, urban villages are fulfilling the housing needs of a vital segment of China's labor force. However, local authorities do not hesitate to demolish them when they see fit. In November 2017, after a fire killed nineteen people in an apartment building with mainly migrant workers as tenants, the Beijing municipal government launched a campaign to demolish "illegal and unsafe structures." As a result of the demolitions, tens of thousands of migrant workers, many of whom had been living in the city for years, were rendered "abruptly homeless in midwinter."[15] To make matters worse, an unnamed local official referred to the migrants as "low-end population" (*diduan renkou*)—deploying an adjective commonly used to describe cheap and poorly made commodities. In Shanghai, the municipal government has been demolishing some housing on the city outskirts where migrants live. Although these areas provide cheap rental accommodations for migrant laborers, they also occupy valuable land, preventing it from being developed. In mid-2016, over 30,000 long term residents and migrants were evicted from Hongqi Village area of Shanghai, which was subsequently demolished.[16]

The social bias and difficult working conditions migrants encounter are worthy of special mention. Many urbanites actively discriminate against the floating population in their cities. City officials often blame spikes in criminal activity or problems of public health squarely on migrants who usually have nothing to do with them. One researcher uncovered a particularly sharp articulation of this bias in a Beijing newspaper commentary praising proposals to segregate members of the floating population into separate areas of the Qingdao public transit network because urban residents allegedly could not stand their foul smell.[17] In terms of their working environment, migrants usually must do the most difficult or dangerous jobs, while enjoying the weakest protections and lowest compensation.

On a more human scale, young workers at a fairly typical factory in the Pearl River Delta described the day-to-day health risks of their long hours working with toxic chemicals in poor conditions as "headache, sore throat, flu and coughs, stomach problems, backache, nausea, eye strain, dizziness and weakness, and aggravated menstrual pain." As one worker explained, "The room is stuffy, and the smells are worse than the smells in the hospital. Those acids make me feel dizzy all the time and I can't make my mind concentrate. Recently I find my head is too painful to describe." Another coworker added that, "we all know our eyesight is becoming weaker and weaker. Sometimes when I leave the factory, I do not dare to glance at the sunlight. I find my vision blurred, and I can't walk a straight line."[18]

The harsh working conditions faced by migrants in factories that make electronic products for Apple, Samsung, HP, Microsoft, and other hi-tech giants have drawn considerable international attention from human rights groups, labor activists, and the media. Exhausting mandatory overtime, brutally long shifts, safety hazards, highly regimented labor discipline, and crowded dormitories are among the most commonly reported abuses. After a series of incidents at the plants of one of the major manufacturers of iPhones and iPads, Foxconn—a Taiwanese company, the largest private employer in the PRC with 1.2 million workers—Apple agreed to enlist the Fair Labor Association, a nonprofit collaboration of businesses, nongovernmental organizations, and universities that promotes adherence to international labor standards, to report on and monitor the working conditions at its supplier facilities in China.[19]

One key aspect of the PRCs' New-Style Urbanization Plan is to encourage migrants to move to small and medium-sized cities by giving those who do so permanent urban *hukou* so they can have access to health, education, and other social services. The aim is to make the more than 250 million current rural residents into urbanites by 2025 by moving them into smaller cities and newly constructed housing, with several hundred million more doing so by 2030, when it is projected that 70 percent of the country's population—more than 900 million people—will be urban. Although the goals of "poverty alleviation," "social equality," and building smarter and greener cities are laudable,[20] they are far from a panacea for China's developmental contradictions. In many cases, economic opportunities have yet to emerge for "new urban residents" who have relocated, either voluntarily or administratively, to their new urban dwellings. In solving one set of problems, entirely new and unforeseen ones are created. Mao phrased it well: "Processes change, old processes and old contradictions disappear, new processes and new contradictions emerge, and the methods of resolving contradictions differ accordingly."[21]

For example, in some smaller cities where modern housing has been built to attract migrants, this "new process" has not always been accompanied by better employment; even the subsidized purchase price for new dwellings has proven to be a financial burden for the relocated population, as have the higher costs of urban living, for example, the price of electricity.[22] One troubling phenomenon of China's hyper-urbanization plan includes the appearance of numerous "ghost cities" (*gui chengshi*)—large districts, or even entire cities, some the geographic size of Chicago, which remain almost completely uninhabited after being constructed at great cost.

One of the most famous and largest such ghost cities, Inner Mongolia's Kangbashi (built to be roughly the size of Chicago), hosted the 2012 Ms. World Beauty Pageant and has served as the backdrop for a skateboarding film, despite being nearly devoid of residents. Others, such as Sichuan's New Beichuan, nearly empty since being reconstructed after the devastating Wenchuan Earthquake destroyed the old county town in 2008, have been less high-profile but equally problematic. Smaller-scale examples include the mostly uninhabited "New Zhengzhou" district in Henan and one of the world's largest shopping malls in Guangdong's Dongguan City, which has yet to attract more than two or three shops. Only time will tell whether the government can reconcile the real need for the development of smaller cities, which are attractive to migrants, with problems like overinvestment in infrastructure (which have produced those ghost cities) to generate local economic growth.[23]

China's top-down urbanization plan also promotes policies that direct *different categories of people* into *different kinds of cities*, which has important implications for migrants (see Box 10.2). China's affluent metropolises are being administratively gentrified to maintain a high standard of living and the "quality" (*suzhi*) of their population. In 2017, both Beijing and Shanghai established population caps at twenty-three million and twenty-five million, respectively. Already near their population limits, both cities' governments have taken measures to decrease their populations—specifically, migrants—including, as noted above, demolishing their housing.

The inflow of new migrants is also set to be regulated more tightly. New *hukou* rules have been introduced by local governments in China's largest cities that require migrants to fill out an application, which is then used to grade them according to their level of education, savings, tax payments, and employment history. Those who meet a certain grade may be given at least temporary urban residency. Those who don't qualify may not be allowed to stay in the city. Smaller cities also are experimenting with a grading system, but the standards for gaining residency there are lower.[24]

Migrants will also be steered to new megaregions. One of Xi Jinping's core plans is the construction of a new metropolitan national capital region named Jing-Jin-Ji composed of the cities Beijing and Tianjin and a large part of Hebei province. The economic hub of this region will be the Xiong'an New Area in Hebei, which Xi has described as a "big strategy for a thousand years" and a "perfect place" that will become

BOX 10.2 MAKING NEW URBAN CITIZENS

China's current macroeconomic strategy is based on "increasing domestic demand" (*kuoda neixu*) to replace excessive reliance on export- and investment-driven growth. But just *where* exactly does "domestic demand" come from? For people to buy goods or services, they need sufficient income to afford these on the market. Would-be consumers must also want to spend money on goods rather than to save it. For China's villagers, neither condition can be taken for granted. As Karl Polanyi put it, free markets and consumers do not arise spontaneously. China's Party-state has taken it upon itself to "engineer" (*gongcheng*) them politically.

The CCP seeks nothing less than to transform rural residents into middle-class consumers through urbanization. As prime minister Li Keqiang described in an article he published in the Swiss newspaper *Neue Zürcher Zeitung* in 2013, "China's ongoing efforts to prudently drive the country's urbanisation—*an endeavor which is expected to unlock the ever-growing market demand of hundreds of millions living in rural areas*" (emphasis added). The economic goal of increasing domestic consumption requires the political solution of moving peasants off the land into the cities. But how?

One solution has been to bring the city to the countryside. Under the banner of "urban-rural integration" (*chengxiang yitihua*), China's state planners have aimed to extend economic opportunities and public services from urban into rural areas. In practice, integration means building small-scale cities and urbanized townships throughout the countryside. Introducing urban development into the countryside is also meant to advance the Party's social objectives of alleviating poverty and narrowing the disparities between cities and the surrounding countryside. If the rural population can become urban citizens without having to move too far, this can even help mitigate migration flows, control population growth in China's megacities, and prevent the expansion of urban slums.

This strategy has been adapted to a variety of contexts. After the 2008 Sichuan earthquake, for example, local governments used the opportunity created by collapsed rural houses to move the peasantry into newly built apartments. In predominantly minority ethnic areas, such as western Sichuan and Inner Mongolia, local governments have moved nomadic and seminomadic Tibetan and Mongolian herders from their pastures into small-scale urbanized settlements. Officially referred to as "ecological migration" (*shengtai yimin*), this process is advocated as a means of protecting fragile ecosystems in the rangelands. No matter who or where you are in China, all roads eventually lead to urban modernity.

Despite ambitious plans and visions of the future, there is trouble in paradise. The construction of small cities does not guarantee their economic viability or desirability as a place to live, especially as jobs and commercial opportunities have too often not followed urbanizing populations. The expansion of urban space has also consumed vast areas of increasingly scarce arable land. Finally, "urban-rural integration" entails training people how to live and consume as urban citizens. Such bio-political engineering is by no means easy and has generated significant tensions between the Party and local residents at the grassroots.

as important to China's future development as the Pudong district in Shanghai and the southern boom city of Shenzhen were during the first decades of the reform era. According to a *Xinhua* news report, Xiong'an was selected as the city of the future because it was a "piece of white paper" and "the most beautiful picture can be painted on it."[25] This vision of urbanization is an uncanny echo of Mao's description of China's population in 1958 just as the Great Leap Forward was beginning as "a blank sheet of paper free from any mark" on which "the freshest and most beautiful pictures can be painted."[26]

The foreign media have been enthralled by the rapid development of a Chinese middle class, which in 2000 made up just 4 percent of urban households, but is predicted to number 630 million people (76 percent of urban households) by 2022.[27] But who are these hundreds of millions of new consumers?

What impact will they have on urban China? These are just some of the questions that arise as this relatively new segment of China's urban population emerges as a major factor in Chinese society and (potentially) politics.. To assess their role, it is necessary to understand a bit about the China's middle class - where they have come from and what they want for themselves.

To be middle class in China today means having an annual income in range of US\$11,500–42,000.[28] Broadly speaking, there are three subgroups among the urban middle class: (1) young professionals working for foreign firms or domestic private sector start-ups; (2) former SOE managers who have converted their companies or professional contacts into private-sector successes; and (3) entrepreneurs from rural or working-class backgrounds who "made it big" in the classic sense as depicted in American popular "rags to riches" discourse. Each subgroup has particular features that make it hard to lump all three together.[29]

Young professionals suffer from a degree of insecurity and uncertainty, which imbues many of them with strong measures of cynicism and a focus on short-term horizons. This leads some to have little loyalty to their employers, jumping from job to job, in many cases several times a year. As one young professional in Beijing explained, "I don't know if I'll have any job a year from now, so I'll change jobs after only three months if the new one pays 500 yuan (US\$60) more per month."[30] Some observers explain these professionals' allegedly self-centered focus by pointing out that more and more rising professionals were raised in one-child families.

Those members of the middle class who come from the ranks of former SOE managers, on the other hand, are less numerous than young professionals in cities like Beijing or Shanghai, but they form the main body of the middle class in many other cities. These are mostly older, usually male, ex-bureaucrats who found a pathway to wealth that led from SOEs to the private sector. Often, this involved taking possession of privatized (or stripped) state assets (see chap. 8). Other times, this entailed leveraging political clout or status into capital to launch private ventures. Nearly always, success rested on connections (*guanxi*) or privileged access to information, capital, or opportunities.

The smallest but most inspiring segment of the new middle class is made up of those workers and farmers who have managed to make their own way in the new market economy, becoming well-off businesspeople through hard work and perseverance. Many of these individuals are in trades in which state managers and yuppies take little interest—for example, recycling, taxi services, waste removal, food service, religious statuary and incense production, and retail. In one widely publicized example, a man laid off from a furniture factory in Jiangsu Province used his severance pay to build fish ponds in several villages, transforming himself into a "goldfish king" and becoming wealthy in the process.[31] These self-made success stories inspire many to believe in the opportunities available in the new market economy, but most realize that these situations are extremely rare.

A second question is how the newly prosperous live their lives. Many reports have stressed the tendency of the wealthiest Chinese urbanites—particularly the superrich millionaires (1.9 million in 2017) and billionaires (819 in 2017)[32]—to consume conspicuously in a manner similar to post–Soviet Russian "oligarchs" or the American "robber barons" at the turn of the twentieth century. Such a tendency is indeed real. But for every tycoon buying frivolous and overpriced luxuries, there are many middle-class yuppies buying their first houses or cars. Because personal consumption was depressed so severely for so long in China, many people view big-ticket purchases (in the 1980s and early 1990s, a television and refrigerator; in the early to mid-2000s, a car and a condominium) as markers of improved living standards. Now the middle class spends more on travel and entertainment, health and exercise, foreign luxury items, more expensive automobiles and housing, and other amenities of a "modern" lifestyle.[33]

There are some cities, notably Shanghai, Beijing, and Guangzhou, where the middle class has attained critical mass, becoming a leading force in urban society. The overall long-term trend, however, is toward growth of the middle class, even as millions of destitute migrants continue to live in the cities, and many former SOE workers and their families remain mired in poverty after being laid off.

Finally, most of the new middle class has not been particularly politically active—at least not in ways that have challenged the CCP or local governments, which is hardly surprising in an authoritarian context such as China's. The middle class has benefited from recent policy and development strategies. They also have the most to lose from instability, whether political or economic. Considering the close ties between many members of the new middle class and the state and party apparatus, their quiescence is even less surprising and looks set to continue for the foreseeable future. As several previous chapters have mentioned, the former CCP leader, Jiang Zemin, made an effort under his "Three Represents" ideology to reach out to the private sector entrepreneurs and employees and even encourage them to join the Communist Party.

The one issue that has shown signs of getting the middle class involved in protests has been environmental protection and pollution control, which is a major problem in urban China. For example, in mid-2015, more than one thousand people took to the streets in Shanghai to show their opposition to a new chemical plant. In the same year, there were demonstrations in Tianjin against a polluting steel mill, and in Wuchuan (in Guangdong province) protests by people who lived near a planned waste incinerator.[34] Research has shown that as people become more affluent, they tend to care more about and act on social issues such as environmental degradation.[35]

URBAN UNIVERSITY STUDENTS

Dating back to the 1919 May Fourth Movement, the 1989 Tiananmen protests, and the Red Guards during the Cultural Revolution, urban university students have been key actors in Chinese politics. But young people in Chinese cities today do not appear as politicized as in the recent past. They are still an important group though, since even their apathy or self-centeredness will influence future trends in political, economic, and social life.

Perhaps the biggest change in the lives of university students since the 1990s has been the end of the **job assignment system** or *fenpei*. From the 1950s into the 1990s, university students were assigned state-sector jobs upon graduation, in much the same way that Chinese workers were assigned to factories, where they were obliged to remain for at least several years. This was in exchange for the free university tuition and housing they had received. Students had little choice over what jobs they were assigned or even where they were located. They could be sent more than a thousand miles away from where they wanted to be, to take up a job in which they were uninterested and for which they were unqualified, but they had no rights to appeal or complain. In practice, given the rigidities of the *danwei* system, initial job assignments often shaped the entire future careers of university graduates. While this system prevented unemployment, it stifled students' prospects and detracted from their dignity and autonomy.

One, perhaps unintended, effect of the *fenpei* system was that students were heavily politicized in opposition to it. This sprang not so much from some idealistic sense of civic engagement as from their desire to have more control over the course of their own lives and careers. Reform of the *fenpei* system was a major goal of the Tiananmen protesters and their allies in 1989, and it was in the aftermath of that conflagration that the CCP leadership decided to dismantle the system.

What has emerged in recent decades is a China that requires university degrees for decent employment and in which university admission has become not only more intensely competitive, with only three out of five students passing the required national university entrance exam (**gaokao**) but also vastly more costly for the many who enroll in private colleges because they don't qualify for the much more prestigious state-run schools.

Furthermore, a significant number of the eight million annual college graduates have difficulty finding employment suitable to their education. Members of this group, which has become known as the **Ant Tribe**, often live in shared crowded quarters, take low-paying jobs to get by, and spend a lot of time just hanging out and being depressed. Most of the un- or underemployed college graduates are from low-income rural and small-city families and have degrees from one of the multitude of relatively new (and lesser quality) mostly private institutions of higher education that have sprung up throughout China as part of the effort to expand university enrollments. But one survey in 2010 found that 30 percent of the "ants" were graduates of prestigious universities, and many had degrees in fields such as health sciences, economics, business, and engineering.[36] This could be an increasingly serious problem as China's economic growth rate slows down. Unemployed educated youth can become a major source of social unrest and political protest, as shown during the "Arab Spring" of 2010–2011.

But young people at last have mastery of their own fates, at least in the sense that no one compels them to take particular jobs. The other major change is that the most lucrative and promising careers are now more often found in private or even foreign companies, rather than in SOEs or government bureaus. These shifts have dramatically reoriented political and social life for urban Chinese under the age of thirty.

The phenomenal success of books and periodicals purporting to be guides to financial and social success is a sign of this transformation. One of the most popular routes to success has been that of studying abroad. Parents are desperate to give their children every advantage in attaining this specific type of success. A book titled *Harvard Girl*, written by the parents of a young Chinese woman who went to Harvard, detailed how to raise successful academic-star children from birth; it became a huge hit in China with sales of over 1.4 million copies.[37] Such parents' guides to helping their children win the new rat race are a relatively recent phenomenon in urban China (although they have been around for decades in Taiwan and Hong Kong) and foretell a sea change in attitudes affecting several generations.

While most urban youth today are best described as apathetic toward politics, they are intensely concerned about their own careers and life prospects. Most undergraduates at Beijing University, China's most prestigious institution of higher education, know little and care less about the events of Tiananmen in 1989 or the Cultural Revolution, both of which played out in important ways on their campus, but they are palpably fearful of graduating and not landing a job. Worse, those not from Beijing are often concerned that they might lose their right to reside in Beijing if they are unable to get a job with an employer capable of sponsoring them for a Beijing *hukou*—no small feat. At the same time, though, in part related to pressures to get ahead in the job market, students have become much more internationalized and cosmopolitan than prior generations.

With so many plum jobs in foreign companies and with English as a mandatory *gaokao* examination field, Chinese urban youth and students are virtually compelled to take an interest in international affairs. Many read foreign media sources and literature; those who work in foreign firms interact regularly with foreign co-workers. In addition, studying abroad has become extremely popular. In 2017, there were about 600,000 Chinese students studying abroad, more than half of whom were in the United States.[38] Some who return with advanced degrees move on fast tracks into leadership positions in certain sectors. They also frequently retain networks of contacts and friends outside China. These both help them succeed in their work and ensure that they keep an eye focused on developments beyond China's borders. The experience of living abroad inevitably also broadens their perspectives on many issues, including political ones.

For successful university graduates, there are many opportunities that earlier generations could not even imagine, while even those at the margins are becoming far more cosmopolitan and globally aware than their counterparts of a decade or more ago, even though none of this has led to increasing political or social activism. Nonetheless, China's middle-class millennials and postmillennials are very active online (see chap. 15), where they express a range of opinions that are often in sync with official policy such as supporting a stronger global role for the PRC and Chinese claims to disputed territories in the South and East China Seas. But many netizens also express views that are contrary to party-state orthodoxy by, for example, expressing strong support for universal human rights.[39]

CHALLENGES FOR URBAN CHINA

By 2030, China's urban population is expected to reach nearly one billion, and the country will have more than two hundred cities with a million or more inhabitants.[40] Chinese cities continue to face a number of critical challenges as rapid urbanization continues to transform nearly every aspect of life in the country. These include environmental problems, inequality, and city planning.

The environmental consequences of rapid modernization, citizen protests against polluting firms, and government policy are discussed in detail in chapter 12. But one city, Datong, can serve to highlight both the urgency of the environmental crisis in urban China and the local government's response.

Datong, a city of roughly three million people in Shanxi province that was once the capital of Imperial China, is home to the PRCs most productive coal mines and was considered one of the country's most polluted cities. The ever-present visible coal dust and soot in air made many visitors choke, possibly linked to the fact that Datong had what is said to be the highest rate of lung cancer in China. At one point, the government presented residents with "evidence" that the prevalence of lung cancer was due to local residents' penchant for consumption of pickled vegetables. Many people in Datong expressed outrage at the government's lack of concern about their air and water quality, even as they worried that enforcement of environmental standards could put additional pressure on mining jobs.

A new mayor, Geng Yanbo, took over in 2008 and began a series of major initiatives to improve life in that "rust belt" city; these included addressing the occupational health and safety concerns of miners and the dire environmental situation. Mayor Geng's plans were supported both by the Hu Jintao's administration with its prioritization of sustainable development and by Xi Jinping's administration with its goal to promote "ecological civilization" in China. In recent years, Datong has made impressive progress in moving toward cleaner ways to extract and burn coal, reduce economic dependence on coal, and develop alternative sources of energy.

In 2005, the city's air quality was ranked 115th out of 117 of all those monitored. In 2012, it was ranked 47 out of 120 cities.[41] In August 2013, Datong hosted the first Solar Decathlon in China, an international event initiated by the U.S. Department of Energy, attended by teams from more than a dozen countries. When Mayor Geng was promoted by the party-state to take over the government of a bigger city, Taiyuan, earlier that year, many citizens of Datong took to the streets or signed petitions begging him to stay.[42]

Social inequality is another major issue in China's cities—indeed, in all of China. Over the last two decades, the PRC has moved from being one of the most egalitarian societies in the developing world to being one of the most unequal (see Box 8.1 in chap. 8, "The Challenge of Inequality in China"). Much of China's inequality is interregional: for example, Shanghai is much richer than Xining, the capital of the far western province of Qinghai. A respected Chinese sociologist observed that, just as many used to speak of first, second, and third worlds, within China there are actually four "worlds": Hong Kong; Beijing, Shanghai, and Guangzhou; all other cities; and rural areas.[43]

There are also grinding disparities within cities (see Box 10.3). Just within Beijing, for example, there are vivid reminders of this inequality in the extreme gaps in living standards between the ten million middle-class citizens and the nine million migrants, many of whom live on the edge of subsistence. These gaps concern policy makers and ordinary citizens alike, but their ultimate impact is not yet clear. Many societies, notably across much of Latin America, have lived with even sharper levels of inequality for decades without constant or overly disruptive political upheaval. In fact, survey

BOX 10.3 INEQUALITY IN CHINESE CITIES

There are four main dimensions of inequality in Chinese cities: (1) the urban core of the city versus its incorporated rural areas; (2) within the state sector; (3) within the private sector; and (4) the newly rich and rising middle classes versus the "new urban underclass."*

The urban-rural divide has always been one of the most salient axes of inequality in China. It was exacerbated and entrenched by the imposition of the *hukou* (household registration) system in the 1950s. As discussed earlier in this chapter, cities in China often incorporate within their municipal boundaries many rural areas where the residents still hold an agricultural *hukou*. These areas are better off than parts of the countryside far removed from a city, but their residents are also, on average, considerably poorer than their urban counterparts within the same municipality. Those who do migrate to the city for work are paid dramatically lower wages than those with urban registrations and face many kinds of blatant discrimination because of their rural origins.

In pre-reform China, most of the benefits that urban residents enjoyed were rooted in the *danwei* (work unit) system. Rather than providing general public goods to all citizens through state agencies, individual work units funded and administered health insurance, pensions, and other social protection measures. This system created considerable inequality among units within the state sector. Broadly speaking, workers in favored industries including steel, resource-extraction enterprises (such as oil fields and coal mining), and defense plants, as well as those who worked in the state or party bureaucracy, enjoyed higher living standards and better benefits than those who worked in light industry, the services, or retail outlets. These sources of inequality among workers in state-owned enterprises persist today despite the erosion of the *danwei* as a factor in urban life. Those employed by the one hundred or so companies directly under the control of the central government, such as Baoshan Iron and Steel in Shanghai, which is the second-largest steel producer in the world, fare much better than employees of the many thousands of SOES that fall under more local jurisdictions.

There is also a glaring divide within the private sector. As noted in chapters 6 and 8, the number of private enterprises in China has skyrocketed during the last decade or so. But these range in size from megamultinational corporations to mom-and-pop stores and street vendors. On the one hand, most of China's newly rich and new middle class work in private companies. On the other hand, sweatshop production of low-end exports is also almost exclusively in the nonstate sector. Private firms employ more migrants under worse conditions and more advanced degree-holders with generous pay packages than do SOEs.

Finally, along with the newly rich and the new middle class, China's cities are also home to a "new urban underclass." This group, which perhaps numbers more than 100 million, consists of laid-off state-owned enterprise workers who have not been able to find gainful employment, most rural migrants, and others who have a slim chance of escaping poverty. In terms of income distribution and access to services, urban China is probably the most highly stratified part of contemporary Chinese society.

research shows that while most Chinese citizens believe that more should be done to help the poor, they are not deeply concerned about socioeconomic inequality since they also believe that life has gotten better and will continue to do so for most people. They are more aggrieved over abuses of power by party-state officials and the lack of procedural justice for aggrieved citizens.[44] Nevertheless, inequality could become a more politically sensitive issue if the economy were to experience a sharp downturn.

Beyond these two big-ticket issues of environmental problems and growing inequality is another major urban concern that should be highlighted—effective and forward-looking city planning that can keep pace with breakneck urbanization. Building subway systems and other rapid transit networks in virtually every major city has been one new focus of urban planning. New attention to the creation or preservation of green space and parks, as well as to aspects of zoning, has also been noteworthy.

In the years ahead, there are numerous issues to be tackled related to the massive increase in urban population. For example, the job market, especially for the eight million or so university graduates each year, will tighten. Environmental problems are a huge challenge, and remedies will often be pitted against the demands for economic growth in both new and old cities.

Another question is whether some key urban areas in China will become "global cities," which is important if the PRC truly wants to join the ranks of the world's great powers. The sociologist Saskia Sassen offered the idea of the "global city" to describe metropolises that serve as critical nodes of interaction in the world economy.[45] The interchange of ideas, capital, people, and goods at these commercial and financial centers is often seen as the key to advancing the agenda of international integration and globalization.

Hong Kong is considered a global city (see chap. 18). Its tourism slogan, "Asia's World City," even echoes this theme. But many say it is losing its place in the lead among Chinese cities. Others, notably Shanghai—but also Beijing and Guangzhou—are beginning to catch up. Some imagine that these cities may challenge even New York or London for global influence in the coming decades, although they have a very long way to go. Cities like Paris or Tokyo may find themselves rivaled or eclipsed more quickly.

China is urbanizing faster than any other society in history. Predictions that more than half of China's population would live in cities by 2015 were wrong. That threshold was actually passed in 2011, four years earlier than estimated, and the trend seems likely to continue accelerating. This is a sea change in Chinese society, one that would stretch any country's ability to manage or control. The stakes are high for the CCP, a party that was brought to power because of its rural roots and is now presiding over a country where the majority—and soon a large majority—of the population is living in cities.

NOTES

1. That said, certain important cities, like Beijing, were planned during the premodern era around *feng shui* (geomancy) principles.

2. See David Bray, *Social Space and Governance in Urban China: The Danwei System from Origins to Reform* (Stanford, CA: Stanford University Press, 2005).

3. For more on Chinese cities during the Maoist era, see John Wilson Lewis, ed., *The City in Communist China* (Stanford, CA: Stanford University Press, 1971).

4. Benjamin L. Read, *Roots of the State: Neighborhood Organization and Social Networks in Beijing and* Taipei (Stanford, CA: Stanford University Press, 2012); Jane Duckett, *The Entrepreneurial State in China* (London: Routledge, 1998); Kenneth Foster "Embedded within State Agencies: Business Associations in Yantai," *China Journal* 47 (2002): 41–66.

5. David Harvey, *The Ways of the World* (Oxford: Oxford University Press, 2016), 1.

6. See "China: Alarming New Surveillance, Security in Tibet," Human Rights Watch, Mar. 20, 2013, http://www.hrw.org/news/2013/03/20/china-alarming-new-surveillance-security-tibet; "Party Paper Lists Six Errors in Chinese Social Management," *Human Rights Journal*, Dui Hua Foundation, Nov. 7, 2012, http://www.duihuahrjournal.org/2012/11/party-paper-lists-six-errors-in-chinese.html.

7. Karoline Kan, "Chengguan, Widely Despised Officers in China, Find Refuge and a Kind Ear," *New York Times*, Sept. 29, 2016, https://www.nytimes.com/2016/09/30/world/asia/china-nanjing-chengguan.html

8. Lu Xiaobo and Elizabeth J. Perry, eds., *Danwei: The Changing Chinese Workplace Historical and Comparative Perspectives* (Armonk, NY: M. E. Sharpe, 1997).

9. Dorothy J. Solinger, "The Minimum Livelihood Guarantee: Social Assistance (just to) to Stave off Starvation," in *Handbook of Welfare in China*, ed. Beatriz Carrillo Johanna Hood and Paul Kadetz (Cheltenham: Edward Elgar, 2017), 144–162.

10. See Ning Tang and Fei Sun, "Shequ Construction and Service Development in Urban China: An Examination of the Shenzhen Model," *Community Development Journal* 52, no. 1 (Jan. 2017: 10–20).

11. Simon Denyer, "Strikes and Workers' Protests Multiply in China, Testing Party Authority," *Washington Post*, Feb. 25, 2016, https://www.washingtonpost.com/world/asia_pacific/strikes-and-workers-protests-multiply-in-china-testing-party-authority/2016/02/24/caba321c-b3c8-11e5-8abc-d09392edc612_story.html?utm_term=.09d898280e33

12. Pun Ngai, *Made in China: Women Factory Workers in a Global Workplace* (Durham, NC: Duke University Press, 2005).

13. The award-winning documentary, *Last Train Home* (2009), depicts the impact of this long-distance migration on one family in Sichuan when the father and mother move to Guangdong to find factory work. https://www.pbs.org/pov/lasttrainhome/

14. Guo Chen et al., "Slums with Chinese Characteristics: A Comparative Study," in *Housing Inequality in China*, ed. Youqin Huang and Si-ming Li (New York: Taylor and Francis, 2014).

15. Chris Buckley, "Why Parts of Beijing Look Like a Devastated War Zone," *New York Times*, Nov. 30, 2017, https://www.nytimes.com/2017/11/30/world/asia/china-beijing-migrants.html

16. Ni Dandan, "Shanghai Migrant Workers Told to Vacate Urban Village," *Sixth Tone*, Jan. 26, 2017, http://www.sixthtone.com/news/1869/shanghai-migrant-workers-told-to-vacate-urban-village

17. Stanley Rosen, "The State of Youth/Youth and the State in Early 21st Century China: The Triumph of the Urban Rich?" in *State and Society in 21st Century China*, ed. Peter Hays Gries and Stanley Rosen (London: Routledge, 2004), 171.

18. Pun Ngai, *Made in China*, 169–170, 172.

19. See http://www.fairlabor.org/affiliate/apple for the FTA's reports on Foxconn.

20. Ian Johnson, "China's Great Uprooting: Moving 250 Million Into Cities," *New York Times*, June 15 2013, https://www.nytimes.com/2013/06/16/world/asia/chinas-great-uprooting-moving-250-million-into-cities.html

21. Mao Zedong, "On Contradiction," Aug. 1937, translation public at https://www.marxists.org/reference/archive/mao/selected-works/volume-1/mswv1_17.htm

22. See Ian Johnson, "Chinese Hit Pitfalls Pushing Millions off Farm," *New York Times*, July 14, 2013, A1, A8.

23. Christian Sorace and William Hurst. "China's Phantom Urbanisation and the Pathology of Ghost Cities," *Journal of Contemporary Asia* 46, no. 2 (Feb. 2016): 304–322.

24. Spencer Sheehan, "China's Hukou Reforms and the Urbanization Challenge," *Diplomat*, Feb. 22, 2017, https://thediplomat.com/2017/02/chinas-hukou-reforms-and-the-urbanization-challenge/

25. Jane Cai, "Can China's President Xi Jinping Realise His 'Perfect' City Dream?" *South China Morning Post*, Apr. 26, 2017, http://www.scmp.com/news/china/economy/article/2090809/can-chinas-president-realise-his-perfect-city-dream

26. Mao Zedong, "Introducing a Co-operative," Apr. 15, 1958, translation public at: https://www.marxists.org/reference/archive/mao/selected-works/volume-8/mswv8_09.htm

27. Dominic Barton, "The Rise of the Middle Class in China and Its Impact on the Chinese and World Economies," Pt. 2, chap. 7, in *US-China 2022: US-China Relations in the Next Ten Years*, China-US Focus, https://www.chinausfocus.com/2022/wp-content/uploads/Part+02-Chapter+07.pdf

28. "The New Class War," *Economist*, July 9, 2016, https://www.economist.com/special-report/2016/07/09/the-new-class-war.

29. Dominic Barton, "Half a Billion: China's Middle-Class Consumers," *Diplomat*, May 30, 2013, http://thediplomat.com/pacific-money/2013/05/30/half-a-billion-chinas-middle-class-consumers/.

30. Personal communication with advertising company junior executive, Beijing 2001.

31. Chen Tao, "Cong Xiagang Zhigong Dao 'Jinyu Wang'" (From Laid-off Worker to "Goldfish King"), *Yuye Zhifu Zhinan* 3 (2003): 14.

32. For the number of millionaires, see Global Wealth Report 2017, Credit Suisse Research Institute, https://www.credit-suisse.com/corporate/en/research/research-institute/global-wealth-report.html; for billionaires, see Hurun Global Rich List 2018, http://www.hurun.net/EN/Article/Details?num=2B1B8F33F9C0

33. Yuval Atsmon et al., "Meet the 2020 Chinese Consumer," McKinsey Consumer & Shopper Insights, March 2012, https://www.mckinsey.com/~/media/mckinsey/featured%20insights/asia%20pacific/meet%20the%20chinese%20consumer%20of%202020/mckinseyinsightschina%20meetthe2020chineseconsumer.ashxr

34. Samantha Hoffman and Jonathan Sullivan, "Environmental Protests Expose Weakness in China's Leadership," *Forbes Asia*, June 22, 2015, https://www.forbes.com/sites/forbesasia/2015/06/22/environmental-protests-expose-weakness-in-chinas-leadership/

35. Ronald Inglehart and Christian Welzel, "How Development Leads to Democracy: What We Know About Modernization," *Foreign Affairs*, Mar./Apr. 2009, 33–48.

36. "China's 'Ant Tribe' Still Struggling," China.org.cn, December 14, 2010, http://www.china.org.cn/china/2010-12/14/content_21536966.htm. The term "Ant Tribe" was coined by Lian Si, then a researcher at Peking University and now a professor at University of International Business and Economics in Beijing. Lian said the unemployed college graduates were like ants in that "They live in colonies in cramped areas. They're intelligent and hardworking, yet anonymous and underpaid" (see URL). Lian wrote two books about the "Ant Tribe" (2009 and 2010) and has also published a book titled *Worker Bees, The Life of*

Young University Teachers (2012) about the difficulties of junior faculty members in Chinese universities.

37. Rosen, "The State of Youth/Youth and the State," 164; Eugenia V. Levenson, "Harvard Girl," *Harvard Magazine*, July–August 2002, http://harvardmagazine.com/2002/07/harvard-girl.html. The book *Harvard Girl*, written by Weihua Liu, was published in China by Writers Publishing House in 2002.

38. "2017 Sees Increase in Number of Chinese Students Studying Abroad and Returning After Overseas Studies," PRC Ministry of Education, Apr. 4, 2018, http://en.moe.gov.cn/News/Top_News/201804/t20180404_332354.html; "Chinese Keep Lion's Share of Int'l Admission by U.S. Higher Education," *Xinhua*, Jan. 29, 2018, http://www.xinhuanet.com/english/2018-01/29/c_136931884.htm

39. "Chinese Online Discussions Challenge Official Ideology—Despite Stricter Censorship," Mercator Institute for Chinese Studies, May 1, 2017, https://www.merics.org/en/china-flash/merics-paper-china-chinese-online-discussions-challenge-official-ideology-despite.

40. McKinsey & Company, "Preparing for China's Urban Billion," Feb. 2009, http://www.mckinsey.com/insights/urbanization/preparing_for_urban_billion_in_china.

41. Chris Luo, "Datong Residents Kneel Down to Plea for Mayor to Stay On," *South China Morning Post*, Feb. 14, 2013, http://www.scmp.com/news/china/article/1150142/datong-residents-kneel-down-plea-mayor-stay. An award-winning documentary about Geng Yanbo, *The Chinese Mayor*, was released in 2015. For the trailer, see https://www.youtube.com/watch?v=gu5I7Ky1xTQ

42. Chris Luo, "Datong Residents."

43. Personal communication with a sociologist from the Beijing Academy of Social Sciences, 1998.

44. Martin Kin Whyte, "China Needs Justice, Not Equality: How to Calm the Middle Kingdom, *Foreign Affairs*, May 5, 2013, https://sociology.fas.harvard.edu/news/china-needs-justice-not-equality

45. Saskia Sassen, *The Global City: New York, London, Tokyo* (Princeton, NJ: Princeton University Press, 1991).

SUGGESTED READINGS

Chang, Leslie T. *Factory Girls: From Village to City in a Changing China*. New York: Spiegel & Grau, 2008.

Eggleston, Karen, Jean C. Oi, and Wang Yiming. *Challenges in the Process of China's Urbanization*. Stanford, CA: Shorenstein Asia-Pacific Research Center, 2017.

Friedman, Eli. *Insurgency Trap: Labor Politics in Postsocialist China*. Ithaca, NY: Cornell University Press, 2014.

Gold, Thomas B., William J. Hurst, Jaeyoun Won, and Qiang, Li. *Laid-Off Workers in a Workers' State: Unemployment with Chinese Characteristics*. New York: Palgrave Macmillan, 2009.

Hurst, William. "The City as the Focus: The Analysis of Contemporary Chinese Urban Politics." *China Information* 20, no. 3 (Nov. 2006): 457–479.

Lee, Ching Kwan. *Against the Law: Labor Protests in China's Rustbelt and Sunbelt*. Berkeley: University of California Press, 2007.

Looney, Kristen, and Meg Rithmire. "China Gambles on Modernizing Through Urbanization." *Current History* 116, no. 791 (Sept. 2017): 203–209.

Miller, Tom. *China's Urban Billion: The Story Behind the Biggest Migration in Human History*. London: Zed Books, 2012.

Read, Benjamin L. *Roots of the State: Neighborhood Organization and Social Networks in Beijing and Taipei* (Stanford, CA: Stanford University Press, 2012).

Solinger, Dorothy J. "The New Urban Underclass and Its Consciousness: (Is it a Class?)." *Journal of Contemporary China* 21, no. 78 (2012), 1011–1028.

Sorace, Christian. *Shaken Authority: China's Communist Party and the 2008 Sichuan Earthquake*. Ithaca, NY: Cornell University Press, 2017.

Sorace, Christian, and William Hurst. "China's Phantom Urbanisation and the Pathology of Ghost Cities." *Journal of Contemporary Asia* 46, no. 2 (Feb. 2016): 304–322.

Teets, Jessica C. and William Hurst. *Local Governance Innovation in China: Experimentation, Diffusion, and Defiance* Abingdon: Routledge, 2015.

Tomba, Luigi. *The Government Next Door: Neighborhood Politics in Urban China* Ithaca, NY: Cornell University Press, 2014.

Wallace, Jeremy. *Cities and Stability: Urbanization, Redistribution, and Regime Survival in China* (Oxford: Oxford University Press, 2014).

Walton, Jonathan. *Intensifying Contradictions: Chinese Policing Enters the 21st Century*. Seattle: National Bureau of Asian Research, 2013.

Whyte, Martin King, ed. *One Country, Two Societies: Rural-Urban Inequality in Contemporary China*. Cambridge, MA: Harvard University Press, 2010.

Wu Weiping, and Piper Gaubatz. *The Chinese City*. New York: Routledge, 2012.

11

Policy Case Study: The Arts

RICHARD CURT KRAUS

China's arts and their political context have changed dramatically since the Maoist period. The arts constitute one of the most open and dynamic aspects of civil society in the PRC, although the cultural arena remains under political scrutiny by the party-state. The arts are near the frontlines of political change in China, and how they fare is a measure for future progress in other areas of public discourse. This section will first introduce the background for the current arts scene, then discuss three topics: the post-Mao relationship between art and politics, the declining effectiveness of party-state censorship, and the party-state's new vigor in promoting culture as a symbol of Chinese nationalism.

BACKGROUND FOR ARTS REFORM

China's recent arts policies have been fashioned by and against two weighty inheritances. One of these is the tradition of Confucian learning and statecraft. Modern leaders look to a past in which the state was an important arbiter of defining what was art, and in which great political figures were often significant poets, calligraphers, or connoisseurs. The bond between art and power was intensified by a second legacy, the communist revolution. Mao and other party leaders won power by force of arms but also by harnessing the arts to mobilize mass support. The victories of the Red Army were accompanied by Party-sponsored songs, novels, dance, ballads, woodcuts, and film.

During three decades of revolution, the Chinese Communist Party (CCP) learned to use the arts as a political weapon. As discussed in chapter 3, a critical moment was the 1942 party rectification campaign in Yan'an. Many sophisticated urban writers, painters, and musicians had joined the party in its Northwest China base. Mao Zedong addressed these artists, demanding that the newcomers to Yan'an learn new skills to produce art that would inspire an uneducated and largely rural audience. Mao charged that they would remain "heroes without a battlefield," as long as they imagined they were producing works for Shanghai intellectuals and were unfamiliar with the needs of their new audience.[1] "If the professional writers and artists regard themselves as masters of the masses, as aristocrats on a superior level to the 'lower classes,' then no matter how talented they may be, they are completely useless as far as the masses are concerned and there is no future for their work."[2] Mao went on to observe "In the world of today, all culture, literature, and art belongs to a definite class and party. Art for art's sake, art that stands above class and party . . . or politically independent art do not exist in reality."[3]

By the time the party came to power in 1949, it had learned to organize and discipline its arts workers. No civil libertarian heritage held back party leaders from "interfering" with artists; both the Confucian and revolutionary traditions regarded energetic cultural intervention as the responsibility of wise leadership. Only an infrequently invoked **Daoist** ideal suggested that the best government was achieved by inaction.

The new government's statist inclinations were reinforced through its first decade by influence from the Soviet Union. China's new cultural institutions, like its political system in general, resembled the Union of Soviet Socialist Republics, its socialist "elder brother." Russian oil painters lectured in Chinese arts academies, as Chinese pianists trained at the Moscow Conservatory.

The peak of centralized control over the arts in China came during the Cultural Revolution and its aftermath (1966–1976). During this protracted political struggle, some arts were dismissed as feudal (such as calligraphy) or bourgeois (such as oil painting), while others were recrafted for a new era of Chinese revolution (see Box 11.1.)[4]

After Mao's death and the arrest of the Gang of Four in the fall of 1976, China's leaders sought initially to restore the system of the early 1950s, which featured a more tolerant and looser party leadership, paying China's intellectuals proper respect as both arts producers and consumers. This initial reform period (which lasted until 1989) was especially influenced by expanded exposure to foreign trade and competition in arts products, and by the party's decision to reduce subsidies to arts organizations, which were called upon to earn more of their own income. The 1980s were filled with cultural controversies, as artists pressed the limits of the post-Mao order, and as citizens reveled in new tastes that had earlier been banned, such as public dancing, more variety in clothing, imported television shows, and recorded music.

The 1989 Tiananmen political crisis stalled momentum for change. Many artists participated in the spring demonstrations and were shocked by the Beijing massacre of June 4. Many who were abroad at the time chose not to return to China; others became cautious in their work, as the harsh climate emboldened leaders who favored heavy-handed tactics in disciplining the arts.

BOX 11.1 WHAT WAS CULTURAL ABOUT THE CULTURAL REVOLUTION?

Political Scientists typically treat the Cultural Revolution as a power struggle over China's future. It is seen primarily as a time when Mao mobilized radical youth, the Red Guards, to attack those among his fellow senior leaders he judged to have betrayed him and who were leading China down the "capitalist road." But over the course of the "decade of chaos" from 1966 to 1976, as the Chinese officially date the Cultural Revolution, political conflict spilled over into nearly every aspect of life in China, including every facet of the arts. Literature, music, painting, drama, film, architecture, and even fashion became ideological battlegrounds that had an impact on all citizens.

Why did Mao and his supporters think a Cultural Revolution in the arts was necessary? Maoists believed that the 1949 seizure of political power and subsequent control of the economy had not truly empowered the working class. They concluded that once-stalwart veteran revolutionaries had been seduced by the attractive yet corrupting culture from China's feudal past or from foreign bourgeois nations. The Maoist prescription was to limit these "sugar-coated bullets" while fostering a new and potent culture that was firmly proletarian in form and content.

Schools were closed in the early period of the movement, both to choke off the flow of bourgeois ideology to students and also to provide a source of Red Guard activists to serve as the shock force of Mao's crusade. When rebels toppled party leaders from power, they typically included among their charges such aesthetic misdeeds as patronizing feudal operas from China's imperial past, supporting capitalist reforms in the arts, or showing an interest in foreign arts.

The Maoist approach to revolutionizing culture encountered several problems in implementation:

- In the course of opposing the "four olds" (old customs, culture, habits, and ideas), Red Guards destroyed many priceless artifacts of traditional Chinese culture. In many cases, the state, and in some cases, local people intervened to protect major monuments, as in Qufu, the birthplace of Confucius. Nevertheless, not only was the scale of the destruction of national treasures caused by the young rebels incalculable, but many personal items, including family genealogies, paintings, books, phonograph records, and religious images, were also lost forever.

- Maoist leaders enforced Cultural Revolution guidelines for the arts hypocritically. While traditional operas were banned, Mao Zedong watched a set of specially filmed performances in his private residence. Lower-level party leaders could watch foreign movies barred to public view. Kang Sheng, a leading Mao ally, was also an arts connoisseur, and he added to his personal collection thousands of paintings, seal carvings, and books that had been seized by Red Guards from "bourgeois" and "feudal" owners.

- Radical leaders were slow to develop new and revolutionary art. Mao's wife, Jiang Qing, a one-time actress before she met Mao in the 1930s, made the radical reform of Chinese opera a personal project. She commissioned new stage works with revolutionary themes, such as *The Red Lantern*, *The Red Detachment of Women*, and *Taking Tiger Mountain by Strategy*. Despite the successes of these works, the development of new pieces progressed slowly, in part because artists feared to cross Jiang Qing. As a result, only **eight model operas** and a few other artistic works gained official approval. For the Chinese people, it was truly a time of cultural famine.

- Other arts reform projects only flourished late in the Cultural Revolution, such as peasant painting, which again went slowly, in part because of the awkward

(Continued)

BOX 11.1 (*Continued*)

need to use formally trained (but ideologically discredited) experts to train new peasant artists.

- The downfall of the pre-Cultural Revolution arts leadership in the CCP shifted influence to new centers of power. One was the army, whose performing arts groups gained new prestige. Even nonmilitary units, such as the Central Philharmonic Orchestra, began to perform in army uniforms as a sign of political allegiance. This afforded some political protection to the musicians, but it was also a sign of the loss of any artistic independence.

Older artists and their children often became targets of the Cultural Revolution as it unfolded on the local level. Many of these came from highly educated families who had initially supported the CCP when it came to power in 1949. But the double blows of the 1957 Anti-Rightist campaign and the Cultural Revolution made it difficult for the Party to draw upon their training and enthusiasm. After Mao's death, Deng Xiaoping was able to tap into the deep cultural resentments of such families as he launched his effort to turn China away from the Maoism in every way, including the arts.

A NEW BALANCE BETWEEN PARTY-STATE AND MARKET

After suppressing the 1989 Tiananmen demonstrations, Deng Xiaoping's solution for the political mess he had made was to push more boldly toward marketizing the economy. His 1992 initiative intensified economic changes underway in the 1980s and resulted in the dramatic remaking of China's cities, transportation system, and consumption habits, as well as reuniting Hong Kong and Macao with China. In contrast to Maoist policies, which explicitly focused on the arts, Deng's economic reforms affected the arts indirectly, yet profoundly.

The economic reforms launched by Deng liberalized Chinese culture by weakening the grasp of party-state patronage, encouraging artists and arts organizations to turn to the marketplace instead of relying upon automatic government subsidies. In addition, a new array of cultural products was introduced in the PRC, not only from across China but also from around the world.

However, the reforms had significant costs, both to artists and art consumers. Some prominent writers, singers, and painters profited enormously from these changes, which also removed limits on individual income. Other artists fared less well, especially folk musicians, dancers, puppeteers, and traditional landscape painters. Many found the process of change to be unnerving and disorienting. Although there are still many government subsidies for the arts, most artists had to find employment outside official circles, give up subsidized housing and other benefits, purchase their own materials for creating art, and, in general, fend for themselves.

A broader critique of the market reforms in culture is that they have rewarded coarseness, sensationalism, and vulgarity, at the expense of higher artistic principles. In the past, the Chinese communist party-state may have set limits for the content of new art but, typically, interfered little with the pursuit of artistic techniques. The exception was during political campaigns such as the Cultural Revolution when the arts were not only totally controlled by the party-state but were also actively used as a propaganda tool to mobilize the masses and send not-so-subtle messages about proper communist attitudes and behavior.

Artists are often quick to protest the cultural destruction associated with the sustained construction boom that began with the economic reforms. Old architecture is vanishing to make way for new housing, shopping malls, and public buildings. Cultural traditions are also collapsing before economic growth. Chinese opera, a national icon of traditional culture, is losing its audience, especially in urban areas, where it cannot face the competition from more modern forms of entertainment, such as video games, television, and pop music.

These trends have elicited serious interest in cultural protection. By the mid-1990s, some began to attempt at least to slow the replacement of distinctively Chinese buildings by new structures of no national character. This has been accompanied by a broader interest in signs of older Chinese culture and art, precisely as it is being destroyed. Corrupt officials in cahoots with real estate speculators make preservation difficult. However, it would be unfair to blame the housing transformation on corrupt officials: Chinese citizens want new, clean, and well-insulated homes with adequate plumbing. The politically motivated destruction of the Cultural Revolution had mostly ended by 1968. In contrast, the present era's economically driven destruction has had few checks since Deng Xiaoping reignited the market reforms in 1992.

It would be a mistake to view these changes as a simple triumph of the marketplace over the party-state, rather than a reconfiguration of the party-state's visible role in producing art. The party-state still maintains a role in overseeing and financing cultural affairs. Indeed, there is a whiff of the ancient Roman strategy of "bread and circuses" in its conscious use of the market to provide greater cultural opportunities, entertainment, and distraction from political controversy.

A WEAKENED CENSORSHIP

The distractions of popular culture are one way the CCP protects its rule. The strong hand of censorship is another. Yet current Chinese censorship is very different from its Maoist predecessor.

Arts censorship began to loosen in the 1980s, gradually becoming more of a recurring annoyance than a central feature of cultural life. Censorship of news is more pervasive, although it too is much looser than in the past. For the arts, control mechanisms and party-state interest vary by genre. Music is probably the least controlled, and film and television the most supervised. Fiction and painting are only loosely monitored. Except for broadcasting and film, China practices a postpublication censorship, which means that a painting might be withdrawn after a show opens, or a book might be cancelled, but not until tens of thousands of copies have been distributed. So, writers and painters calculate the prevailing political climate as shrewdly as they know how, self-censor when necessary, and plunge ahead when the country is in a relatively open period.

The decline of censorship has been uneven, in cycles of loosening and tightening,[5] but generally leaving the censors with less power in the end. This is in part a result of economic change, as there are too many cultural products on the market for anyone to monitor them all. Also, China has never had a Soviet-style corps of professional censors (with the important exception of television and film). In the Maoist years, cultural controversies often began when a local activist or zealous official decided to make a fuss about a particular work. As political life in China became less intense, many people decided that censorship was not worth the trouble or even a bad idea.

Generational change has also consolidated the process, with the retirements, then deaths of the old revolutionaries who founded the People's Republic and had held on to more conservative views of the limits of artistic freedom. In the 1970s and 1980s, debates over individual songs or scenes in films would bubble up to the top of the system, requiring the central party leadership to determine whether a particular work of art was permissible. In the twenty-first century, the scope of censorship is much narrower and is handled at lower political levels. Even so, the opening ceremony of the 2008 Olympics was judged to be so important to China's national image that a top leader is said to have intervened to substitute a prettier child for the little girl whose voice was actually heard singing a prominent song.[6]

The erratic weakening of censorship often assumes forms that Westerners may not expect. For example, one battleground was paintings of nude figures. Figure painting is not an important theme in Chinese painting, and Confucian propriety reinforced communist prudery to suppress naked images for much of the twentieth century. Liu Haisu, an oil-painting master, fled to Japan in the 1920s to escape a warlord who was outraged by his use of naked models in teaching.

After 1949, communist patronage of oil painting as a "modern" art form led again to nude modeling and to renewed attacks on the painters, the models, and the people who viewed the art. In 1965 Mao Zedong intervened on this subject:

> Fundamental training in drawing and sculpture requires models—male, female, old and young; they are indispensable. The prohibitions of feudal ideology are inappropriate. It is unimportant if a few bad things emerge. For the sake of art and science, we must put up with some small sacrifices.[7]

No one dared pursue his encouragement in the ensuing Cultural Revolution. Yet in the post-Mao relaxation of cultural controls, a wave of nude painting spread over the nation in the 1980s, this time with success. The nudes were almost all young women, as the fight over gender equality was another matter. In one case, a painter pulled an abstract oil from his closet and labeled it a "nude" in order to enter it into a hastily arranged exhibition of nude art. The breakthrough of this restricted zone also produced profits for the institutions that organized the shows. Conservative critics denounced the new work as pornographic, but over the course of the 1990s it became another fallen aesthetic barrier, and no longer inspired such controversy.

With Xi Jinping as China's leader, the political cycle of alternating relaxed and strict controls over art entered a tough-minded phase. Xi has taken a firm line, insisting that artists have a political responsibility to promote socialist values and follow the party's guidance. In a 2014 speech notable for his denunciation of the "strange" architecture that has risen in China's cities, Xi demanded that art "be like sunshine from the blue sky and the breeze in spring that will inspire minds, warm hearts, cultivate taste and clean up undesirable work styles."[8] Such lofty but ambiguous aspirations are typical of central pronouncements about culture. Unsurprisingly, China's architects were thrown into a tizzy trying to discern what the leader's publicly stated design preferences might imply for their daily work.

In that same speech, which was given to a gathering of some of China's most renowned cultural figures, Xi echoed Mao's 1942 talks on art and literature during the Yan'an rectification campaign when he said that "literature and art must adhere to the fundamental direction of serving the people and serving socialism. This is a basic requirement put forward by the party on the front of the literature and arts, and it is also the key to determining the future destiny of China's literature and arts." He also bluntly noted that "the leadership of the party is the fundamental guarantee for the development of socialist literature and art."[9] There are, indeed, signs that the arts are coming under increased political scrutiny as part of Xi Jinping's increased emphasis on party control and ideological orthodoxy in Chinese society

What gets censored? In politics, lots of things, such as critical views of China's control of Tibet; it is also taboo to write about the 1989 Beijing protests and massacre. In the arts, no one will dare satirize living political leaders. But you can certainly mock corrupt or sanctimonious officials, if they are suitably local and not famous. Sometimes censorship is a simple editorial cut. The Academy Award winner (Best Director, *Brokeback Mountain*, 2006) Ang Lee's imported movie, *Lust, Caution* (2007), had some steamy moments clipped before its mainland release. In other instances, censorship is more complex. A 2000 Chinese war film, *Devils at the Doorstep*, was banned because it showed too nuanced a view of the Japanese occupation troops. But the ban applied only to theatrical distribution, so the film was available on DVD, and its director, Jiang Wen, continued to work on and act in other movies.

China maintains some limits on foreign culture, although with less success and zeal than in the past. Visiting musical groups need to have their programs vetted before going onstage. The party-state restricts the number of Hollywood movies that can be shown, although this is more to protect China's film industry than to block American ideology. China has both increased Hollywood imports for its own screens and purchased one-third of the movie theaters in the United States, making the once rigid barrier between the United States and China still more porous.

Efforts to control internet access are contentious, and China's government is certainly more activist in directly controlling unfavorable news than most Western governments (see chap. 14). But the "great firewall of China" is erratic and porous. Like many forms of Chinese censorship, control of the internet is reasonably effective toward the masses and less so toward educated or politically connected elites. The party worries less about the elites, who long enjoyed books, performances, films, and news that ordinary people could not access. Computer restrictions are most easily evaded by technically savvy citizens who slip around the firewall, and by bloggers who employ circumlocutions to beat censoring software.

Other countries attempt to create national firewalls (for example, Singapore, Malaysia, and several Middle Eastern countries). In the West, arts controls tend to be private, enforced by the state through intellectual property lawsuits. The main state interest in the West seems to be restricting pornography, terrorist information, and criminal access to computers.

China has far less efficient censorship than many Westerners want to believe. Many artists have boosted their celebrity by playing the system, while assuming the pose of the dissident to Westerners. Book sales in the West can soar if ads claim that the text has been "Banned in China!" even if the book had in fact been sold to a million Chinese readers before being withdrawn.

Many Chinese artists sell "dissident" paintings that mock Mao Zedong to foreign collectors, understanding full well that making fun of Mao is no longer very controversial, and that the CCP backs their success in the international art market.

The artist and architect Ai Weiwei, an extremely well-connected cultural leader and entrepreneur, celebrated for his "birds-nest" conception for the Beijing Olympic Stadium, tweaked the party-state with his criticism of the Olympics, encouraging Western journalists to publicize him as a dissident flirting with political danger. A subsequent police beating, house arrest, and prosecution for vague economic offenses showed this to be true.[10] Ai Weiwei has assumed a special burden as the artist who cannot be silenced. The son of the revolutionary poet Ai Qing, Ai Weiwei spent twelve years in the United States, including a period as a New York City street artist. Some think his projects are more interesting politically than artistically, yet even critics are impressed by his productivity and stubborn defiance. Several works took up the cause of the Szechuan students killed when their cheaply constructed schools collapsed in an earthquake in 2008. Ai has exhibited photographs of himself making obscene middle-finger gestures in front of famous sites and has made statues of the surveillance cameras installed by police outside his home.

Despite and because of the party's harassment, Ai has become the most famous international representative of China's arts world. Ai's golden versions of the heads of zodiac animals looted by the British and French in 1860 calls attention to the issue of the looting of China's arts heritage. Ai's 100 million hand-painted porcelain sunflower seeds in London's Tate Museum, invited viewers to think about the place of labor in China's craft production and about cultural relations between China and the West. Other works have enlarged his soapbox beyond Chinese issues, including a series of works exploring the ongoing migration crisis in Europe and the Middle East,[11] as well as the Fukushima nuclear disaster in Japan. The party's efforts to co-opt Ai Weiwei with official posts and honor have failed.

But for most creators and performers, China is less repressive than Westerners often imagine. As China has become more prosperous, less Maoist, and more like "ordinary" countries, its censorship issues have also become more ordinary.

A NATIONAL QUEST FOR GLOBAL CULTURAL RESPECT

While the post-Mao Chinese party-state leads cultural policy with a lighter hand, it uses cultural symbols for its political purposes. The party continues to invoke the memory of revolution but recognizes that this is no longer an adequate claim to political legitimacy. Instead, the party substitutes a continuously expanding economy, but adds to this a sometimes deft, sometimes heavy-handed manipulation of nationalist cultural symbols.

One sees this in the restoration of once disfavored heroes of Chinese culture such as Confucius or Sun Yat-sen, who can appeal across region and class. China's new prosperity has permitted an astonishing growth in public works, not just railroads, highways, and airports but also prominent cultural infrastructure, such as concert halls and museums in nearly all provincial capitals. The impact of these shining new temples of culture is probably analogous to the wave of cultural construction that swept late-nineteenth-century Europe, where nationalist politics were mixed with a desire to bind citizens together in the consciousness of a newly shared national culture.

China wants its culture to impress not only residents of Wuhan or Shanghai but foreigners as well. This desire stems in part from the tradition of Confucian statecraft, by which China awed lesser nations with its arts and inventions. It also flows from the sense that China has left behind the period of national humiliation, when it was unable to prevent imperialist armies from plundering its temples, homes, and palaces.

In the Maoist era, China enjoyed extensive artistic ties to Eastern Europe until the eve of the Cultural Revolution. China then sought cultural ties with "third world" nations, such as Algeria or Indonesia (with whom China planned a counter-Olympics—the "Games of the New Emerging Forces"—in the early 1960s). But by the end of the Cultural Revolution, China was so culturally isolated that screening Albanian or North Korean films was a major act of artistic exchange.

Maoist leaders viewed foreign culture with suspicion, as uncontrolled or controlled by outsiders. Even foreign artists sympathetic to the revolution were treated with paranoia. China invited the Italian director Michelangelo Antonioni to China to make a three-hour film, *Zhongguo* (China, 1972), which the leftist filmmaker certainly intended to be sympathetic to the PRC. But Antonioni's fondness for filming the picturesque, the antique, and the human-powered was misunderstood by Cultural Revolutionaries as an imperialist belittling of China's backwardness. Few Chinese saw the movie, although it was the subject of a fierce nationwide campaign of criticism in 1974. *Zhongguo* was not shown to a Chinese audience until 2004.

Now Chinese filmgoers have experienced decades of post-Mao Western and Japanese cultural imports, and Chinese citizens have increasingly become world travelers. The sustained economic growth of the past two decades has inspired a new level of national confidence, so the nation's leaders are less likely to bristle at foreign criticism.

At the same time, China wants to promote its art and artists abroad. Chinese media report with special joy the accomplishments of ethnically Chinese performers and artists such as the architect I. M. Pei (American), the cellist Yo-Yo Ma (American), the concert pianist Lang Lang (Chinese), the film directors Zhang Yimou (Chinese) and Ang Lee (Taiwanese), and the actors Bruce Lee (Hong Kong) and Jackie Chan (Hong Kong), whether or not they are citizens of the People's Republic of China. There was great pride in China when the renowned Italian tenor, Placido Domingo, sang the lead role of Qin Shihuangdi, founder of the Chinese empire in 221 BCE, at New York's Metropolitan Opera in Tan Dun's *The First Emperor*. The fact that works by several contemporary Chinese artists are now in great demand by Western collectors and command some of the highest prices in the global arts market is another source of satisfaction.

Even greater national pride was felt when the novelist Mo Yan won the 2012 Nobel Literature Prize. China's intellectuals had longed for this recognition of their nation's cultural prowess for nearly a century. When Gao Xingjian, a dissident writer resident in France, was awarded the prize in 2000, Chinese hopes remained unsatisfied. Gao was mostly unknown within China and the Communist Party dismissed him as a "French" writer. Mo Yan's often bawdy and politically critical novels are popular in China, but his role as leader of the official writer's union led to hostile criticism from some Westerners that he was a party stooge and unworthy of international admiration.

Many recent artistic accomplishments were achieved without party-state support. Nonetheless, most of the recent Chinese stars in the international art market have enjoyed free training in Chinese arts academies. And some of their breakthrough works have been subsidized by the state. This is true, for instance, of Xu Bing's celebrated *Book of the Sky*, a massive installation of "nonsense" Chinese characters, printed from thousands of blocks carved by Xu.[12] The hugely successful Beijing arts district, the 798 Factory, enables artists to exhibit to Chinese and foreign visitors, yet part of its charm is that it is reconfigured from a one-time military electronics factory, a foreign-aid project of East Germany.[13]

Less glamorous, but economically more important, is the low-end art exemplified by the painting sweatshop village of Dafen, Guangdong, which exports millions of cheap oil paintings. Here, the arts harness low-cost labor for export product, much like the shoe industry.

CONCLUSION

China's post-Mao rulers have adopted a new approach to cultural policy, withdrawing from micromanagement of the arts and intervening only in what they regard as key matters. These include limiting the flow of news critical of the PRC, protecting China's film industry against foreign competition, and promoting cultural achievements with nationalist pride. They are managing culture less . . . but better.

Nevertheless, the arts in the PRC remain more political than in the United States, which, unlike most nations, has no ministry of culture to promote or oversee the arts. China's approach to the arts would still seem intrusive to many Americans. Although China's system assures frequent friction between artists and the state, it honors China's inherited practice of government responsibility for the arts.

NOTES

1. Bonnie S McDougall, ed., *Mao Zedong's "Talks at the Yan'an Conference on Literature and Art": A Translation of the 1943 Text with Commentary* (Ann Arbor: University of Michigan Center for Chinese Studies, 1980), 61. An official translation of this speech, which make some changes from the original, can be found at https://www.marxists.org/reference/archive/mao/selected-works/volume-3/mswv3_08.htm

2. McDougall, *Mao Zedong's "Talks at the Yan'an Conference,"* 73.

3. McDougall, *Mao Zedong's "Talks at the Yan'an Conference,"* 75.

4. Richard Curt Kraus, "Art Policies of the Cultural Revolution," in *New Perspectives on the Cultural Revolution*, ed. William A. Joseph, Christine Wong, and David Zweig et al. (Cambridge, MA: Harvard University Council on East Asian Studies, 1991), 219–249.

5. See Richard Baum, *Burying Mao: Chinese Politics in the Age of Deng Xiaoping* (Princeton, NJ: Princeton University Press, 1996), for an analysis of how cycles of opening (*fang*) and tightening (*shou*) characterized Chinese politics in the first two decades of the post-Mao era. This remains an insightful framework for understanding the PRC today.

6. Jim Yardley, "In Grand Olympic Show, Some Sleight of Voice," *New York Times*, Aug. 12, 2008.

7. "*Lu Xun Meishu Xueyuan huifu yong 'mote'er' jinxing renti xiesheng jiaoxue*" (Lu Xun Fine Arts Academy resumes use of "models" for classes in life drawing), *Meishu* (Fine Arts) 16 (May 1978): 46.

8. Alyssa Abkowitz, "Xi Jinping Isn't a Fan of Weird Architecture in China," *Wall Street Journal* (Oct. 17, 2014).

9. The Chinese version of the full text of the speech can be found at http://news.ifeng.com/a/20151014/44928424_0.shtml. For an analysis of Xi's remarks, see Jun Mai, "Chinese President Xi Jinping's Call for 'Socialist Arts' Sparks Fears over Creative Freedom," *South China Morning Post*, Oct. 21, 2016, http://www.scmp.com/news/china/policies-politics/article/1870191/chinese-president-xi-jinpings-call-socialist-arts

10. See the award-winning documentary by Alison Klayman, *Ai Weiwei: Never Sorry* (2012), http://aiweiweineversorry.com/.

11. See Ai's 2017 film about the migration crisis, *Human Flow*, https://www.humanflow.com/.

12. See Jerome Silbergeld and Dora C. Y. Ching, eds., *Persistence-Transformation: Text as Image in the Art of Xu Bing* (Princeton, NJ: Princeton University Press, 2006).

13. Huang Rui, ed., *Beijing 798: Reflections on Art, Architecture and Society in China* (Beijing: timezone 8 + Thinking Hands, 2004).

SUGGESTED READINGS

Andrews, Julia F., and Kuiyi Shen. *The Art of Modern China*. Berkeley: University of California Press, 2010.

Barmé, Geremie. *In the Red: On Contemporary Chinese Culture*. New York: Columbia University Press, 1999.

Clark, Paul. *The Chinese Cultural Revolution: A History*. Cambridge: Cambridge University Press, 2008.

Curtin, Michael. *Playing to the World's Biggest Audience: The Globalization of Chinese Film and TV*. Berkeley: University of California Press, 2007.

Huot, Claire. *China's New Cultural Scene*. Durham, NC: Duke University Press, 2000.

Kraus, Richard Curt. *The Party and the Arty: China's New Politics of Culture*. Lanham, MD: Rowman & Littlefield, 2004.

Link, Perry. *The Uses of Literature: Life in the Socialist Chinese Literary System*. Princeton, NJ: Princeton University Press, 2000.

Lovell, Julia. *The Politics of Cultural Capital: China's Quest for a Nobel Prize in Literature*. Honolulu: University of Hawai'i Press, 2006.

Mittler, Barbara. *A Continuous Revolution: Making Sense of Cultural Revolution Culture*. Cambridge, MA: Harvard University Press, 2013.

Mo Yan. *The Garlic Ballads*. Translated by Howard Goldblatt. New York: Arcade Publishing, 2012.

Rosen, Stanley. "The Chinese Dream in Popular Culture: China as Producer and Consumer of Films at Home and Abroad." In *China's Global Engagement: Cooperation, Competition, and Influence in the 21st Century* eds., Jacques deLilse and Avery Goldstein. Washington, DC: Brookings Institution, 2017, 359–388.

Silbergeld, Jerome. *Contradictions: An Artistic Life, the Socialist State, and the Chinese Painter Li Huasheng*. Seattle: University of Washington Press, 1993.

Wang, Jing. *Brand New China: Advertising, Media, and Commercial Culture*. Cambridge, MA: Harvard University Press, 2008.

Zha, Jianying. *China Pop: How Soap Operas, Tabloids, and Bestsellers Are Transforming a Culture*. New York: New Press, 1995.

12

Policy Case Study: The Environment

KATHERINE MORTON AND FENGSHI WU

In traditional Chinese philosophy, wise leadership was based on achieving a balanced approach to the human-nature relationship known as *tian ren he yi*—harmony between heaven and humankind. The values of moderation and adaptation meant that sustainable forms of agriculture, forestry management, and the protection of biodiversity were in evidence centuries ago. Such practices, however, did not prevent environmental mismanagement. Over time, China's ecological balance became disrupted by excessive land cultivation and the extraction of natural resources in the pursuit of state industrial and military power. This reached a peak during the Mao era when *ren ding sheng tian*—humans must conquer nature—became the new metaphor for understanding the relationship between humans and nature, with devastating environmental consequences.[1]

More recently, nearly forty years of rapid economic growth have placed further pressures on the natural environment. The People's Republic of China (PRC) is now home to some of the most polluted cities in the world, more than 70 percent of its rivers and lakes are seriously polluted, and ecological degradation is widespread. The scale and severity of China's environmental problems threaten the sustainability of its modernization drive. Opportunities to reverse negative environmental trends and transition toward a more sustainable path of development still exist, but the timeframe for taking action is now shorter. Consequently, the Xi Jinping leadership (since 2012) faces a critical policy dilemma: how to meet continuing demands for economic growth while simultaneously solving a rising ecological debt crisis that is already undermining the health and prosperity of the Chinese population.[2] The stakes are high both at home and abroad. At a broader level, the domestic pattern of development inevitably affects the international distribution of resources and the global environment. Xi's administration has prioritized the Belt and Road Initiative (BRI) as the signature global strategy to integrate China's overseas economic activities (see chap. 8).[3] Over the coming years, the direction that China takes in responding to environmental challenges both domestically and along the BRI will have considerable implications for its own future as well as that of the rest of the world.

This case study will discuss China's contemporary environmental challenges within a broader global perspective. It begins with an overview of the PRC's current environmental crisis and its spillover effects beyond its borders. This is followed by a brief review of evolving government responses and civil society initiatives at the grassroots level. Attention then turns to identifying the core challenges that remain, especially in the poorer and more ecologically fragile regions. The final part of the case study discusses the potential for a more sustainable future that takes into account the importance of leadership at both the domestic and global levels.

CHINA'S ENVIRONMENTAL CRISIS IN THE MAKING

Problems of landslides, flooding, deforestation, and increased silt loads in rivers have existed in China for centuries. The uniqueness of the current environmental crisis lies in its scale, severity, and interdependence with the outside world.[4] Most visible to the outside observer are the rising levels of pollution. Following India, China is now the world's second largest emitter of sulfur dioxide (SO_2) emissions—in many cities exceeding World Health Organization recommendations by two to five times.[5] In fact, SO_2 pollution is a precursor of acid rain, which covers roughly 30 percent of the total land area of China. In the major cities of Shanghai, Beijing, and Guangzhou, nitrogen oxide (NOx) emissions have also risen dramatically. As a result of heavy traffic pollution, what these cities are experiencing is similar to Los Angeles–style photochemical smog on a regular basis. The rapid rise in car ownership means that air pollution is likely to get far worse before it gets better. Between 2000 and 2012, the number of cars on the roads in Beijing quadrupled to around five million. In mid-2018, the number stood at nearly six million. On a significant number of days in the year, breathing the air in Beijing is now equivalent to smoking two packs of cigarettes per day. Severe air pollution peaked in January 2013 when a thick noxious smog blanketed the nation's capital for three weeks. Described by some observers as Beijing's "airpocalypse," small airborne particulates (PM 2.5), considered extremely hazardous to public health, surpassed 500 micrograms per square meter, more than twenty times the recommended government safety levels.[6]

Water pollution has also reached record levels. The industrial discharge of toxic substances, such as mercury, phenol, chromium, and cyanide, is largely to blame, together with untreated municipal wastewater and fertilizer runoff. Recent studies confirm the correlation between heavily polluted water and a higher incidence of cancer in the Huai River watershed (Henan, Anhui, and Jiangsu). More than half of the monitored urban river sections in northern China do not meet the lowest ambient standard (grade 5)—the water is officially classified as unfit even for irrigation. Despite efforts to enforce regulatory controls, an estimated three hundred million people (almost a quarter of the Chinese population) still do not have access to clean water.

The trends relating to ecological degradation in China are just as sobering. According to official statistics, 90 percent of China's grasslands have become degraded, and desertification—the gradual transformation of habitable land into desert—now covers one-third of China's land base. Forest resources are scarce (20 percent of the total land area, compared to 33 percent in the United States), and wetlands have been reduced by 60 percent. In addition, almost 40 percent of the nation suffers from soil erosion as deforestation and unsustainable farming practices cause 10,000 square kilometers (about 3,900 sq mi) of lost soil per annum. The sediment discharge from soil erosion is filling up rivers and lakes, thus contributing to the frequency of flooding. At the same time, water scarcity is reaching a critical threshold. China holds the fourth largest freshwater reserves in the world, but they are unevenly distributed, and per capita water use is only one-quarter of the world average. Most of the water supply to major cities depends upon groundwater pumped from aquifers (geological formations that store water underground), but these are drying up or becoming depleted due to the accumulation of salts in the soil. An estimated three hundred cities across China now face severe water shortages.

Transboundary Effects

The spillover effects of China's environmental problems began to attract attention in the early 1990s, when it became apparent that a significant proportion of acid rain in Korea and Japan had its origins in China. Dust and aerial pollutants are now transported as far as the United States, and high levels of toxic pollution in the East China Sea, Bohai Sea, and Pearl River Delta are having a serious impact on regional fish stocks. In 2005, the explosion of a state-owned petrochemical plant in Jilin province, which released tons of toxic benzene into the Songhua River, affecting water supply in Harbin as well as the Russian city of Khabarovsky, placed a spotlight on the need for significant improvements in information disclosure as well as monitoring systems across the Sino-Russian border. A year later, a 106-kilometer-long diesel slick flowing into the Bohai Sea resulted in additional pressure on the Chinese government to establish a regulatory framework for protecting the marine environment.

In an era of global interdependence, it is becoming increasingly difficult to apportion blame for transboundary environmental problems. Foreign firms generate a significant portion of pollutants in China, and an estimated 40 percent of China's total energy demand ends up in exported manufactured goods. Thus consumers in other parts of the world benefit considerably from China's status as a global factory, and it is fair to say they are also one source of the PRC's increasing demand for energy and natural resources, which, in turn, has an impact on the regional and global environment.

At the regional level, it is widely known that the cascade of dams built on the Mekong River in Yunnan province poses serious risks for countries downstream (Laos, Myanmar [Burma], Thailand, Vietnam, and Cambodia). Although less than one-sixth of the Mekong River's total water catchment is located in China, changes in water flows, especially during the dry season, can have negative impacts on irrigation and fisheries downstream. Equally worrying is the destruction of Myanmar's northern frontier forests by Chinese loggers. Following a logging ban imposed by the Chinese government in 1998, the importation of illegal logs from across the China–Myanmar border has increased exponentially to meet the huge demand for timber that comes largely from the almost uncontrolled building boom in the PRC. Although the illicit trade has declined in recent years on account of surplus stocks reducing demand, a formal bilateral agreement to manage sustainable forestry has yet to emerge.

Above all, the BRI has raised the level of alert among environmental experts around the world to a new level, given the focus of this mega-international cooperation initiative is on large-scale infrastructure development (i.e., roads, rails, ports, and energy facilities). Most of the current projects under the BRI blueprint build on the previous waves of Chinese large companies (mostly state owned) "going out" since the beginning of the 2000s (see chap. 8), and therefore the patterns of transboundary pollution, regulation, and social resistance are to some extent easier to trace.[7] However, with the significant scaling-up of the BRI over the past five years, more research needs to be done to expose the more remote and indirect, yet often severe, ecological impact of Chinese overseas investments, including in Africa and Latin America.[8]

Consequences of Climate Change

At the global level, China's rising contribution to global CO_2 (carbon dioxide) emissions from fossil fuel combustion has attracted significant attention. The burning of coal, in particular, pumps millions of tons of chemicals into the atmosphere. Efforts are now underway to invest in alternative sources, and China is becoming a world leader in developing cleaner coal-burning technology, solar panels, and wind turbines.[9] However, energy demand is outpacing reforms; thus, highly polluting coal will remain the primary source of China's energy supply for the foreseeable future. As a consequence, in 2007 China overtook the United States (with 25 percent of the world's total CO_2 emissions) to become the world's biggest emitter (see Figure 12.1).[10] Although per capita emissions are still relatively low (in 2016 China emitted 7.2 tons of CO_2 per capita, compared with 16.5 tons in the United States), they have already reached European Union levels (see Figure 12.2).

Not surprisingly, at the international level, the Chinese government remains committed to the principle of common but differentiated responsibilities based on historic cumulative emissions. It points out that the developed countries did not sacrifice growth for environmental concerns during their "industrial revolutions" and insists that it is the responsibility of richer countries to take the lead in cutting emissions. During recent United Nations Framework Convention on Climate Change talks, China's stance has softened to some degree. It now publicly commits to peak its energy consumption by 2030 and supports legally binding emissions caps post-2020. Under the 2016 Paris Agreement China's nationally appropriate mitigation actions are still contingent upon the transfer of enabling finance and technology from wealthier industrialized states, but it has agreed to provide biannual reports on mitigation action as well as to submit reports on greenhouse gas emissions.

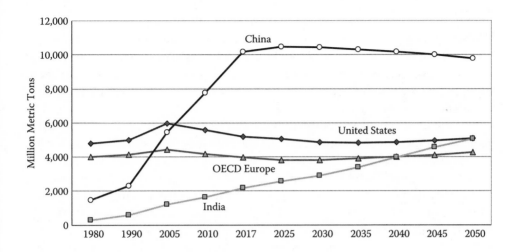

FIGURE 12.1 Carbon Dioxide Emissions (1980–2050)

Source: U.S. Energy Information Administration, *International Energy Outlook 2017*
https://www.eia.gov/outlooks/aeo/data/browser/#/?id=10-IEO2017.

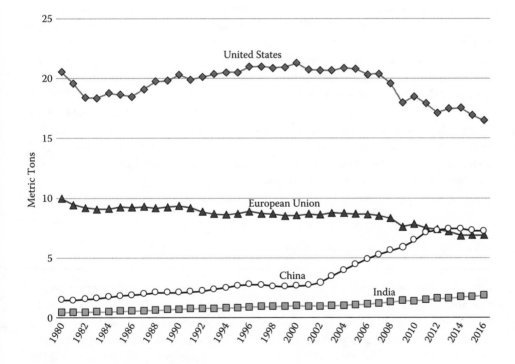

FIGURE 12.2 Carbon Dioxide Emissions per capita (1980–2016)

Source: Carbon Atlas, Global Carbon Project, http://www.globalcarbonatlas.org/

The Chinese government increasingly recognizes that the dire consequences of climate change demand an immediate response. In China's first National Climate Change Assessment Report published in late 2006, it was predicted that the average annual temperature could increase between 1.3 and 2.1 degrees by 2020 and as much as 3.3 degrees by 2050. Major cities in coastal areas will face serious challenges due to rising sea levels, and extreme weather patterns are likely to increase.

The impact of climate change on the Qinghai-Tibetan Plateau in China's far west is particularly worrying for both China and the Asia region. As the largest freshwater reserve outside the polar ice caps, the Plateau is also known as Asia's water tower, or the "Third Pole." For climate change, the Plateau is the equivalent of the proverbial canary in the coal mine that stopped singing (or died) as a warning to miners of dangerous methane gas buildup. The glaciers that feed Asia's great rivers—the Yellow, Yangtze, Mekong, Salween, Indus, Ganges, and Brahmaputra—have shrunk by at least 17 percent over the past decade. While the overall trend is one of glacial retreat, melting is occurring at different rates depending upon variables such as elevation and rainfall. Glacial melt has dramatic adverse effects on biodiversity, people, and livelihoods, with long-term implications for water, food, and energy security. Over the longer term, higher temperatures will increase flooding in the rainy season and reduce water in the dry season, thus affecting food production in the provinces downstream as well as the livelihoods of more than a billion people in China, South Asia, and Southeast Asia. Eventually, water shortages will occur on a massive scale. This is particularly troubling given that Asia already has less freshwater—about 3,920 cubic meters (about 5,130 cu yd) per person—than any other continent outside Antarctica.

In effect, China's current development trajectory represents a fragile balance between human and environmental needs that cannot be sustained over time. Is an environmental catastrophe inevitable, or does the potential exist to shift toward a more sustainable pattern of development? Clearly, much will depend upon China's capacity to adapt. How is the Chinese government responding to the crisis? And to what extent can citizen participation help to alleviate environmental problems?

TAKING ACTION: GOVERNMENT RESPONSES

Over the past two decades, the Chinese government has expressed a growing commitment toward environmental protection: the regulatory and legal frameworks have expanded, with a stronger emphasis upon ecological protection as well as pollution control. Environmental priorities have been fully integrated into the state five-year plans for development, culminating in the thirteenth five-year plan (2016–2020) that signals a turning point in the shift toward a less resource-intensive model of economic growth. Strategically, environmental protection is now considered a pillar industry alongside information technology and biotechnology. The government plans to invest 5 trillion yuan (US$761 billion) in the new-energy sector by 2020.

The most important change to have taken place is at the attitudinal level. During the early stage of economic reforms in the 1980s and early 1990s, environmental issues remained low on the political agenda. Rising pollution and other forms of environmental degradation were seen as an inevitable consequence of moderniza-tion. Environmental protection became a fundamental state policy (*jiben guoce*) in 1993, opening the way for further environmental laws and regulations. There now exists a realization at the highest levels of the Chinese Communist Party (CCP) that the pursuit of economic growth at all costs is no longer environmentally or socially sustainable. At the 2012 18th National Party Congress the concept of "ecological civ-ilization (*shengtai wenming*)" was officially incorporated into the Party Constitution, and ecological imperatives now underpin the broader strategy of building socialism with Chinese characteristics.

As in the case of many other states, China traditionally lacks a centralized reg-ulatory authority capable of mainstreaming environmental concerns into develop-ment policy making. It also experiences the familiar problem of poor interagency coordination. The upgrading of the State Environmental Protection Administration to a cabinet-level Ministry of Environmental Protection in March 2008 has not led to a significant increase in its authority at the central level; and the political status of environmental agencies working at the local level still have limited power to enforce regulations. After the 13th People's Congress in March 2018, the Ministry of Environmental Protection was restructured and transformed into the Ministry of Ecology and Environment (MEE), and its regulatory scope has been expanded from merely pollution control to cover natural conservation, biodiversity, climate adaptation and more. This is an important administrative step to further integrate, upgrade, and eventually mainstream environmental sustainability across all public policies.

Despite implementation problems, governing the environment from above has led to some impressive results. Most notably, China is now leading rather than fol-lowing many industrialized states in the pursuit of more efficient and cleaner en-ergy. It is on track to meet its voluntary target of reducing carbon intensity by unit of GDP between 40 to 45 percent from 2005 levels by 2020. This is largely due to the forced closure of hundreds of inefficient coal-fired power plants and state-owned industries, such as paper and pulp production, copper smelting, and cement pro-duction.[11] Plans are also underway to increase the share of nonfossil fuels in primary energy production to around 20 percent in 2020. China has overtaken the United States in wind energy capacity (41.8 GW of installed turbines in 2011), but it lags far behind in the development of shale gas due to technical and legal barriers. A na-tionwide campaign has helped to promote cleaner production methods in Chinese factories, strict vehicle emissions standards have been imposed in major cities, and reforestation programs are beginning to reap rewards. Since the late 1990s, the State Forestry Administration has planted more than four million hectares (1,618,742.57 ac) of new forest each year, and further measures are in place to expand forest cov-erage by forty million hectares (16,187,425.7 ac) by 2020 from 2005 levels. China is now leading the world in the conservation of natural systems that absorb carbon dioxide from the atmosphere (carbon sinks), as well as in wind, solar, and hydro power production.

Coinciding with the shift toward a market-based economy in China, top-down command and control measures are no longer seen as the only means of protecting the environment. To reduce pollution, market incentives are slowly being used to internalize environmental costs. For example, an environmentally informative labeling plan is now in place to promote green consumerism; a quota system for regulating SO_2 emissions has been set up in some provinces and cities; and new proposals have been introduced to place a monetary value on scarce resources such as water and coal. More ambitiously, to initiate a market mechanism for carbon pricing, new CO_2 trading schemes that create incentives to reduce emissions are operating in seven provinces and cities (Guangdong, Hubei, Beijing, Chongqing, Shanghai, Shenzhen, and Tianjin) with permits issued by local exchanges. Water trading is also taking place in a number of pilot cities with the potential to further develop market tools for the purpose of sharing water resources across jurisdictional boundaries.

ENVIRONMENTALISM FROM BELOW

Citizen involvement in environmental protection is also expanding. The Chinese print and television media play a critical role in channeling public opinion; and new forms of "electronic government" have provided an alternative virtual means of soliciting citizen ideas for environmental improvement.[12] Public participation is demonstrated most clearly in the emergence of environmental nongovernmental organizations (NGOs) that are seeking to bring about changes at the local level.

According to the NGO Center for Research at Tsinghua University, over 3,500 environmental NGOs are now operating across China.[13] Moreover, there are provincial level and cross-regional activism hubs and networks that bring together and enhance local NGOs' capacity and impact.[14] They vary greatly in the scope of their activities, the degree of government autonomy, and access to resources. What they tend to share in common is a strong desire for environmental policy reforms and changes on the ground. To this end, many prioritize the importance of environmental education, including training for government officials. Others focus on advocating alternative solutions for restoring degraded ecosystems, saving endangered species, or improving the effectiveness of pollution control mechanisms. At the community level, small initiatives can gain momentum especially when they bring about visible changes of the environment. A group of environmentalists in Gansu (many of whom are ethnic Tibetans) have helped to protect the habitat of the wild camel, leading to the construction of a new nature reserve in the water sources area of the Yangtze River and the Yellow River; a small NGO advocating the reduction of pesticide use in Yunnan has facilitated a revival in organic farming; in Qinghai a grassroots organization has successfully campaigned against the use of plastic bags in areas on the Tibetan Plateau, thus preempting a nationwide ban that came into effect on June 1, 2008; and in Beijing many groups are working to advance energy conservation among businesses and at the community level.[15]

The problem is that these kinds of initiatives often generate considerable resistance from local vested interests, including bureaucrats and business owners who do not want to do anything that may limit economic growth or lessen profits. This is exacerbated by the fact that the political status of NGOs in China remains unclear. Government regulations on social organizations—first promulgated by the State Council following the student-led pro-democracy movement in 1989—are highly restrictive. A new Charity Law, which came into effect in September 2016, seeks to further regulate the activities of domestic NGOs, requiring formal registration with the Ministry of Civil Affairs, while a separate new law for foreign NGOs requires registration with the Ministry of Public Security and introduces higher levels of surveillance.

The party-state is largely supportive of NGOs whose agenda coincides with its own, which is the case with many aspects of environmental protection. That said, the Chinese authorities are intolerant of any social movement or organization that is perceived to pose a direct threat to the regime or national stability.[16] Consequently, self-censorship remains a unique characteristic of Chinese environmental activism. Although this does not necessarily impede effective action, it does restrict the ability of NGOs to fulfill their creative potential as advocates of environmental protection. In effect, bringing about reforms from below remains limited by the refusal to relinquish control from above.

The extent to which state controls can continue to subdue public grievances over the longer term is a serious question. Social media ensures that environmental disasters—from toxic algae bloom in Lake Tai that turned the water fluorescent green to thousands of dead pigs floating in Shanghai's Huangpu River—are no longer hidden from public view. The Chinese journalist Cai Jing's documentary on the human impacts of pollution ("Under the Dome") was viewed by millions in a short period of time before being blocked by the authorities prior to the National People's Congress in March 2015—a living testament to the severity of the crisis as well as ineffective government controls.

Even more alarming for the party leadership is the fact that thousands of people, armed with facemasks and mobile phones, are now taking to the street to protest against polluting industries across China. According to the conservative estimates of the Ministry of Civil Affairs, there were more than eighty thousand environmental protests in 2012 alone. The majority of protests are still highly localized and limited to rural areas. However, large-scale demonstrations in urban areas, facilitated by the spread of mobile communications, have gained momentum in recent years. Mass protests against chemical factories producing paraxylene—a toxic petrochemical used in the manufacture of polyester, paints, and plastic—took place in the coastal cities of Xiamen in 2007, Dalian in 2011, and again in Ningbo in late October 2012, just before the 18th Party Congress. Seen by many as a victory for people power, the demonstrations caught the attention of the central authorities in Beijing, leading to production suspensions and factory relocations. With the availability of new media and communication technology, some locally rooted protests against industrial projects have been able to gather broader public attention and support from outside. Limited in number, it is nevertheless a promising trend that more NGOs are directly connected with local victim groups helping them to transform their specific grievances into sustainable policy changes, particularly in the field of zero-waste in urban cities.[17]

For those living with the consequences of environmental pollution, the potential exists to seek compensation through legal means, although many have chosen to give up on open confrontation and simply cope with harmful environmental conditions.[18] The Chinese media have reported a growing number of cases in which citizens have filed lawsuits against polluting enterprises, often with the support of legal aid centers. A 2011 landmark case involved mussel farmers in Tianjin who sought compensation via the Maritime Court for environmental harm caused by a coastal oil pipeline spill. The plaintiffs received US$1.9 million. Environmental litigation is still at an early stage of development, but the fact that ordinary citizens are pursuing a legal means of redress suggests a rise in public confidence in China's legal system (see chap. 7). Equally promising is the fact that polluters are facing more serious punitive action. In the wake of a rising tide of environmental disasters, special environmental courts have been set up in Wuxi, Guiyang, and Yunnan with special privileges to introduce innovative procedures. In a high-profile case in Yancheng, Jiangsu, the chairman of a chemical company that had discharged toxic chemicals into the city's water supply, received an eleven-year prison sentence.[19]

LIMITS TO ENVIRONMENTAL REFORM

Taking into account China's level of economic development, the new initiatives described above provide grounds for optimism. In seeking a sense of perspective, however, it is important to bear in mind that the overall strategy for economic development in China is still one of pro-growth, with the aim of quadrupling per capita income by 2020, in spite of the recent rhetoric about the "new normal," which reflects the intention to move the Chinese economy from the investment-labor-resource intensive mode to one based on technology and innovation with a lower growth rate. In addition, current efforts toward protecting the environment are limited by three key constraints: weak implementation at the local level; an overreliance upon large-scale engineering solutions; and a highly centralized decision-making process.

The Implementation Deficit

It is now widely recognized that environmental policies are extremely difficult to implement in China because of weak compliance at the local level. The basic problem is that self-serving officials collude with local enterprises to pursue profits at a cost to the environment. The situation is made worse by the fact that dirty factories are relocating away from large urban cities and into rural areas, where regulatory control is weaker. A sobering example is the village of Xinsi in Gansu province, where more than 250 children are reported to be suffering from lead poisoning—with up to five times the blood-lead levels considered safe by the World Health Organization. Local villagers were unaware of the significant health risks involved in living next to a lead factory, and their children now live with the consequences of severe intellectual impairment.[20]

It is already clear that uneven development is leading to a situation in which the richer regions can more easily adapt. Given that China's poorest regions—including Tibet and Xinjiang—are also the most ecologically fragile, a fundamental challenge for the Chinese government is to ensure that the burden of responsibility for environmental protection does not fall on the shoulders of those who are least able to carry it. Over the longer term, the risk is that sustainability will become the preserve of the rich thus exacerbating preexisting inequities. The Xi administration has elevated the importance of pollution in the evaluation system of bureaucrat and cadre promotion.[21] In late 2015, President Xi created and sent a 120-expert Central Environmental Inspection Team, or the "green team," under the then Ministry for Environmental Protection to all thirty-one provinces to investigate local institutions' environmental policy enforcement. When this Green Team came back to Beijing after two years' work, they held 2,900 businesses and more than 18,000 individuals accountable for violating central-level environmental policy or regulatory mandates.[22] However, the long-term impact of these new top-down measures on the improvement of local environmental law enforcement remains to be seen.

The Engineering Fix

A second major constraint on environmental protection is the continuing reliance on large-scale engineering projects that offset the benefits of alternative solutions. The construction of the highly controversial Three Gorges Dam (*Sanxia*) on the Yangtze River, which has achieved the goal of generating 22.5 GW of electricity (equivalent to fifteen nuclear reactors) but in the process caused significant ecological disruption and the displacement of more than 1.5 million people, is a good example of this trend.[23] Equally controversial is the south–north water transfer program (*nanshui beidiao gongcheng*), first proposed by Mao Zedong in 1952, that aims to alleviate flooding in the south and water scarcity in the north by diverting water from the Yangtze basin to the North China Plain. Three planned routes are designed to connect four river basins with three cities and six provinces. Now in operation, the eastern route is diverting water from the lower Yangtze basin to the city of Tianjin and four provinces of Jiangsu, Anhui, Shandong, and Hebei. A central route connects the Danjiangkou reservoir on the Han river to Beijing (providing up to one-third of the city's water supply) and the two provinces of Henan and Hebei. No final decision, as yet, has been made on the western route linking the headwaters of the Yangtze on the Qinghai-Tibetan Plateau to the Yellow River. Landslides and earthquakes present even the most hardened techno-optimist with a formidable challenge. Pervasive environmental problems include large-scale soil salinization, polluted sewage water intrusion, and adverse effects upon aquatic life along the routes, not to mention the unintended consequences upon the seasonal regulatory capacity of rivers under changing climatic conditions.

China has the highest number of large dams (those above 15 meters [49 ft] high) in the world, numbering 20,000 or almost half of the world's total. With plans to increase total installed hydropower capacity to 380 GW by 2020, there is likely to be a dam-building frenzy in the coming years. As noted by Vaclav Smil, it is not the emphasis upon dam building per se that is the problem. What is of concern is the obsession with scale and the inability to approach the harnessing of natural resources with an appreciation of the environmental and social costs involved.[24] In the case of the Three Gorges Dam, the costs are already apparent. The huge weight of water behind the dam is causing erosion of the riverbank, leading to landslides; the quality of water in the tributaries of the Yangtze has severely deteriorated; and sediment accumulation is greatly reducing the dam's future capacity for power generation and flood control.[25] From an international standpoint, a major concern is the fact that China's infrastructure investments overseas are often equally lax in conforming to environmental and social safeguards.

A Lack of Openness

A third constraint on environmental protection relates to China's highly centralized decision-making process. The relevance of public accountability in the Chinese context lies in its potential to act as a vital check against political excess, and as a corrective to policy interventions that exacerbate rather than alleviate public concerns. Witness the draconian measures taken by local officials to meet national energy-savings targets in 2010, in some instances cutting off power critical to households, businesses, and hospitals.[26] At a minimum, accountability can happen only within the context of an open society supported by the rule of law. The free flow of information is essential for effective policy making to take place. The implementation of a national sustainability agenda relies upon "learning by doing," which requires high levels of transparency across the policy-making system. An open public debate also plays a central role in the negotiation of the difficult trade-offs between individual concerns and social and environmental needs, as perceived by the Chinese people, who are, understandably, mostly concerned about raising living standards for themselves and their family. Above all, a balanced assessment of the complex relationships between poverty alleviation, energy security, and environmental protection cannot be made if decision-making power is highly concentrated; this inevitably increases the risk that powerful vested interests will hold sway over broader public concerns.

National measures on environmental information disclosure, introduced in the PRC in May 2008, are a positive step in the right direction. Under these guidelines, environmental agencies are required to disclose information on enterprises exceeding discharge quotas. For their part, corporations are under the obligation to disclose discharge data within a certain period of time or pay a fine of up to 100,000 yuan (roughly US$14,500). Since 2005, a single NGO—the Institute of Public and Environmental Affairs (IPE)—has made a critical contribution to the facilitation of public access to quality environmental data in China. With the support from a network of local environmental NGOs across the country and sometimes even local state agencies, IPE now publishes highly reliable and updated air, water and industrial pollution data on the web, freely accessible to all. Encouraged by IPE, a new alliance of NGOs is advocating to make data related to all incinerators, power plants, and other heavily polluting factories/projects more transparent and publicly available. However, they face more challenges ahead. Given that the environmental field covers diverse sectors beyond industrial pollution, the state will need to become more tolerant and respond effectively to NGO and the public's demand for accurate information.

IS A MORE SUSTAINABLE FUTURE POSSIBLE FOR CHINA?

Overall, China's approach to environmental governance is a story of both continuity and change. A strong preference for top-down decision making still remains, but it coexists with new forms of nonstate activism that reflect greater pluralism within Chinese society. In the early twenty-first century, Chinese leaders are caught between a continuing desire to control nature via large-scale engineering projects and a new aspiration to chart an alternative development path that reconciles human and environmental needs.

"Ecological civilization" is the most recent metaphor employed by the Chinese party-state for understanding the relationship between humans and nature that promises to transform the processes of industrialization and, in turn, reconnect Chinese civilization with its environmental genesis. It is a key part of former PRC President and CCP General Secretary Hu Jintao's so-called Scientific Outlook on Development and his commitment to creating a harmonious socialist society (see chaps. 4 and 5). The Xi Jinping leadership that took office in 2012–2013 has advanced the notion of combining socialist modernization with ecological progress. How these ideas actually translate into action remains to be seen. This new thinking reflects a deeper cultural aspiration that has yet to permeate through the domestic agenda. For this to happen, further reforms are required to support public participation in environmental efforts. Ultimately, redressing the balance between human and environmental needs is not simply a question of improving efficiency and taking corrective measures; it can be achieved only if the Chinese people who stand to benefit—both rich and poor—are central to the process.

Tipping the balance in favor of sustainability will also require greater cooperation at the international level. A fundamental problem with current Chinese practice is that efforts to protect environmental and human welfare are largely concentrated within China's territorial boundaries. This is not to suggest that China has failed to participate in relevant international treaties and regimes. Rather, it is to make the point that given the transboundary nature of environmental problems, China's growing demands for resources from other nations (see chap. 8) and its emerging role as a champion of international sustainable development, much more needs to be done to enhance environmental cooperation at the international level. In short, the internationalization of state-owned enterprises under the mandate of the government's "go global" strategy and the groundbreaking BRI requires environmental and social safeguards.

Clearly, co-leadership between China, the U.S., Europe, and other leading nations such as Japan is imperative for the purpose of sustaining global environmental stewardship. Transfers of knowledge, funds, and clean technologies from industrialized to developing countries will also remain important in the short to medium term. At the same time, a strong case can be made for a parallel transfer of experience and resources from the PRC to other developing countries that look to China as a model of development. Led by China, a new approach toward South-South cooperation that takes into account climate change may well help to break the unsustainable pattern of economic development that exists globally. In the coming years, the touchstone of the success of China's transition toward a sustainable model of development will be the extent to which it is able to reverse negative environmental trends and demonstrate an alternative vision both within and beyond its territorial boundaries.

NOTES

1. See Judith Shapiro, *Mao's War against Nature: Politics and the Environment in Revolutionary China* (New York: Cambridge University Press, 2001).

2. China's ecological footprint (measured on the basis of human demand on ecosystems relative to their capacity to regenerate) has quadrupled over the past four decades. Today, China has the largest biocapacity deficit amongst all nations. See WWF and China Council for International Cooperation on Environment and Development, *China Ecological Footprint Report 2010: Biocapacity, Cities and Development* (Beijing, WWF and CCICED, 2010).

3. President Xi launched the Silk Road Economic Belt and the 21st-Century Maritime Silk Road soon after he took office, and later these two initiatives were combined and became One-Belt-One-Road first and later the Belt Road Initiative. At least fifty-seven heads of the government attended the BRI summit in Beijing, May 2017.

4. Fengshi Wu and Richard Edmonds, "Environmental degradation in China," in *Critical Issues in Contemporary China: Unity, Stability and Development*, ed. Czes Tubilewicz (London: Routledge, 2017), 105–119.

5. Unless otherwise stated, the statistics used in this case study are taken from the official Chinese environmental yearbooks and the website of the Ministry of Environmental Protection http://www.mep.gov.cn.

6. The U.S. embassy in Beijing posts hourly air-quality readings for the city at http://www.stateair.net/web/post/1/1.html.

7. Elizabeth Economy and Michael Levi, *By All Means Necessary: How China's Resource Quest Is Changing the World* (Oxford: Oxford University Press, 2014); Fengshi Wu and Hongzhou Zhang, eds., *China's Global Quest for Resource: Water, Food and Energy* (London: Routledge Press, 2017).

8. William F. Laurance, for example, a world-renown professor specialized in the ecological impact of roads, has written multiple academic articles to warn the potentially devastating effects of some of the Chinese funded infrastructure projects in Africa or the Amazon region. See William F. Laurance, "China's Growing Footprint on the Globe Threatens to Trample the Natural World," *Conversation*, Dec. 6, 2017.

9. See Keith Bradhser, "China Leading Race to Make Clean Energy," *New York Times*, Jan. 30, 2010; and Worldwatch Institute, "China Leads Growth in Global Wind Power Capacity," May 30, 2012, www.worldwatch.org/china-leads-growth-global-wind-power-capacity.

10. Between 1950 and 2002, China's cumulative CO_2 emissions totaled only 9.3 percent of the world total. Up until the turn of the twenty-first century, the Chinese economy grew without placing a significant burden on energy resources. This has recently changed as a consequence of an investment-led shift back to heavy industry, together with higher levels of consumption growth. Hence, the rapid growth in carbon emissions is a fairly new phenomenon.

11. It is, however, important to recognize that reducing carbon intensity does not guarantee a reduction in overall carbon emissions. Under conditions in which a structural energy mix remains constant, energy intensity declines naturally with economic growth even while absolute energy consumption continues to increase.

12. For example, in the planning stage of the tenth five-year plan (2001–2006), the National Development and Reform Commission was reported to have received over ten thousand suggestions from citizens, many of which were environment-related.

13. Liu Sha, "Environmental NGOs Grow Across China But Still Struggle for Support," *Global Times*, Dec. 6, 2012, www.globaltimes.cn/content/714330.shtml.

14. Fengshi Wu, "Environmental Activism in Provincial China: Comparative Evidence from Guangdong and Guangxi," *Journal of Environmental Policy and Planning*, 15/1 (2013): 89–108; Maria Bondes and Thomas Johnson, "Beyond Localized Environmental Contention: Horizontal and Vertical Diffusion in a Chinese Anti-Incinerator Campaign," *Journal of Contemporary China* 26, no. 106 (2017): 504–520.

15. To date, much of the literature on environmental activism in China has tended to focus on a small number of relatively independent organizations in Beijing such as Friends of Nature or Global Village. Many organizations are also working below the radar in diverse regions of China, as noted in these examples.

16. For how the Chinese authority categorize NGOs and interact with them differently, see: Xiaoguang Kang and Heng Han, "Graduated Control: Research on State-Society Relationship in Contemporary Mainland China," in *State and Civil Society: The Chinese Perspective*, ed. Deng Zhenglai (WorldScientific, 2010), 97–120; Fengshi Wu and Kin-man Chan, "Graduated Control and Beyond: The Evolving Governance over Social Organizations in China," *China Perspectives* 3 (2012): 9–17.

17. H. Christoph Steinhardt and Fengshi Wu, "In the Name of the Public: Environmental Protest and the Changing Landscape of Popular Contention in China," *China Journal* 75, no. 1 (2016): 61–82.

18. Anna Lora-Wainwright, *Resigned Activism: Living with Pollution in Rural China* (Cambridge, MA: MIT Press, 2017).

19. Lucy Hornby, "Chinese Executives Sentenced for Polluting Lake," *Reuters*, June 2, 2009, www.reuters.com/article/environmentNews/idUSTRE5513G820090602.

20. Shai Oster and Jane Spencer, "A Poison Spreads Amid China's Boom," *Wall Street Journal*, Sept. 30, 2006.

21. Sarah Eaton and Genia Kostka, "Authoritarian Environmentalism Undermined? Local Leaders' Time Horizons and Environmental Policy Implementation in China," *China Quarterly* 218 (2014): 359–380.

22. Leigh Wedell, "What Did China's 'Green Teams' Accomplish?" *Diplomat*, Feb, 10, 2018, https://thediplomat.com/2018/02/what-did-chinas-green-teams-accomplish/.

23. Other concerns include silt buildup behind the dam, which is highly likely to stall power generation and place the dam in jeopardy as well as block downstream regions of vital nutrients resulting in the destruction of much of China's finest scenery and wetlands habitat.

24. Vaclav Smil, *China's Past, China's Future: Energy, Food, Environment* (London: Routledge Curzon, 2004).

25. Serious silt buildup in the Three Gorges reservoir is encouraging further dam building in the tributaries of the Yangtze, thus leading to a vicious cycle of ecological degradation without significantly improving energy security.

26. Yuan Duanduan and Feng Jie, "Behind China's Green Goals," *ChinaDialogue*, Mar. 24, 2011, www.chinadialogue.net/article/show/single/en/4181-Behind-China-s-green-goals.

SUGGESTED READINGS

Cai, Jing. *Under the Dome*. 2015. (Video). Available online: https://www.youtube.com/watch?v= MhIZ50HKIpo.

Economy, Elizabeth C. *The River Runs Black: The Environmental Challenge to China's Future.* Ithaca, NY: Cornell University Press, 2004.

Geall, Sam. *China and the Environment: The Green Revolution.* London: Zed Books, 2013.

Liu, Jianguo, and Jared Diamond. "China's Environment in a Globalizing World: How China and the Rest of the World Affect Each Other." *Nature* 435 (June 2005): 1179–1186.

Ma, Jun. *China's Water Crisis.* Translated by Nancy Yang Lin and Lawrence R. Sullivan. Norwalk, CT: EastBridge, 2004.

Marks, Robert. *China: An Environmental History*, 2nd ed. Lanham, MD: Rowan & Littlefield, 2017.

Mertha, Andrew C. *China's Water Warriors: Citizen Action and Policy Change.* Ithaca, NY: Cornell University Press, 2008.

Morton, Katherine. *International Aid and China's Environment: Taming the Yellow Dragon.* London: Routledge, 2005.

Lora-Wainwright, Anna. *Resigned Activism: Living with Pollution in Rural China.* Cambridge, MA: MIT Press, 2017.

Shapiro, Judith. *China's Environmental Challenges.* 2nd ed. Cambridge: Polity Press, 2015.

Stern, Rachel E. *Environmental Litigation in China: A Study in Political Ambivalence.* New York: Cambridge University Press, 2013.

Sternfeld, Eva, ed. *Routledge Handbook of Environmental Policy in China.* New York: Routledge, 2017.

Wu, Fengshi, and Hongzhou Zhang, eds. *China's Global Quest for Resource: Water, Food and Energy.* London: Routledge, 2017.

Yang, Ruby, and Thomas Lennon. *The Warriors of Qiugong.* (Documentary on the Struggle to Save China's Environment.) New York: Thomas Lennon Films and Chang Ai Media Project, 2010.

Zhang, Joy, and Michael Barr, *Green Politics in China: Environmental Governance and State-Society Relations.* London: Pluto Press

13

Policy Case Study: Public Health

JOAN KAUFMAN

Health-care provision and health-care policy are important themes in China's modern history and contemporary politics. From the late nineteenth and early twentieth centuries up to the time of the founding of the People's Republic of China (PRC), China was known as the "sick man of Asia" with high rates of death from infectious and preventable diseases. In fact, the blatant neglect of the public's health was a rallying cry for change at the end of the republican era. One appeal of communism to China's vast rural population was the promise of equitable social-welfare investment, especially for health and education.

During the early years of the new regime, attention to health and other social issues began to pay off, with rapid improvements in reducing mortality rates and increasing life expectancy. Health policy during the Maoist era gave priority to primary care, preventive medicine, sanitation, and equitable access to services that made China's population among the healthiest in the developing world.

But in the 1980s and 1990s, the shift to a marketized economy and fiscal decentralization led to the breaking of the "iron rice bowl," which had guaranteed most Chinese free or inexpensive social services, including health care. By the end of the 1990s, medical expenses topped the list of reasons that rural families gave for falling into poverty.[1] A World Health Organization (WHO) report in 2000 ranked the PRC's health system at number 144 out of 191 countries according to measures such as health-care inequalities, fair financing, and patient satisfaction.[2]

In more recent years, China's response to epidemics like Severe Acute Respiratory Syndrome (SARS) and AIDS have shown how bureaucratic governance of health policy can both adversely affect the control of emerging infectious diseases and contribute to positive change. After the SARS debacle in 2003, the Hu Jintao administration (2002–2012) made medical care financing and reform a key part of their equity-oriented political agenda under the rubric of creating a "harmonious socialist society," which resulted in significant improvements in areas like insurance coverage, changes that have continued to advance in the Xi Jinping era (2012–). However, the health and income improvements that have come with China's rapid economic development in the last decades, combined with thirty-five years of strict population control, have led to new serious challenges related to a rapidly aging population (see chap. 14), lifestyle diseases (diet and smoking), and the health impacts of severe environmental pollution (see chap. 12).

This case study reviews the main phases of public health policy in China since 1949 and highlights achievements, challenges, and future prospects. The SARS crisis is discussed as a major turning point in China's approach to health policy, and the government's response to HIV/AIDS from 1985 to 2018 will be used as a window into how health policy is made and revised in the PRC.

THE MAOIST APPROACH TO PUBLIC HEALTH

Control of infectious diseases, rampant in China before 1949, was an initial priority for the communist government. Preventable infectious diseases such as plague and cholera, vaccine-preventable childhood diseases, and vector-borne diseases such as schistosomiasis (snail fever) and intestinal parasites (worms) sickened and killed millions each year in the precommunist era.[3] A campaign approach to public health, utilizing propaganda and mass mobilization, was developed during these early years of the regime, and "patriotic health campaigns" have been a hallmark of China's approach to health-policy implementation ever since.

One of the first actions of the new regime after 1949 was the launching of a massive campaign to eradicate sexually transmitted diseases, involving both political and health-service approaches.[4] Prostitutes were arrested and sent for rehabilitation and job training, while medical workers diagnosed and treated their sexually transmitted diseases. A mass campaign against opium use, which emphasized treating addicts as victims of the "old society" and imperialism rather than as criminals or deviants, but also made use of coercion (including capital punishment for dealers), had, by 1952, essentially eliminated an epidemic that had plagued China for more than a hundred years.[5]

To bring infectious diseases under control, a combination of political mobilization and investment in public-health projects, such as improving sanitation, the training and deploying of a corps of primary health-care workers to staff subsidized (essentially free) health stations throughout the country, and nutritional improvements brought about by increased agricultural production and improved food supply system set in motion a dramatic "epidemiological transition" during the 1960s and 1970s. As a result, death rates fell to levels seen only in countries with higher per capita incomes.

When the PRC was founded in 1949, life expectancy in China was just thirty-six years. By the mid-1950s, it had increased by about ten years, and at the end of the Maoist era in 1976, life expectancy had risen to sixty-six. Likewise there were dramatic improvements in maternal mortality (death in childbirth) and infant mortality (see Table 13.1), due at least in part to the reduction in the number of births per woman from more than six in the 1950s to a little over half that by 1976. Of course, the politically induced "Great Leap Forward" famine that led to as many as forty-five million deaths was a tragic setback to improving the health of the Chinese people.

China's primary health-care system became a target of the Cultural Revolution after Mao had proclaimed, in 1965, "The Ministry of Public Health is not a Ministry of Public Health for the people, so why not change its name to the Ministry of Urban Health, the Ministry of Gentlemen's Health, or even to Ministry of Urban Gentlemen's Health?. . . In medical and health work put the emphasis on the countryside!"[6] Reflecting a historical tension in China (as in many other countries) about the balance between investing in the urban hospital system versus rural public health, the PRC's health-spending pendulum shifted strongly toward the construction of a prevention-focused equity-oriented public-health approach for the rural poor during the Cultural Revolution and its aftermath, an approach that was often touted as a model for the developing world.[7]

In the urban areas, health insurance for workers and cadres was provided by their work unit. Urban migration was strictly controlled. For rural citizens, because the rural economy was organized into large agricultural production units, the "people's communes," it was possible to allocate a portion of the commune funds to support such an approach, including a rudimentary health insurance system. With basic services provided at the village level by about two million minimally trained community health workers called **barefoot doctors** and a network of clinics and better health facilities and hospitals at higher levels of administration, most rural citizens had access to basic medical care.[8]

In the late 1970s, over 90 percent of rural citizens were covered by a health insurance system called the **Cooperative Medical Scheme (CMS)**. Since rural mobility was restricted by the household registration (*hukou*) system, and insurance coverage was dependent on referral up the tiered chain from village clinic to commune hospital

TABLE 13.1 China's Health, ca. 1950–2016

	ca. 1950	1978–1980	2000	2016	India 2016	U.S. 2016
Life Expectancy at birth (years)	40.1	66.0	71.2	76.3	68.6	78.7
Infant Mortality (per 1000 live births)	250	58.9	28.8	8.6	33.6	5.7
Under 5 Child Mortality (per 1000 live births)	260	79.4	35.0	10.0	41.6	6.7
Maternal Mortality (per 100,000 births)	1500	165	57	27	174	14

Sources: Dean T. Jamison, and World Bank. 1984. China, the Health Sector. Washington, DC: World Bank; Nancy E. Riley, *China's Population: New Trends and Challenges. Population* Bulletin 59.2 (June 2004). Washington, DC: Population Reference Bureau, http://www.prb.org/Source/59.2ChinasPopNewTrends.pdf; "Medical and Health Services in China," *Xinhua*, December 26, 2012, http://news.xinhuanet.com/english/china/2012-12/26/c_132064836_2.htm; Gao Yanqiu, Carine Ronsmans, and An Lin, "Time Trends and Regional Differences in Maternal Mortality in China from 2000 to 2005," *Bulletin of the World Health Organization*, August 25, 2009, http://www.who.int/bulletin/volumes/87/12/08-060426/en/; China Profile, http://www.china-profile.com/data/fig_WPP2010_5q0_Boths.htm; World Bank World Development Indicators.

to county facility, access to higher and more expensive levels of health care was carefully controlled.

The local-level curative health system of basic care was supported by investments in preventive health through the "patriotic health campaigns" that carried out public projects such as insect and snail control and improving access to clean water. These campaigns also educated the public about disease prevention through such means as handwashing, prenatal care, and immunizations.[9]

While few rural Chinese wish for a return to the restrictions and shared poverty of the commune system, which was dismantled in the early 1980s when the country returned to family farming and a market economy (see chap. 8), and few would glorify the quality of China's rural medical-care system in the Maoist era, many long for a return to its equity and emphasis on prevention, and these themes have permeated the current debates on health reform and are reflected in some of the new reform initiatives.

MARKET REFORMS AND HEALTH CARE

After the breakup of the commune system in the early 1980s, the rural CMS was dismantled, and health-care financing was delegated to provinces and local areas, including villages, which turned to the market economy to provide the necessary funds by privatizing much of the health-care system. Since many villages were no longer able to pay them, most barefoot doctors either returned to farming or became fee-for-service private practitioners, which was a blow to providing equitable basic health care in rural China.

As public financing of health care decreased, the unregulated market (especially for drugs and medical tests) steadily increased the price of care. Limited public finances were diverted to cover staff salaries at county- and township-level facilities. Health-care stations at the local level were supported by village governments, but medical staff salaries had to be earned from fees for service and drug sales. By 1993, only 13 percent of rural residents were still covered by rural health insurance.[10] Rural citizens who could afford to do so bypassed township (former commune) facilities for the better county-level care, undermining the tiered referral chain and introducing high levels of health-care inequality in the countryside.

There were also numerous indicators of the reemergence of sharp urban-rural inequalities in the distribution of health-care resources and access. In 1999, of total government health spending, a full 25 percent occurred in just four of China's wealthiest cities and provinces, Beijing, Shanghai, Zhejiang, and Jiangsu. In 2002, 80 percent of medical services were located in cities, although 60 percent of China's population lived in the rural areas.[11] It was precisely this inequitable investment and urban focus of the medical system that became the rallying cry for Mao during the Cultural Revolution. While health reform is now back on the government's policy agenda and reconstructing an equitable health-care system is a stated priority, closing the gap will not be easy.

The health-care system that has been in place since the 1980s when the reform era began, with its focus on patient fee-based financing of curative rather than preventive care, has shifted attention and investments away from vital public health education and public works that reduce both chronic and infectious diseases, like providing clean drinking water, pest eradication, and education for healthy lifestyles. Even with recent improvements in health insurance coverage (see next paragraph), the focus remains on curative services. This threatens the ability to control new emerging and common infectious diseases and to prevent the serious and more costly complications of the diseases that currently are the leading causes of death (see next paragraph) including noncommunicable diseases like cancer, diabetes, heart disease, and tobacco-related illnesses, which now constitute 70 percent of China's disease burden.[12]

Several important demographic trends are shaping current health challenges. Rapidly increasingly urbanization and population aging are accelerating the already serious burden of noncommunicable diseases (NCDs). More than half (57 percent) of China's residents now live in cities and that number will increase to 60–70 percent by 2030 because of the accelerated population movement under China's "New Style Urbanization" plan (see chap. 10) Those without urban household registration are not covered by health insurance in the cities where they live and pay high out-of-pocket costs for health care.

China population is also rapidly aging, the result of thirty-five years of the highly restrictive population policy that has shrunk the proportional size of younger demographic cohorts[13] relative to older ones and the fact that senior citizens are living longer due to better health care. The percentage of the population over sixty years of age is 12.4 percent now and will grow to 28 percent (402 million) in 2040.[14] As the population ages, however, it is not aging healthily: the burden of NCDs is increasing. In 2018, 85 percent of all deaths were due to NCDs.[15] These diseases, diabetes and cancer, especially lung cancer, have been on the rise as a result of poor diets, smoking, and exposure to China's severe air, water, and soil pollution. Ten percent of adults over twenty have diabetes, 23 percent of boys under twenty are overweight or obese, and China ranks number 2 globally (after the U.S.) in child obesity.[16] There are about 315 million (overwhelming male) smokers in China,[17] who on average light up more than 2,000 cigarettes each and account for more than 40 percent of the world's cigarette consumption.[18] The rate of increase in new lung cancer cases has surged in the last ten to fifteen years, with more than 730,000 reported in 2015.[19] That same year it was estimated that one in three men who were then under twenty years old would die of lung cancer.[20] The overall cancer rate in China in general is exploding, with over 4.3 million new cancer patients and 2.8 million deaths in 2015.[21] In fact, environmental pollution is considered the most important factor in the rapidly rising cancer rate. There is a 5.5-year reduction in life expectancy, attributable to air pollution, for those living north of the Huaihai River, which separates north and south China.[22] More than half of China's groundwater is polluted and not fit for human consumption, due to pesticide runoff and heavy metals, which obviously has important health implications.[23]

The Chinese leadership is fully aware of these challenges. An ambitious plan, "Healthy China 2030," was launched in August 2016 that sets goals and targets for health insurance coverage, healthy lifestyle, increased life expectancy (to seventy-nine years), access to drugs, improved community-based prevention and care, and care for the elderly. A series of government reforms that began in March 2018 reflected

China's commitment to reorganizing and coordinating its weak and fragmented health-care governance structure. The newly renamed National Health Commission has been charged with promoting the Healthy China 2030 initiative and will be responsible for formulating national health policies, coordinating and advancing medical and health-care reform, establishing a national basic medicine system, elder care, overseeing public health programs, including health emergencies, as well as family planning services. The commission's director, Dr. Ma Xiaowei, seems well suited to address current health challenges, especially compared with China's previous Minister of Health and Family Planning, Li Bin, who lacked medical credentials.

China signed on to the World Health Organization's International Convention on Tobacco Control in 2003 and has belatedly begun to institute policies to restrict and discourage tobacco use. New regulatory authorities in the pharmaceutical and health-care sector were established, including a reorganized State Drug Administration, which will operate under a new State Market Regulatory Administration (SMRA) that also absorbed the functions of the General Administration of Quality Supervision, Inspection, and Quarantine (AQSIQ), which, among other things managed entry and exit health quarantines, import and export food safety, and food production. Responsibility for implementing tobacco control was moved to the newly renamed National Health Commission and away from the Ministry of Industry and Information Technology where it was poorly implemented.

One of the most important reforms was the establishment of the State Administration for Medical Security Insurance (SAMI) that will regulate and unify different types of medical insurance for urban and rural residents. This entity will be consolidated and eventually unified into a single national system for all citizens not tied to residence (to which it is currently tied). Urban residents with household registrations (*hukou*) have always received health insurance from their work units; rural residents have received health insurance since 2008 through the reestablished CMS (cooperative medical service), which is tied to household registration in their home villages or towns. But China's many millions of rural economic migrants have been denied medical care in the cities where they work because they still hold a rural *hukou*. SAMI is overseeing experiments in provinces and large municipalities that eliminate the *hukou* as a requirement for receiving health insurance and medical care.

THE SARS CRISIS

The deadly Severe Acute Respiratory Syndrome (SARS) epidemic broke out in China in 2002–2003. It was first spread from animals to humans in southern China probably via live-animal markets, a long tradition in Chinese communities that seek the freshest ingredients for cooking and provide an easy mechanism for human infection from animals

When SARS was first detected in Guangdong in November 2002, provincial authorities concealed the gravity of the early epidemic. Between then and January 2003, the outbreak gained momentum in the province, but the epidemic was reported to the World Health Organization (WHO) only on February 11, 2003, and then only after the organization initiated an inquiry, based upon reports received from Hong

Kong's Global Outbreak Alert and Response Network (GOARN). A WHO team was dispatched from Geneva to investigate the outbreak on February 19 but was stonewalled in Beijing. The team was not granted permission to travel to Guangdong until April.

These failures in early acknowledgment and appropriate response during March and April set the stage for China's massive SARS epidemic in the following months and allowed the outbreak to spread to Hong Kong and from there to the world. Through a combination of luck (virus seasonality) and effective person-to-person control measures, the epidemic subsided by the summer of 2003. Toward the end of the worldwide epidemic, of the 8,422 cases and 916 deaths in thirty countries and Hong Kong, 5,327 cases and 349 deaths (63 percent) were in China.[24]

Only when SARS became an international embarrassment for Beijing did the central government intervene. In a dramatic move, the Chinese government fired the minister of health and changed course, instituting a rarely seen transparency and honesty in reporting, and allocating over US$250 million in emergency funding for stopping the spread of SARS. The "loss of face" and the resulting policy reversal set in motion the actions that brought the epidemic under control. This was an example of how political will and national mobilization are required for tackling serious threats to public health and provided lessons for China's response to its AIDS epidemic and other newly emerging infectious diseases like avian influenza.

The SARS epidemic was a wake-up call for China's government on the deterioration of the capacity of China's rural health system. However, the extensive, if weakened health infrastructure, was still able to rise to the occasion once national leadership provided the mandate for action, along with adequate funding.

It is important to note that few countries in the world have as great a capacity as the PRC for national mobilization that extends to the most remote corners of a large nation. During the SARS epidemic, the patriotic health campaign approach of the 1950s and 1960s was resurrected to mobilize the population to self-quarantine, report fellow citizens with fevers, and extol medical personnel, especially nurses, who were at the forefront of the control effort and played an important role in keeping the epidemic from spreading in China's rural areas.[25] This mobilization was precisely what was required to put in place the series of preventive measures that broke the chain of SARS transmission.

China was able to offer some of its own lessons learned from its domestic response to SARS during the West Africa Ebola epidemic in 2014.[26] The PRC's contribution to the global Ebola response, coordinated through the WHO (and other UN agencies) with whom China has worked closely on its own emerging infectious diseases surveillance and reporting efforts since SARS, while mainly humanitarian, also arose from its desire to protect both Chinese citizens and Chinese firms and its growing economic interests in the region. As of November 2014, the PRC had provided four successive waves of humanitarian aid to the West African countries for a total of $123 million, China's largest-ever humanitarian commitment. This included deployment of three expert disease control teams, which collectively totaled 115 people as well as a 59-member Chinese laboratory team (to Sierra Leone) to provide technical support and help the country build its lab-testing capacity. This "soft power" effort by China helped restore its global reputation as a good global citizen following the

SARS debacle a decade earlier and has set the stage for further health aid, which will be orchestrated through the new China International Development Cooperation Agency under the State Council, established in March 2018.

AIDS IN CHINA: EPIDEMIC AND RESPONSE

The lessons the PRC government learned from its SARS experience, especially the cost of its belated response, has had lasting benefits for the control of infectious disease threats in the country. The outbreak, in spring 2013, of a virulent new and fatal strain of avian flu, H7N9, was met with an aggressive and transparent response by the Chinese government, which worked closely with both the World Health Organization and the U.S. Centers for Disease Control (CDC) to quickly identify cases, close live-animal markets, and share viral strains for analysis. These actions limited the spread of the virus, which infected 137 and caused 38 deaths, almost all limited to the region (Shanghai, Zhejiang, Jiangsu) where it originated.

China's AIDS advocates from government, civil society, academia, and their international partners grabbed the opportunity of the PRC's post-SARS aggressive approach to dealing with infectious disease to urge more action to curtail the spread of the HIV virus. They highlighted the problems of official concealment and media control that had initially let SARS spread and the need for transparency, government leadership, and national mobilization that had been effective in dealing with that disease.

AIDS is an infectious disease, though spread less easily than SARS. However, the stigma and embarrassment associated with its two main routes of transmission, sex and drugs, makes AIDS much harder to openly discuss and address, especially in China's morally conservative society. However, there was no question that if not controlled, AIDS would have serious economic and social impacts in China, as tragically evidenced by several sub-Saharan African countries.

Origins of the Epidemic

China's AIDS epidemic began in the early 1980s among needle-sharing intravenous drug users along the southern border with Myanmar (Burma). Myanmar is a major grower of the opium poppies that are the source of heroin. At that time the disease was viewed by the Chinese authorities as a problem limited to a marginal, deviant population and as a largely foreign illness associated with illicit behavior, which could be controlled by testing all foreigners who entered the country.

The government was forced to take action when an AIDS epidemic broke out among paid blood-plasma donors in central China in the mid-1990s. The source of the epidemic was intravenous drug users traveling through the major transportation crossroads of Henan province who earned money by selling their blood at plasma collection stations run by so-called **blood heads**—often with the collusion of local officials—who, in turn, stood to profit by selling what they had collected to medical firms and hospitals that needed the blood for transfusions or the manufacture of drugs derived from blood products. Many poor farmers in Henan and bordering provinces (Anhui, Hunan, Shanxi, Hubei, Hunan) also sold blood at these stations, where blood samples were pooled and red blood cells then reinjected into donors to allow for more frequent donations. The result was widespread HIV infections, which were then transmitted to sexual partners and through pregnancy and delivery to newborns.

A retired doctor, Gao Yaojie, was among the first to investigate and expose the severity of the epidemic caused by these tainted blood-donation practices. Dr. Gao's investigations in the 1990s were widely reported in the Chinese and international press and led to the exposure of a government cover-up by Henan provincial authorities.[27] As the plight of the affected victims in Henan was publicized, it created a flood of sympathy among China's citizens. Previously, there had been little public sympathy for sufferers of AIDS, who mainly tended to be heroin users or commercial sex workers, both highly stigmatized and illegal groups.

The fact that Henan's farmers and their affected children and elderly parents were "innocent victims" helped the AIDS crisis gain public awareness and led to a demand for action. The pressure on the government to respond, along with existing concern about the potential for a political crisis generated by demands for justice by infected farmers, pushed the government to act.[28]

The Government Responds

To address the plight of central China's AIDS-infected farmers, in September 2003, the government announced a free national AIDS treatment program, one of the few countries in the world to do so at that time. This important (and expensive) step was the first of many that moved China out of denial in its response to its AIDS epidemic. Mainly focused on the estimated eighty thousand infected persons, mostly in central China, requiring immediate treatment, the program titled "The Four Frees and the One Care" provided free, domestically produced, antiretroviral drugs to all rural residents and poor urban residents with HIV/AIDS; free voluntary counseling and testing; free drugs to pregnant women living with HIV/AIDS to prevent mother-to-child transmission and HIV testing of newborn babies; free schooling for children orphaned by HIV/AIDS; and care and economic assistance to affected families affected by HIV/AIDS.[29] With this policy, the government squarely recognized the need for treatment and care, not just for disease treatment but also as a means of improving the lives of people and functioning of communities affected by HIV and AIDS.

These actions, and the greater transparency that has accompanied them, were initiated by the administration of CCP general secretary Hu Jintao and PRC premier Wen Jiabao (2002–2012), which defined itself as giving higher priority to helping the poor and being more concerned with equity than their predecessors (see chap. 6). A State Council AIDS Working Committee (SCAWCO) was established in early 2004, chaired by Vice Premier Wu Yi (who had successfully steered the SARS response in 2003), elevating the importance of the AIDS issue at the national level. Following similar moves put in place during the SARS epidemic, the government clearly stated its intention to hold all government officials accountable for their honesty in dealing with AIDS and for ensuring heightened attention, surveillance, and resources for infectious disease control. A strong five-year action plan for dealing with AIDS was published in 2006, and the State Council issued a decree the same year signaling its determination to fight AIDS. Premier Wen Jiabao met publicly with AIDS patients and orphans, including in Henan villages affected by the blood scandal, an unprecedented step for such a high-level official, and one meant to show the government's commitment to confronting the problem.

Trends and Developments in AIDS Policy

There have been many other positive developments in China's AIDS response. As part of both outside funding requirements and donor calls for greater participation of people living with AIDS in the global AIDS response, some urban hospitals have set up patient groups that routinely participate in meetings and workshops on AIDS. In January 2013, China had its first successful AIDS discrimination case when a court awarded compensation to a man who was denied employment as a teacher after he tested positive for HIV.[30]

Chinese leaders have also acknowledged that there is a need for NGOs to play a major role in China's AIDS response, and there are now nearly a thousand such groups, including AIDS orphan charities, patient support groups, and groups that work with victims who shun government services programs, such as sex workers, drug users, and gay men. Many of those affected by HIV/AIDs prefer the confidentiality, flexibility and accessibility that these NGOS provide compared with more official or formal organizations.[31]

For example, in Chengdu, a mostly volunteer group of gay men, the Chengdu Gay Community Care Organization, provides AIDS education outreach and condoms in bars and bathhouses, and has been working with the provincial and municipal health bureaus and foreign donors in their efforts to provide care for infected gay people. Homosexuality was only decriminalized in PRC a short time ago, and the growing tolerance for gay persons has made it easier to involve that community in the fight against HIV/AIDS.[32] This is providing a model for other NGOs working on sensitive issues in China.

In November 2012, then vice premier and soon-to-be premier Li Kejiang said that HIV/AIDS was "not only a medical issue but also a social challenge" that required close collaboration between government organizations and greater participation of NGOs.[33] Early in their first term in power, the Xi Jinping administration signaled their support for increasing civil society's place at the table by reducing the red tape for registering an NGO, which was an important step for expanding the reach of China's AIDS response. However, in January 2017, a law went into effect requiring foreign NGOs in the PRC to officially register with China's Public Security Bureau and placing other restrictions on their operations,[34] This has already affected the work of many foreign NGOs that support local groups such as the Britain-based International HIV/AIDS Alliance that supports AidsCare China, an NGO in Yunnan. While the law is targeted at foreign NGOs operating in China, it has also had a chilling effect on the many Chinese partner organizations who rely on their foreign partners for funding and technical advice.

Peng Liyuan, a popular singer/actress who became China's first lady when her husband, Xi Jinping, became the president of the PRC in 2013, has been the WHO Goodwill Ambassador for Tuberculosis and HIV/AIDS since 2011 and has been a strong advocate for children affected by AIDS, including recording a music video with AIDS orphans for the 25th World AIDS Day in December 2012.[35] The United Nations organization, UNAIDS, presented Peng with an Award for Outstanding Achievement in January 2017.[36]

Even with the national will to tackle AIDS, the changes wrought by four decades of fiscal and political decentralization have made the provincial governments increasingly independent of Beijing, even within the context of China's unitary political system. China's national ministries may set policy and program guidelines, but real control over decisions and budgets rests with provincial and local governments. Sometime provincial governments may actually be ahead of the national curve as when the Guangdong Department of Education removed restrictions against people living with HIV from serving as teachers in September 2013.[37]

In contrast, officials in Henan, where the "blood head" scandal occurred and which still has one of the highest concentrations of AIDS-infected population, have blocked accurate reporting on the disease, as well as some research and prevention efforts, and have been accused of not providing adequate treatment or compensation as required by law to some victims. In August 2012, three hundred AIDS patients protested outside the headquarters of the provincial government,[38] and ninety of them took their protest to the Ministry of Civil Affairs in Beijing the following February.[39] The Henan government has denied any official responsibility in the 1990s scandal, and there has never been a full investigation or report. Because Li Keqiang was the provincial governor and then party secretary in Henan shortly after the crisis took place, some activists blame him for the cover-up and police harassment of those who wanted to expose the truth and are skeptical that there will be an honest accounting during his tenure as premier.[40]

Continuing the Fight

The number of people living with HIV (PLHIV) who are aware of their condition in China has risen steadily from about 26,000 in 1990 to 410,000 in 2000 to 850,000 in 2018, with an estimated 400,000 more who are not aware or have not reported their infection.[41] (The number of PLHIV in the U.S. is 1.1 million).

The largest annual increases in HIV/AIDS cases were in the late 1990s and early 2000s, with the rate of increase slowing considerably as the government became more open and proactive in dealing with the epidemic. Nevertheless, the epidemic continues to spread (see Figure 13.1), with 115,000 new cases in 2015, an 11.6 percent increase over the previous year.[42] There was a reported 14 percent surge in new cases in the first half of 2018, with 40,000 in the second quarter alone, although some of this large increase is attributed to better and more widely available testing.[43]

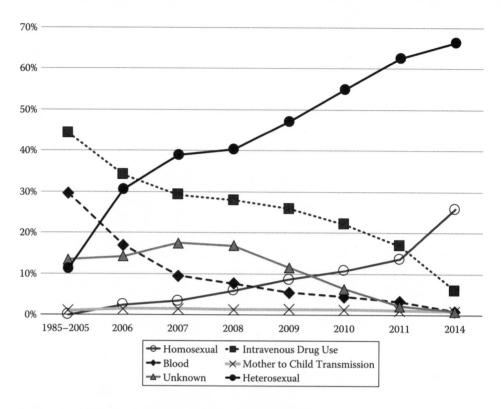

FIGURE 13.1 Sources of HIV/AIDS Transmission in China (1985–2014)

Sources: PRC Ministry of Health, 2012 China AIDS Response Progress Report, 2013; PRC National Health and Family Planning Commission, 2015 China AIDS Response Progress Report, May 2016.

There are several factors that make controlling the spread of AIDS difficult, in-cluding the substantial size of China's young and sexually active population; changing sexual behaviors and norms; massive internal migration; insufficient knowledge about HIV, along with inadequate perceptions of risk among the general population; and the expanding epidemic among hard-to-reach gay men, especially young gay men (reference: UNAIDS). Between 2010 and 2015, there was a 420 percent increase in new AIDS cases among gay men and a 410 percent jump among students aged fifteen to twenty-four.[44] Another group with a large increase in newly diagnosed AIDS was among men over sixty: in 2002, just 2 percent of men newly diagnosed with HIV posi-tive were over sixty; in 2015, it was almost 25 percent, with the most likely explanation being the detection of the virus in men who were infected earlier in their life, although risky sexual behavior among "the Viagra Generation" was also a factor.[45]

As shown in Figure 13.2, the source of new infections has also shifted quite dra-matically. Until recently the largest source of infection was from injecting drug use (IDU), specifically, shared needles by heroin users, 44.2 percent in 2005). In 2014, only 6.0 percent of new infections were IDU related, with the largest share (92.2 percent) coming from sexual transmission, of which 66.4 percent from heterosexual transmis-sion and 25.8 percent from homosexual transmission. Those infected through het-erosexual transmission are mostly female commercial sex workers and their clients.

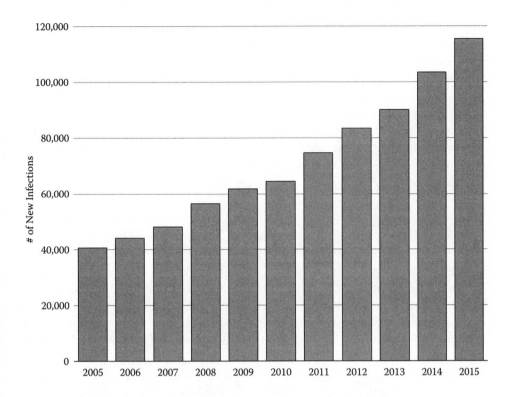

FIGURE 13.2 New Cases of HIV/AIDS in China (2005–2015)

Source: Elizabeth Pisani and Zunyou Wu, "HIV in China: 30 Years in Numbers," in Zunyou Wu, ed., *HIV/AIDS in China: Beyond the Numbers*. New York: Springer, 2017, 133.

The current focus of China's AIDS response, in line with global goals, is to expand early treatment to infected persons and people at high risk as a means of restoring health to those infected and preventing transmission of the virus to sexual partners. Eighty-seven percent of HIV infected people were receiving treatment in 2015, and the mortality rate from AIDS had dropped to 5.6 percent, a 67.8 percent decrease from a decade earlier.[46] Since June 2016, China has provided free treatment to all its citizens with HIV, expanding the program from the earlier free treatment limited only to rural citizens.

The development of China's AIDS policy has been shaped by a combination of both internal and external events. Domestic advocacy from within government and from NGO activists, medical professionals, and academic scholars spurred government action following the SARS crisis. But external pressure from the international community has also been an important factor in pushing for greater attention to AIDS in China. As with many other issues, the international perception of denial, inaction, human rights abuses, and cover-up have threatened China's self-image and spurred internal debate and response, which has often been positive.

Combined with a realization that economic growth and participation in the fruits of globalization depend on good global citizenship, these forces have propelled an uncustomary government accountability on the AIDS issue. The more proactive government AIDS response also points out clearly, however, that the mustering of the party-state's high-level political commitment is the essential requirement in China for implementing responsive national policies and mobilizing local-level action.

The leadership's pragmatic approach to dealing with AIDS has helped push China's government toward increasing tolerance and support for the role of civil society and is an important public policy development. But this tolerance has not always extended to the local level, where officials often distrust or feel threatened by nongovernmental actors and limit their actions. And it is ultimately at the local level where health-care personnel need access to the most at-risk populations that the success or failure of China's response to AIDS response will be determined.

CONCLUSION

Building on the foundation laid by the Maoist era's emphasis on preventative health care and equitable access, China today has generally excellent basic health statistics for a developing country (see Table 13.1). But thirty years of privatization, decentralization, and benign neglect of the rural health system, coupled with new threats from emerging or resurgent infectious diseases, finally pushed the central government to begin the arduous process of fixing a very broken health-care system. Moreover, with modernization and a higher standard of living have come the challenge of addressing chronic disease problems and improving health behaviors such as tobacco use and diet, both of which explain why cardiovascular disease and cancer are the leading causes of death in China.

China's leadership is now engaged in a massive multifaceted health initiative under the rubric of Healthy China 2030, which includes, among other things, plans for a new and more comprehensive medical insurance program, pollution control, an effort to reign in the overuse of drugs and tests as money-earning ploys, regulation of drug costs, instituting rational drug prescribing, and revitalization of a basic prevention approach to public health. By 2016, basic health insurance covered more than 95 percent of the population, gradually extending from only hospitalization (covering about 50 percent of costs) to outpatient services (covering 60–70 percent of costs) and almost fully covering hospital-based childbirth deliveries.[47]

This is a huge achievement but still insufficient to avoid substantial out-of-pocket payments—which in 2016 constituted 30 percent of total health payments—in an increasingly expensive health system where medical tests and drugs are overprescribed and contribute to high health-care costs. The newly established State Administration for Medical Security Insurance is spearheading efforts to reduce out-of-pocket payments and regulate and control drug and medical-test prescribing and costs, which are aimed at further addressing these chronic problems. These problems will only worsen with population aging and the rise in health-seeking that will accompany it.

As discussed earlier, China's rapidly aging population, which is largely due to its achievements in health care, brings with it new health challenges. Twelve percent of China's population was over sixty years of age in 2012, and that percentage will increase to 30 percent in 2050.[48] Chronic diseases (noncommunicable diseases) already constitute nearly 70 percent of China's disease burden, and because of population aging, this number will also increase.[49] The cost of providing earlier treatment for chronic illnesses will also add to the burden and costs of health care especially as the population ages.

China is urbanizing faster than any country in history, not only because of the migration of more than 250 million people from the rural areas to the cities looking for better economic opportunities but also because of the government plans to move another 250 million rural residents to smaller and medium-sized cities by 2025. This will require a vast expansion of urban medical systems as well as increasing urban health risks such as pollution-related illnesses and automobile accidents.[50]

Another health-care challenge for the PRC are the food and drug safety scandals that have endangered or harmed large numbers of citizen and are the major source of public outrage. In 2008, several hundred thousand Chinese children were sickened and six died because a toxic industrial chemical (melamine) had been added to milk powder by manufacturers in order to boost its apparent protein content while reducing the cost of production. As result, the head of a local firm responsible for much of the tainted product and one of his associates were executed, the chairwomen of one of China's largest dairy producers was sentenced to life in prison as were two others, while fifteen others received lesser jail terms. Other food-related scandals have involved "fake eggs, diseased pork, recycled cooking oil, and mislabeled meat."[51] There have also been several scandals of expired or faulty childhood vaccines reaching the market, such as that which occurred in mid-2018 and led to two days of protests by angry parents outside the offices of the National Health Commission in Beijing.[52]

As the SARS and AIDS cases illustrate, national-level solutions to health crises are hard to carry out without the political will to overcome bureaucratic and financial barriers. The ministry-level government agency that has overseen health policy has generally been a weak player on the national, provincial, and local stage, where other priorities, especially economic development, are of greater perceived importance.

The SARS epidemic was an alarm bell for the problems of an inequitable and poorly functioning health-care system. This led first to greater transparency and better international cooperation on infectious disease reporting, then to a strengthened and more open response to HIV/AIDS, and now to a major overhaul of the entire health-care system. As China's economy and global footprint continues to grow, achieving equitable health access and addressing new health threats related to its own economic miracle will be a crucial test for the government. If successful, China could again be a model for the developing world on how to achieve "health for all."

NOTES

1. Li Changming, "China's Rural Health in Economic Transition," Consultative Meeting of the China Health Development Forum, Apr. 2002, Beijing; Tony Saich and Joan Kaufman, "Financial Reform, Poverty and the Impact on Reproductive Health Provision: Evidence from Three Rural Townships," in *Financial Sector Reform in China*, ed. Yasheng Huang, Anthony Saich, and Edward Steinfeld (Cambridge, MA: Harvard Asia Center Publications, 2005).

2. *The World Health Report 2000: Health Systems Improving Performance* (Geneva: World Health Organization, 2000), http://www.who.int/whr/2000/en/index.html.

3. Wang Longde et al., "Emergence and Control of Infectious Diseases in China," *Lancet* 372, no. 9649 (2008): 1598–1605; and Victor Sidel and Ruth Sidel, *Serve the People: Observations on Medicine in the People's Republic of China* (Boston: Beacon Press, 1974).

4. Henderson Cohen and Aiello Zheng, "Successful Eradication of Sexually Transmitted Diseases in the People's Republic of China," *Journal of Infectious Diseases*, 174, supp. 2 (Oct. 1996): 223–229.

5. See Zhou Yongming, *Anti-Drug Crusades in Twentieth-Century China: Nationalism, History and State Building* (Lanham, MD: Rowman & Littlefield, 1999).

6. "Directive on Public Health," June 26, 1965, http://www.marxists.org/reference/archive/mao/selected-works/volume-9/mswv9_41.htm.

7. See, for example, Victor W. Sidel, "Medicine and Health," in *China's Developmental Experience*, ed. Michel Oksenberg (New York, Academy of Political Science, 1973).

8. Victor W. Sidel, "The Barefoot Doctors of the People's Republic of China," *New England Journal of Medicine* 286, no. 24 (June 15, 1972): 1292–1300; W. C. Hsiao, "Transformation of Health Care in China," *New England Journal of Medicine* 310 (1984): 932–936; the 1975 documentary film, *The Barefoot Doctors of Rural China*, http://archive.org/details/gov.archives.arc.46549.

9. For an online collection of posters from these and earlier patriotic health campaigns, see "Chinese Public Health Posters," U.S. National Library of Health, National Institutes of Health, https://www.nlm.nih.gov/hmd/chineseposters/index.html

10. Yuanli Liu and Keqin Rao, "Providing Health Insurance in Rural China: From Research to Policy," *Journal of Health Politics, Policy and Law* 31, no. 1 (2006): 71–92.

11. "Health Care Reform Targets at 900m Rural Residents," *People's Daily*, Nov. 21, 2002, http://english.peopledaily.com.cn/200211/21/eng20021121_107213.shtml.

12. World Bank, *Toward a Healthy and Harmonious Life in China: Stemming the Rising Tide of Non-Communicable Diseases*, Human Development Unit, East Asia and Pacific Region, Washington, DC, 2012. http://www.worldbank.org/content/dam/Worldbank/document/NCD_report_en.pdf.

13. Joan Kaufman, "2016: China's Two Child Policy: Two Little, Too Late," Council on Foreign Relations, Dec. 1, 2016, https://www.cfr.org/blog/chinas-new-two-child-policy-too-little-too-late

14. "The Change We Bring, WHO Progress Report 2016–2017, World Health Organization China Office, 2018, http://www.wpro.who.int/china/publications/2017-the-change-we-bring/en/.

15. China National Plan for NCD Prevention and Treatment (2012–2015), China Center for Disease Control, https://www.iccp-portal.org/system/files/plans/National%20Plan%20for%20NCD%20Prevention%20and%20Treatment%202012-2015.pdf

16. "Neoliberal Science, Chinese-Style: Making and Managing the 'Obesity Epidemic,'" *Social Studies of Science* 46, no. 4 (Aug. 2016): 485–510.

17. "Most Smokers in China Have No Plans to Quit, Study Finds," *South China Morning Post*, Apr. 16, 2018, https://www.scmp.com/news/china/society/article/2096446/most-smokers-china-have-no-plans-quit-study-finds;

18. *Tobacco Atlas*, https://tobaccoatlas.org/topic/consumption/#

19. "Lung Cancer Rising, but Not from Smoking," *China Daily*, Aug. 11, 2018, http://www.chinadaily.com.cn/china/2017-08/11/content_30451525.htm

20. "One in Three Young Chinese Men Will Die from Smoking, Study Says," BBC, Oct. 9, 2015, https://www.bbc.com/news/world-asia-34483448

21. "Cancer in China: More than 7500 Cancer Deaths Per Day Estimated," American Cancer Society, Jan. 26, 2016, http://pressroom.cancer.org/China2015

22. Yuyu Chen et al., "Evidence on the Impact of Sustained Exposure to Air Pollution on Life Expectancy from China's Huai River Policy, PNAS (Proceedings of the National Academy of Sciences), Aug. 6, 2013, 110, no. 32, 12936–12941 (Aug. 6, 2013), www.pnas.org/cgi/doi/10.1073/pnas.1300018110

23. Jonathan Kaiman, "More than Half of China's Groundwater Is Polluted," *Guardian*, Apr. 23, 2014, https://www.theguardian.com/environment/2014/apr/23/china-half-groundwater-polluted

24. Joan Kaufman, "Infectious Disease Challenges in China," in *China's Capacity to Manage Infectious Diseases: Global Implications,* ed. Xiaoqing Lu, (Washington, DC: Center for Strategic and International Studies, 2009).

25. Joan Kaufman, "SARS and China's Health Care Response: Better to Be Both Red and Expert!"; Anthony Saich, "Is SARS China's Chernobyl or Much Ado about Nothing?," in *SARS: Prelude to Pandemic*?, ed. Arthur Kleinman and James L. Watson (Stanford, CA: Stanford University Press, 2006).

26. Yanzhong Huang, "China's Response to the 2014 Ebola Outbreak in West Africa," *Global Challenges* 1, no. 2, Feb. 27, 2017, https://onlinelibrary.wiley.com/doi/abs/10.1002/gch2.201600001

27. Gao Yaojie has been recognized and has won several prestigious awards both abroad and in China for her courageous work associated with HIV/AIDS. Ironically, she was also placed under house arrest, harassed by police, and refused permission to travel abroad at various times by Chinese authorities, who worried about her outspokenness. In 2007, bowing to international pressure, the government allowed her to leave for the United States, where she now lives.

28. Jun Jing, "The Social Origins of AIDS Panics in China," in *AIDS and Social Policy in China,* ed. Joan Kaufman, Arthur Kleinman, and Anthony Saich (Cambridge, MA: Harvard University Asia Center Publications, 2006), 152–169.

29. *A Joint Assessment of HIV/AIDS Prevention, Treatment and Care in China,* State Council AIDS Working Committee (SCAWCO) and UN Theme Group on HIV/AIDS in China, Dec. 2004.

30. "China's First Successful AIDS Discrimination Claim," *Xinhua*, Jan. 25, 2013, ews.xinhuanet.com/english/china/2013-01/25/c_132128163.htm.

31. See Danni Wang et al., "Chinese Non-governmental Organizations Involved in HIV/AIDS Prevention and Control: Intra-organizational Social Capital as a New Analytical Perspective," *Bioscience Trends* 10, no. 5 (2016): 418–423.

32. James Palmer, "It's Still (Just About) OK to Be Gay in China," Apr. 18, 2018, FP (Foreign Policy online), https://foreignpolicy.com/2018/04/17/its-still-just-about-ok-to-be-gay-in-china/

33. "China's NGOs Praised for Role in Fighting HIV/AIDS," *Xinhua*, Nov. 29, 2012, http://news.xinhuanet.com/english/bilingual/2012-11/29/c_132007520.htm.

34. Nectar Gan, "Why Foreign NGOs Are Struggling with New Chinese Law," *South China Morning Post*, June 13, 2017, https://www.scmp.com/news/china/policies-politics/article/2097923/why-foreign-ngos-are-struggling-new-chinese-law

35. "Peng Liyuan Stars in Video for Kids Stricken with AIDS," http://english.sina.com/video/2012/1202/533411.html.

36. "UNAIDS Presents the First Lady of China, Professor Peng Liyuan, with Award for Outstanding Achievement," UNAIDS, Jan. 18, 2017, http://www.unaids.org/en/resources/presscentre/pressreleaseandstatementarchive/2017/january/20170118_first-lady-Peng-Liyua

37. "China's Guangdong Province to Lift HIV Restrictions on Teacher Recruitment," http://www.unaids.org/en/resources/presscentre/featurestories/2013/June/20130613china-teachers/.

38. "AIDS Patients Protest in Henan," Radio Free Asia, Aug. 29, 2012, http://www.rfa.org/english/news/china/aids-08292012150012.html.

39. Bai Tiantian, "Henan AIDS Group Comes to Beijing to Demonstrate," *Global Times*, Feb. 28, 2013, http://www.globaltimes.cn/content/764752.shtml.

40. "AIDS Activism: Bad Blood," *Economist*, Sept. 8, 2012.

41. "China Focus: China spends heavily on HIV/AIDS control," *Xinhua*, Sept. 26, 2017, http://www.xinhuanet.com/english/2017-09/26/c_136640340.htm; "Reported cases of HIV in China are rising rapidly," *Economist*, Jan. 12, 2019, https://www.economist.com/china/2019/01/12/reported-cases-of-hiv-in-china-are-rising-rapidly

42. Elizabeth Pisani and Zunyou Wu, "HIV in China: 30 Years in Numbers," in *HIV/AIDS in China: Beyond the Numbers,* ed. Zunyou Wu (New York: Springer, 2017), 133; and "Increase in Number of HIV Cases in China Raises Concerns," *Financial Times*, Dec. 1, 2016, https://www.ft.com/content/586c3526-b795-11e6-ba85-95d1533d9a62

43. "HIV/Aids: China Reports 14% Surge in New Cases," BBC, Sept. 29, 2018, https://www.bbc.com/news/world-asia-china-45692551

44. Echo Huang, "HIV Infections in China Are Rising Sharply among Students, Gay Men, and Men over 60," *Quartz*, Dec. 1, 2016, https://qz.com/850110/hiv-infections-are-rising-sharply-among-gay-men-men-over-60-and-students-in-china/

45. Pisani and Wu, "HIV in China: 30 Years in Numbers," 130–131.

46. Pisani and Wu, "HIV in China: 30 Years in Numbers,"136; and National Center for AIDS/STD Control and Prevention (NCAIDS), China Center for Disease Control and Prevention, 2015 (unpublished data) as cited in "China-WHO Country Cooperation Strategy 2016–2020," World Health Organization, Western Pacific Region, 2016, http://www.wpro.who.int/china/160321_ccs_eng.pdf

47. Winnie Chi-Man Yip, William C. Hsiao, Wen Chen, Shanlian Hu, Jin Ma, and Alan Maynard, "Early Appraisal of China's Huge and Complex Health-Care Reforms," *Lancet* 379 (Mar. 3, 2012): 833–842.

48. Bradley Yao, "China's Elderly Masses," *U.S. China Today*, http://uschina.usc.edu/article@usct?chinas_elderly_masses_14584.aspx; http://www.ncbi.nlm.nih.gov/pmc/articles/PMC2704564/.

49. World Bank, *Toward a Healthy and Harmonious Life in China*, 2012.

50. World Bank, *Toward a Healthy and Harmonious Life in China*, 2012.

51. "China Food Safety," *South China Morning Post*, https://www.scmp.com/topics/china-food-safety

52. Javier C. Hernández, "Chinese Parents Protest Bad Vaccines for Hundreds of Thousand," *New York Times*, July 30, 2018, https://www.nytimes.com/2018/07/30/world/asia/china-protest-faulty-vaccines.html

SUGGESTED READINGS

Bu, Liping. *Public Health and the Modernization of China, 1865–2015*. New York: Routledge, 2017.

Burns, Lawton Robert, and Gordon G. Liu, eds. *China's Healthcare System and Reform*. New York: Cambridge University Press, 2017.

Duckett, Jane. *The Chinese State's Retreat from Health: Policy and the Politics of Retrenchment*. New York: Routledge, 2010.

French, Paul, and Matthew Crabbe. *Fat China: How Expanding Waistlines Are Changing a Nation*. New York: Anthem Press, 2010.

Henderson, Gail, and Myron Cohen. *The Chinese Hospital: A Socialist Work Unit.* New Haven, CT: Yale University Press, 1984.

Horn, Joshua. *Away with All Pests: An English Surgeon in People's China: 1954–1969.* New York: Monthly Review Press, 1969.

Huang, Yangzhong. *Governing Health in Contemporary China.* New York: Routledge, 2014.

Kaufman, Joan, Arthur Kleinman, and Tony Saich, eds. *AIDS and Social Policy in China* Cambridge, MA: Harvard University Asia Center Publications, 2006.

Kleinman, Arthur, and James L. Watson, eds. *SARS in China: Prelude to Pandemic*? Stanford, CA: Stanford University Press, 2006.

Lu, Xiaoqing, ed. *China's Capacity to Manage Infectious Diseases: Global Implications.* Washington, DC: Center for Strategic and International Studies, 2009.

Sidel, Victor, and Ruth Sidel. *Serve the People: Observations on Medicine in the People's Republic of China.* Boston; Beacon Press, 1973.

Wu, Zunyou, ed. *HIV/AIDS in China: Beyond the Numbers.* New York: Springer, 2017.

14

Policy Case Study: Population Policy

TYRENE WHITE

When the People's Republic was established in 1949, China's population was more than 500 million. By way of comparison, that figure was roughly the same as the total population of Europe at that time, and more than three times the population of the United States. Despite urgent attempts to slow down population growth in the 1970s, the country passed the demographic milestone of one billion people in July 1980. By 2017, China's population had risen to approximately 1.4 billion. This popula-

tion increase alone—approximately 400 million between 1980 and 2017—exceeds the current population size of every country in the world except China and India.

It was numbers like these that led Chinese leaders to implement the so-called one-child policy in 1979, and made them reluctant to repeal it three decades later despite increasingly grave warnings from China's professional demographers that the demographic costs of the policy outweighed the benefits. Despite those costs, which included skewed sex ratios and a rapidly aging population, China's leaders were very cautious about policy reform and delayed major changes to the policy until 2014, and a complete repeal until 2016.

HOW DID THEY GET HERE?

If you ask mainland Chinese why the population grew so large and so rapidly after 1949, they will likely blame Mao Zedong, the leader of the Chinese Communist Party (CCP) who ruled the People's Republic until his death in 1976. His pro-natalist stance and opposition to family planning, they will say, resulted in high rates of population growth for more than two decades. When the Maoist era ended, China's population stood at 930 million, not quite double what it had been at the founding of the PRC. By the time the post-Mao regime began to enforce a serious birth-limitation policy, China's population had grown so much that even a radical program like the one-child birth limit could not prevent its continued increase for decades to come.

There is some validity to this view. Mao's pro-natalist views certainly slowed the implementation of birth-control programs and contributed to the more accelerated growth of the population after 1949. China's demographic challenge did not begin in 1949, however, nor was Mao's view as crude and simplistic as it is usually portrayed. When the CCP came to power in 1949, they inherited an empire that had experienced a fivefold increase in population over the previous three centuries. Around 1650, China's population size topped 100 million for the first time. From that point, it only took another 250 years to pass the 400 million mark (ca. 1900) and just 50 years more to top 500 million.

From the founding of the People's Republic, population pressures received the attention of Chinese Communist party (CCP) leaders. During the first two decades of the Maoist era, however, the proper approach to demographic issues was hotly debated and contested. Initially, Mao and the CCP, resisted any suggestion that a large population constituted a problem. They argued that what appeared to be "overpopulation" was actually the result of the exploitative system of capitalism, and would disappear as capitalism was replaced by socialism and unprecedented wealth was created by the liberated masses. It did not take long, however, for top officials in the CCP to begin to worry about the population pressures. Some began to speak in more practical ways about the burden of population growth on economic development and to recommend that China amend its population policy to provide more support for family planning education and allow the import of condoms and other contraceptive supplies.

Before these first steps could yield any meaningful results, however, the radicalization of domestic politics interrupted the effort, and advocates of family planning were branded as "rightists," or enemies of the revolution. At the same, time, however, the second half of the 1950s was a period of intensified state planning. All institutions and bureaucracies were mobilized to put into place annual and five-year performance plans that would help China achieve its goal of becoming an advanced socialist economy and society. In this context, it was Mao who suggested in 1957 that China should attempt to plan reproduction in the same way it aspired to plan material production. At the time, birth planning (*jihua shengyu*), that is, the attempt to regulate population growth so as to keep it in balance with levels of economic production and growth, was only a goal to be reached at some more advanced stage of socialist development.

As China's population continued to grow rapidly in the 1960s (see Figure 14.1), key leaders such as Premier Zhou Enlai came to believe that birth planning could no longer be postponed. In 1965, Zhou proposed the first national population control target—reducing the annual rate of population growth to 1 percent by the end of the century, and by 1972 he had authorized the creation of an extensive family planning bureaucracy to oversee implementation; provide free access to contraceptives, abortions, and sterilizations; and monitor the enforcement of local birth targets.

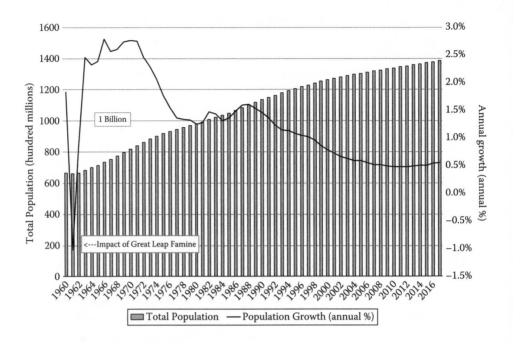

FIGURE 14.1 China's Population (1960–2017)

Source: World Development Indicators, World Bank

Socialist planning thus came to embrace human reproduction in much the same way that it embraced agricultural and industrial production. Local officials who were responsible for meeting grain and steel production quotas now began to receive quotas for babies.

In the early and mid-1970s, the campaign focus was "later, longer, fewer," that is, promoting later marriage, longer spacing between births (three to five years), and fewer births (a two-child ideal and a three-child limit). By mid-decade, the childbearing norm began to tighten; the new slogan was "one is not too few, two is enough, three is too many." In the cities, young couples began to feel pressure to have only one child. In the countryside, they were urged to have no more than two. In 1979, a group of China's top scientists announced that if China were to achieve its economic goals by the year 2000—a goal that the new Deng regime had expressed as achieving a per capita (exchange-rate based) gross domestic product of US$1,000 by the year 2000 (subsequently reduced to US$800 per capita), population had to be contained within 1.2 billion. In turn, this meant that the official birth limit had to be lowered to one child per couple (with some exceptions for special circumstances).

In an extraordinary "Open Letter" to CCP members that was published in all newspapers in September 1980, China's leaders defended the new policy and made it clear the high level of priority they attached to it. They argued that the two-decade delay after 1949 was a fateful mistake. By the time the state began to encourage fertility control, a huge new generation of young people had already been born and was approaching its childbearing age years. As a result, even with naturally declining fertility levels (i.e., the average number of children born to a woman during her reproductive years), demographic momentum meant continued growth of total population size (see Figure 14.1). That growth, which threatened to reach 1.5 billion by century's end if no action was taken, could doom China to poverty and economic backwardness through another generation or more if urgent action was not taken by this generation. To oversee the new policy, a State Family Commission was established in 1981.

IMPLEMENTING THE ONE-CHILD POLICY

The one-child policy was inaugurated just as the Deng regime was about to embark on a far-reaching reform program that gradually transformed China's economy, polity, and society. As previous chapters have described, the socialist economy was decollectivized and marketized; politics was de-radicalized and political institutions revived; society was granted some relief from the all-intrusive party-state that had permeated every aspect of public and private life. Change came in fits and stops, with periods of dramatic change often followed by a partial retreat to safer political ground. This pattern gave Chinese politics a cyclical or wavelike pattern, not unlike the high tides and low tides of the mass campaigns of the Mao era.

Through all of these changes and fluctuations in political atmosphere, the insistence on strict birth control never faltered. It was a constant in an otherwise volatile situation. This does not mean, however, that the content and enforcement of the policy were static. On the contrary, officials at all levels struggled to adapt to a rapidly changing situation to unintended consequences of the policy and, to a lesser degree, international scrutiny and criticism. This translated into several different stages of implementation.

Phase One: Collectivism and Coercion, 1979–1983

In the early years of the program, as the Deng regime fought against the lingering influences of the Cultural Revolution, it was possible to use the tools and institutions of the Maoist era to press for strict enforcement of birth quotas that were handed down to each city, county, neighborhood, and village. Thirty years of Maoism had taught Chinese citizens to be wary of voicing opposition to the latest campaign, taught officials that they could intimidate and coerce anyone who dared to defy them, and taught party leaders at all levels that the failure to meet campaign quotas was one of the most deadly sins of Chinese politics. A poor campaign performance could spell the end of a promising career. All childbearing-age couples, urban and rural, had to receive official permits from the state in order to give birth legally. In addition, provinces and local governments drafted regulations offering economic incentives to encourage policy compliance and imposing stiff sanctions on policy violators. All childbearing-age women were required to undergo periodic gynecological exams to ensure that they were not carrying an "unplanned" pregnancy, and if they were, they were pressed to undergo an abortion immediately. In addition, all CCP members were urged to "take the lead" in implementing the one-child policy by accepting it themselves, urging family members to do so, and in every respect setting a good example for others to follow.

Gaining compliance from those under their jurisdiction took much more than setting a good example, however. In China's cities and towns, growing acceptance of the small-family norm, free access to contraceptives, and tight administrative control in workplaces and neighborhoods had brought the urban total fertility rate down from 3.3 in 1970 to about 1.5 by 1978, a remarkably low level for a developing country, as was the total fertility rate (see Figure 14.2).

With a large cohort of women about to enter their peak childbearing years, the state deemed even this low level inadequate. To further suppress fertility and prevent more second births, state monitoring intensified in workplaces and neighborhoods. Monthly gynecological examinations for childbearing-age women, plus a system of marriage and birth permits provided by the work unit, ensured that anyone attempting to have a second child was caught in a tight surveillance net. Those who escaped the net faced severe penalties, including fines, loss of employment, and perhaps even one's coveted urban household registration (*hukou*).

If changing childbearing preferences and strong mechanisms of state control worked together to induce compliance with the one-child policy in urban China, rural China posed a far more difficult challenge. Like rural populations in other places and times, life in the countryside encouraged higher levels of fertility. Agricultural work requires household labor, and unlike their urban counterparts, even very young children can be put to work in the service of family income. Moreover, while many urban couples could rely on a state pension for retirement support, rural families had no such welfare net. Children were the only guarantee of old-age support, and the most destitute villagers were inevitably those who were alone and childless. Only a son could assure a couple that they would be spared such a fate. Daughters usually married out of the village and, upon marriage, a daughter's first obligation transferred to her husband's family. Even the most devoted daughter could not be counted on to provide either income or assistance.

In addition to these practical considerations, the traditional emphasis on bearing sons to carry on the ancestral line remained deeply entrenched in the countryside. As a result, although rural fertility levels were cut in half between 1971 and 1979 (declining from approximately 6 to 3), much of rural China remained hostile to a two- or one-child limit, including the rural cadres who would have to enforce the policy. When the rural reforms implemented after 1978 began to relax the state's administrative grip on the peasantry, the launching of the one-child policy set the stage for a prolonged and intense struggle over the control of childbearing.

The struggle took a variety of forms, and evolved over time as the unfolding rural reforms altered the local context. In some villages, women who refused to abort an unplanned birth were subjected to meetings where they were berated, intimidated, and threatened into cooperation. In others, medical teams and party cadres swooped in unexpectedly in an effort to catch women who were eluding them. At worst, women were forced onto trucks and taken directly to the township headquarters, where medical personnel would perform an abortion, a sterilization, or insert an intrauterine device (IUD), or some combination of these. The use of some form of birth control

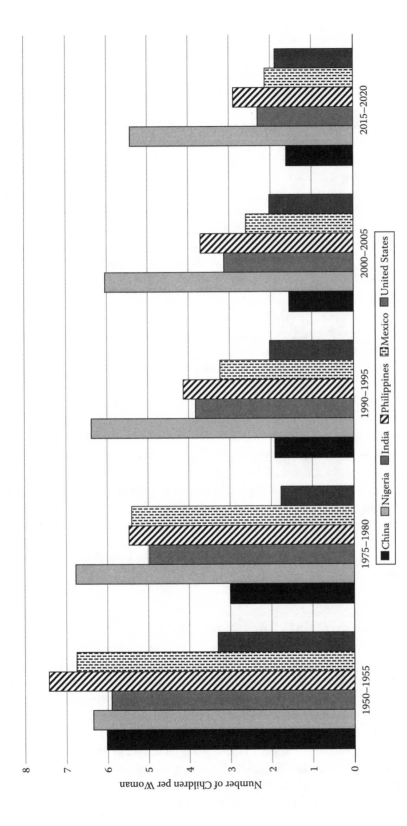

FIGURE 14.2 China Total Fertility Rate in Comparative Perspective

Source: United Nations Population Division, World Population Prospects: The 2017 Revision, Population Database

after the first or second child became mandatory, and in the countryside the preferred method was the IUD, since it was more reliable and not easily removed.

Rural villagers responded with a wide variety of resistance strategies. Enraged family members who came home from a day outside the village to discover that the birth control team had performed abortions on their wives or daughters sometimes beat or killed those responsible. Others bribed local officials to accept their stories when they returned to the village after an absence with an "adopted" child. Subterfuges of this sort were acceptable to rural officials, as long as they did not need to register the new infant as a birth in their jurisdiction. Others used their standing in the village to avoid compliance; many rural officials, or their family members, expected the compliance of others while flaunting the policy themselves. Some officials colluded with village families to hide unauthorized pregnancies, particularly for couples with no sons.

Worst of all, the intense pressure to limit births led to many cases of female infanticide. Absent the one-child policy, most families welcomed the arrival of daughters and sons, though a daughter was described as a "small happiness" and a son as a "big happiness." If only one child was to be allowed, however, many villagers—male and female, young and old—felt it was imperative to have a son, so much so that female infanticide was frequently the result.

There were two possible responses to this volatile rural situation. One was to relax the one-child policy, hoping that more education and support for rural women and children would hold birth rates down and improve cadre-mass relations. The other was to intensify enforcement for a short time, but use widespread sterilization to guarantee that those who already had two or more children would never have another. In the short run, the latter option won out, and a massive sterilization campaign was launched. The key campaign target was to eliminate all third and higher-order births. Once that problem was solved, more pressure could be brought to bear on those who were having a second child without state permission.

The result of this campaign was a fourfold increase in the number of tubal ligations performed in 1983, as compared with the previous years, and large increases across every category of birth control procedures. So severe were the local pressures to meet sterilization targets that many women who had long since completed their intended childbearing, and had been effectively utilizing another form of birth control, were forced to undergo sterilization.

Phase Two: Policy Relaxation, 1984–1989

As the campaign began to play itself out and elite politics took a more "liberal" turn in the mid-1980s, a decision was made to modify the one-child policy to allow for more exceptions. Fearful of a breakdown of authority in the countryside and widespread anger over the one-child limit and the often brutal tactics used to enforce it, leaders in Beijing decided to simply concede the need for a son in the countryside. Henceforth, the rural policy became a one-son or two-child policy. Village couples whose first child was a daughter would be allowed to have a second child, allowed to try again for a son. This concession was made in the hopes of pacifying restless villagers and improving enforcement, but over a period of several years, the net effect of this and other rural reforms was to encourage local governments to unduly relax their enforcement efforts. Village officials who themselves were subject to the birth control policies often colluded with their neighbors to avoid enforcement efforts undertaken by outside teams. As the agricultural reforms destroyed the instruments of control and power that officials had enjoyed in the past, they found it difficult to enforce birth limits and found it easier to report false numbers than fight with neighbors and kin.

The net effect of this policy "slippage" was to weaken central control over the levers of enforcement and to provide support for experts and birth planning officials, who argued that the policy should be more flexible across different regions of China, allowing those in the most impoverished areas with difficult, hilly terrain to have two children, allowing those in average circumstances to have one son or two children, and limiting those in more prosperous areas to only one child. They believed that the same results could be achieved, with less effort and more compliance, than if policy did not respond to the nuances of family need and economic circumstance.

Phase Three: Another Cycle Unfolds, 1989–1995

This more differentiated policy was put into place in the latter half of the 1980s, only to be upset by the events of May–June 1989, which ended in a military crackdown on Tiananmen protesters and their supporters in Beijing and in other cities around the country. The martial atmosphere that returned to Chinese politics for the next two to three years made it possible to once again tighten local enforcement and to carry out another population control campaign. As in 1982–1983, fear about a poor performance justified the revival of campaign methods. Cadres who had been warned off those methods in the mid-1980s were now instructed to use "crack troops" and "shock attacks" to break through resistance and meet the new goals of the 1991–1995 plan period.

The campaign was justified by the results of the five-year plan that ended in 1990. It showed that China's population control targets had been exceeded by a very substantial margin, giving fuel to those who believed that it was acceptable to use coercion in service of the higher goal of achieving the per capita economic goals that had been set for the year 2000. It was also justified by the preliminary results of the 1990 census, which indicated that China's population had grown more quickly (to 1.13 billion) than planned or expected. Even worse, despite the massive effort that went into the census-taking process, it was clear that rural officials were manipulating local data in ways that hid "excess births," which should have been registered in their jurisdiction. They had a strong incentive to do this, since failure on their part would also reflect badly on their immediate superiors. Even when fraud was suspected, therefore, it was rarely investigated by those higher in the political command.

These numbers prompted the conservative leadership in Beijing to tighten enforcement, returning to a strict formula that limited all urban couples to only one child, and all rural couples to one son or two children. Exceptions were granted only to some of China's smaller minority nationalities and to parents whose first child was mentally or physically handicapped to such a degree that they would be unable to function as a healthy, working adult. Local officials were put on notice that they were liable for strict enforcement, and that failure to achieve their performance targets for birth planning would result in economic penalties, administrative sanctions, and even demotions. They were to assume that meeting population targets was just as important to their future career success as meeting key economic goals. Population growth rates, which had been creeping up in the late 1980s, dropped steadily in the 1990s (see Figure 14.1).

This success came at a price, however. Evidence of intimidation and coercion was widespread, particularly in areas that had done poorly prior to 1990. Cadres destroyed crops, homes, and property to force compliance or punish policy violators. Relatives, particularly the elder members of the family, were detained indefinitely until they paid their fines, aborted an unplanned pregnancy, or agreed to sterilization. Rural cadres who sided with their fellow villagers did what was necessary to give the appearance of compliance, but also behaved as they had in the past, like during the Great Leap Forward, when the work was hard and the campaign targets too ambitious—by lying, exaggerating, and dodging, or finding other ways to manipulate the system.

On the one hand, data for the period between 1990 and 1995 indicate a significant improvement in enforcement, as well as a further reduction of the fertility level (see Figure 14.2) With greater pressure on local officials to report impressive results, however, came greater pressure on grassroots personnel to submit fraudulent data. When official reports based on these data claimed that China's fertility level had dropped to an unusually low 1.4, many Chinese demographers were skeptical, reporting their concerns in scholarly journals and other reports.

Phase Four: Policy Stagnation

Over the next two decades (1993–2013), the PRC underwent enormous change, achieving levels of economic development and social change that were unprecedented in their speed and scope. Despite this rapid transformation, however, China's population policy remained unchanged. CCP leaders were repeatedly urged by experts to revise or abolish the one-child policy, and warned of the consequences of failing to act swiftly. Calls for reform were repeatedly rejected, however, overridden by continuing fears of a fertility rebound if the one-child limit was relaxed.

In 1989, when the Deng regime crushed the pro-democracy movement, China still inhabited a world defined by the contours of the Cold War. By 1992 the world had changed dramatically after the fall of the Soviet Union, and the CCP now faced the problem of how to survive in a global order that was dominated by the United States and its allies. Responding to the new challenges, the post-Tiananmen politics of conservatism gave way to a new wave of reform and opening, which rapidly transformed the political, economic, and social landscape of the PRC.

It was in this context that many of China's population specialists began again to challenge the wisdom of the administrative and punitive approach to population control that had been relied on since the 1970s. Leading figures in China's new generation of highly trained demographers and sociologists criticized the assumption that "fewer births is everything," arguing that it led to "short-sighted actions" (such as surprise raids on pregnant women). Frankly acknowledging that China's fertility decline had been induced through the widespread use of coercion, they insisted on the need for a broader and more complex view of population dynamics and a population policy better suited to an overall strategy of "sustainable development." Writing that "the curtain is gradually closing on the era of monolithic population control," these critics went on to discuss the disturbing consequences of that approach (including **sex ratio imbalances** and a rapidly aging population) and the necessity of shifting to a developmental approach which emphasized improvements and investments in the quality of the population.[1] In short, they argued that development was the best route to fertility decline, rejecting in the process the sort of "population determinism" (fewer births is everything) that was so deeply embedded in the PRC's family planning strategy.

This open revolt against the theory and practice of birth planning was unprecedented, and it proved to be the leading edge of a push to reform China's population control program. Like the critique of excess coercion that emerged in 1984, the timely convergence of multiple political developments, both domestic and international, helped to advance the reform agenda in population policy. Domestically, the problem of rural unrest and instability was again preoccupying the leadership, and one of the major complaints of villagers was the use of coercive birth control tactics to collect burdensome and excessive taxes. Not only did new documents on rural taxation explicitly forbid the use of those measures, a family planning document issued in 1995 codified them as seven types of prohibited behaviors: (1) illegally detaining, beating, or humiliating an offender or a relative; (2) destroying property, crops, or houses; (3) raising mortgages without legal authorization; (4) the imposition of "unreasonable" fines or the confiscation of goods; (5) implicating relatives or neighbors of offenders, or retaliating against those who report cadre misbehavior; (6) prohibiting childbirths permitted by the local plan in order to fulfill population targets; (7) organizing pregnancy checkups for unmarried women.[2]

Another factor that was conducive to reform was the shifting discourse on population and development in the international community. When China began to implement its one-child policy in 1979, it was widely lauded by leaders in the international family-planning community, who subscribed to the dominant theory that population growth was a primary, if not *the* primary, impediment to economic growth, and that population-control programs were the solution. By the mid-1990s, another school of thought began to dominate the discourse on population and development. This alternative approach focused on women's reproductive health and rights, and was crystallized in Cairo at the 1994 United Nations International Conference on Population and Development. It emphasized the organic relationship between the elevation of the status of women (especially through increased education and employment outside the home), the elimination of poverty, and declining fertility levels.

The substance of the conference was reported in some detail in the Chinese media and in population journals, and shortly thereafter, the influence of the new international approach on Chinese policy became clear. In China's "Outline Plan for Family Planning Work in 1995–2000," for example, stress was placed on the impact of the socialist market economy on population control, and on the necessity of linking population policy to economic development. This language, though seemingly benign, was noteworthy for its suggestion that population policy should be recalibrated to match China's new social and economic conditions. In addition, the plan placed special emphasis on the role of education, and urged aggressive efforts to increase women's educational level in order to promote lower fertility.

If the Cairo conference was influential in China, it was because there was a constituency ready to seize the opportunity to press home similar views. In the early 1970s, China's leaders, while publicly condemning the orthodox view on limiting population growth, had quietly embraced it. Though framed in Marxist terms, the logic of China's policy was the same—that reducing population growth was a prerequisite for socioeconomic development, and that China could not afford to wait for a development-induced **demographic transition** like that which occurred in Europe and North America. In the post-Mao era, this rationale legitimated the regime's insistence that strict population control was the linchpin of the modernization strategy, even as it came under increased international criticism.

The new language of Cairo—protecting women's rights and taking a more holistic approach to achieving demographic goals—buttressed the position of Chinese population policy reformers. It also provided institutional contacts and resources they could use to experiment with a softer approach to enforcement. The UN's Fourth World Conference on Women, held in Beijing in 1995, strongly reinforced the Cairo message, provoking a new wave of feminist thinking and action, and further encouraging State Family Planning Commission* officials to consider a more client-centered approach that gave greater consideration to women's needs and their reproductive health.

Predictably, however, reform came slowly and remained highly controversial. Faced with the reality of a rapidly aging population at one end of the demographic pyramid, a bulging workforce in the middle that even the fast-growing Chinese economy could not absorb, and at the bottom, sex ratios so skewed that they posed a threat to social stability, family planning professionals were increasingly persuaded that the costs of China's one-child policy had grown too steep. Their arguments and analyses were overridden, however, by conservative political voices that continued to insist on the necessity of a one-child birth limit and warned of a big jump in fertility if the policy was relaxed.

China officially reaffirmed the one-child policy in 2000 and in 2001 passed a long-debated Population and Family Planning Law that upheld the existing policy and gave compliance the force of law.[3] Although the law included provisions that echoed the Cairo and Beijing conference agendas, calling for an "informed choice of safe, effective, and appropriate contraceptive methods" and one provision prohibiting officials from infringing on "personal rights, property rights, or other legitimate rights and interests," it reiterated China's basic approach to population control.

Despite the reaffirmation of the one-child policy, the chorus for reform grew louder after 2000. It was supported by several parallel developments in Chinese politics and public policy during the first decade of the twenty-first century. First, the year 2000 had come and gone, and although China's population had exceeded the original target number of 1.2 billion, the rate of economic growth after 1980 had also exceeded all expectations, suggesting that population growth was no longer a critical threat to China's continued development. Second, young couples entering their childbearing years in the twenty-first century were far more likely than their predecessors in 1980 to desire only one or two children, to prefer to delay childbirth, or to forgo childbearing altogether. Traditional norms and expectations regarding marriage and childbirth had been altered by twenty years of rapid economic development and by the relentless education they had received about the individual and societal costs of childbearing.[4]

With acceptance of a one- or two-child norm on the rise, reformers argued, the regulation of childbirth could be relaxed without fear of a rise in birth rates. And as China began to take a more active role in international institutions after 2000, developing strong links to the global community of nongovernmental organizations (NGOs), the overt use of coercion in enforcing birth planning became an embarrassment to the now highly professionalized state family-planning bureaucracy. Many were convinced that it was time for China to shift more decidedly toward a system of education, rewards, and support for those who chose to have no more than two children and who were willing to space those children four to six years apart. The official government White Paper on "China's Population and Development in the Twenty-First Century" (2000) reflected many of these concerns, embracing an approach to population policy that was consistent with the new international discourse and viewed family planning as just one part of a holistic approach to development.[5]

What the demographic experts were unable to do, however, was to convince China's top leaders that it was "safe" to formally abandon the one-child policy. Fears of a fertility rebound remained, and the necessity of keeping the numbers of births in check continued to outweigh the opinion of specialists that China's population goals could be better achieved, and at a lower social and economic cost, by moving to a universal two-child policy, which gave rewards for compliance rather than penalties for violations. Only in 2012, with the results of the 2010 census in hand and a change of CCP leadership underway, did the one-child policy begin to change.

Phase Five: From One Child to Two

After the 2000 census, demographers and other population experts made several appeals to the CCP leadership to relax or abolish the one-child policy. At the national level, those appeals failed to persuade, but in areas with the lowest fertility rates, local leaders took the initiative to encourage more couples to have a second child. In Shanghai, for example, where exceptionally low fertility rates raised concerns over the rapidly shrinking labor force, residents were reminded that the one-child policy allowed couples to have a second child if both parents were single children. Officials in other localities also publicly reiterated this exception, which was increasingly pertinent as the single-child generation born under the one-child policy after 1979 began to come of age and marry in growing numbers.

Despite the growing number of voices urging policy reform, it took the combined impact of the 2010 census results and the close of the Jiang/Hu leadership era (1993–2013) to provoke real change. Alarms that had been raised repeatedly about rapid aging of the population and sex ratio imbalance in young cohorts were confirmed by the census results, galvanizing the new regime of Xi Jinping to take action. The first indicator of the change to come was the publication in October 2012 of a report prepared by the China Development Research Foundation, an influential think tank closely associated with the Chinese government. The report recommended that relaxation of the one-child limit begin immediately, and that a universal two child policy be put in place by 2015. In November 2013 the first reform was announced, allowing couples to have a second child if *either* of the parents was a single child. This policy change, referred to as *dandu erhai* (single [child], two children), increased substantially the number of couples eligible for a second child, including many rural couples, and was implemented nationwide in 2014. This proved to be a short, interim step toward more fundamental change. In October 2015, China's leaders announced a universal two-child policy (*quanmian lianghai*), the goal of which was to "promote balanced development of the population."[6] This was followed in January 2016 by the enactment of amendments to the Population and Family Planning Law that encouraged a two-child family, eliminated benefits for late marriage and late childbirth, extended maternity and paternity leave, and ceded to individual couples decisions about contraceptive use. Since about two-thirds of childbearing-age women relied on intrauterine devices or tubal ligation, the National Health and Family Planning Commission launched a program offering free surgery to women wishing to remove IUDs or reverse sterilization surgery.[7]

The swift demise of the one-child policy—when change finally came, was perhaps due in part to the limited impact of the *dandu erhai* policy that got underway in 2014. Despite long-standing fears in some quarters that lifting the one-child limit might lead to a substantial rise in the birth rate, preliminary data available for 2014 indicated just the opposite. As a result of the policy reform, approximately 11 million couples became eligible to have a second child. By September of 2015, however, only 1.7 million of those couples had applied to have a second child, comprising only 16 percent of eligible couples. This low response rate belied the results of previous surveys suggesting that as many as 40 percent of one-child couples wished to have a second child, and confirmed the wide gap between expressions of fertility preferences and preparedness to act on that preference. Nevertheless, in 2016 the number of births rose to 18.5 million, more than two million more than in 2015. In 2017 and 2018, however, the number fell to 17.2 and 15.23 million, respectively.For those who had long argued that ending the one-child policy would not result in a big fertility rebound, this was the first clear evidence to support their view.[8]

CONSEQUENCES OF THE ONE-CHILD POLICY

The long debate over the one-child policy began and ended with the same question: did China's development goals make it necessary to adopt or retire the one-child birth limit? In 1979, China's leaders had been persuaded by faulty science that only a one-child birth limit would allow China to meet its modernization goals.[9] Thirty years later, the 2010 census results made a compelling case for change, and the limited relaxation of policy in 2014 quelled any lingering fears that a sudden and sustained baby boom would jeopardize China's economic development.

As in the late 1970s, however, everything still revolved around the numbers, particularly economic projections and demographic analyses. Two sets of numbers were particularly weighty in the decision to end the one-child policy. First, the sex ratio imbalance among newborns had reached alarming levels and showed no signs of abating. Second, fertility rates, which were already very low in 2000, had continued to fall. At the same time, China's population was aging rapidly, increasing the social and economic burden on working-age adults and threatening China's long-term economic vitality.

Sex-Selective Abortion and Sex Ratio Imbalance

Over time and across many different human populations, sex ratios at birth—that is, the number of males born during a given time period compared to the number of females—hover around 103–106 boys for every 100 girls. On occasion, for a limited period of time, this ratio may vary naturally, with a few more or a few less boys for each 100 girls. Data from PRC censuses, however, revealed that China's sex ratio at birth had climbed to unprecedented levels by 2010. They reported a 1990 sex ratio at birth of 111 males per 100 females, a 2000 sex ratio of 117 to 100, and a 2010 sex ratio at birth of nearly 118 males per 100 females. They also revealed individual provinces with sex ratios as high as 130 boys per 100 girls.

From the beginning of the one-child policy, there was concern that the one-child birth limit might result in an imbalanced sex ratio at birth. In the September 1980 "Open Letter" on the one-child policy, for example, several of the most common objections to the policy were aired, including fears that it would lead to female infanticide and abandonment and, consequently, to an imbalance in the sex ratio. These fears were initially discounted, but they proved to be warranted.

In the early 1980s, as the pressure on couples to have only one child grew intense, senior officials became alarmed about the many reports of female infanticide and female abandonment on the part of couples desperate to have a son. The infanticide reports produced a firestorm of controversy at home and abroad, leading the regime to respond in two contradictory ways. First, it denied that there was a widespread problem; census and survey data were used to show that China's sex ratio at birth was well within what was considered to be the normal range and in keeping with China's own population history. Though conceding that incidents of infanticide and abandonment did occur, it was insisted that such cases were rare, and that they occurred only in the most backward regions of the countryside, where the "feudal mentality" remained entrenched. The solution proposed was an education campaign to uproot such backward ideas, but education alone was of little use, given the social and economic realities that privileged male offspring.

By 1984, as reports of female infanticide multiplied and the All-China Women's Federation (ACWF) began to insist that the problem be faced and addressed, the state changed tack. But rather than address the underlying causes of gender bias, it made concessions to rural sensibilities and adjusted the one-child policy to allow single-daughter households to try again—for a son. The intent of this policy change was to legitimize what was already the de facto policy in many rural areas, but it also had the effect of underscoring the unequal status of males and females, especially in the countryside. A woman with a single daughter and no sons might be applauded by local officials, but in the real world of the village she was likely subject to a lifetime of pity and blame, much of it heaped upon her by other rural women who had themselves endured pressures to produce a son. In addition, sonless couples were disadvantaged in village life, stigmatized by their failure to continue the male ancestral line and the potential prey of stronger families and kin groups. Single-daughter households should therefore be given special consideration.

Faced with intense demands from the state, on the one hand, and their peers and elders, on the other, some took the desperate course of female infanticide to preserve the chance to have a son. As the 1980s progressed, however, two alternative strategies emerged. The first was infant abandonment, which increased substantially in the late 1980s and 1990s in response to a tightening of the birth control policies. The second was sex-selective abortion.

By the early 1990s, all county hospitals and clinics and most township clinics and family planning stations had ultrasound equipment capable of fetal sex determination. As private clinics proliferated in the 1990s, they too were equipped with ultrasound technology, providing easy access for a fee. Despite repeated condemnations of sex-selective abortion and attempts to outlaw the use of ultrasound technology for fetal sex identification, easy access to the technology, combined with the lure of lucrative bribes and consultation fees, made ultrasound use very popular.[10] This was especially true in newly prosperous county towns and rural townships, where higher incomes made ultrasound diagnosis possible, but where modest degrees of upward mobility had done nothing to undermine the cultural prejudice and practical logic that favored male offspring.

In the early 1990s, Chinese experts attributed most of the skew in the sex ratio to underreporting of female births, implying that the actual sex ratio at birth remained within, or close to, acceptable norms. While underreporting of female births was certainly a factor, by the late 1990s more candid assessments concluded that sex-selective abortion was widespread and was the main cause of the distorted sex ratio. Moreover, accumulating data indicated that the phenomenon was not just a rural problem, nor was it concentrated in the least educated segment of the population. In other words, son preference was not confined to the rural or backward elements of society. Instead, the combined effect of the one-child birth limit, traditional son preference, and easy access to a technology that allowed couples to make sure they had a son was to tempt people from a wide variety of socioeconomic backgrounds to choose sons over daughters.

The extent to which China's skewed sex ratio at birth can be attributed to the one-child birth limit has been a focus of intense debate. Some who question the impact of China's policy point to evidence of sex ratio imbalance in other countries, as ultrasound technology made it possible to assure the birth of a son. In several cases, increases in the imbalanced sex ratio at birth tracked closely with increased access to the technology that allowed for fetal sex determination. This pattern suggested that there was nothing unique about China's skewed sex ratio. Rather, it was the cultural tradition of son preference that was the primary driver of rising sex ratios at birth.[11] Critics of this interpretation, however, point to the persistence and severity of China's sex ratio imbalance as evidence of the impact of the one-child policy. They note that the sex ratio imbalance grows much worse when one isolates second births and third or higher order births from first births.[12] Since rural couples were permitted to have a second child if the first was a daughter, they had only one chance to give birth to a son. Although the latter comprised less than ten percent of all births recorded in the 2000 census, for example, the sex ratio at birth for this category was an extraordinary 160 males for every 100 females.

Others argue that the incidence of sex-selective abortion is far less extensive than generally believed, and that most of the so-called "missing girls" are not missing at all, but have reappeared in various data sources, including household registration (*hukou*) data, school registration data, and the most recent census data. They point to the bureaucratic and organizational factors that create incentives for skewed reporting of birth data. Close analysis of multiple data sources, however, has led others to conclude that while underreporting did inflate the number of "missing girls," it accounts for only about a quarter of the problem. That still leaves a deficit of more than twenty million girls in China, with a projected decrease of more than 39 million women in the twenty to thirty-nine age range by 2030.[13]

The decision to adopt a two-child policy may help to move the sex ratio at birth back into balance more quickly than might otherwise have been the case, but the deficit of females has already begun to have an impact on marriage markets in China. Rural men of marriage age compete for a limited number of wives from the local area, and as the number of "bare branches" continues to grow, the higher the costs of marriage become. Men whose families are unable to raise enough money are unable to marry, and frequently resort to marriage brokers to help them find brides from other provinces.[14] Despite these and other efforts, however, the number of unmarried men in their late twenties is rising rapidly. While the shortage of women has allowed some brides to marry into a higher economic or social status, others have become more vulnerable to human trafficking, or to abuse in their new homes, where they are far removed from their family support system. Conversely, disadvantaged men are vulnerable to being cheated by marriage brokers, or by the bride and her family. There have been many reports of brides disappearing days after their marriage, once the bride's family had received the compensation they had demanded for their daughter.[15]

CHINA'S AGING POPULATION

Some of the most urgent calls to end the one-child policy came from those who worried about China's rapid population aging. Persons aged sixty-five or older comprised just 4.9 percent of China's population in 1990. By 2050 it will reach 26.3 percent by 2050 and 31.2 percent by 2100 (see Figure 14.3) These numbers did not place China among the nations with the highest proportion of elderly population, but its rate of aging was unusually fast, especially for a country at its level of development, due to the combined effects of rapid gains in life span and low levels of fertility.

Like all of China's population figures, the raw numbers were breathtaking, especially considering China's inadequate pension, welfare, and health-care systems. In 2013, the elderly population numbered approximately 185 million, on its way up to an estimated 284 million by 2025, and 440 million by 2050.[16]

This trajectory of rapidly increasing numbers of elderly persons is a source of grave concern for two reasons. First, the increase in the elderly population will be

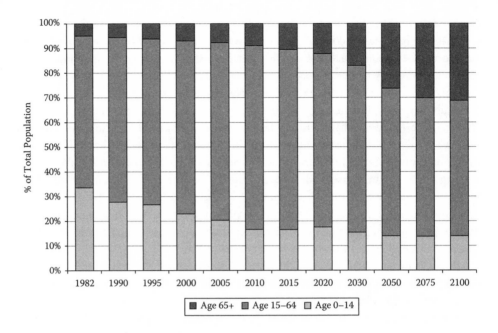

FIGURE 14.3 Age Composition of China's Population (1982–2100)

Sources: For 1982–2015, *China Statistical Yearbook 2017* (Beijing: China Statistics Press), Table 2-4. Accessed online at http://www.stats.gov.cn/tjsj/ndsj/2017/indexeh.htm. For 2020-2100, see the China country profile *World Population Prospects, 2017,* published by the Population Division of the Department of Economic and Social Affairs, United Nations.

accompanied by a decline in the size of the working-age population (ages fifteen to sixty-four), increasing the economic and social burden that will be placed on each worker. China's **dependency ratio**, that is, the working-age population expressed as a proportion of the total population, was manageable during the first two decades of reform, when the working-age population was large enough and young enough to ensure an adequate labor force and to provide essential care for dependents young and old. As the working-age population declines relative to the elderly, however, their ability to maintain current levels of support will be strained.

In 2012, the size of China's labor force began to fall, with 3.45 million fewer workers than the previous year and a projected decline of about 29 million by the end of the decade.[17] A government study estimated that the PRC could lose 200 million workers by 2050 unless the fertility rate increases.[18] In 2009 there were thirteen working-age adults for each elderly person; by 2050, there will be only two. This will place tremendous pressure on the working adult population, as their labor will be expected to generate much of the national wealth needed to care for their elders and their children. This is compounded by the fact that the current mandatory retirement age in China is sixty for men, fifty-five for female civil servants, and fifty for other female workers. Although proposals to gradually raisethe retirement age have been made, not surprisingly, they have been very unpopular. This may explain why a detailed outline of those plans, originally promised for 2017, had not been published by early 2019.The aging population will also place great pressure on the Chinese government, which must find the resources necessary to provide pensions and health care for hundreds of millions of retirees. Although many countries will face similar challenges or are already facing them (e.g., Italy, Germany, and Japan), China is experiencing rapid population aging at a lower level of national wealth and per capita income. As the *Economist* put it, China is unusual because it is "getting old before getting rich."[19] Despite the challenge posed by its aging population, Chinese authorities have worked in recent years to improve and extend the national pension system and the health-care system. Experts worry, however, about the ability of the regime to sustain current levels of economic growth given its already heavy debt burden, the declining numbers of young adults entering the work force, and the necessity of investing heavily in the social welfare system. Already in 2015, China had thirty-six dependents (children aged fourteen and under plus retirees over the age of sixty) for every one hundred workers. By 2050, that number is projected to nearly double, posing unprecedented challenges to the Chinese government.

This looming crisis of population aging was a key factor in the decision to relax the one-child policy, and then repeal it in favor of a two-child limit. As noted earlier, however, the tepid response by married couples to the policy relaxation after 2014 suggests that the reform will lead to fewer additional births each year than had been estimated. While this was a relief to those who feared that policy reform would lead to a baby boom, it was disappointing to those hoping the two-child policy would shore up the shrinking cohort of young workers who will enter the work force after 2030.

THE ONE-CHILD POLICY AS HISTORY

China's one-child policy has been lauded by some for its contribution to slowing world population growth and its contribution to China's rapid economic development. Given the costs and negative consequences of the policy, however, and the sometimes brutal methods of enforcement, it is important to ask if a similar result could have been achieved by different means.

China's approach to population control was set in motion prior to the era of reform that began in 1978, and while nearly every other policy arena underwent a transformation in the decades that followed, population control policy essentially remained static until very recently. The policy has been tinkered with, and sometimes relaxed on the margins, but the possibility of changing China's entire approach to population issues has never gained traction with China's leaders. Indeed, even the new two child policy does not alter China's fundamental approach to population policy—that the party-state, in service of China's development goals, has jurisdiction over childbearing. In their view, economic success, and projected future socioeconomic trends have mitigated the need for a one child birth limit, but not the need for enforcing a two child limit. It may be true that very few of China's childbearing-age couples would plan to have three or more children, given the costs of childrearing, the desire to maintain or improve their economic circumstances, and the lack of adequate support for various child care services. But that does not alter the fact that the Chinese party-state continues to claim sovereignty over childbearing, and that opportunities to have more than the officially mandated limit are still granted by the state and require permission of the authorities.

China claims that the birth limitation program has prevented as many as 400 million births since the mid-1970s, but they offer no explanation for how this number is calculated.[20] Nor does this calculation take into consideration the independent impact of reform and modernization on population growth and fertility. There is abundant historical evidence that fertility rates drop in response to rapid economic development, urbanization, increasing costs of childbearing, the commercialization of agriculture, and improved educational opportunities, especially for women. Changes like these, all of which occurred in China after 1978, may not have been enough to bring down fertility rates as far and as fast as Chinese leaders desired, but it is grossly misleading to suggest that the strict enforcement of a one-or-two child birth limit prevented the growth of the population by an additional 400 million, or that China's "modernization by the year 2000" agenda would have failed without the one-child policy.[21]

The great irony of China's one-child policy is that by the time China embraced it, nearly everything that inspired it was on the cusp of becoming obsolete. The intellectual hubris of the "population control movement" that peaked between the mid-1960s and 1980 would shortly thereafter begin to flounder under the combined challenges of the Green Revolution that brought increased agricultural productivity through technological advance to the developing world, revisionist demographic theories that challenged the orthodox view that population growth impeded development, and feminist and conservative challenges that criticized, respectively, the undue burden put on women by top-down family planning programs and the intrusion of the state into the most private of matters. In the midst of this ferment, China moved to embrace precisely the "numbers is everything" approach that was the core belief of its population controllers, wrapping it in a language of socialist modernization that was the mantra of the party-state. Once in place, and with the full weight of the reform leaders, including Deng Xiaoping, behind it, the legitimacy of the project and the validity of the method were difficult to challenge. The Party had declared that the achievement of "modernization by the year 2000" depended on the successful implementation of the one-child birth limit. Even when it became clear that China would exceed all expectations for economic growth by the year 2000, even when it became clear that the social consequences of the policy were severe, even when "population control" had become a discredited approach to demographic challenges, the policy remained in place. It recedes now as an anachronism, but its social and political consequences will be felt for decades to come.

Beyond the consequences discussed earlier, there is the rage left behind in many Chinese over the party-state's unwillingness to adopt a two-child policy many years earlier, or even more that its claims that government control over childbearing is legitimate and justifiable. There is also residual rage over its reliance on an enforcement system that privileged the rich, allowing them to effectively purchase a second child by paying a large "social compensation fee," while avoiding the pressure, harassment, or outright coercion experienced by ordinary Chinese whose pregnancies were deemed illegal. As the Chinese writer Ma Jian noted in a 2013 Op-Ed in the *New York Times*, however, venting popular anger against the wealthy "plays into the Party's hands" by deflecting public outrage away from "the government's barbaric policy."[22] However one judges the one-child policy—as an economic and social necessity, a barbaric violation of human rights and dignity, or a dual-edged sword, it is important to keep in mind that although the one-child birth limit has disappeared, the state has not conceded its authority to plan China's population growth. The birth limit has changed, but the logic that led to a one-child policy remains in place. As an August 2018 editorial about the important of increasing China's birthrate in the CCP's official newspaper, *People's Daily*, declared, "To put it bluntly, the birth of a baby is not only a matter of the family itself, but also a state affair."[23] Changing demographics, rising popular protest, and global influences have certainly moderated China's approach to family planning, as well as the language used to describe the program, but the Chinese approach to population management remains grounded in the principle of party-state sovereignty over reproduction. Until that principle is repudiated, China's population will remain subject to any childbearing requirement the party-state wishes to impose.

NOTES

1. Gu Baochang and Mu Guangzong, "A New Understanding of China's Population Problem," *Renkou yanjiu* (Population Research) 5 (1994): 2–10.

2. See Tyrene White, *China's Longest Campaign: Birth Planning in the People's Republic* (Ithaca, NY: Cornell University Press, 2006), 232.

3. For the full text of China's Population and Family Planning Law, see *Population and Development Review* 28, no. 3 (Sept. 2002): 579–585.

4. For a wide-ranging discussion of changing patterns of family life, childbearing preference, and childbearing behavior, see Wang Feng, Peng Xizhe, Gu Baochang et al., *Globalization and Low Fertility: China's Options* (Shanghai: Fudan University Press, 2011); Xiaowei Zang and Lucy Liu Zhao, eds., *Handbook on the Family and Marriage in China* (Cheltenham: Edward Elgar Publishing, 2017).

5. PRC State Council Information Office, "China's Population and Development in the 21st Century," (2000), http://www.china.org.cn/e-white/21st/index.htm

6. "Communique of the Fifth Plenary Session of the Eighteenth Central Committee of the Communist Party of China," *Xinhua News Agency* (Beijing), Oct. 29, 2015, reprinted in *Population and Development Review* 41, no. 4 (Dec. 2015): 733–734.

7. Isabelle Attane, "Second Child Decisions in China," *Population and Development Review* 42, no. 3, (Sept. 2016): 733–734.

8. Attane, "Second Child Decisions in China," 519–525. See also Stuart Basten and Quanbao Jiang, "China's Family Planning Policies: Recent Reforms and Future Prospects," *Studies in Family Planning* 45 no. 4 (Dec. 2014): 493–509.

9. On the faulty science used to justify the one-child policy, see Susan Greenhalgh, *Just One Child: Science and Policy in Deng's China* (Berkeley: University of California Press, 2008).

10. For a report on such a business, see "Boys Preferred, Lucrative Trade Remains in Illegal Fetus Gender Identification," *Global Times*, Mar. 31, 2013, http://www.globaltimes.cn/content/769754.shtml#.Uds-wj54ZoM.

11. See Charis Loh and Elizabeth Remick, "China's Skewed Sex Ratio and the One-Child Policy," *China Quarterly* 222 (June 2015): 295–319.

12. See, for example, Quanbao Jiang, Qun Yu, Shucai Yang, and Jesus J. Sanchez-Barricarte, "Changes in Sex Ratio at Birth in China: A Decomposition by Birth Order," *Journal of Biosocial Science* 49, no. 6: 826–841.

13. See Yaojiang Shi and John James Kennedy, "Delayed Registration and Identifying the 'Missing Girls' of China," *China Quarterly* 228 (Dec. 2016): 1018–1038; Yong Cai, "China's New Demographic Reality: Learning from the 2010 Census," *Population and Development Review* 39, no. 3 (Sept. 2013): 371–396; and Steven Lee Myers and Olivia Mitchell Ryan, "Burying 'One Child' Limits, China Pushes Women to Have More Babies," *New York Times*, Aug. 11, 2018, https://www.nytimes.com/2018/08/11/world/asia/china-one-child-policy-birthrate.html

14. Lige Liu, Xiaoyi Jin, Melissa J. Brown, and Marcus W. Feldman, "Male Marriage Squeeze and Inter-provincial Marriage in Central China: Evidence from Anhui," *Journal of Contemporary China* 23, no. 86 (2014): 351–371.

15. Lige Liu et al., "Male Marriage Squeeze."

16. Mark W. Frazier, "No Country for Old Age," *New York Times*, Feb. 18, 2013, http://www.nytimes.com/2013/02/19/opinion/no-country-for-old-age.html; "China's Population: The Most Surprising Demographic Crisis," *Economist*, May 5, 2011, http://www.economist.com/node/18651512.

17. "China to Ease One-child Policy," *Xinhua*, http://news.xinhuanet.com/english/china/2013-11/15/c_132891920.html.

18. Myers and Ryan, "Burying 'One Child' Limits."

19. "China's Predicament: 'Getting Old before Getting Rich,'" *Economist*, June 25, 2009, http://www.economist.com/node/13888069.

20. Martin King Whyte and Wang Feng explore the origins of the 400 million figure in "Challenging the Myths about China's One-Child Policy," *China Journal* 74: 144–159.

21. One example of the intensity of this debate can be found in the journal *Demography*, where several scholars offered harsh criticism of an analysis by Daniel Goodkind, "The Astonishing Population Averted by China's Birth Restrictions: Estimates, Nightmares, and Reprogrammed Ambitions," *Demography* 54 (2017): 1375–1400. For the critiques of this article, see Susan Greenhalgh, "Making Demography Astonishing: Lessons in the Politics of Population Science"; Feng Wang et al., "Is Demography Just a Numerical Exercise? Numbers, Politics, and Legacies of China's One-Child Policy; and Zhongwei Zhao and Guangyu Zhang, "Socioeconomic Factors have been the Major Driving Force of China's Fertility Changes Since the mid-2000s," all in *Demography* 55, no. 2 (2018): 721–731, 693–719, and 733–742, respectively. See also Amartya Sen, "Women's Progress Outdid China's One-Child Policy," *New York Times*, Nov. 2, 2015, https://www.nytimes.com/2015/11/02/opinion/amartya-sen-womens-progress-outdid-chinas-one-child-policy.html

22. Ma Jian, "China's Brutal One-Child Policy," *New York Times*, May 21, 2013, https://www.nytimes.com/2013/05/22/opinion/chinas-brutal-one-child-policy.html

23. Cited in Myers and Ryan, "Burying 'One Child' Limits." For an analysis of this editorial and the online backlash it generated, see Jiayun Feng, "The People's Daily: 'Giving Birth Is not nly a Family Matter but also a National Issue,'" *SupChina*, August 7, 2018, https://supchina.com/2018/08/07/the-peoples-daily-giving-birth-is-not-only-a-family-matter-but-also-a-national-issue/

SUGGESTED READINGS

Banister, Judith. *China's Changing Population*. Stanford, CA: Stanford University Press, 1987.
Banister, Judith, David E. Bloom, and Larry Rosenberg. "Population Aging and Economic Growth in China." Harvard School of Public Health Working Paper, Mar. 2010.

Croll, Elisabeth. *Cultivating Global Citizens: Population in the Rise of China*. Cambridge, MA: Harvard University Press, 2010.

Croll, Elisabeth. *Endangered Daughters: Discrimination and Development in Asia*. New York: Routledge, 2000.

Fong, Mei. *One Child: The Story of China's Most Radical Experiment*. Boston: Houghton Mifflin Harcourt, 2015.

Greenhalgh, Susan. *Just One Child: Science and Policy in Deng's China*. Berkeley: University of California Press, 2008.

Greenhalgh, Susan, and Edwin Winckler. *Governing China's Population: From Leninist to Neoliberal Biopolitics*. Berkeley: University of California Press, 2005.

Hudson, Valerie, and Andrea den Boer. *Bare Branches: The Security Implications of Asia's Surplus Male Population*. Cambridge, MA: MIT Press, 2004.

Johnson, Kay Ann. *China's Hidden Children: Abandonment, Adoption, and the Human Costs of the One-Child Policy*. Chicago: University of Chicago Press, 2017.

Lee, James, and Wang Feng. *One Quarter of Humanity: Malthusian Mythologies and Chinese Realities*. Cambridge, MA: Harvard University Press, 1999.

Riley, Nancy. *Population in China*. Cambridge: Polity Press, 2017.

White, Tyrene. *China's Longest Campaign: Birth Planning in the People's Republic, 1949–2005*. Ithaca, NY: Cornell University Press, 2006.

Whyte, Martin King, Wang Feng, and Yong Cai. "Challenging Myths about China's One-Child Policy," *China Journal* 74: 144–159.

Zhao, Zhongwei, and Fei Guo. *Transition and Challenge: China's Population at the Beginning of the 21st Century*. New York: Oxford University Press, 2007.

15

Policy Case Study: Internet Politics

GUOBIN YANG

The internet is one of the big China stories in the past two-plus decades. When China was first linked to the global internet in 1994, the goal was to propel industrialization and economic development through informationization (*xinxihua*). Neither Chinese leaders nor ordinary citizens could have anticipated how deeply the internet was to transform not only the economy but also politics and society. This is not a linear story of technologically driven change, however, but a complex process of contestation involving multiple actors—the party-state, business firms, and ordinary citizens. The ways in which different actors approach the internet, through policy, marketing, technological design, or everyday use, shape the cultures and politics of the internet over time. In broad strokes, the period from the 1990s to 2012 saw the gradual expansion of citizen engagement and activism on the internet, whereas the period since 2013 is characterized by more intensive and proactive forms of co-optation and control by the party-state. In the first period, the internet changed Chinese politics more than the other way around; in the second period, Chinese politics has caused more changes to the internet. Ultimately, this process has led to the appearance of a cyberpolitics consisting of both new forms of citizen engagement and new forms of party-state domination and governance.

HISTORY OF THE INTERNET IN CHINA

In October 1997, when the China Internet Network Information Center (CNNIC) issued its first survey report on internet development, there were only 620,000 internet users in China. About 88 percent of them were male. As Figure 15.1 shows, internet usage in the PRC expanded rapidly beginning in about 2008, and by the end of 2017, China had 772 million internet users, 47.4 of whom were female. Government support and investment played an essential role in this dramatic growth. From 1997 to 2009, 4.3 trillion yuan (approximately US$673 billion) was invested in the construction of an internet infrastructure, and a total length of 8.267 million kilometers of optical communication networks was built nationwide.[1] Government support, although crucial, is not the only story. As one observer puts it, "China's Internet market is substantially driven by the competitive jockeying among powerful groups in agencies, ministries, government-owned companies, and private bodies, including Internet service providers (ISPs) and Internet content providers (ICPs)."[2] In addition, the rapid growth of the number of internet users reflects the zeal with which ordinary citizens and consumers embraced the new communication technologies. It is through the everyday use of the internet and social media that new social, cultural, and political forms have appeared.

Unlike the history of the internet in the United States, where emails and newsgroups were already common before the invention of the World Wide Web, the development of the Internet in China is a story of the web from the very beginning. In the late 1990s and early 2000s, users in China browsed websites for information and entertainment and to express themselves and communicate with others. Major commercial websites like Sohu, Netease, and Sina provided real-time online chatrooms and bulletin-board forums known as BBS. In 1997, Netease's initiative to offer free web

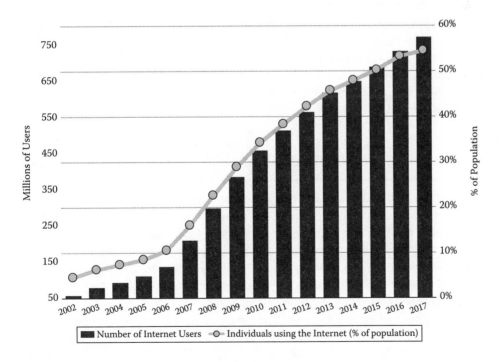

FIGURE 15.1 The Growth of the Internet in China (2002–2017)

Sources: China Internet Network Information Center (CNNIC)

space for individual users to build personal web pages prompted a "fever for personal homepages." Universities around the country operated numerous BBS forums, the best known of which were affiliated with Peking University and Tsinghua University. Among government agencies, the newspaper of the Chinese Communist Party, *People's Daily*, opened a BBS forum in 1999 for users to protest NATO's bombing of the Chinese embassy in Yugoslavia during the Kosovo War. It was later renamed as the Strengthening the Nation Forum (*qiangguo lutan*) and quickly became one of the most popular online forums in China of its time.

The venues of internet access have changed over the years, reflecting both different socioeconomic conditions and the appearance of new technology platforms. In CNNIC's first survey report in 1997, 46.7 percent of users accessed the internet from their work units, while about a quarter had access from home. By December 2000, more than 60 percent of users had home access, about 44 percent accessed it from their work-units, and about 21 percent and 20 percent accessed the internet from internet bars (i.e., cybercafes) and schools respectively. In December 2007, close to half of all internet users in rural areas accessed through internet bars; 23 percent use cellphones for access.[3] By December 2017, 97.5 percent of China's 772 million internet users can access the internet from mobile phones, while 53 percent had desktop-computer access and 35.8 percent had laptop access.[4]

Venues of access matter for understanding internet politics in China. They are not only associated with different user habits, different kinds of gratification, and different forms of social association, but also vary in terms of external oversight. For example, for Chinese teenagers, home access is highly restricted and monitored by parents. To avoid parental surveillance, teenagers prefer to patronize internet bars, which they often see as spaces of socializing and freedom. For migrant workers, internet bars provided affordable venues of access. Yet because of the growing numbers of users who patronize internet bars, and due to the appearance of a public discourse linking these cybercafes with unhealthy if not illegitimate online activities, the bars were subject to intense official scrutiny and control at the height of their popularity in the early 2000s.[5]

NEW EXPRESSIVE AND ASSOCIATIONAL FORMS

How the internet is used and for what purposes often depend on how it is perceived by users. Perception in turn depends on the social and political context as well as users' needs and initial experiences in cyberspace. In the 1990s, public discourse in the PRC saw the internet, computers, and new information technologies as symbols of modernity.[6] Testimonials of personal experiences with the internet, expressed in personal narratives in BBS forums, personal homepages, and blogs, conveyed intense excitement about the social and political implications of the newly available channels of information and communication. They inspired people's dreams and aspirations for freer and more open channels of expression. If many of these dreams have been shattered as the internet turns more and more into a battleground of power and money, they were nonetheless genuine expressions of hope based on people's real experiences with the internet.

It was from these initial encounters with the internet that important new expressive and associational forms appeared, setting off a wave of remarkable online creativity in spite of an expanding internet censorship regime. The broad range of expressive forms include, in roughly chronological order of their initial appearance, BBS postings, live chats, internet literature, blogs, online videos, emoji packages, live-streaming, microblogs, and WeChat messages. The earlier genres of these expressive forms were mostly text-based, whereas the more recent ones tend to be more visual, as in the use of emojis and live-streaming, and contain shorter texts, as in microblogs.

New associational forms fall into numerous categories according to issues, identity, or demographics, ranging from online communities of parenting, gaming, literature, academics of various disciplines, migrant workers, films, American television series, dramas, and automobiles to Hepatitis-B carriers, environmental protection, animal rights, LGBT, and so forth. Due to their public character, there is necessarily a degree of diversity in this universe of virtual forms, but there are also clear patterns of stratification along lines of social class, life-style, or age.

VARIETIES OF ONLINE ACTIVISM

As new expressive and associational forms have appeared in Chinese cyberspace, online activism has also emerged. Online activism, which refers to "contentious activities associated with the use of the internet and other new communication technologies"[7] is comprised of multiple types and issues. It shapes Chinese politics by expanding the possibilities for political participation by individual citizens, nongovernmental organizations (NGOs), and grassroots groups.

NGOs use the internet for publicity, advocacy, and organizing. Among the most well-documented examples are environmental NGOs which have used the internet in anti-dam-building campaigns or in monitoring air and water pollution. Dissidents take to the internet to express political opposition and plead their cause and seek support and visibility overseas.[8] Both NGOs and dissidents were early adopters and savvy users of the internet. For example, in 1997, democracy activists launched what they claimed to be the first "free magazine" edited in the PRC and distributed by email. Its inaugural statement encouraged readers to forward their e-magazine to others, stressing the importance of the internet for disseminating ideas of democracy and challenging information monopoly by the regime.[9] More than ten years later, on February 19, 2011, shortly after Egypt's Hosni Mubarak was forced from office by revolutionary insurgents, anonymous calls for a jasmine revolution in China appeared on overseas Chinese-language websites. They called on citizens to gather at designated spots in thirteen Chinese cities at 2 p.m. every Sunday. The Chinese government acted preemptively by rounding up prominent dissidents and installing heavy police presence. Back in 1997, however, when the influence of the internet was still limited, calls by activists to use the internet to promote democracy drew little attention from the authorities, if only because the e-magazine was circulated clandestinely.

The most influential type of online activism in China is what are often called internet mass incidents (*wangluo quntixing shijian*). These are protest activities that happen when large numbers of postings and responses on a social issue begin to appear and circulate in major online communities, blogs, and microblog platforms. The messages typically mix texts with digital photos and sometimes videos. The online expressions are often highly emotional, with people showing great anger or playfulness depending on the tragic or comic nature of the events. Mass media and international media cover some of the events, thus magnifying their impact.

Although hundreds of internet mass incidents happen every year, the main issues focus on corruption, social injustices done to vulnerable persons, and the abuse of power by government officials.[10] An online protest often happens in response to an offline incident, such as the mysterious death of an individual under police detention. People engage in this kind of online activism because they do not trust official accounts of the incident or because government authorities withhold information. Thus, many internet protests are about the politics of transparency and accountability.

The sites of internet protests change with technologies. In the 1990s and early 2000s, they happened in bulletin board systems (BBS) and online communities. Then they expanded to blogs and microblogs. The most popular microblogging platform is the Twitterlike Sina Weibo, which was launched in August 2009 and was a favorite platform for social networking and protest between 2010 and 2012. Its brief 140-character format and enormous reach (nearly 400 million monthly users in 2017) make it especially hospitable to a kind of muck-raking citizen journalism that is as entertaining to the public as it is nettling to the censorship-prone propaganda officials. Although Sina Weibo remains active, the growing popularity of the so-called super app WeChat, an instant messaging social media platform run by China's dominant internet firm Tencent, means that much of the action has migrated from Sina Weibo to WeChat.

Over the years, Chinese netizens have developed a rich repertoire of humor, puns, and coded language to express protest and evade censorship. "Harmonizing" an online posting means censoring it, which is a not-so-subtle pun on the CCP's mantra that it aims to build a "harmonious socialist society" in China. To be invited to tea by the police means trouble; the term "grass-mud horse" does not refer to an animal but is the homophone of a curse word that is often aimed at officials. Seemingly apolitical issues, such as the sex diaries of a female blogger, a spoof video mocking a big-budget film, or a service blackout in online gaming communities can trigger an internet protest. Although these issues attract attention more for their entertaining contents than politics, they often turn into political discussions.

Sometimes online protests move offline and into the street. When this happens, online activism both retains its own distinct features and merges into the larger landscape of popular contention. Chapter 12 describes the growing number of environmental protests that involve interactions between online mobilization and offline protests.

Since 2013, however, although internet protest events have continued to appear, they are not as frequent as before. Surveys by Chinese internet research and monitoring agencies show that the overall number of online incidents has declined, while the number of online incidents with "positive energy" has increased — "positive" meaning voices in support of party-state policies and priorities. In a 2015 survey, *People's Daily* Online attributed this change to China's new strategy of governing the web by "combining hard with soft power."[11]

Does the growth of internet activism and online cultural and organizational forms amount to the appearance of an incipient digital civil society or digital public sphere in China? Answers will differ depending on people's assumptions and perspectives. If the assumption is that civil society and the public sphere operate autonomously outside of state politics and the market, then the answer would be no. Yet one would be hard pressed to find such a civil society and public sphere anywhere. If we take a historical perspective and view civil society and the public sphere not as absolute categories which either exist or do not exist, but as civic and communicative institutions which are more or less open, then it might be claimed that some form of digital civil society and digital public sphere did appear in China in the past two decades. One might further argue that since 2013, this digital civil society and public sphere have been undermined due to tightening ideological control.

Cyber-nationalism

Cyber-nationalism is a special category of online activism. Unlike other types of online activism, whose targets are located inside mainland China, the targets of cyber-nationalism are usually overseas. Cyber-nationalism also tends to enjoy more political legitimacy and in some cases explicit sponsorship by the state. It is intricately related to China's domestic politics and international relations. Sometimes it is aligned with China's foreign policy agenda. At other times, it may create "pressure to pursue approaches that are more unaccommodating than the leadership's preferences or their assessments of China's national interests would dictate."[12] On still other occasions, it may be used to air social grievances.[13]

Cyber-nationalism originated in the very early days of the internet in China. In 1996, an online campaign was staged to protest against NBC's coverage of PRC athletes at the 1996 Olympic Games because of one reporter's comments about performance-enhancing drug use by Chinese track athletes and female swimmers. Also in 1996, an online protest movement was launched against Japanese ultranationalists' construction of a lighthouse on the Diaoyutai/Senkaku Islands, which are claimed by both China and Japan. In 1998, online protest was combined with offline demonstrations against violence against ethnic Chinese in Indonesia.[14] Websites of civilian military enthusiasts are major sites of cybernationalism.[15]

Chinese cybernationalism took a dramatic turn in 2008, the year of the Beijing Olympics.[16] Protests against CNN's stories in the run-up to the Games critical of PRC policy in Tibet led to the launching of the website anti-cnn.com.[17] Eventually it turned into something of a sustained movement aiming not only to protest negative depictions of China in Western media, but also to proactively shape public opinion of the PRC at home and abroad. In 2010, the website changed its name to m4.cn, m4 meaning the month of April when the anti-CNN protest began. China's young nationalists had by then attained the nickname of "April youth." Besides expanding into a portal site of news and current affairs, m4.cn opened an English website called 4th Media (http://www.4thmedia.org/) in order to reach an international audience.[18]

A more recent wave of cyber-nationalism, represented by the so-called "Diba Expedition" in 2016, manifests some new features. Diba, or King Ba, is the nickname of the most popular online message board run by China's major technology company, Baidu, with a membership in the tens of millions. In January 2016, it served as the central hub for organizing a virtual expedition to the Facebook page of the newly elected Taiwanese president Tsai Ing-wen. Participants in the expedition are dubbed "Little Pink," because one of the websites used for mobilization, a popular online forum of the literary website Jinjiang Literature City (*Jinjiang wenxue cheng*), has pink as its background color. In comparison with earlier cyber-nationalistic protest, the most striking feature of this "Expedition" was the form of participation, which consisted of posting large numbers of emojis, called "emoji packs" (*biaoqing bao*), on Tsai's Facebook page and several news websites in Taiwan. These emojis were used as weapons to attack the pro-Taiwanese independence positions of Tsai's Democratic Progressive Party. But their emotional tone differs from earlier cyber-nationalistic protest. The cyber-nationalistic protests in 2008 were acts of "angry youth" venting rage and resentment against perceived slights to China,[19] but the Diba Expedition emojis posted on Taiwanese websites showed images of fine cuisine, modern city skylines, and impressive scenery in the mainland to convey a sense of national pride. In other words, if anger, resentment, and national humiliation dominated the sentiments in earlier outbursts of Chinese cyber-nationalism, a new-found sense of confident assertiveness has become more salient in recent trends in this form of online activism.

INTERNET GOVERNANCE AND CONTROL

What is often referred to as the Great Firewall of China in Western media discourse is a popular if inaccurate umbrella term for talking about the technological and institutional systems for blocking access to foreign websites deemed harmful to Chinese interests by the party-state. In this sense, the Great Firewall does not capture another, equally important aspect of internet control in China, namely, the censoring of domestic web contents. Instead of talking about the Great Firewall of China, therefore, I examine the evolution of Chinese institutions and practices of internet governance and control.

The basic institutions for internet governance by the party-state were set up in the 1990s with the establishment of new bureaucracies and the issuance of administrative regulations. The initial focus was on the regulation of network security, internet service provision, and institutional restructuring to accommodate this initial wave of informationization. The first major policy framework related to the internet was set out in the "Regulations Concerning the Safety and Protection of Computer Information Systems." These regulations went into effect on February 18, 1994, two months before China established full-functional internet connectivity. They outlined the principles and institutions of governance and designated the Ministry of Public Security as the principal agency in charge. Another major policy document was the "Computer Information Network and Internet Security, Protection and Management Regulations," issued by the Ministry of Public Security in December 1997. It detailed the responsibilities of China's internet service providers (ISPs) and enumerates nine types of information to be prohibited online, including "information that damages the credibility of state organs." A milestone in institutional development was the merging in 1998 of the Ministry of Post and Telecommunications and the Ministry of Electronics Industry into the new Ministry of Information Industry (MII), which became the primary regulatory agency of the information industry. In 2008, MII was renamed as the Ministry of Industry and Information Technology (MIIT).

The evolution of institutions of internet governance and control happened in the context of growing online contention and a heightened sense of a more general governance crisis within the party leadership. A major CCP plenum convened in 2004 passed an unprecedented resolution concerning the strengthening of the party's ability to govern the rapidly changing country. In its own words, "The Party's governing status is not congenital, nor is it something settled once and for all."[20] Among a long list of steps to be taken to improve the party's capacity to manage the rapidly changing country, the decision set out new principles for internet governance in the following terms:

> Attach great importance to the influence of the Internet and other new media on public opinion, step up the establishment of a management system that integrates legal regulation, administrative supervision, self-discipline by the industry, and technical safeguards, strengthen the building of an Internet propaganda team, and forge the influence of positive opinion on the Internet.[21]

The document recognized the fragmented character of party-state organizations involved in the governance of the internet, which led to intra-bureaucracy tensions and conflicts, as well as regulatory loopholes. One example of this was the regulatory spat between the General Administration of Press and Publication (GAPP) and the Ministry of Culture in 2009 over the licensing in China of the popular game World of Warcraft. GAPP asked the internet firm Netease to suspend operation of the game on account of regulatory violations, but Netease claimed that its operation had been approved by the Ministry of Culture.[22]

Efforts to integrate and centralize the institutions of internet governance accelerated after Xi Jinping took over as CCP general secretary in November 2012. In 2013, GAPP was merged with the State Administration of Radio, Film, and Television to form the State Administration of Press, Publication, Radio, Film, and Television (SAPPRFT). In 2014, the Cyberspace Administration of China (CAC) was established as the agency in charge of internet regulation and oversight under the supervision of a CCP leading group (see chap. 6) that is currently called the Central Cyberspace Affairs Commission (CCAC), which is headed by Xi Jinping. In 2018, SAPPRFT was abolished and all its responsibilities moved from the PRC State Council to CCAC, thus strengthening the party's direct control of the internet and reflecting the high priority that the CCP attaches to making sure that China's cyberspace remains subservient to its political and ideological agenda.

Methods of Internet Governance and Control

The evolution of the CCP's determination to control the internet has entailed the institutionalization and innovation of methods of cyberspace governance. Initially, the regime's methods of control and censorship were reactive and often heavy-handed. Forced closure of well-known websites and detention of digital activists was not uncommon. An Amnesty International report in 2004 listed the names of fifty-four individuals who were detained or imprisoned for using the internet in China in ways that were deemed to violate regulations.[23]

Selective blocking of foreign websites, including Twitter and Facebook, and the filtering of online postings are still routine affairs. But, over time, the party-state's approach has shifted to the use of law and proactive methods of "administration," softer means of control, and propaganda offensives. In terms of using the law to enforce internet control, two developments are most notable under the Xi Jinping regime. One was a judicial interpretation issued on September 8, 2013, by the Chinese Supreme People's Court and Supreme People's Procuratorate, which stated that people who post false information on the internet may face up to three years in prison if the posting is viewed more than 5,000 times or retweeted 500 times. This new rule was applied just a few days later when a sixteen-year-old boy in a small town in remote Gansu province was detained for posting a message on Weibo alleging local police brutality, which indeed had been retweeted more than 500 times. He was charged with "picking quarrels and provoking disputes" by posting false information that led to a street demonstration and disrupted social order.[24] Although he was released because of public pressure, this judicial interpretation indicates how detailed and specific Chinese laws can become when it comes to the governance of cyberspace.

The other development was the establishment in 2014 of the National Security Commission headed by Xi Jinping and the issuance of the National Security Law and a draft Cybersecurity Law in 2015 (subsequently passed in 2017).[25] The latter was designed to consolidate and strengthen the fragmented laws and regulations governing cyberspace. As the names of these laws reflect, the CCP increasingly uses language that equates cyberspace security with national security to legitimate internet censorship and surveillance.

Chinese authorities also resort to a broad range of softer approaches to induce voluntary and cooperative behavior in managing cyberspace. First is the use of national campaigns. Campaigns were a distinct feature of Chinese politics in the Maoist era that involved the central government setting a national policy and then charging lower levels with implementing it and holding them responsible for doing so. Although some scholars argue that China has shifted to a more "rational" bureaucratic mode of governance in the reform period, campaigns continue to be used in modified forms.[26] In earlier times, political campaigns focused on issues of economic production, social problems, ideological work, and class struggle. Today, campaigns are launched to tackle new issues, including trends in cyberspace. For example, the anti-vulgarity "special action" campaign launched in January 2009 was a coordinated national movement "to curb the spread of vulgar contents online, further purify the cultural environment of the internet, protect the healthy growth of minor, and promote the healthy and orderly development of the Internet."[27] On the day of its launching, the China Internet Illegal Information Reporting Center (CIIRC), established in 2004 under the sponsorship of the Internet Society of China, publicized the names of nineteen websites allegedly containing "vulgar contents." By February 24, 2009, a total of 2,962 websites had been closed for similar reasons.[28]

A second soft method of control involves efforts to "occupy the internet" by opening party-state accounts on popular social media platforms.[29] In September 2011, the Ministry of Public Security held a national conference to promote the use of microblogs by public security agencies. There were then more than 4,000 official microblog accounts and 5,000 individual police officers' accounts.[30] Since October 2015, *People's Daily Online* has regularly issued a ranking of the performance of party-state media agencies on China's major social media platforms, Sina Weibo, WeChat and Toudiao. These rankings encourage official media agencies to have an active presence on these internet platforms in order to expand their influence, and doing so has become an integral part of their operations. There is little research yet, however, on the effects of these practices on public opinion. A study of one city government's microblogging accounts finds that they do give officials the flexibility to experiment with new ways of engaging the public, but ultimately reinforce existing power structures rather than leading to deeper reforms in local governance.[31] Another study finds that official accounts on social media platforms sometimes appropriate popular elements of fan culture to appeal to users' patriotic sentiments to promote the party-state's nationalist agenda.[32]

A third method is to co-opt internet firms into become self-regulating agents of control. One common practice is to mobilize internet businesses to make pledges to this end. Although such pledges have previously been made about self-regulation for search engines, rumormongering, and so forth, it still came as a surprise to many that on November 6, 2014, the CAC orchestrated a ceremony for twenty-nine major websites to commit to doing so in the management of their user-comments functions.

Fourth, the CCP uses some of its core organizations to engage influential individuals in information technology to get them to help party-state efforts to supervise internet content. For example, at a May 2015 conference of the United Front Work Department—a long-standing institution of the CCP that manages its relations with nonparty groups and individuals—General Secretary Xi Jinping told the participants to strengthen relationships with representatives of new media so that they can help to purify cyberspace. What Xi refers to as "representatives of new media" consist of two types of individuals—entrepreneurs in the internet industry and new media "content producers" (or internet opinion leaders). The goal of reaching out to new media personnel, according to an article on the department's website, is "to achieve the 'two healthys'—to guide and help the representative figures in new media to have healthy professional growth, and to support and promote the healthy development of the new media industry."[33] The article also states that a "healthy" new media entrepreneur would be a patriotic and responsible person who "consciously practices core socialist values" and that a healthy new media sector would be a "clean web environment" which generates positive energy.[34] Apparently following through on Xi's new directive, then head of CAC Lu Wei dined with half a dozen internet public opinion leaders on November 9, 2014.[35]

A fifth example of the party-state's use soft power to manage cyberspace are indirect—even hidden—methods of shaping online opinions. Internet commentators, known by the pejorative nickname of "50-Cent Party" (*wumaodang*), are paid (allegedly 50 Chinese cents (about 8 U.S. cents) per post to participate in online discussion anonymously in support of official agendas. Since its introduction in 2005, this practice has been adopted widely by local governments.[36] In more recent years, the 50-Cent Party has been joined by a so-called "voluntary 50-Cent Army" (*ziganwu*) who volunteer to defend party-state positions without being recruited or paid by officials agencies.[37] The appearance of the voluntary 50-Cent Army signals the increasingly divided and fragmented nature of online discourse, but this is not simply the result of a top-down strategy of divide and rule. Rather, the division reflects deep fractures in Chinese society between those who support the CCP's agenda and those who are critical of many aspects of the party's use of its power.

Finally, at the center of all of the soft methods of internet governance and censorship is a set of discourses on "civility" and "civilization," which are both conveyed by the Chinese term *wenming*. As civilization, *wenming* operates as an ideological discourse that legitimates the governance and administration of society. As civility, it functions as a strategic tool for governance and self-governance, including the governance of the internet. Discourses about civility and civilization have been integral to Chinese modernity since the late 19th century,[38] but they have been elevated to the new height under Xi Jinping by being linked explicitly to Confucian virtues of harmony, propriety, culture, and self-cultivation as the embodiment of China's great civilizational tradition.

Many forms of internet governance and control are undertaken in the name of promoting civility. Thus internet commentators can serve as online civility monitors; national competitions are held to select model websites and internet users for their civil use of the web; online protests can be shut down for being uncivil.

In the service of this discourse on civility, an online opinion industry is thriving. Consisting of both commercial public relations firms and government media and academic research institutions, this industry generates survey reports on the trends in online public opinion by mining the big data of cyberspace discourse. The survey reports track hot-button incidents on social media, including online protests, and provide metrics showing whether a specific incident has generated positive or negative energy and whether the online sentiments associated with it are positive or negative. Positive energy promotes "civilized cyberspace,"[39] whereas negative energy undermines it.

These survey reports may then be used to guide policy making in how to manage online expression or as training manuals to help government officials or business managers better understand and control internet mass incidents and crisis situations. The survey reports also create and naturalize a new vocabulary of internet governance that is being adopted in both official and public media discourse. A distinct feature of these survey reports is the use of metrics to attribute degrees of emotionality, rationality, hopefulness, apathy, and pessimism to internet incidents. This provides a convenient and seemingly scientific approach to measuring the degree of positive (civil) or negative (uncivil) energy in online speech, which could then be deployed for more effective governance and control. These measures ultimately serve to delegitimize online speech that is critical of the party-state because they reflect a vision of cyberspace that sees such expressions as political threats and social pollution to be eliminated.

It is in this context of data-driven governance and surveillance that China's new **social credit system** must be understood. Launched in 2014, the social credit system has been characterized as "an all-encompassing, penetrative system of personal data processing, manifested by the comprehensive collection and expansive use of personal data with the explicit intention on the Chinese government's part of harnessing the ambition and power of big data technology."[40] Still in its pilot stage, the goals of the system are officially said to include "perfecting the socialist market economy system" and "building a socialist harmonious society."[41] Citizens' internet search histories and social media activities can all be collected and used to determine their social credit worthiness. Some forms of offline social behavior—for example, driving infractions—are also used to compile credit scores. It is proposed that those with high scores be rewarded or recognized in some way, whereas those with low rating are to be penalized. For example, there are already reports that individuals with poor social credit have been blocked from buying air tickets or stopped from traveling on high-speed trains.[42] Thus, the cyberspace traces left by PRC citizens are not only part of internet governance and censorship, but can also be used for social surveillance and management more broadly. Described by one China scholar "as a cure-all solution to a multitude of disparate societal and economic problems,"[43] the social credit system is worrisome to many observers because of its potentially unlimited scale in the collection and use by the party-state of citizens' personal information and the lack of protection of their rights and privacy. The enormous size of China's internet and mobile phone users only exacerbates the situation. The more wired and networked Chinese society becomes, the more easily it will be subject to surveillance and control.

CONCLUSION

The history of the internet in China is one of constrained but still creative expression, as well as political contestation. As new social, cultural and political forms appear in Chinese cyberspace, new institutions and methods of governing the internet appear in response or in tandem. This chapter has delineated the main forms of China's internet politics since the 1990s. It highlights the complex contestation among multiple actors, especially the interactions between party-state power and citizens as online activists. It shows that China's netizens are contentious while the party-state is intransigent in exercising its self-proclaimed right to play a leading role in managing cyberspace, but adaptive and skillful in refining its methods and techniques it uses to do so. The general trend in recent decades is the gradual curtailing of citizens' power in using the internet to challenge the party-state. Nevertheless, internet politics in China must be understood as a dynamically unfolding story of contention and control. New information and communication technologies do not inherently favor or forgo either of those developments. In any case, it is no longer possible to understand Chinese politics without studying the politics of the internet.

NOTES

1. "The Internet in China" (White Paper), Information Office of the State Council of the People's Republic of China, June 8, 2010, http://www.china.org.cn/government/whitepaper/node_7093508.htm

2. Ernest J. Wilson III, *The Information Revolution and Developing Countries* (Cambridge, MA: MIT Press, 2006), 223.

3. "Survey of the Internet in Rural Areas," Mar. 2008, http://www.cnnic.net.cn.

4. CNNIC, "The 41st China Statistical Report on Internet Development," Jan. 2018. http://cnnic.net/hlwfzyj/hlwxzbg/hlwtjbg/201803/P020180305409870339136.pdf

5. Jack Linchuan Qiu and Lining Zhou, "Through the Prism of the Internet Café: Managing Access in an Ecology of Games," *China Information* 19, no. 2 (2005): 261–297.

6. Jing Wu and Guoqiang Yun, "From Modernization to Neoliberalism? How IT Opinion Leaders Imagine the Information Society," *International Communication Gazette* 80, no. 1 (2018): 7–29.

7. Guobin Yang, *The Power of the Internet in China* (New York: Columbia University Press), 3.

8. Hualing Fu and Richard Cullen, "Climbing the Weiquan Ladder: A Radicalizing Process for Rights Protection Lawyers." *China Quarterly* 205 (2011): 40–59.

9. Yang, *The Power of the Internet in China*, 91.

10. A recent study by scholars in China surveys 248 internet incidents in 2009 and 274 in 2010. One-third of those in 2009 and half of those in 2010 concern social issues and law enforcement authorities. See Yu Guoming, ed., *Annual Report on Public Opinion in China* (in Chinese) (Beijing: *People's Daily Press*, 2011), 17.

11. "Report on the degree of consensus in internet public opinion for June issued by the Media Monitoring Office of People's Daily Online (*Renmin wang yuqing jiance shi fabu liuyue wangluo yulun gongshi du baogao*), *People's Daily Online*, July 10, 2015), http://yuqing.people.com.cn/n/2015/0710/c210107-27283825.html

12. Jacque deLisle, Avery Goldstein, and Guobin Yang, eds., *The Internet, Social Media, and a Changing China* (Philadelphia: University of Pennsylvania Press, 2016), 4.

13. Liu, Shih-Diing, "China's Popular Nationalism on the Internet. Report on the 2005 Anti-Japan Network Struggles," *Inter-Asia Cultural Studies* 7, no. 1 (2006): 144–155.

14. Guobin Yang, "The Internet and the Rise of a Transnational Cultural Sphere," *Media, Culture & Society* 25 (2003): 469–490.

15. Zhou, Yongming, *Historicizing Online Politics: Telegraphy, the Internet, and Political Participation in China* (Stanford, CA: Stanford University Press, 2006), 216.

16. Jack Linchuan Qiu, "The Changing Web of Chinese Nationalism," *Global Media and Communication* 2, no. 1 (1996): 125–128. http://doi.org/10.1177/1742766506061846; Xu Wu, *Chinese Cyber Nationalism: Evolution, Characteristics, and Implications* (Lanham, MD: Lexington Books, 2007).

17. Lijun Yang and Yongnian Zheng, "Fen Qings (Angry Youth) in Contemporary China," *Journal of Contemporary China* 21, no. 76 (2012): 637–653.

18. See http://www.4thmedia.org.

19. Lijun Yang and Yongnian Zheng, "Fen Qings (Angry Youth)."

20. Central Committee of Chinese Communist Party (CCCCP), "Decision of the Central Committee of the Communist Party of China Regarding the Strengthening of the Party's Ability to Govern." People.com.cn, 2004, http://www.people.com.cn/GB/42410/42764/3097243.html

21. CCCCP, "Decision of the Central Committee of the Communist Party," 2004.

22. Reuters Staff, "NetEase Regulatory Saga Near End—Govt Official," Jan. 4, 2010. https://www.reuters.com/article/netease-wow-idCNTOE60308D20100104

23. Amnesty International, "People's Republic of China: Controls Tighten as Internet Activism Grows" (Jan. 2004), http://www.amnesty.org/ en/alfresco_asset/c176cd3d-a48b-11dc-bac9-0158df32ab50/asa170012004en.pdf.

24. "China Detains Teenager Over Web Post Amid Social Media Crackdown," *Guardian*, Sept. 20, 2013, https://www.theguardian.com/world/2013/sep/20/china-detains-teenage-web-post-crackdown.

25. Available in English at http://www.lawinfochina.com/display.aspx?id=22826&lib=law

26. Elizabeth Perry, "From Mass Campaigns to Managed Campaigns: "Constructing a New Socialist Countryside," in *Mao's Invisible Hand: The Political Foundations of Adaptive Governance in China*, ed. Sebastian Heilmann and Elizabeth Perry (Cambridge, MA: Harvard University Press, 2011), 30–61.

27. "The State Council Information Office and Seven Other Ministries Launch Campaign against Internet Vulgarity" (*Guo xin ban deng qi buwei kaizhan zhengzhi hulianwang disu zhi feng zhuanxiang xingdong*), Jan. 5, 2009. http://news.xinhuanet.com/politics/2009-01/05/content_10606040_1.htm

28. People.com.cn, "Internet Campaign Action to Close Illegal Websites," May 24, 2009. http://news.sina.com.cn/c/2009-02-24/193617279700.shtml

29. Shaohua Guo, "'Occupying' the Internet: State Media and the Reinvention of Official Culture online," *Communication and the Public* 3, no. 1 (2018): 19–33.

30. "Police Urged to Boost Use of Micro Blog," *China Daily*, Sept. 27, 2012. http://www.china.org.cn/china/2011-09/27/content_23498523.htm.

31. Jesper Schlaeger and Min Jiang, "Official Microblogging and Social Management by Local Governments in China," in *China's Contested Internet*, ed. Guobin Yang (Copenhagen: Nordic Institute of Asian Studies Press, 2016), 192–226.

32. Shaohua Guo, "'Occupying' the Internet."

33. Run Zhi, "How to Understand "Strengthening and Improving Our Work Toward Representative Personnel in the New Media Industry? (*Ruhe kandai, lijie "jiaqiang he gaishan dui xin meiti zhong de daibiao renshi de gongzuo?*), People.com.cn, June 4, 2015. http://politics.people.com.cn/n/2015/0604/c1001-27106081.html

34. Run Zhi, "How to Understand?"

35. Kang Jia, "Director of State Internet Information Office Lu Wei Dines Pan Shiyi, Chen Tong and Other 'Big Vs'" (*Guoxinban zhuren Lu Wei yu Pan Shiyi, Chen Tong deng "da V" huican*), *China Youth Daily*, Nov. 9, 2014, http://news.youth.cn/gn/201411/t20141109_6013025.htm.

36. For example, in Sept. 2011, a news release by a county-level department of population and family planning in Hubei province states that it utilizes seventeen internet commentators to monitor internet information. See http://www.hbpop.gov.cn/hbegs/show.asp?id=10939.

37. Rongbin Han, *Contesting Cyberspace in China: Online Expression and Authoritarian Resilience* (New York: Columbia University Press, 2018).

38. Prasenjit Duara, "The Discourse of Civilization and pan-Asianism," *Journal of World History* 12, no. 1 (2001): 99–130.

39. Lu Wei, "Concentrate Positive Energy Online, Build the Chinese Dream Together," Speech at the 13th Chinese Online Media Forum, Oct. 30, 2013; https://chinacopyrightandmedia.wordpress.com/2013/10/30/lu-wei-concentrate-positive-energy-online-build-the-chinese-dream-together/

40. Yongxi Chen and Anne SY Cheung, "The Transparent Self under Big Data Profiling: Privacy and Chinese Legislation on the Social Credit System," *Journal of Comparative Law* 12, no. 2 (2017): 356–378.

41. The State Council, "Planning Outline for the Construction of a Social Credit System (2014–2020)". See English translation at: https://chinacopyrightandmedia.wordpress.com/2014/06/14/planning-outline-for-the-construction-of-a-social-credit-system-2014-2020/.

42. Chen and Cheung, "The Transparent Self under Big Data Profiling," 362.

43. Mareike Ohlberg, Shazeda Ahmed, and Bertram Lang, "Central Planning, Local Experiments: The Complex Implementation of China's Social Credit System." Dec. 12, 2017. MERICS Mercator Institute for China Studies. https://www.merics.org/en/microsite/china-monitor/central-planning-local-experiments.

SUGGESTED READINGS

deLisle, Jacques, Avery Goldstein, and Guobin Yang, eds. *The Internet, Social Media, and a Changing China.* Philadelphia: University of Pennsylvania Press, 2016.

Han, Rongbin. *Contesting Cyberspace in China: Online Expression and Authoritarian Resilience.* New York: Columbia University Press, 2018.

Herold, David Kurt, and Peter Marolt, eds. *Online Society in China: Creating, Celebrating, and Instrumentalising the Online Carnival.* London: Routledge, 2011.

Hochx, Michel. *Internet Literature in China.* New York: Columbia University Press, 2015.

Lei, Ya-Wen. *The Contentious Public Sphere: Law, Media and Authoritarian Rule in China.* Princeton, NJ: Princeton University Press, 2017.

Qiu, Jack Linchuan. *Working-class Network Society: Communication Technology and the Information Have-less in Urban China.* Cambridge, MA: MIT Press, 2009.

Roberts, Margaret E. *Censored: Distraction and Diversion inside China's Great Firewall.* Princeton, NJ: Princeton University Press, 2018.

Wallis, Cara. *Technomobility in China: Young Migrant Women and Mobile Phones.* New York: NYU Press, 2013.

Yang, Guobin. *The Power of the Internet in China: Citizen Activism Online.* New York: Columbia University Press, 2009.

Zheng, Yongnian. *Technological Empowerment: The Internet, State, and Society in China.* Stanford, CA: Stanford University Press, 2007.

Zhou, Yongming. *Historicizing Online Politics: Telegraphy, the Internet, and Political Participation in China.* Stanford, CA: Stanford University Press, 2006.

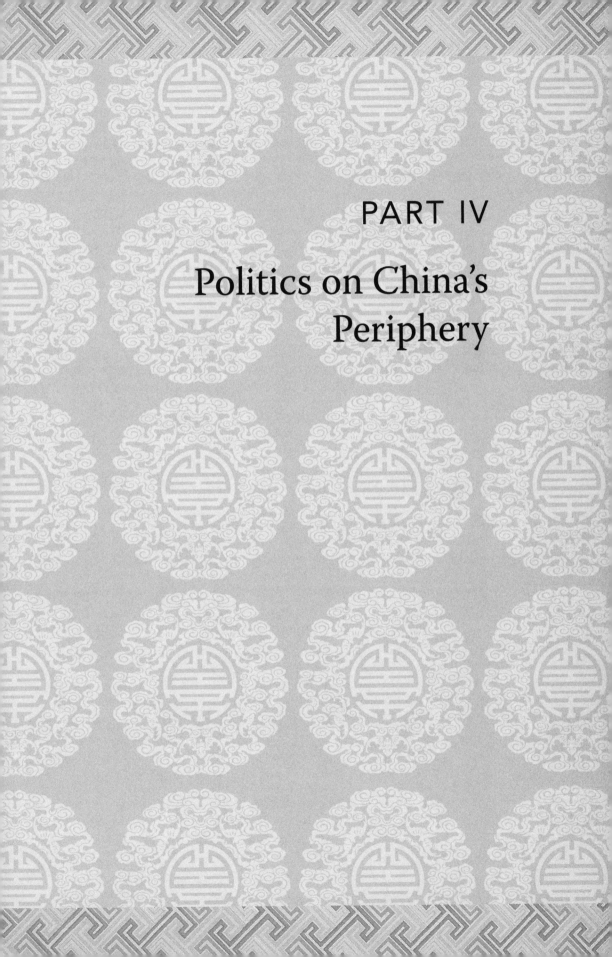

PART IV

Politics on China's Periphery

16

Tibet

ROBERT BARNETT

Most Tibetans in China live up to 2,500 miles from Beijing and at an average altitude of some 14,000 feet above sea level. Numbering 6.2 million within China, according to a 2010 census, they represent less than 0.5 percent of China's population and, as of 2017, 69 percent of Tibetans in central Tibet were still living in rural areas, mainly herding yaks or sheep on semiarid grassland or farming barley and other crops in high-altitude valleys. These statistics suggest a tiny group in a remote area of China that one would expect to be marginal to that country's politics. Yet, in 2008, when China presented its first Olympic Games as a "century-old dream" (*bainian mengxiang*) and "a historical event in the great revitalization of the Chinese nation,"[1] the most telling challenge from within the country to that narrative came from Tibet, where over a hundred protests against Chinese rule took place in the four months before the Games began. These did more than capture the attention of the world's media: they led the PRC to cut off the Tibetan areas—one quarter of China's territory—from the outside world for several months as troops were put in place and reprisals carried out. The Tibet Autonomous Region (TAR) remains the only region or province within China where foreigners are not allowed to enter except with special permission, and in 2012 it became one of only two regions within China where most residents are denied passports and in effect banned from foreign travel. Why did the unrest in Tibet have such a dramatic effect, when a hundred thousand or more protests were known to have occurred in other parts of China that year without such repercussions?

The official Chinese media asserted at the time that the protests were either isolated instances of anti-China agitation instigated by a small number of foreigners and

458 POLITICS IN CHINA

exiles, or that they resulted from Tibetan jealousy of the growing wealth among the ethnic Chinese. These explanations do little to explain the scale of the state's response to unrest in Tibetan areas. Rather, that response suggests that Tibetans have a significance as political actors within China that is disproportionate to their numbers and contrary to the perception of their role as marginal. In fact, if we set aside the small proportion of the Tibetan population in China, the size, location, and history of Tibet should lead us to expect that the area will be politically important. Tibet—used here in its broadest sense to describe the entire **Tibetan Plateau,** the area traditionally inhabited by Tibetans—covers some 970,000 square miles, making it roughly equivalent in size to Western Europe minus Scandinavia. In China, the Chinese word for "Tibet"—*Xizang*—is used to refer only to the western half of the plateau, an area of some 472,000 square miles, which was directly administered by the Dalai Lama's government in the 1940s. This area was taken over by the People's Liberation Army in 1950 and officially renamed the Tibet Autonomous Region in 1965.

The Tibetan Plateau represents 26 percent of current Chinese territory, while the areas traditionally inhabited by Uyghurs and Mongols, two other peoples with long histories of resistance to Chinese rule, cover another third of the PRC's landmass. The importance of the Tibetan area is not just a question of size: the headwaters of many of Asia's most important rivers flow from the Tibetan Plateau, including the Yangtze, the Yellow, the Brahmaputra, the Salween, the Mekong, the Irrawaddy, and the Indus, supplying vital sources of water to lowland China, India, Bangladesh, Myanmar, Thailand, Laos, Vietnam, Cambodia, and Pakistan. In military terms, the Tibetan Plateau is the strategic high ground where Central, South, and East Asia converge. It includes 2,300 miles of international borders with four countries, of which one, that with India, is still disputed and highly militarized, while another, the border with Bhutan, has yet to be settled. The most serious armed challenge that the CCP has faced within its territory since it took over China came from Tibetans in the late 1950s. The only sustained guerrilla attacks China has faced since 1949 were those staged by Tibetans from 1959 to 1974, and China's only war that remains unresolved was the 1962 war with India over Tibet's disputed borders. The recent prominence of Tibet as a factor in China's international relations, particularly those with the United States, is reflected in the fact that since 1987 Beijing has not allowed any nation to open diplomatic relations with it unless that nation states publicly its recognition of China's sovereignty over not just Taiwan but Tibet as well.

Since the late 1980s, Tibet has come to play a new role in China's internal politics too: it has emerged as a proving ground for some of China's highest leaders. Hu Jintao, the leader of the Chinese Communist Party from 2002 to 2012 and China's president from 2003 to 2013, was promoted to the top positions in the nation after he had proved his abilities by serving as the party secretary of the TAR from 1988 to 1992, crushing protests and overseeing the imposition of martial law in the region for thirteen months from March 1989. Guo Jinlong, the party secretary of Beijing from 2012 to 2017, was given that position after working as the party secretary of the TAR, and vice premier Hu Chunhua, a member of the CCP Politburo and a rising star in the party leadership, worked for twenty years as a leader in the TAR.

There are other indications that Tibet and Tibetans are viewed by China's leaders in different ways from other areas and other nationalities within China. The CCP has

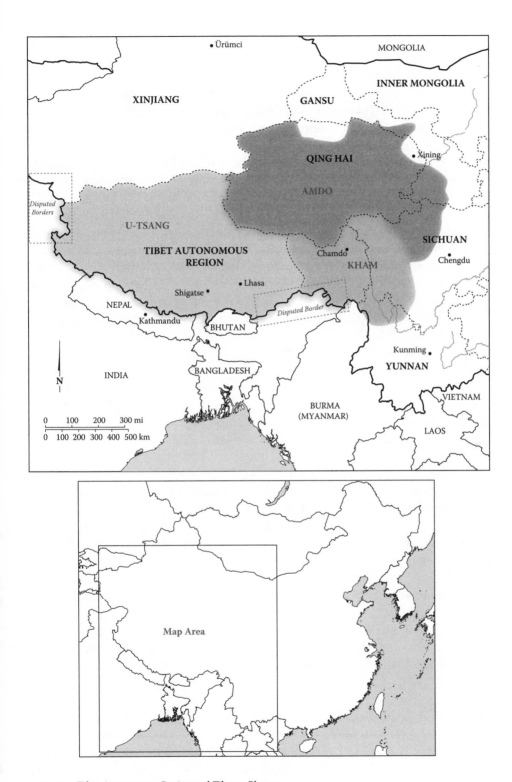

MAP 16.1 Tibet Autonomous Region and Tibetan Plateau

a top-level system of eleven or more specialist committees known as the permanent "Leading Small Groups" (see chap. 6) and "Coordination Small Groups" that guide and oversee policy on the principal political issues in China, and two of those bodies deal with Tibet and Xinjiang respectively. Although the fifty-five nationalities in China that are not ethnically Chinese—PRC officials use the term "Han," apparently because it implies the ethnic Chinese are just one component in a multiethnic country and that Tibetans and other nationalities are also Chinese—are in theory governed according to a single policy, and some nationalities are much more numerous than the Tibetans, there is clearly more concern about Tibet and Xinjiang than the other minorities. Of the 111 "White Papers" —definitive statements released by the Chinese government on a wide range of important policies—since 1991, thirteen have been about Tibet or Tibetans,[2] and six have been about Xinjiang; none of the other nationalities have had a White Paper devoted to them. In 2005 Tibetans became the first nationality to have their own bureau (No. 7) within the United Front Work Department,[3] the CCP organization that runs all nationality and religious affairs in China; among the other nationalities and nationality areas, Xinjiang is the only area besides Tibet that has a bureau (No. 9) specifically assigned to it within the United Front Work Department, and that only since 2017.

These factors suggest that although Tibet is often thought of as geographically peripheral and politically marginal, Tibet and Tibetans have an important role, perhaps even a critical one, in Chinese politics. This may be why China's leaders respond to Tibetan issues, with their complex historical legacies, more nervously than they do to equivalent instances of social or political unrest in China proper—and why their responses to Tibetan problems have so far met with less success than those in almost any other policy domain.

The standard formulation used by Chinese leaders since 1990 to describe their Tibet policy indicates that the Tibet issue is anything but marginal to them: "From a strategic height and an overall point of view," goes the formula, the PRC's policy in Tibet is "crucial to the success of reforms, development, and stability throughout the country."[4] In 2006, Tibet was for the first time declared publicly by China to be one of the nation's "core interests," and in 2008 Hu Jintao said in his annual statement on Tibet that "the stability in Tibet concerns the stability of the country."[5] (Major protests erupted in Lhasa four days later.) In 2015, Xi Jinping re-emphasized this concern, declaring that "governing border areas is the key for governing a country, and stabilizing Tibet is a priority for governing border areas."[6] Such statements, repeated in all China's recent major policy documents on the region, may well mean exactly what they say: Tibet is a crucial political concern for the PRC.

SINO-TIBETAN RELATIONS AND THE ROLE OF THE GIFT

When Xi Jinping visited Lhasa in July 2011, a year before he became China's new leader, he was greeted by floral arrangements laid out in the main square of the city, a hundred feet or more across, that spelled out in Tibetan the words "We thank the Central Party Authorities" (*tang krung dbyang la thugs rje che shu*). Three months later, as if to ensure that the slogan had not been inaccurate, 21,000 cadres were gathered in the same square and told that they would spend the next three years living in teams of four or more in every village in the TAR, where they were to educate the villagers on "Feeling Grateful to the Party for its Generosity." Eight years later, the teams are still in place. Each of the 5,000 work teams (*gongzuo dui*) was instructed to use "vivid teaching materials" to explain to the villagers that "their happy and peaceful life today is because of the leadership of the Communist Party" and to bring them to "consciously love the Party, love patriotism, and love socialism." The teams were given 100,000 yuan (about US$16,000) to spend on gifts for each village, such as new roads, facilities, and meeting halls, as well as one million national flags and posters bearing the portrait of Mao Zedong and the leaders who came after him, which were then given to Tibetan villagers and others to put up in their homes. The focus on thankfulness was not an incidental detail: the cadres were told that "Feeling Grateful to the Party" education was a higher priority than dispensing the money to the villagers.[7]

This cultivation of Tibetan gratitude was a key part of China's long-term response to the protests in Tibet in 2008. It is an approach that has deep historical roots in China's relations with Tibet and Tibetans. If we try to envisage the perspective of Chinese officials and the CCP toward Tibetans over the last sixty years, what we see for the most part is not an effort to destroy or attack Tibetan culture, as some critics have alleged, but the opposite: a long series of "gifts" which has been interrupted only by what the Party now describes as the "errors" of the Cultural Revolution. The nature of these gifts changed according to shifts in political conditions and ideology in China, as did the explanations that went with them. The initial gift to Tibetans was that of "liberation" in 1950; this was followed by the gift of class struggle and the accompanying dispensing of land to the peasantry in 1959. Other gifts were to come: "regional autonomy" in 1965, a classless society in 1966, the household economy in 1980, stability in 1990, the market economy in 1992, and "comfortable housing" for villagers in 2006. Some of these gifts—land distribution in 1959, the ending of class divisions and "old ideas" in 1966, and the household economy in the early 1980s—were aimed at winning over the masses, while others, such as permission to continue traditional social relations in 1951 and the marketization policy in 1992, were carried out at times when the Party needed to make an alliance with local elites. All of these gifts, from the perspective of the Party and the Chinese people, were forms of generosity.

The many uprisings, rebellions, protests, and forms of resistance that have taken place in Tibet over the last sixty years have been interpreted, particularly among foreigners and exiles, as indications that these gifts have been seen by many Tibetans as impositions, oppression, or, at best, flawed policies. Chinese officials and writers, on the other hand, have tended to write about the negative response of many Tibetans to these displays of largesse as signs of backwardness, opportunism, foreign agitation, or, in the final analysis, ingratitude. Either view reflects the influence of ideologies, whether these be Marxism, modernism, or liberal humanism, that train us to assume that certain values will necessarily be shared by others, and that gifts exemplifying those values will be welcomed. It is such perspectives that have scripted repeated cycles of generosity and resentment, or of pride followed by anxiety, in China's policies toward Tibet.

Tibetan-Chinese relations have long been governed by gifts. In the traditional Tibetan view—at least from the mid-seventeenth century, when the **Dalai Lamas,** spiritual leaders regarded as the reincarnations of a fifteenth-century Buddhist master (see Box 16.1), became the political rulers of Tibet and created what we would now call a state—Tibet's political relations were with particular emperors who ruled China rather than with China as a nation. During the Yuan (1271–1368) and Qing (1644–1912) dynasties, those emperors were in any case not Chinese, but were Mongols or Manchus respectively, and presented themselves in the Tibetan context as Buddhist kings or "Dharma-protectors," an important concept in Buddhist societies. The relationship between them and the Dalai Lamas was described in Tibetan texts at the time as that between a patron and a lama, with the emperors giving patronage and protection in return for religious teachings and spiritual empowerment. The emperors' patronage was expressed by their recognition and conferring of titles on the Dalai Lamas, by the appointment of some officials, and by their willingness to send troops when the Tibetans needed them. Material gifts were an important expression of this relationship, functioning both as religious offerings and as signs of wealth, respect, and commitment. The importance with which they were viewed can be seen from the fact that the autobiography of the Fifth Dalai Lama (1617–1682), the most important

BOX 16.1 DALAI LAMAS AND PANCHEN LAMAS

Although all forms of Buddhism recognize reincarnation, only the Tibetans developed a theory that certain highly achieved spiritual masters, or lamas, voluntarily renounce nirvana so that they can be reborn as a human in order to help others. The Tibetans also developed techniques, such as visions in divination lakes, tests of children's previous-life memories, and prayers, which are believed to enable the previous lama's followers to identify the right child as the reincarnation of that *trulku* or reincarnated lama. Such children inherit their predecessor's position and estate.

The longest continuous *trulku* lineage is that of the Karmapa, first recognized in the thirteenth century and now in his seventeenth body. There are at least a thousand *trulku*, or lama, lineages, at least four of which are or were composed only of women. The most famous and influential *trulku* is that of the Dalai Lamas, which began in the late fourteenth century. The Third Dalai Lama (1543–1588) was a leading spiritual master within the Gelugpa school of Tibetan Buddhism and became well known in Mongolia as the teacher of Altan Khan, ruler of the Tumed Mongols. When a Mongol army invaded Tibet in 1642, its leader appointed the Fifth Dalai Lama (1617–1682) as the ruler of Tibet, with the Potala Palace in Lhasa as his seat. The Great Fifth, as he was called, was able to create a unified nation and a governmental system presided over by his successors, or by their regents when they were young, for the next three hundred years.

The Panchen Lamas, first recognized as a *trulku* lineage by the Fifth Dalai Lama in the seventeenth century, were based in Tashilhunpo monastery in Tibet's second largest town, Shigatse, and became the second-most famous teachers in the Gelugpa school. The Panchen Lamas and the Dalai Lamas were sometimes tutors to each other, depending on which was older at the time.

In Tibetan, the word "lama" is used only to describe a highly regarded spiritual teacher, but in Chinese it is used incorrectly to refer to any Tibetan monk. English terms like "Lamaism," "Living Buddha," "Living God," "God King," or "Soul Boy" have no equivalent in Tibetan (there is no creator god in Buddhism, and no belief in the soul) and are technically incorrect, if not derogatory.

of his line, includes details of each gift presented to him by the Qing emperors and other potentates.

When the emperors wrote to Tibetan rulers, their letters were always accompanied by gifts, with each one itemized so as to emphasize its value. "With this decree," wrote the Qing emperor Daoguang to the Tenth Dalai Lama in 1823, "I am presenting you with a 60-*liang* gold-plated silver container for tea-leaves, a gold-plated silver vase, a large goblet, 30 rolls of assorted silk . . . in addition to a jade figure of Buddha, a set of bells and sticks, a jade *ruyi*, a chaplet of coral beads, a python-patterned robe, two boxes of fragrant cakes and a pair of padded mattresses."[8] These were just half of the twenty-four offerings listed in the letter, which, like many of its kind, had no specific purpose other than to convey respect and to record the extent of the emperor's offerings to the Lama.

As the anthropologist Marcel Mauss famously pointed out, gifts are social transactions that are always invested with unstated meanings known to the giver and expected of the recipient. "In theory," he wrote, an act of giving is "voluntary, disinterested and spontaneous" and "the form usually taken is that of the gift generously offered." This is, he argued, a "pretense and social deception," because behind the formal transaction are notions of "obligation and economic self-interest."[9] Notwithstanding what we say to others or tell ourselves, according to Mauss, when we give, we expect something in return. This appears to be even more the case with political gifts, and still more so with those given by one nation or one ruler to another. The Tibetans certainly understood that they should give something in return for the satin and the silk, and so gave religious respect, charismatic status, and limited forms of obedience to the Qing emperors. In particular, the Fifth Dalai Lama declared— though only after first receiving gifts from the new dynasty in Beijing—that the Qing emperor was an emanation of the Bodhisattva Jambeyang, known in Sanskrit as Manjushri. We could call the Tibetan gifts to the Chinese ruler "soft tribute," since they consisted mostly of intangibles like titles, spiritual empowerments, and deference of a sort, but it is clear that these gifts were part of a relationship based on exchange, with relatively little emphasis on hierarchy. It is also clear that the gifts from the Dalai Lamas were of exceptional symbolic value and importance to the Manchu Qing emperors in their quest for legitimacy, especially in their dealings with Buddhist Inner Asia.

MANCHU VIEWS OF TIBET

When China was at the center of the vast land-based empires run by the Mongol Yuan dynasty or the Manchu Qing dynasty, Tibet was viewed as both a part of those empires and at the same time as a distinct political entity. There was none of the flattening of space or persons that conceives of all the people and regions within a territory as co-equal or equivalent, as in a modern nation-state. Traditional leaders in Tibet received imperial orders from time to time, mainly confirmations of appointments, but largely were left to rule as they saw fit; the Ming emperors (1368–1644) did not even include Tibet in their official maps and seem not to have considered it a part of their domain. From the 1720s, the Manchu Qing emperors sent *amban*s, or imperial commissioners, with a small detachment of troops to Lhasa, where they were kept informed of certain kinds of local decisions, such as official appointments and interactions with foreign states. But otherwise the role of these officials from Beijing (who until the twentieth century were always Mongols or Manchus, not ethnic Chinese) was somewhat limited, and there is no trace at all of any concept among Tibetans suggesting that Tibet and China were a single country.[10]

The Manchu rulers in Beijing did not refer to the status of Tibet in modern terms until just before the twentieth century. Prior to that time they described it as a "barbarian" (*fan*) region that was part of their "outer dominions" and administered it until 1861 through a special office, the *Lifanyuan*, sometimes translated as the "Court of Colonial Affairs," while the areas that had been part of China under the Ming were administered directly as provinces.[11] The Manchus were obliged to change this loose, premodern terminology when a British army led by Francis Younghusband invaded Tibet in 1903, supposedly in order to guarantee British trade rights and to avert a rumored buildup of Russian weapons in Tibet. (After massacring some three thousand to four thousand Tibetans, the British found just three Russian-made rifles in the country.) British and other Western officials at the time defined Tibet as a protectorate, a dependency, or a territory under the authority of a suzerain state or "overlord," indicating that, while not a fully independent state, they considered Tibet a distinct nation of some kind.[12]

Younghusband returned with his troops to India within six months of reaching Lhasa, having forced the Tibetans to sign a humiliating surrender agreement, but his escapade had momentous results: it impelled the Qing court to formalize its relationship with Tibet. In 1910 the court, which had determined that Tibet should henceforth be considered part of China's sovereign territory, sent an army to invade Lhasa, planning to disband the Tibetan government and to make Tibet into a Chinese province. The Tibetan army was able to rout the Qing troops and reclaim control a year later, when the collapse of the Qing dynasty left its soldiers with no money and no supplies. But the die had been cast: a century of wars, invasions, and protests, leading to scores or even hundreds of thousands of deaths, would follow as successive Chinese governments sought to enforce the new view of Tibet as part of China's sovereign territory.

The failure of the Qing attempt at full annexation in turn led the Thirteenth Dalai Lama (1876–1933), once he had returned to Lhasa from refuge in British India, to redefine Tibet's status in modern terms. "The Chinese intention of colonizing Tibet under the priest [lama]-patron relationship has faded like a rainbow in the sky," he wrote to the Tibetan people in 1913.[13] He described Tibet as independent, asserting that the relationship between Tibet and China "had not been based on the subordination of one to the other," but on personal ties between the imperial "patrons" and the Tibetan lamas. All remaining Chinese officials and their dependents were expelled from Lhasa, and Tibet, or at least those parts of it that the Dalai Lama's government controlled, became a de facto independent country.

The government of the Republic of China (1912–1949) asserted its claims over Tibet based on similarly modern notions of sovereignty and ownership, but was unable even to gain entry to the region for its officials until 1934, let alone to exercise authority.

From then until 1950 a few Chinese officials were allowed to reside in Lhasa, but with the same status as the representatives of Nepal, Bhutan, and Britain.

It was only when the CCP came to power in China in October 1949 that a government in Beijing had the military resources to enforce the Chinese claim to sovereignty over Tibet, and one year and a week after the CCP took over China, some forty thousand troops of the People's Liberation Army (PLA) crossed the border between China and the territory run by the Lhasa government, taking only a few days to overwhelm the seven thousand or so Tibetan forces stationed at Chamdo, near the current border with Sichuan province.

THE "SEVENTEEN POINT AGREEMENT" OF 1951: THE GIFT OF EXCEPTIONALISM

Even before 1949, echoes of the historical gift relationship between China and Tibet can be detected in the CCP's statements and policies. In its Jiangxi Constitution of 1931, the party, which had been founded a decade earlier, spelled out its policy toward Tibetans and other non-Chinese nationalities, promising them the ultimate gift: the right to "complete separation from China, and the formation of an independent state" once the party obtained power. This commitment, which emulated Lenin's "accommodationist" approach to nationalities in the Soviet Union,[14] was quietly withdrawn in the early 1940s, before it could be implemented. Recollections of this early, undelivered gift had important consequences, particularly among the first Tibetan communists like Baba Phuntsog Wanggyal, once the highest placed Tibetan in the CCP, who was to spend eighteen years in prison for having tried to remind his comrades in 1957 of Leninist principles and the Jiangxi promise, some ten years after these had been silently removed from the Party's list of allowed policies.[15]

But the principle of the gift remained paramount in CCP thinking about Tibet (meaning here the territory ruled by the Lhasa government). Following the military victory of the PLA in 1950, the Party faced the reality of ruling over a people who had had almost no contact with anything Chinese, let alone communist, and yet were being told by their new rulers that they were not only part of China but were themselves Chinese. At that moment, Mao made a bold decision that reflected the legacy he had inherited from the Qing: he decided to promise the Tibetans almost everything they wanted, short of independence. In May 1951, the Tibetan government, which had been rebuffed in its efforts to obtain support from Britain, India, or the United Nations, signed a surrender document in Beijing titled "The Agreement Between the Central Government and the Local Government of Tibet on Measures for the Peaceful Liberation of Tibet," known more often as the **Seventeen Point Agreement**.[16] The agreement stated that although Tibet was now part of China, "the central authorities will not alter the existing political system in Tibet [or] the established status, functions and powers of the Dalai Lama" (Article 4). As for "reforms in Tibet, there will be no compulsion on the part of the central authorities" (Article 11), Tibetan officials were to remain in position, and "religious beliefs, customs and habits of the Tibetan people would be respected, and the lamaseries shall be protected"

(Article 7). The Chinese Communist Party was not mentioned in the agreement, and its representatives were to take only an advisory role in Tibet.

This was a policy of exceptionalism, according to which, in return for a treaty-like document confirming its acceptance of subordinate status, the area ruled by the Lhasa government was to be treated quite differently from the rest of China and given the gift of continuing, status-quo governance and society—in other words, there would be no introduction of socialism or socialist reforms in that area. It was unlike anything else in Chinese Communist history until the 1997 agreement that transferred control of Hong Kong from Britain to the PRC. In return, the Fourteenth Dalai Lama (born 1935) and his government gave China soft tribute in its strongest form: recognition for the first time of China's sovereignty over their territory.

Mao had several reasons for treating Tibet so differently from the rest of China: there were no roads to move supplies and troops there, no party members or cells in place, very few translators, little or no experience of working with Tibetans or Tibetan Buddhism, and almost no indigenous calls for social reform, let alone for occupation. He was also cautious because of the international dimensions of the Tibetan issue. The British had had diplomats residing in Lhasa from 1936 to 1947, as had Nepal, Sikkim, Bhutan, and later, India; American interest in Tibet had begun to increase following a mission sent in 1943 by the Office of Strategic Services (OSS), the predecessor of the Central Intelligence Agency (CIA). Although initial offers of American military support in 1951 had been rejected by the advisers to the Fourteenth Dalai Lama (who was then twenty-one) as too tentative and unreliable, from 1956 the newly formed CIA went on to give covert support to Tibetan resistance forces in Eastern Tibet. Munitions were parachuted into the region and 250 Tibetans were given military training, first on the Pacific island of Saipan and later in the Colorado Rockies, with about fifty of them dropped into Tibet. (From 1959 till around 1970, the agency equipped some two thousand Tibetan guerrilla fighters operating from a secret base in Nepal, from where they made occasional armed sorties into Tibet, reportedly without the knowledge of the Dalai Lama.) The new Chinese rulers of Tibet thus had numerous reasons to choose initially to avoid alienating the existing elite and the middle class in Lhasa, and to treat the region much as the Qing had done a half century earlier: they offered gifts, demanded respect or acquiescence in return, but did not openly interfere in local or internal affairs. At least on the surface, Mao thus initially followed imperial traditions in his approach to ruling Tibet.

1959: THE GIFT OF EXCEPTIONALISM UNRAVELS

From the outset, the annexation of Tibet was explained by Chinese officials, at least to its domestic audience, not as noninterference or exceptionalism but as "liberation." At the time, this term referred not to the freeing of Tibetans from feudal serfdom—that phrase was used by the Chinese to describe traditional Tibetan society only from about 1959 on, so as to avoid antagonizing the elite—but to freeing them from imperialism, by which was meant British or American intervention. The CCP's first substantive dealings with Tibet were thus presented publicly as the gift of being freed from the threat of foreign domination. The Tibetans had no reason to consider that they faced any such threat—there were just six Westerners in the country in 1950, and no nation had offered substantive support to the Tibetans at that time. The only significant request from a Tibetan for China to take over Tibet had come from the Tenth Panchen Lama (1938–1989), one of the most important Tibetan religious leaders, in 1949, but he was then living in exile in China, estranged from the Tibetan government, desperate for China's support in his dispute with Lhasa—and only eleven years old.

Mao's rhetoric was probably not of much importance to Tibetans at the time— what was persuasive and significant to them was the promise in the Seventeen Point Agreement that their government and religious institutions would remain intact. That promise was not, however, sustainable, coming as it did from a political party committed to bringing radical change throughout society if not the world.[17] The monasteries and the aristocrats that were the foundation of the traditional Tibetan order would be allowed to survive in the short term, but it was only a matter of time before they would be displaced, once the inevitable socialist transformation began.

There was another contradiction within China's 1950s policy toward Tibet. Mao's policy of exceptionalism was not offered to Tibetans, but only to "Tibet" as understood in Chinese usage, meaning only the western half of the Tibetan Plateau, the area formerly administered directly by Lhasa. The majority of Tibetans—nowadays about 56 percent—live in the eastern part of the Tibetan Plateau (referred to by the Chinese authorities as the Qinghai-Tibetan Plateau). Those areas, some 628,000 square miles lying to the east of the upper Yangtze River, are called Kham and Amdo in Tibetan and are now within the provinces of Qinghai, southern Gansu, western Sichuan, and the northern tip of Yunnan.[18] The Seventeen Point Agreement had never been intended by Mao to apply to Tibetans who lived in those areas, and there were only short delays before radical socialist changes were imposed there. By 1955 a land-reform campaign—in effect, violent attacks on the landholding classes, including small farmers, herders, and all monasteries—had begun in the eastern Tibetan areas. This led to widespread resistance, uprisings, and military conflict across the eastern plateau, reaching a climax in 1958.

Most of the eastern Tibetan areas had been separate domains or small principalities until the arrival of the PLA, and many of these had not been directly ruled by the government of the Dalai Lamas for decades, if not centuries. But Tibetans in those areas had strong cultural and religious links to Lhasa—Tibetans in all areas of the plateau for centuries had referred to themselves as peoples of the Snow Land, irrespective of which local government or ruler they were under—and it was to Lhasa that thousands fled to avoid the fighting and destruction in the east. The refugees brought with them accounts of the suppression of religion and the bombing of major monasteries, particularly in the Tibetan areas of Sichuan—proof, in Tibetan eyes, that the gift promised to the western Tibetans had been a trick and was not going to last. This news helped trigger the Lhasa uprising of March 10, 1959. It was an armed rebellion, with widespread popular support, but it was suppressed within a few days by the PLA, which had been expecting such a confrontation for several months. The failed uprising led to the flight of the Dalai Lama and some eighty thousand refugees to India, where for several years they struggled to survive in desperate conditions until Indian and Western financial support gradually enabled the exile Tibetan administration to set up orphanages, schools, monasteries, and agricultural settlements.

THE GIFT OF "DEMOCRATIC REFORM"

Inside Tibet, the Party immediately introduced new policies in March 1959 that marked an end to exceptionalism. It renounced the Seventeen Point Agreement (as did the Dalai Lama) and began imposing radical social leveling, which it referred to as "democratic reform" (*minzhu gaige*). It seized land from landlords and monasteries, ended all debts, and disbanded the traditional social system, as it had done some four years earlier in Kham and Amdo and in the rest of China. Its primary allies in Tibet were no longer the elite but the peasantry. This allowed it to present a much stronger argument to explain its mission in Tibet and provided it with credible evidence of Tibetan enthusiasm for the changes: official newsreel footage at the time shows thousands of farmers burning their debt documents and denouncing their former landlords. The mass ceremonies were largely staged, but there were certainly many people who had good reason to feel deeply grateful for the chance to have their own land and to speak out against whatever suffering and financial burdens they had endured under the previous system. The newsreel footage, and fictional reconstructions of it in popular Chinese films—most famously the 1963 epic, *Nongnu* (The Serf), the story of a Tibetan orphan who is freed by PLA soldiers from endless brutality by landlords and lamas—became extremely influential in China and other developing countries, providing powerful images of mass Tibetan gratitude to the CCP for its reforms. The word used by the Chinese authorities to describe this gift was again "liberation," but it now referred to the freeing of the Tibetan peasants from the alleged barbarity of feudalism, serfdom, and the ruling classes rather than to freedom from imperialism.

The new gift, land for the farmers and herders and an end to class privilege, had a hard side too: it was combined with ruthless punishment for those who had rejected or undermined the previous gift of liberation from the supposed foreign threat. In a campaign called the "Elimination of the Rebellion," the Chinese military began a sweep across Central Tibet (it was already carrying out armed reprisals in Kham and Amdo), holding mass struggle sessions to denounce alleged traitors and counterrevolutionaries, and killing or imprisoning those suspected of sympathy for the uprisings, the previous system, Tibetan independence, or opposition to socialism. The Chinese military historian Ji Youquan wrote that some ninety thousand Tibetans were killed or wounded in the campaign in Central Tibet alone.[19] Thousands of others who had not been able to reach the safety of India and were suspected of dissent were sent to labor camps, where many died of starvation or abuse; those caught trying to escape to India were executed; and of those who survived, many were not released until after Mao's death twenty years later. Years afterward, the Tenth Panchen Lama, the highest-ranking lama to have remained in Tibet after the Dalai Lama fled, is reported to have said in an internal speech that 10–15 percent of the Tibetans in Qinghai province had been imprisoned for involvement in the rebellions there, of whom half had died in prison.[20] Only a handful of these, he said, had had any involvement in the resistance movement of the 1950s.

Secretly, the Panchen Lama had tried to stop these atrocities at the time. In 1962, then aged 24, he had sent an internal petition, 120 pages long, to Chairman Mao and Premier Zhou Enlai, begging them to end the extreme abuses that he had witnessed on a tour of the Tibetan Plateau the previous winter. In his appeal, he described the effect on Tibetans in Qinghai of the famines created by the Great Leap Forward: "There has been an evident and severe reduction in the present-day Tibetan population [presenting] a great threat to the continued existence of the Tibetan nationality, which is sinking into a state close to death," he wrote.[21] He went on to describe local policies that were decimating Tibetan society and religion, so that he doubted they could survive. He reported that 97 percent of the monasteries in the TAR had been shut down, and 93 percent of monks and nuns had been forced to leave their institutions and probably made to shed their religious robes.[22]

The Panchen Lama's report was written four years before the Cultural Revolution began, making it impossible that policies of cultural and religious destruction in Tibet were limited to that episode, as most accounts published in China and elsewhere have assumed. The petition led to the Panchen Lama himself being subjected to struggle sessions in Lhasa every day for two and a half months in 1964, and then to fourteen years in prison or under house arrest.

By the early 1960s, the increases in agricultural production that had initially resulted from the new techniques introduced by the Chinese were being offset by increasing tax demands on the Tibetan farmers, partly a result of China's loss of aid from the Soviet Union, and partly a result of the introduction of the commune system. For some farmers, this meant that the gift of land they had received in 1959 had now in effect been taken away from them. In this climate, Beijing made another gift to Tibetans in 1965: local autonomy. Tibet was renamed the "Tibet Autonomous Region" and declared to be autonomous, as had already been done with twelve prefectures and counties in the eastern Tibetan areas. This meant that the TAR and other Tibetan autonomous areas would have a Tibetan appointed as head of the local government—the chairman (*zhushi*)—and that they would have a local legislature. This system remains a major element of China's policies toward Tibetans and other minority nationalities today, but it applies only to governmental bodies, not to CCP organizations. Each governmental office in China has a CCP committee within it whose leader, the party secretary (*shuji*), is the most powerful person in the larger office. Similarly, the TAR, and each of the PRC's autonomous regions, provinces, and other administrative units, are run by their party secretaries, not by their chairmen or directors, and the party secretary of the TAR has never been a Tibetan. All governmental decisions, policies, and appointments are thus overseen by party officials who at the more senior levels are generally ethnic Chinese. The gift to the Tibetans of autonomy has thus remained almost entirely nominal.[23]

THE CULTURAL REVOLUTION IN TIBET

The Cultural Revolution, which began in May 1966, made little difference to thousands of the former elite in Tibet who had already been languishing in prisons or labor camps since 1959, but it caused extraordinary damage to cultural, intellectual, and religious life in the rest of the society. Again, it was presented as a gift to "the people," a term which at that time referred only to peasants, workers, and soldiers. On this occasion, the gift was freedom from the "Four Olds"—old customs, old culture, old habits, and old ideas—that were then seen as a form of oppression. The campaign, widely regarded now as having been a pretext for a factional attack by Mao's supporters on leaders within the party who were suspected of disloyalty to the Chairman, led to a period of radical social leveling, recalled by some as refreshing. But it came at a huge cost: teachers were paraded in the streets and denounced in ritualistic displays of mass political violence; schools were disbanded; disrobed clerics, who were supposed to be celibate, were forced to marry; disgraced aristocrats and intellectuals were paraded through the streets and pilloried; the empty monasteries were pillaged and the buildings wrecked; and almost all literature, art, and film production ceased for ten years except for a short list of ideologically acceptable items. Only thirteen out of more than a thousand monasteries are said to have been left standing in the TAR by the time the violence was over. No one had the option of remaining uninvolved in these activities, and much of the destruction and violence of this period was carried out by Tibetans, under the leadership of Red Guard teams sent to Tibet from different parts of China.[24]

Within a year, the situation had deteriorated into civil war between two Red Guard factions known in Tibetan as Nyamdrel ("the Alliance") and Gyenlok ("the Rebels"), both of which were led by Han Chinese activists. Several armed rebellions took place in 1969, leading to killings and fighting in at least a quarter of the rural counties in the TAR. The most famous of these was the Nyemo revolt, led by a charismatic village oracle, the nun Thrinley Choedron. Inspired by visions of Tibetan warriors from ancient epics, she called on villagers to ransack local government offices in neighboring villages, leading to the slaughter of some fifty Chinese officials and soldiers and the mutilation of Tibetans thought to be sympathetic to them. Historians disagree over whether the revolt was a nationalist movement against the Chinese presence in Tibet, a dispute over the failure of officials to distribute resources, or a conflict deliberately incited by Chinese leaders in the Gyenlok faction against their opponents (the last two explanations are given in official documents from the time).[25] As in the rest of China, the army had to be brought in to regain control, and thirty-four leaders of the Nyemo rebellion, including Thrinley Choedron, were captured and executed.

During the Cultural Revolution the Chinese promoted a new kind of leadership among Tibetans: former serfs—not so different in their background from Thrinley Choedron, except that they espoused atheism—were promoted to leading positions throughout the region. There were few other Tibetans whose loyalty to Beijing could be relied upon, as no one else benefited from the gift of revolutionary violence and cultural destruction then on offer. From 1978 or shortly afterward, "red" leaders of this type throughout China were purged from their positions. In the TAR, however, a significant number of Cultural Revolution leaders were allowed to remain in high positions until 2000 or even later.

THE TURNING POINT

The most violent phase of the Cultural Revolution ended in 1969, but many of its radical policies remained in force throughout China until the death of Mao in 1976, and for some three years longer in Tibet. A turning point came on May 23, 1980, when

Hu Yaobang, then general secretary of the CCP and a protégé of China's paramount leader, Deng Xiaoping, gave a speech in Lhasa that was unique in CCP history. Rather than accusing Tibetans of ingratitude or foreigners of interference, Hu declared that party policy had failed in the TAR. Accusing the Chinese cadres stationed there of having thrown the money entrusted to them by Beijing "into the Lhasa river," Hu declared that Tibetans should be allowed to run their own region and to practice their own cultural traditions. Most of the Chinese living in the TAR at that time— almost all of them were party or government cadres—were told to hand over their positions to local people and to leave the region. Former aristocrats and intellectuals were rehabilitated and local people were encouraged to wear traditional clothes again. Within a few years, people gradually discovered that they were allowed to rebuild the monasteries and temples that had been desecrated or destroyed, and by the next decade more than a thousand of these had been restored.

Hu delivered his speech on the anniversary of the signing of the Seventeen Point Agreement in 1951, signaling that Beijing wished to recall the exceptionalist policies of the early 1950s when Tibet had been treated as if it were truly an autonomous area. This time the gift from Beijing was much more limited than it had been in the 1950s: it consisted of cultural tolerance and a token measure of Tibetan participation in the government of the TAR. But the beneficiaries included almost the entire society: aristocrats were released from prison, the communes were disbanded, private management of land and herds was allowed again, monasteries and temples were gradually reconstructed, and internal travel and pilgrimage became possible. Tibetan-language education was reintroduced in primary schools, and for the first time since the Chinese takeover, individual foreign tourists were allowed to visit the Tibetan capital and certain other areas. In the summer of 1985 several thousand Tibetans were even permitted to travel to India to attend an important Buddhist ceremony known as the *Kalachakra*, conducted by the Dalai Lama. The eastern Tibetans, who had suffered even longer and rebelled more ferociously than those in the TAR, benefited from similar policy relaxations, which were implemented with more commitment and tenacity than in Lhasa, and which were to last much longer than in the TAR.

Even before Hu Yaobang made his historic apology in Lhasa, Deng Xiaoping had opened talks with the Tibetan exiles for the first time since 1959. He met with the Dalai Lama's elder brother in Beijing in February 1979 and later that year allowed the first of four delegations of exile Tibetans to visit Tibet to see conditions there. This led to formal talks between the two sides in 1982 and 1984. When the exile delegates arrived in Tibet, tens of thousands of Tibetans turned out to try to greet them. One of the delegates was able to film the crowd, capturing scenes of abject poverty, desperation, and anguish that were beyond anything outsiders could have envisaged. They were almost certainly beyond anything that Deng and other leaders in China could have imagined either: Beijing probably had little idea of the actual conditions of life on the periphery, consistently misinformed by local satraps there. But the introduction of the "household responsibility" system and the restoration of some elements of religious freedom meant that the situation improved extremely rapidly across the entire plateau after 1980—economically, culturally, and politically—just as it did in China proper.

THE COLLAPSE OF THE 1980S EXCEPTIONALISM

As economic and cultural conditions improved in Tibet, pressure on Beijing to negotiate with the exiles diminished. In 1984, talks between the two sides collapsed, with the Chinese side saying that it would only discuss the return of the Dalai Lama to Tibet, while the exiles reportedly wanted the Chinese to recognize Tibet as having a special status of some kind. By the summer of 1987, there had been no sign of any thaw in relations between the two sides and Sino-Indian relations had also worsened, leading to serious tensions between India and China along the Tibetan border. That September the Dalai Lama turned to the West for open international support. In what was his first political speech in a Western country, in a meeting at the U.S. Capitol in Washington, DC, he presented the Tibet issue for the first time in terms of human rights abuses rather than as a call for independence. In Lhasa the party responded with strident anti–Dalai Lama rhetoric and a public rally at which two Tibetans were sentenced to death. This triggered the first street protests by Tibetans in Tibet ever seen by foreign tourists, leading to the Tibet issue becoming headline news around the world. The protestors in Tibet called for independence and for the Chinese to leave Tibet, although by this time the Dalai Lama was already signaling his willingness to accept a settlement with China that would give Tibet a status short of independence.

The official response in China to the protests was that they had been instigated by the exiles. The Tenth Panchen Lama, who had been released from prison in 1978 and had been reinstated as once again the most important Tibetan lama and official remaining in Tibet, insisted otherwise: he said that the protests had been provoked by "leftist" policies introduced in Tibet. These had been imposed by hard-liners in the CCP who, angered by Hu Yaobang's liberalization in 1980, had wanted to see more restrictions on religion and nationalities. His astonishingly bold interventions were effective at the time, but when he died abruptly in January 1989 at the age of fifty, the Tibetans were left without any leading figure with the stature or courage to openly challenge hard-liners within the Chinese policy elite.

It also left China without any respected intermediary who could speak on its behalf to Tibetans. Street protests and mass arrests continued in Lhasa off and on for nearly a decade, with almost all protestors detained, and many of them tortured while in prison. At least 150 street protests calling for independence took place in or near Lhasa during those years, most of them broken up by police within five or ten minutes. The participants received sentences averaging six-and-a-half years in prison. During those years, four small demonstrations spiraled into major incidents involving hundreds and sometimes thousands of laypeople, in some cases with damage to property and attacks on police. In March 1989 one of these large-scale protests continued for three days; it was in response to this event that Hu Jintao imposed martial law on the region, the first time this had happened in China since the PRC had been established. An estimated 75–150 Tibetans were shot dead during these protests, and about 3,000–4,000 were arrested.

From the perspective of a CCP hard-liner, these developments were similar to what had happened in the 1950s: within eight years of a major gift in the form of exceptional political and cultural concessions, Tibetans had rejected Beijing's generosity by rising up and calling for independence, again with support from the Western world.

This appeared to show that cultural and religious concessions to Tibetans, plus foreign instigation, had led on both occasions to an upsurge in nationalism and unrest that seemed designed to threaten China's unity. This perception become a major force in Chinese nationality policy after the breakup of the Soviet Union in 1991, which was viewed by analysts in the CCP as partly a result of overly relaxed Soviet policies toward non-Russian nationalities. This led in Tibet to a systematic effort by Beijing in the 1990s to reverse the liberalization policies of the previous decade.

THE GIFT OF ECONOMIC DEVELOPMENT

In 1992, a new party secretary was appointed to run the TAR and to introduce these new policies: Chen Kuiyuan, formerly a deputy party leader in Inner Mongolia. Chen set out to identify and truncate the elements of Tibetan culture and religion that he thought fueled "splittism," as Chinese officials term support for the independence of any area within China. This led to two fundamental shifts in policy, announced at a meeting in Beijing in July 1994 called the "Third National Forum on Work in Tibet," chaired by the then-party-secretary of the CCP, Jiang Zemin. The first was a series of decisions that led to an effective ban on worship of the Dalai Lama. Although he had been criticized repeatedly for his political views, his religious status and personal standing had not been questioned since the Cultural Revolution. Initially, the display of his photograph was banned, then possession of such images was outlawed, and soon after, all prayers to him were ruled unacceptable. All officials in the TAR had to repeat four slogans deriding him, while all monks and nuns were required to undergo three months of "patriotic education" that concluded with them having to formally denounce him in writing as a religious leader. Other, more controversial policies were conveyed orally rather than in writing, such as the ban on all Tibetan employees of the TAR government from any form of Buddhist practice, no matter whether they were janitors or bureau heads. The same ban was imposed on their family members too, as well as on all Tibetan students in the TAR who were Buddhists. Older scholars with traditional training were retired early, university textbooks on Tibetan history were rewritten to reduce references to religion or the Dalai Lamas, Tibetans who had traveled secretly to India for their education were banned from working in government-owned companies, and the few examples of Tibetan-medium education in middle schools in the TAR were brought to an end.

The second, much more visible, shift after Chen came to power in Lhasa was the decision to marketize the economy and to boost central investment to the region, a response to Deng Xiaoping's call in 1992 for the country to speed up market reform. The number of individually run businesses in the TAR soared from 489 in 1980 to 41,830 in 1993, and led to an explosion of shops, malls, luxury housing developments, leisure zones, and top-rate transportation facilities in Lhasa and other Tibetan towns. The TAR was given large subsidies in order to develop infrastructure and stimulate urban growth, with the Central Government investing 4.86 billion yuan (over US$670 million) in sixty-two projects in the TAR from 1994 to 2001, while other Chinese provinces gave 3.16 billion yuan (over US$450 million) to support construction in the region. Subsidies from the Central Government as a proportion of Tibet's gross domestic product (GDP) rose from 46.5 percent in 2000 to 71 percent by the close of 2001.[26]

This growth-based strategy emphasized infrastructural and commercial expansion rather than enhancing local education, capacity, or occupational skills, which would have signaled an intention to provide long-term benefit to local residents. It also encouraged migration of non-Tibetans to the region. In December 1992, all intraprovincial checkpoints on roads leading to the TAR were removed, signaling that the region welcomed job-seekers from outside; cheap business loans were announced; business licenses were made easily accessible; all government offices in towns were required to convert street-side frontage into rental units for shopkeepers; and plans were begun to increase the number of towns in the TAR from 31 to 105 by 2010.[27]

The thousands of non-Tibetans attracted to Tibet by these measures lived mainly in towns or along major roads and stayed for only five to ten years, unlike the much larger number of permanent, agricultural Chinese settlers who have repopulated Xinjiang and Inner Mongolia. But the economic and cultural impact of the temporary migrants in Tibetan towns was significant. According to the national census in 2000, of the 223,000 registered inhabitants in the inner Lhasa urban area (the *chengguanqu*), 46 percent of people of peak working age (between twenty-five and forty years old) and a fifth of those under fifteen were non-Tibetans; by 2010, 31 percent of all urban residents in the TAR were non-Tibetans. In 2007 the regional government, though saying officially that there was no migration to the region, announced the construction of a new suburb in Lhasa in 2009 to house 110,000 people, representing an expected 25 percent increase in the city's population.[28]

Even more significant were the political dimensions of the new economic policies. Until 1992, moderate Tibetan leaders in the CCP had been able to argue publicly for alternate, Tibetan-centered approaches to development in their area. But in May 1994 the national newspaper of the CCP, the *People's Daily*, made it clear that criticism of the rapid growth or migration policies was henceforth politically unacceptable:

> Can Tibet remain "special" forever and continue to depend on the state's long-term "blood transfusions"? Is Tibet willing to accept the label of "being special" and stand at the rear of reform and opening up? Backwardness is not terrifying. Being geographically closed is not terrifying. What is terrifying is rigid and conservative thinking and the psychology of idleness.[29]

The 1994 decisions defined Tibet policy for the following decade, and it has barely changed since. Once Hu Jintao, believed to have masterminded or at least endorsed these new policies after spending four years as the party leader in Tibet from 1988, became general secretary of the CCP in 2002, their principles could not be questioned. Tibet may have been granted autonomy, but it was clear that its policies at that time were to be set by Chinese leaders in Beijing and implemented largely by Chinese officials in Lhasa.

In the decade following the Third Forum, further subsidies were given to the TAR. In 1999, the **Open Up the West** drive (also known as the "Great Western

Development")[30] was announced, leading to major construction in western China, including the US$4.2 billion Qinghai–Tibetan railway. Completed in 2006, this sparked a major expansion of tourism in Tibet, almost all of it domestic, followed by a surge in mining, with the environmental hazards that go with it. Investment by the central government in the region reached a total of 310 billion yuan (about US$45.6 billion) between 2001 and 2010, leading to annual GDP growth in the TAR of 10 percent or over for the twenty-five years from 1993, faster than any other province-level entity in China. The quality of urban infrastructure and commodities soared, along with the income of urban residents in Tibet, which rose from 2,208 yuan (under US$300) per capita in 1992 to 30,671 (US$4527) in 2017.[31] The average salaries of government employees in the TAR, most of whom are Tibetans, rose even more dramatically, going from 3,448 yuan (a little over US$500) a year in 1992 to 110,980 yuan (about US$16,380) in 2016,[32] a 3,200 percent increase over twenty-three years, making salaries in the TAR the highest on average of any province or region in China except Beijing. A new and wealthy urban Tibetan middle class had been created.

The average per capita income of rural residents has also increased steadily, going from 653 yuan (under US$100) in 1992 to 10,330 yuan (US$1,525) in 2017.[33] But during the first decade of rising incomes, the focus on urban growth had led to a sharp widening in the gap between urban and rural incomes—average rural incomes in the TAR had dropped to 20 percent of urban incomes by 2002— raising fears among government planners of potential social unrest. In 2005, a new party secretary for the TAR, Zhang Qingli, was sent to Lhasa to carry out programs that aimed to rectify the urban-rural divide, and he did so on an unprecedented scale: between 2006 and 2012, he required or persuaded 2.1 million Tibetan villagers to rebuild their houses along-side major roads in order to improve their access to the modern economy and thus boost rural incomes. By 2017 rural incomes in the TAR had reached 34 percent of the urban equivalent. In Qinghai and Gansu provinces, officials set in motion plans to settle one million Tibetan nomads permanently in villages or towns without their an-imals, supposedly to protect grasslands from being overgrazed. In 2008, the Sichuan government announced that half a million Tibetan herders in Sichuan province were listed for permanent settlement by 2014. The former herders receive an initial cash handout, but it has remained unclear how they will be able to acquire new skills or find any opportunities to generate income in the future.

From Beijing's perspective, this was being done to help Tibetans. Their economy was being developed, their environment was being protected, the rural poor were being moved closer to commercial opportunities in towns, new houses were being provided, and rural children were being brought closer to schools and hospitals. Encouraging migrants to come to work in Tibet was beneficial because "the Tibetan people learn the skills to earn money when a hinterlander makes money in Tibet,"[34] and providing Chinese-medium education at an earlier age improved work prospects. These benefits indeed improved material conditions in significant ways for many Tibetans in the region, not unlike the silk and satin sent to the Dalai Lamas by former Chinese emperors. But the party's gifts lacked the shared cultural understanding of its imperial predecessors, sought radical change in Tibetan customs and society, and were imposed by force.

TIBET ERUPTS

On March 10, 2008, the fifth-ninth anniversary of the 1959 uprising, three hundred to four hundred monks from Drepung monastery near Lhasa staged a brief march, the first public political protest in the city for nearly a decade. Four days later, amid rumors that some of the monks had been ill-treated in prison, gangs of Tibetans beat up Chinese migrants in the streets of Lhasa and burned down about a thousand Chinese-owned shops, killing nineteen people, of whom eighteen were ethnic Chinese. Troops with armored vehicles later took over the city and a number of Tibetans died in the aftermath—the Chinese government admits to three "accidental" deaths of protestors, while the exile Tibetan administration maintains that up to eighty people were shot dead in Lhasa.

Within a week, more than a hundred protests had taken place across the Tibetan Plateau. Beijing insisted that these were coordinated by exiles, but they were more likely a result of people hearing news of events in Lhasa by cell phone or from broadcasts by Voice of America or Radio Free Asia, the two radio stations with Tibetan-language services funded by the U.S. Congress since the early 1990s. Eighteen or so of these incidents after March 14 involved violence by protestors, though in these cases the violence was directed at Chinese government buildings, not at civilians. In at least eleven cases, protestors took over villages and hoisted the forbidden Tibetan national flag, suggesting support for independence, but most protestors called for the Dalai Lama to be allowed to return from exile, a much more moderate demand, given that since at least the early 1990s his objective has been "genuine autonomy" in Tibet rather than independence.

The PRC media, focusing only on the anti-Chinese violence in Lhasa on March 14, presented Tibetans as hooligans who, jealous at the success of Chinese traders, had been stirred up by exile instigators and foreigners, and praised the arrest of the thousand or more Tibetans accused of involvement in unrest. Western media reports focused on the hundred or more incidents that took place across the Plateau rather than on the single riot in Lhasa, viewing them as responses by Tibetans from an unusually wide range of social sectors and regions to Beijing's policies, particularly its anti–Dalai Lama campaigns and its encouragement of migration into Tibet. This led to protests across Europe, the United States, Australia, and other countries that disrupted the progress of the Olympic torch as it was paraded by Chinese police and officials across the world on its way to Beijing for the start of the 2008 Games that autumn. In response, Chinese citizens staged angry counterprotests both at home and abroad, together with internet campaigns, shop-boycotts, and other measures condemning Western criticisms of China's actions in Tibet.

Within Tibet, People's Armed Police paramilitary forces were posted in major towns. In Lhasa, troops remained in position twenty-four hours a day on every street corner in the Tibetan quarter of the city for five years after the 2008 protests. For a year or more after the protests no foreigners were allowed to visit any Tibetan areas without special permission, and as of 2019, foreigners are still allowed entry to the TAR only in accompanied tour groups or with special permits. China's leaders have continued to say that the unrest was a result of exile instigation, unrelated to their policies.

In late 2011, after three years of research by officials to try to identify ways to pre-vent any resurgence of unrest, China introduced new and tighter policies in the TAR, which were gradually imposed in some eastern Tibetan areas as well. These were based on an official assessment that support among Tibetans for the Dalai Lama was not limited to "a handful of splittists," as officials had claimed before 2008, but was rife throughout the rural population and the grassroots residents of Tibetan towns. This was why teams of cadres were sent to live in every village in the TAR and ordered to carry out "gratefulness" education. For the same reason, party committees and security teams were established in each village, cadre teams were stationed perma-nently in each monastery, 670 block-level police stations ("convenience police-posts") were constructed throughout towns, offices called "grid units" (see chap. 10) were set up to manage and monitor every street or block in urban areas, and all households throughout the TAR were divided into groups of five to ten households with a local resident responsible for the political behavior of all the residents in each group. In addition, officials announced profiles of people deemed most likely to have dissident views, known as "key personnel" (*gtso gnad mi sna* in Tibetan or *zhongdian renyuan* in Chinese), including monks, nuns, former prisoners, returnees from abroad and short-term renters. People within these categories were subjected to special monitoring.[35] From 2012, all residents of the TAR were required to hand in their passports, and few new ones have since been issued. At the same time, draconian restrictions were imposed on any Tibetans—but not on Chinese—entering the TAR from other Tibetan areas. In Qinghai, nearly 10,000 extra police were transferred or recruited in October 2015 to run new village-level police stations throughout the province.[36]

These forms of administration and control at the grassroots level in Tibet, which were unprecedented in modern times, were adaptations of the China-wide drive to achieve *weiwen* or "stability maintenance" (see chap. 6) and were designed to identify and incapacitate support for the Dalai Lama and for Tibetan independence. These measures marked a new stage in the emergence in China of what has been described as a **surveillance state**, where administrative, political, and technological tools are developed to micromanage an entire population at the household or even individual level.[37]

Meanwhile, efforts by the exiles to reach a political solution with the PRC collapsed. In 2002, three years after President Bill Clinton called publicly on Jiang Zemin to re-open discussions with the exile Tibetan leader, Beijing had begun a series of talks with representatives of the Dalai Lama. By 2010, after ten rounds, despite some substan-tial concessions by the exiles, these meetings had become increasingly fraught, with Chinese officials using them to make ever stronger denunciations of the exiles and then apparently refusing to reconvene. In May 2011, apparently in part to encourage Beijing to resume the talks, the Dalai Lama formally retired from his position as head of the exile Tibetan government. A young lay Tibetan, Lobsang Sangay (b. 1968), was elected by the exiles to be the head of their administration in India and tried to get the Chinese to agree to talks with his officials rather than with representatives of the now-retired Dalai Lama, a demand which Beijing had rejected for decades and was always certain to refuse.

As the resumption of talks became ever more unlikely, a new form of popular po-litical protest emerged within Tibet, one that could not be dismissed as an act of violence against Chinese citizens or against government property: self-immolation. Between February 2009 and December 2018, seemingly frustrated by the failure of the authorities to respond constructively to the grievances raised by the protests of 2008, around one hundred and fifty-five Tibetans set themselves on fire. About one hundred and twenty of these protestors are believed to have died from their wounds. Their actions indicated the spread of dissent to grassroots communities in Tibet: whereas most Tibetan protestors in the 1980s and 1990s had been monks or nuns in Lhasa or the surrounding areas, most of the self-immolators, including twenty-eight women, were laypeople from small towns, villages, or former herder communities in Kham and Amdo. Most called for the Dalai Lama to be allowed to return from exile and for an end to policies seen as damaging or destroying Tibetan language, religion, or culture.

The authorities in Beijing accused the Dalai Lama and exile activists of organizing, paying, or persuading these individuals to set themselves on fire. Officials in Tibet launched a series of denunciations, arrests, trials, life sentences, and collective punishment for families and villages suspected of supporting the immolations. The Dalai Lama denied any responsibility for the self-immolations and said that he did not encourage the practice, but he also refused to call for the self-immolations to stop, claiming that the situation was too delicate for him to intervene. Beijing continued to denounce the Dalai Lama and gave no sign of any interest in talks of any kind, let alone concessions.

By 2015, China's dramatic increase in global power and influence had led almost all foreign leaders except the U.S. president to stop meeting with the Dalai Lama, even though he had withdrawn from any formal role in government. The wave of self-immolations subsided, but protests and arrests continued, with one study by foreign observers identifying sixty-eight street protests in Tibetan areas between 2013 and 2015 besides the self-immolations.[38] At least ten of these involved more than one hundred participants and, in six cases, security forces opened fire on protestors, leading to unknown numbers of casualties and about five hundred detentions. The protests were quite different from earlier ones: most occurred in small towns or rural townships rather than in cities and were triggered by local environmental disputes and other social or cultural issues not previously treated as illegal by the authorities, reflecting the increase of controls on any actions that might lead to dissent or unrest. As independent reports from Tibet become increasingly rare, it becomes ever harder to know whether the deeply felt concerns that surfaced in 2008 among ordinary farmers, villagers, monks, and townspeople within greater Tibet have continued to spread but are silenced by fears of state violence, or whether Tibetans are gradually being won over by improvements in their economic and material conditions.

CONCLUSION: UNRESOLVED QUESTIONS, PERSISTING TENSIONS

The story of modern China's interactions with Tibetans is threaded through with instances of violence and aggressive policies by the state, but also with traces of Chinese deference to history, exceptionalism, and the practice of giving gifts. The

Cultural Revolution, and much of the decade before it, saw a sustained attempt to destroy or suppress cultural identity, tradition, and religion, but in the early 1950s and since around 1980 the CCP has not attempted the total assimilation of Tibetans that the Qing modernizers had planned in 1910. In other contested areas on China's periphery, the CCP and earlier Chinese governments used mass migration to staunch challenges to their rule: in Xinjiang, the Han or ethnic Chinese population went from 7 percent of the population in 1953 to 39 percent according to the 2010 census, and in Inner Mongolia, the proportion of Mongolians in the population declined to 17 percent in the same period. So far proposals originally made by Mao to arrange the permanent settlement of millions of Chinese in Tibet have not been carried out, and most Chinese migrants to Tibet have been jobseekers in urban areas rather than permanent rural settlers as in Xinjiang or Inner Mongolia. According to official figures, about 90 percent of the registered population of the TAR remains Tibetan. The uprisings of the 1950s may have made some CCP leaders reluctant to rely on population transfer or military force alone to control Tibetans, and, at times, they have tried to secure Tibetan loyalty through beneficence, such as the offer of regional autonomy (token though that seems to be), and by providing economic development. This pattern of intermittent concessions and crackdowns is an index of the strategic and political importance of the Tibetan areas to modern China, and of an unstated, deep anxiety in Beijing about the major challenge presented by Tibetans' memories of their separate history.

China's efforts at winning over its Tibetan subjects seem thus far to have failed, despite a view among many Chinese that their government has been exceptionally generous to Tibetans. The party's gifts have certainly been evident everywhere in Tibetan areas since the 1990s—modern buildings, highways, private wealth, and lavish infrastructure—and at times have succeeded in getting the support or acquiescence of the local beneficiaries. But, unlike imperial-era gifts to Tibet, which had indicated China's respect for the Tibetans' religious leader and had been accompanied by minimal interference in Tibetan life or governance, the more recent gifts from Beijing have been premised on a notion of the backwardness of the recipients and accompanied by attacks on their religious leader and elements of their culture, while encouraging Chinese traders and job-seekers to move into Tibetan areas in significant numbers. Since 2004, Beijing has increasingly sought to reduce Tibetan-medium education in Tibetan schools in order to boost competence in Chinese language—a policy that many fear presages assimilation. Each phase of gift-giving in the modern era has been followed by periods of punishment, and at times the two functions have been carried out simultaneously, as in the post-1996 policy of providing lavish salaries and housing for Tibetan government employees in the TAR while at the same time banning them from any form of Buddhist practice.

Apart from the Great Leap Forward and the Cultural Revolution, which were China-wide phenomena rather than responses to events in Tibet, most of the punitive campaigns were Tibet-specific. Some were a response to rebellions or street protests, but others, such as those of 1994 and 2006, were imposed at times when there were few if any demonstrations. These crackdowns increased during the later 1990s, with some targeting Tibetans in general and others aimed at Tibetan Buddhists in particular, largely separate in nature if not in name from those directed at Chinese citizens as a whole. This may have been partly due to anxieties in Beijing arising from the collapse of the Soviet Union and democratic movements in Georgia, Ukraine, and elsewhere, and to fears about the impact of successful exile activism abroad. But for the most part these crackdowns in Tibet have been reactions to an indistinct sense, often without much evidence, that Tibetans were harboring "splittist" plans to divide the state. Behind these moves by Beijing can be detected a culture of distrust or resentment among Chinese officials, fueled by the perceived failure of Tibetans to recognize the generosity of China's gifts to them.

Should China's policy toward Tibet be considered to be a type of colonialism, the term that the Thirteenth Dalai Lama had used in 1913 to describe Qing rule? Some have argued that colonialism exists only where nations are geographically separate, or where the colonizer is a traditional imperial power that has not itself been colonized in the past, or where a nation extracts more resources from a place than it puts in, none of which can be said with confidence to apply to Tibet. The most frequently encountered arguments in China are that Tibet cannot be a colony because it is a region within the single Chinese state, or that Tibetans are part of the broader Chinese race or culture and so are linked by blood or history to the Chinese people. From this perspective, the disparities in power and wealth between Tibet and China are seen as the unfortunate result of uneven development; China proper is said to have "advanced" earlier and faster than outer China, and the PRC thus compensates outer China when possible, so that, over time, the latter will "catch up" and enjoy the same benefits and lifestyle that China proper has enjoyed. This narrative helps explain why the TAR is often described in the Chinese media as the poorest province-level administrative region in the country (it does indeed have the lowest rate of disposable income per capita—in 2017 the rate was 15,457 yuan, or US$2,282, compared to the national average of 25,974 yuan, or US$3,731).[39] In fact, other statistics, such as the rate of disposable income per household or GDP per capita, show that the provinces of Guizhou and Gansu (and often Yunnan, Ningxia, and Guanxi) are significantly poorer than the TAR.[40] But the perception of the TAR as China's poorest province-level area serves to reinforce the argument that Tibetans need help from their Chinese compatriots.

Critics of these views argue that China's administration of Tibet has many of the typical features of colonial rule: there is a permanent military garrison in the subject areas with soldiers of one ethnicity ruling subjects of another; restrictions on local religion, culture, and discussion are much stricter than in the homeland areas; rules and practices apply to members of the subject ethnicity that do not apply to those of the ruling nationality; public explanations by the mother-state stress the benefits brought to the local population by its policies; the presence of migrants and officials from the ruling ethnic group is considered beneficial to local people, apparently because the ruling group is assumed to be more advanced in some way; local culture and religion are reassessed, with the mother-state deciding which cultural practices are unacceptable and which should be allowed. All of these apply to the Chinese presence in Tibet.

The difference between these two views of the Tibet-China relationship can be seen as the product of a profound divergence over the primary role of the nation-state. The general Chinese view can be described as statist—it is centered on the preeminent importance in people's lives of the modern state, viewed as an impersonal, machinelike institution that strives to benefit the majority of its citizens by maximizing production, distributing goods, enforcing security, and ensuring international prominence for the nation, thus producing for the PRC what from 2004 was described in China as "a harmonious society" and pursuing what since 2012 is usually referred to as "the China Dream" (see chap. 5).

The other view, which is currently found among many Tibetans and foreigners, can be described as a national view. It sees the nation as the primary representative and source of identity for its people, imagining it as an organic, exclusive collectivity that sustains communality through shared culture, language, memory, and religion. In this view, as the nineteenth-century historian-philosopher Ernest Renan put it, "a nation is a soul, a spiritual principle."[41] This view has no necessary relation to ideas of independence or separate statehood; it tends to harden into such a position only if it is repressed or disparaged. The holder of the statist view thinks typically in terms of numbers—things that can be measured, majorities, social norms, and laws—while the national view places value primarily on intangibles, such as heritage, perceptions, and specialness or difference, what the political scientist Benedict Anderson famously called "imagined communities."[42]

In the Tibetan case, a test of where people place themselves on this spectrum is to ask who should participate in a referendum on the future of Tibet, something the current Dalai Lama has called for unsuccessfully several times. The nationalists would say that participants should be Tibetans, defined by birth, language, culture, or a similar shared feature, while the statists tend to say that all citizens of China should vote, since it concerns a part of the state of which they are all equal members. Which criterion is used to decide participation—ethnicity or citizenship—would determine the outcome of any consultation exercise on this issue. The same division underlies debates concerning Tibetan policy and history, too.

The eight-year series of talks between Beijing and the Tibetan exiles from 2002 to 2010 failed in large part because of these clashing perspectives: the Tibetans, with their nation-based vision, saw an entitlement to special treatment for largely cultural and religious reasons, while the statists saw Tibetans as having finally been won over to China to higher levels of prosperity, and therefore not needing any kind of change. Additionally, the statists are considering the welfare and sustainability of the larger unit, and are fearful of making concessions toward real autonomy in Tibet that could then be claimed by other groups in China, such as the Uyghurs in Xinjiang. Chinese statists also find it hard to reconcile themselves to accommodating Tibetan religion, or at least the Dalai Lama, either because the idea of a religious leader having political influence is inherently abhorrent to them, or perhaps because it recalls threats to the state posed by religiously inspired rebels such as the Taiping and the Boxers in the late Qing era, or supposedly by the Falun Gong in the late 1990s. Tibetan exiles in turn antagonize many Chinese by accusing their government of such heinous offenses as "cultural genocide," even though China's policies in Tibet for some forty years have in general been nothing like those of the Cultural Revolution. In addition, the exiles' strategy of arranging for Western leaders to meet the Dalai Lama is seen as provocative and humiliating for China, given his public criticisms of Beijing.

The Dalai Lama has nevertheless made repeated concessions to Beijing's demands. In a formal declaration in 1988 he indicated that his objective was to achieve "association" status for Tibet—essentially an indirect way of retaining independence, as the Chinese were quick to point out—but from 1992 on, he explicitly renounced the pursuit of independence and changed his demand to "genuine autonomy" or "a high degree of autonomy" for Tibet within China. In 2010, he went much farther, conceding that this "genuine autonomy" should operate within the terms allowed by the current Chinese constitution and within the current political system in China.

Given these concessions by Dalai Lama, the Tibetan-China dispute should have been relatively easy to resolve. Although it has lasted for a century, and from the 1950s to the 1970s encompassed military combat, innumerable violent and unnecessary deaths, and cultural destruction on a vast scale, the conflict saw minimal violence in the last four decades, with little evidence of ethnic violence other than the March 14 riot in 2008. The Tibetans' leader has been begging for a diplomatic resolution for thirty years, has conceded to most Chinese demands, and has no military resources or obvious alternatives besides a negotiated settlement. Yet the situation appears to be rapidly deteriorating. As of 2019, the two sides had not met for talks in nine years; the health and survival of the current Dalai Lama, born in 1935, are increasingly in doubt; and no Tibetan leader in the future is likely to have similar standing among Tibetans or to be able to arrange broad Tibetan support for any future settlement with Beijing. In any case, both China and the exiles have already said that they will each choose their own successors to the current Dalai Lama, and so, unless the issue is resolved, there will be two Fifteenth Dalai Lamas, just as there have been two Eleventh Panchen Lamas since 1995.

In terms of simple logic, therefore, one would expect China to seek a settlement before the current Dalai Lama (born in 1935) dies. But there are innumerable forms of internal resistance within Beijing to any change in its approach to Tibet: bureaucratic inertia, embedded interest groups, rising public nationalism, a consensus leadership, and a political culture fiercely opposed to any appearance of concession, among others. An even greater obstacle may lie in the long, divergent histories of belief and ideology between the two sides, with one perceiving its policies as examples of state generosity, and the other seeing them as impositions in which they had no say and for which their nation was made to pay heavily. Until the cycles of gift and retribution in its relations with Tibet are reconfigured by Chinese leaders in a way that takes into account Tibetan memories of a distinct history and a different view of nationhood, China is unlikely to receive the "soft tribute"—loyalty to the Chinese state—that it demands from Tibetans. Meanwhile, Beijing's policies in Tibet remain contradictory and inconclusive, fueling the very nationalism among Tibetans that China's leaders have tried for decades to extinguish.

NOTES

1. Elizabeth C. Economy and Adam Segal, "China's Olympic Nightmare: What the Games Mean for Beijing's Future," *Foreign Affairs* 87, no. 4 (Jul–Aug, 2008): 47–56; and Zhang Weidong, "New Assertiveness and New Confidence?: How Does China Perceive Its Own Rise?—A Critical Discourse Analysis of the People's Daily Editorials and Commentaries on the 2008 Beijing Olympics," *International Journal of China Studies* 3, no. 1 (Apr. 2012): 1–24.

2. The most recent White Paper on Tibet, titled "Ecological Progress on the Qinghai-Tibet Plateau," was issued in July 2018, http://www.china.org.cn/government/whitepaper/node_8006336.htm

3. See Marcel Angliviel de la Beaumelle, "The United Front Work Department: 'Magic Weapon' at Home and Abroad," *China Brief* 17 no. 9 (June 6, 2017), https://jamestown.org/program/united-front-work-department-magic-weapon-home-abroad/

4. "Milestone in Tibet's Reform, Development, and Stability," *Renmin Ribao* (People's Daily), July 19, 2001, http://www.chinahouston.org/news/2001719071430.html. At the Third Forum in 1994 "Jiang underscored the region's importance to all of China and observed that maintaining stability in Tibet was 'crucial to the success of reforms, development, and stability throughout the country'" (Allen Carlson, "Beijing's Tibet Policy: Securing Sovereignty and Legitimacy," *Policy Studies* 4, Washington, DC: East-West Center, 2004, citing "Jiang Zemin on Stability in Tibet," *Xinhua*, July 26, 1994).

5. "Chinese President Stresses Stability, Social Harmony in Tibet," *Xinhua*, Mar. 6, 2008, http://www.nyconsulate.prchina.org/eng/xw/t412955.htm#. The struggle against separatism is also one of the three primary objectives in China's relations with the Central Asian states through the Shanghai Co-operation Organization. Statements on Xinjiang are somewhat similar: "As the country's front line in battling terrorism and separatism, Xinjiang's anti-terrorism fight is of crucial importance to the stability of the whole country" ("No Let-up in Fight against 'Forces of Terror,'" *China Daily*, Mar. 3, 2008).

6. "Xi stresses unity for Tibet, vows fight against separatism," *Xinhuanet*, Aug. 25, 2015, http://www.xinhuanet.com/english/2015-08/25/c_134554681.htm.

7. "Mobilization meeting for the 'Solidifying Foundations and Benefiting the Masses' Campaign," *Xizang Ribao* (Tibet Daily), Oct. 11, 2011, http://cxzy.people.com.cn/GB/194307/15863333.html.

8. Huang Wenkun, Liu Xiaodai, and the Editorial Committee, eds., *A Collection of Historical Archives of Tibet* (compiled by the Archives of the Tibet Autonomous Region), (Beijing: Cultural Relics Publishing House, 1995), item 59-5.

9. Marcel Mauss, *The Gift: Forms and Functions of Exchange in Archaic Societies* (New York: Norton, 1967 [1923]), 1.

10. In Tibetan the words *Rgya* (China) and *Bod* (Tibet) have always denoted separate countries. There was no word in Tibetan that described a China that included Tibet, and in 1951 the Chinese translators at the negotiations over the Seventeen Point Agreement invented a new Tibetan word (*Krung go*, a Tibetanized rendering of the Chinese word for China, *Zhongguo*) to refer to this. The use of *Krung go* for "China" has since been obligatory in Tibetan-language publications within China.

11. Evelyn Rawski, "Presidential Address: Re-envisioning the Qing: The Significance of the Qing Period in Chinese History," *Journal of Asian Studies* 55, no. 4 (1996): 829–850.

12. The British government's position on the status of Tibet was that "Tibet is autonomous and China has a special position there," a restatement of its century-long recognition in the 1914 Simla Convention and other formal treaties or agreements of China's role in Tibet as a form of suzerainty (meaning that it did not have absolute sovereignty). The British renounced that position unilaterally, seemingly without any pressure and without seeking any concession in return, in October 2008, when they first recognized China's claim to full sovereignty over Tibet. British politicians apparently believed that this would endear them to Beijing and improve trade prospects.

13. Melvyn C. Goldstein, *A History of Modern Tibet, 1913–1951: The Demise of the Lamaist State* (Berkeley: University of California Press, 1989), 60.

14. Minglang Zhou, *Multilingualism in China: The Politics of Writing Reforms for Minority Languages 1949–2002* (Berlin: Mouton de Gruyter, 2003), 37–38.

15. See Melvyn C. Goldstein, Dawei Sherap, and William R. Siebenschuh, *A Tibetan Revolutionary: The Political Life and Times of Bapa Phüntso Wangye* (Berkeley: University of California Press, 2004).

16. For the full text of the Seventeen Point Agreement, see http://www.china.org.cn/english/zhuanti/tibet%20facts/163877.htm.

17. See Chen Jian, "The Tibetan Rebellion of 1959 and China's Changing Relations with India and the Soviet Union," *Journal of Cold War Studies* 8, no. 3 (2006): 54–101.

18. The western half of the former Tibetan province of Kham is now in the TAR. The eastern part of Kham, which is now the western part of Sichuan, was recognized by China as a separate province, Xikang, from 1935 to 1955.

19. Ji Youquan, *Xizang pingpan jishi* (Factual Record of Rebellion Suppression in Tibet) (Lhasa: Xizang Renmin Chubanshe, 1993).

20. "The Panchen Lama's Address to the TAR Standing Committee Meeting of the National People's Congress, 28th Mar. 1987" in *The Panchen Lama Speaks* (Dharamsala, India: Department of Information and International Relations [of the Central Tibetan Administration in exile]).

21. The Tenth Panchen Lama, *A Poisoned Arrow: The Secret Petition of the 10th Panchen Lama*, edited by Robert Barnett (London: Tibet Information Network, 1998), 103.

22. Tenth Panchen Lama, *A Poisoned Arrow*, 52.

23. See Cheng Li and Yiou Zhang, "Assessing Institutional Rules in China's Elite Selection: The Case of Ethnic Minority Leaders," Brookings Institution, Apr. 19, 2017, https://www.brookings.edu/opinions/assessing-institutional-rules-in-chinas-elite-selection-the-case-of-ethnic-minority-leaders/

24. For photographs of Tibet during the Cultural Revolution, see "When Tibet Loved China: Rare photos of the Cultural Revolution in the Land of Snows," at http://www.foreignpolicy.com/articles/2013/01/22/when_tibet_loved_china_cultural_revolution.

25. See Melvyn C. Goldstein, Ben Jiao, and Tanzen Lhundrup, *On the Cultural Revolution in Tibet: The Nyemo Incident of 1969* (Berkeley: University of California Press, 2009).

26. Nearly 95 percent of this investment was directed into state-owned enterprises. Andrew Martin Fischer, *State Growth and Social Exclusion in Tibet* (Copenhagen: Nordic Institute of Asian Studies Press, 2005), 59, 71.

27. "Ninth Five-Year Plan," TAR Government, Lhasa, published in English translation by the BBC *Summary of World Broadcasts*, Aug. 5, 1996.

28. "Lhasa Plans Homes for 110,000," *Xinhua*, Nov. 20, 2007. This article gives the 2007 population of "downtown" Lhasa as around 480,000, about four times the figure in the 2000 census for the inner urban area of the city.

29. Liu Wei and He Guanghua, "Looking at Tibet in a New Light," *People's Daily*, Beijing, in Chinese, May 16, 1994, 1, published in translation by the BBC *Summary of World Broadcasts*, May 31, 1994.

30. See David S. G. Goodman, ed., *China's Campaign to "Open up the West": National, Provincial and Local Perspectives* (New York: Cambridge University Press, 2004).

31. *Tibet Statistical Datasheet 1996* and "Tibet lifts 260,000 people out of poverty in past two years," *Xinhua*, Jan. 24, 2018, http://www.xinhuanet.com/english/2018-01/24/c_136921093.htm

32. *Tibet Statistical Yearbook, 2012* (Beijing: National Bureau of Statistics) and *China Statistical Yearbook, 2017* (Beijing: National Bureau of Statistics), Table 4.11: "Average Wage of Employed Persons in Urban Units and Related Indices by type of registration, by time series," via China Data Online. In 2016, the average salary of government employees in the TAR increased by 175 percent over the previous year.

33. *Tibet Statistical Yearbook 2012.* "Tibet Lifts 260,000 People Out of Poverty in Past Two Years."

34. Speech by Chen Kuiyuan, Tibet People's Broadcasting Station, Lhasa, Nov. 28, 1994, published in translation as "Tibet: Chen Kuiyuan in Qamdo Says Prosperity Will Drive Out Religion," BBC *Summary of World Broadcasts*, Dec. 5, 1994.

35. "China: Alarming New Surveillance, Security in Tibet," *Human Rights Watch*, Mar. 20, 2013, http://www.hrw.org/news/2013/03/20/china-alarming-new-surveillance-security-tibet.

36. *Mtsho sngon zhing cen gyis nyen rtog pa stong lnga dang bdun brgya go gsum shor 'then dang gdan zhu byas nas gzhi rim gyi nhen rdog las khungs su mngag rgyu red* ("Qinghai province transfers 5,793 police personnel to grassroots-level police stations"), Qinghai Tibetan Language Broadcasting, Oct. 8, 2015, http://ti.tibet3.com/news/tibet/qh/2015-10/08/content_545020.htm.

37. Qiang, Xiao. "President Xi's Surveillance State," *Journal of Democracy*, vol. 30, no. 1, 2019, pp. 53-67.

38. *Relentless: Detention and Prosecution of Tibetans Under China's "Stability Maintenance" Campaign* (New York: Human Rights Watch, May 2016). None of these protests were reported in official Chinese media during this period. Of 479 known political detainees, 153 were said by foreign or exile observers to have been sent for trial and sentenced on average to 5.7 years in prison.

39. "Shanghai, Beijing and Zhejiang Province Top China's New Per Capita Income List," China Banking News, Feb. 26, 2018, http://www.chinabankingnews.com/2018/02/26/shanghai-beijing-zhejiang-province-top-chinas-new-per-capita-income-list/

40. In terms of GDP per capita, Guizhou (33,127 yuan; US$4,906 in 2016), Yunnan (30,996 yuan; US$4,590) and Gansu (27,587 yuan; US $4,086) have long been poorer than the TAR (34,785; yuan; US$5,152) (National Data, National Bureau of Statistics, http://data.stats.gov.cn/english/easyquery.htm?cn=E0103). Similarly, in terms of disposable income per household (rather than per person), Guizhou and Gansu provinces were significantly poorer than the TAR in 2016.

41. Ernest Renan, "What Is a Nation?" (1882), in *Becoming National: A Reader*, ed. Geoff Eley and Ronald Grigor Suny (New York: Oxford University Press, 1996), 41–55.

42. Benedict Anderson, *Imagined Communities: Reflections on the Origin and Spread of Nationalism* (London: Verso Press, 2016 [1991]).

SUGGESTED READINGS

Barnett, Robert. *Lhasa: Streets with Memories.* New York: Columbia University Press, 2006.

Fischer, Andrew Martin. *State Growth and Social Exclusion in Tibet.* Copenhagen: NIAS (Nordic Institute of Asian Studies) Press, 2005.

Goldstein, Melvyn C. *A History of Modern Tibet*, 3 vols. Vol. 1, *1913–1951: The Demise of the Lamaist State* (1991); Vol. 2, *The Calm before the Storm: 1951–1955* (2009); Vol. 3, *The Storm Clouds Descend, 1955–1957* (2013). Berkeley: University of California Press.

Goldstein, Melvyn C., and Cynthia M. Beall. *Nomads of Western Tibet: The Survival of a Way of Life.* Berkeley: University of California, 1990.

Goldstein, Melvyn C., Dawei Sherap, and William R. Siebenschuh. *A Tibetan Revolutionary: The Political Life and Times of Bapa Phüntso Wangye.* Berkeley: University of California Press, 2004.

Gyatso, Janet, and Hanna Havnevik, eds. *Women in Tibet, Past and Present.* New York: Columbia University Press, 2005.

Kapstein, Matthew T. *The Tibetans*. Malden, MA: Blackwell Publishing, 2006.

Khétsun, Tubten. *Memories of Life in Lhasa under Chinese Rule: An Autobiography*. Translated by Matthew Akester. New York: Columbia University Press, 2007.

Knaus, John Kenneth. *Orphans of the Cold War: America and the Tibetan Struggle for Survival*. New York: Public Affairs, 1999.

Makley, Charlene. *The Battle for Fortune: State-Led Development, Personhood, and Power among Tibetans in China*. New York: Columbia University Press, 2018.

Makley, Charlene. *The Violence of Liberation: Gender and Tibetan Buddhist Revival in Post-Mao China*. Berkeley, CA: University of California Press, 2007

Powers, John. *The Buddha Party: How the People's Republic of China Works to Define and Control Tibetan Buddhism*. New York: Oxford University Press, 2016.

Riedel, Bruce. *JFK's Forgotten Crisis: Tibet, the CIA, and the Sino-Indian War*. Washington, DC: Brookings Institution, 2017.

Shakya, Tsering. *The Dragon in the Land of Snows: A History of Modern Tibet since 1947*. New York: Columbia University Press, 1999.

Schwartz, Ronald D. *Circle of Protest: Political Ritual in the Tibetan Uprising*. New York: Columbia University Press, 1994.

van Schaik, Sam. *Tibet: A History*. New Haven, CT: Yale University Press, 2011.

Virtanen, Riika J., ed. and trans. *A Blighted Flower and Other Stories: Portraits of Women in Modern Tibetan Literature*. Dharamsala: Library of Tibetan Works and Archives, 2000.

Wang Lixiong, and Tsering Shakya. *The Struggle for Tibet*. London: Verso, 2006.

Yeh, Emily T. *Taming Tibet: Landscape Transformation and the Gift of Chinese Development*. Ithaca, NY: Cornell University Press, 2013.

17

Xinjiang

GARDNER BOVINGDON[*]

Once all but unknown to outsiders, Xinjiang has recently come to be seen by many as China's second Tibet. The ethnic riots and the severe police response in the region's capital city of Ürümchi in early July 2009 brought Xinjiang, located in the far northwestern part of China, bordering on Central Asia, and home to most of China's eleven million Muslim Uyghurs, unprecedented coverage in the global media. More recently another cycle of ethnic violence and state repression that began in 2014 has been much in the news. But Xinjiang first claimed international attention two decades earlier. Sympathetic stories about large protests forcibly suppressed by the government splashed across U.S. newspaper pages in the 1990s. Those stories were followed in the 2000s by news of large-scale Han Chinese immigration into Xinjiang, forced linguistic assimilation, and the razing of Uyghur neighborhoods. Another set of stories focused on the nearly two dozen Uyghurs imprisoned by the U.S. government as suspected terrorists in Guantanamo after 9/11, and the **Eastern Turkistan Islamic Movement (ETIM)**, a small Uyghur separatist group supposedly affiliated with al-Qaeda, which the U.S. Government declared to be a terrorist organization in August 2002 (see Box 17.1). A reader of this kind of coverage could be forgiven puzzlement: Are Uyghurs freedom fighters like Tibetans, but without a Dalai Lama to lead them? Or are they religious extremists and terrorists, participants in a global jihad?

Chinese officials, and most Han people, believe that Xinjiang is an integral part of China and that Uyghurs are part of the Chinese nation. They are confident that Uyghurs struggling for independence constitute a tiny fraction of the population and lack popular support. Uyghur activists abroad, and many inside Xinjiang, believe that

[*] This chapter was updated for the third edition by the editor.

BOX 17.1 EASTERN TURKISTAN ISLAMIC MOVEMENT

The Eastern Turkistan Islamic Movement (ETIM) is a small militant organization based in Xinjiang and which is seeking an independent Uyghur state called East Turkistan. The ETIM was virtually unknown to the outside world before August 2002, when the U.S. Deputy Secretary of State Richard Armitage announced in Beijing that Washington had labeled it a terrorist organization. The United Nations quickly followed with a similar designation.

Critics observed that the timing of the designation was strangely convenient, since Washington was, at the time, seeking Beijing's support for, or at least acquiescence to, a military offensive against Iraq as part of the war on terrorism. Furthermore, most of the published information about ETIM seemed to come from Chinese government sources, about which neutral observers raised serious doubts. The U.S. government claimed to have independent information that two ETIM members had plotted to blow up the U.S. embassy in Bishkek, the capital of Kyrgyzstan. Outside experts raised concerns about this claim as well, since the United States appeared to be the Uyghurs' sole hope for outside support of any kind. American officials claimed that some of the twenty-two Uyghurs apprehended in Afghanistan in 2001 and detained in Guantanamo had belonged to ETIM, though the assertion is controversial. (The revelation that the U.S. military had allowed Chinese interrogators into Guantanamo to question the Uyghur detainees raised strong criticism from members of Congress and also elicited fresh doubts about the quality of any information the questioning might have elicited.) Since then the remaining seventeen have been released to the Pacific island nation of Palau (2009), Bermuda (2009), Switzerland (2010), El Salvador (2012), and Slovakia (2013).

Journalists later lent credence to the claim by the United States and Chinese governments that ETIM had received support from al-Qaeda in Afghanistan in the mid-1990s, and that some members met with Osama Bin Laden in 1997 and 1999. At the same time, they reported that Bin Laden and other al-Qaeda fighters had focused attention on the struggles of Muslims in various Middle Eastern countries and Chechnya, saying nothing about Xinjiang. ETIM members reportedly left these meetings chagrined and discouraged.

Soon after the U.S. designation of ETIM as a terrorist organization, Chinese officials began to imply in domestic media that Washington regarded all groups seeking an independent "Eastern Turkistan" were terrorists, despite American officials' insistence that the government was identifying only the one organization. When in December 2003 Beijing promulgated a list of four Uyghur organizations and ten individuals it considered terrorists, other governments declined to designate them as such.

In October 2003, the ETIM leader Hasan Makhsum was killed by Pakistani soldiers in Waziristan, a mountainous region of northwest Pakistan bordering Afghanistan. Internationally verified evidence of the organization's activities dried up after that. Yet when several Uyghurs drove a truck into a phalanx of Han policemen in Kashgar, Xinjiang, in summer 2008, Beijing claimed that the attack had been orchestrated by ETIM, although that was never proven.

Chinese officials also later asserted that ETIM had plotted several attacks on the 2008 Olympics in Beijing, all of which were thwarted. Some analysts regarded the "(Eastern) Turkistan Islamic Party" (TIP) as a splinter group that had emerged in 2005 from the moribund ETIM as more of a terrorist threat. The self-styled leader of TIP, "Commander Abdullah Mansour," broadcast a video in summer 2008 claiming responsibility for several explosions in China (a claim denied by Beijing), and issued another video in May 2009 warning governments against extraditing TIP members to China. There was no way to establish the origins of the videos, the validity of the threat, or how substantial an organization Abdullah actually represented.

In November 2013 Mansour used an audio broadcast to declare that TIP had masterminded the deadly vehicle-ramming attack on pedestrians in Tiananmen Square that had taken place the month before. The government placed the blame on the ETIM. It is not clear whether TIP and ETIM are two separate Islamist organizations or whether, as is likely the case, ETIM has re-formed as TIP. In any case, ETIM/TIP has an active presence in Pakistan, Syria, and Afghanistan, where it was targeted by American bombers in early 2018, and it has been implicated in a number of terrorist attacks outside of China. These have included the August 2015 setting off of explosive devices at a Buddhist shrine in downtown Bangkok, Thailand, that killed twenty (among whom were 6 Chinese tourists) and injured 120 others; the August 2016 car bombing of the PRC embassy in Bishek, Kyrgyzstan, in which only the driver died, and the January 2017 shooting by a Uyghur gunman in an Istanbul, Turkey, nightclub that left thirty-nine people dead and seventy wounded. Such incidents led Britain to put ETIM/TIP on its list of terrorist organizations in July 2016.

Although there is little evidence that ETIM/TIP has carried out attacks in Xinjiang in recent years, Beijing frequently singles them out as responsible for unrest and terrorist acts in the region. In March 2017, the PRCs state commissioner for counterterrorism, Cheng Guoping, said that ETIM/TIP was "the most prominent challenge to China's social stability, economic development and national security."[†]

[†]"Xinjiang separatists biggest challenge to China's security, stability, says official," *South China Morning Post*, Mar. 10, 2017. https://www.scmp.com/news/china/policies-politics/article/2077815/xinjiang-separatists-biggest-challenge-chinas-security

most if not all Uyghurs desire independence, and that Uyghurs constitute a nation of their own rather than a part of the Chinese nation. Many see Xinjiang as a colony of China that must, and one day shall, be an independent country.

THE LAND AND PEOPLE OF XINJIANG

To understand political and economic developments in Xinjiang since 1949, it is essential to first note the importance of its geography and demography. The Xinjiang Uyghur Autonomous Region (XUAR), as it has been called since 1955, is the largest provincial-level unit in the PRC, with one-sixth of the country's total land mass (640,930 sq mi) equal to two-thirds of continental Europe and just a bit smaller than Alaska (see Map 17.1). The region's vastness is compounded by its geological and climatic extremes. It includes two large deserts and four mountain ranges. Summer and winter temperatures can vary by more than one hundred degrees, and annual rainfall in much of the region is a scant six inches. Xinjiang's great size, scarce waterways, and rugged terrain have made transportation unusually difficult for most of its history. But the region is rich in natural resources, which includes 25 percent of the national total of oil and natural gas and 38 percent of the country's coal.[1]

Furthermore, the region has strikingly few inhabitants, given China's enormous population. Roughly twenty-four million people currently inhabit Xinjiang, giving the region a population density of roughly fourteen people per square kilometer (about thirty-six per sq mi), one-tenth the density of China as a whole. But just as China's population density differs widely across the country, with some 90 percent of the

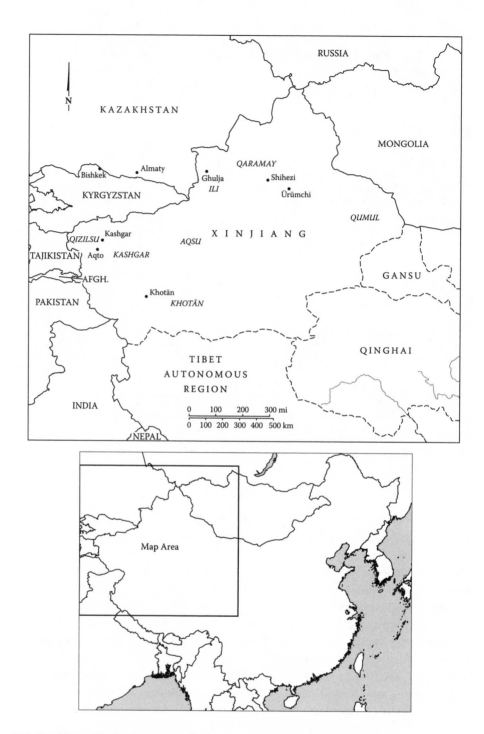

MAP 17.1 Xinjiang Uyghur Autonomous Region

people living on less than 40 percent of the land, human habitation in Xinjiang is very unevenly distributed. Most of the people in southern Xinjiang are crowded into a string of oases ringing the Taklamakan desert, and which are as densely peopled as almost any region in China.[2]

Any would-be ruler seeking to control Xinjiang from afar has faced a fundamental political economy challenge: how to generate enough revenue from a region that is huge, largely desert, sparsely populated, encircled and crisscrossed by high mountains, and remote from any coast, to pay for local administration and satisfy the material wants of its inhabitants. The ethnic and cultural characteristics of those inhabitants have compounded the difficulty for Chinese governors from the Qing dynasty to the present.

Islam first spread from Central Asia to what is now western Xinjiang in the ninth century; it reached the eastern part of the region seven or eight hundred years later. By that time, the vast majority of the population of Xinjiang were Turkic-speaking Muslims While members of this majority differed among themselves in lifestyles, customary dress, and dialect, they did not divide themselves or others into ethnonational categories; instead, they identified themselves as inhabitants of particular oases, as settled people or as herders, and as Muslims. Hence it is conventional to refer to the settled Turkic-speaking population of the region prior to the twentieth century simply as Turki. As discussed later, the name "Uyghur" did not come into common use until the late nineteenth century to refer to one part of the region's Turkic population.

Most Uyghurs practice Sufism, a form of Islam that emphasizes an inner search for God through meditation and chanting, and which rejects possessive materialism. It is considered moderate in its religious practices and beliefs, and its "adherents cherish tolerance and pluralism," which often puts it in conflict with those who hold to and promote—sometimes by violent means—a more radical vision of Islam.[3]

The most important demographic trend in Xinjiang over the last six decades has been the extensive migration of Han Chinese to the region. In 1945, Han made up just 6.2 percent of the total population of Xinjiang, while Uyghurs represented 82.7.[4] In 2016, Han were 36 percent of Xinjiang's population and Uyghurs 49.6 percent.[5] The causes and consequences of this shift are discussed next.

THE INCORPORATION OF XINJIANG INTO QING CHINA

The Qing dynasty Emperor Qianlong conquered the region now known as Xinjiang in 1759, at great expense and after a long, bloody campaign. He did so not principally out of territorial ambition but in order to rid the Qing dynasty of threatening Mongol neighbors. Ruling the new colony proved costly and difficult. In the nineteenth century, prominent Chinese intellectuals urged that the Qing government wash its hands of the region, focusing instead on its vulnerable coast, which was experiencing increasing pressure from the British (see chap. 2). A competing group of intellectuals persuaded the emperor instead to commit further resources to ruling and colonizing the region, arguing that it was a bulwark against more crucial threats from the Mongols, who had conquered China in the thirteenth century.

The Qing government began to promote Han migration into the region from the late eighteenth century in order to "fill out the borders" of its colony and help sustain the military garrisons needed to rule the vast territory. By the early 1800s, Hans comprised nearly one-third of the total population of half a million, though they were mainly concentrated in the area north of the Tianshan Mountains, while more than three hundred thousand Turkis lived mainly in the Tarim Basin south of the mountains. Fearing friction between groups, the Qing initially discouraged Han migration to the Tarim Basin, but after a series of uprisings in the south in the 1830s, Qing administrators came to regard the Muslim population with suspicion and reversed the prior policy, actively encouraging Han farmers to move into the Basin. Although they added to the tax rolls and produced crops to feed the garrisons, the Han migrants could not fundamentally alter the region's desert economy. The huge colony with its legions of imperial soldiers and network of administrators required considerable annual subsidies from the central government.

Despite the military presence and the sustained largesse, Beijing could not maintain a firm grip on the region. In 1864, a warlord named Ya'qub Beg from Kokand, in what today is Uzbekistan, led a Turki uprising that wrested nearly all of the area from Qing control for more than a decade. Russian generals took advantage of the ensuing chaos to occupy and claim for the Russian Empire a strategic swath of territory's northwest. General Zuo Zongtang (immortalized in the "General Tso's Chicken" found in many Chinese restaurants) mounted an expensive expedition in the mid-1870s, which reconquered most of the territory, but it took several more years of careful diplomacy to persuade the Russians to return the region it had claimed.[6]

In 1884, the Qing government transformed the colony into a formal province, which they named Xinjiang, meaning "New Frontier," with the hope of placing it beyond the claims and aspirations of the Russian Empire. Beijing committed to sponsoring new migrants to rebuild the war-torn province and add to its tax base. But the cost of the reconquest and the late Qing's financial difficulties left the court without resources to promote further immigration. Instead, increasing taxes in Xinjiang actually drove some Han immigrants to return to China Proper. One unintended and significant consequence was that substantial numbers of Turkis moved into parts of northern Xinjiang, where they had not previously had large settlements.[7]

XINJIANG UNDER THE REPUBLIC OF CHINA

In the chaos following the fall of the Qing dynasty and the founding of the Republic of China (ROC) in 1912, Tibet lay beyond Chinese influence, and part of Mongolia was "lost" to formal independence even though it was, in reality, under Russian, then Soviet control. Xinjiang fell under the sway of a series of autocratic Han warlords, the last being General Sheng Shicai, who formed much closer ties in the 1930s with the Soviet Union than with the ROC government. During that decade, many Chinese officials and intellectuals alike argued that it was desperately important for China not to lose Xinjiang. With so much of the former Qing territory gone already, they feared the weakening and even the ultimate dismemberment of the country, a worry considerably exacerbated by increasing Japanese encroachment.

The Republican government led by Chiang Kai-shek and the Kuomintang (KMT, or Nationalist) party lacked the capacity to stimulate substantial Han immigration to the region, and attempts by several of Xinjiang's Han warlords to lure migrants by forcing Turkis off farmland and offering it tax-free to Han farmers proved both politically explosive and unsuccessful. By 1940 there were only about 190,000 Han Chinese in Xinjiang, scarcely more than the number in the early 1800s. By contrast, the population of Turkis had grown tenfold to around three million.

The cultural identity of that population had also grown more politicized in the intervening decades. As an assertion of cultural pride, some Turki intellectuals in the late nineteenth century began to refer to themselves by the traditional term "Uyghur," and in the mid-1930s the pro-Soviet government of Sheng Shicai granted the name official recognition, along with different names for other Turkic groups in the province. Sheng's gesture of "recognizing" distinct groups must have seemed magnanimous to many, particularly in contrast to Chiang Kai-shek's assertion that all the peoples of China came from the same root stock, looking and sounding different only because of regional differences in water and soil; but Sheng made the choice under Soviet influence, and clearly intended to avert the emergence of Pan-Turkism—the movement to unite all the Turkic peoples of Central Asia into a single nation—the specter of which had alarmed the Russians for decades. It was no coincidence that the names of the major Turkic groups Sheng recognized in Xinjiang had exact counterparts in Soviet Central Asia.[8]

In the decade before the communist victory in China, Uyghurs settled in the Tarim basin in southern Xinjiang and the Ili River valley in the northwest and made up 80 percent of the provincial population; another four hundred thousand Turkic-speaking pastoralists, now known as Kazakh and Qirghiz (Kyrgyz), roved the grasslands of the Zunghar Basin in the north and the foothills of the Tianshan and Pamir Mountains. Only 5 percent of Xinjiang's inhabitants were Han, still concentrated mostly in the cities of the North.[9]

When Turkis declared an independent Eastern Turkistan Republic (ETR) in northwestern Xinjiang in 1944, it rattled Kuomintang and Communist leaders alike. Chiang Kai-shek sent one of his ablest generals, Zhang Zhizhong, to negotiate a coalition between ETR leaders and the KMT administration in the provincial capital, Dihua (today's Ürümchi, or Urumqi). Five years later, as the civil war was drawing to a close, Mao Zedong dispatched a trusted subordinate to parley with ETR officials; he also sent the CCP's First Field Army to occupy strategic points in the huge province and ensure it would not evade the grasp of the Chinese Communist Party (CCP) once it had won national power.

XINJIANG IN THE EARLY YEARS OF THE PRC

Many Uyghurs had reason to hope that they would enjoy political independence in part or all of Xinjiang after the Chinese civil war. In the late 1940s, Xinjiang's last Han governor under the KMT, Zhang Zhizhong, had speculated publicly about its eventual "decolonization," citing the examples of India and the Philippines.[10] Seeking to outbid the Nationalists and win support among non-Hans for the anti-Japanese war, Mao promised Mongols and Muslims several times in the 1930s that they would be able to decide freely whether to join a federal China under the CCP (explicitly modeled on the Soviet Union) or declare independence.[11] Yet Mao stopped speaking about self-determination in the 1940s, and after the founding of the PRC, CCP leaders expected Uyghurs to be satisfied with limited regional autonomy under a unitary Chinese state. This proved particularly unpalatable to individuals who had lived in the Eastern Turkistan Republic during the latter half of the 1940s.

As the prospect of true autonomy faded, protests in Xinjiang became increasingly strident. At a 1951 conference in Ghulja, the former seat of government of the ETR, a group of Uyghur leaders proposed the establishment of a "Republic of Uyghurstan" with the capacity to regulate all its internal affairs. Local party officials, on instructions from Beijing, hastily convened a meeting to condemn the proposal and make sure that this "incorrect idea" was not spread widely.[12] It gradually became clear that the premise of the system of autonomy proposed by the CCP had never been the protection of regional political rights but instead prioritized maintaining national unity.[13] This fact was amply demonstrated in the organization of the government, the distribution of power, and the nature of the legal system in the Xinjiang Uyghur Autonomous Region, which was officially established on October 1, 1955.

By law, members of local minorities were to hold the top government positions of all autonomous units of the PRC, from the regional level to the county. Government personnel were to be recruited from the several ethnic nationalities in proportion to their weight in the region's total population, though generally slightly favoring non-Hans over Hans. In the first decades of the People's Republic, tens of thousands of Uyghurs and other non-Hans were recruited into Xinjiang's government. But no corresponding laws mandated proportional representation of groups in the party, and the continued appointment of Hans to the most powerful position in the CCP organizations (called the "first secretary of the party committee") at all levels in the region came to appear over time not as a temporary aberration but as Beijing's long-term plan. As the reality of strong party control and continued Han dominance set in, many Uyghurs became deeply and increasingly dissatisfied with their lack of political power. It seemed to them that the Xinjiang Uyghur Autonomous Region was neither truly Uyghur nor autonomous.

HAN IMMIGRATION TO XINJIANG

The leaders of the PRC clearly intended to increase the Han presence in Xinjiang shortly after the CCP came to power in 1949. But the crowded oases settlements could not easily accommodate new colonists, and there was worry in Beijing that Uyghurs' mistrust of Han Chinese would be exacerbated if the two groups were forced to live side by side. Uyghurs had come to resent the intrusion of outsiders who did not speak their language or share their faith, and who, moreover, regarded them with suspicion or disdain.

Beginning in 1949, on orders from Chairman Mao, the top party and military official in Xinjiang, Wang Zhen, demobilized over one hundred thousand soldiers and settled them on a network of paramilitary farms and in small-scale industrial projects throughout the province. The demobilized soldiers were still under the command of the PRC's People's Liberation Army, and military training and preparation were important parts of their routine. In 1954, this network was christened the Xinjiang Production and Construction Corps (XPCC), or as it is commonly called, the **Bingtuan** (from the transliteration of the Chinese for the XPCC) and adopted the motto, "On one shoulder a rifle, on the other a hoe."[14] The *Bingtuan* was charged with both protecting the region from external incursions and guarding against internal rebellion by nationalist Uyghurs. As the organization grew, Wang Zhen chose new XPCC sites at strategic points throughout Xinjiang, often outside existing cities or on marginal land. The aim was to implant millions of Han Chinese and at the same time avoid arousing suspicion. The immigrants farmed and worked in isolated, overwhelmingly Han communities, so their presence, even in large numbers, did not immediately compound tensions with Turkic groups. But frictions developed despite the geographic isolation of the respective communities. In 1980, a conflict between Han XPCC members and local Uyghurs precipitated a major riot in the city of Aqsu.[15]

The party also openly encouraged urban youths in Shanghai and other major coastal cities to move to Xinjiang and help "build the borderlands." The millions of Hans who answered the party's call flowed not only to the *Bingtuan* but also into the cities of northern Xinjiang, fundamentally altering the region's demography over time.

XINJIANG'S ECONOMIC DEVELOPMENT

Since the founding of the PRC, Beijing has consistently directed economic development in Xinjiang with an eye to integrating it more fully into the national territory. Investment or distributive decisions have generally been linked to central goals rather than local needs. In the first decades of the new state, the party steadily weakened Xinjiang's connections with Central Asia, while simultaneously strengthening the region's links to China Proper. The three pillars of Beijing's economic policy for Xinjiang have been industrial development, expansion of agriculture, and sustained support for the large-scale *Bingtuan* farms.

In the Mao era, the central government funded factory construction to give Xinjiang a modest complement of industrial capacities. Yet considering the region "tactically expendable, if strategically useful," the government declined to create anything either too vulnerable or too useful should the region fall under Soviet control. There were reasons to worry that the Soviet Union might covet the region. First, Stalin had supported the Eastern Turkistan Republic in the 1940s, which Mao saw as a plot to make Xinjiang a nominally independent, Soviet client state after the model of Outer Mongolia. The doubling of Soviet forces along the Xinjiang border in the 1960s and a series of Red Army incursions over that decade only increased this concern. Second, from the early 1960s Chinese scientists were working to build the PRC's first atomic bomb in Lop Nor, a remote area in southwestern Xinjiang.[16] Khrushchev had originally offered to help China build a bomb but later reneged on the offer as relations between Moscow and Beijing soured. There were credible reports in the late 1960s that the Soviets considered launching an air strike against Lop Nor in order to destroy China's nuclear weapons program.[17]

The economic priorities of the Mao era brought considerable benefits to Xinjiang. Boons to the region included significant growth in gross domestic product (GDP), nascent industrialization, and infrastructural improvements. Planners set up factories for vehicle repair, machinery, cement, and textiles, as well as facilities for exploiting the area's rich natural resources, especially oil and coal. Agricultural output, and particularly the production of commercial crops such as cotton, increased as a consequence of land reclamation and investment in irrigation, fertilizer, and mechanization. To integrate Xinjiang more tightly with China Proper the government expanded the network of roads, rail, and airports. Moreover, the authorities placed an emphasis on the hiring large numbers of Uyghurs, Kazakhs, and other non-Hans. All of this development was underwritten by enormous subsidies from Beijing.

Economic growth also brought general, if modest, improvement in living standards. State-owned enterprises provided industrial and service jobs in unprecedented numbers. Annual GDP per capita rose from 170 yuan (US$76) in 1952 to 314 (US$128) in 1960, though it had fallen to 229 (US$118) by the end of the Mao era in the mid-1970s.[18]

The drawbacks of Maoist economic policies in Xinjiang included distorted development that favored industry over agriculture and the inefficient use of capital, as in the rest of the PRC. Ill-planned and breakneck development also caused environmental degradation. This included soil deterioration, desertification that often outpaced land reclamation by the XPCC, and a drop in the water table. There is some evidence that nuclear fallout from the testing at Lop Nor contaminated groundwater. Also, in emphasizing economic integration with China Proper and attempting to guard against Soviet aggression by sealing the border, the government kept Xinjiang isolated from natural markets in Central Asia.

In the post-Mao reform era, the PRC government has invested in industrial concerns that directly serve national interests and reflect Xinjiang's comparative advantage in serving the country's needs. In the 1990s, planners began to speak of Xinjiang's economic future in terms of a strategy of "one black, one white": the black stood for oil, the white for cotton. Thus, oil production and petroleum processing have received considerable support, with the goal of exporting the resource to parts of the country where economic expansion has generated almost insatiable demands for energy.

Cotton cultivation in Xinjiang has consistently received both policy and financial support from the central government. In 1998, for instance, Beijing extended a subsidy of 5.5 billion yuan (US$670 million) to the government of the autonomous region to purchase locally grown cotton at below-market prices, which it could then sell for the market price and reap a considerable profit; the 1998 subsidy was equal to Xinjiang's *entire revenue* in 1997.[19] Xinjiang became the largest cotton producer in the country in the 1990s. As part of the ninth Five-Year Plan (1996–2000), the government sponsored the movement of hundreds of thousands of spindles used in cotton production from cities on the coast such as Shanghai, Guangdong, and Tianjin to Xinjiang, seeking at once to unite cotton production and weaving in China's northwest and help enterprises on the coast to shift to producing more capital-intensive and high-technology goods. At the same time, the focus on cotton production and textile manufacture in Xinjiang suits the government's regional political goals. The "ultimate explanation" for the CCP's emphasis on cotton and the development of commercial agriculture, one expert writes, is that it helps sustain the influx of enormous numbers of Han immigrants to "reinforce territorial consolidation."[20]

Beijing has also continued to support the *Bingtuan*, an organization that simultaneously serves the developmental, military-strategic, and immigration goals of the central government. In the late 1990s, the *Bingtuan* was separated from any supervision by the People's Liberation Army and was formally designated as a corporation directly accountable to the CCP and to Beijing rather than to the government of the Xinjiang Uyghur Autonomous Region.[21] As of mid-2013, there were more than 2.7 million *Bingtuan* "soldiers" in Xinjiang, which was about 11.8 percent of the XUAR's total population, working on 3.1 million acres of farmland, and running a vast array of industrial and commercial enterprises, as well as media, educational, and medical institutions.[22]

The *Bingtuan* has become the single largest producer of cotton in Xinjiang and in 2013 accounted for 21.3 percent of the national total.[23] It has economic and trade relations with more than 160 countries and regions, along with exports and imports that totaled US$21.9 billion in 2013, which represented almost 80 percent of Xinjiang's total trade.[24] The transformation of this massive Mao-era highly militarized socialist entity into a profit-making business enterprise in recent decades has been nothing short of astonishing.

By maintaining "one face to the outside world and another domestically"—that is, by operating as a commercial business internationally, under the name "Construction Group" while continuing to sustain some armed militias and large farms—the *Bingtuan* has served the twin aims of Han colonization and regional security much less expensively than the operation of separate self-directed farms and fully military units would have. In the unvarnished language of a self-styled "veteran warrior" of the *Bingtuan* put it, the purpose of the organization is to ensure that "the whole of Xinjiang's territory is forever surnamed 'Zhong'" by which he meant that it will always be part of *Zhongguo*, the Chinese term for China.[25]

The reform era has brought dramatic economic development to Xinjiang. Total GDP rose from 3.9 billion yuan in 1978 (US$2.3 billion) to 1.09 trillion (US$160.7 billion) in 2017, with GDP per capita rising from 313 yuan (US$196) to 44,941 yuan (US$6635) in the same period. In 1978, agriculture accounted for 35.8 percent of the regional GDP, while industry and services made up 64.2 percent. In 2017, agriculture's share of GDP was 14.3 percent with the other two sectors accounting for 85.7 percent.[26] There has also been major expansion of highways, railroads, and airports and other infrastructure improvements.

These achievements have been underwritten by the huge injection of capital by the state. Between 1949 and 2015, the central government's financial grants to Xinjiang totaled nearly 1.7 trillion yuan (US$250 billion), the vast majority of which has come since 1978.[27] In 2010, a "pairing assistance" (*duikou*) system was put in place through which nineteen provinces and directly administered cities in China Proper were "each required to help support the development of different areas in Xinjiang by providing human resources, technology, management and funds."[28] For example, the city of Beijing was paired with several counties in southwestern Xinjiang to provide funding in the amount of 7.3 billion yuan (US$1.1 billion) to support projects that included earthquake-proof housing construction, low-income housing renovation, education, and sanitation.[29]

Agricultural reforms have allowed some Uyghurs (and many Hans) to prosper through specialization. Uyghurs in Turpan and nearby regions profited by cultivating melons and grapes. Uyghur traders prospered, first from internal trade, then from transborder activities. Domestic traders traveled to China's major cities to sell fruits, raisins, walnuts, and shish kebabs. After the borders with Central Asia were reopened in the 1980s, many merchants embarked on the shuttle trade, sending textiles and housewares west and importing steel and other industrial commodities in return.

At the same time, some reform era policies exacted costs for Xinjiang. Reforms of state owned enterprises (SOEs) eliminated at least six hundred thousand jobs between 1995 and 2000.[30] In many cases Uyghurs appear to have been fired before Hans in those enterprises. Hiring patterns in key state industries were (and continue to be) at best discriminatory and often exclusionary.[31] The workforce in Xinjiang's booming oil industry is overwhelmingly Han. Uyghurs have long felt intentionally excluded from the industry. In 1993 Xinjiang Party Secretary Wang Lequan dismissed the charge of bias by claiming dubiously that "all" workers came from oil fields elsewhere in the country, so no locals of any sort were hired.[32] The following year an official in the industry said more candidly that non-Han employees were scarce because "most can't meet the basic standards"[33] due to low levels of education.

In general Uyghurs and other non-Hans face greater difficulty than Hans in finding jobs in the civil service, state-owned enterprises, and the private sector even though Chinese law forbids discrimination based on ethnicity.[34] Some job ads call for people natively fluent in Chinese, which excludes most Uyghurs, or even state that the positions (or most of them) are open only to Hans. One report in 2013 said that half of the 161 jobs advertised on the Civil Servant Examination Information website in the city of Kashgar (which is 90 percent Uyghur) were open only to ethnic Han Chinese or native Mandarin speakers.[35]

It is widely recognized that Uyghurs are as a group less educated than Hans and that this is a serious disadvantage to finding employment in the modernizing economy. There are numerous reasons for the comparatively low rates of educational attainment and thus high rates of unemployment among Uyghurs. Many Uyghur families who make a living through farming, particularly those in predominantly agrarian southern Xinjiang, may place less emphasis on education than their Han counterparts and also feel compelled by economic necessity to keep school-age children home to work in the fields.[36] As school fees have risen in the reform era, poorer families may be financially unable to keep their children in school. Poorly funded schools in southern Xinjiang often lack adequate equipment and are unable to attract and retain good teachers. The strong and increasing emphasis on Chinese-language instruction, even in schools with non-Han majorities, may also have deterred parents who hoped their children would grow up with a strong basis in Uyghur language and culture, and may also have discouraged students with little or no facility in Chinese. Finally, the high Uyghur unemployment rate has clearly sent the dispiriting message to many students that even if they work hard, their prospects are poor, leading many to question the ultimate value of education. In addition, some Uyghurs are by their own account not interested in jobs with long hours and rigid work discipline as required in factories

and other sectors of the modern economy.[37] The Uyghur economist, Ilham Tohti—
who would be sentenced to life in prison in 2016 for allegedly promoting separatism—
conceded in a 2005 lecture (published in 2006) that many Uyghurs are held back
economically by "limited technical skills, conservative thinking, shortsightedness, an
emphasis on manual labor unsuited to the modern market economy, weak competitive spirit, and fatalism."[38]

Yet differences in educational attainment and motivation to work in certain jobs
do not entirely account for disparities in income between Uyghurs and Hans. Recent
research has suggested that despite being better educated as a group than their elders,
young Uyghurs still pay a measurable "cost of being Uyghurs," earning less than Hans
in their age cohort owing to employment discrimination in private enterprises and a
smaller proportion of jobs in the state sector.[39] It is important to acknowledge both
the systemic factors and the individual choices here because many Uyghur dissidents
and international observers attribute all Uyghur problems to discrimination, unfairly
suggesting that the Chinese government has the capacity to change everything with
a few policy adjustments.

As in the rest of China, economic growth in Xinjiang has been accompanied by
growing inequalities. The PRC does not publish statistics comparing incomes among
ethnic groups in Xinjiang. This appears to be a premeditated state policy rather than
an inadvertent omission.[40] Officials might well be seeking to avoid publicizing "negative" information that could be used to criticize the government and the system
of regional autonomy. While state-sponsored reports do acknowledge that "real
inequalities" persist despite the establishment of "absolute legal equality" and take
note of the need "to improve the quality of life 'through balanced development,' "[41]
they studiously avoid putting numbers to those gaps.

But it is easy to find statistics on living standards divided by administrative units
within the XUAR and then to correlate them with population distributions. Uyghurs
predominate in the south and are mostly farmers. Han are the majority population in
the north, and a significant proportion of them live in cities. The visitor to Xinjiang
can see immediately that Uyghur farmers in the south live much simpler lives than do
Han oil workers or agro-industrial combine workers in the north, and several scholars
have remarked on the strong correlation of high incomes and high concentrations of
Hans, and low incomes and Uyghur predominance.[42] The overall economic difference
is actually greater since areas where non-Hans predominate depend more heavily on
agriculture, which generates less income than industry or commerce.[43] Furthermore,
the pattern of state investment in energy exploitation and commercial crop production shows a clear orientation to national rather than regional concerns that certainly
has ethnic consequences.

For example, in 2016, the oil-producing center of Karamay had a per capita GDP of
137,307 yuan (US$20,678), which was similar to that of Beijing and Shanghai; in the
capital city of Ürümchi, it was 69,565 yuan (about US$10,476). However, GDP per
capita in the agricultural Khotän (Hotan) region in the southwest, which is 95 percent
Uyghur, was 9,901 yuan (US$1491), just one ninth of that of Ürümchi, which is about
74 percent Han.[44]

The economic priorities set by officials in the last two and a half decades, notably
the "one black, one white" approach, appear certain to have left Uyghurs, and much of

southern Xinjiang, behind. With state subsidies, growing cotton is profitable for large mechanized *Bingtuan* farms where Hans predominate, while small-scale Uyghur cultivators have ended up worse off. Those farmers confront very high prices for inputs such as seeds, fertilizer, and fuel, and face volatile market demand and prices. In some cases, it costs more to grow cotton than Uyghur farmers take in from selling it. Furthermore, cotton is an extraordinarily thirsty crop. Xinjiang's water table has already dropped sixty meters (nearly two hundred feet) over the last thirty years, and increasing cotton monoculture will almost certainly cause further damage. Farmers have had to dig deeper and deeper wells, and conflicts over water use have increased. Since so many *Bingtuan* units are situated at the sources of the region's major rivers, the organization has "effective control of [Xinjiang's] surface water."[45]

Uyghurs have also complained that Beijing simply carts off the mineral wealth of Xinjiang without adequate compensation, and rumors abound that even a small surtax on the oil sent inland would make every Uyghur rich. It has been suggested that the huge subsidies Beijing has provided Xinjiang for decades are really "a disguised form of payment" for mineral exploitation at below world-market rates set by the central government. In any case, it appears that despite the subsidies and other measures, most of the profits from energy and mineral exploitation in Xinjiang enrich Beijing rather than the region.[46]

Since the late 1990s, Xinjiang has been a central part of two major state-led economic initiatives. The first was the "Open the West" campaign, unveiled in 1999 to promote development of twelve provincial level regions that had not benefited as much from the market reforms and opening up to the global economy as areas closer to the coast.[47] The focus of the campaign has been on developing transportation, energy, including hydro-electric power, and telecommunications, improving education, promoting environmental protection, and attracting foreign investment. Key aspects of the initiative are included in the 13th Five-Year Plan (2016–2020). The 6.35 trillion yuan (US$914 billion)[48] injected into the western regions between 2000 and 2016 certainly has stimulated development, but it has not achieved the campaigns goals of eliminating the gap with eastern China or, in the case of Xinjiang, of significantly narrowing the inequalities between Uyghurs (or other minorities) and Hans. Instead, the benefits of the initiative in Xinjiang appear to have been directed mostly to the Han population.

The second central government program in which the XUAR figures prominently is the even more ambitious Belt and Road Initiative (BRI, see chap. 8). The "Road" part of the BRI refers to a "New Silk Road" that is to connect the PRC with Central Asia and beyond. Xinjiang, was, of course, at the heart of the original Silk Road that began in the Han dynasty (207 BCE–220 CE) and ran from eastern China to southern Europe.[49] Xinjiang is seen as being a vital transportation, commercial, and logistics hub of the BRI. One of the first major steps to that end was the completion in 2017 of a new 2,768 kilometer (1,720 m.) freeway linking Beijing with Ürümchi.[50] Boosting economic growth and modernization in the XUAR is among the stated goals of the BRI; it is also portrayed as promoting "the solidarity of ethnic groups."[51] But it remains to be seen whether the BRI benefits both Uyghurs and Hans alike or if, as with earlier state-led developmental policies that have been applied to Xinjiang, it is yet another example of, as one scholar put it, "Han economic imperialism."[52] There is also the question of how the region can become a flourishing center of transcontinental trade when, as discussed later in this chapter, ethnic tensions are palpable, and the Uyghur population is experiencing an unprecedented level of repression as part of a multifaceted state-led crackdown said to be necessary to thwart Islamist-inspired terrorism.[53]

POLITICAL DEVELOPMENTS XINJIANG FROM THE 1980S TO 2009

When then CCP General Secretary Hu Yaobang visited Tibet in May 1980, he was horrified to find many Tibetans living in dire poverty and profoundly alienated from the government, despite decades of substantial financial support from Beijing. Hu proposed to remedy both problems by enacting "ample autonomy." He ordered that two-thirds of the cadre positions there be filled with Tibetans and a large number of Han cadres be retired or transferred to China Proper.[54] After convening a meeting with members of the Xinjiang Party Committee in July of that year, Hu approved a proposal along similar lines, mandating that the party appoint non-Hans as first party secretaries at various subregional levels and stipulating that the ratio of minority cadres in Xinjiang be raised to over 60 percent.[55] Hu pushed these changes through despite ferocious resistance from Han officials in the XUAR.

In Xinjiang, more than seven thousand Han cadres were transferred to China Proper in 1981 alone, and in the early part of the decade all top-ranked Han cadres in the villages of southern Xinjiang reportedly moved to cities or other administrative positions. Some two hundred thousand Hans left Xinjiang between 1979 and 1993, although new immigration more than replaced that number. At the same time, despite the substantial nativization of party and government in Xinjiang and Tibet in the wake of Hu Yaobang's directives, Beijing continued to select only trusted Han officials as first secretaries of the regional party committees, as it had done with very few exceptions in prior decades.

The liberalization of cultural policies, including increased protection for religious freedom, and the nativization of administrative ranks under Hu Yaobang pleased many Tibetans and Uyghurs, even if those changes did not extinguish criticism of Beijing. A sizable number of Tibetans reportedly said they "had never had it so good," and Uyghur peasants and traders avowed a satisfaction with the party that Uyghur nationalist intellectuals found disconcerting. At the same time, Han cadres in both Xinjiang and Tibet deeply resented Hu, feeling that his policies called their political contributions into question, rewarded local anti-Han prejudice, and threatened the very security of Hans living in the regions.[56] One Han official in Xinjiang reportedly fulminated that the author of these proposals was a "traitor" aiming to "create an East Turkestan . . . surrendering Xinjiang to the Soviet Union and Turkey."[57]

When a series of major protests, including several led by Uyghur university students, rocked Xinjiang in the mid-to-late 1980s, Hu's accommodationist policies were held responsible. He was removed as CCP general secretary in 1987 by paramount leader Deng Xiaoping, although Hu's alleged soft line on the burgeoning democracy movement in Beijing figured more prominently in his dismissal than the unrest in Xinjiang.

The generally peaceful demonstrations of the 1980s in the XUAR gave way to more violent ones in the following decade, possibly as a consequence of the prior severe reprisals against expressions of Uyghur nationalism. Nearly one hundred Uyghurs staged an armed uprising in Baren in southwestern Xinjiang in April 1990. In 1992, several buses were bombed in one day in Ürümchi; five Uyghurs were executed for the attack. In 1997, large numbers of Uyghurs marched in the streets of Ghulja to protest against religious and political repression, and after the police responded harshly, the protests turned violent and the police, in turn, suppressed the protestors with brutal force. Shortly afterward, more bus bombings occurred in the region's capital. Hard-liners in Beijing and Ürümchi pointed to violent events in the 1990s as further evidence that the liberal policies of Hu Yaobang had been a mistake. Many hard-liners in the current party-state leadership maintain the same perspective today, which is one reason that Beijing has continued to refuse to negotiate with external parties or accommodate local demands.

After Hu's ouster, Xinjiang's leaders reversed the nativization initiative and again promoted the recruitment and retention of Han cadres. The party stepped up calls for Han cadres to work in Xinjiang beginning in the late 1990s.[58] In 1996 the CCP promulgated "Document Number 7," a top secret order for authorities in Ürümchi to "train a number of minority cadres who can determinedly defend the nation. . . . At the same time . . . train a large number of Han cadres who love Xinjiang . . . and then relocate them to Xinjiang." It also instructed the Autonomous Region's Party Committee to place greater restrictions on religious practices, insist that non-Han officials demonstrate loyalty to country and party or face dismissal, and extend the *Bingtuan* (meaning targeted Han immigration) into Xinjiang's south.[59] The document set the tone for policies in the region for the first decade of the 2000s, which combined strong support for economic growth with rigorous political control and intolerance for dissent.

THE JULY 2009 CRISIS AND ITS AFTERMATH

The frequency of protests fell dramatically in the early 2000s, and the economy continued to grow at a rapid clip. Nevertheless, Xinjiang remained a contentious place and a political headache for Beijing. The most obvious concern for China's leaders has been to avert the emergence of widespread, sustained ethnic violence. A second concern, with the situation of Tibet in mind, has been to prevent the "internationalization" of the "Xinjiang problem." Both of these concerns became a reality with the outbreak of major riots in Ürümchi in July 2009.

Most observers agree that the riots were touched off by a brawl that took place in late June in Guangdong province, some two thousand miles distant from Ürümchi, where substantial numbers of young Uyghur men and women had gone to take factory jobs beginning in 2006.[60] On June 25, responding to a rumor that several Uyghur men had raped two Han women at the Xuri Toy Factory in the city of Shaoguan— a story later repudiated by one of the women supposedly involved—Han workers stormed a dormitory where Uyghur workers lived. Armed with crude weapons such as iron bars and long knives, the Han workers attacked the occupants indiscriminately and a huge brawl ensued; several videos of the violence that surfaced on the internet showed no evidence of a police response. Two Uyghurs were killed and hundreds injured, according to official reports, though some Uyghur and Han workers at the factory believed the death toll was higher. In the days following, only one person was arrested: the man held responsible for spreading the false rumors of the rape.[61]

Within days, Uyghur blogs and websites published news of the violence and what many regarded as an inadequate government response; some also argued that the labor recruitment system was compulsory rather than voluntary, focused on rural Uyghur women, and aimed at inducing Uyghurs to assimilate. In the first days of July, Uyghurs in Ürümchi used text messages and the web to disseminate plans for a peaceful demonstration. On July 5, roughly one thousand Uyghurs, several waving PRC flags, marched through the streets of Ürümchi to People's Square to protest the killings and the government's handling of the Shaoguan episode.

Party officials in Beijing and Ürümchi responded to the demonstration with police action as they had to previous such protests, first mobilizing police with riot gear and later, after some delay, sending in paramilitary **People's Armed Police (PAP)** forces with automatic weapons. Still at issue is when, where, and to whom they responded. Official accounts later described police and PAP forces patrolling the streets to stop violent attacks by Uyghurs on Han civilians. Uyghur expatriate organizations and eyewitnesses claimed by contrast that the police had used lethal force against peaceful protestors and even children. By the next morning the government had promulgated news of a curfew from 9:00 p.m. to 8:00 a.m., shut down internet and cell-phone service, ostensibly to prevent the spread of rumors and further violence, and continued to bring PAP forces into Ürümchi.

In the wake of the 2008 protests in Tibet (see chap. 15), Beijing had enforced a media blackout and refused to allow foreign journalists to travel to the TAR. That choice later came to be regarded both inside and outside China as a poor one, inviting suspicions that the government had much to hide and preventing it from making a plausible case that police had responded appropriately. In a striking departure from the previous year's strategy, on July 6 Beijing invited a group of foreign reporters to Ürümchi to investigate and report on events there firsthand. They were all housed in the Hoi Tak Hotel, which reportedly had the only working internet connection in the XUAR at the time. At one point a group of journalists walking down a street were accosted by roughly two hundred women who demanded that the government release their male relatives detained after the protests. International journalists wrote numerous stories from Ürümchi investigating the extent of the violence and trying to clarify the causes. These reports not only praised the government for being more open to journalists but also produced graphic evidence of police handling unarmed protestors roughly, kicking them, striking them with batons, and even punching them in the face.

Unexpectedly, on July 7, the second day of the reporters' visit, bands of Han citizens armed with homemade weapons organized to patrol the streets. The Han vigilantes drew considerable attention; international media reported their complaints that they did not trust Beijing or local police forces to protect Han residents. The vigilantes are said to have attacked Uyghurs they found on the streets in several locations, but no casualty figures were released. Foreign journalists took note that police were conspicuously scarce as the Han citizens roamed; indeed, Ürümchi Party Secretary Li Zhi was observed standing on a police car leading a group in chants of "down with Rebiya [Kadeer]," the Washington, DC–based president of the World Uyghur Congress (WUC), an international organization headquartered in Germany, whom the authorities blamed for organizing and triggering the riot via a series of phone calls to relatives in Ürümchi (see Box 17.2).[62]

The violence and tension were serious enough that on July 8, the PRC President and CCP General Secretary Hu Jintao returned early from Italy, where he had been scheduled to take part in the G-8 summit. By Friday, July 10, the violence had stopped, but in the name of avoiding further conflict, the government posted placards announcing that all Ürümchi mosques would be closed for Friday prayers and ordering men to pray at home. Groups of Uyghurs gathered angrily before a number of mosques and the government relented, allowing several to open. On the same day a smaller group of Uyghur protestors took to the streets to demand the release of those who had been detained. Even though the protestors were marching peacefully, riot police set upon them with truncheons and fists, an episode captured memorably by BBC video cameras.[63]

By July 11 there were no further reports of violence, even though the government announced that more than fourteen hundred people had been detained in connection with the events. With the heavy police presence, the city became quiet but remained extremely tense throughout the summer. A month later the government announced the trials of some two hundred suspects in connection with the riots and said that there would be a "drastic increase in security" in preparation for the trials.[64]

Even after having invited foreign journalists to investigate the riot, Beijing attempted to maintain control of the narrative, pronouncing officially that 197 people had died and over 1,700 been wounded in the violence of July 5.[65] Officials also quickly moved to assign blame, taking two different and seemingly contradictory tacks. They attributed the riot to outside agitators like Rebiya Kadeer for meddling in an otherwise peaceful region. They also asserted that Rebiya and the WUC had ties to the Eastern Turkistan Islamic Movement (ETIM), the group linked to al-Qaeda by the United States, though this claim faded over time. Officials later asserted that simultaneous eruption of violence in fifty different sites in the city proved it had been premeditated. They also announced that women in "long Islamic robes and head coverings" had directed the rioters, and that one even distributed clubs[66]—propositions hard to square with the several PRC flags carried by the marchers and the absence of obviously "Islamic" dress in the videos of the protest or episodes of violence caught on surveillance cameras.

While officials publicly continued to blame Rebiya, on July 8 police also detained Ilham Tohti, a charismatic Uyghur professor at the Central University for Nationalities(Minzu) University in Beijing, for a few weeks after Xinjiang's governor Nur Bekri publicly blamed Tohti's blog *Uyghur Online* for contributing to the riot by spreading what he termed rumors about violence against the protesters.

Tohti, an economist, had long voiced sharp yet carefully reasoned criticisms of Chinese policies in the XUAR in his lectures and on his blog. His most well-known lecture was delivered at Minzu University and later widely disseminated via his blog, in which Tohti noted that some of the region's most powerful economic interests, the petroleum and mining companies guided by Beijing, undervalued resources extracted in

BOX 17.2 REBIYA KADER

Rebiya Kadeer (Rabiyä Qadir) is a complex and controversial figure: a shopkeeper turned millionaire; the mother of eleven children; a delegate to a national-level advisory body to the government of the PRC, later imprisoned in China for "revealing state secrets"; a businesswoman and philanthropist turned independence movement leader; a human rights activist accused by Beijing of supporting terrorism.

Born in 1947 into a poor Uyghur family in Altay in northern Xinjiang, Rebiya entered business in the in late 1970s with a single laundromat. Through a series of increasingly bold ventures, she managed to build an international trading company that made her one of the richest people in China by the early 1990s. She used some of her wealth to help other Uyghur women get a start in business through her foundation, the 1,000 Families Mothers Project. In recognition of her achievement, she was appointed to the PRC government advisory body in 1993, and in 1995 was a representative of China at the United Nations Conference on Women in Beijing.

Following the large-scale Uyghur protests in early February1997, her husband, Sidik Rozi Haji, who had emigrated to the United States, heaped criticism on Chinese policies in Xinjiang. The Communist Party subsequently stripped her of her passport and prevented her from conducting international trade. In her capacity as a delegate in the national advisory body, Rabiyä also spoke critically about Beijing's rule in Xinjiang and was summarily removed from her position. She later sent newspaper clippings to Sidik in the United States. As she prepared to hand a file on Uyghur political prisoners to a U.S. congressional delegation in 1999, police took her into custody, and she was subsequently charged with "revealing state secrets." Sentenced to ten years in prison, she was released and deported in 2005 after strong pressure from Washington.

For years Uyghurs in diaspora had lamented the lack of a leader with the charisma or international stature of the Dalai Lama. When Rabiyä arrived in Washington in 2005, she was quickly touted as the Uyghurs' great new hope. Nominated five times for the Nobel Peace Prize, awarded the Norwegian Rafto Prize (often taken as a harbinger of a future Nobel winner) in 2004, energetic and articulate, she has done much to raise the profile of Uyghur organizations and concerns outside Xinjiang. In 2006 she was elected president of the World Uyghur Congress (WUC), an international organization that claims to represent the interests of Uyghurs in Xinjiang and elsewhere. She held that position until 2017. In April 2018, she started a hunger strike to protest not only the detention of more than thirty of her relatives but more generally the severe crackdown on Uyghurs that began in 2016, declaring that "I will stop the hunger strike when the United Nations and other international organizations stand up with Uyghur people against Chinese brutal and harsh policy."[‡]

At the same time, she has made some embarrassing gaffes and leveled exaggerated charges against Beijing that have damaged her credibility and that of the organizations she heads. After the July 2009 riots, she held a press conference during which she presented a picture supposedly showing police cracking down on Uyghur demonstrators; within hours it was revealed to have been an image from an unrelated protest in south China.

Given that the Dalai Lama has been unable to wrest political concessions from Beijing through years of trying, despite his fame and international support, it seems unlikely that Rebiyä will have much impact on politics in Xinjiang. However, China will only enhance her influence among Xinjiang Uyghurs and globally if it continues to bring her international attention and sympathy as it did in 2017 when it denounced her planned visit to Taiwan, saying that "It is a well-known fact that Rebiya Kadeer is among the heads of the separatist 'East Turkistan' forces" and that "The invitation . . . is intended to make trouble and will certainly harm cross-Strait relations."[§]

(Continued)

BOX 17.2 (*Continued*)

‡"Rebiya Kadeer to go on hunger strike to protest against treatment of Chinese minorities," Australian Broadcasting Company, Apr. 19, 2018, http://www.abc.net.au/news/2018-04-20/rebiya-kadeer-to-go-on-hunger-strike-chinese-minorities-uighurs/9675376

§"Mainland opposes Uygur separatist visiting Taiwan," Xinhua, Feb. 8, 2017, http://www.xinhuanet.com/english/2017-02/08/c_136041276.htm

Xinjiang and therefore paid very little in local taxes in the service of national economic objectives. Further, instead of contributing to regional economic development as the Xinjiang government had claimed, the companies actually "segregated" their enterprises from the local economy and effectively provided Beijing with hidden transfer payments at the expense of locals. To remedy this, Tohti explicitly pleaded for official recognition of Uyghurs' rights to a share of the proceeds from mineral exploitation, as well as constitutionally granted rights to political autonomy to safeguard their collective interests, but he also lamented that Uyghurs would receive neither because the current division of power and resources advantaged those powerful interest groups.

Both the condemnation of Rebiya and Tohti's detention in July 2009 implicitly acknowledged that dissatisfaction inside Xinjiang, and not just foreign agitation, had been a factor in the protest. After all, neither an outspoken expatriate leader in Washington nor a professor in Beijing could simply will large numbers of Uyghurs into the streets of Ürümchi, particularly given the official forceful response to previous protests.[67]

But a fresh spate of violence in Ürümchi in late summer 2009, and Beijing's responses to it, revealed the power of another discontented constituency in Xinjiang: the millions of Hans who called the region home. Rumors of Uyghurs leaping out of shadows and stabbing Hans with syringes began to circulate in August, and by early September near-hysterical concern about "syringe attacks" (quite out of proportion with the tiny number of verified episodes) was rife throughout Xinjiang and beyond.[68] On September 3 there was another march on People's Square, this time by some ten thousand Hans shouting that the Xinjiang government was incapable of protecting the population and demanding that Xinjiang Party Secretary Wang Lequan resign. The demonstration unquestionably caught Beijing's attention, and Ürümchi's party secretary and police chief were fired two days later. Wang Lequan, who had served an extraordinary fifteen years in the XUAR's top party position on the strength of having "maintained stability" with a firm hand, had clearly lost the confidence of the CCP leadership. Wang was transferred to a party post in Beijing in April 2010 and was replaced by Hunan Party Secretary Zhang Chunxian, an official known not for political crackdowns but for his media savvy.[69]

In May 2010, Hu Jintao convened a "Xinjiang Work Group" in Beijing. The Work Group handed Zhang Chunxian a set of policies ostensibly aimed at resolving the economic and security problems in Xinjiang. These included the "pairing" of provincial-level regions in eastern China with various locales in Xinjiang for the provision of technical assistance and fiscal grants described earlier; the declaration of a Special Economic Zone to attract foreign investment in Kashgar; massive infrastructural investments in roads and airports; a substantial increase in the taxes on local mining and petroleum production to direct more of the benefits of resource exploitation to the region's inhabitants; and increased subsidies to the salaries of cadres and other noncommercial workers to be financed by those increased taxes.[70]

There is little doubt that these policies have contributed to Xinjiang's economic growth. Between 2011 and 2017, the XUAR's GDP expanded by an average of 9.6 percent per year compared with 7.9 percent for the PRC as a whole. In the same period, urban per capita income rose from 13,644 yuan (US$2004) to 30,775 yuan ($4522) and rural incomes from 4,643 yuan (US$682) to11,045 yuan (US$1622), while average staff and worker annual wages in modern sectors of the economy increased from 32,361 yuan (US$4755) to 64,630 yuan (US$9495) between 2010 and 2016.[71]

As noted earlier,there are no statistics comparing average Han and Uyghur incomes over this period, but given that the former predominate in salaried jobs and urban areas, it is safe to conclude that most of the benefits of growth have continued to flow to Hans. While one scholar has mocked Beijing's post-2009 Xinjiang policies as an "economic band-aid" incapable of winning over disaffected Uyghurs, another has argued that this was never their primary purpose. Instead, the policies were intended to address Xinjiang's "Han problem": the problem of convincing longtime Han residents unsettled by July 2009 to stay, and also of drawing more "human capital"— meaning educated and skilled Han migrants—to the region.[72] The announcement in 2013 of a plan for "leapfrog development" focused on four cities in XPCC-controlled areas and the celebration of a mass wedding for fifty XPCC couples "lured to Xinjiang to realize their dreams" lend credence to this conclusion.[73] So, too, does the fact that in 2010, in the aftermath of the 2009 riots, the total Han population in the XUAR dropped for the first time since 1978, if only by ten thousand, and that it started to grow again the following year.[74] In 2016, the Han population of Xinjiang dropped by about thirty-four thousand (4 percent) over the previous year to its lowest level in a decade,[75] a reflection of the intensification of the cycle of violence and repression that has gripped the XUAR in the Xi Jinping era.

XINJIANG IN THE XI JINPING ERA

Since Xi Jinping came to power in 2012–2013 the situation in Xinjiang has become dramatically more severe for the Uyghur population as part of the campaign to eradicate the "three evil forces" of "separatism, extremism, and terrorism" that were identified as the source of ethnic troubles in the region.[76] This was set in motion by a series of violent incidents, including a suicide crash of a jeep driven by a Uyghur into a crowd of pedestrians in Beijing's Tiananmen Square (October 2013), the slaughter of thirty-one civilians by eight knife-wielding Uyghurs at the railway station in Kunming, Yunnan (March 2014), vehicle-ramming attacks in Ürümchi that killed more than three dozen Han and injured 90 (May 2014), and ethnic clashes in the southern Xinjiang city of Yarkand that left more than one hundred people dead, mostly Uyghurs shot by police (August 2014).[77] The party-state responded with a far-reaching crackdown, which it said was necessary to stem the violence and the threat to local and national security posed by Islamist separatists inspired by global jihadism.

The crackdown was launched during Xi Jinping's first-ever visit to Xinjiang as China's top leader in late April 2014 during which he said, while visiting local SWAT teams, that "the police are the 'fists and daggers' in the fight against terrorism."[78] A day after Xi left, assailants wielding knives and explosives killed three people and injured seventy-nine outside the Ürümchi train station. In the following week, a "strike hard" campaign targeting alleged terrorist cells was implemented. One of the first displays of the campaign's "success" was the mass trial and sentencing of fifty-five people on terror charges—including three who were sentenced to death— in front of seven thousand people in a stadium in northwestern Xinjiang. Later that year, as if to send a message to other Uyghur intellectuals who might challenge party-state policy in the XUAR, Ilham Tohti, the economist who was first detained after the 2009 riots, was sentenced to life in prison after a two-day trial Ürümchi in which he was convicted of promoting separatism.[79]

In August 2016, Chen Quanguo, who had been the CCP secretary of Tibet since 2011, was appointed to take over the same position in the XUAR. Chen quickly proceeded to implement a number of security policies that he had pioneered in Tibet. A "grid-management system" (see chap. 16) divided cities into squares containing about five hundred people, each with a state-of-the art police station to keep watch over the residents. A web of checkpoints with facial or iris recognition scanners that most people have to pass through several times a day as they go about their business has been set up. Police patrols are ubiquitous, as are PAP armored cars on the roads. High-resolution surveillance cameras dot the urban landscape. Everyone is supposed to have a GPS tracker in their automobiles and an app on their cell phone that transmits information to the authorities about who they talk to, their social media presence, and their internet surfing habits.

Under Party Secretary Chen small teams composed of local officials and police visit individual households collecting personal information under the guise of "researching people's conditions, improving people's lives, winning people's hearts." But their real purpose is to be on the lookout for signs of extremist beliefs or behavior "such as not drinking alcohol, fasting during Ramadan and sporting long beards."[80] The information gathered by this and other means is used to measure a person's level of "trustworthiness," that is, political reliability, which can determine the degree of surveillance to which someone is subjected and can even serve as the basis for extralegal detention. One NGO, China Human Rights Defenders, marshalled evidence based on Chinese government data that showed nearly 228,000 people were arrested in Xinjiang in 2017, about one-fifth of all arrests in China, even though the region has only 1.5 percent of the PRC's total population.[81]

In March 2017, at the same time that he said "Just as one loves one's own eyes, one must love ethnic unity; just as one takes one's own livelihood seriously, one must take ethnic unity seriously," Xi Jinping declared the central government's resolve to build a "great wall of steel" around Xinjiang in order to bring "lasting peace and stability to the region."[82] This followed a massive show of force when thousands of weapon-bearing members of the People's Armed Police paraded through the streets of several XUAR cities. During one of these parades, Xinjiang's deputy party secretary told his audience that "We shall load our guns, draw our swords from their sheaths, throw hard punches and relentlessly beat, and strike hard without flinching at terrorists" and that "With the caring and strong leadership of the Communist Party Central Committee, where President Xi Jinping serves as the core . . . the strong support of 23 [million] people from all ethnic groups in Xinjiang, and with the powerful fist of the People's Democratic Dictatorship, all separatist activities and all terrorists shall be smashed to pieces."[83]

Severe restrictions have also been placed on Islamic religious and Uyghur cultural practices. Some neighborhood mosques have been closed. Large ones are monitored by the police and their minarets—the distinctive towers adjacent to mosques from which the faithful are called to prayer—have been demolished. More than two dozen Islamic names are no longer allowed to be given to newborns. The use of the Uyghur language as a medium of instruction in schools has been drastically reduced, and some Uyghur wedding and funeral customs have been banned.

The most alarming turn of events has been the construction of large numbers of "reeducation camps" in many parts of the XUAR that are holding an estimated five hundred thousand to a million Uyghurs who are subject to intense indoctrination to imbue them with love for the party and the country, including cultural and linguistic assimilation.[84] There have also been credible reports of waterboarding and other physical mistreatment of those being held. Detentions, which are indefinite in length, are not determined by a judicial process but are solely based on decisions by local political authorities and the police.

In August 2018, when the United Nations Committee on Elimination of Racial Discrimination called for an investigation into the camps, the PRC denied they existed. But by October of that year, in the face of clear and mounting evidence of the scale of the centers, the authorities in the XUAR acknowledged their existence claiming that they are part of "a vocational education and training program" whose "purpose is to get rid of the environment and soil that breeds terrorism and religious extremism and stop violent terrorist activities from happening." Most trainees, it was noted, had "been able to reflect on their mistakes and see clearly the essence and harm of terrorism and religious extremism. They have notably enhanced national consciousness, civil awareness, awareness of the rule of law and the sense of community of the Chinese nation. They have also been able to better tell right from wrong and resist the infiltration of extremist thought." Furthermore, the job training they received had enhanced their employment prospects in the modern sector so that they are able "to become more proactive in shaking off poverty."[85] The influential editor of the state-run *Global Times* declared that "The West just cares about finding faults with China and accusing us with nonexistent wrongdoings. They put pressure on China on the global stage and try to mess up the governance of Xinjiang. In fact, those Western forces don't care about the well-being of Xinjiang residents at all."[86]

The bottom line is that in recent years Xinjiang has become a neo-totalitarian police state[87] based on a massive infusion of security personnel and security-related funding into the region. This surveillance state uses cutting-edge technology and big data to carry out what one commentator has called "a vast experiment in 'predictive policing,' whereby the authorities are able to assess an individual's identity and ethnicity, social interactions, use of social media, and physical movement to ascertain their relative 'threat' to the state and better direct operations of security forces."[88] The fact that this predictive policing is aimed specifically at one ethnic group—the Uyghurs—raises the specter of racial profiling at best and, at worst, the potential for policies that in effect constitute a form of apartheid or even ethnic cleansing.[89]

THE FUTURE OF XINJIANG

Chinese leaders have several reasons for wanting to keep a firm hold of Xinjiang. First, Xinjiang represents a large piece of Chinese territory in a strategically vital part of the country. From the time of the Sino-Soviet split of the 1960s until 1991, Xinjiang was a buffer protecting China from the Soviet Union. With the collapse of the Soviet Union and Beijing's successful negotiation of friendly relations with Russia, the fear of a major military threat in that region has disappeared. But given the XUAR's proximity to areas where Islamist forces are active, Beijing sees Xinjiang as vital to its national security. Second, the region has some of the country's largest remaining reserves of coal, oil, and natural gas, which are important resources needed to fuel China's continued economic growth. Third, Xinjiang provides a vital link to Central Asia and beyond. A pipeline connects Xinjiang to the even richer oil deposits of China's neighbor, Kazakhstan, and Beijing has begun construction of a pipeline from Turkmenistan to tap that country's rich natural gas holdings. The Belt and Road Initiative makes the location all the more important to the PRC's economic priorities and regional diplomacy.

In sum, China will not willingly relinquish or even substantially lessen its control of Xinjiang, and the PRC has developed sufficient economic, political, and military capacity that neither Uyghurs nor any outside power could force it to do so. Nevertheless, despite the central government's overwhelming tactical advantage, it would be unwise to ignore the signs of profound and pervasive discontent among Uyghurs. For even though they have little chance of gaining independence, they will remain a restive population with deep resentments about how they are treated in their own homeland.

It is by no means clear how the crisis in Xinjiang can be resolved or significantly reduced. Many Uyghurs and foreign observers argue that party-state's rigid assimilationist policies and draconian repression have precipitated the protests and violent episodes of recent years. In contrast, Chinese officials claim that the lax PRC policies of the 1980s allowed separatist organizations and Islamic extremists to grow in number and become more influential in the region. Careful analysis of the modern political history of Xinjiang demonstrates that the former view is more plausible. Organized protest and violence emerged in the region long before the 1980s. Furthermore, dissatisfaction since then has not been confined to Islamists and separatists advocating violence; ordinary Uyghurs have expressed growing discontent with Chinese rule in the XUAR. Although some protests and violence are driven by real material grievances, economic growth will not eliminate the discontent: for most Uyghurs the deepest roots of their discontent are in what they see as an assault on their ethnic and religious identities. Nor will more rigorous political and social control eliminate the desire or ability of Uyghurs to express it. Unfortunately, there is little evidence that China's current leadership has contemplated serious alternatives.

NOTES

1. "Xinjiang's Natural Resources," http://www.china.org.cn/english/MATERIAL/139230.htm.

2. Stanley W. Toops, "The Demography of Xinjiang," in *Xinjiang: China's Muslim Borderland,* ed. S. Frederick Starr (Armonk, NY: M. E. Sharpe, 2004), 241–263.

3. Megan Specia, "Who Are Sufi Muslims and Why Do Some Extremists Hate Them?," *New York Times,* Nov. 24, 2017, https://www.nytimes.com/2017/11/24/world/middleeast/sufi-muslim-explainer.html

4. Anthony Howell and C. Cindy Fan, "Migration and Inequality in Xinjiang: A Survey of Han and Uyghur Migrants in Urumqi," *Eurasian Geography and Economics* 52, no. 1 (2001), 123.

5. *Xinjiang Statistical Yearbook 2017* (Beijing: China Statistics Press, 2017), 96.

6. James A. Millward, *Beyond the Pass: Economy, Ethnicity, and Empire in Qing Central Asia, 1759–1864* (Stanford, CA: Stanford University Press, 1998), 197.

7. James A. Millward and Nabijan Tursun, "Political History and Strategies of Control, 1884–1997," in Starr, *Xinjiang,* 65–67.

8. James A. Millward, *Eurasian Crossroads: A History of Xinjiang* (New York: Columbia University Press, 2007), 206–210.

9. Toops, "The Demography of Xinjiang," 244–245.

10. Gardner Bovingdon, "The History of the History of Xinjiang," *Twentieth Century China* 26, no. 2 (2001), 95–139.

11. Walker Connor, *The National Question in Marxist-Leninist Theory and Strategy* (Princeton, NJ: Princeton University Press, 1984), 80–81 and chap. 4 passim.

12. Zhu Peimin, *Ershi shiji Xinjiang shi yanjiu* (Research on the History of Xinjiang in the Twentieth Century) (Urumci: Xinjiang renmin chubanshe, 2000), 335.

13. Baogang He, "Minority Rights with Chinese Characteristics," in *Multiculturalism in Asia,* ed. Will Kymlicka (Oxford: Oxford University Press, 2005), 68.

14. On the XPCC (*Bingtuan*), see Uyghur Human Rights Project. "The Bingtuan: China's Paramilitary Colonizing Force in East Turkestan," April 26, 2018. https://docs.uhrp.org/pdf/bingtuan.pdf; Yuchao Zhu and Dongyan Blachford, "'Old Bottle, New Wine'? Xinjiang *Bingtuan* and China's ethnic frontier governance," *Journal of Contemporary China,* 25, no. 97 (2016), 25–40; Thomas Matthew James Cliff, "Neo Oasis: The Xinjiang Bingtuan in the Twenty-first Century," *Asian Studies Review* 33 (2009), 83–106; James D. Seymour, "Xinjiang's Production and Construction Corps, and the Sinification of Eastern Turkestan," *Inner Asia* 2 (2000), 171–193. On the *Bingtuan's* motto, see Nick Holdstock, *China's Forgotten People: Xinjiang, Terror, and the Chinese State* (London: I. B. Tauris, 2015), 37.

15. Michael Dillon, *Xinjiang: China's Muslim Far Northwest* (London: RoutledgeCurzo, 2004).

16. See John W. Lewis and Xue Litai, *China Builds the Bomb* (Stanford, CA: Stanford University Press, 1991).

17. See various documents at "The Sino-Soviet Border Conflict, 1969: US Reactions and Diplomatic Maneuvers," in *A National Security Archive Electronic Briefing Book,* ed. William Burr, June 12, 2001, http://www.gwu.edu/percent7Ensarchiv/NSAEBB/NSAEBB49/. Decades later, it also emerged that in 1964 President John F. Kennedy had proposed to Khrushchev that the U.S. and the USSR send two bombers to Xinjiang and jointly destroy the nuclear outpost, but Khrushchev declined; see Gordon H. Chang, "JFK, China, and the Bomb," *Journal of American History* 74 (1988), 1287–1310.

18. Calla Weimer, "The Economy of Xinjiang," in Starr, *Xinjiang: China's Muslim Borderland*, 169.

19. Becquelin, "Xinjiang in the Nineties," 82–83.

20. Becquelin, "Xinjiang in the Nineties," 83.

21. Cliff, "Neo Oasis," 87–89.

22. "Historical Witness to Ethnic Equality, Unity and Development in Xinjiang," White Paper, Information Office of the State Council, People's Republic of China Sept. 2015, http://english.gov.cn/archive/white_paper/2015/09/24/content_281475197200182.htm; and "The History and Development of the Xinjiang Production and Construction Corps," White Paper, Information Office of the State Council, People's Republic of China, Oct. 2014, https://en.people.cn/n/2014/1005/c90785-8790958.html

23. "The History and Development of the Xinjiang Production and Construction Corps."

24. The History and Development of the Xinjiang Production and Construction Corps"; PRC National Bureau of Statistics, http://data.stats.gov.cn/english/easyquery.htm?cn=E0103.

25. Wang Lixiong, *Wode Xiyu, nide Dong Tu* (My Western Regions, Your Eastern Turkistan) (Taibei: Dakuai wenhua chuban gu fen you xian gong si, 2007), 21.

26. "Human Rights in Xinjiang - Development and Progress,"White Paper, Information Office of the State Council, People's Republic of China June 2017, http://www.xinhuanet.com//english/2017-06/01/c_136331805.htm; PRC National Bureau of Statistics, http://data.stats.gov.cn/english/easyquery.htm?cn=E0103.

27. "Historical Witness to Ethnic Equality, Unity and Development in Xinjiang," http://english.gov.cn/archive/white_paper/2015/09/24/content_281475197200182.htm

28. Shan Wei and Weng Cuifen, "China's New Policy in Xinjiang and its Challenges," *East Asian Policy* 2, no. 3 (2012), 61.

29. Liu Yong, "An Economic Band-Aid: Beijing's New Approach to Xinjiang," *China Security* 6, no. 2 (2010), 37.

30. Weimer, "The Economy of Xinjiang," 179.

31. Becquelin, "Xinjiang in the Nineties," 85, 90.

32. Barry Sautman, "Preferential Policies for Ethnic Minorities in China: The Case of Xinjiang," *Nationalism and Ethnic Politics* 4 (1998): 97. The author met a number of workers in the oil industry between 1995 and 2002, many of whom who had grown up in Xinjiang.

33. K. Chen, "Muslims in China Hate Beijing a Bit Less—Recent Economic Gains Temper Calls for Revolt," *Wall Street Journal*, Oct. 21, 1994, A10.

34. "Job Discrimination Against Ethnic Minorities Continues in Xinjiang, United States Congressional-Executive Commission on China, Mar. 31, 2011, https://www.cecc.gov/publications/commission-analysis/job-discrimination-against-ethnic-minorities-continues-in-xinjiang

35. Andrew Jacobs, "Uighurs in China Say Bias Is Growing," Oct. 7, 2013, https://www.nytimes.com/2013/10/08/world/asia/uighurs-in-china-say-bias-is-growing.html

36. An official government report acknowledged this problem in 2001. See "Guanyu zhengque renshi he chuli xin xingshi xia Xinjiang minzu wenti de diaocha baogao," *Makesi zhuyi yu xianshi* (Feb. 2001), 34–38. Cited in Becquelin, "Staged Development in Xinjiang," 358–378.

37. Author's field notes 1997, 2002.

38. Ilham Tohti, "Xinjiang Jingji Fazhan Yu Minzu Guanxi" (Xinjiang's Economic Development and Relations among Minzu), *Weiwu'er zai xian (Uyghur online)*, 2006, available at https://wenku.baidu.com/view/8288a76ba98271fe910ef983.html

39. Xiaowei Zang, "Age and the Cost of Being Uyghurs in Ürümchi," *China Quarterly* 210 (2012); "Uyghur—Han Earnings Differentials in Ürümchi," *China Journal*, no. 65 (2011).

40. Such statistics are closely guarded, even in the most peaceful and least politicized of the autonomous regions, such as the Guangxi Zhuang Autonomous Region in southern China. Guangxi officials told a foreign researcher in the 1990s that they were forbidden even to study differences in Han and Zhuang incomes, as the topic was "too sensitive"; Katherine Palmer Kaup, *Creating the Zhuang: Ethnic Politics in China* (Boulder, CO: Lynne Rienner, 2000).

41. Shannon Tiezzi, "China Doubles Down on Economic Development in Troubled Xinjiang," *Diplomat*, May 7, 2014, https://thediplomat.com/2014/05/china-doubles-down-on-economic-development-in-troubled-xinjiang/

42. Toops, "The Demography of Xinjiang," 261–262.

43. Weimer, "The Economy of Xinjiang," 177.

44. Hong Kong Trade and Development Council (HKTDC) Research, Mainland China Provinces and Cities, http://china-trade-research.hktdc.com/business-news/article/Facts-and-Figures/Mainland-China-Provinces-and-Cities/ff/en/1/1X39VTST/1X06BOQA.htm; and *Xinjiang Statistical Yearbook 2017*, 90.

45. Cliff, "Neo Oasis," 272–277. Figures on dropping water table from Eric Hagt "China's Water Policies: Implications for Xinjiang and Kazakhstan," *Central Asia—Caucasus Analyst* (2004), http://www.cacianalyst.org/?q=node/1358.

46. Comment on subsidies as "disguised payments" from Minxin Pei, "Self-Administration and Local Autonomy: Reconciling Conflicting Interests in China" in *The Self-Determination of Peoples: Community, Nation, and State in an Interdependent World*, ed. Wolfgang F. Danspeckgruber (Boulder, CO: Lynne Rienner, 2002), 315–332. For analysis of relative benefits to Xinjiang and Beijing, see Weimer, "The Economy of Xinjiang," 174.

47. Qunjian Tian, "China Develops Its West: Motivation, Strategy and Prospect," *Journal of Contemporary China* 13 (2004), 611–636.

48. "New five-year plan brings hope to China's west," Xinhua, Dec. 27, 2016, http://english.gov.cn/premier/news/2016/12/27/content_281475526349906.htm

49. See James Millward, *The Silk Road: A Very Short Introduction* (New York: Oxford University Press, 2013).

50. Faisal Kidwai, "Xinjiang rides high on Belt and Road Initiative" Aug. 8, 2018, http://www.chinadaily.com.cn/a/201808/08/WS5b6a649ba310add14f384a0c.html

51. Liu Xin, "Xinjiang continues counter-terror measures to ensure safe Belt and Road," *Global Times*, July 22, 2018, http://www.globaltimes.cn/content/1111801.shtml

52. David Bachman, "Making Xinjiang Safe for the Han? Contradictions and Ironies of Chinese Governance in China's Northwest," in *Governing China's Multiethnic Frontiers*, ed. Morris Rossabi (Seattle: University of Washington Press, 2004), 156.

53. Mihir Sharma, "The Hole at the Heart of China's Silk Road," Bloomberg Opinion, Aug. 7, 2018, https://www.bloomberg.com/view/articles/2018-08-07/xinjiang-is-key-weakness-in-china-s-belt-and-road-plan

54. Melvyn C. Goldstein, *The Snow Lion and the Dragon: China, Tibet, and the Dalai Lama* (Berkeley: University of California Press, 1997), 65.

55. Zhu Xiaomin, "Jiefang hou zhi 20 shiji 80 niandai Xinjiang Yily fan fenlie douzheng jiaoxun qianxi" (A Preliminary Analysis of the Lessons from the Struggle against Separatism in Xinjiang's Ili from the Revolution through the 1980s), *Zhonggong Yili zhou wei dangxiao xuebao* (2006), 61–63.

56. Zhu Xiaomin, 61–63. Information about Tibet from Tsering W. Shakya, *The Dragon in the Land of Snows: A History of Modern Tibet since 1947* (New York: Columbia University Press, 1999) 400, 410.

57. Cited in Dillon, *Xinjiang: China's Muslim Far Northwest*, 36.

58. Deng Liqun, *Deng Liqun zishu: shi'er ge Chunqiu* (Deng Liqun in His Own Words: Twelve Seasons) (1975–1987), (Hong Kong: Da Feng chubanshe, 2006), 205–208.

59. CCP Central Committee, "Document #7: Record of the Meeting of the Standing Committee of the Politburo of the Chinese Communist Party Concerning the Maintenance of Stability in Xinjiang." English translation published by Human Rights Watch (1996).

60. A concise chronology of events can be found on the BBC website, http://news.bbc.co.uk/2/hi/asia-pacific/8138866.stm. The best English-language account of the events is James Millward's "Introduction: Does the 2009 Ürümchi Violence Mark a Turning Point?," *Central Asian Survey* 28, no. 4 (2009), 347–360. The following paragraphs largely follow that account.

61. See James A. Millward, "Introduction: Does the 2009 Ürümchi Violence Mark a Turning Point?," *Central Asian Survey* 28, no. 4 (2009).

62. Millward, "Introduction," *Central Asian Survey* 28, no. 4 (2009), 354.

63. Video available at http://news.bbc.co.uk/2/hi/asia-pacific/8141657.stm.

64. Cai Ke and Lei Xiaoxun, "200 to Face Trial for Day of Carnage," *China Daily*, Aug. 24, 2009, http://www.chinadaily.com.cn/china/2009xinjiangriot/2009–08/24/content_8605477.htm.

65. China's official Xinhua News Service also set up an English-language "Urumqi Riot" website to promulgate its version of events abroad: http://www.chinaview.cn/urumqiriot/.

66. Barbara Demick, "China Says It Has Evidence Deadly Uighur Uprisings Were Coordinated," *Los Angeles Times*, July 21, 2009.

67. Tohti's lecture was originally posted at http://www.uighurbiz.net/html/2008/0324/8137.html (cited July 29, 2009); link now defunct. On Tohti's influence on his students, see Ananth Krishnan, "The Road to a Better Life," in *Chinese Characters: Profiles of Fast-Changing Lives in a Fast-Changing Land*, ed. Angilee Shah and Jeffrey Wasserstrom (Berkeley: University of California Press, 2012), 133–144. On his July 2009 detention, see Edward Wong, "Intellectuals Call for Release of Uighur Economist," *New York Times*, July 15, 2009. Radio Free Asia Uyghur service reported Tohti's detention and the closure of his website on July 9, 2009, http://www.rfa.org/uyghur/xewerler/tepsili_xewer/ilham-tohti-nezerbentte-03252009051627.html?encoding=latin. Tohti was quietly released along with two prominent Chinese democracy activists in Aug. 2009, apparently as a goodwill gesture in advance of President Obama's first trip to China later that year.

68. Thomas Cliff, "The Partnership of Stability in Xinjiang: State–Society Interactions Following the July 2009 Unrest," *China Journal*, no. 68 (2012), 96.

69. Cliff, "The Partnership of Stability in Xinjiang," 80, 87, 90.

70. Cliff, "The Partnership of Stability in Xinjiang," 100–105.

71. PRC National Bureau of Statistics, http://data.stats.gov.cn/english/easyquery.htm?cn=E0103; "Xinjiang's economy expands 7.6 pct in 2017," Xinhua, Jan. 25, 2018, http://www.xinhuanet.com/english/2018-01/25/c_136924235.htm; and Basic Statistics for the People's Livelihood, Xinjiang, China Yearly Macro-Economic Statistics, China Data Online, http://chinadataonline.org/

72. Liu "An Economic Band-Aid: Beijing's New Approach to Xinjiang": 41–65; Cliff, "The Partnership of Stability in Xinjiang," 83–86.

73. Mao Weihua, and Shao Wei, "Three Goals to Realize 'Leapfrog' Development," *China Daily*, http://www.chinadaily.com.cn/cndy/2011-06/01/content_12621481.htm; "Circling the Wagons," *Economist*, May 25, 2013; Li Laifang, Zhang Hongchi, and Pan Yin, "Graduates Lured to Xinjiang to Realize Dreams" *People's Daily Online*, June 11, 2013, http://english.people-daily.com.cn/203691/8280757.html.

74. *Xinjiang Statistical Yearbook, 2017*, 90.

75. *Xinjiang Statistical Yearbook 2017*, 96.

76. See "Xinjiang to crack down on 'three evil forces,'" *China Daily*, Mar. 6, 2012, http://www.chinadaily.com.cn/china/2012-03/06/content_14766900.htm

77. See Jonathan Kalman, "Islamist group claims responsibility for attack on China's Tiananmen Square," *Guardian*, Nov. 25, 2013, https://www.theguardian.com/world/2013/nov/25/islamist-china-tiananmen-beijing-attack; Shannon Tiezzi, "China Executes 3 for Deadly Kunming Attack," *Diplomat*, Mar. 24, 2015, https://thediplomat.com/2015/03/china-executes-3-for-deadly-kunming-attack/; "Urumqi car and bomb attack kills dozens," *Guardian*, May 22, 2014, https://www.theguardian.com/world/2014/may/22/china-urumqi-car-bomb-attack-xinjiang; Emily Rauhala, "China Now Says Almost 100 Were Killed in Xinjiang Violence," Aug. 4, 2014, http://time.com/3078381/china-xinjiang-violence-shache-yarkand/

78. "China's Xi says Xinjiang is front line on terrorism, hails police," Reuters, Apr. 29, 2014, https://www.reuters.com/arti,cle/us-china-xinjiang-idUSBREA3S03D20140429

79. "Five facts about Ilham Tohti, award-winning activist jailed in China," Amnesty International, Oct. 20, 2016, https://www.amnesty.org/en/latest/campaigns/2016/10/five-facts-about-ilham-tohti-uighur-activist-jailed-in-china/

80. "Apartheid with Chinese characteristics: China has turned Xinjiang into a police state like no other," *Economist*, June 10, 2018, https://www.economist.com/briefing/2018/05/31/china-has-turned-xinjiang-into-a-police-state-like-no-other

81. "Criminal Arrests in Xinjiang Account for 21% of China's Total in 2017," China Human Rights Defenders, July 25, 2018, https://www.nchrd.org/2018/07/criminal-arrests-in-xinjiang-account-for-21-of-chinas-total-in-2017/

82. "China's Xi calls for 'great wall of iron' to safeguard restive Xinjiang," Reuters, Mar. 9, 2017, https://www.reuters.com/article/us-china-security-xinjiang/chinas-xi-calls-for-great-wall-of-iron-to-safeguard-restive-xinjiang-idUSKBN16H04J; Tom Phillips, "China: Xi Jinping wants 'Great Wall of Steel' in violence-hit Xinjiang," *Guardian*, Mar. 10, 2017, https://www.theguardian.com/world/2017/mar/11/china-xi-jinping-wants-great-wall-of-steel-in-violence-hit-xinjiang. The full conversation in Chinese that Xi Jinping had with the Xinjiang delegation to the National People's Congress meeting in Mar. 2017 in which he made these remarks can be found at http://m.news.cctv.com/2017/03/10/ARTIHyDZXYT5wKGA5VKT3FVt170310.shtml

83. Tom Phillips, "Chinese troops stage show of force in Xinjiang and vow to 'relentlessly beat' separatists" Reuters, Feb. 20, 2017, https://www.theguardian.com/world/2017/feb/20/chinese-troops-stage-show-of-force-in-xinjiang-and-vow-to-relentlessly-beat-separatists

84. James Millward, "'Reeducating' Xinjiang's Muslims," *New York Review of Books*, Feb. 7, 2019, https://www.nybooks.com/articles/2019/02/07/reeducating-xinjiangs-muslims/?utm_medium=email&utm_campaign=NYR%20Xinjiang%20Roma%20Paris&utm_content=NYR%20Xinjiang%20Roma%20Paris+CID_9f7831cbd83cb966b47cc6dd74dfe1ad&utm_source=Newsletter&utm_term=Reeducating%20Xinjiangs%20Muslims

85. The quotes come from "Full transcript: Interview with Xinjiang government chief on counterterrorism, vocational education and training in Xinjiang," Xinhuanet, Oct. 16, 2018, http://www.xinhuanet.com/english/2018-10/16/c_137535821.htm?mc_cid=ace3de327f&mc_eid=c8292ef9bf

86. Gerry Shih, "China defends its 'people-oriented' Muslim reeducation program as job training," *Washington Post*, Oct. 16, 2018, https://www.washingtonpost.com/world/asia_pacific/china-defends-its-people-oriented-muslim-reeducation-program-as-job-training/2018/10/16/521964a8-d12b-11e8-a275-81c671a50422_story.html?utm_term=.41c30a7c9d63

87. Michael Clarke, "In Xinjiang, China's 'Neo-Totalitarian' Turn Is Already a Reality," *Diplomat*, Mar. 10, 2018, https://thediplomat.com/2018/03/in-xinjiang-chinas-neo-totalitarian-turn-is-already-a-reality/

88. Clarke, "In Xinjiang, China's 'Neo-Totalitarian' Turn Is Already a Reality."

89. "Apartheid with Chinese characteristics"; Josh Rogin, "Ethnic cleansing makes a comeback—in China." *Washington Post*, Aug. 2, 2018, https://www.washingtonpost.com/opinions/global-opinions/ethnic-cleansing-makes-a-comeback--in-china/2018/08/02/55f73fa2-9691-11e8-810c-5fa705927d54_story.html?utm_term=.0e9aca87c5a7

SUGGESTED READINGS

Bovingdon, Gardner. *The Uyghurs: Strangers in Their Own Land*. New York: Columbia University Press, 2010.

Cliff, Tom. *Oil and Water: Being Han in Xinjiang*. Chicago: University of Chicago Press, 2016.

Gladney, Dru C. *Dislocating China: Reflections on Muslims, Minorities, and Other Subaltern Subjects*. Chicago: University of Chicago Press, 2005.

Goodman, David S. G. *China's Campaign to "Open up the West": National, Provincial, and Local Perspectives*. New York: Cambridge University Press, 2004.

Hayes, Anna, and Michael Clarke, eds. *Inside Xinjiang Space, Place and Power in China's Muslim Far Northwest*. New York: Routledge, 2015.

Hillman, Ben, and Gary Tuttle. *Ethnic Conflict and Protest in Tibet and Xinjiang: Unrest in China's West*. New York: Columbia University Press, 2016

Holdstock, Nick. *China's Forgotten People: Xinjiang, Terror, and the Chinese State*. London: I. B. Tauris, 2015.

Jacobs, James. *Xinjiang and the Modern Chinese State*. Seattle: University of Washington Press, 2017.

Kaltman, Brian. *Under the Heel of the Dragon: Islam, Racism, Crime, and the Uighur in China*. Athens: Ohio University Press, 2007.

Lipman, Jonathan N. *Familiar Strangers: A History of Muslims in Northwest China*. Seattle: University of Washington Press, 1997.

Millward, James A. *Eurasian Crossroads: A History of Xinjiang*. New York: Columbia University Press, 2007.

Starr, S. Frederick, ed. *Xinjiang: China's Muslim Borderland*. Armonk, NY: M. E. Sharpe, 2004.

18

Hong Kong

SONNY SHIU-HING LO

FROM BRITISH CROWN COLONY TO SPECIAL ADMINISTRATIVE REGION OF CHINA

Hong Kong, with a total area of a little over 420 square miles (less than one-quarter the size of Rhode Island) and a population of about seven million, became a special administrative region (SAR) of the People's Republic of China (PRC) on July 1, 1997. For about 150 years prior to that it was a colony of Great Britain. The territory became a British colony in three phases after the first Opium War between United Kingdom and the Qing dynasty in 1839–1842. The first phase included Hong Kong Island (about 50 sq mi), which was ceded to Great Britain in perpetuity according to the terms of the Treaty of Nanjing. Britain also took control in perpetuity of Kowloon (eighteen square miles) in 1860 as part of the Convention of Peking (Beijing) that ended the **Second Opium War**. In 1898, the largest part of Hong Kong, the New Territories (368 square miles) was *leased* for ninety-nine years from Qing China to the United Kingdom in the Second Convention of Peking (The Convention for the Extension of Hong Kong Territory).

For more than a century, the British government directly governed Hong Kong by sending governors and expatriate civil servants from London and indirectly ruled the territory through the co-optation of local elites, in both the urban and rural areas. The co-optation of Hong Kong elites took the form of appointing them to various consultative bodies and conferring upon them honors and titles such as the Members of the British Empire (MBE) and Order of the British Empire (OBE). A **Legislative Council (LegCo)** was established in colonial Hong Kong in 1843, but it always played a subordinate role in the executive-dominant system. Prior to 1985, the governor appointed all members of the Legislative Council.

In 1979, when the British governor of Hong Kong, Sir Murray MacLehose, visited Beijing, the Chinese leader Deng Xiaoping told him that the PRC would take back all of Hong Kong by 1997, when the U.K.'s lease on the New Territories was set to expire. MacLehose did not inform the people of Hong Kong of this message, but he conveyed Deng's remark that the Hong Kong people should put their hearts at ease about their future.

In 1982, British Prime Minister Margaret Thatcher visited Beijing and began negotiations with the PRC on Hong Kong's sovereignty. The negotiations got off to a rocky start, but eventually Thatcher made an important concession by exchanging sovereignty over Hong Kong for Beijing's promise of a high degree of autonomy for the territory after the British departure. The **Sino-British Joint Declaration** (formally, the Joint Declaration of the Government of the United Kingdom of Great Britain and Northern Ireland and the Government of the People's Republic of China on the Question of Hong Kong) was signed in Beijing in December 1984 and set out the terms for the formal transfer of sovereignty on July 1, 1997.

The Joint Declaration was based on the principle of "**One Country, Two Systems**" for Hong Kong, which was to become a special administrative region (SAR) of the People's Republic of China. This principle meant that, although Chinese sovereignty over Hong Kong would be recognized, Beijing promised that it would not impose socialism or direct communist party-rule on the SAR, and the capitalist system and way of life would not be changed for at least fifty years. A similar formula was applied to the nearby Portuguese colony of Macao in its return to Chinese sovereignty in 1999 (see Box 18.1).

"ONE COUNTRY, TWO SYSTEMS"

In 1990, the Chinese government promulgated the **Basic Law**—a mini-constitution for the Hong Kong Special Administrative Region (HKSAR) based on the "One Country, Two Systems" principle. The Basic Law provided a blueprint for maintaining Hong Kong's legislative, administrative, judicial, social, and economic autonomy under Chinese sovereignty. But it also empowered the Standing Committee of the PRC's National People's Congress to interpret the provisions of the Basic Law, thus giving China final say on all matters related to Hong Kong. In fact, final decisions about such matters rest with the highest levels of the Chinese Communist Party, which has a special Leading Small Group on Hong Kong-Macao Affairs headed by a member of the party's Politburo Standing Committee (see chap. 6 for more on Leading Small Groups).

After the British became aware of the Chinese plan to take back the sovereignty of Hong Kong, they decided, rather belatedly in the view of many, to implement political reform in the territory by introducing direct elections to some of the seats in the local advisory bodies called District Boards. In 1985, the British introduced *functional* constituency elections to the Legislative Council. This meant that certain occupational or interest groups, such as business, law, finance, health care, education,

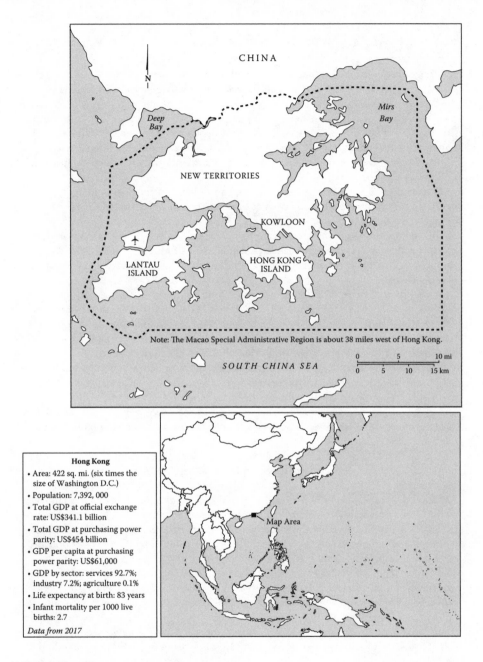

Note: The Macao Special Administrative Region is about 38 miles west of Hong Kong.

Hong Kong
- Area: 422 sq. mi. (six times the size of Washington D.C.)
- Population: 7,392, 000
- Total GDP at official exchange rate: US$341.1 billion
- Total GDP at purchasing power parity: US$454 billion
- GDP per capita at purchasing power parity: US$61,000
- GDP by sector: services 92.7%; industry 7.2%; agriculture 0.1%
- Life expectancy at birth: 83 years
- Infant mortality per 1000 live births: 2.7

Data from 2017

MAP 18.1 Hong Kong

labor, and engineering, were to select representatives to the law-making chamber. The main objectives of these elections were to introduce an element of democracy into the Hong Kong legislative process and to encourage political participation by important functional groups.

The British attempted to accelerate democratization in Hong Kong by toying with the idea of introducing directly elected seats from *geographical* constituencies to LegCo in 1987. This would have given all citizens of Hong Kong, not just the members

BOX 18.1 MACAO: THE OTHER SAR

Many people do not realize that there is another former colony besides Hong Kong that was returned to Chinese sovereignty and became a special administrative region (SAR) of the People's Republic of China in the late 1990s. Macao, a one-time colony of Portugal on the coast of China, about thirty-seven miles southwest of Hong Kong, returned to Chinese sovereignty in 1999. Macao is only eleven square miles in area, and has a population of a little over half a million, but it is one of the most densely populated places in the world. Macao has some similarities to the HKSAR but also many fundamental historical, political, and economic differences.

The Portuguese first established a presence in Macao in the sixteenth century as a haven for shipwrecked sailors and then as base for trading with imperial China. Portugal gradually extended its activities in and control over Macao, and from the early seventeenth century to the mid-nineteenth century, Portugal's relations with China were tense and fluctuating, with both sides claiming sovereignty over Macao. In the 1840s, Portugal was able to assert full colonial control over Macao, as the Qing dynasty was in its period of rapid decline.

After Portugal became a democracy in 1974, it began to renounce its claims on its colonies. In 1976, China and Portugal agreed that Macao was a Chinese territory under Portuguese administration. The two countries reached agreement in April 1987 on the return of Macao to Chinese sovereignty, which formally took place on December 20, 1999. Beijing wanted to settle the question of Hong Kong's sovereignty before that of Macao.

Like Hong Kong, the Macao SAR has a Basic Law as a mini-constitution that grants it a great deal of autonomy, except in defense and foreign affairs. In all matters, the government of Macao, headed by a chief executive, is subordinate to that of the PRC. Despite one very high-profile corruption case in which a former senior government official was arrested in 2007 and sentenced to a long prison term, the Macao government has been relatively clean.

The SAR's first chief executive, Edmund Ho Hau-wah, a former banker, remained quite popular through his second term, which ended in late 2009. However, there was a mismatch between Ho's ability to lead Macao and the bureaucratic structure underneath him. Although there are signs of improvement, the Macao bureaucracy has been traditionally hierarchical, unresponsive, and slow to react to socioeconomic and political change, reflecting perhaps the persistence of the legacy of Portuguese rather than British colonialism.

But, in many ways, Macao's undemocratic but consultative and overwhelmingly pro-establishment political system is more akin to that of the PRC than to its Hong Kong counterpart. Like the HKSAR, the Macao Special Administrative Region (MSAR) has an executive-led administration that dominates the legislature, which also has a majority of pro-government and pro-Beijing members. Political parties operate only before an election and are disbanded afterward. Interest groups are mainly dominated by pro-Beijing trade unions and neighborhood associations. Although there have been some working-class protests, civil society in Macao is relatively weak compared to Hong Kong, and its democracy movement is small and ineffective. There is also a lack of an independent mass media critical of the administration.

In March 2009, a tough national security law took effect in Macao after it was approved by an overwhelming majority of members of the Legislative Assembly. Civil society did not rise up against the bill, unlike the Hong Kong case with Article 23 of the Basic Law. In fact, many legal scholars in Macao supported the law. Critics argue that it outlaws ambiguous "preparatory acts" of treason, secession, and subversion—offenses that can bring a minimum of three years and a maximum of twenty-five years of imprisonment. Some Hong Kong democracy supporters fear that the enactment of the law is an attempt by the PRC to pave the way for "Macaonizing" the HKSAR in the future. To Beijing, however, its smooth enactment was one of the major achievements of the Edmund Ho administration in Macao.

The unique thing about Macao is the importance of **casino capitalism** in its economy—and therefore in its politics, as well. Macao developed as one of the main gambling havens in East Asia during the Portuguese colonial era. But Macao's casino sector has undergone significant expansion and transformation since the 1990s because of the growth of tourism in South China and the influx of foreign investment in the gambling industry, including huge sums by Las Vegas companies. The Macao SAR is now home to the world's largest casinos, and its gambling revenue now exceeds those of Las Vegas and Atlantic City, New Jersey, combined.

During the 1990s, gang warfare between underground **triad organizations** over access to casino turf, particularly the VIP rooms where rich businesspeople gambled, became commonplace. The arrest in November 1999 and imprisonment of one of the most flamboyant triad bosses helped to decrease the gang violence by sending a strong message that China intended to crack down hard after Macao reverted to Chinese sovereignty. In mid-2008 Beijing suddenly tightened the number of mainland visitors who were allowed to gamble in Macao, partly because of the need to control money laundering, cross-border crime, and illegal immigration. The central government was also concerned about the vicious competition among casino operators and the danger of an overgrown industry. The retrenchment policy initiated by Beijing and followed by the Ho administration has not really seriously affected gambling proceeds since Macao's casino sector relies much more on gamblers from Hong Kong and elsewhere than on those from the PRC. In July 2009, Fernando Chui Sai-on was elected as the Chief Executive of Macao, receiving 297 out of 300 votes from the Chief Executive Election Committee. As with Edmund Ho, Chui has emphasized Macao's need to focus on economic development rather than political reform, while forging ahead with the scheme of integrating with the mainland economically. Chui had been the secretary for social affairs and culture for ten years. As an experienced leader, Chui has realized the importance of improving the livelihood of the Macao people and maintaining Macao's casino capitalism as a driving force that brings about employment and economic prosperity.

In August 2017, a strong typhoon named Hato attacked Macao, killing ten people and plunging the city into chaos. The People's Liberation Army (PLA) Garrison in Macao had to be deployed to help the Macao government clean up the destroyed construction materials and debris caused by Hato. The Fernando Chui administration was criticized for poor preparation. The head of the Macao Observatory resigned as it was severely criticized for failing to alert the members of the public on the dangers of the strong typhoon. Although the Macao government invited a mainland delegation of experts to look into the ways in which Macao could learn from the typhoon, and even though it later published a report on the remedial measures that would be taken to prepare for any future typhoon, the weak capacity of the Macao administration in coping with sudden crises was fully exposed. It remains to be seen how the Macao bureaucracy can really enhance coordination among government departments to tackle any crisis, and how the disciplinary forces would be capable to tackle another typhoon without the need for the Macao government to request the mobilization of the PLA Garrison. Most importantly, the crisis consciousness of the members of the public on how to prepare for any new typhoon remains to be instilled; the education of the Macao citizens has to be enhanced to protect Macao from being plunged into chaos by another strong typhoon in the future.

The Hato attack on Macao was followed by the Legislative Council elections in September 2017, when five democrats were directly elected. They were Antonio Ng, Jose Coutinho, Au Kam-sun, Agnes Lam, and Sulu Sou. The young Sulu Sou, however, was later suspended from office for his unauthorized protest near the residence of Chief Executive Edmund Ho over a donation made by Macao Foundation to Jinan University in 2016. Fortunately, Sou returned to the legislature after paying a fine of MOP40,800 for his unlawful gathering as ruled by the Court of First Instance. Obviously, the political space in Macao is limited and the democrats have to learn how to conduct and augment their pro-democracy activities within the constrained political circumstances.

of the designated functional constituencies, at least one vote for a legislator. But because of Beijing's opposition, this was postponed to 1991. As a result of these changes, between 1991 and the turnover in 1997 more pro-democracy supporters were directly elected to the legislature. Although they did not constitute a majority in LegCo, the PRC government viewed them as a political menace and therefore attempted to apply the brakes on democratic reforms in Hong Kong.

However, when the last British governor of Hong Kong, Christopher Patten, arrived in 1992, he was determined to accelerate the pace and scope of democratic reform. Patten also adopted a confrontational approach to dealing with Beijing concerning the issue of political change in Hong Kong. Although his political reform package was approved narrowly by LegCo in 1993, Beijing was determined to thwart his plans. To do so, in 1996, it replaced LegCo with a handpicked Provisional Legislative Council that would handle transitional matters straddling the period from the July 1, 1997 turnover until new elections were held in 1998.

Despite the efforts of local supporters of greater democracy as well as Governor Patten to reform the legislature, the top policy-making body in Hong Kong, the **Executive Council**, was still composed of nonelected elites, including businesspeople and senior civil servants. In the 1980s, the British proposed that some Executive Council members be elected from among LegCo members. This bold idea was, as expected, rejected by the PRC, which wanted to maintain a powerful executive-led government in Hong Kong. Beijing's bottom line was clear: Hong Kong democrats would not be allowed to capture a majority of the seats in LegCo, and LegCo would remain less powerful than the Executive Council.

The judiciary in Hong Kong under British rule was basically independent of any control or interference from the executive, and equality before the law was a strictly observed norm. Moreover, the colonial government was constantly checked by the Independent Commission Against Corruption, which was set up in 1974 to tackle the serious problem of corruption within the bureaucracy, and by the Audit Commission, whose findings were often critical of departmental misuse of government funds. Although Hong Kong was not a Western-style democracy where the chief executive is directly elected by citizens through universal suffrage or chosen by a directly elected legislature, it had some of the trappings of a democratic system, including freedom of speech, press, and assembly; judicial independence; the rule of law; and internal checks and balances on public maladministration.

Political parties did not emerge in Hong Kong until shortly after the Tiananmen tragedy in China in June 1989. A wide range of parties, mostly split along pro-Beijing or pro-democracy lines, has been formed since then, but none has been able to capture a majority of seats in the Legislative Council,[1] which following the 2016 election has representatives from eighteen different political groups (and thirteen independents) among its seventy members. The major pro-Beijing parties are the Democratic Alliance for the Betterment and Progress of Hong Kong (DAB) and the Business and Professionals Alliance for Hong Kong (BPA).The main pro-democracy parties are the centrist Democratic Party and the professional-oriented Civic Party. New parties, including Younginspiration and Demosistō, represent growing, if still relatively small, support for Hong Kong independence from China.

The Chinese Communist Party (CCP) has traditionally operated in Hong Kong in a secretive manner. An underground CCP organization was established in colonial Hong Kong and was under the local supervision of the PRC's New China News Agency (*Xinhua*), which acted as the public cover for communist activities in the territory. The New China News Agency conducted activities beyond its media functions. It also engaged in intelligence gathering and united front work (i.e., building support for the PRC) targeted at the business, political, professional, grassroots, and religious sectors of Hong Kong society. After sovereignty over Hong Kong reverted to China, an official PRC Liaison Office was established to oversee Beijing's interests in the SAR.

The Basic Law gives responsibility for Hong Kong's defense to the government of the PRC. A 6,000-troop-strong garrison of the People's Liberation Army (PLA) is stationed in the SAR. It plays no active role in local police or security functions, although it does engage in joint exercises and liaison work with the Hong Kong police, for example on matters relating to terrorism. The PLA Hong Kong garrison also has a public relations function for the PRC as an important symbol of Chinese sovereignty.

Hong Kong prospered economically under British rule. It was (and still is) considered to have one of the freest market economies in the world. In 2017, it had a gross domestic product (GDP) per capita (at purchasing power parity) of $61,540, compared with US$59,532 in the United States and $443,279 in Japan. It is one of the world's great financial and commercial centers, and one of the PRC's main concerns in exercising its sovereignty over the HKSAR is to preserve its economic vitality.

FROM TUNG TO LAM: THE HKSAR'S FIRST FOUR CHIEF EXECUTIVES

The Basic Law of the HKSAR established the position of **chief executive** to be the head of the government. The chief executive must be a Chinese citizen, at least forty years old, and have lived in Hong Kong for twenty years or more. He or she is elected for a five-year term by an Election Committee, which currently consists of eight hundred members elected or appointed from various sectors of society, such as commerce, finance, labor, the professions, religion, and government. The composition of the Election Committee is closely controlled by Beijing, and the candidate elected has to be approved by the government of the PRC.

The first chief executive of the HKSAR was Tung Chee Hwa, who served from 1997 to 2005. Tung was a very wealthy shipping industry tycoon with strong ties to the PRC when he was tapped by Beijing to run Hong Kong. Although he was popular when he first took office, his term was quite politically turbulent. Tung implemented civil service and housing reforms that antagonized many career bureaucrats and the middle class. His civil service reforms included cuts in the number and salaries of civil servants, an increase in the number of key government leaders (called principal officials) directly appointed by the chief executive, and changes in how government contracts were given to the private sector. Many civil servants who had a vested interest in the status quo inherited from the colonial administration strongly opposed Tung's reform plans.

Tung's housing reforms embraced the idea of expanding the number of residential units built each year, intentionally driving down the sky-high prices on the Hong Kong housing market, but unintentionally affecting the interests of the many in the middle class who had speculated heavily in the property sector. Tung's reforms also coincided with the start of the Asian financial crisis in 1997–1998, which hit Hong Kong hard and plunged many middle-class citizens into economic difficulties as their assets declined drastically in value.[2]

The controversies stirred by Tung's civil service and housing reforms were compounded by his effort, with Beijing support, in September 2002 to pass and implement a tough antisubversion law under the terms of **Article 23** of the Basic Law, which deals with the security of the HKSAR. Many SAR citizens felt that security was adequately protected by existing Hong Kong laws governing treason, subversion, and the theft of state secrets; they feared that the new antisubversion law, if enacted, would be used to undermine civil liberties in Hong Kong. Other Hong Kong people believed that additional measures were needed to prevent espionage and subversion aimed against the PRC from occurring in the SAR. Not surprisingly, opposition to the anti-subversion law was strongest among those who identified themselves most closely with Hong Kong, while support for the law was strongest among those who identified with China (see Box 18.2).

The heated political controversy over Article 23 lasted until September 2003, when Tung announced that the so-called National Security (Legislative Provisions) Bill would be withdrawn and not reintroduced until public consultations were held. No timetable for reintroduction of the bill was mentioned. The bill's withdrawal was clearly due to strong public opposition that culminated in protests by half a million citizens on July 1, 2003. Shocked by the massive and unexpected public outcry against the bill, the PRC moved to calm the crisis by setting up a committee led by a CCP Politburo member to look into the situation. None of Tung's successors have moved to reintroduce the antisecession legislation, although Beijing clearly still wants to see such a law passed and enacted.[3]

To rescue Tung's declining popularity in 2003, Beijing decided to introduce two policies that would be beneficial to Hong Kong. One was the Closer Economic Partnership Arrangement (CEPA), which gave preferential treatment to Hong Kong companies that conducted business in the mainland. The other was the Individual Visit Scheme. This allowed individuals from mainland China to visit Hong Kong, whereas previously they had to be part of a tour group. It was hoped that this would stimulate the tourism industry in the HKSAR. Both policies were designed to offset the political alienation toward the PRC that many Hong Kong people were feeling at the time. The measures apparently worked well, since public attitudes toward the government and Chief Executive Tung improved after they were implemented.

Nevertheless, in March 2005, Tung tendered his resignation to the central government in Beijing, citing health reasons. Rumors were rife that he had lost the support of China's new leaders, including CCP general secretary and PRC president Hu Jintao and Premier Wen Jiabao. Tung had been supported by the former Chinese leader Jiang Zemin. With the gradual retirement of Jiang from the Chinese political arena in 2002–2003, Tung lost his main patron in Beijing.

BOX 18.2 NATIONAL IDENTITY IN HONG KONG

Although almost all Hong Kong people culturally identify themselves as Chinese, their political identities are divided between those who see themselves primarily as Chinese or as Hong Kong nationals. In 2007, a decade after Hong Kong returned to Chinese sovereignty, a poll conducted by Hong Kong University revealed that 55.2 percent of HKSAR residents identified themselves as "Chinese or Chinese in Hong Kong," while 43.2 percent said they considered themselves either as a "Hongkonger" or "Hongkonger in China." In a similar poll in June 2018, those who chose a Chinese identity had dropped to 29.8 percent, while 67.5 percent identified as Hongkongers.* Thirty-eight percent of respondents said they were proud to be PRC citizens, 57 percent said they were not proud of their citizenship, with the number dropping to only 16 percent among those between the ages of eighteen and twenty-nine.

Identity is a very important factor in Hong Kong politics and is reflected in different views on political reform in the HKSAR. Those citizens who tend to support the democrats are more likely to identify themselves as Hong Kong persons, whereas those who tend to vote for the pro-Beijing party in elections are more likely to be Chinese identifiers. Similarly, those people who strongly oppose the SCNPC interpretations of the Basic Law tend to be Hong Kong identifiers, while those who support the SCNPC interpretation are more likely to be Chinese identifiers. Moreover, those citizens who tend to support the double direct elections—universal suffrage in the election of the chief executive and the direct election of the whole legislature—are more likely to be Hong Kong identifiers, whereas those who side with a more gradual and piecemeal approach to political reform tend to be Chinese identifiers.

In recent years, the expression of local identity ("localism") in Hong Kong has taken the forms of antigovernment protests and nativism, which is an ideology that prioritizes the interests of native inhabitants over those of nonnatives, which in the HKSAR means those from the mainland. The emergence of nativist organizations can be traced to the opposition against the HKSAR government's plan to implement a Beijing-backed "moral and national education" secondary school curriculum starting in 2012. Students, teachers, and parents as well as pro-democracy groups accused the government of attempting to "brainwash" the younger generation. Students formed an interest group named "Scholarism," which helped organize a series of large public rallies and held a three-day hunger strike just prior to the September 2012 LegCo elections. In the face of such visible opposition, the government decided to delay the implementation of the controversial curriculum. Scholarism emerged as the leading organization in the 2014 Umbrella Movement protests in Hong Kong.

The rise of localist activism in Hong Kong is a testimony to the heightened political awareness and strong Hong Kong identity of the younger generation. This has been on display when, for example, young people have carried the flag of British-controlled Hong Kong at public rallies and in parades as a symbol of their view that things were better under British rule, especially in terms of government and politics. The pro-Beijing media has accused these young people of harboring "pro-colonial" sentiments. Indeed, some Hong Kong people do have nostalgia for certain aspects of the British era, but many more are worried about the "mainlandization" of Hong Kong, particularly the gradual erosion of civil liberties, pluralism, respect for human rights, and the rule of law.

An extreme form of localism in Hong Kong takes the form of supporting Hong Kong independence from China. Originally, a very tiny group of young Hong Kong people imagined such a possibility. But after HKSAR government leaders, notably the former chief executive C. Y. Leung, the pro-Beijing local media, and officials in Beijing severely criticized these "independentists," organizations supporting this radical notion have been ironically been expanding their membership and activities in the community. In

(Continued)

> **BOX 18.2 (Continued)**
>
> ───────────────────────────────
>
> August 2018, the Hong Kong government set in motion an attempt to legally ban the pro-independence Hong Kong National Party led by Andy Chan Ho-tin. To Beijing and its supporters in the HKSAR, this variant of localism is subversive and should be outlawed in order to safeguard the national security and territorial integrity of the People's Republic of China.

Patron-client relations between the Chinese leaders and the HKSAR chief executive persist and, in fact, are very much a part of Hong Kong's overall political culture. The chief executive is the client who needs the endorsement and support of patrons in Beijing, which confers legitimacy and authority on the Hong Kong leader.[4] Under the chief executive, there are, in turn, a whole range of clients, including the members of the top policy-making body, the Executive Council, the appointed members of various advisory and consultative committees, and influential business and other pro-establishment elites. Friends and followers of the chief executive are rewarded for their support with various favors and preferential treatment.

After Tung Chee Hwa's resignation, Beijing endorsed the American-trained (Harvard Kennedy School, MPA) civil servant Donald Tsang (Tsang Yam-kuen) as the new chief executive to serve out the remainder of Tung's term. Tsang had served in a sequence of high-level posts dealing with finance and administration in both the colonial and SAR governments. He was elected to a full five-year term as chief executive by the Election Committee on March 25, 2007, with 649 votes compared to 123 for his rival, Alan Leong of the pro-democracy Civic Party. This was the first time in the history of the HKSAR that the chief executive election had a candidate with political party affiliation. Leong's electoral participation was supported by moderate and mainstream democrats. The more radical democrats opposed the highly restricted "small circle election" and regarded Leong's participation as legitimizing an undemocratic electoral process.

In his first term of office, Donald Tsang steered clear of controversial matters. But after his reelection in 2007, some of his initiatives became more contentious. The most notable example was his expansion of the Principal Officials Accountability System (POAS), first established by the Tung administration to appoint loyal political supporters as the secretaries in charge of important policy areas in the Hong Kong government. The POAS was designed in part to protect the chief executive from being directly criticized for policy mistakes. The appointees also formed a loose coalition that could strengthen the system's legitimacy among important sectors of Hong Kong society. Tung's POAS system handled appointment to all the key positions in the HKSAR government, such as the chief secretary for administration (the second most powerful office) and the secretaries of finance; justice; commerce; industry and manpower; economic development; education; and the environment, health, and welfare.[5] These principal officials were hired on contractual terms, unlike civil servants who had permanent employment, and the length of their contract could not exceed the term in office of the chief executive who nominated them for appointment. In other words, they were political, rather than professional appointments.

In the summer of 2008, Donald Tsang expanded the POAS by adding seventeen undersecretaries and political assistants to the list of positions under its authority. But the fact that some of Tsang's appointees held foreign passports, including Singaporean, British, and Canadian, as well as their exorbitant salaries, aroused immediate public disapproval. Those undersecretaries who had foreign passports quickly renounced their non-Chinese citizenships. But the high salaries of the POAS appointees remained a source of public anger. Overall, the POAS became a patron-client mechanism for rewarding Tsang's supporters rather than a system of appointing HKSAR principal officials on the basis of their merits and talents. Tsang's expanded POAS proved to be as controversial as Tung's initial civil service reforms.

Toward the end of his second term in 2012, Tsang's image was tarnished by a scandal involving a businessman who had reportedly offered him a luxurious apartment across the border in Shenzhen. As a result of the scandal Tsang was not appointed as a vice chairman of the Chinese People's Political Consultative Conference (CPPCC), an honor that had been bestowed on Tung Chee Hwa soon after he stepped down in 2005. In July 2018, the Court of Appeal ruled that Tsang had concealed a conflict of interest and rejected his appeal against his conviction for misconduct in public office. Tsang's previous twenty-month sentence was reduced to twelve months, but the court verdict tarnished the reputation of the former Chief Executive.

On March 25, 2012, the HSKAR had its most hotly contested chief executive election. The top two vote-getters were both pro-Beijing and pro-establishment: Leung Chun-ying, or C. Y. Leung, won 689 out of 1,050 valid votes cast by members of the Election Committee; Henry Tang got just 285 votes even though had been staunchly supported by many important and wealthy business people. The third candidate, Albert Ho, from the pro-democracy Democratic Party, managed to get only 76 votes.

The electoral result was significant in several aspects. The central government in Beijing originally supported Tang but later changed its position to favor Leung on March 14 after Tang was plagued by a series of scandals, including extramarital affairs and illegal construction at his house. It was revealed that Leung, too, had had illegal work done on his home, and there were accusations of involvement of Hong Kong gang (triad) members in his campaign.

During an election forum Tang let it be known that in mid-2003, when the Executive Council was debating the proposed antisubversion law, Leung had spoken of the need to take strong measures against protestors who demonstrated outside the Legislative Council. Tang's remark shocked many Hong Kong people, who already had suspicions about Leung. Some of his critics claimed he was an underground member of the Chinese Communist Party in Hong Kong. Leung adamantly denied that he was a member of any political party, but deep distrust toward him had already been sown among a public that did not have the right to vote for their chief executive and could only watch the scandals and controversies swirling around the two pro-establishment candidates.

Leung's administration got off to a rocky start. His appointee as secretary for development, Mak Chai-kwong, resigned after just twelve days in office following charges of financial fraud, and this came after the departure of two Executive Council members, one due to potential conflicts of interest and the other because of a police investigation into the failure of a commodities exchange he had founded.

Rumors were rife in the Hong Kong media that China planned to replace Leung with someone more competent. Although Beijing denied that it had such a plan, it was certainly concerned about the increasing unhappiness of Hong Kong people with the HKSAR government: A poll taken in June 2013 showed that only 13.3 percent of those surveyed were satisfied with the political situation in Hong Kong, down from a high of nearly 60 percent on the eve of the 1997 takeover.[6] Beijing saw the 2012 chief executive election as a negative phenomenon that split the pro-establishment camp while giving a golden opportunity for the political opposition in Hong Kong to undermine the legitimacy of the HKSAR government.

In March 2017, Carrie Lam Cheng Yuet-ngor was elected as the fourth chief executive of the HKSAR with 777 votes, defeating a former Financial Secretary John Tsang (365 votes) and a former court judge Woo Kwok-hing (21 votes). Beijing favored and supported Lam as she had been observed carefully as a politically reliable and loyal chief executive, while Tsang and Woo tended to be far more politically liberal, which was unacceptable to the central government. After her electoral victory, Lam focused on how to improve the livelihood of the Hong Kong people. She also maintains a politically obedient attitude toward Beijing, especially on the central government's national security position of regarding any remarks and actions in support of "Hong Kong independence" as politically undesirable and unacceptable. In mid-2018, an invitation made by the Foreign Correspondents Club in Hong Kong to Andy Chan Ho-tin, the founder of the pro-independence Hong Kong National Party, to speak at the club on the topic of "A Politically Incorrect Guide to Hong Kong under Chinese Rule" was criticized by both the Chinese Foreign Ministry and the HKSAR Chief Executive, raising new fear about the future of freedom of speech in Hong Kong.[7] Around the same time, such fears were amplified when the Hong Kong police sought to use a law on the book to ban the party on the grounds of national security and seeking to undermine China's territorial integrity.[8] The emergence of groups advocating that Hong Kong declare its independence from the PRC has become a worry for Beijing and a source of tension in HKSAR politics.

INTERPRETING THE BASIC LAW

Four specific interpretations of the Basic Law by the Standing Committee of the National People's Congress (SCNPC), which is the PRC body formally charged with authority over the HKSAR, were particularly controversial during the Tung, Tsang, and Leung administrations.

The first concerned the Basic Law's stipulation on the right of abode of mainland Chinese nationals in Hong Kong, which says that PRC citizens are allowed to live, work, and vote in Hong Kong under certain circumstances. In January 1999, the Court of Final Appeal, the highest judicial authority in Hong Kong, ruled that the right of abode also applied to children of Chinese nationals residing in the SAR. After the ruling, the HKSAR government estimated that 1.67 million mainlanders would flood into the territory and asked the SCNPC to review the matter.[9] In June 1999, the SCNPC overturned the decision of the Court of Final Appeals and allowed the HKSAR to invoke more restrictive measures on the right of abode.

Supporters of the SCNPC interpretation believed that it was necessary to stabilize Hong Kong by stemming the influx of a large number of mainland Chinese, a position, according the public opinion polls, favored by a majority of HKSAR residents. Opponents of the SCNPC ruling argued that it amounted to political interference with judicial independence of the Court of Final Appeal, and that the size of the projected influx of Chinese nationals was an exaggeration. They were most concerned about the implications for the preservation of the rule of law in Hong Kong.

The second interpretation of the Basic Law by the SCNPC that proved controversial in Hong Kong occurred in April 2004, nine months after five thousand protesters had taken to the streets to protest the Tung administration's effort to pass the antisubversion law. In the aftermath of the success of those protests, Hong Kong democrats began to press for the direct election by universal suffrage of the chief executive in 2007 and of the entire legislature in 2008. The SCNPC settled the matter by ruling that such elections would violate the Basic Law. This hardline interpretation of the Basic Law coincided with the reelection in Taiwan of President Chen Shui-bian of the pro-independence **Democratic Progressive Party** (see chap. 19). Clearly, the SCNPC interpretation of the Hong Kong Basic Law reflected Beijing's determination to prevent the "Taiwanization" of HKSAR politics through the introduction of more democratic elections procedures for either the executive or the legislature.

The third controversial SCNPC interpretation of the Basic Law took place in April 2005, a month after Chief Executive Tung's resignation. Some members of the Hong Kong legal community pointed to Article 46 of the Basic Law, which states that the chief executive's term of office is five years, and therefore argued that Tung's successor should serve a full five-year term. Originally, the HKSAR government adopted this legal interpretation; nevertheless, after the HKSAR Secretary for Justice Elsie Leung visited Beijing, the Hong Kong government sided with Beijing's view that Tung's successor should serve only *the remainder* of his term before standing for reelection for a full five-year term, which is how the SCNPC ruled. The PRC was eager to establish the precedent that, in the event of any sudden resignation of the chief executive, they would have time to assess the new leader's performance before committing to a five-year term.

Opponents of each of these three interpretations of the Basic Law by the SCNPC believed they were based more on political considerations than on purely legal grounds. They saw them as a reflection of a worrisome trend away from the legal tradition inherited from the British that emphasized the rule of law over politics and toward the PRC's legal system in which politics can trump the rule of law (see chap. 7). The clash between these two fundamentally different legal cultures remains another source of tension and controversy in Hong Kong politics.

POLITICAL REFORM IN HONG KONG

In November 2005, the Tsang government published a document on political reform in the HKSAR. The government's proposals included an expansion, in 2007, of the Election Committee that selects the chief executive from 800 to 1,600 members. It also proposed that LegCo be expanded to from 60 to 70 members in 2008, with 6 elected by Hong Kong's local advisory boards, called District Councils, which are made up of both elected and appointed members. But the reform package did not gain the required two-thirds support of Legislative Councilors when it was presented to LegCo on December 21, 2005. It was rejected by a 34 to 24 vote with one abstention. Pro-democracy legislators opposed the reform proposals because they did not address their demand for the direct election of the chief executive by universal suffrage in 2012.

The HKSAR government tried to lessen the democrats' opposition to its reform package by proposing that the appointed District Councilors would gradually be phased out and replaced by elected members. The democrats rejected this concession, however. This tussle over political reform further deepened the mutual distrust between the democrats and both the Tsang administration and Beijing.

In order to demonstrate to the public that the HKSAR government had not abandoned political reform, in mid-2007 the Tsang administration began a three-month public consultation process on the question of constitutional development in Hong Kong. In December 2007, Tsang submitted a report to Beijing saying that the Hong Kong public generally supported democratization of the electoral process with the eventual goal of universal suffrage in choosing the chief executive and the members of the Legislative Council. Many in Hong Kong wanted this to be implemented in 2012, but others wanted to move more slowly. Tsang concluded that these political reforms would have a greater chance of being accepted by the majority of Hong Kong people if they were set for 2017.

In response to the report, the SCNPC reached a decision on December 29, 2007, stating that the chief executive and the Legislative Council would *not* be chosen by universal suffrage in 2012; that LegCo would retain the half-and-half ratio of members returned from geographical constituencies and functional constituencies in the 2012 elections; and that any amendment to the method of electing the chief executive must be reported to the SCNPC for approval. But the SCNPC did rule that the chief executive would be chosen by universal suffrage in 2017 and, following that "the election of the Legislative Council of Hong Kong Special Administrative Region may be implemented by the method of electing all members by universal suffrage."[10]

In 2010, key elements of Tsang's 2005 reform package were implemented: LegCo was to be expanded to seventy members and the Election Committee that chooses the chief executive to twelve hundred members. Radical democrats again rejected the reforms as not going far enough. But the changes were approved by LegCo because of a split within the pro-democracy parties, with the centrist Democratic Party backing the government (and Beijing-approved) proposal. During the campaign waged by both supporters and opponents of the reforms there was an unprecedented televised debate between Chief Executive Tsang and Audrey Eu, the head of the pro-democracy Civic Party.

In the 2012 LegCo elections, pro-democrats managed to win twenty-seven out of seventy seats in the legislature. Although the mass media portrayed this as a "failure" for the pro-democracy parties, the reality was that the democrats had succeeded in winning more than one-third of the seats in the legislature. Given that government bills need the endorsement of two-thirds of LegCo members, the democratic front was able block the passage of legislation, including political reform bills it regarded as too conservative. In this sense, the democratic front (also referred to as "pan-democrats") in Hong Kong came to constitute a "negative" veto inside the Legislative Council against the power and influence of the government. As such, pan-democrats in the HKSAR have been far more politically influential and powerful than the local mass media have portrayed.

Another very important outcome of the 2012 LegCo elections was that the radical democratic coalition—People Power—won 9.8 percent of the votes and three directly elected seats, while the more established Democratic Party won only six seats in its worst showing since 1994. The People Power coalition was supported by many young Hong Kong people with a very strong sense of local identity. This reflected a momentous shift among pan-democrats to a more radical and confrontational agenda.

At the same time, the pro-Beijing forces did not perform well in the voting for the directly elected LegCo seats in 2012, winning just 34 percent of the votes. The fact that their allies got well below half of the total votes in direct elections probably made Beijing more than a bit nervous about allowing the HKSAR to have a fully directly elected legislature, not to mention a chief executive chosen by universal suffrage.

FROM OCCUPY CENTRAL TO THE UMBRELLA MOVEMENT

The planning for an act of civil disobedience in the city's main business district to pressure the HKSAR government and the PRC to fulfill the promise of choosing both the chief executive and LegCo by universal suffrage in the next round of elections was begun in early 2013 by the legal scholar Benny Tai Yiu-ting, the sociologist Chan Kin-man, and a Baptist minister, Chu Yiu-ming. They originally planned for a short-term nonviolent protest that they called "Occupy Central with Love and Peace," which was to take place in October 2014. They quickly gained the support of other organizations, notably the student groups, particularly the Hong Kong Federation of Students (HKFS) and "Scholarism," an organization formed in 2011 to protest plans to introduce a Beijing-guided school curriculum.

In August 2014, the SCNPC approved a plan by which two or three candidates for chief executive who had the support of at least half of a Nominating Committee's twelve hundred members would be presented to all eligible HKSAR voters in the election scheduled for March 2017. It further declared that the chief executive "shall be a person who loves the country [China] and loves Hong Kong" and that "the method for selecting the chief executive by universal suffrage must provide corresponding institutional safeguards" to "maintain long-term prosperity and stability of Hong Kong and uphold the sovereignty, security and development interests of the country."[11] Beijing also affirmed its right of final approval and appointment of the new chief executive.

The pan-democrats found this electoral model to be unacceptable and "pseudo-democratic," and, in protest on September 26, 2014, pro-democracy university students boycotted their classes, and led by the HKSF and Scholarism took over the Civic Square outside the HKSAR Government, triggering the beginning of the **Occupy Central** protest. Scholarism leader, then eighteen-year-old Joshua Wong, was among the seventy-four protesters immediately detained by the police. In response, more citizens flocked to the Central District to support the democracy movement. On the afternoon of September 28 police used tear gas, pepper spray, and batons to disperse the crowd of protestors, many of whom raised their umbrellas to protect themselves from the eye irritants. This signaled the transition from Occupy Central to the so-called **Umbrella Movement** that lasted for seventy-nine days until December 15.[12] During that time, protests spread to other areas of Hong Kong such as Mongkok and Causeway Bay, two bustling shopping districts in the HKSAR.

The Umbrella Movement was politically significant in several regards. First, it failed to pressure the central government in Beijing and the Hong Kong administration to make any concession on the scope and pace of political reform. A meeting between the student activists and the government leaders was held on October 21, but it came to nothing as both sides did not want to project an image of being "soft" by making any concessions.

Second, the disorganized and chaotic nature of the Umbrella Movement, which was intentionally or unintentionally taken over by radical student activists, illustrated the deeply fragmented feature of the pan-democratic forces in Hong Kong. The three leaders of Occupy Central had badly miscalculated the situation and turned themselves in at the central police station on December 3, while many mainstream democrats remained relatively silent and inactive throughout.

Third, the government wisely adopted a wait-it-out strategy to let public opinion change in such a way as to discredit the entire Umbrella Movement. While the shopkeepers and business people were against the movement from the beginning because of its negative economic impact, pro-government groups launched a media campaign to discredit the protests. Many ordinary citizens who had felt some sympathy for the demonstrations and had recoiled at the use of force by the police grew tired of the disruption, which not only affected traffic but also threatened the social stability and economic prosperity of Hong Kong,

Fourth, the central government in Beijing saw the movement as an attempt at undermining the national security of China and the authority of the Hong Kong government. Its position was clear: the people of Hong Kong, including the pan-democrats, should accept the August 2014 electoral plan of the Standing Committee of the National People's Congress. In the aftermath of the Umbrella Movement, it seems clear that the democrats cannot easily use a sociopolitical campaign to exert pressure on China to make concessions on the pace and scope of political reform because Beijing still sees full democratization in Hong Kong as a possible wedge for undermining the authority of the CCP on the mainland as well as endangering the national security of the PRC.

Although the Umbrella Movement failed in its most immediate objectives, it triggered unprecedented public political discourse. Every night during the protests, occupiers discussed and debated politics among themselves and with interested citizens. They also produced a remarkable range of politically inspired artworks of all kinds, many of which drew on the umbrella symbol of the movement, that attracted large crowds. In the end, the Umbrella Movement had the important effect of raising the political awareness, interest, and participation of a part of the public in ways that are bound to influence Hong Kong politics in the future.

THE 2016 LEGCO ELECTIONS

The September 2016 Legislative Council election resulted in an increase in number of antiestablishment legislators, from twenty-seven to twenty-nine seats, and a decline from forty-three to forty for the pro-establishment side (and one independent). But the most surprising part of this outcome was that among the victorious antiestablishment candidates were six young so-called "localists" who advocated Hong Kong independence from the PRC. One important reason for the victory of the localists was the continuing refusal of the PRC to make any concession on Hong Kong's political reform.

But two events in the months before the election also influenced the outcome. The first was the sudden disappearance of five Hong Kong booksellers between August and December 2015 and the speculation that that they had been kidnapped by Chinese national security agents and brought to the mainland to be charged with for distributing politically sensitive books about China.[13] The books in question touched on issues such as corruption and sex scandals among the party elite and the personal ambitions of Xi Jinping to prolong his rule in China along the lines of Russian leader Vladimir Putin. All five booksellers reappeared in the first half of 2016, saying they had gone to the PRC voluntarily and confessing to engaging in illegal activities in the PRC. But in June 2016, one of the booksellers, Lam Wing-kee, said at a press conference that he and the others had been abducted by Chinese agents and forced to confess, charges that were denied by Beijing, which said that Lam "is a Chinese citizen" who "violated China's laws on the mainland," and that "Relevant authorities in China are authorized to handle the case in accordance with the law."[14] The whole saga deepened the worries of many in Hong Kong about the PRC's encroachment on the territory's founding principle of "One country, Two systems," including respect for the rule of law and independence of the judicial system in the HKSAR.

The second event that influenced the 2016 LegCo election was a large-scale riot that took place in the Mongkok district on February 8 and 9 of that year. The immediate cause was a crackdown on unlicensed street vendors selling popular foods during the Chinese Lunar New Year holiday. When student localists came to the vendors' defense, violence between protesters and the police broke out, leading to the arrest of many activists. Many young Hong Kong people were angered by what they saw as the unreasonable treatment of some hawkers in the Mongkok district and the "excessive" use of force by the police on the localists. This, in turn, stimulated many of them to go to the polls on September 4, 2016, and vote for localist candidates.

The 2016 Legislative Council elections marked a generational change in the political landscape of Hong Kong. Some pro-Beijing veteran politicians decided not to run for reelection, while several prominent pan-democrats also withdrew from politics. The six elected localists averaged little more than thirty years of age.

But the new localist legislators-elect decided to challenge the authority of the central government in Beijing during the oath-taking ceremony on October 16, 2016. Baggio Leung and Yau Wai-ching took the lead by displaying a banner that said "Hong Kong is not China," in English and, again in English, mispronouncing China as "Jeena," a derogatory term used by the Japanese to refer to the country and the Chinese people during the Sino-Japanese War of 1937–1945. Beijing saw these moves as insulting and totally unacceptable. The Standing Committee of the National People's Congress proceeded to interpret the Basic Law as meaning that an official oath must be taken as written or the elected candidate will be disqualified from assuming office. The Hong Kong High Court then ruled that Leung and Yau could not be seated as legislators. Subsequently, two more localists and two radical pro-democrats were also disqualified for oath-taking violations. In four special elections (by-electionso held in March 2018 to fill the vacancies, the pro-democrat and pro-Beijing camps each won two seats. Two LegCo seats remained unfilled pending legal appeals of the disqualifications.

With the benefit of hindsight, the localists and radical democrats elected to the Legislative Council in 2016, but were disqualified from taking their LegCo seats, might have displayed political immaturity by using the symbolic oath-taking ceremony to challenge Beijing so directly and therefore losing the opportunity to make their views heard and votes counted in the HKSAR legislature. Many among the more moderate antiestablishment forces were dismayed by this turn of events, which revealed the profound mutual distrust that persists within and ultimately weakens that side of the political spectrum in Hong Kong.

HONG KONG: SEMICOLONY OR SEMIDEMOCRACY?

Under the prevailing situation in which the interpretation of the Basic Law is under the final jurisdiction of the SCNPC, and political reform ultimately depends on the will of the central government in Beijing, it could be said that the Hong Kong political system remains largely semicolonial. The executive branch is more powerful than the legislature, and even in LegCo, pro-government and pro-Beijing elites can check the influence of the pro-democracy legislators. Advisory bodies and consultative committees are filled through political appointments with people who favor the go-slow status quo, whereas pro-democracy voices are politically excluded or marginalized.

But antiestablishment parties are very visible and increasingly successful in electoral politics, and most elections are quite competitive and run according to democratic procedures. There are also important nonparty democratic elements in Hong Kong. Interest groups and the mass media, both of which are part of the SAR's strong civil society representing a wide variety of political views, are active and influential.

In general, business interest groups tend to be far more influential than the pro-democracy groups because of the conservative nature of the HKSAR administration. Workers are particularly well-organized and have their interests represented by two rival unions, the pro-Beijing Federation of Trade Unions (FTU) and the pro-democracy Confederation of Trade Unions (CTU). The FTU usually forms an alliance with the pro-Beijing DAB party in Legislative Council and other elections, whereas the CTU constantly supports the democratic camp in elections. Both trade unions compete fiercely for labor support whenever issues affecting working-class rights and interests surface. The CTU tends to mobilize disgruntled workers to protest against the government, but the FTU tries to moderate protests in order to avoid undermining the HKSAR authorities. In the wake of the Umbrella Movement of 2014, student and youth organizations have become particularly active and vocal.

All in all, Hong Kong has also maintained its long tradition of a lively, independent press. There are some concerns about media self-censorship in Hong Kong when it comes to reporting about political issues, especially by those outlets whose owners eye the lucrative China market and whose proprietors and editors are the targets of political co-optation or pressure by PRC officials in the HKSAR. But many newspapers and other media sources, especially the increasing important cyberspace radio programs and Internet news organizations, often voice strong criticisms of both the HKSAR and the PRC governments.

Public oversight of the government remains strong in some important regards, perhaps due to the British legacy of having a robust and respected Independent Commission Against Corruption (ICAC). Although the ICAC was plagued by internal management problems before the handover of Hong Kong, its performance remains relatively stable and commands the support of an overwhelming majority of the Hong Kong people. Other mechanisms that provide checks and balances against the abuse of power within the HKSAR political system include the Office of the Ombudsman and the Audit Commission. The ombudsman, who is appointed by the chief executive, serves as a public "watchdog" and handles complaints by individuals or organizations concerning maladministration by government departments and agencies; it also has some investigative powers of its own. The Audit Commission checks the budgets and expenditures of government departments. The HKSAR civil service remains relatively honest, capable, competent, and politically neutral.

And there is probably no more vibrant symbol of the democratic spirit in Hong Kong than the annual candlelight vigil held in Victoria Park every June 4 to commemorate the Tiananmen Square protests in Beijing on that date in 1989. Although official and organizer estimates vary, the event draws tens of thousands of participants every year.

After the Occupy Central and Umbrella Movements, the Mongkok riot, and the disqualification of two legislators-elect and then four other legislators, the political atmosphere in Hong Kong appears to have taken a turn for the worse. The chief executive elected in 2017, Carrie Lam, has vowed to tackle livelihood issues before any discussion on political reform, but some young Hong Kong people who are imbued with postmaterialist values, notably human rights, social justice, and democracy, see her as a political puppet of Beijing and have started using the term "authoritarianism" to describe Hong Kong's political system.

Objectively speaking, Hong Kong's political system remains far more pluralistic than China's. If soft authoritarianism as a type of political system is defined as the occasional repression of dissident and use its power to impose its will, Hong Kong's polity appears to be drifting slowly, with resistance from many members of the public, in that direction. Recent court decision that have punished activist protestors and politicians, such as the re-jailing of Joshua Wong in early 2018 on charges stemming from his role in the 2014 Umbrella Movement,[15] and mounting attacks by the HKSAR establishment and Beijing on Occupy Central's founder, Benny Tai,[16] are very disconcerting.

Overall, it may be said that contemporary Hong Kong has elements of both a semicolonial and a semidemocratic political system. The interaction of these two opposing tendencies will shape Hong Kong's future political development. How this will play out is quite unpredictable, except to say that much depends on the impact on the HKSAR cycles of tightening and loosening that have characterized politics in the PRC for much of the post-Mao era.[17]

NOTES

1. Suzanne Pepper, *Keeping Democracy at Bay: Hong Kong and the Challenge of Chinese Political Reform* (Lanham: Rowman & Littlefield, 2008), chap. 12.

2. Lo Shiu-Hing, *Governing Hong Kong: Legitimacy, Communication and Political Decay* (New York: Nova Science, 2001).

3. Ng Kang-chung, "Fear and Loathing: Which Way Forward for Article 23 National Security Law in Face of Stiff Opposition in Hong Kong?." *South China Morning Post*, Nov. 22, 2017, https://www.scmp.com/news/hong-kong/politics/article/2121035/fear-and-loathing-which-way-forward-article-23-national; and Stuart Lau and Tony Cheung, "Beijing Signals Impatience at Hong Kong's Delay in Enacting National Security Law," *South China Morning Post*, Nov.16, 2017, https://www.scmp.com/news/hong-kong/politics/article/2120195/beijing-signals-impatience-hong-kongs-delay-enacting

4. Bruce Kwong, "Patron-Client Politics in Hong Kong: A Study of the 2002 and 2005 Chief Executive Elections," *Journal of Contemporary China* 16, no. 52 (2007): 389–415.

5. Christine Loh and Richard Cullen, "Political Reform in Hong Kong: The Principal Officials Accountability System, The First Year (2002–2003)," *Journal of Contemporary China* 14, no. 42 (Feb. 2005): 153–176.

6. Hong Kong University Public Opinion Programme, http://hkupop.hku.hk/english/.

7. Kelly Olsen, "Hong Kong's Autonomy in Focus Amid Calls to Cancel Speech by Pro-independence Politician," CNBC, Aug. 8, 2018, https://www.cnbc.com/2018/08/09/hong-kong-autonomy-in-focus-over-talk-by-pro-independence-politician.html

8. Austin Ramzy, "Hong Kong May Ban Political Party That Seeks Independence From China," *New York Times*, July 17, 2018, https://www.nytimes.com/2018/07/17/world/asia/hong-kong-ban-independence-party.html

9. Sonny Lo, *The Dynamics of Beijing-Hong Kong Relations: A Model for Taiwan?* (Hong Kong: Hong Kong University Press, 2008), chap. 3.

10. "Decision of the Standing Committee of the National People's Congress on Issues Relating to the Methods for Selecting the Chief Executive of the Hong Kong," Adopted by the Standing Committee of the Tenth National People's Congress at its thirty-first meeting on Dec. 29, 2007, http://www.npc.gov.cn/englishnpc/Law/2009-02/26/content_1473392.htm

11. "Full text: NPC Standing Committee Decision on Hong Kong 2017 Election Framework," *South China Morning Post*, Aug. 31, 2014, https://www.scmp.com/news/hong-kong/article/1582245/full-text-npc-standing-committee-decision-hong-kong-2017-election

12. Samson Yuen, "Hong Kong After the Umbrella Movement: An Uncertain Future for "One Country Two Systems," *China Perspectives*, 2015, no. 1 (Mar. 2015), 49–53.

13. Alex W. Palmer, "The Case of Hong Kong's Missing Booksellers," *New York Times*, Apr. 3, 2018, https://www.nytimes.com/2018/04/03/magazine/the-case-of-hong-kongs-missing-booksellers.html

14. Phila Siu and Tony Cheung, "Bookseller Lam Wing-kee Is a Chinese National Who Broke Mainland Law and Beijing Has the Right to Deal With Him, Ministry Declares," *South China Morning Post*, June 17, 2016, https://www.scmp.com/news/hong-kong/politics/article/1976912/bookseller-lam-wing-kee-chinese-national-who-broke-mainland

15. James Griffiths, "Hong Kong Activist Joshua Wong Jailed Again," CNN, Jan. 17, 2018, https://www.cnn.com/2018/01/17/asia/hong-kong-joshua-wong-jailed-intl/index.html

16. Suzanne Pepper, "Free Speech: Hong Kong's New Limits, New Punishments, and the Fate of Academic Benny Tai," *Hong Kong Free Press*, Apr. 29, 2018, https://www.hongkongfp.com/2018/04/29/free-speech-hong-kongs-new-limits-new-punishments-fate-academic-benny-tai/

17. See Richard Baum, *Burying Mao: Chinese Politics in the Age of Deng Xiaoping.* (Princeton, NJ: Princeton University Press, 1996).

SUGGESTED READINGS

Kwong, Bruce Kam-kwan. *Patron-Client Politics and Elections in Hong Kong.* New York: Routledge, 2010.

Lee, Leo Ou-fan. *City between Worlds: My Hong Kong.* Cambridge, MA: Belknap Press of Harvard University Press, 2008.

Lo, Sonny. "Casino Capitalism and Its Legitimacy Impact on the Politico-administrative State in Macao," *Journal of Current Chinese Affairs: China Aktuell* 18, no. 1, (2009): 17–49.

Lo, Sonny. *The Dynamics of Beijing-Hong Kong Relations: A Model for Taiwan.* Hong Kong: Hong Kong University Press, 2008.

Lo, Sonny Shiu-Hing. *Hong Kong's Indigenous Democracy.* London: Palgrave, 2015.

Lo, Sonny Shiu-Hing. *Political Change in Macao.* London: Routledge, 2008.

Lo, Sonny Shiu-Hing, *The Politics of Policing in Greater China.* London: Palgrave, 2016.

Lui, Tai-lok, Stephen W. K. Chiu, and Ray Yep, eds. *Routledge Handbook of Contemporary Hong Kong.* New York: Routledge, 2018.

Manion, Melanie. *Corruption by Design Building Clean Government in Mainland China and Hong Kong.* Cambridge, MA: Harvard University Press, 2004.

Pepper, Suzanne. *Keeping Democracy at Bay: Hong Kong and the Challenge of Chinese Political Reform.* Lanham, MD: Rowman & Littlefield, 2008.

Tsai, Yongshun, *The Occupy Movement in Hong Kong: Sustaining Decentralized Protest.* New York: Routledge, 2018.

Tsang, Steve. *A Modern History of Hong Kong.* London: I. B. Tauris, 2007.

19

Taiwan

SHELLEY RIGGER

In the summer of 2007, young people in Taiwan discovered an online game called "Click Click Click." The game is simple: visit a website (www.clickclickclick.com) and click a button. The site credits your click to your country; the winner is the country with the largest number of clicks when the game ends. In the first round of the game, netizens from eighty-four countries outclicked Taiwanese; in the next three rounds, Taiwan inched up to fifty-eighth place. Then, in round six, Taiwan caught fire. Taiwan's cyberspace lit up with websites and online videos exhorting young people to get on the site and "Click Click Click" for Taiwan. Taiwan leapt to third place, then second, then, in round seven, to first. Taiwanese logged 1.3 *billion* clicks in seven days.

Taiwan is an island of twenty-three million people; the winning total represented fifty-five clicks for every man, woman, and child in the country—in a game that few Taiwanese over thirty had ever heard of. How did Taiwan pull off this remarkable feat? And why?

The how is straightforward: once Taiwanese decided to get into the game to win, they launched an all-out assault. They used every available technology—word of mouth, viral video, email, text messaging—to promote the game. They blanketed the web with videos and graphics that urged "clickers" on. In the virtual world of the internet, "Click Click Click" became a war fought by anime-style cartoon girls dressed (barely) in the national flags of the leading countries—Taiwan, Japan, and Hungary. As the competition heated up, amateur programmers built robot programs to run up vast numbers of clicks. When the game sponsor changed its software to stop the bots, Taiwan's programmers developed new ones.

Winning the game turned out to be a matter of human mobilization and technical skill—two things Taiwan is very good at. But why did so many people devote so many hours to an activity that most people would consider utterly pointless?

The "Click Click Click" craze is a testament to the power of fads, no doubt, and a tribute to the technical savvy of Taiwanese youth. But it also reveals a deep desire for international recognition that permeates Taiwan's society.

Taiwan is different from other countries; it is controversial even to *call* it a country. It has a government—democratically elected in free, fair, competitive elections—that makes and enforces laws, collects taxes, and sustains a modern military, but it does not have a seat in the United Nations or an embassy in a major world capital. Newspapers in mainland China refer to its government as the "Taiwan authorities," and put scare quotes around its leaders' titles: "president" Tsai Ing-wen and "premier" Lai Ching-de.

Although it is small geographically and demographically, Taiwan is one of the world's largest economies—it ranks in the top twenty in both gross domestic product (GDP) per capita and total trade and has the world's sixth-largest foreign exchange reserves—but Taiwan's national economic statistics are not reported by the World Bank. It was not until 2009 that it gained participant—not member—status in the World Health Organization, under the name "Chinese Taipei," and it is forbidden to join international agreements (it complies voluntarily with many conventions, even though it is denied the benefits of participation). The leading U.S. high-tech companies depend on Taiwanese firms for engineering and manufacturing services, but a Taiwanese political leader can set foot in the United States only if he or she is on an approved stopover en route to another destination.

Isolation makes Taiwanese work overtime to remind the world that "we are here." Their efforts range from the "Click Click Click" wars to the Taiwan government's quixotic campaign to participate in United Nations-related groups—an effort that is now in its third fruitless decade.

Taiwan's exclusion from the world community is a product of history, but it is sustained and reinforced by the PRC government's unrelenting determination to deny the island international recognition. Beijing's position is that Taiwan is part of China, and since the People's Republic of China (PRC) is the legal government of China, Taiwan's international representation should be channeled through Beijing. Although the PRC has never governed Taiwan, its National People's Congress includes deputies claiming to represent the island, and Beijing requires international organizations to secure its permission before conducting any business regarding Taiwan. China calls this "exercising sovereignty"; Taiwanese call it "diplomatic strangulation."

Taiwan's unique international position makes it a fascinating place to study, while its complex relationships with the world's major powers make it an important geostrategic player. It also is an economic powerhouse whose influence far exceeds its size. And it is an intriguing case for students of politics: a culturally Chinese society that overcame colonization and authoritarianism to create a free-wheeling liberal democracy.

TAIWAN TO 1945

Taiwan is a volcanic island about 120 kilometers (75 mi) off the coast of southeastern China. At just under 36,000 square kilometers (13,892 sq mi) in area, it is larger than Belgium but smaller than Switzerland. From the perspective of comparative islands, Taiwan is about 15 percent the size of Britain. The island is mountainous, with peaks up to 4,000 meters (13,100 ft). Most of Taiwan's population lives on a broad plain on the west coast and in the northwestern basin where the capital, Taipei, is located. On the northeast coast, the mountains plunge straight into the sea; the southeastern plain is narrow and remote. With high mountains occupying most of the island, Taiwan's inhabited area is one of the most densely populated places in the world.

Four thousand years ago, Austronesian-speaking settlers from other Western Pacific islands began living in Taiwan. Their descendants, who belong to more than a dozen distinct groups, are collectively referred to as Taiwan's indigenous peoples (*yuan zhu min*). There are about 530,000 indigenous people living in Taiwan today.

Beginning in the sixteenth century, indigenous peoples were joined by settlers from mainland China. Most came from Fujian, the Chinese province directly across the **Taiwan Strait**, the part of the Pacific Ocean that separates the island from the mainland. Eventually, the Aboriginal people living along the western plain were either assimilated or displaced, and the region sprouted stable communities of Chinese migrants. In the mid-1500s, a passenger on a Portuguese ship passing by Taiwan called the island "Ilha Formosa," or beautiful island, giving it a name Europeans used for centuries.

In 1623, Dutch traders established a commercial colony in southwestern Taiwan. In the north, Spanish colonists launched a parallel operation with forts at Tamsui and Keelung. The local Chinese called the Spanish fort of San Domingo the "Red Hair Fort" in recognition of the Europeans' extraordinary hairiness and odd coloration.

In the early 1600s, the pirate Zheng Zhilong operated a large fleet in the Taiwan Strait. When the Dutch expelled him from his base in Taiwan, Zheng put his pirate armada in the service of the Ming empire. The Ming was overthrown and replaced by the Qing dynasty in 1644, but Zheng Zhilong's son, Zheng Chenggong, remained loyal to the Ming. Acting in the name of the Ming, Zheng Chenggong drove the Dutch out of Taiwan. He used his naval forces to keep Taiwan out of Qing hands for two more decades, but in 1683, forces led by Zheng Chenggong's grandson fell to defeat at the hands of the Qing admiral Shi Lang.

This historical episode bears uncanny parallels to events four hundred years later. In 1945, forces of the Republic of China (ROC) under Chiang Kai-shek took the island from a foreign colonizer (Japan). Within a few years, a new government (the PRC) came to power in mainland China, but Taiwan's leaders remained faithful to the ROC. Under the Chiang family "dynasty" until the late 1980s, ROC loyalists struggled to recapture the mainland while resisting Communist efforts to bring Taiwan under PRC control. Where the twentieth century diverges from the seventeenth is in the absence (to date) of a modern-day Shi Lang who brings the island back under the control of the mainland government.

Between these episodes of change and resistance, Chinese settlements on Taiwan expanded, first under the Qing, then under Japanese colonial rule. Japan seized

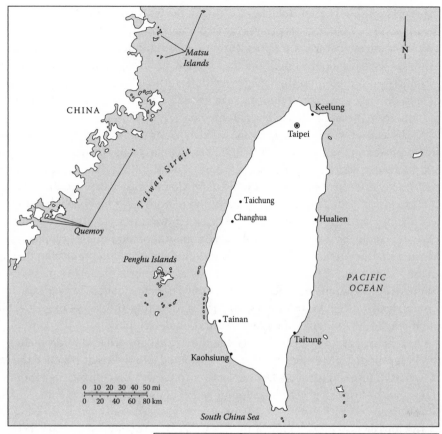

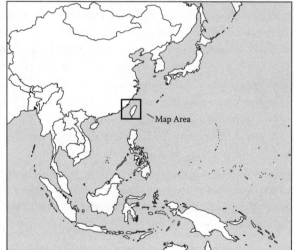

Taiwan

- Area: 13,892 sq. mi.
- Population: 25,545,000
- Total GDP at official exchange rate: US$572.6 billion
- Total GDP at purchasing power parity: US$1.189 trillion
- GDP per capita at purchasing power parity: US$49,800
- GDP by sector: services 62.1%; industry 36.0%; agriculture 1.8%
- Life expectancy at birth: 80.4 years
- Infant mortality per 1000 live births: 4.3

Data from 2017.

MAP 19.1 Taiwan

Taiwan as war booty after it defeated China in the Sino-Japanese War in 1895. It used the island to demonstrate its prowess as a colonial power, building an extensive transportation infrastructure and agricultural processing industries. In the 1930s, at the height of its expansionist ambition, the colonial authorities launched a campaign to assimilate Taiwanese into the Japanese nation. Although the effort failed, Japan's influence on Taiwan was profound, and can be seen today in everything from cuisine to fashion, from literary tastes to law enforcement.

At the end of World War II in 1945, Taiwan was ceded to the ROC, which was still in power on the mainland. The ROC's ruling party was the Kuomintang (KMT), and its leader was Chiang Kai-shek. Chiang and the KMT had been engaged in a civil war with Mao Zedong and the Chinese Communist Party (CCP) more or less continuously since 1927, though the attention of both sides had been diverted to the war against Japan from 1937 to 1945. At first, Taiwanese were glad to see the era of Japanese colonialism end, but the ROC administration and military forces were exhausted by years of war and acutely aware of the islanders' long subjection to China's enemy. They treated the Taiwanese more as a conquered people than as liberated compatriots. Relations between the long-time residents (called **Taiwanese**) and the new arrivals (called **Mainlanders, or '49ers**, denoting the year—1949—that large numbers of KMT followers fled to Taiwan) soon deteriorated.

On February 28, 1947 tensions between the two groups erupted into violence when protests over police violence in Taipei mushroomed into riots that engulfed the island. When ROC forces returned a few weeks later to reestablish control, they rounded up thousands of suspected rioters, including much of Taiwan's political elite. Thousands were killed.[1]

The uprising—which is known today as the **2-28 Incident** (February 28)—set in place the themes that dominated Taiwan politics for the next four decades: a highly repressive single-party authoritarian regime under the Kuomintang, disproportionate political influence for the '49er minority, and a single-minded focus on reinstating the ROC on the mainland. The needs and preferences of Taiwan's people were set aside; their energies and talents were to be harnessed to a grand mission: rescuing China from the "communist bandits" (*gongfei*), as the CCP was called.

Two years after the 2-28 Incident, ROC forces on the mainland lost to Mao's Red Army. With the PRC newly declared on the mainland, only Taiwan and a handful of outlying islands remained under ROC control. Nonetheless, the ROC government, with massive economic aid and strong security guarantees from the United States, set to work building Taiwan into an economic and military powerhouse that it imagined would one day be strong enough to battle back and reclaim mainland China.

TAIWAN UNDER AUTHORITARIAN RULE

In its heyday—roughly 1950 to 1980—KMT rule was a unique mixture of authoritarianism, rapid economic development, and popular mobilization. The ROC based its legitimacy on a democratic claim; its constitution established a five-branch, dual-executive electoral democracy with a full complement of civil liberties. To avoid implementing this system in Taiwan, the KMT invoked martial law and suspended the constitution. National elections, too, were postponed, because the ongoing "communist rebellion" made it impossible for Chinese living on the mainland to participate, and (the KMT argued) it would be unfair to have the whole ROC governed by people living in a single province (Taiwan). National representatives who were elected in mainland China in the 1940s and had followed Chiang and the KMT to Taiwan—including the National Assembly members who chose the ROC president—were to remain in office until elections could be held in their home provinces.

Challenging this restrictive political system was risky. The 2-28 Incident had shattered Taiwan's native-born leadership; when it was over, few Taiwanese dared to oppose the KMT openly. Because the slightest whiff of anti-government activism could result in a long prison term, the KMT's most vocal opponents were Taiwanese exiled to Japan and the United States. Nor were '49ers exempt from political repression. The KMT had been fighting communism in its ranks for decades, and the purges continued even after the party moved to Taiwan. Civil liberties, including freedom of speech, were minimal. Intense repression in the 1950s and 1960s earned those decades the nickname "White Terror" (as Chiang Kai-shek's purge of the CCP in the late 1920s was also called; see chap. 2), but politics remained closed well into the 1980s. It was not until 1984 that a leading American scholar raised the possibility that Taiwan might be shifting from "hard to soft authoritarianism."[2]

Retaking mainland China was too great a task for Taiwan's '49ers (about 15 percent of the island's population) to accomplish alone: that mission would require active support and participation from the Taiwanese majority. To win over the Taiwanese, the KMT used both economic and political means. In the early 1950s, it carried out a non-violent land reform that paved the way for economic progress in the rural areas. It encouraged competitive local elections as a way of legitimating local government and identifying talented leaders. It nurtured export-oriented industrialization by promoting state-sponsored heavy industries and small- and medium-sized family firms.

The combination of successful policies, a well-developed prewar infrastructure, hardworking and nimble entrepreneurs, and ready access to the U.S. market drove double-digit economic growth and rapidly rising living standards and inspired the phrase "Taiwan's economic miracle"[3] (see Figure 19.1). In 2017, Taiwan had a GDP per capita (at purchasing power parity) of $49,800, comparable to that of Germany, Australia and Denmark. The Taiwan model of development is also noted for policies that promoted relatively high levels of socio-economic equality.

As Taiwan's economy began to soar, the KMT's political might began to wane. By the mid-1970s, recovering the mainland was a distant dream, not least because many countries had recognized Beijing as the legitimate government of China. In 1971, Taiwan lost its seat in the UN; a year later, U.S. President Richard Nixon visited China. In 1979, the ROC lost its most important diplomatic partner when the United States decided to recognize the PRC. The United States said it would not challenge Beijing's view (which the ROC government at that time shared) that Taiwan is part of China (but the U.S. did not express agreement, either). Washington continued to support Taiwan in unofficial ways—even selling weapons to the ROC military and

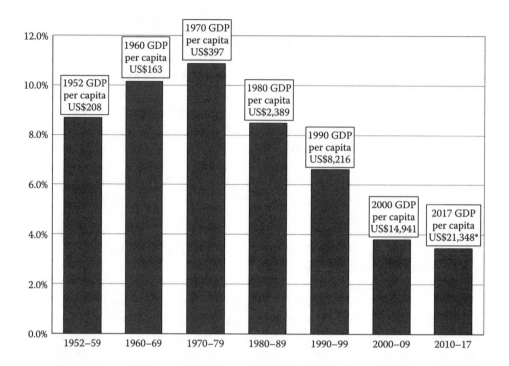

FIGURE 19.1 Taiwan's Economic Growth by Decade

* The GDP per capita figures are based on foreign currency exchange rates. At purchasing power parity, Taiwan's GDP per capita in 2017 was US$49,800.

Sources: National Statistics Taiwan.

maintaining a quasi-diplomatic presence in the form of the American Institute in Taiwan—but the loss of U.S. formal diplomatic recognition reinforced the growing sense that the KMT-led state was losing legitimacy.

As the idea of retaking the mainland faded, so too did the justification for suspending the ROC constitution. Seeing the change in the international climate— and feeling their growing economic clout—Taiwanese citizens began challenging the authoritarian system.

THE TRANSITION TO DEMOCRACY

In 1975, Chiang Kai-shek died, and power passed to his son, Chiang Ching-kuo. The young Chiang had the foresight to recognize that history was turning against the ROC, and he launched a controlled unraveling of the authoritarian system aimed at rebuilding the KMT's battered legitimacy.[4] Chiang Ching-kuo expanded the number of Taiwanese in the party leadership and opened some seats in the national legislative bodies to direct election, while opposition activists probed the ruling party's tolerance for dissent. While some ideas remained out of bounds (including communism and Taiwan independence), calls for democracy and justice for the Taiwanese majority met with an increasingly permissive reaction.

The reform process snowballed in the 1980s after an attempt to shut down the opposition in 1979 failed. Opposition politicians began running coordinated campaigns for local and national elected office—and winning. In 1984, Lee Teng-hui, a Taiwan-born politician educated in Japan and the United States, became Chiang Ching-kuo's vice president. When Chiang died four years later, Lee became the ROC's first Taiwan-born president.

In the early stages of democratization, the formation of opposition political parties was still banned under the terms of martial law. The KMT's opponents operated under the informal rubric of *dangwai*, or "outside the party." In 1986, *dangwai* politicians took the next step, and founded the **Democratic Progressive Party (DPP)**. Although the move technically violated martial law, the event went unpunished, and only ten months later, Chiang Ching-kuo terminated martial law. Within a few years, national legislative bodies were subjected to complete reelection, bringing into office a new generation of politicians elected by the people of Taiwan. In 1996, Lee Teng-hui added "first directly elected president" to his list of breakthroughs.

In 2000, the DPP candidate won the presidential election, ending the era of KMT rule. Single-party authoritarianism was gone, replaced by a fully functioning liberal democracy, complete with civil liberties and regular, competitive elections. Taiwan has been called "the First Chinese Democracy,"[5] both to make a comparison with the persistence of authoritarian rule on the mainland and to make the point that Confucian culture is not incompatible with democracy, as some scholars claim.

Taiwan's democratic transition reinvigorated its domestic politics, and it also attracted international support. Taiwan's transformation into a democracy reinforced America's commitment to protect the island from being absorbed against its will into a communist-led PRC.

TAIWAN POLITICS TODAY

The ROC constitution adopted in 1947 is still the blueprint for Taiwan's political system. A directly elected president heads the national government and appoints a premier, who, in turn, names the Executive Yuan* (cabinet). The Executive Yuan is responsible for implementing the decisions of Taiwan's national lawmaking body, the Legislative Yuan. There is also a Judicial Yuan (to manage the courts), a Control Yuan (to supervise public officials), and an Examination Yuan (to run civil service examinations).

Taiwan's political institutions are a hybrid of presidential and parliamentary features. In theory, Taiwan's constitution divides power between the president and premier, with the president in charge of international affairs (including relations with the PRC) and the premier responsible for domestic matters. In practice, however, Taiwan's presidents have played the dominant role.

* "Yuan," which literally means "board," as in "executive board," is adopted from the imperial Chinese system of government. The imperial government had a number of boards, such as the Board of Rites and the Board of Punishments, which advised the emperor. Sun Yat-sen adapted the terminology to the institutions of the constitutional republic established after the fall of the Qing dynasty in 1912.

In 2000, Taiwanese voters elected their first non-KMT president, the DPP's Chen Shui-bian. Chen won a three-way race in which the KMT vote was divided between two prominent conservatives, Lien Chan and James Soong. Chen's 39 percent vote share provided only a weak mandate, and representatives of Lien's KMT and Soong's newly formed People First Party (PFP) held a solid majority in the Legislative Yuan. During the eight years of Chen's presidency, this conservative majority stonewalled many of Chen's legislative proposals.

In early 2008, Taiwan held legislative and presidential elections. The KMT won both, ending the era of divided government. Still, the Chen years exposed a serious flaw in Taiwan's constitutional order. Divided government is possible in all presidential and dual-executive systems, but most have institutional devices to resolve conflicts between the executive and legislative branches. The United States has the presidential veto and the legislative override, for example, and the French system has a formalized structure for "cohabitation" in which the premier (representing the legislative majority) takes the lead during periods of divided government. Taiwan has nothing similar.

In the early 2000s, many Taiwanese hoped to use constitutional amendments—or even a new constitution—to resolve this and other institutional problems. But like many other issues, constitutional reform became entangled in the hot-button debate over Taiwan's international status. The PRC has had four constitutions in its sixty-year history, reflecting the fundamental political changes the country has experienced. But Beijing feared Taiwan would use a new constitution to establish a new country. Given President Chen's appetite for challenging Beijing—and Beijing's thin skin on the issue—many observers feared constitutional reform on Chen's watch could lead to a military confrontation. To prevent a crisis, the Legislative Yuan set a high threshold for constitutional amendment, effectively ending the constitutional reform debate.

Ma Ying-jeou, a KMT politician with law degrees from New York University and Harvard University and a former mayor of Taipei, was elected president in 2008 and 2012. The KMT kept its legislative majority, but efficient government remained elusive. Even with the KMT in charge of all three, cooperation among the presidential office, Executive Yuan, and Legislative Yuan was difficult. Disagreements within the ruling party abetted the DPP's efforts to derail presidential initiatives. In 2016 both branches switched hands again, to President Tsai Ing-wen's DPP, but it, too, found governing difficult. Taiwan's experience under Ma and Tsai reveal its political system to be highly sensitive to public opinion, even minority opinion. Compared to the decisive, authoritative leadership Taiwanese remember from the days of the Chiangs and Lee Teng-hui, today's politics can seem exasperatingly slow and ineffectual.

THE INDEPENDENCE DEBATE

Taiwan is the only country in the world that has all the attributes of a state—government, population, territory, military forces—except international recognition. As it is often said, Taiwan has de facto independence, but not de jure (legal) independence. It lacks recognition because Beijing insists it is a province of China, and "China" is the PRC. To have diplomatic relations with China—a rising global power—states must repudiate Taiwan. It is also important to acknowledge that Taiwan has not always been clear and consistent in its own message to the world about its status.

During the authoritarian era, the ROC wanted to be recognized as the government of all China. It refused to accept the existence of two Chinese states—the ROC and the PRC. It viewed the PRC as an illegitimate regime imposed by force on the Chinese people.

During the transition to democracy, many islanders began to question this characterization. While '49ers tended to accept the KMT's perspective, many Taiwanese thought defending the interests of the island and its people was more important than overthrowing communism and "saving" the mainland. Some people believed so strongly in putting Taiwan first that they advocated Taiwan independence and the permanent renunciation of unification. They wanted the international community to recognize that Taiwan was not—and never would be—part of a nation-state that also included mainland China.

Taiwan independence is anathema to Beijing. Although the two sides have lived apart for almost seventy years, the PRC government does not like to admit they are separated; divorce is unthinkable. Chinese leaders insist that they will use any means necessary—including military force—to block Taiwan independence. In 2005, the PRC's National People's Congress passed legislation authorizing military action if the nation's leaders decide independence is imminent. China has hundreds of short-range ballistic missiles aimed at the island, backing up its threat.

Taiwanese are well aware of China's determination, and they take the danger seriously. For that reason, no more than 10 percent of Taiwanese have ever said they want to pursue independence right away. The percentage that want immediate unification is even lower—below 5 percent. What Taiwanese *do* want is to maintain the status quo—to have the benefits of de facto independence (economic freedom and democratic self-government) without the risks of de jure independence. There is no longer a big difference between '49ers and Taiwanese on this issue; nearly everyone now agrees that maintaining the status quo—*de facto* independence—is Taiwan's best option (see Table 19.1).

TABLE 19.1 Survey on "Taiwan Public's Views on Current Cross-Strait Relations" (2017)

"Regarding relations between Taiwan and mainland China, which of the following positions do you lean toward?"

Unification as soon as possible	Maintaining status quo and move toward unification	Maintaining status quo and deciding on independence or unification later	Maintaining status quo indefinitely	Maintaining status quo move toward independence	Independence as soon as possible	No response
2.2%	10.3%	33.2%	25.1%	17.2%	5.0%	6.8%

85.8%
◄——— Those favoring some variant of the status quo ———►

Source: Election Study Center, National Chengchi University, Taipei, Taiwan. For a chart showing the trend in the above responses since 1992, see the "Trends in Core Political Attitudes Among Taiwanese" at esc.nccu.edu.tw.

The fact that few Taiwanese are interested in pushing for de jure independence is good news for Beijing, but the declining enthusiasm for unification makes Chinese leaders nervous. What will they do if Taiwan makes a sudden lunge for independence?

In fact, it would even be difficult to recognize what steps would constitute "independence." Clearly, a declaration of independence by Taiwan would do the trick. Short of that, changing the name (from ROC to, say, Republic of Taiwan) or adopting a new national flag (Taiwan still uses the original flag of the ROC founded in 1912) also would indicate a change. Other gestures—including constitutional reform—are more ambiguous. In 2008 Taiwanese voters considered a ballot measure instructing the government to seek UN membership under the name "Taiwan." The measure failed, but if it had passed, would it have constituted an act of independence? The answer is subjective, but Beijing believed it was necessary to oppose the measure—as it opposes all gestures toward independence—just in case.

RELATIONS WITH THE MAINLAND

Since its democratic transition, Taiwan's relationship with mainland China has changed radically. Under the authoritarian system, Taiwan treated the PRC as enemy territory, but democratization ushered in a more relaxed view. In 1987, Taipei lifted the ban on travel to the mainland that had been in place since the 1950s and thousands of Taiwanese made the trip. Many were '49ers hoping to reunite families divided by the civil war, but many others were Taiwanese who went as tourists.

The visitors included entrepreneurs who saw in China's fast-changing economy an investment opportunity. Rising wages and land prices on the island were starting to suffocate Taiwan's traditional manufacturers, but marrying China's low costs to Taiwan's know-how and global connections offered a way forward. Taiwanese manufacturers soon became a leading force in the Chinese economy, and investment in the mainland became a critical factor in Taiwan's economic growth. As the second decade of the century began, the two were among each other's top trading partners, and Taiwan was almost certainly the first or second largest source of direct foreign investment in the PRC economy.[6]

The flood of Taiwanese visiting and investing in the mainland brought the two sides closer than they had been in four decades. President Lee declared the civil war over in 1991 and replaced the goal of recovering the mainland with peaceful unification. Representatives of the two sides began meeting in the guise of unofficial bodies to discuss issues ranging from the exchange of mail to criminal extraditions.

Those conversations eased people-to-people relations and economic cooperation, but they also exposed profound differences in the two sides' goals. Beijing's idea of unification was to make Taiwan a province of the PRC under its "one country, two systems" formula, but when Taiwan's leaders spoke of unification, they had in mind a marriage of equals. Subordinating a democratic Taiwan to a communist PRC was unacceptable to a society that had only recently thrown off single-party authoritarianism. Eventually, the talks broke down.

Relations deteriorated further in the second half of the 1990s. Lee was growing anxious that Taiwan would be roped into a unification it did not want, so he looked to the international community to confirm the island's separate status. In 1999, he stunned Beijing by calling the cross-strait connection a "special state-to-state relationship." Fearing that Taiwan was on the verge of permanently discarding its Chinese identity, Beijing tightened its stranglehold on Taiwan's diplomacy. Economic ties between the two sides continued to develop, but political relations turned icy.

Campaigning for the presidency in 2000, the DPP candidate, Chen Shui-bian, called for increased economic engagement between Taiwan and China, but PRC leaders (as well as many Taiwanese voters) were convinced his real goal was Taiwan independence, a stance that had been part of his party's platform since 1991. As president, Chen found himself stonewalled by Beijing and by a Legislative Yuan dominated by his opponents. In response, he hardened his position, especially after his reelection in 2004. The PRC was especially agitated when Chen described the situation in the Taiwan Strait as "one country on each side." The result was eight years of stagnation in cross-strait political relations.

The combination of hot economics and cold politics drove competing trends in Taiwan's public opinion. During Chen's presidency, the people of Taiwan became ever more convinced that the island's economic prosperity depended upon taking advantage of the economic opportunities on the mainland. At the same time, though, fewer and fewer citizens of Taiwan felt themselves to be Chinese, and the sense that Taiwan should remain politically separate deepened.

By 2008, unification had become so unpopular that even the KMT presidential candidate, Ma Ying-jeou, promised not to move toward it during his term. He reiterated that position before his 2012 reelection. Ma's position revealed the extent to which the status quo—neither independence nor unification—had become the consensus preference of Taiwan's people. There was little the PRC could do to counter this trend, except promote economic and social integration and hope that Taiwan would return to the fold someday. To that end, Beijing worked with Ma to expand cross-strait economic cooperation. In 2008, the two sides began allowing direct flights, and two years later they adopted an Economic Cooperation Framework Agreement that reduced trade and investment restrictions and created a structure for managing economic relations.

Ma's first term saw rapid improvement in cross-strait relations. In addition to relaxing travel and economic restrictions, the two sides exchanged high-level visits, culminating in a historic meeting between Ma and PRC president Xi Jinping in late 2015 in Singapore. While most Taiwanese welcomed the reduced tension, many wondered whether Taiwan might have conceded too much. According to his opponents, Ma's willingness to compromise with Beijing was naïve at best. At worst, they averred, his actions revealed an openness to unification that put him outside the popular mainstream.

Early in Ma's second term, growing concern about Beijing's influence sparked a series of protest movements. At the same time, a longstanding rift between the president and the speaker of the legislature, also a KMT member, widened into open conflict. These two processes collided in the spring 2014 **Sunflower Movement**. Young protesters who were unhappy about the way the KMT was handling cross-Strait trade liberalization invaded the legislative chamber. They camped out there for 24 days until the speaker negotiated their departure.

As the 2016 presidential election approached the KMT was in deep trouble—so deep, in fact, that it had difficulty finding anyone willing to run. When its first nominee turned out to be far more China-friendly than the electorate, the KMT was forced to replace her just three months before the election. The DPP candidate, Tsai Ing-wen, had lost to Ma in 2012, but public opinion had shifted in her direction by 2016. Tsai promised to preserve the status quo, by which she meant maintaining good relations with the mainland while resisting pressure to move quickly. After eight years of fast-paced rapprochement, many voters believed it was time to slow down, and Tsai was elected with 56 percent of the vote, making her the first female leader of a modern Chinese-speaking state.

Taiwan's smooth relations with the PRC during the Ma years were welcome in Washington, where policymakers had found the ill will and lack of communication between Taipei and Beijing during the Chen years dangerously destabilizing. But the steady expansion of the PRC's economic muscle and military ambition during the Ma era sparked debates in the U.S., too. Some experts said Washington should reduce its assistance to Taiwan and encourage the island to be more "realistic." Others advocated continuing arms sales and other forms of engagement with Taiwan, especially in view of the PRC's growing might.

Tsai's inauguration brought a sharp change in cross-Strait relations. Initially, the mainland leadership said it would "listen to her words and observe her deeds," but when she refused to succumb to its demand to accept the "1992 Consensus," a vaguely worded agreement-to-disagree Beijing had used to justify its negotiations with Taipei during the Ma era, the PRC increased the pressure on Taiwan. Talks ceased, and Beijing pulled back its economic outreach to Taiwan. It also began squeezing Taiwan's international space, even demanding that foreign airlines change their websites to identify Taiwan destinations as "Taiwan, China."

POLITICS AND ELECTIONS

During the authoritarian period, Taiwan's twenty-five local governments were the focal point for political competition. As the result of a recent reorganization, Taiwan now has twenty-two municipalities, including thirteen counties, three cities, and six special municipalities, as well as two tiny islands near the mainland's Fujian coast. Each municipality has an elected executive and council and various sub-municipalities (townships, towns, villages, and wards), most of which elect their leaders, as well. Since the early '90s, Taiwanese have elected their national legislature, too. The current system was adopted in 2005. It calls for 113 legislative seats: 73 elected from geographical districts and 34 by party-list proportional representation (lists must include at least 50 percent women). Six seats are reserved for Taiwan's indigenous peoples.

Before the DPP was founded, nearly all local politicians were KMT members, but the party in each municipality was divided into local factions. Although all were affiliated with the KMT, when it came to local elections, factions competed fiercely. Local factions might cooperate to help KMT candidates in national elections, but when opposition politicians began challenging the KMT in significant numbers, factions found ways to leverage those opposition candidacies for their own advantage. Local politics was an important training ground and venue for democratization, and as the scope of elections expanded, voters and politicians were well-prepared.

Taiwanese have participated in elections since the 1940s, so it is not surprising that they are skilled in the arts of campaigning and voting. During the period of one-party rule, campaigns revolved around "vote pulling." Candidates cultivated influential supporters—vote brokers—who mobilized their personal networks in support of those candidates. Successful candidates rewarded their vote brokers and supporters with targeted benefits—everything from public works projects to funeral wreaths. In small-town Taiwan, knowing a public official was a big deal, and politicians spent a huge amount of time and money serving their constituents.

To supplement this personalized politicking, Taiwanese politicians also used high-visibility techniques such as sound trucks, campaign flags, and rallies. As the island's population has grown and politics has become more sophisticated, parties and candidates have added mass media—TV advertising, media tours, endorsements—to their repertoire. Today, all these elements come into play in elections, and candidates spend their days racing from TV studios to stadium rallies to wedding feasts. In the 2008 Legislative Yuan election, one candidate in Taipei City followed garbage trucks through his district, shaking hands with voters as they came out to dispose of their trash (residents are required to put their trash directly in the truck at a scheduled time) (see Box 19.1).

As in most countries, many of the issues voters care about are local. Economic development, law and order, and public services top the list in municipal elections. In national elections—legislative and presidential contests—Taiwanese voters pay attention to party affiliation, too. For a long time, the KMT was the "establishment" party in Taiwan. It got credit for many of Taiwan's successes—especially its strong economic performance in the high-growth era—and while its opponents have tried to paint it as a pro-unification party, the party's platform is centrist. In his successful 2008 and 2012 campaigns, for example, President Ma promoted "Three No's": no independence, no unification, and no armed conflict—in other words, the status quo—with the PRC. He also promised to make it easier for Taiwanese to do business in the mainland.

The 2016 elections ended the KMT's decades-long dominance. The DPP won the presidency and captured its first-ever legislative majority. It added those wins to the thirteen out of twenty-two top municipal posts it had won in 2014. The KMT struggled to overcome multiple deficits: lack of confidence in its mainland policy, a sluggish economy, divisions in the top leadership, and an aging leadership; nonetheless, it recovered much of the lost ground in local elections in 2018. Meanwhile a new political party that leans towards independence—the New Power Party (NPP) emerged out of the Sunflower Movement. It won only a handful of seats, but it attracted a great deal of buzz—suggesting the future might belong to the Sino-skeptics.

The DPP is known for promoting democratization, but it also has a reputation as a pro-independence party. The party's position is more subtle and moderate than this characterization implies, but perception is what matters in politics, and until recently, many Taiwanese voters perceived the DPP as recklessly pro-independence. Even now, Tsai Ing-wen's refusal to accept Beijing's precondition for a more normal

BOX 19.1 TAIWAN'S "HOT AND NOISY" POLITICS

In 2004, Taiwan's presidential election made headlines worldwide when the incumbent president and vice president were shot while campaigning for reelection. President Chen Shui-bian, grazed by a bullet across his midsection, said he felt something when he was hit, but he went on waving to the crowd for several minutes. When he finally looked down, he realized he was bleeding. Then he noticed Vice President Annette Lu bleeding from her knee. About that time, he noticed a bullet hole in the car window.

The incident provoked a tsunami of conspiracy theories, mostly because the official account seemed so implausible. How could two politicians be shot in front of thousands of people without anyone—even the candidates themselves—noticing? It's easy to understand why so many people scoffed at Chen's story, but if you've ever been to a Taiwanese campaign rally, you won't find it quite so hard to believe.

Although security procedures have tightened since, Chen and Lu were following standard Taiwanese campaign protocol on March 19, 2004: they were standing in an open Jeep, each secured by a seat belt, driving through a tightly packed crowd with firecrackers raining down on them. The air was full of smoke, the noise was deafening, and there were explosions going off everywhere. No one could have heard a gunshot in the din.

Both candidates said they initially assumed their injuries were nothing unusual: just the typical dings from out-of-control bottle rockets. (Television cameramen trailing the candidates in another car reported smelling their own hair burning as smoldering fireworks-wrappers fell from the sky.) It was only later, when the adrenaline wore off, that Chen and Lu recognized the nature of their wounds.

Crushing crowds and earsplitting noise are the sine qua non of Taiwanese political rallies. They are required, both literally and figuratively, to meet the Chinese definition of fun: re'nao ("hot and noisy"). A candidate who cannot provide them—along with a robust selection of food vendors and color-coordinated tracksuits for the staff—cannot expect to win an election.

Politics in Taiwan is a combination of door-to-door sales and traveling circus. The real mystery is how so many politicians make it to Election Day in one piece.

relationship—the 1992 Consensus—is a source of concern for those who still believe the wisest course of action is to cultivate good relations with the mainland.

Beyond the two major parties, political parties have come and gone, but so far, none has become a major force in Taiwan politics. The most important of the small parties are the People First Party (PFP), the Taiwan Solidarity Union (TSU), and the New Party, all of which grew out of splits in the KMT, and the NPP. In the 2016 legislative elections, the DPP won sixty-eight seats, the KMT thirty-five, the NPP five, and the PFP three. The New Party and TSU were shut out.

CONCLUSION

Taiwan's prosperous economy and successful democracy should make it a model for developing countries, but its troubled relationship with China has left it isolated, its achievements largely ignored. The two sides depend on one another economically, and they have learned to communicate despite their differences. Nonetheless, those differences are profound. The PRC hopes to incorporate Taiwan into a Chinese nation-state with Beijing as its capital, while Taiwanese want to preserve their island's democracy. After decades of arguing about identity—how to think of themselves in relation to China—Taiwanese seem to have settled on civic nationalism, the idea that their shared commitment to freedom and democracy is what defines them, as the heart of what makes their society distinctive and separates them from the PRC. As long as China retains its nominally communist party-state political framework, to remain democratic Taiwan will need at least de facto independence. Resolving the standoff in the Taiwan Strait will require patience, flexibility, confidence, and goodwill on both sides. In the meantime, Taiwan will continue to look for international affirmation and support wherever it can find it—whether in the UN General Assembly or on the "Click Click Click" website.

NOTES

1. The most complete English-language account of these events is Tse-han Lai, Ramon Myers, and Wou Wei, *A Tragic Beginning: The Taiwan Uprising of February 28, 1947* (Palo Alto, CA: Stanford University Press, 1991).

2. Edwin A. Winckler, "Institutionalization and Participation on Taiwan: From Hard to Soft Authoritarianism?" *China Quarterly* 99 (1984): 482–499.

3. Taiwan's economic development model is analyzed in detail in two books: Thomas B. Gold, *State and Society in the Taiwan Miracle* (Armonk, NY: M. E. Sharpe, 1986); and Robert Wade, *Governing the Market: Economic Theory and the Role of Government in East Asian Industrialization* (Princeton, NJ: Princeton University Press, 1990).

4. Accounts of Taiwan's democratization include Linda Chao and Ramon H. Myers, *The First Chinese Democracy: Political Life in the Republic of China on Taiwan* (Baltimore, MD: Johns Hopkins University Press, 1998); Yun-han Chu, *Crafting Democracy in Taiwan* (Taipei: Institute for National Policy Research, 1992); Peter Moody, *Political Change on Taiwan: A Study of Ruling Party Adaptability* (New York: Praeger, 1992); Shelley Rigger, *Politics in Taiwan: Voting for Democracy* (London: Routledge, 1999); Denny Roy, *Taiwan: A Political History* (Ithaca, NY: Cornell University Press, 2003); Hung-mao Tien, *The Great Transition: Political and Social Change in the Republic of China* (Stanford, CA: Hoover Institution Press, 1989).

5. Chao and Myers, *First Chinese Democracy*.

6. It is impossible to state with certainty exactly where Taiwan ranks among international investors in China because a very large portion of inbound investment flows through offshore channels, including the Cayman Islands, British Virgin Islands, Hong Kong, and Panama. Of this, a substantial—but unknowable—portion originates in Taiwan.

SUGGESTED READINGS

Andrade, Tonio. *How Taiwan Became Chinese: Dutch, Spanish and Han Colonization in the Seventeenth Century*. New York: Columbia University Press, 2008.

Bush, Richard. *Uncharted Strait: The Future of China-Taiwan Relations*. Washington, DC: Brookings Institution, 2013.

Copper, John F. *Taiwan: Nation-State or Province?* 6th ed. Boulder, CO: Routledge, 2018.

Fell, Dafydd. *Government and Politics in Taiwan,* 2nd ed. New York: Routledge, 2018

Gold, Thomas B. *State and Society in the Taiwan Miracle.* Armonk, NY: M. E. Sharpe, 1986.

Goldstein, Steven M. *China and Taiwan Today.* New York: Polity, 2015

Goldstein, Steven M., and Julian Chang, eds. *Presidential Politics in Taiwan: The Administration of Chen Shui-bian.* Norwalk, CT: EastBridge, 2008.

Hsiao, Li-hung. *A Thousand Moons on a Thousand Rivers.* Translated by Michelle Wu. New York: Columbia University Press, 2000.

Kastner, Scott L. *Political Conflict and Economic Interdependence across the Taiwan Strait and Beyond.* Stanford, CA: Stanford University Press, 2009.

Keliher, Macabe. *Out of China or Yu Yonghe's Tale of Formosa: A History of Seventeenth-Century Taiwan.* Taipei: SMC Publishing, 2003.

Rigger, Shelley. *Why Taiwan Matters: Small Island, Global Powerhouse.* Boulder, CO: Rowman & Littlefield, 2011.

Roy, Denny. *Taiwan: A Political History.* Ithaca, NY: Cornell University Press, 2003.

Tucker, Nancy Bernkopf. *Strait Talk: United States-Taiwan Relations and the Crisis with China.* Cambridge, MA: Harvard University Press, 2009.

Tucker, Nancy Bernkopf, ed. *Dangerous Strait: The U.S.-Taiwan-China Crisis.* New York: Columbia University Press, 2008.

Wachman, Alan. *Why Taiwan? Geostrategic Rationales for China's Territorial Integrity.* Stanford, CA: Stanford University Press, 2007.

Timeline of Modern Chinese Political History

1760s–1790s	"High Qing"—the height of glory for China's last imperial dynasty.
1839–1842	The First Opium War; ends in an humiliating defeat for the Qing dynasty and the signing of the Treaty of Nanjing (1842), the first of the "unequal treaties" imposed on imperial China by Western powers.
1850–1863	The Taiping Rebellion nearly overthrows the Qing and leaves more than 20 million dead before it is suppressed.
1856–1860	The Second Opium War; China's defeat leads to more unequal treaties.
1860s	Empress Dowager Cixi, widow of Xianfeng emperor, becomes the "power behind the throne" formally occupied by her infant son and the most powerful leader in China—a position she retains until her death in 1908.
1860s–1890s	The Self-Strengthening Movement involves efforts to save the Qing by modernizing the economy and the military while preserving traditional Chinese values.
1894–1895	China defeated and humiliated in the first Sino-Japanese War; loses influence in Korea and control of Taiwan to Japan.
1898	The Hundred Days Reform is proclaimed by the emperor, promising wide-ranging institutional changes, but the movement is crushed by the Empress Dowager Cixi, who places the emperor under palace arrest.
1899–1900	The Boxer Rebellion breaks out in northern China and is suppressed by Western military forces. The Boxer Indemnity further weakens the Qing dynasty financially.
1905	The imperial examination system is abolished as part of a last-ditch futile reform effort to save the Qing dynasty. Sun Yat-sen establishes the *Tongmenghui*, or "Revolutionary Alliance" and calls for the overthrow of the Qing and the establishment of a republic.
1908	The Empress Dowager dies, but not before she moves to put another child emperor on throne, the three-year old, Puyi, who would be China's last emperor.
1911	Revolution breaks out in many parts of China; Sun Yat-sen becomes provisional president of a republican government before it comes to national power.

1912	The "Last Emperor" abdicates and the Republic of China is established.
1912–1916	General Yuan Shikai takes control of the Republic and tries to establish a new dynasty with himself as emperor.
1912	Sun Yat-sen founds the Kuomintang (KMT, Nationalist Party) to oppose Yuan's usurpation of power in the Republic of China.
1916–1927	The Warlord era, which begins in the political vacuum left by Yuan Shikai's death in 1916. The Republic of China exists in name, but power is, in fact, held by numerous regional military leaders.
1919	The May Fourth Movement begins with protests against the terms of the Versailles Treaty that grants Japan control of former German concessions in China and the weak leaders of the Republic of China, ushering in a period of political and cultural ferment.
1921	The Chinese Communist Party (CCP) is founded with advice and assistance from the Moscow-based Comintern (Communist International).
1924	The KMT and the CCP agree to a united front to oppose the warlords.
1925	Sun Yat-sen dies; Chiang Kai-shek takes over leadership of the KMT.
1926	The KMT-CCP united front begins the Northern Expedition from southern China in a military campaign to subdue the warlords and reunify China.
1927	Chiang Kai-shek turns against the CCP and unleashes the "White Terror," driving surviving communists underground or deep into the countryside. The CCP establishes the first of its major rural base areas in Jinggangshan.
1927–1937	The "Nanjing Decade": Chiang Kai-shek consolidates his position as the most powerful leader of the Republic of China and relocates the country's capital to the central Chinese city of Nanjing (Nanking).
1928–1934	The KMT carries out a series of "extermination campaigns" against CCP base areas. The CCP headquarters is relocated to a remote area in central China, which is called the Jiangxi Soviet.
1931	Japan begins its aggression against China, taking control of Manchuria in the northeast and establishing a puppet state, "Manchukuo," with China's "Last Emperor" as a figurehead ruler.
1934–1935	The Long March: the CCP is driven out of its Jiangxi Soviet base area by Chiang Kai-shek's forces and undertakes a 6,000-mile trek to the northwestern sanctuary in Yan'an; during the Long March, Mao Zedong moves to the top ranks of the CCP leadership.
1935–1945	The Yan'an period: a crucial decade in the development of the CCP, during which Mao Zedong becomes Chairman of the party and consolidates his political and ideological power; the CCP also greatly expands its popular support for its resistance against Japan and its program of reform in Yan'an.
1937	Japan invades China Proper, setting off World War II in Asia; Chiang Kai-shek and the government of the Republic of China are driven to the far southwest and set up a wartime capital in Chongqing (Chungking). The Rape of Nanjing: Japanese forces carry out horrific atrocities against hundreds of thousands of Chinese civilians when they occupy the capital of China.
1945	World War II ends
1946	The Chinese Civil War begins again after a temporary "truce" during the war against Japan and futile efforts by the United States to negotiate a KMT-CCP coalition government.

1949	The CCP wins the Civil War and founds the People's Republic of China (PRC) with Chairman Mao as the leader and Beijing as its capital. Chiang Kai-shek and the government of the Republic of China retreat to the island of Taiwan.
1950	The United States and its allies block the PRC's effort to assume the "China" seat in the United Nations claiming it still rightfully belongs to the Republic of China. The People's Liberation Army invades Tibet; The Seventeen Point Agreement leaves the Dalai Lama in charge in exchange for Tibet's acknowledgment that it is part of China.
1950–1952	The period of the "New Democracy" in the PRC, which promises a mixed economy and a somewhat inclusive polity, although under the firm control of the CCP. Land reform and other revolutionary programs begin.
1950–1953	The Korean War: China fights the United Nations forces under the United States to a stalemate.
1953–1957	China follows the Soviet model of development under a First Five-year Plan that involves a centralized economy, the nationalization of industry and commerce, and the collectivization of agriculture.
1956–1957	The Hundred Flowers Movement: Mao invites criticism of the CCP's rule over China in order to shake up the bureaucracy and prevent discontent from boiling over.
1957	The Anti-Rightist Campaign: in reaction to unexpectedly harsh criticism of the Hundred Flowers, the CCP strikes hard against critics.
1958–1960	The Great Leap Forward: Mao's utopian campaign to accelerate economic development and bring true communism to China by relying on the labor power and revolutionary fervor of the masses; China is plunged into the worst famine in human history and a deep industrial depression.
1959	An uprising in Tibet against Chinese rule is crushed; the Dalai Lama flees to exile in India.
1961–1965	Mao retreats to the "second line" of leadership and turns economic policy-making over to Liu Shaoqi and Deng Xiaoping.
1962–1964	Mao grows increasingly unhappy with the policies that Liu and Deng have implemented to recover from the Leap and set China on a course of sustained economic growth. The Sino-Soviet split emerges: Mao concludes that the Soviet Union has betrayed communism and "restored" capitalism that benefits the party elite and exploits the working classes.
1964	China detonates its first atomic bomb.
1966	Mao launches the Great Proletarian Cultural Revolution, an ideological campaign to get China off the "capitalist road" down which he believes Liu, Deng, and other top party leaders have led it.
1966–1968	The Red Guards emerge as Mao's mass ally in the Cultural Revolution and carry out a reign of terror against anyone and anything judged to be remnants of capitalism or imperial China. Liu Shaoqi and Deng Xiaoping are among those purged.
1968–1969	Mao concludes that the Red Guards and other rebels have gone too far and instructs the army, under his loyal subordinate, Lin Biao, to restore order. More than 20 million former Red Guards are sent for re-education in the countryside.

1969–1971	A period of military ascendency in Chinese politics; Lin Biao is named as Mao's successor.
1971	Sino-American détente begins after a long period of hostility since the founding of the PRC in 1949. National Security Advisor Henry Kissinger makes a "secret" trip to Beijing (July 1971) to prepare the way for President Richard M. Nixon's historic visit in March 1972.
	Lin Biao is killed in an airplane crash following an alleged coup to overthrow Mao, who had grown unhappy with Lin as his chosen successor.
	The People's Republic of China assumes the "China" seat in the United Nations General Assembly and Security Council, replacing the Republic of China (on Taiwan).
1972–1975	A momentous period of transition and tumult in Chinese politics:
	Radicals led by Mao's wife, Jiang Qing, fill part of the political vacuum left by Lin Biao's demise.
	Deng Xiaoping is restored to power to balance the leadership and help long-time premier, Zhou Enlai, manage the economy.
	China's relationship with the United States and the global community deepens.
1975–1976	The "showdown" between the radicals and more moderate CCP leaders intensifies.
1976	Zhou Enlai dies in January.
	A political unknown, Hua Guofeng, is unexpectedly named to succeed Zhou as acting premier in a move by Mao, who is in deteriorating health, to balance power between radical and moderate leaders.
	The Tiananmen Incident: A mass outpouring of mourning for Zhou Enlai turns into a protest against Jiang Qing and other radicals and is suppressed.
	Deng Xiaoping is blamed for the Tiananmen Incident and again ousted from the party-state leadership.
	Hua Guofeng is made PRC premier and first vice chairman of the CCP, clearly emerging as Mao's successor.
	Mao Zedong dies in September.
	Jiang Qing and her closest radical associates (the Gang of Four) are arrested by Hua Guofeng with the support of senior party leaders.
	Hua Guofeng becomes chairman of the CCP.
1977	Deng Xiaoping is restored to his party and state positions by Hua Guofeng and gradually pushes Hua aside to become China's paramount leader, although he never assumes the top offices himself, assigning them instead to loyal lieutenants.
1978	A meeting of the CCP Central Committee in December marks the start of the era of economic reform and opening to the world.
1979	The Democracy Wall Movement calls for greater political freedom but is suppressed.
	Deng Xiaoping enunciates "The Four Cardinal Principles" as the political and ideological framework for economic reform.
	The United States and China establish formal diplomatic relations.
	One-child policy introduced.
1980	Zhao Ziyang, a loyal protégé of Deng Xiaoping, replaces Hua Guofeng as premier of the PRC.
1981	Jiang Qing and other members of the Gang of Four are sentenced to prison in a show trial.

Hu Yaobang, another Deng protégé, replaces Hua Guofeng as chairman of the CCP; the title of the head of the party is changed to general secretary in 1982.

Deng Xiaoping replaces Hua as chairman of the Central Military Commission, thereby becoming the commander in chief of China's armed forces.

CCP issues the "Resolution of Certain Questions in the History of Our Party since the Founding of the PRC," which blames Mao's political and ideological mistakes for the disasters of the Great Leap Forward and the Cultural Revolution, but concludes that his achievements far outweigh his shortcomings.

1983   Party conservatives carry out an "Anti-Spiritual Pollution" campaign against Western ideas they feel are contaminating Chinese society.

1986   Student pro-democracy demonstrations in Beijing; supported by many Chinese intellectuals

1987   Party conservatives carry out an "Anti-Bourgeois Liberalization" campaign against democratic ideas that they see as a challenge to party rule.

Hu Yaobang is forced by Deng to resign as general secretary because he is said to be too sympathetic to calls for more democracy; Zhao Ziyang becomes general secretary and Li Peng becomes premier.

1989   Hu Yaobang dies in April.

Students gather in Tiananmen Square to pay their respects to Hu Yaobang, regarded by many as a political reformer.

The student gathering turns into huge demonstrations and protests against corruption and for democracy, eventually drawing millions of people from nearly all walks of life and spreading to other cities during the spring.

June 4th: The People's Liberation Army is ordered to clear the Square and does so with massive force, resulting in the deaths of a large number of protesters.

Zhao Ziyang is forced to resign as CCP general secretary by Deng because of his sympathy and soft line toward the demonstrations; he is replaced by Jiang Zemin, party secretary in Shanghai, who also becomes chairman of the Central Military Commission.

China enters a period of retreat from political and economic reform.

1989–1991   The collapse of communist regimes in Eastern Europe and the Soviet Union alarms China's leaders.

1992   During his Southern Inspection Tour of China's most prosperous region, Deng proclaims that economic reform must again become the country's highest priority.

1993   Jiang Zemin becomes president of the PRC, reviving the practice (abandoned after Mao turned the position over to Liu Shaoqi in 1959) that the leader of the party also serves as president of the country.

1997   Deng Xiaoping dies; in the preceding few years, he had allowed Jiang Zemin to consolidate his own power.

Hong Kong returns to Chinese sovereignty after nearly 150 years as a British colony.

2002–2004   Jiang Zemin retires. Hu Jintao becomes CCP general secretary (2002), PRC president (2003), and Central Military Commission chair (2004).

2007–2008   Hu Jintao reelected to all of his leading positions, with his second and final terms scheduled to end in 2012–2013.

2008	Large scale unrest occurs in Tibet and is forcefully suppressed.
	Beijing hosts the Olympic Games.
2009	Large-scale unrest occurs in Xinjiang and is forcefully suppressed.
	China celebrates the 60th anniversary of the founding of the People's Republic.
2010	Jailed Chinese dissident Liu Xiaobo is awarded Nobel Peace Prize
2012-13	Xi Jinping becomes CCP general secretary (2012), PRC president (2013), and Central Military Commission chair (2012).
	Xi launches far-reaching anticorruption campaign
2014	China relaxes one-child policy, allowing couples to have two children if one of the parents is an only child.
	Occupy Central and Umbrella Revolution protests in Hong Kong against slow pace of political reform.
	China surpasses the U.S. as the world's largest economy based on Purchasing Power Parity GDP, although is still second by a large measure according to GDP at market exchange rates.
	Xi Jinping acknowledges that China is in a period of a "new normal" of lower economic growth.
2016	China ends the one-child policy, but couples are still limited to two children.
	Severe political crackdown begins in Xinjiang in response to an increase in ethnic clashes and terrorist attacks
	Xi Jinping designated as the "core leader" of the CCP, putting him on a par with Mao Zedong and Deng Xiaoping
	Chinese president Xi Jinping and Taiwan president Ma Ying-jeou meet in Singapore in the first such meeting between the two sides since the end of the Chinese Civil War in 1949
2017	Imprisoned Nobel Peace Prize laureate and Chinese dissident, Liu Xiaobo, dies in prison.
	Xi Jinping is elected to his second five-year term as CCP general secretary and chair of the Central Military Commission at the 19th Party Congress, which also enshrines "Xi Jinping Thought on Building Socialism with Chinese Characteristics for the New Era," in the party constitution.
2018	The National People's Congress reelects Xi Jinping as PRC president and abolishes term-limits for the position, which leads to speculation that Xi may hold on to power longer than his expected retirement in 2022/2023.
	The PRC government significantly tightens and expands the crackdown on ethnic unrest in Xinjiang, including setting up "re-education camps" that were estimated to hold as many as a million Uyghurs.

Glossary

Note: This glossary does not include identifications of individuals. For lists of top leaders of the People's Republic of China, see Table 3.1 (1949–1976) and Table 4.1 (since 1976).

1911 REVOLUTION. The process that began on October 10, 1911 ("Double 10"), with a series of mutinies and rebellions in several Chinese cities and culminated in the abdication of the **Qing** emperor and the founding of the **Republic of China** in February 1912.

2–28 INCIDENT. Events on Taiwan that began on February 28, 1947, when tensions between **Mainlanders** and **Taiwanese** erupted into widespread violence. Protests by Taiwanese over police brutality in Taipei turned into riots that engulfed the island. When **Kuomintang** (KMT) troops arrived from the mainland to reestablish control, they rounded up suspected rioters, including much of Taiwan's political elite. Thousands were killed. Paved the way for KMT dictatorship in Taiwan when Chiang Kai-shek's forces retreated to the island after losing the **Chinese Civil War**

'49ers. See Mainlanders.

7,000 CADRES CONFERENCE. A large gathering of officials from different institutions and administrative levels in the PRC in early 1962 to assess efforts at recovery from the **Great Leap Forward.** Mao offered a very restrained self-criticism, but also reasserted the correctness of the Great Leap policy line. The CCP leadership rallied around the Chairman, but Liu Shaoqi gave a speech critical of the Leap, which Mao later claimed caused him to begin to doubt Liu's political reliability.

ADMINISTRATIVE VILLAGE. The unit of governance in rural China; technically, a "grassroots" unit below the formal government structure of the PRC. An administrative village is made up of one or more **natural villages**. There are about 600,000 administrative villages in China.

ALL-CHINA WOMEN'S FEDERATION (ACWF). One of China's official **mass organizations**. The stated mission of the ACWF is "to represent and to protect women's rights and interests, and to promote equality between men and women." It is a national organization with branches at every level of government. Like other mass organizations, the ACWF operates under the leadership of the CCP.

ANARCHISM. From the Greek term meaning "without rulers"; a political philosophy that rejects all formal state authority as tyrannical and harmful to individuals. Anarchists believe society should be organized into small, voluntary, and cooperative self-governing units. Anarchism was popular in the first decades of the twentieth century among some

Chinese intellectuals looking for a radical solution to problems of late imperial and early republican China.

ANT TRIBE. Refers to young college graduates in China who cannot find suitable employment and live in crowed, shared accommodations, take low-paying jobs, and spend a lot of time just hanging out.

ANTAGONISTIC CONTRADICTION. A Marxist-Leninist concept that refers to differences between opposites that have no common ground and can only be resolved by force, compared with **nonantagonistic contradictions**, which can be resolved by discussion, debate, education, and other non-coercive means. For example, the contradiction between the **bourgeoisie** and the **proletariat** is antagonistic.

ANTI-RIGHTIST CAMPAIGN. Launched by Mao Zedong and the CCP in 1957 in response to the unexpectedly harsh criticism of the party's rule during the **Hundred Flowers Movement.** It deeply touched intellectuals and other segments of the urban population in particular, and resulted in the extensive use of the "rightist" label, which would curse people so designated for the rest of the Maoist era. Many "rightists" were sent to the countryside for reform through labor, in many cases for more than two decades. Even more fundamentally, the campaign sent a chill of fear through society, especially among intellectuals.

ARTICLE 23. Of the **Basic Law** of the **Hong Kong Special Administrative Region** (HKSAR) that gives the HKSAR government the power to enact laws on security issues such as treason and subversion against the government of the PRC, theft of state secrets, and the formation of political organizations with foreign ties. In 2002, the HKSAR government proposed enacting a tough new anti-subversion law under the terms of Article 23. The proposal created much controversy and protest by those who thought it would decrease democracy in Hong Kong. The government, in consultation with the PRC, withdrew the proposal after massive public demonstrations against it.

ASIAN FINANCIAL CRISIS OF 1997–1998. Began in Thailand in July 1997 and spread to most of the other countries in East and Southeast Asia. Among the causes were bad government economic policies, overinvestment, and real estate speculation. The International Monetary Fund (IMF) helped bail out the worst hit countries. Hong Kong was seriously affected by the crisis, but China was not because of its controlled currency and other economic controls.

ASIAN INFRASTRUCTURE INVESTMENT BANK (AIIB). A China-led initiative established in 2016 to provide financing for infrastructure construction (e.g., transportation and communications, energy and power, water supply and sanitation) with a focus on partnerships with countries that are part of the PRC's **Belt and Road Initiative**.

AUTONOMOUS REGION (AR). Administrative units of the PRC with a high concentration of **ethnic minorities** and which are granted a limited degree of autonomy in economic, cultural, social, and other matters, but remain politically and militarily subordinate to the central government. China has five autonomous regions: Guangxi Zhuang AR, Inner Mongolia AR, Ningxia Hui AR, **Tibet** AR, and **Xinjiang Uyghur** AR.

AUTARKY. Economic independence and self-sufficiency.

BAOJIA SYSTEM. A system of community mutual surveillance first developed in China during the early **imperial period** and based on grouping together a number of households that are responsible for maintaining law and order by watching and informing on each other. Chiang Kai-shek tried to revive the baojia system in the **Republic of China** during the 1930s.

BAREFOOT DOCTORS. Paramedics trained (usually by medical teams of the **People's Liberation Army**) to attend to the primary and preventive medical needs of people in China's rural areas during the Maoist era, especially in the early 1970s. Barefoot doctors were selected from among local residents, and the term "barefoot" refers to **peasants** in **South China** who worked without shoes in the rice paddies. They also promoted hygiene and family planning.

BASE AREA. A region in the Chinese countryside under the control of the **Chinese Communist Party** during the Civil War against the **Kuomintang**. The CCP had numerous base areas in the period 1927–1945, the best known of which were the **Jiangxi Soviet** and **Yan'an.**

BASIC LAW. The so-called mini-constitution of the **Hong Kong** Special Administrative Region of the PRC. It is based on the **"One Country, Two Systems"** principle and provides a blueprint for maintaining Hong Kong's legislative, administrative, judicial, social, and economic autonomy under Chinese sovereignty. But the Basic Law empowers the **Standing Committee of the National People's Congress** of the PRC to interpret the provisions of the Basic Law, thus giving China the final say on all matters related to Hong Kong.

BEIDAIHE. An oceanside resort city near **Beijing** where the CCP leadership often holds important mid-summer meetings.

BEIJING. The capital of the **People's Republic of China**, and one of four **directly administered cities**. Beijing literally means "Northern Capital." During the **Nanjing Decade** it was renamed Beiping, or "Northern Peace."

BEIJING MASSACRE. The military assault ordered by the leadership of the **Chinese Communist Party** on pro-democracy protesters in and around **Tiananmen Square** on June 4, 1989. Also called June 4, or simply 6–4.

BEIJINGOLOGY. An approach to the study of Chinese politics that emphasizes the analysis of the top leadership of the Chinese Communist Party, which is based in the national capital, **Beijing**. The term is an adaptation of "Kremlinology," which refers to efforts to understand politics in the Soviet Union (and, to a somewhat lesser extent, Russia today) by analyzing the words and actions of the top leaders who work in the compound of buildings in Moscow called the Kremlin.

BELT AND ROAD INITIATIVE (BRI). The PRC's ambitious plan to link China to Central Asia, South Asia, Africa, and even Europe through Chinese supported infrastructure development, such as maritime ports, airports, and highways. Formally called the Silk Road Economic Belt and the 21st-Century Maritime Silk Road. The "Silk Road" refers to the original Silk Road that began in the Han dynasty (207 BCE–220 CE) and ran from eastern China to southern Europe.

"BIG BANG." An approach to economic development, especially in countries going through a postcommunist transition from a **planned economy** to a **market economy**, that carries out widespread fundamental reforms simultaneously or in rapid succession. See **gradualism.**

BIG CHARACTER POSTERS (*DAZIBAO*). Handwritten posters of oversized Chinese characters, often written on newspapers or large sheets of paper that make a strong public political statement. Although they have an earlier history in China, they were used most extensively during the **Cultural Revolution**, particularly by **Red Guards**, most often to denounce some person or group's ideological mistakes.

BINGTUAN. Chinese pinyin abbreviation for **Xinjiang** Production and Construction Corps (XPCC), established in the early 1950s as places to live and work for demobilized soldiers and their families; designed to promote economic development and **Han** settlement in the far western region of China inhabited largely by **Uyghurs**. *Bingtuan* were initially mostly farms directly under the control of the **People's Liberation Army**. They are now largely civilian organizations and are involved in a wide range of economic enterprises.

BLOOD HEADS. People in China who bought blood from poor farmers and resold it for a handsome profit to blood-products companies in the mid-1990s. They often used unsanitary equipment and methods, which led to widespread HIV infections in donors and which were, in turn, transmitted to sexual partners and newborns. The problem was most severe in Henan and adjacent **provinces** in central China where there were many "AIDS villages" in which a large percentage of the population was infected.

BLUE SHIRTS. A clique of the **Kuomintang** that favored **fascism** as an ideology for the **Republic of China** in the 1930s. They were a paramilitary organization that drew inspiration from Benito Mussolini in Italy. The Blue Shirts were active in implementing Chiang Kai-shek's **New Life Movement**.

BOURGEOIS LIBERALIZATION. A term widely used by the CCP in the late 1980s to criticize intellectuals and others who were thought to be advocating political reforms that would challenge party leadership. The **Tiananmen Square** protests of 1989 were said to have been caused, in part, by the spread of bourgeois liberalization. See also **spiritual pollution**.

BOURGEOISIE. In Marxist theory, the ruling class in capitalist society. The bourgeoisie owns the means of production and employs and exploits the **proletariat** from whose labor they extract profits. It is not only the economically dominant class, but it also controls the state, which it uses as an instrument to protect its own power and property as well as to suppress the working class. Synonymous with the capitalist class. Mao applied the term more broadly to refer to those who used their authority for self-interest and to claim special privilege and higher status. There could be a bourgeoisie and bourgeois **ideology** even after private property had been abolished during the **socialist transformation** and the bourgeoisie as an economic class no longer existed. See also **class struggle, proletariat**.

BOXER PROTOCOL. The peace treaty that the **Qing dynasty** was forced by foreign powers to sign in September 1901 after the suppression of the **Boxer Uprising**. Of all the Protocol's humiliating provisions, the most disastrous for China was a staggering indemnity to pay the cost of the war for the foreign powers, which proved a crushing burden to the imperial government's already crippled economy.

BOXER UPRISING. Also known as the Boxer Rebellion, or the Righteous Harmony Society Movement; took place in **North China** in 1899–1900. The name "Boxers" refers to the martial arts mastered by the rebels, which supposedly gave them protection against harm, even from bullets. The rebellion was aimed at Christian missionaries, Chinese Christian converts, and, initially, the **Qing dynasty**, but its causes lie more deeply in the deteriorating economic conditions in the rural areas, compounded by natural disasters. The Empress Dowager Cixi at first ordered the suppression of the rebellion, but then embraced it as an anti-imperialist movement. It was subdued by the intervention of Western forces after the Boxers attacked foreign diplomatic buildings in **Beijing**. See also **Boxer Protocol**.

BRICS. Brazil, Russia, India, China, and South Africa, as an informal grouping of five large emerging economies.

BUILDING SOCIALISM WITH CHINESE CHARACTERISTICS. One of the two key components of **Deng Xiaoping Theory** (the other being the **Four Cardinal Principles**). The term conveys the idea that China must adapt both the theory and practice of **socialism** in its quest for modernization because of its relative economic "backwardness." This involves using whatever means are necessary, even capitalist ones, to promote development. There are, in turn, two components to building socialism with Chinese characteristics: reform of the economy by increasing the role of the market while reducing that of the state; and opening to the outside world by expanding China's involvement in the global economy. See also **cat theory; primary stage of socialism**.

BUYUN EXPERIMENT. Elections that were held in 1998 in which all the voters in the villages that were part of Buyun **town** (in Sichuan **province**) went to the polls to directly elect the town leaders. This experiment with **direct elections** got much publicity at the time, but the central government soon ruled them unconstitutional and no such elections have been held since.

CADRE. Any person in a position of authority. In China, not all cadres belong to the communist party and not all party members are cadres. The term encompasses officials from the very highest leaders to the lowest ranking and includes people in leadership positions in all types of institutions and settings, not just political.

CADRE EXCHANGE SYSTEM. A system of personnel management used in China in which leading **town** cadres, such as the town head and party secretary, are transferred to a different locality every three to six years. This system is meant to prevent cadres from developing local networks that might dilute their allegiance to higher-level authorities or provide opportunities for corruption.

CAMPAIGN. See **mass mobilization campaign.**

CAPITALISM. A type of economic system in which the means of production are, for the most part, privately owned and operated for profit. Economic activity is based on a free **market economy** in which the state plays a limited role in determining such things as production, distribution, investment, prices, supply and demand, and the allocation of labor. In **Marxism**, capitalism is the stage of human social and economic development that comes after feudalism and before **socialism**. It is a decisive period in history in which the **bourgeoisie** is the ruling class and the **proletariat** comes into being. Capitalism ends (and gives way to **socialism**) when the proletariat rises in revolution and overthrows the bourgeoisie.

CAPITALIST ROADER. A label given to **cadres** in China who were accused of betraying socialism and advocating or following policies that it was alleged would lead to a restoration of capitalism in the country.

CASINO CAPITALISM. A system in which an economy and the government become heavily dependent on gambling in private casinos. **Macao** is an example of casino capitalism.

CAT THEORY. Based on Deng Xiaoping's famous saying that "it does not matter if it is a white cat or a black cat, as long as it catches mice"; in other words, it is results that matter when determining whether a policy is correct. The comment was made in a July 1962 speech on restoring agricultural production in the aftermath of the **Great Leap Forward** famine. Mao interpreted Deng's meaning as being that ideology did not matter in policymaking, and this statement was used against Deng in the **Cultural Revolution** as evidence that he was a **capitalist roader**. See **Deng Xiaoping Theory.**

CENTRAL ADVISORY COMMISSION. Established by Deng Xiaoping in 1982 as a CCP organization with little power, whose purpose was to ease elderly senior leaders into retirement by removing them from important positions, yet allowing them to retain some public visibility and prestige in an advisory capacity. It was abolished in 1992.

CENTRAL COMMISSION FOR DISCIPLINE INSPECTION (CCDI). The CCP organization charged with monitoring and punishing abuses of power, corruption, and other wrongdoings committed by party officials. Lower-level party organizations, including provincial, municipal, and county-level bodies, also have discipline inspection commissions that report directly to the commission one level above them.

CENTRAL COMMITTEE. The third-highest level of leadership in the **Chinese Communist Party**. It is elected every five years by the **National Congress of the CCP** and meets annually for about two weeks. The Central Committee elected in 2017 consisted of 376 regular and alternate members who are high-ranking CCP **cadres** from around the country.

CENTRAL CULTURAL REVOLUTION GROUP (CCRG). Became the *de facto* ruling body in China after the purge of Liu Shaoqi and other top leaders in 1966, although its power and that of all organizations was eclipsed by Mao's personal authority at the height of the **Cultural Revolution**. The CCRG was dominated by ideological radicals like Mao's wife, Jiang Qing, who was the effective leader of the group. It suspended operations in September 1969.

CENTRAL MILITARY COMMISSION (CMC). The most important military organization in China. Technically, there are both a CCP CMC (formally, the Military Commission of the **Central Committee**) and a PRC Central Military Commission; in fact, the two bodies overlap completely in personnel and function. CCP general secretary and PRC president Xi Jinping is the chairman, which makes him the commander in chief of China's armed forces. All the other members are from the military. Sometimes referred to in English as the Military Affairs Commission.

CENTRAL PARTY SCHOOL. Formally called the Party School of the Central Committee of the Communist Party of China; located in **Beijing**; the highest-level institution for training CCP leaders. Party leaders from around the country take courses there for periods ranging from a couple of months to a couple of years on **Marxism-Leninism** and its Chinese adaptations, as well as in subject such as comparative political systems and theories, public administration, economics, law, and various policy-related subjects. Being the head of the school is an important position within the party leadership, particularly for rising stars, and has been held at various times since 1949 by such important figures as Liu Shaoqi, Hua Guofeng, Hu Jintao, and Xi Jinping. Mao Zedong headed the school in 1942–1947, when it was located in **Yan'an** and while he was consolidating his political and ideological authority within the party.

CENTRAL SPECIAL CASE EXAMINATION GROUP. Established in 1966 during the **Cultural Revolution** as the organ of an inner-party inquisition that directed the ferreting out, arrest, and torture of suspect **Central Committee** members and other officials. It was formally dissolved in December 1978.

CHARTER 08. A document signed by more than three hundred Chinese intellectuals and political activists, issued as a blueprint for democratic reforms in December 2008. Its leading signatories were detained and sometimes jailed, including Nobel Peace Prize laureate, Liu Xiaobo.

CHIEF EXECUTIVE. The head of the government of the **Hong Kong** Special Administrative Region of the PRC. The chief executive must be a Chinese citizen, at least forty years old, and have lived in Hong Kong for twenty years or more. He or she is elected for a five-year term by an Election Committee that consists of several hundred members elected or appointed from various sectors of society, such as commerce, finance, labor, the professions, religion, and government. The composition of the Election Committee is closely controlled by the central government in Beijing and the candidate elected has to be approved by the government of the PRC. The **Macao** SAR of the PRC is also headed by a chief executive.

CHINA DEMOCRACY PARTY. Formed in 1998 as an open opposition party by former **Tiananmen Movement** activists. The party was initially allowed to register and open branches nationwide, but fearing that it was becoming too popular, the CCP banned the organization and arrested most of its leaders.

CHINA DREAM (*ZHONGGUO MENG*). A phrase popularized by Xi Jinping starting in November 2012 just as he was taking over as general secretary of the CCP and meant to convey the goals of the PRC to become a moderately well-off society by 2021, the one-hundredth anniversary of the founding of the CCP, and a fully-developed prosperous society by 1949, the one-hundredth anniversary of the establishment of the PRC.

CHINA PROPER (OR INNER CHINA). A somewhat imprecise geographic term that refers to the **provinces** of eastern and central China that became part of the Chinese empire early in its history and is largely populated by the majority ethnic **Han** Chinese.

CHINESE CIVIL WAR. The conflict between the **Kuomintang** (KMT), led by Chiang Kai-shek, and the **Chinese Communist Party** (CCP), led after 1935 by Mao Zedong. There were two phases of the Civil War: 1927–1937, beginning when Chiang Kai-shek unleashed the **White Terror** against the communists to the formation of a **united front** between the KMT and CCP to fight the Japanese after the **Xi'an Incident**; and 1946–1949, from the resumption of KMT-CCP hostilities following the surrender of Japan in World War II to the victory of the CCP and the founding of the **People's Republic of China**.

CHINESE COMMUNIST PARTY (CCP). Founded in 1921; it has been the ruling party of the **People's Republic of China** since 1949. It had 89.6 million members as of mid-2018, making it by far the largest political party in the world, but still a small minority of the Chinese population, which is consistent with its self-proclaimed role as a **vanguard party**. Also referred to as the Communist Party of China (CPC).

CHINESE COMMUNIST YOUTH LEAGUE (CCYL). A **mass organization** of the CCP for people aged fourteen to twenty-eight. It is a training ground for future party members and leaders. In mid-2018, the CCYL had about 80 million members. Some of China's current top leaders advanced their political careers by working as in key positions in the CCYL. See also *tuanpai*.

CHINESE PEOPLE'S POLITICAL CONSULTATIVE CONFERENCE (CPPCC). An advisory body to the PRC's **National People's Congress (NPC)**. Its more than 2000 delegates come from China's eight **"democratic parties," mass organizations**, ethnic minorities various sectors of society (such as literature and the arts), and independents, as well as **Hong Kong** and **Macao**. Although the majority of members of the CPPCC are noncommunists, the organization is bound by its charter to accept the leadership of the CCP, and it has always been headed by a high-ranking party leader.

CHONGQING. A city in southwestern China to which Chiang Kai-shek and the **Kuomintang** retreated after the Japanese invasion in 1937. It became the wartime capital of the **Republic of China**. Today it is one of the four **directly administered cities** of the PRC.

CIVIL SERVICE EXAMINATION SYSTEM. The system for selecting imperial bureaucrats that was first established in the Han dynasty (206 BCE–220 CE) and lasted until 1905, when it was abolished as part of a futile reform effort to save China's last dynasty, the **Qing** (1644–1912). The exams mainly tested knowledge of Confucian texts and required years of intensive, highly specialized studying to prepare for multilevel examinations that few passed.

CIVIL SOCIETY. The social space occupied by private organizations and associations composed of civilians who join together to pursue a common purpose *other than the direct pursuit of political power* and which operate independently of government authority. Most simply, it consists of those associations that exist and operate in the space between the family and the state.

CLASS STRUGGLE. The idea that exploited and exploiting classes are constantly engaged in conflict, for example poor peasants and landlords or the **proletariat** and the **bourgeoisie.** It is one of the central ideas of **Marxism**. Mao's elaborations on the Marxist theory of class struggle, especially that it continues even during the **socialist transformation** and after the elimination of private property, are defining features of **Mao Zedong Thought** as a variety of Marxism. It is also considered by the current leadership of the CCP as one of Mao's ideological errors and a cause of the **Cultural Revolution**.

"CLEANSING OF CLASS RANKS" CAMPAIGN. One of the most violent parts of the **Cultural Revolution**, which in 1968–1969, together with subsequent suppressions in 1970–1972, probably killed at least 1.5 million people. The targets were troublesome rebel elements or others who had earned the displeasure of local authorities during the **Cultural Revolution**, as well as ordinary criminals, imaginary counterrevolutionaries, and the usual suspects with "bad" class backgrounds.

COLLECTIVES. A type of rural organization established in 1956–1957 in the second stage of the **socialist transformation** of the Chinese countryside that followed the formation of **cooperatives** in 1954–1955. Collectives were much larger—250 families—than the earlier cooperatives and more socialist in their organization; the collective not only owned the land, but members were paid only according to their labor with no account made of the amount of land or other resources that families had put in. Only a small portion of the collectively owned land was set aside for private cultivation. Also called Higher-Level Agricultural Producer Cooperatives (HLAPCs).

COLLECTIVE IDENTITY. A sense of belonging to a specific group based on some shared characteristic, for example, race, religion, economic class, culture, language, or gender.

COLLECTIVE OWNERSHIP. A type of public ownership of property in a socialist economy that is between state (government) ownership and private ownership. In theory, the property is owned jointly by a group of people and is operated in their common interest rather than for the profit of any single individual. In China, rural land is collectively-owned by the entire village and is contracted out to individual families or used for other purposes such as building a collectively-owned factory.

COLLECTIVIZATION. The transformation of private property, particularly land, into some type of public ownership. In China, the collectivization—or **socialist transformation**—of agriculture unfolded in three major stages that involved establishing **cooperatives** (1954–1955), **collectives** (1956–1957), and **people's communes** (1958).

COMMUNES. See **people's communes.**

COMINTERN (COMMUNIST INTERNATIONAL). The organization established in Moscow in 1919 with the goal of supporting and spreading communist revolutions to other parts of the world. It worked both with existing communist parties and sent agents to help establish such parties where they did not exist. Comintern agents were important in the founding and development of the **Chinese Communist Party,** though its influence diminished as Mao Zedong rose to power.

COMMUNISM. In Marxist theory, the highest stage of human social development. It is the goal of and follows the **socialist transformation** of society. It is fundamentally egalitarian; power is in the hands of the producers, and the state withers away since there is no need for coercion in a truly classless society. Although reaching communism is the stated goal of all Marxist-Leninist political parties, including the Chinese Communist Party today, no country has ever claimed that it has achieved communism. The term is also often used as a synonym for **Marxism-Leninism.**

COMMUNIST PARTY-STATE. A type of political system in which a communist party, ideologically committed to some variant of **Marxism-Leninism,** has a monopoly of power and claims the right to exercise the "leading role" over the economy, culture, and other aspects of society, including politics.

COMMUNIST PERIOD. Chinese history during which the **Chinese Communist Party** has been in power from the founding of the PRC in 1949 to the present.

"COMMUNITY" OR *SHEQU.* A relatively new form of the lowest level of urban administration in China, first introduced in the 1990s to provide services for and as a means of control of workers laid off from **state-owned enterprises**. The *shequ* is intended to take over many of the functions that were formerly the responsibility of **work units** and **neighborhood committees**.

CONFUCIANISM. The philosophy based on the teachings of Confucius (551–479 BCE) and his disciples and interpreters that emphasizes proper and righteous social behavior, respect for and obedience to parents, deference to elders and superiors, the preservation of social harmony, and the value of education. Politically, it stresses that good government must be based on morality, including that of the ruler, not harsh laws. Confucianism has deeply influenced the history and culture of China, as well those of the other countries in East Asia.

CONTRADICTION. A crucial concept in **Mao Zedong Thought** (with roots in Marxist theory). It refers to the interacting opposites inherent in all things such that each part of the contradiction cannot exist without the other (the "unity of opposites"). It is also the interaction of those opposites that is the source of change and development, for example, in society, as well as in nature. For Mao (and Marx), the most fundamental contradiction in society is that between classes, such as between landlords and **peasants** and between the **bourgeoisie** and the **proletariat**, whose interaction takes the form of **class struggle**. See also **antagonistic contradiction and non-antagonistic contradiction**.

COOPERATIVE MEDICAL SCHEME (CMS). The system of health care in rural China in the 1960s and 1970s during the Maoist period that provided free or almost free basic-level preventive and curative services. About 90 percent of rural residents were covered. The CMS collapsed with the coming of **decollectivization** at the start of the **reform era**, leaving most rural residents uninsured until a new, but more limited form of health insurance was put into place in the early 2000s.

COOPERATIVES. The first form of socialist organization introduced in the Chinese countryside in 1954–1955. Cooperatives consisted of twenty-five to fifty families. Land, although still technically owned by the farmers, as well as tools and draft animals, were pooled. Members were paid partly on the basis of how much work they did and partly according to how much property they had contributed to the cooperative. Agricultural production was under the direction of cooperative officials. Formally called lower-level agricultural producers cooperatives (LLAPCs). See **cooperativization**.

COOPERATIVIZATION. The process of establishing the rural cooperatives that was carried out in China in 1954–1955 in the first phase of the **collectivization** of the Chinese countryside and the agricultural economy.

"CRITICIZE LIN BIAO AND CONFUCIUS" CAMPAIGN. This had little to do with either Lin Biao or Confucius; launched by Mao in 1974 because of his growing unhappiness with Zhou Enlai's policies and the political reliability of the **People's Liberation Army**. Lin Biao and Confucius were surrogates for criticism of alleged ultra-rightist mistakes by Zhou (who was attacked indirectly) and the PLA leadership. Although sometimes called a "second **Cultural Revolution**," it lasted less than a year and caused much less (though not insignificant) disruption.

COUNTY. The level of administration in the PRC below the **provinces** (and **autonomous regions** and **directly administered cities**) and above the **town**.

CROSSING THE RIVER BY FEELING THE STONES A method of gradual policy implementation in the PRC that involves experimentation and adjustment before widespread adoption.

CULTURAL REVOLUTION. Formally the "Great Proletarian Cultural Revolution," a political campaign and mass movement launched by Chairman Mao Zedong in 1966 to stop China from following both the bureaucratic Soviet model of socialist development and the Western "capitalist road" down which he had concluded some of his closest comrades were leading the country. There is a scholarly difference of opinion as to whether the Cultural Revolution occurred during the relatively short span of 1966–1969 or engulfed the whole decade of 1966–1976, including up to and just beyond Mao's death in September 1976. In either case, the Cultural Revolution was a terribly destructive period that combined elements of a witch hunt, a crusade, an inquisition, a reign of terror, armed conflict, and cut-throat palace politics. See **big character posters; Central Cultural Revolution Group; Central Special Case Examination Group; Central Special Case Examination Group; "cleansing of class ranks" campaign; eight model operas; May 7th Cadre Schools; "Four Big" Rights; May 16 Directive; Red Guards; revisionism; Revolutionary Committees; struggle meeting; work teams**.

DALAI LAMA. The spiritual leader of Tibetan Buddhism; from the seventeenth century to 1959 also the head of the government of **Tibet**. "Lama" is a general term referring to a teacher of Tibetan Buddhism. Dalai Lamas are believed to be the reincarnation of their predecessors. The current Dalai Lama (b. 1935) is the fourteenth in a line of succession that goes back to the late fourteenth century. In 1959, an invasion of Tibet by China's **People's Liberation Army** forced the Dalai Lama to flee to India (where the Tibetan government in exile still remains). He won the Nobel Peace Prize in 1989.

DANGWAI. Literally, "outside the party"; the general rubric applied to opponents of the **Kuomintang** (KMT) in **Taiwan** in the early 1980s, when the formation of formal opposition political parties was still banned under the terms of **martial law**. The fact that this was allowed by the KMT, then under the control of Chiang Kai-shek's son, Chiang Ching-kuo, was seen by some as an encouraging sign that democratization might be beginning. In 1986, *dangwai* politicians founded the **Democratic Progressive Party (DPP)**.

DAOIST/DAOISM/(TAOIST/TAOISM). An ancient Chinese school of thought and practice that combines elements of philosophy, religion, and folk beliefs. Dao (or Tao) literally means "the Way," and Daoism emphasizes harmony between humans and nature, the wholeness of the universe, spontaneity over thought, simplicity and truth, the rejection of worldly worries and desires, and achieving transcendence through the cultivation of moral character.

DECOLLECTIVIZATION. The process of dismantling the **people's communes** and establishing the **household responsibility system** in the Chinese countryside in the early 1980s that was a key part of the **market reforms** introduced by Deng Xiaoping when he came to power in the post-Mao era.

DEMOCRACY WALL. The name given to a 650-foot stretch of wall near **Tiananmen Square** in **Beijing**, where in late 1978–early 1979 there was an eruption of political posters by intellectuals criticizing Mao's mistakes and the neo-Maoist **"whateverist" faction**, as well as calling for democratization. Democracy Wall was shut down and several leaders of the movement were arrested after it had served Deng Xiaoping's purpose of isolating his leftist political opponents in the party leadership.

DEMOCRATIC CENTRALISM. The Leninist principle of how a communist party is to be organized and operate internally. The core idea is that the party should encourage open discussion and debate (democracy) while a matter is being decided, but once the leadership has made a decision, then all members are expected to accept and follow it (centralism). It stipulates that the individual party member is subordinate to the party organization and that lower-level party organizations are subordinate to higher-level organizations. In the practice of **communist party-states** such as China, the centralism part of the principle has far outweighed the democratic part. See also **inner-party democracy**.

DEMOCRATIC PARTIES. Refers to the eight non-communist political parties in the PRC that play a limited consultative role in the legislative process. They must swear allegiance to the CCP and do not compete with or challenge the CCP in any meaningful way. These parties have a total membership of about seven-hundred thousand.

DEMOCRATIC PROGRESSIVE PARTY (DPP). One of the two major political parties in **Taiwan**, the other being the **Kuomintang** (KMT). The DPP was established by **Taiwanese** opposition (*dangwai*) politicians in 1986 with independence for Taiwan as a major part of its platform. The DPP has won the presidency of the **Republic of China** in 2000, 2004, and 2016. The party is still more cautious about ties with the PRC than is the KMT, but it no longer proposes outright independence for the island.

DEMOGRAPHIC TRANSITION. Describes the "natural" shift in a country from high birth rates and high death rates to low birth rates and low death rates as a consequence of economic development and modernization.

DENG XIAOPING THEORY. The official name given by the **Chinese Communist Party** to the **ideology** of Deng Xiaoping. Deng Xiaoping Theory was added to the CCP's constitution in 1997 as a formal part of the party's guiding ideology. It can be said to consist of two main parts: **Building Socialism with Chinese Characteristics**, which involves the reform of the economy, including introducing elements of capitalism, and opening the country economically and in other ways to the outside world; and the **Four Cardinal Principles**, which lay out the political framework of Party leadership and the ideological conditions for reform and opening up. See also **cat theory**.

DEPENDENCY RATIO. The size of the working-age population (15–64) expressed as a proportion of the total population. The young (birth–14) and the elderly (over 65) are considered to be dependent on the working age (productive) population. Because of the **one-child policy**, China has a rapidly aging population, which will sharply increase its elderly dependency ratio in the decades ahead. This is a challenge to the government in terms of providing elder care and social security.

DEVELOPMENTAL STATE. A government, usually an authoritarian one, that is strongly committed to and uses its power to promote national economic development.

DIBAO OR "MINIMUM LIVELIHOOD PROTECTION." Implemented to provide subsidies to all individuals with incomes below locally determined poverty lines in urban China after the extensive welfare elements (the **iron rice bowl**) of the **work unit** system were eliminated in the **reform era**.

DICTATORSHIP OF THE PROLETARIAT. The idea (first proposed by Marx) that after the **proletariat** (the industrial working class) has seized political power from the **bourgeoisie** (the capitalists), it—or in the Leninist variation, the communist party on behalf of the proletariat—will have to exercise strict control over the bourgeoisie and others who seek to overthrow the proletarian state. See also **people's democratic dictatorship.**

DIRECT ELECTIONS. An electoral system of choosing political officeholders in which the voters directly vote for the people or party that they want to see elected. Contrast with **indirect elections**.

DIRECTLY ADMINISTERED CITY/DIRECTLY ADMINISTERED MUNICIPALITY. (*ZHIXIASHI*) Any of four cities in China that are under the direct jurisdiction of the central government: **Beijing, Chongqing**, Shanghai, and Tianjin. They have the same administrative standing as **provinces.**

DYNASTIES. The series of hereditary monarchies that ruled China from 221 BCE until 1912 CE. There were a dozen or so major Chinese dynasties, which lasted from under twenty years (the Qin) to two hundred (Tang, Ming, Qing), three hundred (Song), or four hundred (Han) years.

EASTERN TURKISTAN ISLAMIC MOVEMENT (ETIM). A small militant **Uyghur** separatist group in the **Xinjiang Uyghur Autonomous Region** that was supposedly affiliated with Al Qaeda. The United States Government declared it to be a terrorist organization in August 2002. The Chinese government regards the ETIM as a major threat to its internal security.

ECOLOGICAL CIVILIZATION. Part of former PRC president and CCP leader Hu Jintao's so-called **Scientific Outlook on Development** and **harmonious socialist society**, which are the hallmarks of his administration's platform and his contribution to the guiding **ideology** of the CCP. It emphasizes paying attention to the environmental consequences of economic growth and supports giving higher priority to **sustainable development**.

EIGHT IMMORTALS (OR EIGHT ELDERS). Eight very senior leaders of the CCP, including Deng Xiaoping and Chen Yun, who wielded great power in the 1980s and into the 1990s, even though they had mostly retired from their official positions.

EIGHT MODEL OPERAS. The most famous of the very limited number of stage works approved for public performance during the **Cultural Revolution** by Jiang Qing. As with all authorized works of the time, they had revolutionary themes that praised the heroism of workers, peasants, and soldiers and highlighted the infallible leadership of the Chinese Communist Party. The titles of some of them are: *Red Detachment of Women, Taking Tiger Mountain by Strategy*, and *On the Docks*.

ELITIST COALITION. A group of current Chinese leaders who prefer to giving priority to promoting development in the fastest growing and most modern parts of the country and are less concerned about problems such as inequality and environmental degradation. The elitist coalition represents the interests of entrepreneurs, the emerging middle class, and the coastal region. See also **populist coalition; princelings**.

ETHNIC MINORITIES (OR NATIONAL MINORITIES). China's fifty-five non-**Han** ethnic groups that range in size from 16 million (the Zhuang) to under 3,000 (the Lhobo). See also **Tibetan; Uyghur**.

EXECUTIVE COUNCIL (ExCo). The advisory body that assists the **chief executive** of the **Hong Kong Special Administrative Region (HKSAR)** in policy making. In that sense, it serves as the chief executive's cabinet. Members are appointed by the chief executive from among senior civil servants, members of the **Legislative Council**, and notable public figures, such as a university president.

EXPORT-LED GROWTH (ELG). A strategy of economic development that stresses using exports produced by comparatively inexpensive labor to pay for technology imports that fuel modernization and shift the composition of gross domestic product, first from agriculture to industry, and then to services. China's rapid economic growth has largely followed an ELG approach, but the global financial crisis that began in late 2008 forced the government to shift to a strategy that put more emphasis on domestic consumption.

EXTERMINATION CAMPAIGNS. Efforts by Chiang Kai-shek to destroy the **Chinese Communist Party** by military force. There were five such efforts between 1930 and 1934. The Fifth Extermination Campaign in 1934 drove the CCP out of their **Jiangxi Soviet** base and forced them to undertake their year-long **Long March**.

EXTRATERRITORIALITY. A concept in international law in which foreigners or international organizations are exempt or immune from the local laws of the country in which they are present. It may be applied to specific places, such as territorial concessions under the control of a foreign power. It may also mean the extension of the jurisdiction of a nation's laws to its citizens abroad, in which case if such a citizen committed a crime in a foreign country, she or he would be subject to the laws of his or her home country, not the country in which the crime was committed. Extraterritoriality was included in many of the **unequal treaties** imposed on the **Qing dynasty**.

FACTION. An informal group of individuals who are united by some common bond and whose purpose is to maximize their power, especially that of their own leader. Factions may be motivated by shared ideology, policy preferences, personal loyalties, or simply the desire for power.

FALUN GONG. Literally, "Dharma Wheel Practice"; a spiritual sect that combines elements of Buddhism and **Daoism** along with breathing exercises and meditation founded in 1992 by Li Hongzhi, a worker and musician turned spiritual leader. It gained tens of millions of followers from all walks of life both inside China and abroad. The Chinese government began cracking down on the group in 1999, which led to a silent protest by 10,000 Falun Gong followers outside **Zhongnanhai,** the CCP leadership compound in **Beijing**. The government then labeled the group as a dangerous religious cult and banned it. The ban remains in effect and the Falun Gong movement in China has been driven underground.

FASCISM. An ideology that exalts national glory and strong authoritarian government under a single party and a single leader. It is highly militaristic. Fascism is firmly anti-communist and believes in mutually beneficial economic cooperation between the state and the private sector.

FLOATING POPULATION. The rural-to-urban migrant population, numbering about 250 million, who have moved to China's cities in search of jobs since the 1980s. It is the largest population migration in history. Most migrants have insecure, low-paying jobs in the construction or service industries. In some of China's largest cities, they make up as much as a quarter or a third of the total population.

"FOUR BIG" RIGHTS. The right to speak out freely, air views fully, hold great debates, and write big-character posters; included in the 1975 constitution of the PRC—the so-called **Cultural Revolution** constitution because of its many radical features. These rights were removed when the constitution was thoroughly rewritten in 1982 after the Maoist era had ended.

FOUR CARDINAL PRINCIPLES. The ideological guidelines for economic reform spelled out by Deng Xiaoping in a speech in March 1979. In that speech he said, in pursuing modernization it was necessary for China to: (1) uphold the socialist road; (2) uphold the dictatorship of the proletariat; (3) uphold the leadership of the Communist Party; and (4) uphold Marxism-Leninism and Mao Zedong Thought. The CCP still emphasizes the Four Cardinal Principles as part of its guiding ideology.

FREE CHINA. The area of southwest China not under the control of the Japanese or the communists during World War II, but under the authority of the **Republic of China**. Its capital was **Chongqing.** The term was frequently used by the United States and its allies during the Cold War to refer to **Taiwan** in contrast to the People's Republic, which was called "Red China."

GANG OF FOUR. A label first applied by Chairman Mao Zedong in May 1975 to his wife, Jiang Qing, and her radical Shanghai colleagues, Zhang Chunqiao, Yao Wenyuan, and Wang Hongwen as part of a warning to them to stop their secretive factional maneuverings within the party leadership: "Practice Marxism-Leninism, and not revisionism; unite and don't split; be open and aboveboard, and don't intrigue and conspire. Don't function as a gang of four, don't do it any more, why do you keep doing it?" The label was then publicly applied to them as part of a campaign of denunciation after their arrest in October 1976. The "Gang of Four" was put on trial in 1980 and sentenced to long prison terms for their political crimes.

GAOKAO. Literally "high test," this is the National Higher Education Entrance Exam held annually to determine university admissions in the PRC. Students' scores determine whether they can go to college and the college they can attend, and thus have a huge impact on future career prospects. The stakes are enormous and the pressure is intense, and Chinese students spend years of intense studying in preparation.

GENERAL LINE. The overall policy direction set by the leadership of the CCP.

GINI INDEX. A statistical measure of the inequality of income distribution in a country. It ranges from 0 (perfect equality) to 1 (perfect inequality). China's Gini Index has been going up during most of the **reform era**.

"GOING OUT STRATEGY." China's push to purchase overseas firms, mines, and resources, locating its own companies overseas, and listing Chinese firms on global stock markets to acquire foreign capital. This strategy began in the 1990s, but has accelerated dramatically since the mid-2000s.

GRADUALISM. An approach to economic development that implements reform in a cautious, step-by-step manner. China's economic reform are often characterized as being gradualist, in contrast to the **"big bang"** approach of rapid and multifaceted change undertaken by the former Soviet Union and many Eastern European countries after the fall of the region's **communist-party states**. But there have been "big bang" aspects to China's reform, such as the wave of privatization of state-owned and collective enterprises in the 1990s. See also **crossing the river by feeling the stones; segmented deregulation**.

GREAT LEAP FORWARD. Mao's utopian push in 1958-60 to accelerate China's economic development to quickly catch up with the industrial powers and its ideological advancement into the era of true **communism**. The Leap was a **mass mobilization campaign** under party leadership that involved a radical reorganization of society, relied on labor power, and emphasized human will and revolutionary fervor to reach ever higher levels of production. It ended in one of the worst famines in human history and an industrial depression that wiped out nearly all the economic gains of the CCP's first years in power. See also **people's communes; Lushan Conference**.

GREAT PROLETARIAN CULTURAL REVOLUTION. See **Cultural Revolution**.

GREAT WALL. Built as a fortification by various Chinese **dynasties,** beginning with the **Qin** (221–206 BCE), to keep "barbarians" from the north from invading China. Its stretches from the coast northeast of **Beijing** about 4,000 miles (6,400 km) to the west.

OPEN UP THE WEST. A campaign launched by the PRC in the late 1990s to steer more resources to the western part of the country, including **Tibet** and **Xinjiang**, in the effort to narrow the gaps between those regions and China's coastal provinces, which had benefitted much more from **reform era** policies. Also known as the "Great Western Development Drive."

GREATER CHINA. Usually refers to the PRC (particularly the southern **province** of Guangdong), **Hong Kong**, and **Taiwan**—and sometimes Singapore—particularly the close economic integration within the region.

GUANXI ("connections"). Specifically, informal interpersonal relationships or networks. *Guanxi* can be based on a wide variety of connections between people, such as native place, school ties, or common acquaintances, and imply both trust and reciprocity.

GUERRILLA WARFARE. A method of warfare in which small, highly mobile units made up of fighters called guerrillas who attack, harass, distract, or demoralize larger and stronger forces of the enemy. Guerrillas often rely on the support of civilians to provide them with food, medicine, shelter, and intelligence. The word guerrilla is derived from the Spanish meaning "little war." Mao Zedong is considered one of the major theorists of guerilla warfare.

HAN. The largest ethnic group in China, comprising about 92 percent of the Chinese people in the PRC. The name comes from the Han dynasty (206 BCE–220 CE), considered the greatest of China's early dynasties.

HARMONIOUS SOCIALIST SOCIETY. The core of former leader Hu Jintao's political platform, reflecting the proclaimed policy goals of his administration. It emphasized righting some of the imbalances and problems of China's rapid economic growth since the 1980s, including income and development inequalities—especially between city and countryside—environmental degradation, and the collapse of the health care system.

HIGH QING. The period during the latter half of the eighteenth century when the **Qing dynasty** was at the height of its cultural, political, and economic glory.

higher-level agricultural producer cooperatives (HLAPCs). See **collectives**.

HONG KONG. A special administrative region of the PRC, formally known as the Hong Kong Special Administrative Region (HKSAR). It is a small area (420 square miles) located on the far southern coast of China with a population of around 7 million. But it is also a dynamic financial and commercial center and has a standard of living that is comparable to the United States and Japan. Hong Kong became a **special administrative region** of the **People's Republic of China** on July 1, 1997. For about 150 years prior to that, it was a colony of Great Britain. See **Basic Law: chief executive; Executive Council; Legislative Council; "One Country, Two Systems."**

HONG KONG SPECIAL ADMINISTRATIVE REGION (HKSAR). See **Hong Kong.**

HOUSE CHURCHES. Unofficial and officially illegal places of Christian worship that may range from tiny gatherings in rural villages to very large urban congregations. House churches (or underground churches) are illegal because they are not affiliated with the state-approved religious organizations such as the Protestant "Three-Self Patriotic Movement" or the "Chinese Catholic Patriotic Association."

HOUSEHOLD RESPONSIBILITY SYSTEM. The basic form of organization in China's rural economy since the early 1980s when the **people's communes** were abolished. In this system, individual households contract for "use rights" to the land, which is still owned by the village, and families make the decisions about crops, investment, savings, labor allocation, and marketing. There were brief experiments with this type of organization in the aftermath of the **Great Leap Forward**, but they were stopped by Mao, who regarded them as a "sprout of capitalism." See **decollectivization**.

HUKOU SYSTEM. Household registration system, first implemented in the mid-1950s as a way to control the movement of China's population and to prevent the massive rural-to-urban migration that plagued many developing countries. Each individual had either an "agricultural" or a "non-agricultural" registration (*hukou*), which dictated where he or she could, for example, live, work, go to school, receive health care, and get and use ration coupons. The system was very effective in achieving its purposes, but was criticized for the way it reinforced and compounded urban-rural inequalities to the great disadvantage of those with agricultural registrations. The *hukou* system began to break down in the 1980s with **decollectivization, market reform**s, and the need for labor mobility. All citizens of the PRC still must have a *hukou* registration. The system is being reformed, but is not likely to be abolished.

HUNDRED DAYS REFORM. A period in mid-1898 when the emperor issued edicts ordering far-reaching changes to save the **Qing dynasty** from further decline. Among the proposed reforms were modernizing the **civil service examination system**, the entire educational system, and the institutions of government. The reforms were brought to a halt when the Empress Dowager Cixi ordered the arrest of the reformers and put the emperor under palace arrest.

HUNDRED FLOWERS MOVEMENT. Launched by Mao Zedong and the CCP in 1956 to "let a hundred flowers bloom, let a hundred schools of thought contend" as an invitation for freedom of discussion and debate about progress and problems in the first years of communist rule in China. The criticism was much more severe and extensive than the leadership expected, with the result that much of it was labeled by Mao as "poisonous weeds" (**antagonistic contradictions**) rather than "fragrant flowers" (**non-antagonistic contradictions**). The movement was shut down in 1957 and followed by the **Anti-Rightist Campaign**, which suppressed and punished hundreds of thousands of people, mostly intellectuals.

IDEOLOGY. A systematic or comprehensive set of values and beliefs ("ideas") that provide a way of looking at and understanding the world or some aspect of it.

IMPERIAL PERIOD. Chinese history from the establishment of the **Qin dynasty** in 221 BCE to the fall of the **Qing dynasty** in 1912 CE.

INDIRECT ELECTION. An electoral process in which persons elected to office are chosen, not by voters at large, but by members of a body that has previously been elected, sometimes directly and sometimes also indirectly. In China, for example, deputies to the **National People's Congress** are elected by the **people's congresses** at the provincial level, not by all the voters in the **province**. In the United States, senators were elected by state legislatures before 1913, and in many countries today, for example, South Africa, the president is indirectly elected by the national parliament rather than by all voters. See also **direct elections**.

INNER-PARTY DEMOCRACY. Means allowing more open discussion and debate and more competitive elections *within* the Chinese Communist Party. It is aimed at enhancing the democratic aspect of **democratic centralism** without undermining the key principle of centralized leadership. According the China's current leaders, one of Mao Zedong's biggest mistakes was violating and destroying inner-party democracy in the CCP.

IMPERIALISM. The domination of one people or state by another. Imperialism can be political, economic, cultural, or religious and may or may not involve the direct colonization of the weaker people or state.

IRON RICE BOWL. The cradle-to-grave benefits and lifetime employment that were guaranteed to workers in **state-owned enterprises** and to a somewhat lesser extent to peasants in **people's communes** during the Maoist era. One major objective of the **market reforms** begun in the early 1980s was to "smash" the iron rice bowl, which was considered to have been a costly drag on enterprise and commune finances as well as a disincentive to labor productivity and efficiency.

JIANGXI SOVIET. Also known as the Chinese Soviet Republic; the **base area** headquarters of the **Chinese Communist Party** from 1931 to 1934, located deep in the countryside of central China. The CCP was forced to abandon the Jiangxi Soviet because of the **extermination campaign** carried out by Chiang Kai-shek's KMT army; to escape the CCP embarked upon the **Long March** in October 1934.

JOB ASSIGNMENT SYSTEM. Or *fenpei* system. A method of labor allocation used in China from the 1950s into the 1990s in which university students were assigned state sector jobs according to national needs upon graduation. This was in exchange for the free university tuition and housing they had received. Students had little choice over what jobs they were assigned or even where they were located.

JOINT VENTURES. Companies that are partly owned by private foreign investors and partly owned by the Chinese government or a Chinese firm. When the PRC first opened to the world economy in the 1980s, all foreign investment had to be in the form of a joint venture, the share of foreign ownership was limited to less than 50 percent, and the Chinese partner was always a **state-owned enterprise** or other government entity. Now there are no such limits, although some sectors of the economy (especially the financial sector) remain restricted or even off-limits to foreign involvement.

KOREAN WAR. Fought in 1950–1953 with the PRC and its ally, North Korea (the Democratic People's Republic of Korea), on the one side (with limited Soviet support) and, on the other side, the United States (acting under the authorization of the United Nations) and its ally, South Korea (the Republic of Korea). It began with North Korea's invasion of South Korea, which then led to the intervention of, first, the United States and then the PRC. It ended in a truce that left the political situation on the Korean peninsula essentially unchanged. For the PRC, the outcome was a victory, despite very heavy casualties (including one of Mao's sons), because it had fought the United States to a stalemate. The Korean War enhanced the legitimacy of the PRC internationally and the CCP nationally.

KOWTOW. Literally, "knock head," also known as the "three kneelings and nine prostrations"; an act of submission performed by almost anyone who came into the presence of the Chinese emperor, or, more generally, by any commoner in the presence of an imperial official.

KUOMINTANG (KMT). Literally, "National People's Party"; also referred to as the Nationalist Party; founded by Sun Yat-sen in 1912 to oppose the usurpation of power in the **Republic of China** by the **warlord** Yuan Shikai. The KMT was taken over by Chiang Kai-shek after Sun's death in 1925. It then fought and, in 1949, lost a Civil War with the **Chinese Communist Party**, after which it fled to **Taiwan**, where it headed an authoritarian government until democratization began in the 1980s.. The KMT in now one of the two major political parties in Taiwan. See also **Democratic Progressive Party.**

LAND REFORM. The process of redistributing land from those who own a lot to those who have little or none. Land reform can be legal and peaceful, with landlords compensated for their property; or it can be extremely violent, with the land seized by force and without compensation. In China, most of the land reform carried out by the CCP in their **base areas** before 1949 and in the PRC in the early 1950s was of the latter type.

LEADING SMALL GROUPS. Informal decision-making bodies set up by the CCP to deal with important issues that cut across bureaucratic and organizational boundaries. There are about twenty such groups at the national level, including, for example, leading small groups on foreign affairs, finance and economics, cyberspace, and state security. Some leading small groups are more or less permanent and some are temporary. The main purpose of these interagency executive committees is to better coordinate implementation of policies among various top decision-making bodies such as the **Politburo**, the **State Council**, the **Central Military Commission**, and the Ministry of Foreign Affairs.

LEGALISM. An influential school of Chinese thought that, unlike **Confucianism**, emphasizes strict laws and harsh punishments as the only sound basis for government. Its "golden age" was during the **Qin dynasty** (221–206 BCE), when scholars were persecuted and books were burned.

LEGISLATIVE COUNCIL (LegCo). The legislature of the **Hong Kong** Special Administrative Region (HKSAR). It was first established while Hong Kong was a British colony. LegCo has seventy members with thirty-five chosen from geographical constituencies through **direct elections**, and thirty-five elected by functional constituencies such as industry, financial services, labor, education, sports, performing arts, culture, and publishing. It plays an important role in Hong Kong politics and governance, but it is limited in its power because of the executive-dominant nature of the political system, which gives great authority to the HKSAR **chief executive**.

LETTERS AND VISITS *(XINFANG)*. The process Chinese citizens can use to lodge a complaint by making a petition to the authorities. Rather than going through the formal court system, petitioners seek official mediation through the Letters and Visits Offices to resolve problems such as local **cadre** abuse, labors disputes, and property rights.

LONG MARCH. The epic and somewhat mythologized year-long, 6,000-mile trek of the Chinese Communist Party and supporters through some of China's most difficult terrain from their **Jiangxi Soviet** base area in central China to **Yan'an** in the northwestern **province** of Shaanxi. More than 100,000 people began the Long March in October 1934 but less than 10,000 made it to Yan'an in October 1935. It was during the Long March that **Mao Zedong** moved into the very top ranks of party leadership. See also **extermination campaigns.**

LOWER-LEVEL AGRICULTURAL PRODUCER COOPERATIVES (**LLAPCs**). See cooperatives.

LUSHAN CONFERENCE. An expanded meeting of the CCP **Central Committee** held in August 1959 to assess the progress and problems of the **Great Leap Forward**. Chairman Mao Zedong reacted furiously to criticism of the Leap by Defense Minister and high-ranking party leader Peng Dehuai. As a result, Peng and others were purged as part of an anti-rightist campaign within the party, and some of the radical aspects of the Leap were intensified until the reality of the famine forced a major policy shift in 1960.

MACAO. A **special administrative region** of the PRC. It is located on China's far southern coast about thirty-seven miles southwest of **Hong Kong**. It is only eleven square miles in area, and has a population of a little over half a million. Macao became a special administrative region of the **People's Republic of China** on December 20, 1999. For about 150 years prior to that, it was a colony of Portugal, which first established its influence there in the sixteenth century. It is one of the world's great centers of casino gambling, which greatly influences its economics, politics, and relationship with the PRC. See also **casino capitalism**.

MADE IN CHINA 2025. A comprehensive plan to make the PRC into a global hi-tech powerhouse in areas as advanced information technology, aerospace and aviation, new energy vehicles, railway transportation, shipping, and pharmaceuticals and medical equipment. The plan also aims to upgrade the quality of China's industrial products to world-class standards in order to avoid the **middle-income trap**.

MAINLANDERS (**or** '49ERS). People on **Taiwan** who came to the island in the late 1940s as part of the **Kuomintang**'s retreat from the CCP's impending victory in the **Chinese Civil War** and their descendants. See also **Taiwanese**.

MANCHUS. A non-**Han** ethnic group native to what is now the **Northeast** of the People's Republic of China, formerly known as Manchuria. They conquered China in 1644 and established the **Qing dynasty**.

MAO ZEDONG THOUGHT. The official name given by the **Chinese Communist Party** to the **ideology** of Mao Zedong. Often referred to by foreigners as "Maoism."

MARKET ECONOMY. An economy in which market forces such as supply and demand and the profit motive (the "free market") rather than government policies and actions are the major determinant of economic outcomes. See also **capitalism; market reform**.

MARKET REFORM. The process of making the transition from a **planned economy** to a **market economy** through policies that reduce the role of the government and increase the influence of market forces. It also involves a reduction in the amount of state- and **collective ownership** of property and other assets and increases private ownership.

MARTIAL LAW. A system of administration, usually invoked by a government in emergency circumstances, in which the constitution is suspended and military force is used to maintain order.

MARXISM-LENINISM. The ideological foundation of **communism** and **communist party-states**. It is based on the ideas of Karl Marx (1818–1883), particularly his emphasis on the role of classes and class struggle in history, and V. I. Lenin (1870–1924), notably his prescription for the organization of a revolutionary political party and his theory of **imperialism**.

MASS INCIDENTS. Protests, demonstrations, riots, and other forms of social unrest involving more than a handful of people. Causes of mass incidents in China include shady land deals that enrich developers (and sometimes cadres) but don't adequately compensate villagers, environmental problems, ethnic tensions, forced demolitions of housing and relocation of occupants, corrupt or abusive officials, police brutality, and labor disputes.

MASS LINE. The Maoist theory of leadership (or **work style**) that emphasizes that officials must always remain in close touch with those they lead. It rejects both leaderless, spontaneous action by the masses and leadership that is aloof or divorced from the masses. It is one of the principles of **Mao Zedong Thought** that the current leadership of the CCP holds to be valid.

MASS MOBILIZATION CAMPAIGN. A style of policy implementation used by the **Chinese Communist Party** that combines leadership and direction from above and the mobilized involvement of people on the local level to achieve specific objectives; an example would be the **land reform** campaign that was launched in 1952.

MASS ORGANIZATIONS. In the PRC, associations that represent the interests of a specific constituency, but which are under the leadership of the CCP. The major mass organization include the **All-China Women's Federation (ACWF), Chinese Communist Youth League (CYL)**, the All-China Federation of Trade Unions, and the All-China Federation of Industry and Commerce.

MATERIALISM. The view that all things are based on matter, not ideas or ideals ("idealism"). **Marxism** offers a materialist view of history ("historical materialism") that sees change as based largely on stages of economic development and its impact on the class structure of society. References to Marxist materialism basically refer to the primacy the theory gives to economic aspects of human existence, sometimes called economic determinism.

MAY 16 DIRECTIVE **(1966).** Formally, "Circular of the Central Committee of the Communist Party of China on the Great Proletarian Cultural Revolution," marked the official announcement of the launching of the **Cultural Revolution** in May 1966,.

MAY 7TH CADRE SCHOOLS. Established in 1968 during the **Cultural Revolution** to train urban **cadres** to follow the **mass line** in carrying out their duties. The bureaucrats were sent, for periods ranging from a couple of months to several years, to work and live among the masses, mostly in rural **people's communes**, while also engaging in political study and self-criticism. The name of the cadre schools came from a directive the Chairman Mao Zedong issued on May 7, 1966 to the **People's Liberation** that, in addition, to preparing to fight a war, it should become a "big school" by having soldiers engage in a wide-range of civilian activities, including agricultural production.

MAY FOURTH MOVEMENT. Roughly 1915–1924, a crucial period in China's political, social, and cultural development. The name of the movement is taken from the events of May 4, 1919, when students and others gathered in **Beijing** and other cities to protest the terms of the Versailles Peace Treaty giving Japan control of former German concessions in Shandong **province** following World War I. The major themes of the movement were national independence, dignity, and salvation. Many intellectuals were radicalized by the events of the time, one result of which was the founding of the **Chinese Communist Party** on July 1, 1921. See also **Twenty-One Demands.**

MEIJI RESTORATION. The period beginning in 1868 when power in Japan fell into the hands of a modernizing elite who, in the name of the Emperor Meiji (reigned 1852-1912), embarked the country up the path of industrialization and political reform that would transform the country into, first, a regional and then a world power.

MIDDLE-INCOME TRAP. The situation in which a country achieves notable progress in economic development but then is unable to reach the next level of becoming a high-income, advanced economy

MISSING GIRLS. In some countries, including China, there are many millions fewer females than there should be given natural sex-balance ratios. See also **one-child policy; sex ratio imbalance**.

NANJING DECADE. The period from the establishment of the capital of the **Republic of China** at Nanjing by Chiang Kai-shek and the **Kuomintang** in April 1927 to the takeover of the city by Japanese forces in late 1937. It is considered by many to be a time of relative peace and development for China. Nanjing literally means "Southern Capital."

NATIONAL CONGRESS OF THE COMMUNIST PARTY OF CHINA. Party congress have more than 2,200 delegates chosen in **indirect elections** by CCP organizations around the country. According to the constitution of the CCP, the national congress has the power to elect top leaders of the party, but most of its proceedings are symbolic and ceremonial, and the decisions it makes have already been approved by the CCP's higher-level organizations, including the **Central Committee**, the **Politburo**, and the **Standing Committee**.

NATIONAL PEOPLE'S CONGRESS (NPC). The national parliament or legislature of the **People's Republic of China**. It consists of more than 3,000 deputies, is elected every five years, and meets annually for about two weeks in March. According to the PRC constitution, the NPC has significant powers, such as electing the president and declaring war. While more active in recent years in shaping legislation and serving as a forum for discussion of important issues, it still operates within the framework of party leadership and is not a truly independent branch of government.

NATIONAL SUPERVISION COMMISSION. The highest state anticorruption agency of the PRC, with the same administrative ranking as the **Supreme People's Court** and the **Supreme People's Procuracy**. The National Supervision Commission's operations are integrated with the CCP's **Central Discipline Inspection Commission**.

NATIONALIST PARTY. See **Kuomintang**.

NATURAL VILLAGES. Small rural communities in China that have emerged "naturally" over a very long period of time. In most cases, the PRC puts several natural villages together to be governed as a single **administrative village**.

NEIGHBORHOOD COMMITTEE. A quasi-official unit of urban administration in China that functions below the **street office** and may encompass between 100 and 1,000 families. Neighborhood committees are made up of three to seven members, headed by a director, and carry out a variety of functions in the area under their jurisdiction, including organizing volunteer security patrols or cleanup squads, posting official announcements, hearing residents' complaints and conveying them to higher levels, and even dispute mediation. The committee members are generally elected to fixed terms by residents. Neighborhood committees are being replaced by **communities** (*shequ*). Also call residents' committee.

NEO-AUTHORITARIANISM. A school of political thought in China that borrows from traditional Chinese tenets of meritocracy, **legalism**, and hierarchy as the basis of a new form of party dictatorship. This school of thought is referred to as China's "New Right" and favors elite rule by **technocrats**, a strong military, and a **socialist market economy**.

NEOLIBERALISM. An economic philosophy, and the policies that go along with it, that emphasizes free market **capitalism**, a limited role for the state in managing the economy, and unrestricted international trade.

NEW CULTURE MOVEMENT. A period of great intellectual ferment in China in the 1910s–1920s when intellectuals attacked Confucianism as the source of the nation's problems and lauded science, as well as democracy and other Western ideas. A wide range of philosophies from radical and liberal to conservative and reactionary were debated on college campuses. The movement included a language revolution that promoted a vernacular (*baihua*) writing style, in which the written language is the same as the spoken language, to replace literary Chinese (*wenyan*), a difficult grammatical form that was an obstacle to increasing the rate of general literacy. See **May Fourth Movement**.

NEW DEMOCRACY. The early period (1949–1952) of rule by the CCP after the founding of the People's Republic, when the party promised to go slow in the undertaking the **socialist transformation** of China and to maintain a mixed economy of both state and private ownership of property and include non-communists in a limited role in governing the country.

NEW LIFE MOVEMENT. An effort by Chiang Kai-shek in the 1930s to resurrect Confucianism in the **Republic of China** in order to revive traditional values and cultivate civic virtue. It was part of an attempt to both bolster the legitimacy of his rule and to offer an alternative to communism.

NEW NORMAL. Refers to the fact that China's days of double-digit economic growth ended with the Global Economic Crisis of 2007–2008 and that the country would have to adjust its expectations to the reality of more moderate rates of expansion.

NEW SOCIAL STRATA. Includes groups in Chinese society that have been created during the process of **market reform** and internationalization, most importantly private entrepreneurs, managers and technical staff who work for foreign enterprises, as well as professionals, intellectuals, and others who are self-employed or work outside the public sector of the economy. The **Three Represents** theory was an ideological rationalization for allowing members of these strata to join the CCP.

NEW SOCIALIST COUNTRYSIDE. An initiative introduced in 2006 by Hu Jintao to promote rural development through investment, subsidies, and improved social services in order to reduce the rural-urban gap, which had widened over the previous decade.

NOMENKLATURA. A Russian term meaning "name list"; refers to several thousand high-ranking leadership (or **cadre**) positions in the party, government, and military, as well as large business firms, key universities, and other institutions that must be approved by the CCP **organization department** at the relevant level. This personnel management system was adopted from the Soviet communist party. Control of the cadre appointment process is one of the CCP's most important sources of power.

NON-ANTAGONISTIC CONTRADICTION. A Marxist-Leninist concept that refers to differences that can be resolved through debate, discussion, and other non-coercive means because the opposing sides are still part of the "people" who support the revolution, **socialism**, and the CCP. In the PRC, also called "contradictions among the people." See also **contradiction; antagonistic contradiction.**

NORTH CHINA. The area between **Beijing** in the north and the **Yangtze River** in central China.

NORTHEAST. The three **provinces** of northeastern China: Heilongjiang, Jilin, and Liaoning; formerly called Manchuria.

NORTHERN EXPEDITION. Began in southern China in 1926 as a joint military campaign by the KMT-CCP **United Front** to advance against **warlord**-held cities with the goal of defeating the warlords and taking control of the government of the **Republic of China**. Drew to a close in late 1927 when **Chiang Kai-shek** and the KMT established the capital of the Republic at Nanjing and technically brought an end to the **Warlord era**. See also **White Terror**.

OCCUPY CENTRAL. The protests that took place in downtown Hong Kong ("Central") in September 2014 to pressure the governments of the **Hong Kong Special Administrative Region** (HKSAR) and the **People's Republic of China** to live up to the promise to allow direct elections for both the HKSAR's **chief executive** and **Legislative Council** (**Legco**). The protests turned into the **Umbrella Movement** after the police used force to disperse the protesters.

ONE-CHILD POLICY. The official population policy of the PRC from 1979 to 2016. It stipulated that, with some exceptions, couples may have only one child. The policy was implemented in various stages and by various means, ranging from coercion to monetary fines to education. As a result, China's population growth rate decreased dramatically, but there is debate about whether it was the one-child policy or other factors that were the primary cause of fertility decline. The policy has also had important unintended consequences such as a **sex ratio imbalance** ("**missing girls**") and a rapidly aging population in terms of the percentage of people over the age of sixty-five, which will put a strain on China's inadequate pension, welfare, and health care systems.

"ONE COUNTRY, TWO SYSTEMS." The principle, first enunciated by Deng Xiaoping in the early 1980s, and agreed to in essence in the **Sino-British Joint Declaration** of 1984, under which Hong Kong became a **special administrative region** (SAR) of the PRC. This meant that, although **Hong Kong** would become part of the PRC, **socialism** would not be implemented there and its capitalist system and way of life would not be changed for fifty years. The principle also applies to **Macao**, the other SAR of the PRC. It has been proposed by the PRC as the basis of an agreement for reunification with **Taiwan**, but Taiwan has not shown any interest in those terms.

ONE-LEVEL-DOWN MANAGEMENT SYSTEM. A system of personnel management used in China in which **cadres** at each level have the authority to appoint their own subordinates. For example, the head of a county government can appoint the head of the town government without seeking approval from higher authorities at the municipal or provincial levels.

OPEN RECOMMENDATION AND SELECTION. A process of selecting state and party officials that has been implemented in some towns and cities in China to increase competition, public input, and transparency in such appointments through the use of means such as written exam, candidate forums, telephone hotlines, and even televised debates. It does not involve **direct elections** and the CCP **organization department** still has ultimate authority over the process.

"OPEN SEA" NOMINATIONS. A process of selecting candidates for **villager representative assembly** in whichvillagers nominate the candidates with **town** or village party branch interference.

OPERATIONAL CODE. The sum of beliefs of political leaders about the nature of politics and political conflict, the possibility of bringing about change, and the strategy and tactics required to achieve political objectives. The operational code of a leader influences decision-making and therefore has policy consequences. Perceptions of the "enemy" are an important part of an operational code. See also **ideology**.

OPIUM WAR (**1839–1842**). The war between Britain and Qing China, caused by the clash between British insistence on being able to sell opium in China and Chinese efforts to halt the trade. It ended in a humiliating defeat for China and contributed significantly to the weakening and ultimate downfall of the **Qing dynasty**. A **Second Opium War** was fought with much the same outcome in 1856–1860. See also **Treaty of Nanjing; unequal treaties**.

ORGANIC LAW OF VILLAGERS COMMITTEES. First introduced in 1988 and revised in 1998; the legislation under which elections for local leaders take place in China's rural villages. An "organic law," in general, is a fundamental or basic law that specifies the foundations of governance, in this case, in China's villages.

ORGANIZATION DEPARTMENT. The arm of the CCP in charge of reviewing and approving all personnel appointments of leading cadres for positions that are on the *nomenklatura* list. There are organization departments at most levels of the CCP from the top (the **Central Committee**) down to the county.

OUTER CHINA. A somewhat imprecise geographical term that refers to the vast but sparsely populated area to the west of **China Proper** and which was incorporated into the Chinese empire later in its history. The area has a large concentration of non-**Han ethnic minorities**.

PARTY CONGRESS. See **National Congress of the Communist Party of China.**

PATRON-CLIENT RELATIONS. Or clientelism; involve exchanges between a more powerful patron and a less powerful client. The patron may offer resources (such as land or a job) or protection to the client, while the client provides various services, including labor, personal loyalty, and political support to the patron.

PEACEFUL EVOLUTION. A term used by the PRC to suggest that the West (particularly the United States) is trying to peacefully undermine socialism and the rule of the CCP in China so that it evolves toward capitalism and democracy.

PEASANTS. People who produce food from the land, using traditional farming methods, and who comprise an agricultural class dependent on the subsistence farming on a small amount of farmland. In the 1920s, Mao identified three groups of peasants in China: poor peasants who owned little or no land of their own and had to hire out their labor to work on land owned by others; middle peasants who can support themselves by working their own land; and rich peasants who (unlike landlords) still have to work on their land, but are also able to hire others to work for them. **Mao Zedong Thought** is, in part, characterized as a variant of **Marxism-Leninism** because of the important place it gives to poor peasants as a class in taking a leading role in the revolution to seize political power and in the **socialist transformation** of society.

PEOPLE'S ARMED POLICE (PAP). China's paramilitary force that is primarily responsible for internal security. It is estimated that there are about 1.5 million members of the PAP and is directly responsible to the **Central Military Commission**. It was the PAP that responded in force to the ethnic unrest in Tibet and Xinjiang.

PEOPLE'S COMMUNES. The form of rural production and living that was established in 1958 during the **Great Leap Forward**. The communes virtually eliminated private property in the countryside and created larger (5,000–25,000 families) and more radical and egalitarian forms of living than the **collectives** that preceded them. They were designed to be comprehensive, self-reliant units that would pave the way to **communism** through agricultural, industrial, and ideological development. Although the people's communes were significantly scaled back in size, function, and authority after the failure of the Great Leap, they remained the highest unit of economic and social organization in the Chinese countryside until the beginning of the reform era in the early 1980s. See also **decollectivization**.

PEOPLE'S CONGRESSES. The legislative bodies of all levels of government in the PRC from the **National People's Congress** at the top and extending down to district people's congresses in the urban areas and town people's congresses in the rural areas. The people's congress is constitutionally empowered to supervise the work of the **people's government** at its level. Only town and district people's congresses are directly elected by all voters; other levels of people's congress are chosen by **indirect elections.**

PEOPLE'S DAILY. The official newspaper of the Central Committee of the **Chinese Communist Party**.

PEOPLE'S DEMOCRATIC DICTATORSHIP. A Chinese Communist variation on the Marxist idea of **dictatorship of the proletariat**. It is meant to convey that classes besides the proletariat, including the peasantry, revolutionary intellectuals, and other groups supportive of party leadership, are part of the "people" in whose name dictatorship is exercised over the "enemies" of socialism. It is also meant to imply that the "people" are able to enjoy democracy. Article 1 of the constitution of the **People's Republic of China** defines the country as "a socialist state under the people's democratic dictatorship led by the working class and based on the alliance of workers and peasants."

PEOPLE'S GOVERNMENT. The executive branch of the government at all formal levels of the PRC political system, as in provincial people's government or town people's government. See also **people's congress**.

PEOPLE'S LIBERATION ARMY (PLA). The combined armed forces of the **People's Republic** of China, including the army, navy, and air force.

PEOPLE'S REPUBLIC OF CHINA (PRC). The formal name of China since the **Chinese Communist Party** came to power in October 1949.

PERMANENT REVOLUTION. In **Mao Zedong Thought**, the idea that there will always be a need for revolution if human society is not going to stagnate, although the form of that revolution changes as society develops. Mao concluded that even after the overthrow of capitalism and during the **socialist transformation** of China, the permanent revolution would still take the form of class struggle between the **proletariat** and the **bourgeoisie**.

PINYIN. The system of romanization (or transliteration) used in the **People's Republic of China** to make the pronunciation of Chinese characters accessible to people unfamiliar with the language.

PLANNED ECONOMY. Or centrally planned economy, or command economy. An economic system that is controlled by the central government, which makes all important decisions concerning production, investment, prices, and distribution of goods and services. It relies on bureaucratic plans and commands, rather than the free market, to regulate the economy. Planned economies were key features of **communist party-states** such as the Soviet Union. The economic reforms introduced in China since the early 1980s have greatly reduced, but by no means eliminated, the role of planning.

PLENUM. Or plenary session. A meeting of the CCP **Central Committee**, normally held annually between the elections of the Central Committee by the **National Party Congress**, which convenes every five years.

POLITBURO. Or Political Bureau. The second-highest level of leadership in the **Chinese Communist Party**. It consists of twenty-five members and generally meets monthly. See also **Standing Committee**.

POLITICAL-LEGAL COMMITTEES (*zhengfa weiyuanhui*). CCP committees that have the power to oversee legal institutions, including the courts and public security organizations at most every level of the PRC political system.

POPULIST COALITION. A group of current CCP leaders, mostly of humble origins, who want to shift China's policy priorities to address some of the serious problems, such as vast economic inequalities and environmental degradation, that has resulted from the growth-at-any-cost strategy pursued for much of the last four decades. The populists often voice the concerns of vulnerable social groups such as farmers, migrant workers, and the urban poor and support greater attention to the development of the inland regions of the country. See also **elitist coalition**; *tuanpai*.

PRAGMATIST FACTION. Or practice faction; a group of CCP leaders who early in the post-Mao era supported a return to a less ideological approach to policy-making under the slogan "practice is the sole criterion for testing truth." They were led by veteran cadre Chen Yun and were strong advocates of restoring Deng Xiaoping to power after he had been purged by Mao in April 1976. They were opposed by the neo-Maoist **"whateverist" faction**.

PREDATORY STATE. A government that preys on its people and the economy for the benefit of those in power.

PRESIDIUM OF THE NATIONAL PEOPLE'S CONGRESS. The organization that presides over each session of the **National People's Congress** of the PRC. It sets the agenda and determines the process for legislation to be considered by committees and voted on by the Congress. The Presidium also decides on the candidates for election to China's top leadership positions, including president, vice president, and the chief justice of the **Supreme People's Court**, although, in reality, these candidates are determined beforehand by the **Central Committee** of the CCP.

PRIMARY STAGE OF SOCIALISM. Or initial stage of **socialism**. Declared by the CCP in the early 1980s to be where the PRC was in terms of its level of ideological and economic development. This provided justification for using aspects of capitalism and the market economy to promote China's economic development. It was said that one of Mao's biggest mistakes was to skip or compress this primary stage of socialism by eliminating all elements of capitalism (like the profit motive) and moving too fast from the mid-1950s on in implementing China's **socialist transformation**.

PRINCELINGS. An informal group, or **faction**, of current CCP leaders who are children of revolutionary heroes or high-ranking officials. They are mostly associated with the **elitist coalition** in Chinese politics.

PROLETARIAT. The industrial working class in a capitalist society, which Marx saw as the most exploited class in history and the most revolutionary. Mao used the term more broadly to refer to an **ideology** embracing revolutionary change that empowers the working masses. See also **bourgeoisie; class struggle**.

PROVINCE. A level of administration in the PRC just below the central government. China has twenty-two provinces.

PUBLIC SECURITY BUREAU. The chief law enforcement agency in Chinese cities and most other locales. Its main functions are policing and maintaining social order, but it also performs other duties such as supervising the household registration system (*hukou system*). Local public security bureaus are under the authority of the Ministry of Public Security in Beijing.

QIN DYNASTY. China's first imperial dynasty (221–206 BCE); regarded as the beginning of the Chinese empire and Chinese imperial history, even though Chinese cultural history dates back another 2,000 years. The Emperor Qin established the dynasty after defeating and unifying a number of small independent kingdoms. See also **Legalism**.

QING DYNASTY. Imperial China's last dynasty, the **Manchus,** established by a non-**Han** ethnic minority in 1644 and overthrown by the **1911 Revolution** that led to the founding of the **Republic of China** in 1912.

RAPE OF NANJING (NANKING). Also known as the Nanjing Massacre. Occurred during a six-week period beginning in December 1937 when Japanese forces killed an estimated 200,000 to 300,000 Chinese and raped tens of thousands women in their takeover of the city of Nanjing, the capital of the **Republic of China**.

RECTIFICATION CAMPAIGN. A **Chinese Communist Party** method of enforcing compliance of its members with the prevailing party **ideology**, policies, and leadership. The method was used both before the CCP came to power (most famously, in **Yan'an** in 1942) and afterward.

RE-EDUCATION THROUGH LABOR (*LAODONG JIAOYANG OR LAOJIAO*). An administrative sanction Chinese **public security bureaus** (police) impose, without judicial process, to detain people for up to four years. It is used to punish those accused of minor crimes, but has also been wielded against political targets, including democracy activists, ethnic dissidents in **Tibet** and **Xinjiang**, "**house church**" adherents, and **Falun Gong** followers. Abolished in 2014.

RED CAPITALISTS. Refers to member of the CCP who are also private entrepreneurs.

RED AND EXPERT. The Maoist ideal for scientists, technical personnel, and other intellectuals: to combine both ideological commitment to **communism** and knowledge of their field in the service of the country, the people, and the revolution.

RED ARMY. Founded in August 1927 as the armed force of the **Chinese Communist Party**. It was the predecessor to the **People's Liberation Army.**

RED GUARDS. Organizations of students committed to carrying out Mao's call for a **Cultural Revolution**. They first emerged in **Beijing** high schools and universities beginning in June 1966, but soon became a nationwide movement, though never under any kind of central direction. The Red Guards were responsible for the massive destruction of property and cultural artifacts as well as widespread brutal psychological and physical persecution of alleged class enemies. They engaged in increasingly violent factionalism and armed clashes until Mao decreed that order be restored in 1968 by the **People's Liberation Army**. The Red Guards were disbanded and more than 20 million of them were sent to the countryside to labor with and learn from the peasants.

REFORM AND OPENING UP (*GAIGE KAIFANG*). The official phrase used in the PRC to refer to the post-Mao **reform era** that began in 1978. "Reform" refers to the **market reform** of the economy. "Opening up" refers to greater engagement by the PRC in the global economy.

REFORM ERA. The period in China since the late 1970s when Deng Xiaoping first introduced the dramatic economic changes that took the country in a very different direction from where Mao Zedong had led it. The reform era is said to have formally begun in December 1978 at the **plenum** of the CCP **Central Committee**. See also **Building Socialism with Chinese Characteristics**.

REFORM THROUGH LABOR (*laodong gaizao or laogai*). A prison system used mostly to incarcerate those convicted of serious crimes in the PRC. The *laogai* camps are often located in more remote parts of the country, the living conditions are harsh, and the labor, whether in fields, mines, or factories, that inmates have to perform is hard.

REGIONAL POWER HIERARCHY. The idea that there is an implicit ranking, rather than a balance, in the power relationship among countries in a region. The **tributary system** of imperial China in which other countries could trade with China as long as they recognized China's political and cultural supremacy was a regional power hierarchy. Some scholars believe that the recent rise of China marks the emergence of another regional power hierarchy in East Asia.

RENT-SEEKING. Refers to seeking monetary gains ("rents") through political rather than economic activity. Rent-seeking may be legal (lobbying by interest groups for a larger share of the pie) or illegal (bureaucrats manipulating government regulations in order to profit themselves).

REPUBLIC OF CHINA. The government of China following the overthrow of the **Qing dynasty** in the **1911 Revolution** until the founding of the **People's Republic of China** in 1949, following the conclusion of the **Chinese Civil War**. Toward the end of the Civil War, more than a million supporters of the ruling party of the Republic of China, the **Kuomintang**, and its leader, Chiang Kai-shek, fled to the island of **Taiwan**, where, with American support, they were able to establish a stronghold. The government of **Taiwan** still officially calls island the Republic of China (ROC).

REPUBLICAN PERIOD. Chinese history from the establishment of the **Republic of China** in 1912 to the founding of the **People's Republic of China** in 1949.

RESOLUTION ON CERTAIN QUESTIONS IN THE HISTORY OF OUR PARTY SINCE THE FOUNDING OF THE PEOPLE'S REPUBLIC OF CHINA. A major document published by the CCP in 1981 as the authoritative (and still largely upheld) assessment by the post-Mao leadership of the party's achievements and shortcomings since 1949. The Resolution acknowledged that Chairman Mao Zedong had made serious mistakes, but concluded that his achievements were greater than his failings. It also contained an assessment of **Mao Zedong Thought** that distinguished between those aspects that were wrong or taken to extremes and those that remain relevant today to the party's guiding **ideology**.

RETURNEE. A Chinese citizen who returns to work in the PRC after going abroad for advanced education.

REVISIONISM. A alleged betrayal of **Marxism-Leninism** by revising its core principles. The CCP accused the Communist Party of the Soviet Union of revisionism and the label was also applied to Mao's opponents in the **Cultural Revolution**.

REVOLUTIONARY COMMITTEES. These were created in 1968–1969 as the provisional organs of government to replace those destroyed by the **Cultural Revolution**. They consisted of representatives of the party, the army, and the "masses" and were established at the provincial, municipal, and other subnational levels of administration. They were also established as the leading body in schools, factories, **people's communes**, and other institutions. Initially, the military was usually the dominant force on these committees since it was their responsibility to restore and maintain order after the chaos of the Cultural Revolution. The Revolutionary Committees remained the primary sub-national administrative organs of the PRC until they were replaced by **people's governments** in the late 1970s.

RIGHTFUL RESISTANCE. A type of grassroots protest in which the participants invoke national laws when they seek redress for abuses by local officials. Rightful resisters believe that the legal system and the national leadership are on their side. The PRC government usually permits this kind of protest, but some rightful resistance pushes the legal limits and sometimes goes beyond, in which case the it meets with swift state repression.

SCIENTIFIC OUTLOOK ON DEVELOPMENT. The general rubric under which former CCP leader Hu Jintao's contributions to Chinese communist **ideology** is put. It incorporates the goal of creating a **harmonious socialist society**.

SECOND OPIUM WAR. Fought in 1856–1860 between Qing China and Great Britain, which was joined by France. The cause had less to do with opium per se as with Western frustration with the lack of progress more generally by the **Qing dynasty** in implementing the terms of the **Treaty of Nanjing**, which ended the first **Opium War** in 1842. The war resulted in another humiliating defeat for the Qing and the imposition of another **unequal treaty**, the Treaty of Tianjin, which further opened China to foreign merchants and missionaries, legalized the opium trade, and ceded a second part of **Hong Kong** (Kowloon) to Britain.

SECRETARIAT. An important CCP organization that handles the Party's routine business and administrative matters. Secretariat members meet daily and are responsible for coordinating the country's major events and important meetings as well as top leaders' foreign and domestic travels.

SEGMENTED DEREGULATION. An approach to economic reform that implements new policies over time in different sectors of the economy or different parts of the country. The implementation of **Special Economic Zones (SEZs)** in China is an example of segmented deregulation. See also **gradualism**.

SELF-STRENGTHENING MOVEMENT. A series of efforts undertaken roughly between 1861 and 1898 to save the **Qing dynasty** after it had been seriously weakened by external conflicts and internal rebellion. The movement was led mostly by powerful provincial **Han** Chinese leaders and aimed to strengthen China through economic and military modernization. Its approach was captured in the idea that Western techniques could be adopted for their "use" (*yong*) while Chinese learning could be preserved as the "essence" (*ti*) of the nation. See also **Hundred Days Reform**.

SEVENTEEN POINT AGREEMENT. Formally, The Agreement Between the Central Government and the Local Government of **Tibet** on Measures for the Peaceful Liberation of Tibet; the surrender document signed in May 1951 by the **Dalai Lama**'s government and the PRC after the invasion of Tibet by China's **People's Liberation Army**. The agreement acknowledged that Tibet was part of China, but also stated that the Dalai Lama's position would not be changed and that Tibet's religion and customs would be respected.

SEVERE ACUTE RESPIRATORY SYNDROME (SARS). A highly contagious, potentially fatal virus that first broke out in southern China in 2002–2003 and eventually led to 774 deaths worldwide. Chinese officials initially covered up or downplayed the severity of the epidemic, but were forced to confront it when it spread outside the country. The experience is considered to have been a wake-up call to the PRC government that it had to deal more proactively with potential and real epidemics, such as HIV/AIDS.

SEX RATIO IMBALANCE. An unnatural ratio between males and females in a population, particularly as reflected at the time of birth. The natural gender balance is 105 boys for every 100 girls. The PRC's 2010 census revealed a sex ratio at birth of nearly 118 males per 100 females and also showed that some individual provinces had sex ratios as high as 130 boys per 100 girls. One cause of this serious imbalance lies in the country's **one-child policy**. Many rural couples desperate to have a boy because of customary son-preference and economic necessity have resorted to female infanticide, abandonment of baby daughters, and more recently sex-selective abortion made possible by widely available and inexpensive ultrasound tests. See **missing girls**.

SHEQU. See **"community."**

SINIFICATION. The process of being sinified, that is being absorbed by, assimilated to, or deeply influenced by Chinese (Sino) culture, society, or thought. In the **imperial period**, both the Mongols and the Manchus were sinified after they had conquered China and established ruling **dynasties**. Likewise, Mao Zedong is said to have sinified **Marxism-Leninism** by adapting it to China's particular circumstances as an economically poor peasant society.

SINO-BRITISH JOINT DECLARATION. Formally known as the Joint Declaration of the Government of the United Kingdom of Great Britain and Northern Ireland and the Government of the **People's Republic of China** on the Question of **Hong Kong;** signed in December 1984. It specified the terms under which the PRC would take over the sovereignty of Hong Kong on July 1, 1997. Hong Kong had become a British colony in stages during the nineteenth century. See **Opium War; Treaty of Nanjing; unequal treaties**.

SINO-JAPANESE WAR (1895). Sparked by competition between Qing China and imperial Japan over influence in Korea. Ended in a particularly humiliating defeat for China since Japan was viewed with disdain in the traditional Chinese worldview. One result of the war was that **Taiwan** became a colony of Japan and remained so until the end of World War II. The invasion and occupation of much of eastern China by Japan from 1937 to 1945 is referred to as the second Sino-Japanese War.

SINO-SOVIET SPLIT. The ideological conflict between the **Chinese Communist Party** and the Communist Party of the Soviet Union that began to appear in the late 1950s. The split involved a number of issues, including major differences over how to assess the international situation during the Cold War and how to deal with the United States. Each side accused the other of betraying **Marxism-Leninism**. Hostilities reached the point of military clashes along the Sino-Soviet border in 1969. Relations between the two countries were normalized in the 1980s. See also **revisionism**.

SMALL AND MEDIUM ENTERPRISES (SMEs). Enterprises of a certain scale in the PRC as determined by some combination of number of employees, capital, or the value of assets and sales volume. Since 1997, all SMEs in China have been privatized, leaving only large enterprises owned by the state. SMEs are one of the most dynamic sectors of the Chinese economy in terms of growth and innovation.

SOCIAL CREDIT SYSTEM. A system of mass surveillance being developed by the Chinese government that uses technology and big data to assign individuals a numerical "social credit" ranking based on their public behavior and cyber-space activities. Those with poor social credit scores may face sanctions, such as being denied the right to purchase high-speed rail tickets. See also **surveillance state**.

SOCIALISM. In Marxism, the stage of human history between **capitalism** and **communism**. See **socialist transformation**.

SOCIALIST DEMOCRACY. The type of democracy that the PRC says it is practicing and perfecting. It is said to be democracy for all the "people," unlike democracy in capitalist countries, which favors the rich and powerful. How socialist democracy operates in practice is determined by the CCP. See also **people's democratic dictatorship**.

SOCIALIST EDUCATION MOVEMENT. A movement in the PRC in 1962–1965 aimed at ideologically reinvigorating village **cadres** and combating corruption. It only reached about one-third of China's villages. Mao Zedong and Liu Shaoqi had some differences over how the movement should be conducted, which became another source of Mao's growing unhappiness with Liu on the eve of the **Cultural Revolution**.

SOCIALIST LEGALITY. How the PRC refers to the nature of its legal system, implying that it is different from (and better than) "capitalist legality," which is seen as heavily weighted in favor of the rich. In contrast, socialist legality is said to serve the needs of all the "people." Like other important areas of Chinese society, the CCP claims the right to exercise a "leading role" in the legal system.

SOCIALIST MARKET ECONOMY. The official designation given by the PRC to its current economic system. The implication is that the economy combines elements of both **socialism** and the free market (**capitalism**), but that the socialist or public aspect plays the leading role.

SOCIALIST TRANSFORMATION. The process of moving the country from **capitalism** to **socialism**, notably through the abolition of most private ownership, the nationalization of industry and commerce, and the collectivization of agriculture. Once socialism has been established, the ideological goal is to develop it further and prepare for the ultimate transition from socialism to **communism**.

SOFT POWER. The use of noncoercive means, such as diplomatic, cultural, and economic influence, by a state to advance its interests and influence other nations; contrast to hard power, which involves use of military means or threats and other forms of coercion.

SOUTH CHINA. The area between the **Yangtze River** in central China and the country's southern borders.

SOUTHERN INSPECTION TOUR. Or Southern Journey. An inspection tour undertaken by Deng Xiaoping in 1992 to investigate firsthand the situation in China's most economically dynamic region in Guangdong **province**, bordering **Hong Kong**. Deng concluded that China needed to make economic reform and opening to the world its highest priority again after a period of retrenchment following the **Beijing Massacre** of 1989.

SPECIAL ADMINISTRATIVE REGION (SAR). Administrative units of the PRC that have a significant degree of local autonomy in all matters other than foreign relations and defense. China has two special administrative regions: the **Hong Kong** SAR, a former British colony that returned to Chinese sovereignty in 1997; and the **Macao** SAR, a former Portuguese colony that reverted to China in 1999. SARs are much more self-governing than are the **autonomous regions** of the PRC, such as **Tibet** and **Xinjiang**. But ultimate authority resides in **Beijing**.

SPECIAL ECONOMIC ZONES (SEZs). Areas of the country that are allowed to implement incentives designed to attract foreign investment by firms that will produce goods for export. Such incentives may include tax holidays, low rents, guaranteed supply of materials and utilities, and inexpensive labor. The benefits to the host country include job creation and the transfer of technology and management skills. China's first SEZs were established in the early 1980s, followed by a rapid expansion of similar "open cities" and "development zones" in many parts of the country, but especially along the coast.

SPIRITUAL POLLUTION. A term that was widely used in China in 1983–1984 during a campaign against ideas and influences, mostly from abroad, which, according to the CCP, contaminated the thinking and threatened the well-being of the Chinese people. It was a vague term that was applied to everything from democracy to pornography. See also **bourgeois liberalization**.

STANDING COMMITTEE (CCP). Formally, the Standing Committee of the **Politburo** of the **Central Committee**, the most powerful leadership organization in the PRC. It has seven members, headed by the general secretary, Xi Jinping.

STANDING COMMITTEE OF THE NATIONAL PEOPLE'S CONGRESS (SCNPC). The body responsible for any issues that require congressional consideration when the full **National People's Congress** is not in session It generally convenes every two months, with each meeting lasting about one week.

STATE-OWNED ASSETS SUPERVISION AND ADMINISTRATION COMMISSION (SASAC). The PRC government organization that oversees enterprises that remain under state control. SASAC covers five sectors of the economy—telecommunications, petroleum and refining, metallurgy (steel and other metals), electricity, and military industry.

STATE CAPITALISM. An economic system in which the government plays a dominant role in guiding the market and owns or controls assets that represent a significant share of the country's total gross domestic product.

STATE COUNCIL. The cabinet of the central government of the PRC. It is led by the premier, and consists of vice premiers; state councilors, who are senior government leaders with broad responsibilities; ministers or commissioners, who head functional departments such as the Ministry of Foreign Affairs and the National Population and Family Planning Commission; and a secretary-general who manages the day-to-day business of the Council.

STATE FARMS. Huge agricultural enterprises run the by PRC central government. They are usually located in more remote parts of the country such as the **Northeast** and **Xinjiang**. They are run much like **state-owned enterprises**. The number of state farms has been reduced in the **reform era**, but, as of 2017, there were still 1758 of them, employing about 2.7 million people farming more than 15,953,123 acres of land.

STATE-BUILDING. The process of establishing and strengthening the formal institutions and processes of government at the national and subnational levels.

STATE-OWNED ENTERPRISE (SOE). A company that is owned and operated by some level of state administration. By the mid-1950s, all businesses in China had been nationalized and brought under the authority of state planning. SOEs received production quotas from the state, were supplied with all the inputs needed for production from the state, and had to sell its output to the state at fixed prices. Managers were appointed by the state. SOEs were not allowed to fail, and if they got into financial trouble, the state would bail them out. The economic reforms, particularly since the 1990s, have greatly reduced the number of SOEs in China and have streamlined those that still exist, as well as making them accountable for their bottom line. Tens of millions of workers have been laid off from closed or reformed SOEs. See also **iron rice bowl**; **work unit**.

STREET OFFICE. The lowest official unit of formal urban administration in China. Chinese cities are divided into districts, which in turn are divided into sub-districts called street offices. The street office staff are government **cadres,** and there is usually a branch of the public security bureau at the street office-level. See also **neighborhood committee**; **community** (*shequ*).

STRUGGLE MEETING. A technique used by the **Chinese Communist Party** in which a person is subjected to intense criticism ("struggled") and sometimes physical punishment because of alleged political or ideological mistakes. The purpose is to elicit a confession ("self-criticism"), repentance, and compliance. Struggle meetings were used during **rectification campaigns**, **land reform**, the **Anti-Rightist Campaign**, and most extensively during the **Cultural Revolution**.

SUNFLOWER MOVEMENT. The peaceful occupation of Taiwan's legislative chamber in spring 2014 by young protesters who were unhappy about the **Kuomintang**'s liberalization of trade with China, which they perceived as weakening Taiwan's economic and potentially political independence. They camped out there for twenty-four days until the speaker negotiated their departure.

SUPREME PEOPLE'S COURT. The court of highest jurisdiction in the PRC. The SPC exercises ministry-like bureaucratic authority over the lower judiciary, which includes provincial high courts, intermediate courts, and basic courts. The SPC is headed by a chief justice (president), a first grand justice (vice-president), and eleven second grand justices. There are more than 300 other lower level justices who hear cases in smaller panels. The chief justice is elected by the **National People's Congress** and can serve no more than two five-year terms.

SUPREME PEOPLE'S PROCURACY (PROCURATORATE). The national-level organization responsible for both prosecution and investigation in legal matters. In some ways, its functions are similar to the U.S. Department of Justice, and its head, the procurator general, is roughly equivalent to the attorney general. There are procuratorial offices at the subnational levels of government, including provincial and county levels.

SURVEILLANCE STATE. A country in which administrative, political, and technological tools are used to keep and gather information about and keep watch on its citizens. See also **social credit system**.

SUSTAINABLE DEVELOPMENT. Emphasizes the environmental consequences of economic growth and modernization and takes into account the imperative of maintaining resources and a livable world for current and future generations. See also **ecological civilization**.

TAIPING REBELLION. A large-scale rebellion from 1850 to1864 against the **Qing dynasty** led by a Christian convert, Hong Xiuquan, claiming to be the younger brother of Jesus Christ whose mission was to establish the Taiping ("Great Peace) Heavenly Kingdom on earth. Because of deteriorating economic and social conditions and its promise of radical changes, the rebellion gained a huge number of followers from among China's peasants. It conquered most of **South China** up to the **Yangtze River**, before it was undone by its own internal intrigues and discord and suppressed by armies led by powerful provincial **Han** Chinese leaders. The death toll from the rebellion is estimated to have been about 20 million. Although it did not succeed, the Taiping Rebellion greatly weakened the Qing dynasty.

TAIWAN. An island about 110 miles off the coast of southeastern China. At the conclusion of the **Chinese Civil War** in 1949, the defeated forces of Chiang Kai-shek's **Kuomintang** fled to Taiwan. With American support, the KMT was able to continue governing Taiwan as the **Republic of China**. Taiwan is now an economically developed democracy that still calls itself the Republic of China and is *de facto* a separate and distinct political entity from the **People's Republic of China**. The PRC claims that Taiwan is rightfully a **province** of China.

TAIWAN STRAIT. Or Formosa Strait. The 110-mile-wide stretch of water between the PRC and the island of **Taiwan**. It has been the site of several military and political crises, most seriously in the 1950s, and remains one of the strategically fragile parts of the world, despite much improved relations between the PRC and the island.

TAIWANESE. Refers generally to all the people who live on **Taiwan**, and more specifically, to those whose ancestors came to the island before 1945 or so. Taiwanese make up about 84 percent of the population of Taiwan, compared with the 14 percent who are **Mainlanders**, although these are much less important sources of **collective identity** than in the past.

TECHNOCRATS. Political leaders who were trained as engineers or scientists before beginning their careers in government and politics. In China, almost all top leaders are technocrats, though an increasing number have training in economics, political science, or law.

"TEN THOUSAND CHARACTER LETTERS." A series of four underground pamphlets written by CCP intellectuals between 1994 and 1997 that were critical of the direction economic reform was taking in China. The authors complained of the decline of the state sector, rising foreign and private investment, and the loosening hold of communist **ideology** over society. This group of critics was referred to as China's "New Left."

THREE GORGES DAM. On China's **Yangtze River,** the largest dam and hydroelectric power station in the world. It was begun in 1994 and mostly completed by 2006 at an estimated cost of $39 billion. Its purpose is not only to provide a source of much needed clean energy to southwest China, but also to permit large ships to sail all the way from Shanghai on the coast to **Chongqing** and to greatly improve flood control and irrigation. Critics of the dam point to the ecological and archaeological damage caused by the creation of gigantic artificial lakes, which also forced the relocation of 1.5 million area residents, mostly poor farmers. The construction of the dam was controversial both internationally and in China, but much of the internal dissent was suppressed.

THREE PRINCIPLES OF THE PEOPLE. The political philosophy developed by Sun Yat-sen that became the core ideology of the **Kuomintang** party. The Three Principles are: Nationalism, Democracy, and People's Livelihood.

THREE REPRESENTS. Former CCP leader Jiang Zemin's contribution to Chinese communist **ideology**. It means that the CCP should always represent China's advanced productive forces, advanced culture, and the interests of the overwhelming majority of the Chinese people. In essence, this was a reaffirmation of the absolute priority given by **Deng Xiaoping Theory** to economic development by any means, but it also an ideological justification for allowing private entrepreneurs (capitalists) to be members of the CCP. Jiang's theoretical contributions were formally inscribed in the party (2002) and state (2003) constitutions.

THIRD PLENUM. The milestone meeting of the CCP **Central Committee** in December 1978 that is considered the beginning of China's reform era by setting economic development as the nation's top priority and signaling a clear break with the Maoist past.

TIANANMEN INCIDENT. Events in April 1976 when hundreds of thousands of Chinese citizens spontaneously gathered in **Tiananmen Square** to demonstrate their affection for the popular premier (prime minister) Zhou Enlai, who had died in January. Not only were wreaths and poems lauding Zhou posted, but so, too, were scathing criticisms of Chairman Mao and his radical wife, Jiang Qing. After Jiang Qing ordered the removal of the wreaths that honored Zhou, people overturned a police vehicle and burned an official command post on the edge of the Square. The Square was finally emptied with a brief spasm of violence, but no one died and there were few arrests. The events were at first labeled as a "counterrevolutionary incident" and blame was placed on Deng Xiaoping, who was removed from his leadership positions by Mao. After Mao's death and Deng's consolidation of power, the official judgment of the "Tiananmen Incident" was reversed and it was called patriotic and revolutionary.

TIANANMEN MOVEMENT. The largest mass protest in the history of the **People's Republic of China**, which took place in the spring of 1989. It began in **Beijing**, with university students gathering in **Tiananmen Square** in early April to commemorate the death of former party leader, Hu Yaobang, who they regarded as a reformer sympathetic to their desire for greater political freedom. The protesters set up camp in the square, and at one point attracted more than a million citizens from many walks of life expressing a wide range of grievances, including official corruption. The movement was crushed when the leadership of the CCP ordered the **People's Liberation Army** to clear the Square on June 4th, resulting in a large loss of civilian life, known as the **Beijing Massacre**.

TIANANMEN SQUARE. The largest urban public space in the world (100 acres), located in the center of **Beijing**, adjacent to the front entrance of the Forbidden City, the one-time imperial palace. Tiananmen literally means "Gate of Heavenly Peace."

TIBET. A huge, sparsely populated area in China's far west located in the Himalaya Mountains; it is the highest region on Earth, with an average elevation of 14,000 ft above sea level. About 96 percent of its inhabitants are **Tibetan.** Its capital is Lhasa. Tibet was invaded by the **People's Liberation Army (PLA)** in 1951 and incorporated into the PRC. A major uprising against Chinese rule in 1959 was crushed by the PLA and the leader of Tibetan Buddhism, the **Dalai Lama**, fled to exile in India. In 1965 it was formally named the Tibet **Autonomous Region** (TAR). There has been extensive economic development in Tibet in recent years, and also extensive immigration by **Han** Chinese. The situation in Tibet remains politically volatile with frequent episodes of ethnic unrest.

TIBETAN. One of China's fifty-five **ethnic minority** groups. There are altogether about 6.2 million Tibetans in China, 2.4 million of whom live in the Tibet Autonomous Region; the remainder—the majority—live mostly in areas called (in Tibetan) Kham and Amdo, which are now part of the **provinces** of Qinghai, southern Gansu, western Sichuan, and the northern tip of Yunnan.

TIBETAN PLATEAU. A region in the far west of China that includes the Tibet Autonomous Region and parts of Qinghai, Gansu, Sichuan, and Yunnan. It makes up about 30 percent of all of China's area.

TOTALITARIANISM. A term used to describe a type of political system in which a single political party under a charismatic leader attempts to exercise total power over society and will use any means, including terror, to do so.

TOWN AND TOWNSHIP. The lowest levels of formal government administration in rural China. Towns have a higher percentage of population with non-agricultural registrations (see *hukou* **system**) than do townships.

TOWNSHIP AND VILLAGE ENTERPRISES (TVEs). Rural industries that are technically owned collectively by the township (**town**) or village and are not part of the state **planned economy**. TVEs expanded rapidly in the 1980s and were an important part of rising living standards in the countryside and of China's spectacular economic growth more generally. Beginning in the mid-1990s, most TVEs were privatized.

TRADING STATE. A country whose international commerce dramatically increases its national power. China is a contemporary example of a highly successful trading state.

TREATY OF NANJING. Signed by the **Qing dynasty** and Great Britain in 1842 to end the first **Opium War**. It was the first of the **unequal treaties** forced upon imperial China by foreign powers from that time to the early twentieth century. Its main purpose was to open China to foreign trade. It also gave Britain the first part of what would become its colony of **Hong Kong**.

TRIAD ORGANIZATIONS. Secret society criminal gangs that are active in Chinese communities in many parts of the world, especially in **Hong Kong** and **Macao**.

TRIBUTARY SYSTEM. The arrangement by which outsiders were allowed to conduct trade and other foreign relations with the Chinese empire, involving the giving of gifts (tribute) recognizing the superiority of and submission to the Chinese emperor.

TUANPAI. (Literally, "League Faction"). An informal group of current CCP leaders who advanced their political careers through the ranks of the **Chinese Communist Youth League (CCYL)**. They are mostly associated with the **populist coalition** in Chinese politics.

TWENTY-ONE DEMANDS. A set of demands made by imperial Japan on the government of the **Republic of China** in January 1915, giving Japan territorial and other concessions in China. The weak response by the Chinese government led to widespread student protests, including those on May 4, 1919, which, in turn, gave rise to the **May Fourth Movement**.

UMBRELLA MOVEMENT. Protests that took place in Hong Kong in September-December 2014 after police used force to break up crowds that had gathered earlier in the **Occupy Central** demonstration. The movement was named for the umbrellas that Occupy Central protestors used to protect themselves from tear gas and pepper spray used by the police.

UNEQUAL TREATIES. The numerous agreements signed under military or diplomatic pressure in the nineteenth century by the **Qing dynasty** and foreign powers on terms that were very unfavorable to China and included economic, territorial, and other concessions that greatly weakened the imperial system.

UNITARY STATE. A type of political system in which all sub-national units of administration (**provinces**, states, etc.) are subordinate to the central government. The PRC is a unitary state. Compare with a federal system, like the United States, in which sub-national levels of government have considerable power.

UNITED FRONT. The communist party concept of joining together with other groups, even your adversaries, to fight against a common enemy and to achieve a common goal. There were two united fronts in China in the first half of the twentieth century: the First United Front joined the **Kuomintang** and the **Chinese Communist Party** in 1924–1927 to fight against the **warlords** and unify the **Republic of China.** The Second United Front (1937–1945) again brought the KMT and CCP together in order to fight the Japanese invasion of China. See also **Northern Expedition; Warlord era**.

URBAN ADMINISTRATIVE AND LAW ENFORCEMENT BUREAU. The organization charged with enforcing local ordinances, involving a range of issues such as sanitation, environmental regulation, occupational safety, and licensing regulations. The Bureau is in charge of **URBAN MANAGEMENT OFFICERS (*chengguan*)**, the uniformed, but unarmed para-police force that patrols the streets in almost every Chinese city.

URBAN MANAGEMENT OFFICERS (*chengguan*). See **URBAN ADMINISTRATIVE AND LAW ENFORCEMENT BUREAU**.

URBAN VILLAGES. Areas of former farmland in or near cities that have been converted into low cost and often substandard rental housing for migrant workers.

UYGHUR. One of China's fifty-five **ethnic minorities**. Uyghurs are a Turkic ethnic-linguistic group who practice Islam. Most of China's 11 million Uyghurs live in the **Xinjiang** Uyghur **Autonomous Region**. There are also large populations of Uyghurs in other parts of Central Asia, notably Kazakhstan, Kyrgyzstan, and Uzbekistan.

VANGUARD PARTY. The Leninist idea that a communist party should consist only of the most ideologically advanced and committed communists who are capable of leading the revolution to overthrow the old society and guiding the **socialist transformation** of the country once political power has been seized. The CCP considers itself a **vanguard party**.

VILLAGE. The basic social unit in rural China, made up of both **administrative villages** and **natural villages**. Villages are technically self-governing, although they fall under the jurisdiction of a nearby **town**. Village population is typically around 1,000 to 2,000. See **village committee; villager representative assembly (VRA)**.

VILLAGE COMMITTEE. The governing body in China's rural **administrative villages**. It consists of three to seven members, including the chair of the committee or village leader, vice chairs, an accountant, a female member who deals with family planning and women's affairs, and a person in charge of public security. In most of rural China, the village committee is directly elected by all eligible voters. Ultimately, the village committee is subordinate to the authority of the village communist party branch.

VILLAGER REPRESENTATIVE ASSEMBLY (VRA). Monitors the work of the village committee, according to the **Organic Law of Villagers Committees**. Every five to fifteen households elect one representative to the VRA, which reviews annual village budgets, investment plans, and the implementation of national policies on the local level.

VOLUNTARISM. The concept that human willpower and determination can overcome any obstacles, or that the subjective can conquer the objective. **Mao Zedong Thought** is often said to put a great deal of emphasis on voluntarism, particularly the power of the masses when motivated by revolutionary spirit (and mobilized by the communist party) to achieve extraordinary economic or political results. Such voluntarism is contrasted with Marxist **materialism**, which emphasizes the objective limits, particularly economic, of human action at any given point in history.

WARLORD. A person with power over a part of a country based on control of military forces who are loyal to the warlord rather than to the central government.

WARLORD ERA. The years from 1916 to 1927 in China when political power was in the hands of regional or provincial military leaders (**warlords**) and the central government of the **Republic of China** was relatively weak.

"WHATEVERIST" FACTION. A group of CCP leaders who in the early post-Mao era in 1977 pledged to "support whatever policy decisions were made by Chairman Mao" and to "unswervingly follow whatever instructions were given by Chairman Mao." The group, which have been called "neo-Maoists" because of their desire to continue some aspects of Maoist policies and **ideology** and preserve the Chairman's reputation included Hua Guofeng, Mao's successor as party chairman. They were politically opposed by the **pragmatist faction**. The "whateverist" faction was gradually pushed aside after Deng Xiaoping returned to power in 1978.

WHITE TERROR. The suppression of the **Chinese Communist Party** by Chiang Kai-shek that began in April 1927 during the **Northern Expedition**. The terror nearly wiped out the CCP and forced most of the survivors to retreat to the remote countryside. Marks the beginning of the first stage of the **Chinese Civil War** between the KMT and the CCP.

WORK TEAMS. Small groups of party **cadres** who are sent by the leadership to investigate, guide, and report on a situation. Work teams were sent to university campuses in **Beijing** at the outset of the **Cultural Revolution** in June 1966 to guide the **Red Guards**, but wound up clashing with the rebel youth. The teams were withdrawn in August 1966 and later accused of having tried, under the authority of Liu Shaoqi, to suppress the Red Guards.

WORK UNIT (*DANWEI*). The place of employment for most urban Chinese citizens, particularly during the Maoist period when the work unit provided not simply jobs, but also housing, health care, education, daycare, pensions, restaurants, shopping, and vacation resorts, for their members. These benefits, along with permanent employment, made up the **iron rice bowl** that was a feature of urban life in Maoist China. Work units were also important means of social and political control. Their importance has declined considerably during the **reform era**, but they still exert some influence on urban life for some citizens.

WORK STYLE. In CCP terminology, the method of leadership that **cadres** use in carrying out their responsibilities and exercising their authority, particularly in relation to the masses. See also **mass line**.

WORLD TRADE ORGANIZATION (WTO). The international body based in Geneva, Switzerland, that regulates commerce among its 164 member states. Countries have to apply for accession to the WTO. China acceded to the WTO in 2002 after agreeing to a large number of conditions to make its economy more open to trade. Formerly called the General Agreement on Tariffs and Trade (GATT).

XI'AN INCIDENT. The kidnapping of Chiang Kai-shek in the northern city of Xi'an by Marshall Zhang Xueliang, a **warlord** ally of Chiang in December 1936. Zhang's purpose was to force Chiang to agree to a **united front** with the **Chinese Communist Party** to fight the Japanese, who were extending their aggression in China. Chiang did agree, but never really put his heart or forces into the fight against the Japanese, preferring instead to focus on what he thought was the more dangerous communist threat.

XI JINPING THOUGHT ON SOCIALISM WITH CHINESE CHARACTERISTICS FOR A NEW ERA. The official designation of Xi Jinping's contributions to Chinese Communist ideology, which was formally inscribed into the party constitution in October 2017. It builds on his idea of the **Chinese Dream** and emphasizes both achieving balanced and sustainable economic growth and strengthening the leadership of the **Chinese Communist Party**.

XINHUA. The New China News Agency (NCNA), the official news service of the PRC.

XINJIANG. An **autonomous region** of the **People's Republic of China**, with its capital in Ürümchi. It is a huge, sparsely populated area in China's far west bordering Central Asia. It is formally called the Xinjiang **Uyghur** Autonomous Region. About 64 percent of its population of 24 million consists of non-**Han ethnic minorities**, the largest of which are Uyghur Muslims, who make up 48 percent of the population. Oil and cotton have been the basis of recent economic development in the region. But it has also been the site of protest, sometime violent, by Uyghurs who oppose Chinese rule and ethnic conflict between Uyghur and Han residents. The central government has responded to these conflicts with harsh repression.See also *Bingtuan*.

YAN'AN. The area in the northwestern **province** of Shaanxi where the **Chinese Communist Party** established their headquarters and most successful **base area** from 1935 to 1945. It was in Yan'an that Mao Zedong fully consolidated his ideological and political domination of the CCP.

YAN'AN ROUND TABLE. The small group of core CCP leaders around Mao Zedong that was formed in the **Yan'an** base area in the 1940s. The Round Table was shattered as Mao turned against his former close comrades in the decades after the CCP came to power, most significantly during the **Cultural Revolution.**

YANGTZE RIVER (YANGZI). The longest river in China (nearly 4,000 miles) and the third longest in the world. It runs from its source in the far western **province** of Qinghai to the East China Sea near Shanghai. See also **Three Gorges Dam**.

YOUNG PIONEERS. A **mass organization** to which almost all students in the PRC aged seven–fourteen belong. The purpose of the Young Pioneers is to create positive feelings about the party, educate them about party goals, and organize students to engage in service projects consistent with party policies.

YUAN. The base unit of China's official currency, the *renminbi* ("people's currency"), which is denominated in 1, 5, 10, 20, 50, and 100 *yuan* bills.

ZHONGNANHAI. (Literally, "Central and Southern Seas") The large walled comp of buildings in the heart of **Beijing** near **Tiananmen Square** where the **Chinese Communist Party** has its headquarters and where many of its top leaders both live and work.

Index